LABOR RELATIONS AND PUBLIC POLICY SERIES

NO. 25

UNION VIOLENCE: THE RECORD AND THE RESPONSE BY COURTS, LEGISLATURES, AND THE NLRB

by

ARMAND J. THIEBLOT, JR.

and

THOMAS R. HAGGARD

with the assistance of

BEVERLY BURNS

INDUSTRIAL RESEARCH UNIT
The Wharton School, Vance Hall/CS
University of Pennsylvania
Philadelphia, Pennsylvania 19104
U.S.A.

Second Printing, 1984
Copyright © 1983 by the Trustees of the University of Pennsylvania
MANUFACTURED IN THE UNITED STATES OF AMERICA
Library of Congress Catalog Number 83-81085
ISBN: 0-89546-040-8
ISSN: 0075-7470

Foreword

Much has been written concerning violence in America, but little of it has been about the use of force, threats, and physical assaults in strikes and other labor confrontations. These appear, however, to be regular and often predictable occurrences. I first encountered such violence personally in 1960, then as a management negotiator, when the late president of a major AFL-CIO union stated before a strike "you can all look forward to a blood bath in these communities," and indeed there was widespread violence throughout the strike.[1] Later, as an expert witness in litigation involving the United Aircraft Company (now the United Technologies Corporation), strike violence as a union tactic was unfolded in clear view, as set forth in one of the cases described in Chapter VII of this volume. The clarity of the comment by the authors of a perceptive law article, published almost twenty years ago, became very apparent:

> An assault is an assault and a battery is a battery. In every jurisdiction in the United States these common-law torts are actionable, civilly and criminally. One is not privileged to strike the landlord, the policeman, or the professor except in self defense. If one disagrees with an opponent he should seek legal redress—except in labor disputes. The mystique of labor law is that strike violence is an aberration so strange and perplexing that ordinary standards of assault and battery simply will not do. The theory seems to be that, since violence is a traditional part of labor disputes, tradition sanctions its use.[2]

The article which began with this quotation, plus my own experiences and observations, led me to raise with my colleagues the question of whether there was indeed evidence of continuing and quite common use of violence by labor unions and whether the legal system dealt properly with such violence. Obviously, these questions required considerable and careful research which could not have been undertaken without either proper funding or competent and experienced researchers. It was not until 1978 that funding was found through a

---

[1] H. NORTHRUP, BOULWARISM 88-89 (1964).

[2] F. Stewart and R. Townsend, *Strike Violence: The Need for Federal Injunctions*, 114 U. PA. L. REV. 459 (1966).

grant from the Foundation for the Advancement of the Public Trust,
Inc., of Arlington, Virginia, which has underwritten other studies in
the labor relations field. This grant, for which we are especially
grateful to Samuel S. Crutchfield, the Foundation's executive director,
enabled us to proceed with a four-year study and to secure the services
of Thomas R. Haggard, Esq., Professor of Law, University of South
Carolina, and Dr. Armand J. Thieblot, Jr., Associate Professor of
Management, University of Maryland. Professor Haggard received
both his undergraduate and his law degree from the University of
Texas, Austin, and is a member of the Texas and South Carolina bars.
He is a frequent contributor to law journals and is the author of *Compulsory Unionism, the NLRB, and the Courts* (1977), No. 15 in the Wharton Industrial Research Unit's Labor Relations and Public Policy
Series. Professor Thieblot received his undergraduate degree from
Princeton University, and his M.B.A. and Ph.D. degrees from the
Wharton School, University of Pennsylvania. He previously authored
Negro Employment in Finance (1970), Volume II, Studies of Negro
Employment; *Welfare and Strikes* (1972), No. 6, Labor Relations and
Public Policy Series; and *The Davis-Bacon Act* (1975), No. 10, also of
the latter series.

As this study progressed, parts of it were published in the form of articles in a number of journals. The legal chapters, which were authored
by Professor Haggard, appeared in similar form in the *Nebraska Law
Review,* the *Houston Law Review,* the *South Carolina Law Review,* and
the *Kentucky Law Journal.* In addition, the case study of the Memphis
police and fire strikes, authored by J. Daniel Morgan, Esq., and the
undersigned, was first published in the *Labor Law Journal.* We are
grateful to Mr. Morgan and to these journals for their cooperation.

This study, *Union Violence: The Record and the Response by Courts,
Legislatures, and the NLRB,* is published as the twenty-fifth monograph in the Labor Relations and Public Policy Series, which the
Wharton Industrial Research Unit inaugurated in 1968 as a means of
examining issues and stimulating discussions in the complex and controversial areas of industrial relations and the regulation of labor-management issues. Twelve of these monographs, as well as major
portions of this and the previous one, deal with various aspects of the
National Labor Relations Board's (NLRB) procedures and policies.
The other ten explain significant and controversial issues such as
welfare and strikes; opening the skilled construction trades to blacks;
the Davis-Bacon Act; the labor-management situation in urban school
systems; old age, handicapped, and Vietnam-era antidiscrimination
legislation; the impact of the Occupational Safety and Health Act; the
effects of the AT&T-EEO consent decree; unions' rights to company

information; and *Operating During Strikes*. Because of the scope of, interest in, and significance of this study, we are also publishing it in a clothbound edition as our Major Study No. 59.

A number of people deserve acknowledgment for their help in producing this book. The manuscript was edited by Patricia L. Dornbusch, the Industrial Research Unit's Chief Editor. The indexes were prepared by Patricia L. Dornbusch and Robert L. Walker. Administrative matters were handled by the Unit's office manager, Mrs. Margaret E. Doyle. Patricia Sabalis, J.D., 1981, Helen T. McFadden, J.D., 1982, and Mary T. Layton, J.D., 1983, University of South Carolina Law School, served as research assistants to Professor Haggard. Beverly Hall Burns, Esq., J.D., University of Michigan Law School, and Assistant Professor, Glassboro State College, Glassboro, New Jersey, researched the material and wrote the draft of Chapter II. The Industrial Research Unit's former librarian, Harriet Liedman, M.S., researched newspapers and periodicals to obtain information for Part II. Fact checking of Part II was done by Philip W. Northrup and Ronald Turner, students at the University of Oregon and University of Pennsylvania law schools, respectively.

In addition to the grant from the Foundation for the Advancement of the Public Trust, Inc., which underwrote the research and writing, additional funding was supplied by grants from the Campbell Soup, Rollin M. Gerstacker, Gulf Oil, and A.O. Smith foundations, by the Mobil Oil Corporation, and by membership contributions from the ninety-five corporations that constitute the Industrial Research Unit's Research Advisory Group. Publication of this book was financed by the continuing generous grants from the J. Howard Pew Freedom Trust in support of the Labor Relations and Public Policy Series. Editing was financed by grants from the John M. Olin Foundation.

As in all works published by the Wharton Industrial Research Unit, the authors are solely responsible for the research and for all opinions expressed, which should not be attributed to any organization with which they are affiliated, to the grantors, or to the University of Pennsylvania.

HERBERT R. NORTHRUP, *Director*
Industrial Research Unit
The Wharton School
University of Pennsylvania

Philadelphia
July 1983

TABLE OF CONTENTS

LIST OF TABLES

CHAPTER VI

PART ONE

Introduction

CHAPTER I

Scope and Purpose of Study

It is impossible to write about strikes and labor disputes without becoming immersed in the language of conflict and aggression. Labor bargaining, for example, is often described as "economic warfare." When negotiations break down, final resolution is sought through the "aggressive conflict" of strikes and lockouts—physical actions "of a forceful nature intended to harm the other party so that he will be compelled to respond in a described manner.[1] To "strike work" is to stop doing it; but "to strike" also means "to lash out at, or cast a blow against,"[2] and it is in this context that the word has come to be used most frequently in labor relations.

These descriptions are apt, for the history of collective labor relations shows that strikes and lockouts have often been bloody. Through the years, practically no method of coercive or intimidative behavior has been overlooked as a means of getting the message across or convincing the other side of its wisdom. Newspaper accounts and judicial records are full of examples of murder, assault with intent to kill, destruction of property, arson, sabotage, mayhem, shooting, stabbing, beating, stoning, dynamiting, intimidating, threatening—in short, physical, verbal, and psychological abuse of every sort—carried out in the name of collective bargaining in order to gain economic advantage.

Far from being an interesting but irrelevant aspect of collective labor relations, such violence and bloodshed continue to the present day. In many industries, a strike in 1984 is almost as likely to result in fatalities, injuries, or destruction of property as it would have been in 1934 or even in 1904.

Much of the labor violence of the past was associated with the original efforts to organize workers in the major industries in manufacturing, transportation, construction, and mining. Those organizing drives are now safely behind us, and their violence will not be repeated. Some of the conditions that allowed it to occur, however, remain. Decreases

---

[1] C. KERR, LABOR AND MANAGEMENT IN INDUSTRIAL SOCIETY 168n (1964).
[2] WEBSTER'S 7TH NEW COLLEGIATE DICTIONARY 869 (1972).

that have occurred in labor violence have resulted from changes in the social construct or from moral imperatives; but the record indicates that the net effect has been weak, and it has not been supported by changes in law.

Labor laws and their interpretations by the courts have failed to curtail or circumscribe overt violence,[3] and application of criminal law is hampered by the collective nature of much of it and the inability to fix blame on particular individuals. The end result is that violence continues, and can occur in a modern strike or organizational drive just as easily as it did at the turn of the century.

The popular fascination with death, destruction, and violence in general is strong. It is reflected in the subject matter of not only the news but also the entertainment media. This being the case, it is surprising that the violence associated with labor relations has not attracted more attention, especially considering its persistence. Neither the fact of labor violence, nor its causes, nor its impact on collective bargaining have been much analyzed.

What little attention has been given to the topic focuses most often on popular accounts of the battles for organization and recognition that took place from fifty to one hundred years ago—before either the National Labor Relations (Wagner) Act of 1935 (NLRA) or the Norris-LaGuardia (Anti-Injunction) Act of 1932 had become law. Admittedly, those were dramatic times. A new social order was emerging, and it gave the union movement almost irresistible force; but it was an irresistible force pitted against the weight of tradition, the power of law, and the privilege of enterprise—themselves almost immovable objects. The level and the nature of the violence that arose in those early titanic clashes were impressive, and the damages sometimes seemed like the result of war.

The scenario of labor confrontation was frequently one in which strikers, or workers seeking recognition for their union, took part in mass action and were treated by police authorities and company guards as a mob in civil disobedience—as, indeed, they were under the laws of the time. Under the circumstances, the results were often bloody.

To pick a random example, when a crowd of demonstrators marched in the streets of Pittsburgh in 1877 to dramatize its demands for a union, it was fired upon by National Guardsmen, and twenty-six men died.[4] In another instance, at the Colorado Fuel and Iron Company in 1913, the well-known Ludlow Massacre occurred. There, local law en-

[3] J. HUNT, EMPLOYER'S GUIDE TO LABOR RELATIONS 84 (1979).
[4] J. FINLEY, THE CORRUPT KINGDOM 120 (1972).

forcement, the National Guard, and eventually the United States Army were all involved in incidents which culminated in at least sixteen deaths, including those of two women and eleven children who were suffocated in a fire set by troops.[5]

THE MYTHOLOGY OF STRIKE VIOLENCE

Events such as those described above were dramatic and brutal, and because the unions bore the brunt of them, their retelling through the years has given rise to the myth that employers were the primary cause of the violence then—and that they still are now. In the early confrontations, despite the fact that complicated motivations were involved on all sides, the blame for the bloodshed has almost always been fixed on the mindless intransigence of owners and on the overreaction of authorities who were held to be their minions.

Union organizers were said to be "driven to violence" by the owners' antipathy toward unionism, and by their stubbornness in refusing to accommodate the new directions that society was taking. The owners were also blamed for using injunctions, black lists, and yellow-dog contracts, for hiring detectives and private guards, for employing "professional imported strikebreakers" (scabs), for controlling "puppet" sheriffs and other lawmen, and for a variety of other tactics supposedly used to "bust the union."[6]

Under this view, which has gained adherents over the years among academics, legislators, and the general public, the road to labor peace is well marked: curtail the ability of employers to "bust the union," and violence will cease. As one academic author put it only a few years ago:

> In the past, where the regular police were unable to cope with the [strike] situation it was a common practice to swear in company police and even strikebreakers as deputy sheriffs, with the power to carry arms and arrest strikers. These practices have now [1959] virtually disappeared, however, and serious or widespread violence is in all probability a thing of the past.[7]

Unfortunately, the author was wrong. Employers cannot create their own arresting authorities in the modern day, but the road to labor peace has not been opened. Serious and widespread violence continues.

A related part of the myth of the employer as the cause of labor violence is that an active defense by an employer, whether physical or

---

[5] Seidman, *The Borders of Violence,* in UNIONS, MANAGEMENT, AND THE PUBLIC 243 (2d ed. E. Bakke, C. Kerr, and C. Anrod eds. 1960).

[6] SENATE COMM. ON EDUCATION AND LABOR, VIOLATIONS OF FREE SPEECH AND RIGHTS OF LABOR. S. REP. No. 6, 76th Cong., 1st Sess. (1939).

[7] L. REYNOLDS, LABOR ECONOMICS AND LABOR RELATIONS, 291 (3d ed. 1959).

economic, is threatening to the success of an organizing drive or strike, and therefore justifies the use of violence in retaliation. Thus, if an employer deploys armed guards or patrol dogs to protect its property, or if it tries to hire nonunion workers or to continue operations to protect its economic position, its "threatening" actions "drive" the unionists to retaliate—and if violence happens to occur, the employer or its company must bear the blame for it.[8]

Those seeking to blame strike violence on the employer have undertaken arduous searches for possible scapegoats. Some have offered up "the criminal law [which] favors the employer" or the police and judiciary who are partial to the employer's side in labor disputes.[9] Others have gone further afield to such improbable sources as "lawyers representing an employer or an employers' association [who] can charge a larger fee when there is more trouble to be dealt with."[10]

In these incidents, as in the looting and burning during the civil rights riots of the mid-1960s or the confrontations of the Vietnam peace movement a few years later, popular opinion seems to have held that a vigorous defense *causes* offensive violence and must therefore be responsible for it. To go back to Ludlow,

> the Colorado Fuel and Iron Company, in its demonstration of might, brought in a specially armored railroad car to transport its guards and strikebreakers. It was aptly dubbed "The Death Special."[11]

The fact that the railroad car was "armored" rather than "armed," and therefore a defensive rather than an offensive device, was not seen as a reasonable distinction. The crowd saw the armored car as visible evidence of the employer's willingness to mount a spirited defense and that alone was sufficient excuse to test it by force.

A One-Sided Issue

Most issues have two sides, but because labor relations struggles are typically characterized as contests between human beings, on the one hand, and bloodless corporations, on the other, portrayals of violence in labor history are remarkably one-sided. For example, many people who have studied the history of the United States can remember the incidents at Ludlow, Homestead, and Pullman, or the Molly Maguires, all of which have been called "massacres," and several of which have

---

[8] A similar logic was found during the antiwar riots of the early 1970s. At that time it was often said that when policemen wore shields and helmets to protect themselves from demonstrators, they infuriated the demonstrators and incited them to riot.

[9] SEIDMAN, *supra* note 5, at 242.

[10] KERR, *supra* note 1, at 176.

[11] FINLEY, *supra* note 4, at 123.

been the subject of popular movies. Very few people, however, could tell you what happened at a place called Herrin.

Yet at Herrin, in Williamson County, Illinois, on June 21, 1922, occurred one of the most brutal and least excusable massacres in American history. Twenty-three unarmed strikebreakers, who had surrendered their employer's redoubt under a white flag of truce and had been promised safe conduct out of the county were set upon by their captors and butchered. Some had their throats cut, some were hanged. Six men were made to crawl to a small cemetary at the edge of town and dig their own graves before, hands tied, they were shot and mutilated.[12]

Brutality by strikers of the level seen at Herrin has fortunately always been rare and is certainly not likely to be repeated in modern times. But the same can also be said of the intransigence and overreaction of employers such as that seen at Ludlow. Neither example should condition reactions to present-day labor violence, but in fact, Ludlow—because its memory is regularly refreshed—does, whereas Herrin—which remains relatively unknown—does not.

PERSPECTIVE

It is not our intention to lay all of the blame for labor violence at the feet of the unionists, nor to apologize for the sometimes brutal and often brutish actions of the mineowners, industrialists, sheriffs, or militiamen of previous generations. Little would be gained from such an exercise, for a complete reading of the history of the period shows that there were excesses and brutishness on both sides. But the popular concept of employer action as the root cause of industrial violence is based on the continuance of a myth that was inaccurate even when it first arose. Perpetuation of the myth as an excuse for present-day labor violence engenders an atmosphere of tension and an expectation of trouble during strikes, potentials which are often self-fulfilling. Furthermore, it works to prevent legal action that would restrain such violence.

Before continuing, it should be made clear that not all present-day employers are blameless in initiating labor violence, nor are all instances of strike violence initiated or perpetuated solely by strikers or unionists. Common sense, observation of the frailties of the human condition, and analyses of the complexity of motivations possible in

---

[12] FINLEY, *supra* note 4, at 133. *See also Loyalty Survives at Site of '22 Massacre*, New York Times, March 13, 1978, at D5.

any confrontation mitigate against any such eventuality.[13] Motivations for initiating threats, force, and violence are, however, more commonly found on the offensive side of any conflict situation. Lacking clear evidence to the contrary, the aggressors—in the case of labor disputes, typically the unionists—must bear the greatest responsibility. Some of the fault must also lie with the courts and legislatures which have moved to constrain employers' defenses and options much more readily than they have moved to circumscribe strikers' behavior.

PURPOSEFUL VIOLENCE

The pattern of strike violence in the modern setting indicates that the search for its motivations cannot be limited simply to finding scapegoats—to passing it all off as a defensive reaction, or characterizing it as high-spirited, spur-of-the-moment roughhousing such as that which characterizes barroom brawls. Dispassionate analysis reveals that much labor violence is deliberate and perpetrated by strikers to achieve identifiable ends. Much of it seems to be used purposefully as one of the tools of collective bargaining.

The widespread belief in the efficacy of violence, even among those who find it uncivilized and morally abhorrent, is strong. An old saying goes, "A Smith and Wesson beats four aces," and many people believe it. Unfortunately, history has repeatedly demonstrated that the powers of authority or law to constrain concerted violence are weak, especially when the violence is conducted under the protective cover of moral protest, or when it involves large numbers of people in civil disobedience. In these circumstances, a properly positioned adversary may use violence to advance a position, overcome an opponent, or bring public and political notice to grievances without concern for the legal boundaries which otherwise would restrain the action.

Such deliberate use of violence has certainly been found in industrial settings. Incidents discussed in later chapters show that unions have at various times employed violence with a number of apparent purposes, among which are:

---

[13] There is one recent incident, for example, in which the president of a Richmond, Virginia, trucking company apparently paid nonunion employees to sabotage, shoot into, and in other ways damage his own trucking equipment during a Teamsters' strike, and then contrived to fix the blame on the union (through perjured testimony). The object was to bolster the company's case for damages resulting from a secondary boycott. Damages of $806,096 were collected by the company, whose management was also severely censured by the courts. Great Coastal Express, Inc. v. International Brotherhood of Teamsters, _____ F.2d _____ (4th Cir, 1982); *cert. denied,* _____ U.S. _____ (1983). Other such instances either are extremely rare, or have managed to escape the attention of the courts and newspaper.

1. *As an organizing tool,* to engender fear and force compliance with union demands for recognition. (See, for example, Chapter IV, *Meadow Creek Coal Company, 1948.*)

2. *As a bargaining device,* to cause personal or economic harm at costs that exceed the costs of settlement on the union's terms. (See Chapter VI, *Fires in Denver.*)

3. *As an attention getter,* to generate public and political pressure for a quick settlement. (See Chapter V, *Memphis Police and Firefighters Strikes of 1978.*)

4. *As an enforcement mechanism,* to insure solidarity among strikers. (See Chapter VII, *J. L. Popowich & Sons Co., 1971.*)

5. *As a warning,* to demonstrate to employers the consequences of contracting with nonunion companies. (See Chapter VI, *Kalkaska.*)

6. *As a disruptive tactic,* to prevent nonunion companies from working during strikes. (See Chapter III.)

7. *As a form of communication,* to demonstrate "leadership" or "independence," often with respect to internal union affairs. (See Chapter VI, *Roofers Local 30.*)

8. *As a means of generating fear,* to create an aura of "respect" for the meanness of the union, so as to condition future as well as current bargaining. (See Chapter IV, *Coal Strike of 1981,* or Chapter VII, *Violence in Jurisdictional Disputes: FASH, 1978.*)

Purposeful strike violence is not necessarily coordinated by union leaders; in some cases it is not even desired by them, but the results are often the same. Furthermore, the possibility of violence in strikes is enhanced by the setting in which they take place. Crowds in confrontation easily turn violent. Some bargaining relationships, for example those involving mineworkers, truck drivers, building trades workers, and firefighters, have traditions of violence which cause new outbreaks to be expected during negotiations, creating tension on both sides and an early breaking point. Additionally, violence in labor relations settings has typically been excused when it occurs during mass picketing or long strikes, and this again increases its likelihood.

A *University of Pennsylvania Law Review* article commented that

an assault is an assault and a battery is a battery. In every jurisdiction in the United States these common-law torts are actionable, both civilly and criminally. One is not privileged to strike the landlord, the policeman, or the professor except in self-defense. If one disagrees with an opponent he should seek legal redress—except in labor disputes. The mystique of labor law is that strike violence is an aberration so strange and perplexing that ordinary standards of assault and battery simply will not do. The theory seems to be that, since violence is a traditional part of labor disputes, tradition sanctions its use.[14]

To take an extreme example, with respect to the massacre at Herrin, described above, two juries refused to convict the accused slayers, despite the brutality of the event and ample eyewitness testimony.[15] It was held that the guards' behavior before surrendering under flag of truce was such that whatever they got, they deserved.

Influence of the Strike Setting

Certain combinations of factors increase the possibility that violence will break out in any particular strike setting. Many such factors exist, but preliminary analysis suggests that the following are among the most important:

1. *Characteristics of the industry.* The possibility of violence increases when the ratio of union to nonunion workers is close to even; when concentration ratios within the industry are low, *i.e.,* no individual firm nor small number of firms dominates the industry; when the number of independent operators is high; when mechanization or automation is advancing rapidly; and when the industry's products are easily inventoried.

2. *Characteristics of the work and workers.* The possibility of violence increases when skill requirements are low; when employment is decreasing in the particular firm or industry, but not in general; when the available labor pool is large; when prestrike wage rates are high compared with other jobs of similar skill requirements; when union wage rates are high compared with nonunion rates in the same industry; and when local unemployment is above average.

3. *Characteristics of the workplace and product.* Violence becomes more likely when nonstriking employees work alone and are easily singled out (as, for example, are truck drivers); when workplaces are isolated or difficult to protect; when company machinery or equipment is unprotected or easily sabotaged; and when the general public perceives the product to be important or indispensible.

---

[14] Stewart and Townsend, *Strike Violence: the Need for Federal Injunctions,* 114 U. PA. L. REV. 459 (1966).
[15] *Loyalty Survives, supra* note 12.

4. *Characteristics of the union.* Violence becomes more likely when internal bickering for leadership is occurring in the union; when the union has a tradition of violent behavior; and when individual local or national union leaders have demonstrated a propensity toward violence.

5. *Characteristics of the dispute.* The possibility of violence increases when issues being bargained involve demands for union security rather than wages or fringe benefits; and when owners attempt to continue operations during the strike.

6. *Characteristics of public support and environment.* The possibility of violence increases when political intervention in the dispute seems imminent; when government provides food stamps, welfare, and other forms of public support to strikers; when law enforcement is weak, or law enforcement officials are disinclined to act; and when the media applaud or do not discourage violence.

No such enumeration can fully explain or anticipate labor violence. In any strike, local factors influence the choice of bargaining tactics. Furthermore, there is no easy way to sort out the priorities attached to various factors when they are in conflict with each other. Nevertheless, analysis of the factors can yield some perception of the likelihood of violence in a particular strike situation.

DEFINITIONS OF VIOLENCE

In subsequent chapters, many examples of labor violence are examined, and it is well to start out with some attention to what is meant by the term "violence." Definition of this term is complicated by the fact that perceptions of violence are colored by attitudes and conventions which are not fully definable. A pat on the shoulder, for example, is usually a friendly gesture, but might also be construed as aggravated assault if the recipient had a broken clavicle. Among the cases presented in this book are instances of brutal violence and intimidation that have been excused by authorities as roughhousing and normal interpersonal behavior in confrontation settings, and other cases in which trivial actions like pushing someone away from one's nose were interpreted as violent behavior.

Because of these problems of subjective sensitivity, courts have sometimes hesitated to act against violence (and the legislatures have hesitated to prohibit it) for fear of chilling first amendment rights or of overreacting. Physical violence is relatively easier to identify and categorize than psychological violence is; but even in the case of purely physical violence, identification is dependent not only on the behavior but also on the motivations of the perpetrators.

Psychological violence—threats, and intimidation or coercion carried out by verbal means—is no less real than physical violence, but it usually requires recognition not only of behavior and motivation on the part of the perpetrator, but also of the reasonableness of reaction on the part of the victim. It is therefore much more difficult to identify, prosecute, or proscribe.

The courts at various times have attempted to deal with the problem of definition by fleshing out the definitions of violence provided by lexicographers so as to give useful meaning to the word. They have not been entirely successful. The first group of cases below are those in which the courts have provided definitions of violence dwelling on its physical aspects; the second group contains cases in which the courts seemed to emphasize more strongly the combination of physical and nonphysical activities; and the third group is of cases in which the courts' attention centered on intimidation and other forms of non-physical violence.

Violence as Unwarranted Exercise of Physical Force

Anderson-Berney Bldg. Co. v. Lowry. In this case, the court defined violence as: "physical force unlawfully exercised; abuse of force; that force which is employed against common right, against the laws, and against public liberty."[16]

People v. McIlvain. In this case, the court found that violence consisted of the "unjust or unwarranted exercise of force, usually with the accompaniment of vehemence, outrage or fury."[17]

International Longshoremen's & Warehousemen's Union v. Ackerman. "The word 'violence' employed in the section surely has its ordinary legal meaning: 'The abuse of force. That force which is employed against common right, against the laws, and against public liberty.' 'Violence is synonymous with physical force . . .' Bouvier's Law Dictionary, Rawle's 3rd Revision."[18]

Landry v. Daley. "The words force or violence are not so obscure as to fail to advise the public of the prohibited conduct. In common parlance, force means 'power, violence, compulsion, or constraint exerted upon or against a person or thing.' The word 'violence' imparts a similar meaning. It means 'the exertion of any physical force so as to injure or abuse.' [footnote to Webster, New International Dictionary,

---

[16] Anderson-Berney Bldg. Co. v. Lowry, 143 S. W. 2d. 401 (1940).

[17] People v. McIlvain, 55 Cal. App. 2d 322, 130 P. 2d. 131 (1942).

[18] International Longshoremen's & Warehousemen's Union v. Ackerman, 82 F. Supp. 65 (D. Hawaii 1948).

3d ed. 1963] . . . Given a reasonable and natural construction, these terms connote either physical attack upon person or property, or physical aggression reasonably capable of inspiring fear of injury or harm to a person or property."[19]

Commonwealth v. Nadolny. "The Oxford Dictionary (Vol. 12, page 221), inter alia, defines violence: 'to inflict harm or injury upon; to outrage or violate.' . . . Webster's New International Dictionary, 2nd ed., defines the word 'violence,' inter alia: 'Injury done to that which is entitled to respect, reverence, or observance; profanation . . . outrage. . . .'"[20]

Violence as Unwarranted Interference with the Rights of Others

People v. Flummerfelt. "The terms 'violence' and 'force' are synonymous when used in relation to assault, and include any application of force even though it entails no pain or bodily harm and leaves no mark."[21]

Boecker v. Aetna Casualty & Surety Co. "No particular degree of force is required to constitute violence. Violence is broadly defined in Webster's New International Dictionary 2d Ed., as 'the exertion of any physical force considered with reference to its effect on another than the agent.'"[22]

State v. Hawkins. "According to accepted definitions, 'violence' may consist of violent, menacing, turbulent, and threatening action or procedure. (Webster's Intern. Dict., 3rd Ed.), and particularly so if the actor possesses the obvious means of inflicting injury or death."[23]

Violence as Including Intimidation

United Aircraft Corporation v. International Association of Machinists, et al. "To intimidate is to inspire with fear, to overawe or make afraid. Fear may be inspired without physical violence or spoken threats, moral intimidation may be accomplished by a menacing attitude and a display of force which may coerce the will as effectually as actual physical violence. The gathering of strikers in considerable numbers at the entrance of a factory with threatening attitude toward employees, who must run the gauntlet of a hostile picket line in going to and from work, may overawe and make them afraid by a show of force which

---

[19] Landry v. Daley, 280 F. Supp. 938, 954 (N.D. Ill., E.D.), *app. dism.* 393 U.S. 229 (1968).

[20] Commonwealth v. Nadolny, 163 Pa. Super. Ct. 517, 518, 63 A. 2d. 129, 130 (1949).

[21] People v. Flummerfelt, 153 Cal. App. 2d 104, 105, 313 P. 2d 912, 913 (1957).

[22] Boecker v. Aetna Casualty & Surety Co., 281 S.W. 2d 561, 564 (1955).

[23] State v. Hawkins, 418 S.W. 2d 921 (Mo. 1967).

itself is intimidating. The well considered authorities all hold that the conduct of a strike may be such as to constitute intimidation though there is no use of force or physical violence." [There follow ten citations to precedent for the opinion.][24]

None of these definitions is totally acceptable, in part because the fact of violence will always contain some components of subjectivity. For the purpose of identifying acts of violence for this study we have adopted the following definition:

> Violence is the nonprivileged physical interference with the person or property of another, or the threat, express or implied, of such interference.

This definition is intended to include such physical acts as beatings or sabotage, and also the objectional aspects of mass picketing such as blocking ingress or egress to a struck plant, prohibiting nonstriking or nonunion employees from exercising their right to work, and such non-physical violence as threats, intimidation, and moral coercion. It is intended to exclude purely "competitive" or "economic" injuries as might be sustained, for example, by a company struck at a strategic time. It also excludes the consequences of refusals by striking employees to work or perform services, even if those services might be considered important or critical. (Such actions, though they might be morally reprehensible, are not of themselves violent, in our view.)

OUTLINE OF THE CHAPTERS

The following parts of this study are concerned with four main goals: firstly, with demonstrating the pervasiveness of labor violence and evaluating its apparently deliberate use during strikes; secondly, with examining the characteristics of violence used by selected unions or in particular strikes; thirdly, with reviewing the legislative and judicial reactions to violence; and lastly, with presenting recommendations as to how its use might be diminished in the future.

Evidential Materials   (Parts Two and Three)

Although the use of violence in strikes is a widespread problem, there exists no formal, centralized collection of information on specific incidents. In Parts Two and Three, information has been collected from three major sources: case files of the National Labor Relations Board (NLRB) (Chapter II); incident summaries from an ongoing but recent data base maintained by the National Right to Work Legal Defense Foundation (NRTWLDF) (Chapter III); and reports in the popular

---

[24] United Aircraft Corporation v. International Association of Machinists, et al., 133884,5 Conn. Supp., 68 L.R.R.M. 2488 (1978).

press, personal interviews, and field studies performed by the authors (Chapters IV–VII). These chapters compose the evidential section of the study which demonstrates the continuing use of violence as a tactic in labor relations and illustrates the apparent deliberateness with which it is used.

Overview of the Law and Its Reaction (Part Four)

The violence that has been part of the American labor movement since its very first stirrings has differed somewhat in degree, but has been consistent in substance from the very beginning. The legal responses to it, however, have been various both in approach and in legal theory throughout the years. To date, none have been particularly effective.

The first reported instance of labor violence arose in 1799 in connection with a strike among the cordwainers of Philadelphia. The record in that case discloses numerous acts of misconduct, including the throwing of a tack-studded potato through a shop window, barely missing the head of the proprietor who had hired a "scab." This incident was a quaint but lethal way of making a bargaining demand.[25] The perpetrators of this mischief were prosecuted under the so-called "criminal conspiracy doctrine" which, whatever other kinds of union activity it might have encompassed, clearly did proscribe labor conspiracies to commit overt acts of violence against recalcitrant employers and nonunion employees. Most of the criminal conspiracy cases, at least, involved misconduct of that kind; and the doctrine thus perhaps represents the first specific response to the problem by American law.[26]

Eventually, the criminal conspiracy doctrine fell into disuse; but the problem of labor violence did not. The fifty-year period between 1880 and 1930 was especially marked by acts of violence committed by both sides in connection with the many strikes and lockouts of that era, some of which took on the dimensions of "small wars."[27] In one two-year period, 1902–04, approximately 200 people were reported killed and over 2,000 injured in acts of labor violence.[28] During this era, injunctions and general tort damage actions became the prevailing legal response to acts of violence by labor unionists.

---

[25] Nelles, *The First American Labor Case,* 41 YALE L.J. 165, 176 (1931).

[26] *See generally,* T. HAGGARD, COMPULSORY UNIONISM, THE NLRB, AND THE COURTS—A LEGAL ANALYSIS OF UNION SECURITY AGREEMENTS 11-17 (1977).

[27] *See generally,* J. BRECHER, STRIKE! (1972); S. LENS, THE LABOR WARS (1973); Taft & Ross, *American Labor Violence: Its Causes, Character, and Outcome* in 1 VIOLENCE IN AMERICA: HISTORICAL AND COMPARATIVE PERSPECTIVES 221 (1969).

[28] NATIONAL COMMISSION ON THE CAUSES AND PREVENTION OF VIOLENCE, VIOLENCE IN AMERICA 288-289 (1969).

Federal and state legislatures were not entirely happy with what they perceived to be a pro-management bias on the part of the judiciary, and in the 1930s, legislation was passed curtailing the use of injunctions against labor unions for strike and picket line violence. (The federal Norris-LaGuardia Act, and its state counterparts, are discussed in detail in Chapter VIII.)

By the 1940s, the temper of Congress had changed somewhat, however, and two important federal laws dealing with union violence were passed. The first was the Anti-Racketeering (Hobbs) Act of 1946, which purported to overrule an earlier Supreme Court decision generally exempting labor union violence from the federal anti-extortion statute. This legislation, and the judicial response to it, is covered in Chapter IX.

In 1947, the Taft-Hartley Act amendments to the NLRA also represented a significant new legal response to the problem of union violence. First, although the process had certainly begun under the prior act, the 1947 amendments continued to indirectly encourage the use of private arbitration as a means of resolving industrial disputes. One of the recurring issues that these arbitrators have been called upon to face is whether an employee who has engaged in some kind of strike or picket line misconduct could be discharged "for cause" under the collective labor agreement. This issue is discussed in Chapter X.

The Congress that passed the Taft-Hartley amendments was also concerned with the direct federal response to this discharge-for-cause issue. Under the NLRA, before the amendments, there had been a tendency on the part of the NLRB and the courts to treat some kinds of strike violence as being affirmatively "protected" against employer reprisal. The congressional reaction to this, together with the administrative and judicial interpretations of it, is also covered in Chapter X.

The Taft-Hartley Act Congress also made labor union violence an "unfair labor practice" and thus subject to the administrative jurisdiction of the NLRB. The laws relating to this statutory provision are extensive, and perhaps provide the best indication of the true scope and nature of the union violence in this country. The issues raised by this statutory provision are discussed in detail in Chapter XI.

In addition to the legal responses mentioned above, there are also a number of state and federal criminal laws, of both a specific and a general nature, which touch upon the problem of labor union violence. Common law tort actions are, of course, also still available to those injured by such misconduct. These matters, and a few others, are discussed in Chapter XII.

Despite what thus appears to be a plethora of state and federal laws dealing with the matter, the problem of labor union violence seems to persist. And the question is, why? To be sure, the law can never be expected to eradicate completely man's tendency toward physical force as the successor to the failed persuasive power of logic—or always to provide a full measure of justice to its victims. But even if that is conceded, one is still left with the uneasy feeling that the law in this country does not address the problem of labor union violence with the vigor that it should. The attitude seems to be that "boys will be boys"; that a certain amount of "animal exuberance" is to be expected in the emotionally supercharged atmosphere of a labor dispute; that while this is to be regretted, the law should not overreact and run the risk of "chilling" the exercise of the employees' right to organize and strike; and that, indeed, a certain amount of "minor violence" is simply a traditional and thus acceptable part of the American industrial relations scene.

Conclusions and Recommendations (Part Five)

That the law generally reflects an attitude of indifference to the effects of labor violence is the thesis of this book. Its conclusion is that the law as applied has been ineffective in curtailing the actuality or the impact of labor violence (see Chapter XIII), and that it will continue to be ineffective until legislative and judicial attitudes change or are forced to change (Chapter XIV). Our recommendations (Chapter XV) follow accordingly.

PART TWO

Violence Overview

CHAPTER II

NLRB Case Documentation[1]

One of the few places where documentation of strike violence can be found in the public record is in the files of cases heard by the National Labor Relations Board (NLRB). Prior to 1947, the law did not differentiate labor violence from other kinds of violence, with the exception of the largely ineffective provisions of the Anti-Racketeering Act of 1934.[2] Control of it was therefore left almost entirely to the states' ordinary criminal provisions, which do not categorize crimes by the setting in which they take place.

In 1947, the Taft-Hartley Act amendment—also known as the Labor Management Relations Act—was added to the National Labor Relations Act (NLRA). Among other things, this act contained a section making certain kinds of strike violence an unfair labor practice.[3] This new section of the NLRA opened up the possibility of civil remedies as well as criminal prosecutions in cases involving strike violence.

Despite the new possibilities, the majority of incidents of labor violence have continued to go unreported for a number of reasons. In the first place, the NLRB's procedures are complicated and time consuming. Secondly, the remedies available under them are often no more than a cease and desist order which may come months or even years after the incident occurred. Thirdly, an obvious case of violence might go uncontested after the first determination by the administrative law judge or trial examiner, and so would not be part of the NLRB case record reported here. For these and other reasons, the majority of incidents of labor violence go unreported.

---

[1] The analysis of the NLRB cases presented in this chapter was performed by Beverly Hall Burns, J.D., assistant professor of labor relations and collective bargaining, Glassboro State College, New Jersey, and a member of the Michigan Bar.

[2] The Anti-Racketeering Act of 1934 Ch. 569, 48 Stat. 979 (1934), current version at 18 U.S.C. 1951 (1976) is covered in detail in Chapter IX.

[3] The Labor Management Relations Act, or as it is most commonly known, National Labor Relations (Taft-Hartley) Act (NLRA), 29 U.S.C. 158 (1976). Sections 8(a)(1) and 8(a)(3) identify unfair labor practices, including the use of violence, by employers. Section 8(b)(1)(A) identifies violence by labor unions as an unfair labor practice. See Chapter XI for an extended analysis.

The basic procedure in an unfair labor practice case that includes violence is as follows:

1. A charge is filed by an employer, employee, labor organization, or other interested party. It is filed with the regional office of the NLRB in the area in which the alleged unfair labor practice took place.

2. A regional office investigation is carried out. If the investigation indicates that an unfair labor practice has in fact occurred, a complaint may be issued.

3. If a complaint is issued, a hearing will be held by an administrative law judge (referred to as a trial examiner until the early 1970s), who submits a report of his findings and recommendations to the NLRB.

4. If there is no appeal by either party after a twenty-day period, the recommendations of the administrative law judge become final.

5. If there is an appeal, the NLRB will hold a hearing and may affirm, overrule, or modify the administrative law judge's recommendation.

6. The NLRB may remedy unfair labor practices by issuing orders requiring violators to cease and desist, or it may require certain affirmative actions as well—including compensation for losses sustained by the injured parties, posting or public display of NLRB orders, etc.

7. The NLRB's determinations may be appealed by either party through the federal court system.

Records of the initial hearings, those by the administrative law judges, are not readily available to the general public; therefore, only those cases that have been appealed for hearing by the NLRB (step 5, above), result in publicly available reports and orders. It is from these cases that the information in this chapter was generated.

Obviously, this is not a comprehensive account of strike violence. As noted, many incidents are not brought to the NLRB at all. Additionally, the findings of the administrative law judges are not necessarily appealed. Furthermore, the cases presented here are not typically the most heinous ones. Certain types of violence, such as murder, are well handled by criminal authorities and offer little realistic possibility for civil remedy. Therefore, the cases in this chapter offer insight into only a small slice of the violence committed during strikes and organizing drives. The majority of them have to do with mass picketing and its consequences—especially acts committed with or against automobiles, harassment and intimidation of nonstriking employees, and various forms of property damage.[4]

The cases reviewed in this chapter number about fifty-five. Although the total number of cases involving section 8(b)(1)(A) of the NLRA heard by the NLRB since 1947 exceeds three hundred, these fifty-five comprise the record pertinent to the purposes of this book. The others either do not contain reference to physical damage or violence, or involve violence that occurred between unions or between union members and their officers.

THE NLRB CASES: A HISTORY OF VIOLENCE REPEATED

The Sunset Line and Twine Company was a small company located in rural California north of San Francisco. For seven years it had bargained with the International Longshoremen's and Warehousemen's Union (ILWU), which represented its one hundred employees, and for seven years it had avoided a strike. But negotiations in 1947 failed to bring about a new contract agreement, and a strike began in September of that year. The plant remained closed for two weeks, then reopened with a staff of supervisors, newly hired workers, and four women who had decided to abandon the strike and return to work.

The walkout turned violent on the day the company reopened. A new employee, fifty-two years old and in training to be a salesman, arrived at the plant with two of the nonstriking employees in his car as passengers. As the car entered the company premises, the union's business agent stepped into its path and the new salesman braked to a stop.

"The windows of the car were closed, doors were locked, the motor was running. Placing one hand on the car's radiator ornament, with the other [the business agent] motioned to the pickets nearby and said: 'Open the door and pull them out.' "[5]

Fortunately, the door lock held and no bloodshed ensued. But the first of eight incidents which were later determined to be unfair labor practices on the part of the union had occurred. Other tactics seen during the next month included:

1. intimidating and threatening with bodily harm employees who were entering and leaving the plant, or who had already left the plant premises;

---

[4] Many additional incidents covering the broader range of strike violence are found in Chapter III and in later sections of this chapter.

[5] Longshoremen's and Warehousemen's Union and Sunset Line and Twine Co., 79 N.L.R.B. 1487, 1948 (1948).

2. distributing tacks in the company's parking lot;

3. laying hand upon and threatening an employee with bodily harm;

4. blocking entrance to the plant, threatening employees seeking to enter the plant, and shaking and assaulting one of the employees;

5. engaging in mass picketing, attacking and damaging automobiles, and interfering with police seeking to escort employees into the plant;

6. other mass picketing incidents.

One such incident took place in mid-October. The company, which had received information leading it to expect some trouble, had asked for assistance from the local police. On the morning of October 15, 1947, about thirty men from the police and sheriff's departments were at the plant by 6:00 A.M.

> By the time the first car with nonstrikers arrived, shortly before 7 A.M., a crowd of between 200 and 300 had accumulated in the streets and on the sidewalk portion of the driveway leading into the parking lot.
> The first car . . . was blocked by the crowd.
> When the car started to drive in "they jostled the car back and forth and crowded officers right on top of the car."
> When the second car carrying nonstrikers arrived . . . a member of local 6 but not a striker, hit the window of the car with his fist and shattered it. The third car was . . . "shaken violently" by the crowd from both sides.
> Sheriff Patteson made several arrests, and had to threaten the use of a gas bomb if the crowd didn't clear the driveway.[6]

Mass picketing; taunting and harassment of nonstrikers; blocking entrance to the plant; swelling the ranks with union members from other plants; scuffling with police—these are not examples of extraordinary violence. Two things made them worth mentioning: firstly, the Sunset Line and Twine Company case was the first case heard by the NLRB that involved an alleged violation of section 8(b)(1)(A) of the NLRA; secondly, the strike violence seen in this case is characteristic of many of the 300 or more cases that have followed it.

Section 8(b)(1)(A) of the NLRA forbids restraint and coercion of workers' rights, and makes violence, threats of violence, and intimidation unfair labor practices. The charges in this case were filed on October 21, 1947, just months after adoption of the Taft-Hartley amendment to the NLRA, and the case was decided the following year with a

---

[6] *Id.* at 1500-02.

finding that an unfair labor practice had indeed taken place. The union was ordered to cease and desist from such practices.

In several respects, this first decision in 1948 and the one made most recent to the time of writing, in 1981, are similar. In 1981, the NLRB upheld unfair labor practice findings against the International Association of Machinists and Aerospace Workers (IAM) in the *Wolf Machine Company* case.[7] In both cases, the companies were struck after routine negotiations had broken down. In both cases, aggressive acts of violence occurred both on the picket line and away from it. Both cases involved mass picketing; and in both cases, replacement workers and nonstrikers were the targets of harassment.

In the *Wolf Machine Company* case, for example, activities directed against four young men who worked as replacements during the strike were as follows:

> In a house in a nearby town, Norwood, there lived four young men who worked as replacements. The lady of the house, Mrs. Custer, mother of two of these employees, and Danny Miles, one of her sons, testified that on the evening and during the night of October 8, a car with four or five persons drove back and forth in front of their house shouting obscenities and yelling threats at its occupants. Miles said he clearly recognized [the chief steward].
>
> According to Mrs. Custer, the car came by, and circled the block about six or seven times between 6 P.M. and 2 A.M. . . . "They started yelling out vulgarities and screaming out scab, scab, scab, scab . . . They pulled the car into the drive the first time and they threatened to kill us . . . They said "We're going to kill you Norwood punks. . . ."[8]

The scene described is from the 1981 case but it could have taken place just as easily in 1947. Additional similarities between the first and the last in the series of NLRB cases are the use of police intervention, the repetition and escalation of aggressive and violent behavior, the directing of violence by large numbers—groups, or even mobs—against individual nonstrikers or replacements, the involvement of union officials in the activities, and the apparent intimidating purposes to which the activities were directed.

The following section analyzes the types of violence that have occurred commonly throughout the NLRB cases; following that, the contexts in which violence seems to have occurred most frequently are discussed; and finally, conclusions are drawn based upon the discussion of the cases.

---

[7] District 34, International Association of Machinists and Aerospace Workers and the Wolf Machine Company, 254 N.L.R.B. 282 (1981).

[8] *Id.* at 284.

COMMON THEMES OF VIOLENCE IN THE NLRB CASES

At the outset, it must be made clear that the NLRB, in deciding its cases, was concerned with determining if unfair labor practices had occurred based on standards of proof involving "restraint" and "coercion" of employees. The focal pont here is somewhat different. For our purposes, violence embraces not only acts of restraint or coercion, but also other acts of force which might be physical or psychological, extortionate or repressive.[9]

These acts may, and often do, result in physical injury or property damage; but they need not, for the callous use of power or force may do psychological damage in the form of intimidation and repression, although coming short of physical harm or property damage. In *Sunset Line and Twine,* the NLRB characterized violence that falls short of physical injury as "an inimical superior force" which clearly conveys an "unspoken threat."[10]

Physical Confrontation

Perhaps the most dramatic of the varieties of violence portrayed in the cases is the clearly physical confrontation represented by incidents such as those described in the *Susan Evans* case, decided in 1964.[11] There, the violence was related not to a strike over unfinished contract negotiations but to picketing by the International Ladies' Garment Workers' Union (ILGWU), which was moving to represent workers at Susan Evans, Inc., a clothing manufacturing company.

A delivery boy named Irwin, of "very limited education and . . . wholly unable to appreciate the perils that faced him,"[12] arrived at the plant one day and upon trying to enter, was shoved back repeatedly by a picket. With the last shove, the picket "stamped Irwin's foot. A scuffle ensued, in which this picket threw Irwin to the ground and twice banged his head on the sidewalk."[13]

The union's hired organizer broke up the fight with the admonition to "let him go this time. He is pushing his luck."[14] Indeed, the phlegmatic Irwin apparently was "pushing his luck," for a week later he was assaulted again, battered, and his arm was broken.[15]

---

[9] See Chapter I, *supra,* for definitions and discussion of "violence."
[10] Sunset Line and Twine, 79 N.L.R.B. at 1500-02.
[11] Dressmakers Joint Council, International Ladies' Garment Workers' Union and Susan Evans, Inc., 146 N.L.R.B. 559 (1964).
[12] *Id.* at 565.
[13] *Id.* 561.
[14] *Id.*
[15] *Id.*

NLRB cases make frequent reference to such physical attacks on nonstrikers, and the common thread seems to be that the strikers find their strength in masses, while the danger to the nonstriking individual is in being caught alone by the strikers. The attacks have been directed most often at individuals or, at most, at a pair or trio of nonstrikers, while the attackers may number in the dozens or more.

Consider, for example, the similarity in "style" of the attackers in the *Evans* case, above, to those in *Long Construction Company,*[16] a case heard and decided at approximately the same time.

In *Long,* the violence apparently arose out of a dispute between the International Union of Operating Engineers (IUOE) and the employer, a Memphis, Tennessee, construction company.

> Seventy-five to 100 men . . . appeared at the jobsite. . . . The leader of the group initially walked over to employee Ray Garrett and "grabbed" him, and with 40 or 50 men of the group following, Garrett was taken down by the equipment shop where he was assaulted and knocked unconscious. A second employee, trying to take refuge in a nearby house trailer, was also knocked unconscious. The foreman who tried to help was hit with a pair of "knuckles." At the same time, the father of one of the assaulted employees was "being shot at by some men of the group."[17]

In *Evans,* in *Long,* and in many of the other cases discussed here, the power was clearly in numbers—numbers of attacking pickets whose assaults were directed at single nonstrikers.

In other cases, however, the power to do physical violence lay in the use of a weapon: perhaps a club,[18] or a baseball bat,[19] or in more than one instance, a gun.[20] In the *Holiday Press* case,[21] for example, a gun was pulled and fired at a nonstriker by a picket who had followed the employee from the plant. First, the pickets hurled a rock at the employee's car while it was halted at a stop sign. Moments later, when the employee stopped at a liquor store, one of the followers "pulled out a pistol and aimed it in [the nonstriker's] direction. [We] heard three shots fired."[22]

---

[16] International Union of Operating Engineers Local 513, et al. and Long Construction Company, 145 N.L.R.B. 554 (1963).

[17] *Id.* 558-59.

[18] Plastic Workers Local 929 et al. and Doughboy Recreational, Domain Industries, Inc., 200 N.L.R.B. 419 (1972).

[19] United Automobile, Aerospace, and Agricultural Implement Workers of America, UAW, Local 552 and Delavan Corp., 239 N.L.R.B. 312, 315 (1978).

[20] Lithographers and Photoengravers International Union, et al. and Holiday Press, a Division of Holiday Inns, Inc., 193 N.L.R.B. 11 (1971); and United Mine Workers District 31 et al. and Blue Ridge Coal Corp. et al., 129 N.L.R.B. 146 (1960).

[21] Holiday Press, 193 N.L.R.B. at 18.

[22] *Id.*

In *Milwaukee Independent Meat Packers Association,*[23] the weapons included pipes, bricks, chains, and rocks. One victim testified as follows:

> They had chains and pipes and stuff like this in their hands, and they were throwing rocks, and one of the occupants from the black Buick—I think he came out and threw a brick through my back windshield, and that came through just missing my shoulder and hitting the thing. And there was one man on my side of the car beating the window with a brick trying to get in.
>
> Another man came in on the passenger side—looked in, and he had about a thirty-inch pipe, and he smashed out my window on my passenger side of the car.
>
> He looked in, and he said: so, you want to—something to the effect that you want to take my job, you Mother F'er, and he reached in and opened up the door, and he pulled the lock up, and he pulled open the door and came in with the pipe, and he swung once, and I believe he was aiming at my head, but I sort of swerved back and hit the steering wheel busting the steering wheel, and then he stated something like—well, he was still swinging the pipe, and he swung a second time, and he was just about on top of me. He was like kneeling on the passenger seat, and at this time he might have been saying something. I don't know, but anyway, he swung, and I put my hand up to block it, and my hand was struck.
>
> I was still trying to fight the guy in the car. I still had my seatbelt on, and he said I should teach you a lesson, and he started busting up the inside of the car.
>
> He hit the tape player and stuff, and about this time I got my seatbelt off and got the door open and got out of the car, and once I got out, he was still in there, and he was ripping out my tape player and all these other good things.
>
> This guy with the pipe was just taking his time and just walking with my tape player back to the black Buick, and he asked me, he said: He swung the—he swung the pipe or, you know, he sort of threw it, you know, as they were getting back in the car, and he said—he called me like a chicken shit, son of a bee, and at this time I was on the sidewalk, and the pipe just missed me.[24]

The nonstriking employee had two broken fingers on the hand hit by the pipe, and the repair bill for his car was $1,500.

There are many, many more examples of highly confrontational, physical violence. Some are discussed in later chapters in the context of a particular union's history of violent behavior. Others can be typically represented by the following vignettes:

1. Cars of arriving employees were "hit with fists, picket signs, eggs, and rocks." The cars were "rocked back and forth in an

[23] Local 248, Meat & Allied Food Workers and Milwaukee Independent Meat Packers Association, 222 N.L.R.B. 1023 (1976).
[24] *Id.* at 1030-32.

effort to tip them over, while the driveway entrance and its approaches were showered with nails."[25]

2. A car full of pickets crashed a closed plant gate "at about 30-35 miles per hour, striking [a security guard] and knocking him to the ground."[26]

3. In the early morning hours of Halloween, 1977, pickets smashed the window of a moving vehicle, threw debris, rolled a chunk of timber up to block the company gate, broke windows of a company trailer and then set it afire by throwing flaming torches into it. They clubbed out the windows of an employee's car, then cut her hand, fingers, and arm. Finally, they beat her, breaking two of her ribs.[27]

4. A nonstriking employee, followed from work by a car full of pickets was beaten into unconsciousness with a tire iron and "woke up in a hospital with stitches being taken in his hand, arms, and both legs."[28]

5. A nonstriking employee was accused by a striker of taking the striker's job away from him; then the striker hit the nonstriker in the face and broke his jaw.[29]

6. A picket tossed a lighted cigarette through an open car window and the cigarette burned a nonstriking employee in the eye.[30]

7. At a Youngstown, Ohio, newspaper where American Newspaper Guild members were on strike after a breakdown in contract negotiations, the newspaper continued to publish and attempt to sell its product. One Sunday, the paper "opened its doors at 10:30 for the purpose of selling newspapers to the public. During the course of the next hour and 15 minutes numerous incidents occurred outside the front entrance when papers were forcibly grabbed from the purchasers, torn up, and strewn over the street and the sidewalk. In some instances, the purchasers were shoved, shouldered, jostled, roughed up, struck, threatened and chased."[31]

---

[25] Delavan, 239 N.L.R.B. at 314.

[26] *Id.* at 315.

[27] *Id.* at 317.

[28] Holiday Press, 193 N.L.R.B. at 19.

[29] United Steelworkers of America and Wright Line Division of Barry Wright Corp., 146 N.L.R.B. 71, 74-75 (1964).

[30] International Woodworkers of America, Local 3-3 and Western Wirebound Box Co., 144 N.L.R.B. 912, 920 (1963).

[31] American Newspaper Guild et al. and Vindicator Printing Company, 151 N.L.R.B. 1558, 1562 (1965).

How was such physical, confrontational violence combatted? The cases give little indication that it was actively fought at all. Indeed, because many of the incidents were quickly executed, it can be argued that little could have been done to prevent this sort of activity. In occasional cases, a supervisor or fellow nonstriker has attempted to aid the victim.[32] In a few more cases, although not in a large number, the NLRB reports indicate that police were asked to intervene.[33]

The indication of the NLRB accounts is that police have not necessarily been effective in curbing physical violence or in preventing its escalation. Furthermore, in the United Mine Workers (UMW) and International Brotherhood of Teamsters (Teamsters) cases discussed below and elsewhere in this study, the suggestion is that police presence at a picket site often results in nothing more than the violent activity taking place in some other location which the police cannot protect simultaneously with the picket site.

In the *Wright* case,[34] for example, local police were routinely used as escorts for nonstriking employees entering and leaving the plant. The picket line often numbered as many as seventy-five, and police were either present or called immediately to the site during incidents in which company officials were mauled, one nonstriker was beaten in the head, and others were pushed and shoved. While the actual presence or quick availability of police did not prevent the violence, it did appear to at least divert the strikers from more intense violence.[35]

In *Vindicator Printing,*[36] the police strategy was purported to be one of "neutrality." One day during the strike, the vice president of the company phoned the chief of police to ask for assistance because of congestion caused by cars and people in front of the building where picketing was going on. The police chief did not dispatch assistance, but rather suggested to the company official that it was, to a certain extent at least, the company's doing that the congestion existed, as it had been rumored that the company was bringing in outside distributors for its paper.

Indeed, the police chief had a solution to offer: limit the number of papers that the outside distributors would be issued to five. The company official accepted this "mediation" and for the rest of that day, at least, there was no further trouble, although subsequently, further confrontation and violence resulting in damage occurred.[37]

---

[32] *See, e.g.,* Long Construction Co., 145 N.L.R.B. 558.
[33] *See, e.g.,* Vindicator Printing Company, 151 N.L.R.B. 1558.
[34] Wright Line Division, 146 N.L.R.B. 73.
[35] *Id.* at 74.
[36] Vindicator Printing Company, 151 N.L.R.B. 1558.
[37] *Id.*

The administrative law judge (trial examiner) in this case took note of the police department's approach in a footnote:

> The record indicates that the police department maintained an attitude of *neutrality* throughout the strike and that no arrests were made even when assaults and other serious acts of misconduct occurred in the presence of police officers, as for example during the main mass picketing period from August 19 through 24 and during the incidents on September 13 [when customers as nonstrikers were assaulted].[38]

Although police intervention may not have been highlighted in some NLRB opinions, it seems to have been largely ineffectual where it does appear; and in many cases, the victims had to deal with violence and physical confrontation without help from the police.

In *Holiday Press,* for instance, a nonstriker arriving for work on his motorcycle was blocked by a 240-pound striker who stationed himself in the motorcycle's path. Lacking even the metal armor of an automobile for protection, the nonstriker found discretion to be the better part of valor. Confronted by the burly striker, he spun the cycle around and sped off, but found entrance through another gate.[39]

Similarly, in *Sunset Line and Twine,* when strikers flung open the door of a car that was about to be driven across the picket line and dared a female nonstriker to leave the car, she in turn double-dared the striker to come into the car, slammed the door shut, and proceeded through the picket line. On cross-examination before the trial examiner, the nonstriker was asked if she wanted to fight with the picket. She replied that she did, and that "if she had struck me the first lick I would have hit her, too."[40]

Nevertheless, the majority of cases indicate that nonstrikers or other victims who are able to contend with physical violence or the threat of it in the assertive way evidenced above are rare. Indeed, the reaction of the employee in the following incident, taken from the *Susan Evans* case, may be the more typical response to being victimized by union violence.

The Susan Evans plant had been raided by organizers for the International Ladies' Garment Workers Union (ILGWU), in an episode that the trial examiner characterized as a "wild melee." Three company employees were kidnapped and taken under forcible escort to the union offices where they were "interviewed" by the union's chief organizer who told them if they cooperated with the union, the union would try to get them jobs and if not, they would never work in the garment district again. "Wherever you are," the organizer vowed, "we

---

[38] *Id.* at 1561. (Emphasis added.)
[39] Holiday Press, 193 N.L.R.B. at 17.
[40] Sunset Line and Twine, 79 N.L.R.B. at 1437.

will come and get you and pull you out of the place wherever you are working." Eventually, the three were allowed to leave the union office, and two returned to work. The third, however, "was in such a state . . . that he was unable to return to work immediately. His hands were shaking so that he could not safely operate his cutting machine."[41]

This last incident introduces a second element, along with the physical, to the violence portrayed in the NLRB cases: violence in the form of psychological intimidation, extortion, and repression, where no physical injury is done. The cases discussed in the following section give further support to the intimidating nature and effect of some labor union violence which falls short of physical harm, but which achieves its purpose by engendering fear.

Psychological Intimidation

Psychological intimidation in the form of cumulative minor acts of violence, threats, and extortion pervades the NLRB cases. In many of these cases, no single incident taken by itself would be considered especially violent; but when taken together and viewed in the context of strike confrontation they can form an atmosphere of intimidation through fear. In some cases, the union objective is achieved through the cumulative effect of many apparently minor incidents. In others, the same effect is achieved through the extortionate practice of convincing the target, usually through example, that the threats made are real. An example is provided by the case involving a strike against Doughboy Recreational Domain Industries,[42] an Arkansas manufacturer of swimming pools and pool accessories.

In that case, at least one company employee was "convinced" to sign a union card after being told he "would be sorry" if he did not. The union extorted compliance with its activities from other employees by recording license plate numbers and threatening to track down the vehicles' owners,[43] by threatening one employee with clubs and sticks to "prevent" him from going to work,[44] by threatening to burn the plant down,[45] and by phoning one employee who had reported for work and telling her that she "should not have [done so]" and that she "would be sorry."[46] Other employees were brought to compliance

---

[41] Susan Evans, 146 N.L.R.B. at 561.
[42] Doughboy Recreational, Domain Industries, 200 N.L.R.B. 419.
[43] *Id.* at 421.
[44] *Id.*
[45] *Id.*
[46] *Id.* at 422.

after warnings that the union "was talking about burning homes of nonstrikers as well as the home of the plant manager."[47]

In none of these small incidents was physical violence actually reported, but the cumulative effect of the threats intimidated the employees and had the force of psychological violence. The threats were effective because all of the participants knew that every one of the actions threatened in their cases had actually been carried out in other strikes. The trial examiner had little difficulty finding unfair labor practices among the twenty-six separate charges which included both threats and extortion.[48]

In another example of psychological intimidation as a form of picket line violence, the union in the *Austin Company* case managed to prevent a certain employee from going to work three days in a row by applying extortionate psychological pressure.[49] The union was actually striking the Dow Chemical Company in Bay City, Michigan, but the Austin Company furnished construction and maintenance services to the Dow plant there, which was continuing to operate during the strike. One day during the strike, an Austin employee attempted to enter through a reserved gate, and was told by the union to "take a vacation for a day." The employee left promptly.

On the second day, he returned to attempt again to gain entry to the plant. The union agents suggested that since he had taken off the day before, "Why don't you take today off, too." He did. Finally, on the third day the frustrated employee again approached the pickets, and offered the promise that if they would let him in, he would not do work of striking employees. The picket's response was to lie down in front of his car and ask what he intended to do at that point. "Do you think I'm crazy?" he said. Then, for the third time, he left.[50]

At Giles and Ransome, a Pennsylvania retailer of earthmoving machinery, a union certification drive resulted in a strike.[51] A nineteen-year-old employee who wanted to go to work was told that he might "never reach the age of 21" if he continued his efforts.[52] Union agents told another nonstriker that he would be blacklisted by the union and prevented from working any union jobs if he crossed the picket line.[53]

Another example is found in the *Lavino* case.[54] E.J. Lavino & Co., a

---

[47] *Id.*

[48] *Id.* at 420-21.

[49] District 50, Allied and Technical Workers Local 14055 and Austin Co., 198 N.L.R.B. 1184 (1972).

[50] *Id.* at 1184-85.

[51] Local 542, International Union of Operating Engineers and Giles and Ransome, Inc., 139 N.L.R.B. 1169 (1962).

[52] *Id.* at 1172.

[53] *Id.* at 1173.

[54] Teamsters Local 115 and E.J. Lavino & Co., 157 N.L.R.B. 1637 (1966).

Philadelphia-based processor of manganese ore, was struck by the
Teamsters in 1966. Six of the thirty-five bargaining unit employees, as
well as the supervisors, had opted not to join the strike. The union
threw up its picket lines and steadfastly refused to let anyone pass
unless escorted by the Philadelphia Police Department's special "labor
squad."

> Pickets . . . blocked supervisor Manning's car . . . when he tried to enter
> without the labor squad. On one such occasion he and Supervisor Green-
> wald were threatened by striker Barrett, who picked up a brick and threat-
> ened to throw it through the car's windshield if they tried to enter without
> the labor squad. Barrett, holding a stick or a club in his hand, specifically
> told Greenwald not to try to get out through Allegheny Avenue but to go
> back and out with the labor squad.[55]

Here, as in *Giles and Ransome* and in *Austin,* no physical injury
resulted, but the coercive nature of the psychological intimidation is
clear. It is also clear from the NLRB record of other cases that the
supervisors and other employees who were kept from working by the
force of threats had every reason to fear that the violence being
threatened might actually be carried out. The union agents, in fact,
used the actuality of violence to lend power to their threats.

For example, early in the strike at Lavino, a nonstriker approaching
the picket line was asked where he was going. When he responded, "to
work," one picket hit him on the head while another went to the trunk
of a car, took out a piece of lumber, a hammer, a hatchet, and a
crowbar. The nonstriker was attacked with the hammer, and the other
weapons were used to knock out the windows of his car.

The nonstriker was hospitalized for a week as a result of the beating,
and the union used the incident to repress opposition to the strike from
other nonstriking employees. "That afternoon [the union stewards]
stood outside the plant and yelled to the nonstrikers, 'You saw what
happened . . . this morning. We're going to get you this afternoon.' "[56]
In the face of such circumstances, threats made could hardly be considered idle or merely rhetorical.

Nonstrikers and supervisors have not been the only targets. Threats
have been used internally, to maintain "solidarity" and to keep pickets
and other union members in line; suppliers, customers, and even casual
passers-by have also been threatened or intimidated. Typically, such
behavior is not found in the NLRB cases, because it is considered to be
outside the purview of "unfair labor practice," and is left to the
criminal and civil authorities. But the *Eastern Camera and Photo Cor-*

[55] *Id.* at 1640.
[56] *Id.* at 1641-42.

poration case is one which involves intimidation of customers.[57] The strike involved picketing at a retail store. Customers were shouted at and called names by the pickets as they entered and left the store. One customer was challenged to fight by the pickets, but he declined. Then, "after thinking about the matter, [he] went to a police station 'to find out how much abuse and challenge' he had to take from the pickets."[58] He also returned to the store to tell the management of the treatment customers were receiving at the hands of the pickets. On his return, the same picket made similar comments and a similar offer to fight. This time, the customer simply stood and said, "Well, go ahead and hit me." At this point, the psychological intimidation turned physical. The picket who had volunteered to fight "put down his shoulder, charged into [the customer] and knocked him aside."[59]

In this case, the trial examiner had found no violation of the labor statute, but the NLRB reversed that decision, noting that "customers who crossed the picket line were subjected to threats, bumping, pursuit down the street, and actual assaults" which added up to an unfair labor practice.[60]

One of the more vivid examples of the accumulation of a series of petty incidents into a concerted pattern of psychological intimidation is provided by the *Jamestown Sterling* case.[61] The United Furniture Workers of America (UFWA) had struck Jamestown Sterling, a furniture manufacturer, in the early 1960s, but the strike was not totally effective, and the plant remained open. Activities of the union during the strike included the following:

1. Respondents [the union] engaged in mass picketing in numbers estimated in excess of 100 in front of the office and employees' entrance to the plant and told the nonstrikers to go home.

2. Respondents engaged in mass picketing, formed a shoulder-to-shoulder formation, and engaged in shoving and kicking to keep the employees from entering.

3. A nonstriking employee was kicked by a union agent as he entered the plant.

4. A nonstriking employee was struck by a striker in the parking lot across the street from the plant.

---

[57] District 65, Retail, Wholesale & Department Store Union and Eastern Camera and Photo Corp. et al., 141 N.L.R.B. 991 (1963).

[58] *Id.* at 992.

[59] *Id.*

[60] *Id.* at 995.

[61] United Furniture Workers of America et al. and Jamestown Sterling Corporation, 139 N.L.R.B. 1279 (1962).

5. A nonstriking employee was threatened with physical harm by a striker as he left the plant.

6. A union agent told the company president that "If I had a gun I would shoot you."

7. A nonstriking employee was operating a high lift truck and its operation was blocked by a group of strikers.

8. A group of strikers surrounded a nonstriking employee's car and kicked the fender of the car.

9. A striker spat in a nonstriking employee's face when he left the plant.

10. A union agent threatened a company official: "I will meet you somewhere and punch you in the nose again."

11. ". . . ingress to the loading platform at Sterling was temporarily blocked by strikers so that a truck driven by Victor Anderson could not reach the platform on either December 19 or 20 . . . The blocking consisted of placing a car in the driveway and, after the car was moved by direction of a police officer, the driveway was blocked by placing railroad ties."

12. A company official was struck in the face when he went to the assistance of another nonstriking employee.

13. A nonstriking employee was kicked as he attempted to enter the plant.

14. Another nonstriking employee was kicked as he attempted to enter the plant, and the strikers attempted to prevent him from entering the plant, saying, "I ought to push your face in."

15. A nonstriking employee was shoved and his attempt to enter the plant impeded.

16. A union agent and unidentified strikers threw stones at employees working in the lumber yard of the plant.

17. A company official was kicked by the union's agent as he attempted to enter the plant.[62]

In addition to these incidents, the trial examiner noted other activity which in his opinion was "beyond the scope of the complaint,"[63] but which surely might have contributed to the cumulative inhibitory ef-

---

[62] *Id.* at 1282-83.
[63] *Id.* at 1283.

fect of the union's behavior. These other activities included name calling, threats of blackballing and of slowdown, threatening gestures made with a knife toward the tires of a nonstriking employee's auto, and a high level of generalized threats and obscene gestures.

It is obvious that many of these incidents, if looked at in isolation, would be minor in nature. It seems equally obvious, however, that when a union and its agents commit such a multitude of acts, albeit minor ones, within a relatively short time period,[64] the effect on participants and observers is apt to be a chilling one.[65]

In the *Milwaukee Independent Meat Packers Association* case, discussed earlier in terms of its physical violence, some acts did not result in physical harm; but consider the effect that the following conduct, also drawn from that case, would have on nonstrikers, particularly in light of the physical violence that did occur:

1. On one day, the strike captain climbed into the car of a nonstriking employee and told him that the union "cuts peoples' legs off," destroys homes, and shoots at trucks, "and we'll get you, too."[66]

2. The union persistently copied the license numbers of employees hired to replace the strikers, then posted the names and addresses of persons to whom the cars were registered at the union hall.[67]

3. Nonstrikers were threatened with words and weapons including large iron meathooks: "You know we use knives . . . and we'll show you how. . . ."[68]

4. To a pregnant employee, an agent said, "I'll see she never has that baby."[69] To another nonstriker: "Don't go into [that] plant or you'll never get home in one piece."[70]

5. A salesman was threatened with having his eyes cut out and his head cut off.[71]

---

[64] The acts took place in the fall and early winter, with the bulk of them occurring during a one-week period in December. *Id.* at 1282-83.

[65] It should be remembered here that the NLRB cases are not the most fertile ground for uncovering evidence of the effect of violent behavior, whether substantial or *de minimum.* The board need not determine such effect in order to find a violation.

[66] Milwaukee Independent Meat Packers, 222 N.L.R.B. at 1026.

[67] *Id.* at 1025.

[68] *Id.* at 1027.

[69] *Id.*

[70] *Id.* at 1028.

[71] *Id.*

6. An employee was told that if he went to work during the strike "his throat would be cut and he would be sent back to Chicago in a pine box."[72]

Although the NLRB does not discuss this cumulative nature of violence or picket line misconduct, there is recognition of its effect in such cases as *General Electric Company,*[73] in which the recording of license plate numbers by the union and its agents was commented upon by the trial examiner:

> Automobile license numbers of nonstriking employees were recorded. At the same time threats were voiced by pickets that "We will get you" and "We have your license number." . . . In the context of the threats and violence on the picket line it would have been reasonable for the nonstriking employees who were not cooperating with the strikers to have anticipated that the taking of the license numbers was for the purpose of identifying them for reprisals.[74]

Although the effect was noted, the trial examiner failed to find a violation of the law. This is one of the most serious failings of current labor law and its administration, for it frequently allows aggressive, violent, intimidative, and extortionate acts and threats to go unnoted within the context of collective bargaining. Some unions have built up reputations as being "tough" and prone to violence, and they rely upon these reputations to force settlements on their own terms. Some of these unions are proud of their ability to establish a "reign of terror" over the industry or area they "control."[75]

THE WORST OFFENDERS

Not all strikes are equally likely to be violent, nor are all unions equally prone to aggressive behavior. We have cataloged elsewhere some of the circumstances in which labor disputes tend to be more violent because of the characteristics of the demands being made, the environment in which the disputes take place, the nature of the industry, and the identity of the participants.[76] Many of those factors can be found in the cases litigated under section 8 (b) of the NLRA.

Among the nontrivial cases heard by the NLRB (and which did not involve intraunion activity or matters beyond our scope) were many which were part of a string of cases involving a single union or a single

---

[72] *Id.*

[73] Local 761, International Union of Electrical, Radio & Machine Workers and General Electric Company, 126 N.L.R.B. 123-24 (1960).

[74] *Id.* at 124.

[75] *See, e.g.,* Chapter IV, *infra.*

[76] *See* Chapter I, *supra.*

industry. A large proportion of the cases concern a few groups which have been before the NLRB repeatedly on violence-related charges. Principal among them are the United Mine Workers of America (UMW), the International Brotherhood of Teamsters, Chauffeurs, Warehousemen and Helpers of America (Teamsters), and several workers' unions in Puerto Rico. There have also been repeated appearances by construction industry unions, meatcutters, machinists, and, in recent years, various health care employees' unions, as well as others.

The violent activities associated with two of these groups, the UMW and the Teamsters, are covered in greater detail in Chapters IV and and VII of this study, where information from sources in addition to the NLRB hearings is used. To avoid unnecessary duplication they are not treated in detail here. But the patterns of violence found in each group are interesting, and are outlined below. The situation in Puerto Rico is also described.

The United Mine Workers

The following are representative examples of violence drawn from the NLRB case files involving strikes by the UMW and other mine-workers' unions:

1. *mass picketing* with its attendant problems, including for example, the invasion by 150 pickets of a mine where only three employees were present;[77]

2. issuing personal *threats of death or "trouble,"* including threats to a truck driver surrounded by 300 pickets that he would be beaten with a bulldozer clutch;[78]

3. *shooting, and the use of gunfire* to impress dissidents, such as shooting bullets through a man's house in the middle of the night;[79]

4. *killing or wounding,* including several deaths, among them a

---

[77] United Mine Workers District 2 et al. and Mercury Mining and Construction Corp. et al., 96 N.L.R.B. 1410 (1951). *See also,* District 11, United Mine Workers and Frank R. Hahn, 235 N.L.R.B. 757 (1978); District 20, United Mine Workers and Harbert Construction Corp., 192 N.L.R.B. 565 (1971); United Mine Workers District 31 and Bitner Fuel Company, 92 N.L.R.B. 953 (1950); and Burgreen Contracting Company, Inc. and Southern Labor Union, Local 101 and UMW District 20, 195 N.L.R.B. 1067 (1972).

[78] United Mine Workers District 2 et al. and M.F. Fetterolf et al., 103 N.L.R.B. 1572 (1953).

[79] United Mine Workers District 50 et al. and Tungsten Mining Corp., 106 N.L.R.B. 903, 919 (1953).

policeman who was trying to restore peace in a fracas occurring away from the strike site;[80]

5. *abduction or kidnapping,* such as the assault on a nonstriking female employee and her subsequent imprisonment in a scale house by pickets;[81]

6. *injuring or beating,* such as occurred when a throng of picketers dragged a nonstriker from a car in which he was a passenger, assaulted him, and broke his nose;[82]

7. using *explosives,* including the throwing of dynamite or some such substance at a group of mine officials, injuring one of them;[83]

8. destroying cars or trucks, forcing drivers to dump loads of coal, throwing nails on roads, throwing bricks through windshields, pouring molasses into gas tanks, slashing tires, etc.

The above list is exhaustive neither as to types of violence represented in the cases nor as to the individual cases in which it occurred. The items selected are merely representative, in our subjective evaluation, of the types of violent activities which appeared most frequently in the hearings brought before the NLRB concerning the UMW.

Violence by the UMW seems to center around mass picketing, intimidation of individual nonunion or nonstriking miners by means of threats, beatings, or destruction of their cars and trucks, bombings and sabotage of mine equipment, and assaults with weapons of different degrees of deadliness. Whether it occurs during strikes or organizational drives, most of the violence is directed against nonunion employers or employees, because unionized firms rarely try to continue to operate when a strike is in progress.

Teamster Violence

Representative examples found in the NLRB cases of the types of violence engaged in by the Teamsters during labor disputes include the following:

1. *following nonstrikers* on or off the job and forcing them off the

[80] United Mine Workers of America, Local 7425 et al. and Union Supply Company, 90 N.L.R.B. 436 (1950).

[81] United Mine Workers of America, District 31 et al. and B.H. Swaney Inc. et al., 95 N.L.R.B. 546 (1951).

[82] United Mine Workers District 31 et al. and Blue Ridge Coal Corp. et al., 129 N.L.R.B. 146 (1960).

[83] United Mine Workers District 2 and Solar Fuel Company, 170 N.L.R.B. 1581 (1968).

road;[84] intimidating their customers;[85] damaging their cars or trucks;[86] and assaulting them;[87]

2. engaging in *mass picketing,* and telling nonstrikers, for example, "We are Teamsters and we cannot be responsible for what happens to your car";[88]

3. *assaulting strikebreakers* by finger punching them, knocking them down, kicking them, and beating them;[89]

4. issuing *death threats* while brandishing weapons.[90]

The Teamsters, like the UMW, tend to use violence related to their trade. Many of the examples in the cases are of forceful acts or dangerous harassment directed against trucks and their drivers on the road and away from whatever protection might have been offered at the terminal or primary job site. Compared with the UMW, the Teamsters seem to be more mobile and tend to operate in smaller groups, except in those instances where the strike is against an industrial company rather than a trucking firm. At industrial sites and terminals where mass picketing was used, the nature of the violence was similar to that found in the mining regions.

Puerto Rican Labor Unions

Tactics such as those seen in the UMW and Teamsters cases discussed above have been repeated and expanded upon by unions in Puerto Rico.[91] The bulk of the cases involve a single union, the *Unión Nacional de Trabajadores* (National Workers' Union—*Trabajadores*), although the *Tronquistas* (Teamsters), the *Unión de Periodistas Artes Graphicas y Ramas Anexas* (the Newspaper Guild), the *Unión de Operadores y Canteros de la Industria del Cemento de Ponce* (Union of Stonecutters and Operators of the Cement Industry of Ponce—Cement

---

[84] Teamsters Local 536 and the Connecticut Foundry Company, 165 N.L.R.B. 916 (1967).

[85] Local 456, International Brotherhood of Teamsters, Chauffers, Warehousemen, and Helpers of America and Strauss Paper Company, 149 N.L.R.B. 49 (1964).

[86] Teamsters Local 115 and E.J. Lavino & Co., 157 N.L.R.B. 1637 (1966).

[87] Teamsters Local 783 and Coca Cola Bottling Company of Louisville, 160 N.L.R.B. 1776 (1966).

[88] Teamsters, Chauffeurs, Helpers and Taxicab Drivers, Local 327 and Hartmann Luggage Company, 173 N.L.R.B. 1403-04 (1968).

[89] Local 810, International Brotherhood of Teamsters, Chauffeurs, Warehousemen and Helpers of America and Russell Plastics Technology, Inc., 235 N.L.R.B. 40 (1978).

[90] General Truck Drivers, Warehousemen & Helpers of America Local 5, and Union Tank Car Co., 172 N.L.R.B. 137 (1968); 178 N.L.R.B. 431 (1969).

[91] *Unión de Tronquistas* (Teamsters) and Associated Federal Hotels International, 193 N.L.R.B. 591 (1971).

Workers), and the International Association of Machinists and Aerospace Workers (IAM) are also players in this collection of cases.

The most graphically described of these Puerto Rican cases shows violent behavior clearly designed to repress both employees and patrons of an employer, the Associated Federal Hotels International.[92] There, the *Trabajadores,* which represented most of the hotel's 400 employees in a resort area of Puerto Rico, struck over an unresolved grievance. The violence associated with the strike included a mass invasion of the hotel's casino by strikers armed with sticks, clubs, and metal pipes, and attacks on the hotel property, and on nonstriking employees, hotel supervisors, and guests.

The NLRB's trial examiner reconstructed the casino incident from the credited testimony of witnesses:

> At or about . . . midnight . . . a group of people came bursting into the hotel lobby armed with metal pipes, sticks and clubs, shouting "to the casino" and heading for the casino door. . . . The casino was full with patrons, and the gambling in progress at the gaming tables, when the casino was thrown into an uproar of shouting, violence and confusion, as a group of the intruders from the lobby burst through the casino door and the inner corridor and ran around the circular arrangement of the gaming tables with pipes and sticks, striking at croupiers, hitting some, and some of the patrons unable to dodge the blows, knocking over tables and chairs and strewing chips all over the place. At the same time rocks were thrown from outside through the casino windows showering glass and rocks inside. In general the employees and guests of the casino were put in terror of the physical injury inflicted on some. Three of the croupiers were injured by the attackers. . . . Croupier Gonzalez Comacho saw at least one of the women patrons of the casino hurt, when hit on the leg by a blow aimed at a croupier who evaded it.[93]

The violence, which had begun suddenly on the heels of an unsuccessful meeting between the company and the union over the grievance, ended just as abruptly when the casino's assistant manager got a pistol from the cashier's drawer and fired two shots into the carpet.[94] Although the incident lasted for only a few minutes, there was an understandably large impact on the hotel's operations. The casino was in shambles,

> guests were on the floor or under tables, some hurt, some crying; several croupiers were hurt; one of the intruders . . . was hurt and stretched out on the floor; tables, chairs and stools were overturned and some broken; gambling chips having the value of money were strewn all over the place; and broken glass was everywhere.[95]

---

[92] *Id.*
[93] *Id.* at 595.
[94] *Id.*
[95] *Id.* at 592.

That day and the next, almost fifty hotel guests checked out prematurely.

The cases discussed here involving the *Trabajadores* were all decided in a single year, 1975, and three of the four involved organizational activity. In the *Jacobs Constructors Company* case,[96] the *Trabajadores* were attempting to organize the engineering and construction company. Among the tactics employed were:

1. threats to a project superintendent that his "face would be busted" if he went to work;[97]

2. use of bands of strikers mingling among employees and carrying pipes and sticks, in order to back up the no-recognition, no-work position;[98]

3. threats by hammer-wielding union agents.[99]

In *Catalytic Industrial Maintenance Co., Inc.,*[100] forty-eight separate incidents of either physical or psychological intimidation were charged as violations of section 8(b)(1)(A). Included among these were:

1. blockage of a tanker full of a volatile explosive destined for the construction site, so that it did not arrive at a safe location inside the construction site fence until three days later when police escorted it in;

2. repeated bomb threats;

3. promises to "cut" the personnel manager;

4. battery of a utility supervisor who was punched in the jaw;

5. threats made over a public address system that the plant would be blown up with all the workers in it;

6. rock throwing and damage to cars;

7. mob marches with participants armed with clubs and other weapons.[101]

In the administrative law judge's opinion, this last incident was "a serious confrontation" in which consequences were avoided only by the intervention of police.

---

[96] *Unión Nacional de Trabajadores,* et al. and Jacobs Constructors Company of Puerto Rico, 219 N.L.R.B. 405 (1975).
[97] *Id.* at 407.
[98] *Id.* at 408
[99] *Id.* at 409.
[100] *Unión Nacional de Trabajadores* and *Comité Organizador Obreros en Huelga de Catalytic* and Catalytic Industrial Maintenance Co. Inc., 219 N.L.R.B. 414 (1975).
[101] *Id.* at 423-24.

In *Macal Container Corporation,*[102] the *Trabajadores* again were attempting to organize, this time employees of a manufacturer of paper boxes. In the process, the union president pushed the company president down a flight of stairs at the plant and in response to pleas of the injured man's wife that he had a heart condition and "could die" unless they left him alone, one of the union men said, "F--- him, let him die." The couple managed to escape, but both required prolonged hospitalization.[103]

The union also did its best to dissuade a potential buyer of the company: "The street is lonely at night." "Don't forget, sometimes you have to walk alone in the street." "Don't go in the factory or you might come out in a coffin."[104]

In still another incident, an employee who wanted to go to work was flatly informed, "This is *Unión Nacional* and we kill people. So leave."[105] The employee took the hint.

In the last of the *Trabajadores* cases to be discussed here, the union had just been certified as the bargaining agent for the employees of the Carborundum Company of Puerto Rico. Bargaining on the first contract was halted when the president of the union stated at the bargaining table, "I'm about to start slapping people here."[106]

The company, expressing fear about continuing negotiations in the face of this and similar threats, made an agreement with a union official to continue negotiations in the Department of Labor's San Juan office. A meeting date was set, but it never occurred. On the morning of the day it was to take place,

> [the union president] and three union agents entered the employer's plant against the instructions of the plant guard. Once inside . . . they physically attacked and beat a supervisor and an employee. As the four union officials left the scene of the beatings, [one of them] stated, "This one we are about to kill," referring to [a particular employee] who was slumped on the floor.[107]

The board here, as it has also done in UMW and Teamster cases, felt compelled at least to take note of the violent proclivity of the *Trabajadores:*

---

[102] *Unión Nacional de Trabajadores* et al. and Macal Container Corp., 219 N.L.R.B. 429 (1975).

[103] *Id.* at 431.

[104] *Id.* at 432.

[105] *Id.* at 433.

[106] *Unión Nacional de Trabajadores* et al. and the Carborundum Company of Puerto Rico et al., 219 N.L.R.B. 862 (1975).

[107] *Id.* at 863.

This labor organization, by its brutal and unprovoked physical violence in this case and by its extensive record of similar aggravated misconduct in other recent cases, has evinced an intent to bypass the peaceful methods of collective bargaining contemplated in the Act and commonly accepted and practiced by labor organizations and employers throughout the country. It has consistently exhibited an utter disregard for the orderly and lawful processes available under the Act, and has instead deliberately resorted to self-help through violence.[108]

The case involving the Puerto Rico Newspaper Guild and *El Mundo, Inc.,* predates the *Trabajadores* cases discussed above, but the tactics used by the union are similar, if not as aggressively violent, and their cumulative nature may well have achieved the desired effect. The union had been recognized and a strike ensued at an impasse in bargaining. The company charged the union with twenty separate violations of section 8(b)(1)(A), including:

1. an incident in which a striker shouted, "We won't let you in" to an employee attempting to go to work, then rushed toward the nonstriker's car, brandishing a large rock over his head. The nonstriker left;[109]

2. an incident in which a circulation district manager and supervisor were prevented from leaving the plant without signing union cards. When they repeatedly refused to sign, they were held as captives in the plant for fifteen days before being taken out by helicopter;[110]

3. a later incident in which a car carrying the district manager was attacked by about fifteen strikers swinging sticks, rocks, and metal pipe. The strikers then stoned the car and its occupants, breaking all the windows of the car.[111]

Similar violence was seen in a later case involving another Puerto Rican union, the Cement Workers, in a strike against the Puerto Rican Cement Company. The union used mob attacks, assaults, and fire-bombings to intimidate nonstriking employees. Specifically:

1. pickets marched "with shovels, sticks, rakes and other equipment susceptible of being used as a weapon. Several pickets paraded on a company road near the plant gates carrying shovels,

---

[108] *Id.*
[109] Puerto Rico Newspaper Guild Local 225 and El Mundo, Inc., 201 N.L.R.B. 423-24 (1973).
[110] *Id.* at 425.
[111] *Id.* at 426

heavy street brooms and large pieces of timber that best could be characterized as clubs";[112]

2. a nonstriker was beaten: "While one of the strikers grabbed [him] and put an arm lock around his neck, another slugged him in the eye and hand";[113]

3. the union, which kept explosives in a truck near the picket site, was accused of firebombing nonstrikers' homes.[114]

Finally, in the *General Electric* case,[115] the union vandalized buses hired by the company to bring employees into the plant. The company had boarded up the bus windows in hopes of avoiding damage and injury, but the strikers repeatedly pelted employees with stones as they disembarked.[116] On another day, the bus was firebombed when the strike leader's right-hand man

> threw a can of inflammable liquid into the bus through its door and nearby open window, drenching it and a number of its occupants. [A second striker] threw a lighted object at the part of the bus that had been drenched with the liquid. The bus immediately burst into flames. At least four identified non-strikers, besides other unidentified persons, were burned as a result of the flames which engulfed the inside of the bus.[117]

CONCLUSIONS

Incidents of violence occur with depressing regularity in the NLRB's hearings on section 8(b)(1)(A) cases. The cases are conducted in a manner similar to court proceedings on testimonial evidence, much of which is graphically explicit. Examination of the cases, therefore, yields valuable insight into not only what goes on in the name of organized activity on the picket line, but also what impression it makes on the participants.

The examples provided by the NLRB cases are only a small sample of the violence which other evidence assures us is a routine part of the collective bargaining process. Because of the civil nature of NLRB proceedings and the limited remedies available, incidents at both ends of the spectrum of violence are eliminated. Minor cases or cases which

---

[112] *Unión de Operadores y Canteros de la Industria del Cemento de Ponce* and Puerto Rican Cement Co., Inc., 231 N.L.R.B. 171, 173 (1977).

[113] *Id.* at 175.

[114] *Id.* at 176.

[115] International Association of Machinists and Aerospace Workers et al. and General Electric Company Circuit Protective Devices Dept., Caribe Plant Operations, et al., 189 N.L.R.B. 50 (1971).

[116] *Id.* at 53.

[117] *Id.* at 55-56.

contain only a small number of incidents would probably never be brought; cases involving serious incidents—murder, for example—for which culpability is clear are usually handled by the criminal courts; and finally, cases that contain findings of fact about violent incidents are ajudicated by administrative law judges, whose determinations are not part of the case record unless they are contested by one side or the other.

Nowhere in the 300-or-so cases heard by the NLRB is there a deep analysis of the nature of violence or its causes and cures. Indeed, that is not the duty of the NLRB. It is concerned with a lesser standard of conduct: whether the activity in question has coerced or may coerce or restrain employee behavior in the exercise of rights under the NLRA. Clearly, activity need not rise to violence in order to restrain or coerce, and for that reason, perhaps among others, the substantive discussion of labor union violence by the NLRB, trial examiners, and administrative law judges in these cases is minimal.

Nevertheless, where they occur, the graphic portrayals of aggression, intimidation, repression, injury, destruction, and property damage found in the cases focus attention on the use of violence as a deliberate tactic in collective bargaining situations, and hint at the totality of the practice.

Some of the cases illustrate direct and harmful physical force. Others show that the accumulation of many minor acts, none of which is particularly heinous by itself, can result in psychological violence that is as intimidative, extortionate, or repressive as physical force.

The cases also illustrate that although the specific tactics—for example, the use of explosives, or shooting at nonstrikers' homes—may differ from one union group to another, the broad goal in each case is to control opposition, to instill fear, to sway behavior, and to establish the union as a powerful entity in the eyes of co-workers, the employer, and the public.

The cases also suggest that the intervention of police or other civil authorities has been of limited success in quelling union violence. This indication may be due, in part, to the cases simply not taking note of instances in which police were notably successful, or to the inability of the police to provide protection away from the central focus of the strike. But it is also true that in at least some instances, civil authorities have adopted such a "neutral" attitude toward the picket line activity that they refused to make arrests even after nonstrikers were attacked by identifiable individuals in plain sight.[118]

---

[118] *See* notes 30 and 35, *supra*, and accompanying text.

Finally, the cases show no significant change in either the quantity and quality of labor violence or its treatment by the NLRB, the trial examiners, and administrative law judges, from the very first case heard in 1947 to the most recent one. The two factors are related. Violence unpunished is violence encouraged, and we can expect a continuation of it for as long as that situation remains.

The problem, of course, does not all lie with the procedures of the NLRB, or with the quality of its administration of the labor relations acts. A good portion of the blame must be shouldered by the laws themselves, and by their lack of recognition of a problem which is as old as organized labor.

CHAPTER III

Recent Incidents of Strike Violence: A Listing

The line of cases heard and adjudicated by the National Labor Relations Board (NLRB) under section 8(b)(1)(A) of the National Labor Relations (Taft-Hartley) Act (NLRA) demonstrates, if nothing else, that violence is no stranger to strikes and walkouts. Almost every variety of physical force and psychological intimidation is illustrated in them, including fearsome threats and such criminal acts as murder, attempted murder, aggravated assault, assault, battery, abduction and unlawful detention, arson, malicious mischief, trespassing, and vandalism.

The cases show many examples of violence used to intimidate or coerce nonstrikers, replacement workers, managerial or supervisory personnel, nonunion individuals, customers, suppliers, and others who are either part of the bargaining confrontation or able to bring pressure on the negotiations. Fear for personal safety, fear for the safety of others, and fear for the security of property were exploited with apparent deliberateness to influence the outcome of the economic contest of the strike.

The illustrations of violence in the NLRB cases do have some limitations, however. It is, for instance, difficult to tell from a reading of the cases how extensively it is used in strikes. The NLRB cases containing reference to strike violence number only about fifty-five, and cover a period spanning almost thirty-five years. Lacking evidence to the contrary, it might be argued that the violence seen in them represents only aberrations from the normal processes of labor negotiations.

OTHER SOURCES OF INFORMATION

Chapter II pointed out that the NLRB is limited by its complicated hearing process and by the remedies it can provide, and that as a result, the NLRB's line of cases is drawn from a narrow cross section of the violence that actually occurs in strikes. Some other source of information on labor violence that is broader in scope is therefore needed.

49

Additional accounts of individual incidents do exist in court records and newspaper reports, but until recently there was no compilation which allowed estimation of the scope of the violent activity in routine labor relations across the spectrum of unions and industries.

The National Right to Work Legal Defense Foundation (NRTWLDF) is an educational foundation associated with the National Right to Work Committee. As part of its work in defending the rights of individuals as they may be impaired by labor relations laws or practice, the foundation collected reports from the popular press of violent activities associated with labor disputes. In 1981, it began to compile its collection into a computerized violence data base.

The data base is an ongoing project of the foundation and contains records of incidents that have occurred since an arbitrary starting date of 1975. In early 1982, a printout of that data base was made, and the results were made available to the authors of this study. Statistical materials contained in this chapter, unless noted to the contrary, are all drawn from that printout.

Because of the nature of the collection process, the foundation's data base is somewhat haphazard. Nevertheless, it shows no evidence of bias. All of its records are drawn from the popular press or from public documents—and it is the only known sampling that fulfills the need to establish the scope and frequency of violent occurrences during strikes.

Overall, the printout shows records of 2,598 incidents of violence associated with labor relations and occurring between 1975 and 1981. All of the incidents received coverage by the press and were brought to the attention of either the foundation or its clipping services. The entire printout is too lengthy to reproduce here, but because we shall be drawing some inferences and conclusions from it, we will describe it more fully and point out some of its strengths and weaknesses before proceeding.

The Foundation's Violence Data Base

The violence data base is a series of records of violent events involving labor union members or labor union officials. Each individual record summarizes a separate incident or a related series of incidents from information found in magazine articles, newspapers, television news program transcripts, or trade association journals.

One of the weaknesses of this or any catalog of violent events is the determination of what constitutes a separate event or incident. If two men on a picket line each throw a rock, one might argue with equal logic that a single violent event has occurred or that two violent events have occurred. The same problem exists with respect to one picket throwing two different rocks, or with respect to a thrown rock that both breaks a window and injures a person: how many violent events have occurred in each situation?

The counting task in the violence data base is further complicated by the fact that the information used is from secondary sources—that is, newspaper accounts and similar reports—which may not consistently decide these questions, and which may describe the same activity from different perspectives using different words, or may describe it on different days. The worst situation is one in which relatively minor violent activities, none of which merit special press coverage, occur throughout a lengthy strike. In such a case, the likelihood is great that the accumulative violence of the strike would be overlooked.

The method selected by the foundation to overcome this classification problem, though far from perfect, is adequate. The foundation normally followed whatever classification system was used by its sources unless unrelated types of violence occurred. Thus, if a newspaper reported "vandalism, arson throughout 6-month strike," that was counted as a single incident, because no reasonable way existed to identify the separate components of the incident. But if the source reported, "nonstrikers' cars were vandalized in the company parking lot, and shots were fired into a supervisor's home," that might have been counted as two incidents, one covering the vandalism and the other covering the shooting.

Naturally, this method leads to both undercounting and overcounting: undercounting, because many different but unidentifiable violent acts were undoubtedly involved in the report covering six months of a strike; overcounting, because reports covering different aspects of the same confrontation might be treated as independent events.

Through cross-referencing, multiple accounts of singular acts were usually screened from the listing. Therefore, if six different newspapers had reported on the dynamiting of a construction trailer on the same day during the same strike, five of the reports would have been screened out. On the other hand, because the foundation is interested in attribution of violence to individual unions, if the sources identified different labor organizations as being involved in the same incident, it would have been recorded as a listing to each organization so identified. Thus, if both the area building trades council and members of, say, the International Brotherhood of Electrical Workers (IBEW) were implicated in the dynamiting, the incident would have been recorded in the data base for each organization.

On balance, the listings appear to be relatively accurate in reporting major incidents—such as a bombing or a shooting—but less accurate in reporting minor incidents. Several other constraints might also be noted:

1. The data base is ongoing, and therefore incomplete. The files are updated continuously, not only with new information, but also with newly found information on incidents going back to 1975. (The number of listings in the data base grew by 60 percent in the six months preceding the March 1982 printout used here, but future growth will undoubtedly be slower.)

2. The listing includes incidents concerning intraunion and interunion violence, which is not directly pertinent to this study.

3. In a very few of the listings, incidents are reported for which no details of violence are presented, or for which the activity reported would not fit our definition of physical or psychological violence—for example a passive sit-in by pickets who perhaps impeded but did not deny access to the plant by nonstrikers.

4. Incidents in which strikers were the greater victims of violence (*e.g.,* when a picket seeking to block a nonstriker's car was run over by it) are also included.

5. In spite of the foundation's best efforts to avoid double counting, at times the same incident does appear to have been counted twice.

Despite these problems, the foundation's data base provides the best compilation available on the quantity and severity of violence in contemporary labor relations. In the tables that follow, we have not attempted to correct or modify individual records to account for minor discrepancies. Where it appears that the information might be misleading, we have included footnotes containing explanations. The names used for labor organizations in the tables and elsewhere in this chapter are sometimes abbreviated or descriptive. The official counterparts for these names are listed in Appendix A.

Information in the Data Base

Each record in the data base contains the information listed in Table III-1. (Unless otherwise noted, the source of information for all tables in this chapter is the NRTWLDF Data Base.)

Extent of Violence

The foundation's data base printout contains 2,598 records of incidents of violence involving labor unions for the years 1975 through 1981. The total number of incidents occurring each year is shown in Table III-2. Although the table indicates that violence is generally on the upswing, it is likely that some earlier incidents were overlooked, so it is probably safer to conclude simply that violence is not demonstrably decreasing with the passage of time.[1]

TABLE III-1
Data Base Record Structure

Information	Sample
Record number	1639 _____
Union involved and local chapter	Steelworkers, Local 3178
State and city of incident	PA, Muhlenburg
Year, month, and day of incident	81 [unreported]
Employer	Empire Steel Casting
Property damage? (Y = yes; N = no)	Y
details	Company foreman had his home bombed.
Injury? (Y = yes; N = no)	N
details	
Yes/No items:	
Private employer?	Y
Arrests made?	N
Convictions reported?	N
Police on the scene?	N
Strike in progress?	Y
Union officials involved?	N
Source and date of information	Reading *Eagle*, 03/30/81

TABLE III-2
Incidents of Violence by Year, 1975-1981

Year	Number
1975	386
1976	230
1977	234
1978	248
1979	483
1980	442
1981	575

---

[1] Both the economic and the political climates in which bargaining takes place changed with the recession and high unemployment rates in 1982. Under our general theory of violence, other things being equal, we expect that the incidence of violence that will be reported for the year 1982 will probably be lower than it was during the immediately preceding years. At the time of writing, we have no way of statistically testing this theory.

Involvement of Different Labor Organizations

Judging from the listings, violence seems to be an inherent part of labor relations and the collective bargaining process, or at least its use is widely distributed. The 2,598 incidents in the data base involve 131 different unions or labor associations. Furthermore, of the 44 U.S. unions with more than 100,000 members, 38 were involved in at least one violent incident in the listings.[2] Of the six which were not, four are civil service public employee unions: the American Federation of Government Employees (AFGE), with 260,000 members; the American Postal Workers Union (APWU) with 252,000 members; the National Association of Letter Carriers (NALC), with 227,000 members; and the National Association of Government Employees (NAGE) with 150,000 members.

The other two unions for which no incidents were reported are the American Federation of Musicians (AFM), with 330,000 members, and the Brotherhood of Maintenance of Way Employees (BMWE), with 119,000 members. All of the remaining large unions and labor organizations were involved in at least one incident, although they were not equally involved, of course. The ten for whom the greatest number of incidents were reported account for 51 percent of all incidents of known origin, and the twenty involved in the greatest number of incidents account for 74 percent.[3] Table III-3 lists those twenty unions in decreasing order of number of incidents.

Violence Index

Because there are so many more teamsters than there are, say, bakery workers, we would expect to find a larger number of incidents associated with the former, so it might perhaps be unfair to characterize the Teamsters as the most violent union based solely on the count of incidents in which teamsters participated. Table III-4 lists the twenty largest unions and the number of incidents in which each was involved. It shows that the Teamsters, in fact, rank first in both counts, but that the number of violent incidents otherwise is not always proportional to membership. On the basis of membership alone, if the National Education Association (NEA), for example, were involved in violence at the same rate as the Teamsters, it would have to have been involved in about 380 incidents instead of the 80 found in the data base.

---

[2] Membership based on reports submitted to the U.S. Department of Labor. U.S. DEPARTMENT OF LABOR, BUREAU OF LABOR STATISTICS, DIRECTORY OF NATIONAL UNIONS AND EMPLOYEE ASSOCIATIONS, 1977 (1979).

[3] In 205 of the 2,598 listings, the labor organization involved is not identified. This leaves 2,493 incidents of known origin.

TABLE III-3

*Twenty Labor Organizations Most Frequently Involved
in Violent Incidents, 1975-1981*

Rank	Organization[a]	Number of Incidents
1	Teamsters	384
2	Mine Workers (UMW)	204
3	Steelworkers (USW)	130
4	Auto Workers (UAW)	128
5	State, County and Municipal Employees (AFSCME)	116
6	Machinists (IAM)	104
7	Food and Commercial Workers[b] (UFCW)	83
8	Teachers (NEA)	80
9	Fire Fighters (IAFF)	78
10	Building Trades Councils[c]	70
11	Electrical Workers (IBEW)	68
12	National Union of Hospital and Health Care Employees	57
13	Laborers (LIUNA)	51
14	Oil, Chemical and Atomic Workers (OCAW)	51
15	Operating Engineers (IUOE)	50
16	Carpenters (CJA)	45
17	Teachers (AFT)	40
18	Service Employees (SEIU)	37
19	Iron Workers (BSOIW)	36
20	Steel Haulers (FASH)[d]	32

[a] The full names of the unions listed in this table are found in Appendix A.

[b] Includes incidents attributed separately to Meatcutters and to Retail Clerks before merger of the two organizations into the Food and Commercial Workers Union.

[c] The Building Trades Councils are not "unions," but strikes in the construction industry are frequently carried out in the name of a council. Nineteen of the seventy incidents involving councils also involved some identifiable construction union, and to that degree, the total number of violent incidents may be overstated. On the other hand, the remaining fifty-one incidents represent undercounting of incidents which would otherwise be attributable to individual building trades unions.

[d] The Fraternal Association of Steel Haulers is not a labor organization, *per se*, but rather an association of independent owner-operators which shares some characteristics, such as collective bargaining, with labor unions.

Alternatively, if the United Mine Workers of America (UMW) were involved in violence to the same degree as the NEA, in proportion to its membership the UMW would have been involved in only about 12 incidents, instead of the 204 found in the data base.[4]

---

[4] Actually, the membership numbers used here, drawn from the Bureau of Labor Statistics' *Directory* (*see* note 2 *supra*), are suspect in the sense that significant over-reporting of membership is present in them, as well as distortion from union to union. *See* A. J. THIEBLOT, AN ANALYSIS OF THE DATA ON UNION MEMBERSHIP, (1978). Nevertheless, the figures should be sufficiently accurate for general conclusions to be drawn.

TABLE III-4
*Membership Size (1977) and Incidents
of Violence Noted, 1975-1981*

Organization[a]	Membership (in thousands)	Incidents of Violence
Teamsters	1,889	384
Teachers (NEA)	1,887	80
Auto Workers (UAW))	1,358	128
Steelworkers (USW)	1,300	130
Food and Commercial Workers[b] (UFCW)	1,209	83
Electrical Workers (IBEW)	924	68
Machinists (IAM)	917	104
Carpenters (CJA)	820	105[c]
State, County and Municipal Employees (AFSCME)	750	116
Laborers (LIUNA)	627	51[c]
Service Employees (SEIU)	575	37
Clothing and Textile Workers (ACTWU)	502	10
Communications Workers (CWA)	483	21
Teachers (AFT)	446	40
Hotel and Restaurant Workers (HERE)	432	11
Operating Engineers (IUOE)	420	50[c]
Ladies' Garment Workers (ILGWU)	365	16
Musicians (AFM)	330	0
Mine Workers (UMW)	277	204
Transportation (UTU)	265	8

[a] The full names of the unions listed in this table are found in Appendix A.

[b] Figures are for the combination of the Meatcutters and the Retail Clerks.

[c] These figures may be understated by some portion of the seventy unallocated incidents in which the building trades council was involved.

In most cases, the largest unions figured most heavily in the violence listings. In addition to those listed in Table III-4, the United Association of Journeymen and Apprentices of the Plumbing and Pipe Fitting Industry (PPF) (228,000 members), the International Association of Bridge, Structural and Ornamental Iron Workers (BSOIW) (179,000 members), the Oil, Chemical and Atomic Workers (OCAW) (177,000 members), the International Association of Fire Fighters (IAFF) (174,000 members), and the Amalgamated Transit Union (ATU) (150,000 members) were each involved in more than twenty incidents.

Five other groups had high participation in violence—to the extent of being involved in more than twenty incidents—but could not be included in Table III-4 either because they are not membership groups as such, or because membership figures are not accurately available, or because the unions are reported to be small. Those five are: various building trades councils (70 incidents), the Hospital and Health Care Employees (57 incidents), the United Farm Workers (UFW) (44 in-

TABLE III-5

Violence Relative to Union Membership
(in unions with over 100,000 members, 1978–1981)

Organization[a]	Violent Incidents	1977 Membership (thousands)	Violent Incidents Per 10,000 Members
Teamsters	384	1,889	2.03
Mine Workers	204	277	7.36
Steelworkers	130	1,300	1.00
Auto Workers	128	1,358	.94
State, County and Municipal Workers	116	750	1.55
Machinists	104	917	1.13
Food and Commercial Workers	83	1,209	.69
Teachers (NEA)	80	1,887	.42
Fire Fighters	78[b]	174	4.48
Building Trades Councils	70	N.A.	N.A.
Electrical (IBEW)	68	924	.74
Hospital and Health Care	57	100[c]	5.70
Laborers	51[d]	627	.81
Oil, Chemical and Atomic Workers	51	177	2.88
Operating Engineers	50[d]	420	1.19
Carpenters	45[c]	820	.55
Teachers (AFT)	40	446	.90
Service Employees	37	575	.64
Iron Workers	36[d]	179	2.01
Steel Haulers	32	100[c]	3.20

[a] The full names of the unions listed in this table are found in Appendix A.
[b] May contain some incidents better attributable to local firefighting unions.
[c] Estimated.
[d] May be understated by some proportion of construction trade incidents attributed to building trades councils.

cidents), the Fraternal Association of Steel Haulers (FASH) (32 incidents), and the Newspaper Guild (24 incidents).

The building trades councils, umbrella groups for the construction unions, have no definable membership as such. Of the remaining four, the FASH is not an employee association, so its membership is not available. The Hospital and Health Care Employees probably number under 100,000, the Newspaper Guild has on the order of 32,000 members, and the Farm Workers (UFW) were reported to number only about 12,000 members in 1977. Based on this, the Farm Workers may hold the distinction of having the most violent union for its size in the country, and the Newspaper Guild is not far behind. (This comment reflects only on the quantity of violence, not on its severity.)

In order to examine relative violence—that is, violence with respect to membership size—more closely, Table III-5 was constructed. It shows the number of violent incidents per ten thousand members for the twenty unions that had more than 100,000 members each, and that were involved in the largest number of incidents.

As the table demonstrates, on this basis the United Mine Workers (UMW) has the greatest involvement in violence relative to its size, with over seven incidents per 10,000 members. (By comparison, the average for all of the unions in the data base with over 100,000 members was 1.2.) Second most involved is the Fire Fighters, whose involvement in 78 incidents—fewer than shown by the National Education Association (NEA), the United Auto Workers (UAW), the United Steelworkers (USW), the Food and Commercial Workers (UFCW), or the International Association of Machinists (IAM)—was perhaps magnified by the relatively small size of the union's membership.

Special note should again be made of the Hospital and Health Care Employees, the Steel Haulers, the Farm Workers, and the Newspaper Guild (the last two of which are not listed in Table III-5). If the Hospital and Health Care Employees number fewer than 100,000, then their union would have a violence index of at least 5.7, which would place it no lower than second on the list, after the Mine Workers' union. The Hospital and Health Care Employees would be followed by the Fire Fighters, and then by the Steel Haulers—again assuming that the Steel Haulers number under 100,000. With their very small reported memberships, the Farm Workers' union and the Newspaper Guild would show violence indices of 36.7 and 7.5, respectively, but the figures are too easily distorted by the low membership numbers to allow confidence in them.[5]

The ten organizations which appear to have the worst records of relative violence are listed in Table III-6.

Violence by Industrial Grouping

Some industries, because of the nature of the work involved in them, are more physical than others. Construction work, for example, is

---

[5] One additional organization, the Professional Air Traffic Controllers' Organization (PATCO) was involved in several incidents—thirteen—during the 1981 strike, which, combined with its small membership of 14,000 would cause it to be ranked high on the list. The same comments that apply to the United Farm Workers and to the Newspaper Guild apply here, along with the additional notes that PATCO no longer is active, and that, subjectively, all of its reported violence was *de minimus*.

TABLE III-6

*Ten Large Unions or Labor Organizations
with Greatest Relative Involvement in Violence,
1975–1981*

Organization[a]	Violent Incidents Per 10,000 Members
Mine Workers	7.36
Hospital and Health Care Employees	5.70[b]
Fire Fighters	4.48
Steel Haulers	3.20[b]
Oil, Chemical and Atomic Workers	2.88
Teamsters	2.03
Iron Workers	2.01[c]
Transit Workers	2.00
State, County and Municipal Employees	1.55
Operating Engineers	1.19[c]

[a] The full names of the unions listed in this table are found in Appendix A.

[b] Estimated minimum.

[c] May be understated by some proportion of construction violence attributed to building trades councils.

more physical than retail selling. It seems reasonable to assume that the more physical industries attract stronger and generally rougher employees, who might be expected to participate more easily in acts of violence during strikes. As seen in Table III–7, this is not always the case. Table III–7 shows the number of incidents associated with each union or labor organization, arranged by industry. Unions in the state and local government area—not usually considered to involve highly physical occupations—were near the top of the list, right behind those in transportation and above those in contract construction.

Table III–7 shows the great divergence that exists among the various unions in the listing, and also reveals some surprising facts about the settings in which violence takes place. Again, it should be remembered that the severity of violence is not under consideration here, but only the number of incidents. Nevertheless, it is surprising that government employees figure so strongly in the listing. A positive note is that the United Rubber, Cork, Linoleum and Plastic Workers of America (URW), who at one time had a reputation for aggression and violence, are represented in very few of the incidents, and the same is true of the International Longshoremen's Association (ILA).

Examining the data on a relative basis, as was done earlier, is instructive again here. Assuming that a base of approximately 22.5 million union members involved in 2,598 incidents of violence is "nor-

TABLE III-7

Total Number of Incidents by
Industry and Organization[a]
1975–1981

	Incidents

MANUFACTURING

1. Food and kindred products 104
Bakery Workers (BCTW)	11
Beer Bottlers[b]	1
Brewery Workers	4
Cannery Workers[b]	1
Food and Commercial Workers (UFCW)	83
Grain Millers (AFGM)	4

2. Textiles and Apparel 26
Clothing and Textile Workers (ACTWU)	10
Ladies' Garment Workers (ILGWU)	16

3. Lumber and Wood 3
Woodworkers (IWA)	2
Lumber Workers	1

4. Furniture 15
Cabinet Makers and Millmen	1
Furniture Workers (UFWA)	10
Upholsterers (UIU)	4

5. Paper 14
Paperworkers (UPIU)	13
Pulp and Paper	1

6. Printing and Publishing 39
Graphic Arts (GAIU)	4
Newspaper Guild	24
Printing and Graphic Communications (PGCU)	8
Typographical (ITU)	3

7. Chemicals and Petroleum 56
Chemical Workers (ICW)	4
Oil, Chemical and Atomic (OCAW)	51
Plastic Workers[b]	1

8. Rubber 8
Rubber Workers (URW)	8

9. Stone, Clay, and Glass 10
Cement, Lime, and Gypsum Workers (CLGW)	3
Glass and Ceramic Workers	1
Glass Bottle Blowers (GBBA)	1
Flint Glass Workers (AFGW)	1
Pottery Workers[c]	4

10. Primary and Fabricated Metals 144
Boilermakers (BBF)	5
Molders (IMAW)	9
Steelworkers (USW)	130

11. Machinery (Non-Electrical) 113
Die Sinkers (DSC)	1

TABLE III-7 (continued)

Independent Truckers Association	16
5. Communications	22
Broadcast Employees (NABET)	1
Communication Workers (CWA)	21
6. Trade..	2
Butchers, Food Handlers	1
Retail and Wholesale Trade (RWDSU)	1
7. Finance and Insurance	1
Office and Professional (OPEIU)	1
8. Services..	134
Health Care (various)	9
Hospital and Health Care Employees	57
Hotel and Restaurant Workers (HERE)	11
Motion Picture Operators[b]	1
University Professors (AAUP)	1
Service Employees (SEIU)	37
Theatrical Employees	12
Barbers[d]	3
Laundry Workers (LWUI)	1
Culinary Bartenders[b]	2
GOVERNMENT	
1. Federal	13
Air Traffic Controllers (PATCO)	13
2. State and Local	403
State, County and Municipal Employees (AFSCME)	116
Teachers (NEA), Teachers (AFT), and "teachers"	140
Fire Fighters and other "firemen"	84
Police and other "patrolmen"	41
Refuse Collectors (various)	7
Social Workers[b]	1
Other civil service and municipal employees	14
OTHERS, UNCLASSIFIABLE, AND UNKNOWN	157
TOTAL	2,598

[a] The full names for the organizations listed are found in Appendix A.

[b] The names of these organizations are taken directly from the NRTWLDF Violence Data Base. They have not been confirmed, and the incidents of violence associated with them may be misallocated.

[c] Merged in August 1980 to form Glass, Pottery, Plastics and Allied Workers International Union (GPPAW).

[d] Merged into United Food and Commercial Workers International Union, September 1, 1980.

mal," then relatively few industries are subjected to abnormally high levels of violence.

Some of the individual unions with bad violence records are not critical factors in their industries. For example, although the

Newspaper Guild, in the printing and publishing industry, is involved in violence at a rate about six times higher than the norm, it is a relatively small union (32,000 members) and one which does not dominate the industry. The same can be said of the United Farm Workers (UFW) (12,000 members). The UFW participates in violence at about thirty times the rate of unions in general, but it is a small union in an industry not characterized by unionization. Another union in the same situation is the now-defunct Professional Air Traffic Controllers' Organization (PATCO).

Industries that do seem to be characterized by high levels of union violence are led by mining and quarrying, especially coal mining. The United Mine Workers of America (UMW) is an important force in that industry and has engaged in violence at about six times the average rate. Three other troubled industries are contract construction, transportation (particularly over-the-road transportation), and state and local government.

Table III–8 presents this information in tabular form. A violence index greater than 100 (in the last column in Table III–8) indicates an industry in which the principal labor organizations engage in greater than normal violence.

TABLE III-8

Violence Index by Industry Grouping

Industrial Grouping and Union[a]	Violent Incidents[b]	Membership (thousands)	Violence Index[c]
MANUFACTURING			
Food and Kindred Products			
Bakery Workers (BCTW)	11	168	55
Food and Commercial Workers (UFCW)	83	1,209	58
Others	10		
Textiles and Apparel			
Ladies' Garment Workers (ILGWU)	16	405	34
Others	10		
Pulp and Paper			
Paperworkers (UPIU)	13	301	36
Printing and Publishing			
Newspaper Guild	24	32	636
Others	15		
Chemicals and Petroleum			
Oil, Chemical and Atomic Workers (OCAW)	57	177	246

TABLE III-8 (continued)

Industrial Grouping and Union[a]	Violent Incidents[b]	Membership (thousands)	Violence Index[c]
Others	5		
Primary and Fabricated Metals			
Steelworkers (USW)	130	1,300	85
Other	14		
Non-Electrical Machinery			
Machinists (IAM)	104	917	96
Others	9		
Electrical Machinery			
Electrical Workers (IUE)	11	298	31
Electrical Workers (UE)	19	163	99
Electrical Workers (IBEW)	68	924	63
Unspecified	11		
Transportation Equipment			
Autoworkers	128	1,358	80
Production Workers	15		
Others	4		
Other Manufacturing	37		
NONMANUFACTURING			
Agriculture and Fishing			
Farm Workers (UFW)	44	12	3,110
Mining and Quarrying			
Mine Workers (UMW)	204	277	627
Contract Construction			
Building Trades Councils	70		
Carpenters (CJA)	45	820	47
Iron Workers (BSOIW)	36	179	170
Laborers (LIUNA)	51	627	69
Operating Engineers (IUOE)	50	420	100
Plumbers (PPF)	27	228	100
Roofers (RWAW)	18	28	545
Others	22		
Transportation			
Teamsters	304	1,889	172
Steel Haulers (FASH)	32		
Transit Workers (ATU)	30	140	181
Independent Truckers Assn.	16		
Others	47		
Communications			
Communication Workers (CWA)	21	498	36
Services			
Hospital and Health Care	57		
Hotel and Restaurant (HERE)	11	452	20
Service Employees (SEIU)	37	101	167
Theatrical Employees	12		
Other	17		
Other Nonmanufacturing	4		

TABLE III-8 (continued)

Industrial Grouping and Union[a]	Violent Incidents[b]	Membership (thousands)	Violence Index[c]
GOVERNMENT			
Federal			
Air Traffic Controllers (PATCO)	13	14	788
State and Local			
State, County and Municipal Employees (AFSCME)	116	750	131
Teachers (NEA), Teachers (NFT) and other "teachers"	140	2,333	51
Fire Fighters and other "firemen"	84	174	409
Police and other "patrolmen"	41		
Other civil service employees	22		
Others, Unidentifiable, and Unknown	157		
TOTAL	2,598	22,500	100

[a] Only industrial groupings with more than ten reported incidents of violence in the listing are identified. The full names for the organizations in the listing are found in Appendix A.

[b] Estimated from *Directory of National Unions and Employee Associations, 1977,* U.S. Department of Labor, 1979, and other sources.

[c] Index based on comparison of violent incidents per 10,000 members compared with national average = 100.

Table III-9 shows the ten groupings which account for more than two-thirds (68 percent) of all the incidents in the data base, and thus shows where trouble is most likely to occur during strikes.

SEVERITY OF VIOLENCE

Discussion in this chapter so far has centered on the number of violent incidents from the data base which involved various unions. The nature of the violence—its severity, or "quality"—has yet to enter the discussion.

Descriptions of various incidents are highly condensed in the data base, but enough information is present to allow some tentative conclusions about the quality of violence engaged in by different unions. Firstly, the quality of violence does vary significantly from one union to another. Secondly, unions showing the largest number of incidents are not necessarily the most brutal. And thirdly, the nature of the violence in any given strike frequently reflects the tools of the trade of the striking union.

TABLE III–9

*Ten Groupings which Account for
Two-Thirds of the Data Base Incidents*

Groupings	Incidents
Trucking	468
Construction	225
Mining	206
Education	140
Government services, except public safety	139
Public Safety (fire and police)	134
Food, commercial, and related	131
Steel	130
Automobiles	128
Electrical machinery[a]	109

[a] Includes some unions which have extensive membership in contract construction as well as in electrical machinery manufacturing.

To give some idea of the nature of the violence found in the data base, Table III–10 capsulizes all of the incidents involving a particular union, the United Food and Commercial Workers International Union (UFCW), including those associated with the two unions that merged to form the UFCW during the data-collection period—the Amalgamated Meatcutters and Butcher Workmen of North America (Meatcutters), and the Retail Clerks International Association (Retail Clerks). The UFCW was chosen arbitrarily to illustrate the varieties of ordinary, or normal, violence found in the data base. The violence that characterizes various other unions will also be examined.

Among the eighty-three incidents described in Table III–10, thirty-nine involved property damage, twelve involved threats of property damage (such as spreading nails in a road), twenty-one involved personal injury (including one killing which may have been related to a strike), and thirty-one involved threats of injury. There are examples of customers being blocked from stores, nonstrikers being assaulted, damage being done to the homes of nonstrikers, and a number of instances of damage being done to automobiles trying to cross picket lines. Four incidents involved bombs or firebombs; and there were three cases of arson, and nine cases involving either guns or shooting. Union adherents seemed to be victims of the confrontation on seven occasions. All told, there were reports of thirteen arrests, one of a nonstriker, the rest of strikers.

In some unions, the severity of violence is greater than that portrayed in the incidents in Table III–10; in others, it is milder. Some-

TABLE III–10

Data Base Incident Listing, 1975–1981, for
United Food and Commercial Workers International Union
and Predecessor Unions

Meatcutters

1. Union official ran over and tried to kill company official.[1]
2. During strike, refrigeration units turned off by vandals during night.[2]
3. Employees and customers often harassed by strikers; store entrance blocked.[3]
4. Truck windshield smashed by pickets; driver dragged from truck and beaten; hospitalized.[4]
5. Shots fired into truck of nonstriker; threats made to the nonstriker.[5]
6. Vehicles and homes damaged during strike by shots fired into them.[6]
7. During strike, nonstriker beaten inside plant.[7]
8. Truck of nonunion employee slightly damaged when explosive device went off in it.[8]
9. Shots fired into home of nonstriking union member.[9]
10. Pickets threw objects at bus carrying nonstrikers.[10]
11. Striker threw eggs and possibly a bottle at a truck.[11]
12. Windshield broken of plant truck driving through picket line; driver of truck hit picket after rock broke his windshield.[12]
13. Scuffle between unruly pickets and police.[13]
14. Company truck driver injured when picket threw brick into truck.[14]
15. Pickets broke windows of three cattle trucks entering plant.[15]
16. Shots fired at two company trucks.[16]
17. Rocks thrown, nails strewn on road, truck windows broken; throughout strike, strikers threatened nonunion employees.[17]
18. Rocks thrown by strikers who broke windows, damaged cars.[18]
19. Pickets threw bottles, logs, rocks, and nails at police and at nonunion employees.[19]
20. Strikers blocked company entrance, pounded on entering cars; pickets taunted non-union workers, yelling obscenities.[20]

---

[1] Meat Industry, 2/1/77
[2] Spencer *Reporter*, 9/18/79
[3] Alexandria *Town Talk*, 8/23/77
[4] West Point *Militant Truth*, 6/1/78
[5] *Id.*
[6] *Id.*
[7] *Id.*
[8] Rocky Mount *News*, 12/16/75
[9] *Id.*
[10] Durham *Sun*, 9/26/78
[11] *Id.*
[12] Omaha *World Herald*, 5/21/77
[13] *Id.*
[14] *Id.*, 3/8/77
[15] *Id.*
[16] *Id.*, 6/20/79
[17] *Id.*, 5/26/77
[18] *Id.*, 9/26/80
[19] *Id.*, 12/13/77
[20] *Id.*

TABLE III-10 (continued)

21. Unruly pickets tried to turn over car of nonstriker.[21]
22. City council member threatened to kill nonunion employees to settle strike.[22]
23. Strikers threw eggs and shouted at nonstriking workers.[23]
24. Rock throwing and tire slashing reported throughout strike; threats and personal injury also reported.[24]

Retail Clerks

25. Nonstriker beaten so severely that psychomotor epilepsy developed.[25]
26. Nonstriking worker's house set afire by arsonist; children suffered minor injuries.[26]
27. Customers and nonunion employees threatened with bodily harm by pickets.[27]
28. Two people injured when pickets threw rocks at and fought with nonstriking employees.[28]
29. Nonstriking employees badly harassed and intimidated by strikers.[29]
30. Cars damaged, tires slashed and other vandalism reported; bomb threats to grocery stores, and harassment of customers.[30]
31. Metal pipe thrown through window of store; strikers attempted to prevent customers from entering the store.[31]
32. Son of local union president poked holes in meat at struck store; strikers attempted to prevent customers from entering the store.[32]
33. Strikers attempted to prevent customers from entering store.[33]
34. Fire set in large outdoor trash compactor at store.[34]
35. All windows broken at fourteen stores of nonunion company.[35]
36. Car of union business manager firebombed in store parking lot.[36]
37. Pickets very disorderly at times; blocked entrances.[37]

United Food and Commercial Workers
(Merger of Meat Cutters and Retail Clerks)

38. A man was called "scab" and beaten so severely by strikers that psychomotor epilepsy resulted.[38] (See also incident #25.)
39. Striker scratched a woman's car.[39]

---

[21] *Id.*, 2/13/78
[22] *Id.*, 3/5/78
[23] *Id.*, 3/21/79
[24] Sioux Falls *Argus Leader*, 7/24/75
[25] *Chicago Tribune*, 2/6/80
[26] Thomasville (GA) *News*, 5/25/79
[27] Louisville *Times*, 4/26/78
[28] Joplin *Globe*, 10/1/77
[29] Winn Dixie Inc., company pamphlet, n.d.
[30] Reno *Evening Gazette*, 2/26/77
[31] Tri-Community *News*, 8/16/78
[32] *Id.*
[33] *Id.*
[34] *Id.*
[35] Philadelphia *Inquirer*, 10/4/79
[36] Memphis *State Defender*, 5/28/77
[37] Norfolk & Western Railroad, company press release, 9/11/78
[38] Chicago *Tribune*, 2/5/80 (See also incident #25.)
[39] Millbrae *Sun & Leader*, 2/13/80

TABLE III-10 (continued)

40. Truck and car damaged, rocks thrown, and various vandalism reported; also, threats to nonunion workers.[40]
41. Nonstriking union members forcibly barred from voting in union election.[41]
42. Tires slashed on seventeen cars in parking lot of a struck store.[42]
43. Pickets attempted to damage vehicles crossing picket line; minor injuries during strike; nonstrikers threatened.[43]
44. Nonstriker suffered minor injuries when attacked by union members.[44]
45. Two company officials threatened a union organizer.[45]
46. Picket hit by car crossing picket line.[46]
47. Nonstrikers threatened and intimidated.[47]
48. Pipe bomb found in company parking lot during strike.[48]
49. Rocks, bottles, sticks, and other objects thrown at cars crossing picket line.[49]
50. Picket hit by car entering plant; minor injury.[50]
51. Rocks and other objects thrown at homes of nonstrikers.[51]
52. Strikers placed burning straw in road, causing an oncoming car to swerve and overturn.[52]
53. Nonstriker stopped by man who pointed a gun at him and threatened him.[53]
54. The word "scab" painted on home of nonstriker.[54]
55. Rock thrown by pickets broke windshield of car; the driver, a nonstriking employee, received an eye injury.[55]
56. Bullets fired by union members heavily damaged a nonstriker's car.[56]
57. Cars of nonstrikers were sprayed with paint, and their tires slashed.[57]
58. Nonunion employees and pickets threatened each other.[58]
59. Strikers followed nonstrikers to their homes and threw objects at their cars.[59]
60. Pickets attempted, and several times succeeded, in blocking entrance to struck plant.[60]
61. Car window broken, nonstriker's eye injured by broken glass.[61]
62. Nonstriker pointed gun at striker.[62]

---

[40] Gilroy *Dispatch*, 2/25/80
[41] Escondido *Times Advocate*, 5/17/81
[42] Denver *Rocky Mountain News*, 10/24/81
[43] *Id.*
[44] Hartford *Courant*, 7/27/80
[45] Des Moines *Register*, 12/11/81
[46] *Id.*
[47] *Id.*
[48] *Id.*
[49] Allegan (MI) *News & Gazette*, 11/6/81
[50] Kalamazoo *Gazette*, 10/28/81
[51] Allegan (MI) *News & Gazette*, 11/6/81
[52] Kalamazoo *Gazette*, 10/28/81
[53] Allegan (MI) *News and Gazette*, 11/6/81
[54] *Id.*
[55] *Id.*
[56] Kalamazoo *Gazette*, 11/21/81
[57] *Id.*
[58] *Id.*
[59] *Id.*
[60] *Id.*
[61] *Id.*
[62] Omaha *World Herald*, 9/8/80

TABLE III–10 (continued)

63. Two strikers damaged a car during a strike.[63]
64. Nonstriker driving to work was shot at twice by a man in another car.[64]
65. Rocks thrown at cars of nonstriking employees, and a windshield was broken; just after leaving plant, nonstrikers were threatened.[65]
66. Knife wounds inflicted during fight resulted in death (information ambiguous on cause of fight).[66]
67. Roofing nails strewn on pavement along roads leading to struck plant.[67]
68. Nonstriker's car tires slashed, window broken; house windows also broken.[68]
69. As strikers threw rocks at nonstrikers, a nonstriker shot and wound a striker.[69]
70. "Vandalism" reported when unruly pickets shouted and blocked entrance to struck plant.[70]
71. Twelve cars of nonunion employees damaged by thrown objects.[71]
72. Woman who visited a friend at a struck plant was run off the road, and her car was damaged by strikers; one thrown rock hit the woman in the shoulder.[72]
73. A barn near a struck plant was burned, as was company equipment; nails spread on road.[73]
74. Strikers deflated car tires, put ketchup in a mail box; store owners of struck stores received harassing calls.[74]
75. Customer harassed by pickets and told not to shop at store.[75]
76. A nonstriker's car windshield was broken as she crossed the picket line.[76]
77. Striker went to struck stores, painted on, and stole one of store's signs.[77]
78. Store manager carried gun into store; he also attempted to grab a picket sign.[78]
79. Assistant manager took two picket signs and temporarily refused to return them.[79]
80. Car of nonstriker pelted with eggs thrown by pickets.[80]
81. A woman in a van tailgated a nonstriker during a strike.[81]
82. A store manager was assaulted; he received a skull fracture and suffered loss of hearing.[82]
83. Government official says "Head start pickets have resorted to violence."[83]

[63] *Id.*
[64] *Id.*
[65] *Id.*, 9/9/80
[66] *Id.*, 9/20/80
[67] *Id.*, 9/11/80
[68] *Id.*, 9/8/80
[69] *Id.*, 10/28/80
[70] *Id.*, 10/15/80
[71] *Id.*, 10/28/80
[72] Nashville *Banner*, 9/30/80
[73] Seattle *Times*, 3/9/81
[74] Goldendale *Sentinel*, 3/26/81
[75] Tri City *Herald*, 11/9/81
[76] *Id.*, 11/20/81
[77] *Id.*, 11/9/81
[78] *Id.*
[79] *Id.*
[80] *Id.*, 11/20/81
[81] *Id.*
[82] *Id.*, 11/13/81
[83] Toledo *Blade*, 1/30/81

times it reflects the particular tools of the trade involved. Table III–11 gives a few samples which seem to characterize the violence associated with various unions. In most cases, we have not mentioned psychological violence or minor incidents such as harassment; additionally, we have not included incidents which seem to be common to all, or at least most, violent strike situations, such as mass picketing, spreading tacks or nails on roadways near struck plants, damaging cars trying to pass through picket lines, and simple assaults on nonstrikers, strikebreakers, or company supervisors.

TABLE III-11

Incidents Representative of the Violence
Associated With Various Unions During Strikes, 1975–1981 [a]

State, County and Municipal Employees (AFSCME)
Pickets used bus to block entrance to school for retarded children; name tags removed from 50 corpses at county morgue; nonstrikers assaulted; pickets attempted to block hospital entrances; bomb threats made by phone to hospitals; 2 dogs belonging to prison guard poisoned; water valve to prison turned off; telephone poles near prison chopped down; flaming torch thrown onto porch of a state health department official; bus driver killed during municipal employees' strike; fire hydrants opened and tampered with; 192 of city's 260 trash trucks vandalized and put out of service; sewage valves tampered with, causing sewage to flow into river; 16 dumpsters of trash set on fire during sanitation strike.

Teachers (AFT)
School food-supply trucks attacked; eggs thrown, entrances blocked, and obscenities shouted by pickets; tires of substitute teachers' cars slashed.

Building Trades Councils
Nonunion construction projects burned by arsonists; trucks burned; power poles cut; member of rival union shot and killed; nonunion construction projects bombed, damaged, destroyed, or vandalized; nonunion workers threatened, assaulted; construction equipment damaged, destroyed, vandalized; $100,000 worth of machinery belonging to open shop firm damaged; $1,000,000 worth of damage done to nonunion worksite; nonunion project blocked by 1,000 pickets; $75,000 worth of equipment at nonunion site destroyed by firebombing.

Carpenters (CJA)
Cement trucks damaged by gunfire; wife of struck company's personnel manager shot in head while at home; portable office burned; 4 nonunion workers assaulted by mob of union members.

Communications Workers (CWA)
Telephone cables cut (fifty-one total reported; thirty-two in a single incident); trucks firebombed; gun fired into plant; homes of nonstrikers fired upon.

[a] Official names for the organizations listed in this table are found in Appendix A. Sources for individual incidents are included in the NRTWLDF Violence Data Base listing.

TABLE III-11 (continued)

Electrical Workers (IUE)

Pole-mounted electrical equipment shot into; wires cut; machinery damaged; $75,000 worth of equipment destroyed by firebomb at nonunion site.

Steel Haulers (FASH)

Trucks burned, shot into, tires slashed; truck driver shot in neck; nonstriking driver shot and wounded; shots fired at convoy; truckers shot at; paint splattered on windshields.

Firefighters (IAFF)

300 fires set during 3-day strike; striking firemen suspected of setting fire to abandoned warehouse and an apartment building; 2 deaths blamed on inexperience of replacements for strikers; 5 deaths resulted from a fire because there were not enough nonstriking firemen to get to the fire; the number of fires doubled during strike; shots were fired into the car of an emergency-vehicle dispatcher; shots fired into home of fire protection board president, and into car of board member; firebomb thrown onto porch of another fire protection board member; firefighting equipment sabotaged before walkout; car of fire chief firebombed; of fifteen serious fires during strike, only one of them was not the result of arson; hotel burned down as strikers harassed volunteers putting out the fire; fire hydrants sabotaged; striking firemen parked car on hoses at fire.

Furniture Workers (UFWA)

Truck loaded with furniture dumped, contents burned; shots fired at homes and cars of nonstrikers; bricks thrown at trucks.

Hospital and Health Care Employees

Pickets beat drums day and night outside nursing home; hospital entrances blocked; 2 deaths attributed to hospital strike; Molotov cocktails thrown at doctor's residence; windows of nursing home broken; patients needing emergency care turned away by pickets; bullet shot at the hospital broke a window; paint and acid thrown on cars of nonstrikers; doctor crossing picket line hit in head by rock.

Hotel and Restaurant Employees (HERE)

Tacks spread on road leading to hotel; drums beaten and other disturbances created; nonunion restaurant bombed; Las Vegas strip blocked.

Electrical Workers (IBEW)

Main trunk of cable company cut; wires cut and conduit vandalized; telephone lines to plant cut before strike began; power lines cut; chains thrown on transformers; electrical poles toppled; poles cut; power substation vandalized.

Independent Truckers Association

Shots fired at trucks driving on highway; windshield shattered by gunfire; truck windows broken by rocks; shots fired at tank trucks, others.

Ladies' Garment Workers (ILGWU)

Nonstrikers' homes damaged; arson (three incidents on the same day during strike) caused $350,000 worth of damage.

Industrial Workers (NIW)

Pipe bomb thrown into front yard of nonstriking employee; windows broken in home of nonstriker; six shots fired into home of a nonstriking employee; two Molotov cocktails thrown at door of nonstriking employee's home. (All incidents occurred during the same strike.)

TABLE III-11 (continued)

Iron Workers (BSOIW)

Man who returned to work before strike ended shot in head; $2,000,000 worth of damage done to equipment belonging to two nonunion companies; executive beaten when he refused to pay "gratuities" to union members; five nonunion employees beaten with iron pipes and pick handles.

Laborers (LIUNA)

Two workers for nonunion company beaten; supervisor beaten; foreman beaten; man running for union post beaten to death by five masked men.

Machinists (IAM)

Man applying for work at struck plant stabbed by strikers; entrance to plant blocked for seven days; pipe bomb caused $5,000 worth of damage to company executive's home; shots fired into nonstriker's home, home of company manager, home of company service manager, and home of next door neighbor of nonstriking employee; a horse and a pony, both owned by a company supervisor, shot; many windshields broken, tires slashed.

Molders (IMAW)

Shots fired into nonunion employee's home; homes of ten nonunion employees hit by gunfire; two strikers attempted to burn plant.

Teachers (NEA)

Cars of nonstrikers damaged; school entrances blocked; substitute teachers received threatening letters; school board members harassed.

Newspaper Guild

Newspaper delivery trucks firebombed; gasoline exploded under building; fire set in newspaper office lobby; headquarters of struck paper damaged by bomb; advertisers threatened; newsboys intimidated.

Oil, Chemical and Atomic Workers (OCAW)

Arson caused $250,000 worth of damage; severed pig's head found on nonunion employee's doorstep; company equipment sabotaged; two security guards kidnapped by strikers, one shot in jaw; tires of emergency vehicle flattened; supervisor shot and killed by striker; gas valves tampered with, service disrupted; security employee assaulted by striker, his family threatened; gas pumps bombed at filling station; picket shot, wounded while walking picket line.

Operating Engineers (IUOE)

Engines of cranes belonging to nonunion contractor filled with sand; cranes burned after contractor gave up union shop; engines of thirty pieces of heavy construction equipment damaged during strike; thousands of dollars worth of damage done to construction vehicles and equipment.

Policemen (various unions and locals)

Shots fired at national guardsmen filling in for strikers; police cars vandalized, sabotaged, damaged in various ways; keys to 200 police cars stolen; pipe bomb blown up in entrance to mayor's home.

Printing and Graphics (PGCU)

Presses broken up; supervisor beaten; printed materials burned; nonstriker beaten.

Paperworkers (UPIU)

Vandalism; rocks thrown at cars.

TABLE III-11 (continued)

Plumbers (PPF)
Plumber working on Saturday beaten by union men; nonunion construction sites damaged, destroyed.

Production Workers (PSS)
Cabs burned, windshields smashed, tires slashed (many instances). Hand grenade thrown into company headquarters; car of striking local union president bombed; gunshots fired into homes of two company managers.

Railway Carmen (BRC)
Bombs planted beside electrical transformer poles at plant; bomb exploded inside struck plant.

Railway Clerks (BRAC)
Train windows broken; supervisors clearing derailment pelted with rocks; tracks tampered with; boxcars set afire.

Service Employees (SEIU)
Cabs followed, firebombed; shots fired into homes of nonstrikers; school for the blind vandalized; a compound smelling like gas dumped outside two restaurants, a children's hospital, and another building; paint remover sprayed on cars of nonstrikers; firebomb found on top of roof of psychiatric ward; kindergarten bus stopped from entering school.

Steelworkers (USW)
Company supervisor's home, cars damaged; strikers supported KKK members burning cross near a plant employing black guards; union members beaten by nonunion workers, picket trailer damaged; rocks and other things thrown at police (many instances); building next to quarry blown up with twenty tons of TNT; hundreds of plant windows broken during strikes; home of company foreman bombed; car of nonstriker riddled with bullets; nonstriker beaten severely; shots fired into homes of strikers; company security guard shot and killed and another wounded by two strikers; house of union member who returned to work set afire; fire caused $200,000 worth of damage to plant pump house.

Teamsters
Trucks and cars set on fire, damaged, punctured, shot at, riddled, burned, exploded, spray painted, vandalized; trucks and cars hit by rocks, cans and bottles, bricks, concrete blocks, hammers, lead pipes, baseball bats, acid, Molotov cocktails, bullets, bombs, ball bearings, other cars and trucks; air hoses, tires, haudraulic lines, upholstery, radiator hoses, and power lines cut; tires punctured, flattened, cut, slashed, slit, deflated, shot, ice picked; homes of nonunion drivers shot at, torched, destroyed; violence and threats used to coerce company into putting dead people on payroll; nonunion employee's dog hanged and found with a sign reading "This happens to scabs"; nonunion employees, nonstrikers, supervisors, company managers, strikers, dissident unionists, and union rivals beaten, battered, assaulted, shot at, spat upon; nonstriker shot in leg, leg was amputated; nonstriker shot and killed; striker shot and killed; company owner shot to death after his company became open shop; labor attorney shot to death by Teamster union delegate; for four days, a nonstriker received a threatening call every twenty-five minutes; time bomb found at struck nursing home.

Theatrical Employees
Fires set in nonunion theaters (seven instances); screens slashed; bomb planted in theater; theaters vandalized.

TABLE III-11 (continued)

Transit Workers (ATU)

Tires punctured, bus garage vandalized; pickets tried to stop nonunion bus drivers from transporting handicapped children; cabbie driving handicapped child to school assaulted by pickets; three vans carrying emotionally disturbed children surrounded by pickets; pickets smashed windows of taxis taking handicapped children to school; girl shot and critically wounded on bus driven by nonstriker.

Transportation Union (UTU)

Cabs, cab company offices burned.

Electrical Workers (UE)

After throwing rock at company truck, striker shot to death; cars and homes of nonstrikers vandalized, shot at.

Auto Workers (UAW)

Company vehicles and cars and trucks of nonstrikers damaged or destroyed in various ways; brake lines cut, brake fluid drained; 300 shots fired into plant; cars and homes of company supervisors, managers, and executives, and of nonunion employees and nonstrikers shot at, damaged; strikers went on rampage damaging $150,000 worth of company property; dog completely skinned and hung from pole near plant with note reading "scab;" flaming arrow shot at nonstriker as he transported company goods.

Farm Workers (UFW)

Crops destroyed; striker shot to death in grower's field; produce trucks sabotaged; nonstrikers assaulted; car windshields broken.

Mine Workers (UMW)

Bombings, vandalism of equipment, and other property damage; nonunion miners assaulted; nonunion company office leveled by explosion; much mining equipment damaged; 75 persons opened fire on mine, UMW member shot to death; striker threw explosives at security guard, and security guard shot the striker; nonstriking employee killed when shots fired into car; railroad tracks, trains, trestles dynamited; one person killed and two wounded when shots were fired into bus carrying nonunion employees; nonunion members' homes bombed; two pickets shot to death while protesting use of nonunion coal; convoy of trucks hit by barrage of gunfire; 20 power poles to mine cut, electricity lost; pickets surrounded independent coal trucker and made him dump coal; striking miners burned an office trailer and a dump truck; 138 tires of vehicles on company property flattened; security guard shot in leg; security guard beaten near plant; 1,500 UMW members stormed nonunion coal company, trapping 50 employees in building; coal auger worth $100,000 dynamited; nonunion employee shot and killed, and another wounded, by UMW member.

CONCLUSIONS

Records in the data base are too numerous to allow the conclusion that violence in strikes is either unusual or unintended. The period covered, 1975 to 1981, saw very few high-visibility national walkouts, and was generally free from emotionally charged nonwage issues. The cathartic effects of Watergate had ended the era of stridency and confrontation associated with Vietnam and the peace movement and with the earlier civil rights riots. In labor relations, the years between 1975 and 1981 were years of relative tranquility. Yet, 2,598 incidents of violence were recorded.

The nature of the incidents that took place reveals the fatuity of two of the favorite excuses for strike violence—that it is the natural outcome of boisterous men in confrontation, or that it is a defensive reaction to the intimidation of employers and their security guards. One does not follow a person home and shoot into his house as an expression of boisterous exuberance, and one does not skin pet dogs and hang them up with signs reading "scab" as a defensive measure against employer attack. The violence in strikes is real, and a large portion of it can have no other purpose than to intimidate and to coerce.

When the quantity and severity of violence are viewed in combination, certain unions appear to be more violent than others. Subjectively, the most vicious violence seems to be done by the Mine Workers, Fire Fighters, truck or taxi drivers, Steelworkers, and various construction workers. State, County, and Municipal Employees, and Hospital and Health Care Employees, while not quite as bad, can also show extraordinary nastiness at times.

Although the evidence of Chapter II and this chapter makes it quite clear that violence in strikes is a serious problem, and one which is not improving over time, the chapters cover too many different unions and strike situations to illustrate effectively the way in which violence is used with apparent deliberateness to achieve specific labor goals. Part III of this book focuses on several specific unions and evaluates specific strikes or organizational campaigns.

PART THREE

Case Examples

CHAPTER IV

Coal Mining and the UMW: The Legacy of Violence

Mining coal has always been difficult, dangerous, and dirty work; and until World War II, those who did it were also poorly paid. Understandably, it appealed to few intellectuals or social philosophers. The men who have worked in the coal pits have generally been as rough and ready a lot as could be found anywhere in American industry.

Even before the union organizational efforts in the 1880s and 1890s, the coal fields were known for their violence and bloodshed. The work, the workers, and the age itself were physical and unrefined, and violence was an expected part of it. Therefore, when early union campaigns to organize the coal fields turned out to be brutal and bloody, few people were surprised.

Violence was common to the early union drives in many industries besides coal mining, but in most of them it set no precedent for modern practice. Industries accommodated to the new status of workers, and most unions, as they matured during the middle years of this century, relied less and less on physical force and coercion and more and more on negotiations and political pressures to achieve their purposes. In a few cases, however, particularly in those involving arduous but relatively unskilled work, the unions continued their old ways. Despite all the changes that have taken place through the years in the technology, structure, and environment of coal mining, the United Mine Workers of America (UMW) still relies on bloodshed, dynamite, and intimidation to coerce acceptance of the union's demands. Not only has violence continued to be characteristic of UMW strikes and organizing efforts, its use has acquired the sanctity of tradition. Throughout the coal mining regions even today, when the UMW talks of strike, men look for ways to arm themselves.

POSTWAR ORGANIZATIONAL DRIVES AND STRIKES

The years from 1941 to 1945, while the country was preoccupied with war, provided a sharp break in the industrial environment and in the patterns and practices of union organization.

During the depression years of the 1930s, John L. Lewis, the ruthless, autocratic, and highly effective head of the UMW, had been occupied with consolidating his leadership within the union and with organizing the larger mining companies and captive mines of the northern Appalachians. He had spearheaded a series of often bloody organizational drives which had succeeded in signing up most of the operators in the prime regions of West Virginia, Pennsylvania, Ohio, and Illinois.

When the United States entered the war and the demand for both steam coal and metallurgical coal became intense, Lewis changed tactics. He used his control over the union and the base he had built to win economic gains for the union. He defied both court orders and presidential directives in staging a series of wartime work stoppages—three of them in one two-month period in late 1941. His brinksmanship won the enmity of many, but it also convinced the country that the miners meant business. By war's end, union miners had obtained a closed shop agreement, had doubled their hourly pay rate, had negotiated a system of royalty payments to fund a pension and retirement plan, had expanded their compensable workday without changing their working time, and had achieved a number of other substantial gains. Miners had become among the best paid of industrial workers, and by 1948 they would head the list.

But when the war ended, the advantageous contracts so recently won proved painful for both UMW members and union operators. In the late 1940s, the demand for coal slumped sharply. What business there was began to flow to the smaller, nonunionized mines in the southern part of the Appalachian chain. Because the union contract mandated high labor costs, union operators had to charge high prices, and found themselves at a decided competitive disadvantage.

By the end of the decade, it began to look as though the UMW was going to be unable to hold on to its gains, much less sustain its momentum. The Kentucky-Tennessee region was the hardest hit. With few captive mines in the area, the regional market was dominated by the government-subsidized Tennessee Valley Authority (TVA), which bought coal at the lowest spot prices. Unionized operators were losing business on price, and the UMW miners were frequently working only two or three days a week, while their nonunion counterparts, despite generally lower wages, were working more and taking home more pay. Dissatisfaction with the UMW was growing on all sides.

Unwilling to lower the contract wage rate, abandon the royalty payment to the pension fund, or compromise productivity-limiting conditions in its contract, the UMW denied unionized operators the possibility of lowering the cost differential between union and nonunion coal. The unionized mines were in danger of losing all their TVA business, which was the largest available, by far. The UMW, therefore, sought to preserve its strength, and perhaps to pick up some new members, by embarking on a campaign to eliminate the lower priced competition by eliminating the nonunion mines. An organizational drive was begun in 1949, and it was to continue sporadically over the next two decades. It was a drive that was punctuated repeatedly by dynamite, gunshots, and other outbreaks of violence.

Characteristics of the Campaign

The UMW set out to do no less than establish sovereignty over the entire eastern coal field region. Nonunion firms were to be allowed to operate only with the permission of the union. Those who tried otherwise would be "struck" by the union and shut down. Firms and their employees who happened to be organized by some labor organization other than the UMW could expect the same treatment. In the two-dimensional world of the UMW, any coal which was not UMW coal was "scab" coal.

Obstacles: the Product. Coal from the same geological formations is undifferentiated: one lump of it is much like another. Its quality is not affected by the personalities or skills of the miners, or even by the method of extraction. For any given technology of extraction, the manhours required per ton of output are about the same, so the final price is highly dependent on hourly wage rates.[1]

On the open market, nonunion mine operators in the Appalachians and particularly in the Kentucky and Tennessee areas enjoyed substantially lower labor costs per unit of output than did the union operators. The goal of the UMW was to eliminate the differential by closing down the nonunion firms, by forcing them to recognize the UMW, or by making nonunion coal as expensive as union coal.

Obstacles: the Miners. During the postwar campaign, the UMW was at a disadvantage in that it had to work from the top down and force unionization on the nonunion miners. A good many of the nonunion miners liked their independent status. They often worked longer for less money than their union counterparts, but at least they had only one

---

[1] Closely aligned with wages are productivity differences experienced between union and nonunion mines. The UMW contract contains many productivity restrictions. Some of them—like the prohibition of gasoline powered engines underground—are included in the name of safety, but modern nonunion operators contend that most are simply to mandate increased UMW employment and manning levels. Some modern, nonunion mines are able to pay wages equal to or better than contract rates and still sell coal at lower prices than comparable union mines because of the productivity differences in the contract.

set of bosses, and had no dues to pay. The ethnic stock in the Kentucky and Tennessee regions was different from that in Illinois and Pennsylvania, and for whatever reasons it lacked the desire for unanimity of purpose and solidarity that the miners in those regions or in West Virginia had.[2] Left to their own devices, to the lure of the higher union wages, or simply to the blandishments of the UMW, these men would (and did) vote repeatedly in supervised elections to retain their nonunion status. To get them into the fold, the UMW had to force unionism on them by signing up not the miners, but their employers.

Organizing Tactics. The tactics chosen by the UMW to organize the nonunion mines were therefore the tactics of intimidation: the UMW sought to establish a reign of terror in the coal fields, using bullets, clubs, and dynamite. Violence was directed against property and people in attempts to frighten mine operators into coercing their employees to join the union. Tactics included, but were not limited to:

1. Mass picketing and intimidation: roving caravans; "striking" nonunion mines; and beleaguering mine property.

2. Attacks on mine owners and operators, nonunion miners, members of non-UMW unions, independent contractors, transporters, customers, suppliers, and others. Assaults on individuals included verbal abuse, threats, beatings, shootings, and bombings; vandalism of automobiles, homes, and personal property; and threats to and intimidation of families.

3. Sabotage or destruction of mining equipment.

4. Attacks on transporters of nonunion coal and interdiction of the movement of goods.

Cases illustrating each of these tactics can be found in the files of the National Labor Relations Board (NLRB) and in various court records. A few representative cases are described below.

Mass Picketing and Intimidation

In the organizational campaign which began in the late 1940s, the UMW was, in the words of one of its leaders, "out to unionize all the nonunion mines in the territory."[3] The intimidation provided by mass picketing—by long caravans of cars loaded with burly miners, or by throngs numbering in the hundreds amassing on a mine's access road or at its gate—is intense at any time, but doubly so when the target is

---

[2] J. E. FINLEY, THE CORRUPT KINGDOM, 137 (1972).
[3] United Mine Workers of America, 92 N.L.R.B. 916, 918 (1950).

weak or feels defenseless. Most of the nonunion mines in the area were small-scale operators, employing only a few dozen, or up to a few hundred, men. The mass picketing effort was directed against these mines.

Western Kentucky Coal Company, 1949. The UMW's intentions were clear early in this campaign:

> Six mines in western Kentucky were visited in two days by a crowd of approximately 2,000 under the leadership of the Respondents [UMW] [to] organize the Western Kentucky Coal Company and other companies, [who were told] that they were not going to be permitted to operate until they signed up with the United Mine Workers; and that the Western Kentucky and other companies were running coal that was scab coal in competition with union coal, and that it would not be permitted any more. The drive would be continued until they were all organized.[4]

Here, as throughout the campaign, the UMW provided its own definition of "scab" coal. In most unions, a "scab" is one who crosses picket lines to produce at a struck plant. To the UMW, however, a scab was anyone who was not an active member of the UMW: nonunion miners were "scabs" when their nonunion mine was "struck" by the union; miners who were members of rival unions were "scabs" all the time.

In addition, the UMW was taking no chances that its intentions might be unclear. When it delivered its message to Western Kentucky, it reportedly did so with 2,000 men to back it up. Most of the mass movements reported were somewhat smaller, but large enough to have had an impact. Another example involves the drive on the Meadow Creek Coal Company.

Meadow Creek Coal Company, 1948. The Meadow Creek Coal Company was located in central Tennessee. The miners there were an independent lot, and had twice previously, in 1944 and in 1946, voted overwhelmingly against affiliation with the UMW in NLRB-supervised elections. In 1948, while the UMW was active in the region, it decided to make a forceful effort to organize Meadow Creek. Some 200 members of the UMW met at Sparta, Tennessee, where they formed a motorcade and advanced on the mine, arriving at the time of the afternoon shift change. Then, they

> blockaded Meadow Creek's private road and stationed guards between the intersection of the road with the public highway and the mine . . . . The mob, some of which were armed, intercepted Meadow Creek employees and by persuasion and threats of bodily harm to them and their families if they did not do so, urged them to join the UMW.[5]

---

[4] *Id.*

[5] United Mine Workers of America v. Meadow Creek Coal Co., 263 F.2d, 52, 55 (6th Cir., 1959).

The invasion of the mine was led by international representatives of the UMW, who contributed verbal threats to shut down the mine if its employees did not join the union. The initial effort was successful only in closing the mine for as long as the union mob remained in force. The mine reopened as soon as the mob left. Later in the same year, however, the UMW renewed its effort. Another meeting was called and another march to the mine was staged. Meadow Creek had closed in anticipation of the incident, but fifteen to twenty of the union miners found three employees of a Meadow Creek affiliate, whom they forced from their cars, threatened with pistols, and verbally abused, calling them scabs and telling them their days of operating without a union were ended.

Further attacks took place against Meadow Creek and transporters of its coal (see *Meadow Creek Coal Company,* p. 92), and finally, the mine's owner, W. T. Ray, signed on with the UMW, thus forcing his employees into the union. (As it turned out, although the UMW had won a substantial victory, its fruits were short-lived. Costs required by the union contract made Meadow Creek noncompetitive for the TVA work. The mine closed for lack of business within a couple of years, and subsequently won a damage suit against the UMW for the 1948 campaign.)[6]

Mercury Mining and Construction, 1951. The use of mass picketing to extort recognition of the union from independent mining companies was also the case at the Mercury Mining and Construction Company. For example, one day 150 pickets staged a mass invasion of a mine where only three employees were present. On this occasion, as on many others, the police were summoned. The NLRB's trial examiner, after recounting the incident, noted that "this display of force was staged for the purpose of forcing [the employer] to sign agreements with the union,"[7] and called the tactics "typical [of] methods and techniques recently utiiized by the Respondents in their organizational activity."[8]

Attacks on Employees

The cases involving Meadow Creek and Mercury Mining provide examples of threats and force used under the cover of mass picketing to intimidate employees (and extort employers) during the campaign. Many other cases exist. Some of the violence was directed very per-

---

6 Finley, *supra* note 2, at 140.
7 United Mine Workers of America District 2 et al. v. Mercury Mining and Construction Corp et al., 96 N.L.R.B. 1389 (1951).
8 *Id.* at 1392.

sonally against individuals who declined to sign on with the union. An example is found in an NLRB report covering the organizational drive on Tungsten Mining Corporation.

Tungsten Mining Corporation, 1953. An employee who had been repeatedly harassed by the union for going to work at the mine was at home in bed one night when he "heard a [sound] like somebody shot in a barrel . . . 'A car got near my house and slowed up and shot the side of my house . . . Three shots came through the beaver board . . . through the door.' "[9] The UMW was, in fact, often willing to move the scene of violence away from the workplace. Another example was found in the effort to organize the Blue Ridge Coal Corporation.

Blue Ridge Coal Corporation, 1952. The UMW was attempting to organize the employees at Blue Ridge Coal, in West Virginia. One afternoon during the strike, a nonunion miner, driving a truck, turned down a coal road and was soon forced to stop by a car full of union representatives. "Six men got out of the car and asked him where he was going, then grabbed him by the throat."[10] As he started to back his truck away, a union agent "grasped the steering wheel and the truck partially overturned when it rammed into the bank along the road."[11]

Police were often called to be on duty during union activity at the Blue Ridge Corporation, but their presence on the picket sites could not always stop violence; and moreover, the violence sometimes followed the nonstrikers to their homes or into their personal affairs. One day, for example, two nonstrikers were far from their workplace and engaged in entirely personal business when they stopped to buy some groceries. In the store, they were confronted by two union agents, one of whom was accompanied by his wife. The union representative picked up a hatchet, handed it to his wife, and she proceeded to brandish the weapon and threaten to "chop out the brains" of one of the nonstrikers.[12]

Although there is no evidence that this particular threat was ever carried out, at least one violent threat was dramatically executed a few days later in another incident. An employee on his way to work was stopped by ten or twelve strikers and was told, "If you come over this hill another time you had better have your guns with you because we have got guns [and] we will kill you."[13] Several days later, as the man left the mine, he was shot in the arm from ambush.

---

[9] United Mine Workers of America District 50 et al. v. Tungsten Mining Corp., 106 N.L.R.B. 903, 919 (1953).

[10] Blue Ridge Coal Corp. v. United Mine Workers, 129 N.L.R.B. 146, 159 (1960).

[11] *Id.*

[12] *Id.* at 160.

[13] *Id.* at 161.

Another nonstriking employee, named Kelly, met the following fate:

> During the later part of June, about 10 of the nonstrikers adopted the prac-
> tice of living in a shanty on the Marra mine property during the workweek
> and leaving only on the weekends. A number of these men were from the
> vicinity of Buchannon, in the adjoining county. On the evening of Sunday,
> June 29, a car containing seven of the nonstrikers was proceeding from
> Pepper along the Grafton Coal road on the way to the Marra mine. Paul
> Gooden was the driver of this automobile. He testified at length, in a frank
> and completely credible manner, as to the events which occurred that
> evening.
>
> According to Gooden: As he and his co-workers came within about 1,000
> feet of the mine entrance, the car was stopped by a large group of people
> who thronged across the road. One of those who stopped the car asked if
> Gooden and his companions were bound for the Marra coal mine.
>
> When Gooden gave a noncommital response, one of those who had come up
> to the car started hitting him in the mouth. Gooden put his car in gear and
> started to move away. As he did so, rocks were hurled at the automobile
> and several shots were fired. He proceeded on through the crowd until he
> reached a point some distance beyond Brownton.
>
> By that time most of the glass on his car, including the windows, lights, and
> windshield, was broken and a bullet had gone through a front tire. He also
> discovered at this stage that two of his passengers, Lloyd Kelly and Corder
> Liggett, were missing from the car. Gooden estimated that there were at
> least 200 people in the crowd along the road to the mine. . . .
>
> It was at this point that Gooden had lost two of his passengers. Liggett had
> jumped from the car and run out through the crowd. Lloyd Kelly, the other
> one, was dragged from the car and severely beaten. Kelly testified that as
> the car stopped, Myers shouted "Drag them out of the car and beat them
> up," whereupon four or five others whom Kelly did not know pulled him
> out of Gooden's car and struck him about the face and mouth.
>
> According to Kelly, his assailants quit only when Myers told them they had
> gone far enough and ordered them to carry Kelly into a shanty along the
> side of the road. Kelly's nose was broken during the assault and his injuries
> kept him off work for approximately 3 weeks.[14]

Besides this direct, physical approach, the evidence from the Blue
Ridge case shows that the UMW also relied on the cumulative effect of
relatively minor incidents to intimidate employees into joining the
union. At one time or another during the drive, pickets:

1. threatened to kill and dynamite a carpenter who continued
   to work;[15]

2. threw stones at, injured, and threatened to kill a nonstriking
   employee who refused to stop hauling coal;[16]

---

[14] *Id.*
[15] *Id.* at 165-66.
[16] *Id.* at 166.

3. threatened a nonunion member that "If we have to, we can spill some blood to keep you from going in there;[17]

4. intimidated others with such threats as "Let's go down over the hill and kill the scab . . . We ought to take a gun and go down and kill them at the tipple."[18]

This form of "persuasion" had effects on some nonstriking and nonunion employees. For example, in one incident, a nonunion employee was met by 150 pickets and told to sign a card "or somebody just may kick the ___ out of you." Another picket then appeared with a club; the nonunion employee then saw the wisdom of signing a card, and did. He later testified that at that moment, "I would have signed anything."[19]

Osborne Mining Company and Affiliates, 1954. Yet another example of the UMW's methods of convincing reluctant employees to join the union is found in the drive on the Osborne Coal Company.

During 1954 and 1955, the UMW made repeated attempts to organize a number of independent operators who were working the reserves of the Osborne Mining Company under subcontract. As discussed later by the court of appeals, the early stages of violence were fairly mild:

> The facts of this case as found by the District Judge, present a frightening picture of violence and intimidation. Osborne had been pressured more than once to sign a union contract, and company employees had been solicited at their homes and other places by the Union in an unsuccessful attempt to get them to join the Union . . . In early July, 1954, the Union then visited the pit which was the workplace of practically all of the employees, asked the employees to join the Union, promising that if they did not join the Union the next visit would not be peaceful.[20]

Attacks on Employers

Sometimes, the UMW's threats failed to provide a satisfactory result. One tactic employed by the UMW at such times was to direct the violence against the employer in cases such as those described below.

Osborne Mining Company Affiliates, 1955. Early in 1955, a group of 200 to 300 UMW miners descended on Newcomb, Tennessee, to visit the Boots and Cox mine, which was an affiliate of the Osborne Mining Company. They immediately confronted the operator.

---

[17] *Id.* at 168.

[18] *Id.* at 171.

[19] United Mine Workers of America v. Osborne Mining Co., 279 F. 2d 716 (6th Cir. 1960).

[20] *Id.*

Boots, 65 years of age, was beaten severely by the mob, Cox was also beaten and kicked. The mine was closed a week, whereupon Boots and Cox signed a contract with the union.[21]

No trouble occurred thereafter.[22]

The quick success of this direct approach encouraged its repetition at other Osborne-affiliated operations. At the Frost and Parish Mine, the mob assaulted the two operators and attacked several of their employees, "leaving them prostrate in a muddy pool at the bottom of the pit."[23]

At another Osborn affiliate, the Van Huss Mine, the scene was similar. The mob

attacked Van Huss and buried him under a pile of dirt. They forced his employees to beat and curse him. His clothes were stripped off and he was thrown into a pool of water where he was doused up and down. One of his employees was treated in the same manner.[24]

According to another account of the same incident,

[an] old man named Van Huss was hit by a band of marauders. His workers were made to strip him naked, whip his bare buttocks, and "baptize" him in a nearby pool.[25]

Violence of this nature is humiliating, degrading, intensely personal, and effective. After the above incident, in combination with a blockade of the parent company's tipple, Osborne closed his mine. While some of the other affiliates also shut down, a few signed the industry contract. Osborne later sued the UMW and won settlements totalling $215,000, but he did not reopen his mine, and the miners lost their jobs.[26]

Swaney and Cleghorn, 1951. The extortionate behavior directed against two mine employers, B.H. Swaney and L.E. Cleghorn, took place during general organizing activity in 1951. The union sought to shut down the neighboring mines owned by these two individuals while the drive was pending.

At the Cleghorn mine, operations had to be shut down one morning after about forty cars drove up to the mine tipple and blocked entrances. "About 125 men got out of these cars and came on to the tip-

---

[21] *Id.* at 722.
[22] *Id.* at 722.
[23] *Id.* at 722.
[24] *Id.* at 722.
[25] FINLEY, *supra* note 2, at 1480.
[26] *Id.*

ple property cursing and threatening the employees and forcing them to discontinue their work."[27]

On another day, Cleghorn attempted to keep the mine operating, and in the presence of a number of his employees, he was threatened by the District 31 organizer: "We want everybody to shut down until this strike is over. If you don't shut down, these boys are liable to get pretty rough with you."[28]

The activity escalated from threats to more destructive violence. One day, a female employee at Cleghorn was assaulted and thrown against a screen door, "then forced into the scale house where she was imprisoned by the pickets."[29] When Cleghorn himself tried to rescue her, he was beaten and "at the time of the hearing, about a year after the assault, there was still a small lump on his back where he was kicked by the pickets."[30]

In another incident, this one at the Swaney mine, the activities of the pickets became even more violent. "Three or four trucks which had been blocked sought to drive through to the tipple. As they passed through, the pickets rocked the trucks, breaking the windshields of two of the trucks, one of the rocks about the size of an average fist breaking through the windshield and striking the seat next to the driver."[31]

On another day, an employee "crippled in one of his legs" was "pulled backwards off his chair and dragged" outside where his clothes were ripped off and he was severely beaten.[32] He managed to drag himself away as about sixty union members overran the scalehouse area, hurling slate, rocks, and lumps of coal at employees. One employee was knocked down, and had two teeth kicked out. The pickets tore the telephone from the wall and rammed the door of the storage house, tearing the door from its hinges.[33]

In NLRB hearings in the case involving these mines, trial examiners, administrative law judges, and indeed the NLRB itself have usually remained relatively noncommital about the behavior of unions and their use of violence (due in part to the lack of necessity for them to discuss the cases in terms of violence but merely in terms of restraint and coercion), but in the hearings on this case, the trial examiner condemned

---

[27] United Mine Workers of America, District 31, et al. v. B. H. Swaney, et al., 95 N.L.R.B. 546, 559 (1951).

[28] *Id.* at 559.

[29] *Id.* at 560.

[30] *Id.*

[31] *Id.* at 563–64.

[32] *Id.* at 565.

[33] *Id.* at 556.

the behavior as "mob violence," saying it would be difficult to envision more positive evidence of restraining, coercive activity.[34]

Strike Violence

In the early postwar years, much of the violence associated with the UMW took place during organizational campaigns. As those campaigns wound down in the 1950s, however, the violence did not stop. In fact, very little changed in regard to either the tactics of the union or the targets of its violence. In 1958, 176 coal companies declined to sign that year's National Bituminous Coal Wage Agreement between the UMW and the industry bargaining agent, the Bituminous Coal Operators Association (BCOA). Most of the holdouts argued that they could not meet the pay scale required by the contract and retain their TVA contracts. A new "strike," directed against the marginal operators who had failed to sign, began in the spring of 1959.

Woodrow Smith Mine, 1959. One of the early targets was the Woodrow Smith Mine.

> Mine worker convoys began to patrol the roads. Twenty cars rolled up before the small mine of Woodrow Smith on Stinking Creek in Knox County, Kentucky. Smith was told to sign or else. He began to shout his defiance. A group chased him up a small hillside near the mine. State police arrived too late. They found Smith's body with six bullets in it.
>
> The first truck driver was killed a few days after Smith was murdered. The message to all mineowners and drivers was unmistakable. The Kentucky National Guard came into the area, but was no match for snipers and dynamite. Frightened operators pooled their resources and set up a radio transmitter near Hazard, to send out strike bulletins and give advance warning of raids. The transmitter lasted only a few days until another dynamite blast ripped it apart.[35]

Solar Fuel Company, 1966. The case involving this company is included to show the use unionists made of a tool of the miner's trade—explosives. In *Solar Fuel,* explosives were just a part of a long series of threats, violence, and mass picketing which took place over a three-month period of organizational activity. In its NLRB complaint, the employer cited thirty-three separate incidents which had occurred during the period despite the existence of a state court injunction which was to have limited the number of pickets in one location at any time to no more than fifteen.[36]

One morning, several mine officials were conferring outside the mine as nonstrikers arrived for work. "An unidentified picket threw an ex-

---

[34] *Id.*

[35] FINLEY, *supra* note 2, at 148–49.

[36] United Mine Workers District 2 and Solar Fuel Company, 170 N.L.R.B. 1581 (1968).

plosive which hit [one of the officials] on the leg, exploded and caused three puncture wounds in his left thigh and temporary loss of hearing."[37] Shortly after the explosion, witnesses said they could see blood seeping through the official's clothing. More traditional weapons were also enlisted: in one case an employee reported that a union agent "called me names and [held] a large knife and was shaking the knife, also."[38]

It is noteworthy that in this case, unlike some others, the union did not deny that the incidents occurred or that the perpetrators were agents of the union. Rather, the UMW argued that the behavior could hardly have intimidated or coerced employees to behave in a particular way, because the company "did not lose one single day of production." Indeed, the union argued in its brief, "What could be more peaceful in a labor strike than to conduct picketing in such a manner as to continue to permit the employer to conduct his business?"[39]

Attacks on Other Organized Miners

The UMW had precise ideas about what constituted the proper union for miners in the coal fields, and the rival organizations that arose from time to time were treated with the contempt usually reserved for free enterprise. Thus, when mine operators turned to the more reasonable Southern Labor Union (SLU) as a way of avoiding the excesses of the UMW, problems were bound to arise.

One such incident involving the Southern Labor Union occurred at the White Oak Coal Company, in Tennessee. Another took place at the Mears Coal Company, in Pennsylvania.

White Oak Coal Company, 1959. The White Oak Coal Company, in Campbell County, Tennessee, was visited by 200 men led by UMW representatives who told the owners that no more coal would be mined.[40] The problem arose because the mine's employees were negotiating to be represented by the independent Southern Labor Union. The night before the representation election was to be held, all of White Oak's strip mining equipment—two power shovels and a bulldozer—was destroyed by dynamite in an apparent attempt to convince the owners they were negotiating with the wrong union.

Mears Coal Company, 1967. In Dixonville, Pennsylvania, the Mears Coal Company was involved in a labor dispute in 1967 with its employees, who were represented by the Southern Labor Union. The UMW, without invitation from either party, decided to enter into these

---

[37] *Id.* at 1585.
[38] *Id.* at 1588.
[39] *Id.* at 1589.
[40] United Mine Workers v. White Oak Coal Co., 318 F.2d 591 (6th Cir. 1963).

negotiations. A band of UMW members interrupted an SLU meeting, where they seized the SLU president, struck him violently on the back of his head, and knocked him to the ground.[41] In later findings, the Court of Appeals for the Sixth Circuit noticed that "no one attempted to prevent or discourage the assault, nor was any effort made to disperse the crowd at that time."[42]

Attacks on Transportation

Coal is of little value to a customer until it is delivered to him. Independent coal companies seldom do their own hauling, preferring instead to hire independent truckers or to use the common carriers of the railroad system. Therefore, one obvious way to shut down an independent operator is to interdict its delivery process by shutting down or frightening off the coal transporters. Thus, trucks, railroad tracks, and trestles were frequent targets of UMW violence during strikes and organizing drives.

Meadow Creek Coal Company, 1948. At the Meadow Creek Coal Company,

> truck drivers were told [by UMW members] "to get the hell out of here" and not come back until the contract was signed. Some of the mobsters climbed aboard the running board of the truck and told the driver that his would be the last load of coal to leave the mine until a union contract was signed by the management. [A UMW representative] went to a coal dealer . . . who had been hauling coal from the mine in two trucks prior to [the organizational drive], and threatened to blow up his place of business if he ever sold the coal which had come from Meadow Creek.[43]

A district court found that the drivers or owners of more than 500 trucks used in doing business with Meadow Creek had been placed in such fear of bodily harm that they would not return to the mine until the contract was signed. Furthermore, Meadow Creek's spur line to the main railroad was destroyed by dynamite under circumstances which led the court to conclude that it was reasonable to fix blame for the incident on the UMW.[44]

Osborne Mining Company, 1954. A write-up by the Court of Appeals for the Sixth District details the tribulations of hauling coal during the UMW organizing drive at the Osborne Mining Company:

> A truck driver hauling coal from the [Osborne] pit was fired upon by two men with pistols in an attempt to stop him. Later, a group of 200 to 300 men

---

[41] NLRB v. United Mine Workers of America, 614 F.2d 872 (3rd Cir. 1980).
[42] *Id.*
[43] United Mine Workers of America v. Meadow Creek Coal Co. 263 F.2d 52, 57 (6th Cir., 1959).
[44] *Id.*

assembled at Jellico [Tennessee]. They stopped trucks carrying coal into Jellico and dumped the coal in the streets and parking lots. One driver hauling coal to Osborne was assaulted by one or more of the riotous group. Another driver hauling Osborne coal was chased on foot through the Osborne tipple, and his truck was dumped in a nearby lot by the mob. One or more members of the group forced an elderly gentleman to unload coal into the street by hand, though the truck was equipped with a mechnical dumper . . . Large numbers of nails were found on the roads used by trucks hauling Osborne coal.[45]

Various Mines. Incidents of violence directed against third-party coal transporters are so numerous that it is difficult to choose one over another. A few samples follow:

1. Railroad tracks and bridges were dynamited, as were tipples, trucks, and other equipment. On eight different occasions, the railroad track spur leading to the tipple was dynamited.[46]

2. Truck drivers and owners were warned not to deliver coal to mines being pressured.[47]

3. Trucks were stopped and ordered to be turned around or to dump their loads.[48]

4. A crusher operator was ambushed and shot at while on his way home, after finding a barricade of trees and timber on the public street which barred passage of his truck. Another employee was assaulted, beaten, and rendered unconscious by the use of brass knuckles.[49]

5. An independent trucker hauling coal was ambushed. Two tires were shot out, and one bullet entered his truck.[50]

6. A truck was dynamited at the owner's home at midnight. Later, another truck was exploded at the home of a new driver for the trucking company.[51]

7. A railroad trestle serving a nonunion mine was destroyed by dynamite.[52]

---

[45] United Mine Workers of America v. Osborne Mining Co. 279 F.2d 716, 722–723 (6th Cir., 1960).
[46] Flame Coal Co. v. United Mine Workers of America, 303 F.2d 39 (6th Cir., 1962).
[47] Gilchrest v. United Mine Workers of America, 290 F.2d 36 (6th Cir., 1961).
[48] *Id.*
[49] *Id.*
[50] *Id.*
[51] *Id.*
[52] *Id.*

8. Bullets were shot into trucks and truck tailgates were left open, allowing coal to fall onto the highway.[53]

9. Truck drivers were threatened until they finally quit, even though they were given permits by local authorities to operate.[54]

Summary

In the litany of examples taken from the Kentucky-Tennessee organizational drive and related UMW activities, several facts are clear. Firstly, the intent of the UMW was to deny nonunion employees or the members of rival labor organizations the right to choose their own union or to abstain from joining one if they so wished. Secondly, although individual tactics varied slightly from case to case, they were all violent. Thirdly, the targets of violence were anyone who could influence a mineowner or operator to force its workers to join the union.

Violence was employed throughout the UMW organizing campaign in a systematic and comprehensive way. It included the threats or fact of bodily harm, intimidation through mob action, and destruction of personal property. It was done under the direction of UMW officers. Early in 1950, the NLRB concluded that the UMW international was acting in conjunction with the local district officers as a "united joint leadership," and was therefore implicated in specific acts of violence in the organizational campaign.[55] Furthermore, compensatory and punative damages were frequently assessed against the international union, and in at least one case, the international reimbursed a local union member a substantial sum and commended him for his efforts when he was wounded by the irate relative of a nonunion miner who had been subjected to UMW abuse.[56] The conclusion is therefore inescapable that the violence in these campaigns was not spontaneous or reactive, but was directed and condoned by the union's leadership.

In reviewing the Kentucky-Tennessee organizing campaign, the Court of Appeals for the Sixth Circuit described it in this way:

> The campaign was conceived and prosecuted on a grand scale. Spectacular and varied methods were employed. Mass picketing was instituted at the tipple sites, on the highways, on railroad sidings and at the mines. Pickets, sometimes numbering more than a thousand men, roamed throughout the area in motor convoys. The persuasion of sheer numbers was supple-

---

[53] United Mine Workers of America v. Sunfire Coal Co. 313 F.2d 108 (6th Cir., 1963).

[54] United Mine Workers of America v. White Oak Coal Co., 318 F.2d 591 (6th Cir., 1963).

[55] United Mine Workers of America, 92 N.L.R.B. 916 (1950).

[56] United Mine Workers of America v. Meadow Creek Coal Co., 263 F.2d 52 (6th Cir., 1959).

mented by more violent and forceful methods. Trucks were stopped at the tipples, and on the way to and from them; their loads were dumped onto, and off, the highway. Mine and tipple workers were beaten. Strong threats of violence were made to the independent truck drivers to persuade them to discontinue transporting coal from the mines to the tipples.

After April 30, 1959, when mass picketing was substantially discontinued because of a federal court injunction, the pattern of coercion took a different turn. In fulfillment of a prophetic warning to truckers and others that "when the leaves come out on the trees" more convincing methods would be employed, the Flame tipple was put under gunfire from the nearby hills almost daily.[57]

Although not stressed in the examples chosen, many of the violent incidents involving the UMW occurred in the face of restraining orders issued by various courts. The union's short-term considerations seemed to overwhelm any longer view. Although defiance of court orders might have consequences, they would come later, and in the meantime if an owner could be persuaded to sign the contract, the union's goals would be achieved. This view may have won a number of battles for the union, but with the luxury of hindsight, we can now see that many of them were Pyrrhic victories.

INVOLVEMENT OF LEGAL AUTHORITIES

Many times during the UMW organizational drive, quick and effective police involvement prevented a nasty situation from developing into something worse. In other cases, police probably would have provided protection from the UMW mobs had they been able to arrive on the scene in time. (Roving caravans can cover a broad geographic territory, and are hard for the police to keep up with because they often split up, feign movements, send out decoys, or create confusion in other ways.) In many other cases, however, lack of clear determination on the part of the police, the judiciary, or other authorities to protect the UMW's targets encouraged the union to greater defiance of the law and greater violence.

Legal authorities are often loath to interfere in labor disputes for fear of being accused of taking sides in the conflict. Even though much of this organizational drive bore no relationship to a labor dispute as recognizable under the National Labor Relations (Taft-Hartley) Act (NLRA), local authorities seemed confused by the fact that a labor union was involved, and sometimes remained aloof.

For example, when equipment of the Clinfield Coal Corporation—a nonunion Tennessee operation—was found dynamited during the

---

[57] *Flame Coal Co. v. United Mine Workers of America*, 303 F.2d 39, 41 (6th Cir., 1962).

height of the organizational drive in 1949, at a time when nonunion mines throughout the region were being blown up by the UMW, a federal circuit court held that circumstantial evidence would not serve, and declined to hold the UMW responsible for the damage.[58] In another case, at the Osborne Mining Company in 1954, it was found that law enforcement officials were helping the perpetrators of the violence rather than protecting its victims:

> Coal trucks were stopped by a deputy sheriff . . . who was a member of the union, on warrants charging them with operating trucks with improper equipment and without a . . . license.[59]

Although these charges were later dismissed by the district court, which considered the example to be a serious abuse of the legal process inspired by union activity, the union's purpose of stopping the trucks had been achieved.

VIOLENCE DURING CONTRACT NEGOTIATIONS

Historically, the coal industry has had a centralized collective bargaining structure. Since 1950, when the Bituminous Coal Operators (BCOA) became an association, the pattern of bargaining has been such that if the contract is not signed between the UMW and the BCOA, the union mines are closed until an agreement is reached.

Because of this procedure, and because no union operator would dare to continue operating during a strike, strikers have little with which to occupy themselves during a walkout. This creates a curious situation because there is no need for the striking miners to picket their own employers. So, by tradition, they have devoted most of their energies to trying to close down, illegally, the nonunion operators who are not even members of the BCOA, and to shut off production of coal which if produced would diminish the effectiveness of their strike.

So common has this practice become in the coal fields that no one outside of courtrooms even bothers to maintain the fiction that the interdiction of the nonunion operations is an "informational" or "organizational" effort: everyone calls them "strikes." This adds an important dimension to the violence, because the overwhelming majority of it is targeted at firms or individuals who have no control over the settlement of the negotiations in progress. It also tends to leave the unionized operators in an ambivalent economic position about the use of violence, although the moral imperatives may remain.

---

[58] United Mine Workers of America v. Patton et al., 211 F.2d 742 (4th Cir., 1954).
[59] United Mine Workers of America v. Osborne Mining Co., 279 F.2d 716, 721 (6th Cir., 1960).

Since 1950, most of the BCOA-UMW contracts have been negotiated on a three-year time interval. Rarely has a new contract been
signed without a strike, and rarely has a strike been nonviolent. In the
sections which follow, the two most recent strikes are evaluated. They
are not the longest, nor the bloodiest, but they illuminate the fact that
the UMW has not outgrown its dedication to violence as a bargaining
device.

THE COAL STRIKE OF 1977–1978

The contract which had been in effect between the UMW and BCOA
expired at midnight on December 6, 1977. No one was surprised when
the miners walked off their jobs: throughout their history, unionized
soft-coal miners had prided themselves on their "no-contract,
no-work" policy. As one account put it:

> the UMW had so overused the strike weapon by 1977 that the occurrence
> of yet another national strike in December was taken for granted and pre-
> pared for by all concerned—the government, the public, and industries
> dependent on coal, as well as by the immediate parties to the dispute.[60]

The strikers may not have known that they were starting on what
would be the longest national coal walkout in history, but under the circumstances, they must have known it would be lengthy. The power of
the UMW to put public and political pressure on bargaining by simply
curtailing the flow of coal from union mines was not what it once was;
and without that kind of external pressure, successful negotiations
would require either a willingness to compromise—never a great likelihood with the UMW—or a long, slow process of economic attrition.

On their side, the BCOA firms felt boxed in. The market for coal was
strong, and, thanks to the Organization of Petroleum Exporting Coun-
tries (OPEC), prices could increase without affecting demand. But to
the unionized companies, production costs were already high relative
to those of the nonunion firms and to those of the western surface
mines. The BCOA firms feared for their competitive positions if they
agreed to an expensive new contract without relief from productivity-
restricting labor practices.

Strike Environment, 1977

In the fall of 1977, production of soft coal was at record levels, but
the relative importance of the product to the national economy had
been declining for half a century. In 1923, coal provided for 60 percent

---

[60] J. A. Ackerman, *The Impact of the Coal Strike of 1977–1978*, 32 INDUSTRIAL AND
LABOR RELATIONS REVIEW, 178 (1979).

of energy consumed in the United States; but by 1977, it was providing less than 20 percent.[61]

Furthermore, at least part of the record-setting levels of production could be attributed to inventory building. All three of the major customers for coal—steel mills, electric utilities, and heavy industrial plants—had been building their stockpiles, both as a matter of general prudence in an industry beset by wildcat strikes, and in anticipation of a possible nationwide walkout. As the strike began, electric utilities had ninety-six days' supply on hand, coke plants had seventy-nine, and general industrial plants had fifty.[62] With stockpiles this large, only cold weather, a long strike, and a nearly complete shutdown of the coal fields could hope to evoke national emergency measures or economic pressures outside of the coal-producing and coal-using industries. The country's soft economic underbelly, its transportation system, no longer relied on steam or the coal needed to produce it.

The chances that a nationwide strike would close down the entire industry were also remote. Although few if any union mines would try to remain open in the East, union mines there no longer constituted the whole industry. Between 1972 and 1977, national agreement tonnage—that is, tonnage covered by the contract between BCOA firms and the UMW—had fallen from over 68 percent to under 52 percent of total United States coal production. Structural changes were taking place within the industry in both the East and the West.

In the western coal fields, surface mining techniques are the rule rather than the exception. The relatively newer technology of strip mining was developed after the era of great organizational efforts by the UMW. Furthermore, the people who work the strip mines are not really "miners," in the traditional sense, but are heavy equipment operators. As a consequence, many of the western surface mines are nonunion or are organized by the International Union of Operating Engineers (IUOE), and the miners employed there respond to different stimuli than do the eastern deep miners. The western mines are from two to four times more productive than their eastern counterparts, and account for ever-increasing proportions of coal production. From less than 2 percent of coal production in 1923, surface mining had grown to account for more than 60 percent of it by 1977.[63]

In the eastern fields, too, the structure was changing—but for different reasons. The series of petroleum crises during the early 1970s had created additional demand for coal and allowed its price to rise

---

[61] NATIONAL COAL ASSOCIATION, COAL FACTS 59 (1979).
[62] U.S. DEPARTMENT OF ENERGY, COAL SUPPLEMENT NO. 1 TO WINTER DATA BULLETIN OF DEC. 21, 1977 (December 10, 1977).
[63] COAL FACTS, *supra* note 61, at 54, 55.

significantly. These factors encouraged both the opening of new mines and the reopening of abandoned ones. From a low of 6,100 in 1969, the total number of active mines grew to more than 7,000 by 1977. Many of these newly started or reopened mines were marginal in character and relied on the cost savings possible through nonunion operation for their existence. This result may also have been encouraged by the dismal record of wildcat walkouts in the unionized sector. During the middle 1970s, wildcat strikes were responsible for production losses of more than one full working day per month. (See Table IV-1.)

TABLE IV-1
Work Stoppages in the Bituminous Coal Industry
1950-1976

Year	Number of Work Stoppages	Percent of Total Work Time Lost
1950–59 (mean)	314	2.4
1960–69 (mean)	184	1.1
1970–76 (mean)	947	5.1
1970	500	1.8
1971	606	11.8*
1972	963	1.4
1973	1,039	1.4
1974	996	7.6*
1975	1,139	3.0
1976	1,383	3.7

Source: U.S. Department of Labor, Collective Bargaining in the Bituminous Coal Industry. (BLS Report 514, 1978).
*Renegotiation of national agreements.

The structural environment of the coal fields as the negotiations broke down in December 1977 did not cause the violence which was to follow, but it certainly was a contributing factor. The BCOA operators, already working at a competitive disadvantage, were not likely to settle quickly on an expensive new contract. The major coal users had stocked up in anticipation, and if they could rely on a continued flow from the nonunion mines, they could operate indefinitely.

The trend toward nonunion operations was threatening the security of the grip in which the UMW had held the eastern coal fields since the 1920s. The mood was generally unsettled, as evidenced by the number of wildcat strikes that had occurred. To win the strike on their terms, the unionists would have to shut down not only the union mines, but also the nonunion ones—at least in the East where the manpower was available to do it. But their efforts were likely to be resisted by an increasingly strong nonunion segment.

In the strike, both sides held their ground, and the strike dragged on to record-setting lengths. An overview of its chronology and a hint at the bargaining issues involved is presented in Table IV-2. As can be inferred from that table, economic issues were not a major concern. The great sticking point involved the union's right to stage wildcat walkouts between contracts. The BCOA firms considered control of such walkouts to be of great importance.

TABLE IV-2
Chronology of the 1977–1978 Coal Strike

October 6, 1977	National contract negotiations begin. In addition to wages, issues for the UMW were recognition of the right to wildcat strike, and restoration and protection of pension and welfare benefits. For the BCOA, issues were stability, through elimination of wildcat strikes, and increased productivity through changed work rules.
December 6, 1977	Strike begins.
February 5, 1978	UMW president announces "tentative agreement" to the BCOA "last ditch" offer. The proposed contract included most basic BCOA stability and productivity alternatives, most UMW wage increases, and pension protection benefits.
February 6, 1978	Members of the UMW's bargaining council arrive in Washington and picket union headquarters to protest the proposed contract, the terms of which none of them had yet seen. UMW president physically prevented from entering headquarters.
February 12, 1978	Bargaining council officially rejects agreement following disagreement with union leadership.
February 1978	Public and political pressures for government intervention mount. After February 12, government takes active role in structuring new agreement.
February 24, 1978	President Carter announces strike settlement based on a pattern contract conceding economic issues to UMW but retaining for BCOA most "sensitive" elements of stability and productivity packages.
March 5, 1978	Union rank and file reject second contract.
March 6, 1978	President Carter announces intention to invoke Taft-Hartley. Union calls for government takeover of mines.
March 13, 1978	Back-to-work order issued and generally ignored.
March 14, 1978	Third tentative agreement, arrived at by private negotiations, announced.
March 24, 1978	Agreement ratified by rank and file, 57 percent to 43 percent.
March 27, 1978	Work resumed under new contract. Elimination from the agreement of most productivity and stability items (which were contained in the first agreement) deemed victory.

Source: C. Perry, The Decline of the United Mine Workers (to be published in late 1983 by the Wharton Industrial Research Unit).

Initial Activities

The strike began at midnight on December 6, 1977. Although the weather was unseasonably cold in the eastern coal fields during the next several days, it was not severe enough to prevent an early outbreak of violence. In Louisville, Kentucky, and in other places, trouble began on the first day. Under a headline, *Pickets roam snowy coal fields trying to shut non union mines,* the local newspaper reported on a roving caravan of fifty pickets in cars and pickups traveling among nonunion mines and tipples and trying to close their operations.[64]

During that first week, many caravans, sometimes including up to 400 people and coordinated by citizen's band radios, were spotted moving through the coal regions of Kentucky, Tennessee, Ohio, Pennsylvania, Indiana, Virginia, West Virginia, and Alabama.[65] Some of the throng carried clubs, others wore motorcycle helmets or their mining helmets.[66] They stopped trucks and forced drivers to dump their loads; they threw rocks at cars believed to be driven by nonunion miners trying to go to work; they interfered with coal transfers at power generating plants; and they held mass demonstrations at one nonunion mine after another.[67]

Picketing and intimidation were not the only activities of the roving caravans. Two days after the strike began, an explosion destroyed a $90,000 drilling machine at the M&M Coal and Land Development Company, a small nonunion mine in Pennington Gap, Virginia.[68] The tradition of violence which had characterized coal strikes since before the turn of the century was again beginning to evolve.

By the time the Taft-Hartley Act was invoked ninety-five days later, there would be a total of two killings, two assaults, thirty-five bombings, the taking of one hostage, and seventy-one other "disruptions" involving such things as sabotage of railroads, gunfire directed against people, trains, and motor vehicles, property damage, and other incidents of violence serious enough to be noted by the Department of Justice.[69] These are summarized below in Table IV–3.

The statistics in Table IV–3 yield two clear points. The first is that

---

[64] *Pickets roam snowy coalfields trying to shut non union mines,* Louisville Courier Journal, Dec. 7, 1977, at B-3.

[65] *Striking Ohio miners invade E. Kentucky,* Louisville Courier Journal, Dec. 13, 1977, at A-1.

[66] *Roving UMW pickets protest at Sterns,* Louisville Courier Journal, Dec. 13, 1977, at A-1.

[67] *Supra,* note 64.

[68] U.S. Department of Justice, United Mine Workers Strike—Coal Industry, Event Track 77-13, Incident Summary, December 8, 1977, through March 5, 1978 (pre Taft-Hartley) (mimeographed).

[69] *Id.*

Union Violence

TABLE IV-3
*Incidents of Coal Strike Violence
Prior to Taft-Hartley Injunction
(December 6, 1977—March 5, 1978)*

Type of Incident		Location		Targets of Violence	
Assault, fatal	2	Illinois	7	Nonunion mining company	38
Assault	2	Kentucky	44	Rail company	34
Bombings	35	Virginia	18	Independent coal hauler:	
Hostages	1	Pennsylvania	14	truck	19
Disruptions	71	Indiana	9	riverboat	2
		Alabama	6	Nonunion employee	
Total	111	W. Virginia	7	property	8
		Tennessee	1	Police or state trooper	3
		Ohio	5	Utility company	2
				Highway destruction	1
		Total	111	UMW local office	1
				Not identified	1
				Total	111

Summary	
Total incidents	111
Deaths	2
Injuries	9
Property Loss	$4.23 million

Source: U.S. Department of Justice, United Mine Workers Strike—Coal Industry, Event Track 77-13, Incident Summary, December 8, 1977, through March 5, 1978 (Pre Taft-Hartley) (mimeographed).

violent incidents did not occur with equal frequency in all geographic areas covered by the strike. In fact, well over two-thirds of the total occurred in only three states: Kentucky, Virginia, and Pennsylvania. The second point is that all the violence was related to, and usually directed against, individuals who, or companies that, were not actually parties to the contract or participants in the strike. Nonunion mining companies, railroad companies, and independent trucking companies hauling nonunion coal bore most of it.

Other violent incidents, which were not noted by the Department of Justice, occurred during the strike, as well. The department generally did not give notice to mass picketing, verbal intimidation, or coercion not resulting in physical injury (such, for example, as is involved in forcing a truck driver to dump a load of coal in the middle of the street), although these were precisely the type of incidents that gave the strike its atmosphere of pervasive violence.

Table IV–4, derived by adding accounts of violence from selected local newspapers to the Department of Justice incident report, shows totals for the occurrences of various types of violence.[70] The data in the table lead to the conclusion that the overwhelming majority of strike violence was directed against nonunion and independent mines or against independent transportation companies. It also provides the additional information that the majority of strike violence was concentrated in two time periods: the first during the first few days of the strike, and the second during the period beginning in mid-February, when government intervention was imminent and when internal bickering was taking place in the union.

Analysis of the violence occurring during this strike will be aided by evaluating three major questions: who were the targets of violence and why? what caused the geographic variance in the amount of violent activity? and, why did most of the violence occur during the two identified time periods?

The Targets

Employers of striking mine workers were not the principal targets of violence. As discussed earlier, employers of the strikers were too well conditioned to try to operate during a strike. As Table IV–5 shows, all but seven union mines—and absolutely all of those located in Appalachia—immediately ceased operations when the strike began. In addition, some nonunion mines closed down without first being the object of special violence or persuasion. For some owners, remembrance of past confrontations with the UMW was sufficient. For example, one nonunion miner from Ohio had this reaction:

> We put down our tools the day the strike started . . . Union miners are a mean bunch, and we are afraid of them. But it makes me mad that they involve me in their gripes.[71]

Even with these "voluntary" closings, however, more than 1,800 nonunion mines remained in operation, and it was toward these that

[70] Files of the following were examined or sampled: Cincinnati Enquirer, Associated Press, *U.S. News & World Report*, Indianapolis Star, Louisville Courier Journal, The New York Times, Philadelphia Evening Bulletin.

[71] *Where a Drawn-Out Strike Pitted Neighbor Against Neighbor*, U.S. NEWS AND WORLD REPORT, Mar. 6, 1978, at 16.

TABLE IV-4
Incidents of Violence and their Targets as Reported by the Popular Press during UMW Strike, 1977–1978

Time Period (1977–78)	Type of Incident				Total	Target of Violence				
	Intimidation	Coercion	Assault	Other		Nonunion or Independent mine, tipple, or loading dock	Rail, truck, or barge transport	Police or other authority	Non-UMW official or employee	UMW official or employee, other, or not specif'd
12/6–12/8	1	–	–	1	: 2 :	2	1	–	–	–
12/9–12/15	8	34	9	10	: 61 :	11	3	–	–	2a
12/16–12/22	5	–	1	5	: 12 :	5	1	2	1	–
12/23–12/29	2	–	–	5	: 7 :	2	2	1	–	–
12/30–1/5	2	3	3	11	: 19 :	9	6	1	1	1b
1/6–1/12	4	3	2*	6	: 15 :	4	5	–	2	2c
1/13–1/19	4	4	2	10	: 20 :	7	8	–	–	–
1/20–1/26	–	5	2	2	: 9 :	–	3	1	–	–
1/27–2/2	2	–	2*	2	: 6 :	2	–	1	–	2d
2/3–2/9	–	1	–	7	: 8 :	4	5	1	2	–
2/10–2/16	4	4	2	7	: 20 :	7	8	–	–	–
2/17–2/23	4	10	15	20	: 49 :	8	22	3	3	3e
2/24–3/2	7	2	8	6	: 23 :	5	11	–	–	2f
3/3–3/9	1	1	1	–	: 3 :	–	1	–	1	2g
3/10–3/16	3	–	3	2	: 8 :	2	4	–	1	–
Total					246					

Source: popular press, various; and U. S. Department of Justice, Incident Summary.

Notes: *Fatal
aPower company; company store
bPower company transformer
cRetired miners
dUnion man; school
eTwo power companies; manufacturing plant
fPower company; union official
gAmong UMW miners; cameraman

the UMW's initial attacks were directed. Throughout coal fields in Virginia, Pennsylvania, Alabama, and Illinois, UMW members moved against the independent nonunion operators.[72] Union mobs were so large that local authorities did not even try to stop the violence; at best, they tried to control it. The UMW's initial purpose was obviously to close down as many of the remaining nonunion operations as possible so as to increase the effectiveness of the work stoppage. It is perhaps instructive to examine typical examples of the violence that accompanied some nonunion closings. The following two short cases were chosen because they are representative of ordinary situations that occurred during the strike.

Ohio Power Company. During the first week of the strike, fifty to seventy-five pickets from the UMW appeared at the Ohio Power Company's terminal in Massac County, Illinois, a nonunion operation, and refused to allow Ohio Power's employees to enter the terminal. Local authorities were on hand at the time of the first incident, and no damage or bloodshed occurred. Four days later, however, a stronger force of between 150 to 200 UMW miners stormed the terminal, paying no attention to the local police who made some show of trying to confront them. To ensure their safety, the Ohio Power Company employees were evacuated to a towboat on the nearby Ohio River, leaving only a supervisor in the facility to observe the miners. Having broken the windows of all of the vehicles in the parking lot, the strikers forced their way past state police who were standing in the doorway of the main entrance, and began ransacking and vandalizing buildings and machinery inside the plant's fence.

Unable to contain the violence, the state police recommended to the supervisor that the operation be shut down. When this was done, UMW pickets supplanted the police and stood guard at the gates of the terminal to discourage employees and terminal officials from reentering. Ohio Power managers wishing to visit the terminal were obliged to do so by riverboat, but even that route was dangerous, as windows in the boat were shattered by gunfire.

Despite the gunfire, the disregard of police authority, the forced closing of a nonunion mine, intimidation of employees, and damage amounting to over $40,000 to the terminal, the incident was not reported by the Department of Justice.[73]

Westvaco Resources. Another example representative of the union's tactics early in the strike took place in Luke, Maryland, where a West-

---

[72] *Supra* note 68, at 8.

[73] The source of this example has requested anonymity. However, accounts in such newspapers as the Southern Illinoisan include much of the information as discussed, and the files are in the Wharton Industrial Research Unit library.

vaco Corporation papermill plant was located. The plant was fueled by coal extracted by nonunion surface miners located within a few miles of the mill and owned by a subsidiary, Westvaco Resources. Four days after the strike began, on December 12, 1977, two UMW representatives arrived at the local coal operation for the purpose of shutting down the mine. Approximately fifty strikers accompanied the UMW leaders. Their initial request was polite, but it was refused by the mine supervisor who stated that his mine not only fueled the mill, but also supplied fuel for heat and water in surrounding communities.

The pickets went away unsatisfied and returned in force a week later. Carloads of men, most in cars with out-of-state license plates, arrived at the entrance to the mill's wood yard and threatened to set fire to it if the mine was not shut down. The mill's supervisor felt discretion required him to comply, and he also stopped all truck transportation between the mill and the plant.

While this confrontation was in progress, another band of pickets was visiting the company's scale house, located about a mile away. These pickets threw stones and rocked vehicles until they learned that the coaling operation had been successfully shut down.

The pickets then moved next door to the R.A.K. Coal Company, which was still operating, and burned a building. The pickets prevented local fire department personnel from reaching the site and held them at bay until enough state police arrived to force passage for the fire trucks. These incidents, too, escaped the notice of the Department of Justice.[74]

Initial Success

The previous examples are representative of the UMW's original focus of violence against nonunion operators early in the strike. That their tactics were moderately successful can be seen from Table IV–5. Success was particularly great in the Appalachian region, where the number of non-UMW mines in operation (and, therefore, mines which by right should not have been affected by the strike) fell from more than 3,000 before the strike began, to 1,800 when the strike started, to a low of fewer than 1,150 two weeks later.

Transportation Companies

As the strike progressed and the number of closed mines stabilized, the UMW diverted some of its attention to transportation companies

---

[74] This account is taken from signed affadavits from Westvaco Resources' employees, and a complaint filed with the NLRB.

TABLE IV-5

Number of Mines Operating During the UMW Strike, 1977–1978

Date of Count	Coal Mines in Operation			
	Appalachian Region		Total United States	
	UMW	Other	UMW	Other
Before Strike	1,529	3,058	1,651	3,334
December 8	0	1,704	7	1,853
December 22	2	1,133	8	1,275
January 5	1	1,234	15	1,275
January 19	0	1,230	17	1,381
February 2	0	1,275	17	1,429
February 16	2	1,310	20	1,488
March 2	3	1,370	21	1,573
March 16	16	1,667	34	1,884
March 23	14	1,742	34	1,954
After Strike	1,419	2,850	1,496	3,119

Source: U. S. DEPARTMENT OF ENERGY, COMPREHENSIVE OVERVIEW OF WINTER ENERGY DATA BULLETINS. WINTER 1977–1978. (Coal Supplement No. 17, 1978.)

and other transporters of coal. A typical effort was to destroy or sabotage railroad spur lines leading to nonunion mines. Another was to confront a truck driver and force him to dump his load of coal in the middle of the street or alongside the road. Many such actions occurred in Kentucky, where the following representative example was recorded by the Department of Justice:

At approximately 11:25 p.m., an explosion caused by an unknown source occurred at the C&O railroad bridge number 27,1, also known as the wall trestle, Louisa, Lawrence County. There were no injuries sustained, and estimated damage to the trestle was approximately $35,000. The bridge was expected to be out of operation for at least six to seven days.[75]

One more example typifies the scene:

Norfolk and Western Railway Company, Roanoke, Virginia, advised the Richmond office of the FBI that sometime between 12:45 p.m., December 20, 1977 and 11:20 a.m., December 21, 1977, a Norfolk and Western freight train approached bridge and was unable to stop which resulted in the derailment of four engines and one coal car. No personal injuries reported.[76]

[75] *Supra* note 68, at 21.
[76] *Id.* at 7.

Damage to trucking companies occurred as well. In a three-day siege in southern Indiana, UMW members firebombed two independent coal-hauling trucking companies in Boonville.[77] The *Louisville Courier Journal* carried a vivid account:

> Two truck drivers said a horde of men and women swarmed over a hill of coal on the Bland lot and attacked their trucks, smashing windows with axes and puncturing tires with icepicks.[78]

Fires were then started by the UMW members, doing property damage estimated at $500,000.[79] The trucking firm had previously been granted a temporary injunction to allow it to haul coal unmolested from the mine to the railroad, but injunctions seem to carry little weight in strikes.

Geography

Although a few violent incidents were reported in communities west of the Mississippi River during the strike, most of the violence was focused on the underground mines and surrounding communities located east of the Mississippi River. Violence occurred in all coal-mining states within that region. In Kentucky, at the Barton Mining Company in Floyd County, a generator and mine fan valued at $16,000 were dynamited.[80] In Alabama, "a thousand UMW strikers, most of them from Ohio, drove automotive caravans into Jackson County," resulting in mine offices burned down, nonunion miners bloodied, and mine vehicles smashed.[81] Table IV–6 shows that although the correlation is not perfect, states with the middle range of proportions of non-union to union mines in an area tended to be subjected to greater levels of violence than areas in which mines were either heavily union or mostly nonunion.

Timing

As already pointed out, the total number of incidents of violence during the strike followed what statisticians call a bimodal distribution—meaning that it peaked at two times: early in December, and again in late February (see Table IV–1). The reasons for the early violence—that which occurred during the first two weeks of the strike—have already been sufficiently described. The reasons for the

---

[77] *Id.* at 13.
[78] Louisville Courier Journal, Jan. 7, 1978, np.
[79] *Id.*
[80] *Supra* note 68, at 8.
[81] *Id.*

TABLE IV–6
Violence by State:
UMW Coal Strike, 1977–1978

Mines in Operation, Week Prior to Strike			Percent UMW	Strength of UMW[a]	Incidents of Violence	Level of Violence[b]
State	Total	UMW				
TN	217	2	0.9	L	1	L
OH	286	44	15.4	L	17	L
KY	1,345	230	16.9	M	112	H
PA	765	185	24.2	M	28	H
IN	52	18	34.6	M	21	H
AL	224	95	42.4	H	16	L
IL	72	47	65.3	H	17	L
WV	1,095	760	69.4	H	14	L

Source: U. S. DEPARTMENT OF ENERGY, WINTER ENERGY SUMMARY, and information supporting Table IV–3.

second wave of violence are most likely associated with the development of public and political pressures for government intervention and with reinforcement of communications between the union rank and file and its bargaining leadership. It may also have been in anticipation of and reaction to the Taft-Hartley injunction.

Ineffectiveness of Legal Authority: Political Intervention

Government involvement, whether by a district court issuing an injunction or by the president invoking the Taft-Hartley cooling-off period, seems to have always provoked UMW members, causing an increased tendency on their part to use violence as a tactic to demonstrate their disapproval. Although the trait is not specific to the UMW, organized miners seem to enjoy thumbing their noses at authority.

The presence or absence of police also contributes to the frequency with which violence occurs, and the 1977–78 strike was no exception. Throughout the coal fields there were many examples of police inaction, some of them cited above, which allowed mass picketing to develop, which allowed a confrontation to turn into a riot, or which failed to take appropriate measures against obvious violations of the law.

Although these individual actions (or inactions) are often inexcusable, and although they undoubtedly add to the total carnage and destruction, the true harm is done in another quarter—in the feeling of helplessness and vulnerability they engender in the smaller mine owners and independent coal haulers. The inaction of authorities, although admittedly due at least in part to the wide geographic area and large number of separate work locations to be protected, is one of the principal reasons why so many nonunion mines shut down when a strike begins. It also allows the union caravans and mass picketers to choose their targets and move without restraint. In fact, it might be said that the past pattern of police inactivity and ineffectiveness during coal strikes has determined the union's strategy of violence.

The actuality or anticipation of political intervention in strikes must also bear its share of responsibility for the prevalence of violence. For example, in Kentucky, where the *Louisville Courier Journal* was filled daily with descriptions of violent events inspired by UMW members, Governor Julien Carrol responded by investigating not the union's excesses but rather the unsupported charges of police brutality lodged by local unionists.[82] This had the double impact of not only diverting attention, but also discouraging the police from carrying out their duties.

Summary and Conclusions

The coal strike of 1977–78 provides a dramatic example of the use of violence as a deliberate strike tactic. Chapter I suggested that strike violence has been used at various times by unions as an organizing tool, as a bargaining device, as an attention getter, as an enforcement mechanism, and as a communications measure. In this strike, violence was used in all of these ways except as an organizing tool.

It is a discouraging fact, but the concerted violence of the UMW during strikes seems to work, at least in the short term. The final settlement in the strike left unsettled several critical questions involving labor productivity and stability, and it may have accelerated the trend toward nonunion operation; but there is no gainsaying the fact that the settlement of the violent 1978–78 strike was substantially on the union's terms.

THE COAL STRIKE OF 1981

Strikes are a tradition with the UMW. The last settlement without one had been in 1964. So even though progress was remarkably smooth as the contract talks proceeded during early 1981, both sides, and the end consumers of coal, began their preparations. Power com-

---

[82] *Carrol Orders Probe of Charges in Mine Clash,* Louisville Courier Journal, Dec. 16, 1977, np.

panies and heavy industries in the East built up stockpiles of record quantities; miners in the eastern coal fields talked openly about the pleasures of having a few weeks off after the hard winter to take advantage of the bass season and the other joys of spring; union coal companies made preparation for closing as they always do during strikes, and nonunion companies began to set up defenses at their mines and homes.

As the 1981 contract went out for ratification by rank-and-file UMW members, the ritualistic preparations began. The contract was the best the UMW had ever gotten, providing a 36 percent increase in wages, a new dental plan, new contributions of $100 million a year for a pension plan for widows, a prohibition of Sunday work, and asking only one minor concession in return—the elimination of a legally tenuous "royalty" paid by union firms for processing nonunion coal. (In the preceding sixteen years this royalty had contributed $54 million to the pension fund, an amount equal to roughly one-half of one year's contribution under the new system.

But tradition is strong in the coal fields. At union halls in Virginia, West Virginia, Kentucky, Pennsylvania, and throughout the rest of the twenty states where the UMW has representation, officials and rank-and-file members postured for newsmen, burned copies of the proposed contract, and denounced it as an insult and a sellout.

For their part, the nonunion operators girded themselves for a possible repetition of 1977. At the Paramont Mining Corporation in western Virginia, some company officials spent the night organizing convoys of their coal trucks and fitting the lead trucks with five-foot long magnets to sweep up the nails and spikes that were expected to be scattered on the roads. Others strung the mine's perimeter with cow bells on fishing line to warn that intruders were approaching.[83] Throughout the fields, miners and mine owners armed themselves, or prepared to shut down for the duration of the strike "to avoid trouble."[84]

In several particulars, there were major differences from the previous strike. By 1981, UMW coal accounted for less than half (44 percent) of the total U. S. production. Only a decade earlier, it had constituted more than 70 percent, and as recently as the beginning of the 1977 strike, it had still provided more than half (52 percent) of the nation's coal. The decreased proportion was largely the result of higher productivity in the western surface mines, but some of it was also attributable to the changing ownership structure in the East. By striking for 111 days in 1977, union miners had succeeded in driving even more

---

[83] Richmond Times-Dispatch, Mar. 28, 1981, at B-1, and Apr. 7, 1981, at B-1.
[84] Cincinnati Enquirer, Mar. 28, 1981, at A-4.

of the smaller union operators out of business or causing them to price themselves out of their market.[85] Not all of those mines were reopened, but when they did, many of them reopened as nonunion operations.

The number of union mines in Appalachia had diminished substantially, and the proportion of union miners had shrunk accordingly, but the smaller number of union mines was not a controlling factor in the relative mildness of this strike. After all, there were still 160,000 UMW members who could participate in the strike. But the political winds had also begun blowing from a different and more conservative direction. In the event of trouble, many of the nonunion operators now would have easier access—in some cases for the first time—to the political system and its protective police arm.

In western Virginia, for example, at the start of the strike, "increased numbers of state police patrolled coal-hauling roads where scores of nonunion coal companies conducted business more or less as usual.[86] Virginia's governor, John Dalton, was said to have "angered many miners by sending a large contingent of state troopers to the coal fields before the strike began." The troopers "maintained a high profile, patrolling busy streets regularly.[87] All of this was in sharp contrast to the situation at the start of the 1977 strike. For example, in Wise County, Virginia, a mine owner beset by mass picketing during the first few days commented: "Basically, it was pretty peaceful. There were about 30 or 40 state troopers there within a few minutes."[88]

Perhaps it was the increased police protection and increased political support for the nonunion mine owners, perhaps it was the large stockpiles of coal and lack of a real or fabricated national emergency; perhaps it was even the time of the year and the bass season; or perhaps it was just that the strike issue was a complicated one that did not translate well into slogans, but something made this strike unlike previous strikes, for it commenced in a relatively nonviolent manner.

First Two Weeks: March 27 to April 10

On the first day of the strike, there were no strike-related injuries reported from any of the twenty states in which the UMW has mines. In fact, very little activity of any sort was reported—only a few scattered groups of pickets at nonunion operations in eastern Kentucky and southern West Virginia.[89] The first "serious" violent incident was not reported by the eastern press until the strike was almost a week

[85] Richmond Times-Dispatch, Apr. 7, 1981, at B-3.
[86] Richmond Times-Dispatch, Mar. 28, 1981, at B-1.
[87] Pittsburgh Press, Apr. 3, 1981, at B-2.
[88] Richmond Times-Dispatch, Apr. 7, 1981, at B-1.
[89] Cincinnati Enquirer, Mar. 28, 1981, at A-4.

old. It involved a Harlan County (Kentucky) nonunion mine foreman who was fired upon by pickets.

According to a newspaper report, "a state police detective said 19 bullet holes were counted in the [foreman's] truck's cab, windows and body, and the two rear tires were shot out."[90] Other papers reported that "a truck windshield was broken at one of the [Harlan] pits,"[91] and ". . . a foreman's truck was shot at as he drove by a picket line. He was slightly injured by flying glass."[92] It is likely that the understatement of the incident by these other papers was a deliberate effort to avoid inflaming passions and heating up the level of confrontation; if so, those papers performed a valuable service and may have helped to keep the strike from degenerating to the open warfare level seen so frequently in the past.

A barroom murder, adjudged by the local police to have been strike-caused but not strike-related (a nonunion miner was shot to death by a union member following an argument which probably would not have taken place but for the strike) marred the second week. But overall in the early stages of the strike, most incidents were minor ones involving scattered picketing, a few slashed tires, a few scattered nails along mine access roads, a few vehicles shot at, and some windows knocked out. Except for the murder, it was small change stuff by the traditional standards of mining strikes.

The Middle Period: April 11 to May 15

As the strike dragged on and the possibility of an early settlement diminished, a pattern developed in the violence. Overall, there were fewer and less-brutal incidents than there had been in 1977, but the targets were about the same: nonunion companies that continued to operate, independent truckers, transportation companies that served the coal fields, security forces, and individual nonunion mine employees and their families. Most of the trouble occurred in specific contested areas, where the number of nonunion mines had been growing but was not yet large enough to merit political consideration and protection.

Coal industry estimates when the strike began put the level of organization at 53 percent to 96 percent of production in most of the eastern coal fields, but at 40 percent in Virginia and 18 percent in eastern Kentucky.[93] In the highly organized areas, with rare exception,

---

[90] Pittsburgh Press, Apr. 2, 1981, at A-1.
[91] Pittsburgh Press, Apr. 2, 1981, at B-2.
[92] Cleveland Plain Dealer, Apr. 2, 1981, at 5-B.
[93] Richmond Times-Dispatch, Apr. 13, 1981, at B-4.

production stopped when the strike started, so there were no targets for mass picketing, and no foci for violence. In other areas, particularly in Virginia and Kentucky, the possibilities for violence were much greater.

Virginia's governor had elected to give nonunion firms the full protection promised them by law and had dispatched 150 to 200 state troopers to the coal counties. For this decision, he was widely criticized by community-service organizations and church groups aligned with the Southwest Virginia Strike Support Committee, all of which claimed that the presence of the troopers created an "atmosphere of intimidation and fear."[94] Nevertheless, because of the governor's action, nonunion mines stayed open and the region remained relatively calm.

It was not the same in Kentucky. Although the eastern counties were mostly nonunion, Governor John Y. Brown adopted a position of what he called "strict neutrality." To at least some of the nonunion mine operators, this seemed to mean that strikers could do anything they wanted to do during the strike without being hindered by police intervention.[95] As a result, Pike County, in eastern Kentucky, came to be known as the "Little Big Horn" of the 1981 strike. The newspapers reported the following events:

April 12   In Shelbeana, shots were fired at pickets at a railroad yard.[96]

April 16   In Pikesville, rocks were thrown at passing coal trucks.[97]

April 23   A convoy of 10 coal trucks heading for a nonunion mine was ambushed and a gun battle ensued during which three truckers and a union member were wounded.[98]

April 24   Governor Brown rejected a plea for state police protection, saying "We're not going to camp on one side or the other."[99]

April 25   A convoy of 45 coal trucks, 2 steel-hauling trucks, and 1 security vehicle, traveling without police escort, was

---

[94] *Id.*

[95] Louisville Courier-Journal, May 10, 1981, at A-1.

[96] Louisville Courier-Journal, Apr. 12, 1981, at A-19.

[97] Cleveland Plain Dealer, Apr. 16, 1981, at 10-A.

[98] Richmond Times Dispatch, Apr. 23, 1981, at E-4.

[99] Pittsburgh Press, Apr. 24, 1981, at A-1.

ambushed in Pike County and fired upon. Eleven trucks and the security vehicle were hit.[100]

May 4   At Pine Mountain, "several empty trucks" were damaged by gun-toting vandals.[101]

May 7   In Harlan County, nails were scattered and rocks and bottles were thrown at a convoy.[102]

May 8   A picketer was wounded by shots fired from a truck convoy near New Cumberland.[103]

May 9   Gunshots knocked out a transformer in eastern Kentucky, and pickets attacked a coal truck at an Ohio River loading dock.[104]

In the three weeks prior to May 10, while the police were maintaining "neutrality," seven persons were wounded by gunfire in or near Pike County as a direct result of the strike. A Kentucky judge issued a call for independent coal truckers to postpone hauling and observe a one-week "cooling off" period, apparently oblivious to the fact that the truckers were the targets rather than the perpetrators of the violence, and were not parties to the dispute.

To sum up this middle period of the strike, most of the violence, as in earlier strikes, was directed against parties one or two steps removed from the actual labor dispute. Nonunion mines, having no contract with the UMW and no direct relationship with the BCOA, were definitely not part of the bargaining process; but their continued operation during strikes was felt by the UMW to be a threat. Therefore, the nonunion mines were the prime targets.

The independent truckers and the transportation companies which move the nonunion coal to market are two steps removed from the bargaining, because their only contact with the labor dispute is through their contracts to haul commodities to or from mines which are not themselves parties to the labor dispute either. But by the same logic, the UMW sees the independents as "scabs"—as the enemy.

Most of the violence occurred in eastern Kentucky, a region in which the balance of labor representation was tipping in favor of nonunion operators. The region was also one in which the government enforced

---

[100] Richmond Times Dispatch, Apr. 25, 1981, at A-7.
[101] Pittsburgh Press, May 4, 1981, at A-2.
[102] Pittsburgh Press, May 7, 1981, at A-8.
[103] Pittsburgh Press, May 8, 1981, at A-12.
[104] Pittsburgh Press, May 9, 1981, at A-1.

"strict neutrality," although as one nonunion mine operator protested, "the concept of neutrality toward breaking the law is not found in any statute or practice in our society."[105] On the other hand, little violence was reported in western Virginia, where a similar economic demography was developing, but where Governor Dalton had increased the state police patrols for the duration of the strike.

Attitudes toward violence by the actual parties to the strike—the BCOA and the UMW—seldom are helpful, and this strike was no different. The BCOA, whose members are infrequent targets, typically remains aloof, getting through most strikes by issuing occasional mild denunciations. One month into this strike, B. R. Brown, chief negotiator for the BCOA, said only: "I don't have any comment on the violence, but it should not be condoned."[106] As for the union, UMW leaders, when they have not been actively and publically agitating for violence, have always denied its existence: "The only violence by miners I know of has been provoked," said UMW President Sam Church, "following a sniper ambush of a convoy of coal trucks the day before."[107]

The Windup: May 15 to June 8

Bargaining talks began again in earnest during the second week of May. A number of issues were being bargained, of which the most frequently mentioned was the "union standard" clause, under which the BCOA signatory firms were to agree to pay UMW scale for any non-mining work. The fact that this provision had been written into previous contracts only to be struck down as illegal by the courts leads to the conclusion that it probably was included and argued over for internal purposes by both sides.

Although some observers interpreted the resumed talks as an indication that the strike would soon be over, others were of the opinion that it might drag on for many months because of the nature of the leadership on both sides, the issues on the table, and the obvious lack of any convincing national emergency. Judging from the amount and character of violence in the coal fields, the participants were as divided in their opinions as the observers were.

In Virginia and Kentucky, the pattern of violence remained about the same as it had been during the preceding two months, probably in-

---

[105] Letter from T. H. Callahan, president of Zapata Fuels, Inc., parent company of Triple Elkhorn Mining Co., to John Y. Brown, governor of Kentucky, *as reported in* Richmond Times-Dispatch, May 10, 1981, at A-1.
[106] Pittsburgh Press, Apr. 26, 1981, at A-2.
[107] *Id.*

dicating that the participants there were expecting the strike to continue. But mass picketing and violence broke out in Pennsylvania, West Virginia, and Ohio in areas which had previously been quiet, indicating a pattern of increased agitation in anticipation of the strike's end similar to that which had characterized the 1977 strike.

In Virginia, a game was developing between the state police and the UMW; groups of strikers assembled and disbanded, led their trooper escorts on pointless all-night drives in caravans, painted broom handles to resemble gun barrels and pointed them out of windows, and generally tried to confuse the authorities with multiple feints and parries. The police occasionally retaliated by arresting pickets on such charges as littering (for throwing rocks in the road), indecent exposure, and unlawful assembly.[108] This type of activity held the amount of real violence down, but it was not a stable situation, and could have turned ugly with little provocation. Fortunately, nothing serious developed.

In Kentucky, on the other hand, the incidents were more brutal; the situation was already ugly. Near Pikesville, the ambushing of coal truck convoys continued. On May 24, two trucks of a convoy of fifteen were struck by gunfire, one of them sixteen times and the other six, and a driver was wounded. No arrests were made.[109] About a week before this ambush, a ninety-foot Chessie System railroad trestle serving three mines was suspiciously destroyed by fire in Floyd County.[110] No arrests were made in that incident, either.

In both of these states, the trends established earlier were being continued, but according to various newspaper reports, problems involving firebombings, attacks on coal trucks and other vehicles, intimidation of individuals, and mass picketing were also surfacing in new locations which had not previously experienced much trouble. In Boone and Preston Counties, West Virginia; in St. Clairsville, Ohio; in Indiana, Pennsylvania; in Garret County, Maryland; and elsewhere, violence flared. Incidents in these locations were serious (one of them resulted in damage estimated at more than 200,000), but fortunately they did presage the end of the strike.

Late in May, a new contract was suddenly negotiated, substantially on UMW terms. It was quickly sent out for ratification, and the rank and file approved it by a two-to-one margin on June 7. Although coal production remained disrupted for a few more weeks because of picket lines thrown up by mine construction workers and honored by many

---

108 Richmond Times-Dispatch, May 14, 1981, at B-9, and May 21, 1981, at C-1.
109 Louisville Courier-Journal, May 24, 1981, at B-10.
110 Pittsburgh Press, May 18, 1981, at A-2.

UMW members (after a one-day return to work to qualify for a $150-per-man bonus for reporting to the first shift after ratification), the 1981 UMW strike was over.

Regardless of what actually motivated the final settlement, the general impression left on the public was that the miners had once again gotten their way by using the strong-arm tactics for which they are famous.

CHAPTER V

Public Service Employees—
Firefighters, Police, and Medical Care Workers

Inherent in the nature of strikes is that they are economic contests. By withholding their services, strikers inflict economic damage or bring economic pressure to bear on their employers, who would otherwise be able to gain profits by producing goods and services. The economic counterbalance is the pressure on the strikers resulting from the fact that their wages have stopped.

Unfortunately, in strike situations, economic pressure often goes hand-in-hand with physical harm, so the boundary between economic contest and physical confrontation is poorly defined. Strikes are not expected to be purely passive, but neither are they expected to be violently antagonistic. How much physical activity—and more specifically how much violence—should society be asked to condone in the name of economic contest?

In the numerous cases that have come before them involving strikes and labor disputes, the National Labor Relations Board (NLRB) and the courts have sometimes looked at individual incidents objectively and sometimes subjectively; they have sometimes evaluated the intent of the perpetrators and sometimes not; and they have sometimes looked for distinctions and sometimes for similarities between activities held to be either violent or nonviolent within the context of labor law.

Many courts have settled on the notion that "Congress must have contemplated that minor acts of misconduct would go hand-in-hand with most strikes,"[1] but regardless of whether this observation is accurate, it is not helpful; it merely shifts the argument to one of determining whether specific acts of violence are "minor" or not. Even the Supreme Court has been willing to contemplate that a "trivial rough incident" or a "moment of animal exuberance" does not convert otherwise peaceful picketing into violence,[2] thus opening the subject to addi-

---

[1] Chevron U.S.A. v. NLRB 81 3rd Cir. 1982 (1948), *cit.* Republic Steel Corp. v NLRB 107 F.2d 472, 479 (3d Cir. 1939).

[2] Milk Wagon Drivers v. Meadowmoor Dairies, Inc., 312 U.S. 287, 293 (1941).

tional disputation and making control of strike violence more difficult by sanctioning some, but not all, violence.

These problems are exacerbated when those on strike are employed in jobs that vitally affect the public interest or safety. When policemen, firemen, air traffic controllers, prison guards, hospital and health care employees, or other such workers go on strike, an additional distinction must be drawn which sets their strikes apart from those by industrial workers, teachers, coal miners, or professional football players.

Strikes by workers in jobs that affect the public interest are inherently non-economic contests. By withholding their services, these employees are not denying profits to their employers but rather are directly denying services needed by their employers' customers or clients—services that cannot be inventoried or easily substituted. When strikes involve employees charged with protection of public safety they are inherently violent. It is not sophistry to suggest that denial of protection is itself a form of violence.

The normal freedom of employees to withhold work should not be extended to employees whose jobs are vital to the public safety. These jobs, whether they are in the public sector or the private, are unique. When a fireman refuses to fight fires because of a contract dispute, his action does not result in denying revenue or profit to the city which employs him; in fact, it saves the city his wages. It does, however, result in subjecting the citizens of the city to increased hazards of fire. Furthermore, those hazards usually continue for the duration of the strike, because firemen are specialized, require considerable training, and cannot be replaced easily.

In such settings, the refusal to perform needed sevices shares many characteristics with criminally extortionate behavior. Nevertheless, large numbers of employees in critical public service and public safety jobs are members of collective bargaining associations; and when negotiations reach an impasse, some of them go on strike, whether such action is prohibited by contract, or even whether there are restraining orders or injunctions against it.[3]

Furthermore, evidence of the past several years has increasingly indicated that strikes by public service and public safety employees are

---

[3] Perhaps the best known recent example of a public employees' union with a nonstrike provision in its contract striking in defiance of the law is that of the Professional Air Traffic Controllers Organization (PATCO). The government's response to the union's tactic—firing the strikers regardless of the cost to the government or the inconvenience to users of the air traffic control system, was not contemplated by the strikers because it had never been done before. All parties knew the strike was illegal, but experience had suggested to the controllers that the law would be set aside as it had always been before, and the "bluff" of firings would be called with the usual impunity. See Herbert Northrup, *The Rise and Demise of PATCO*, ms. submitted to a journal.

becoming more common and that such strikes can and frequently do go beyond nonperformance of duties. In 1975, for example, the Bureau of Labor Statistics noted that there were 252 work stoppages by municipal workers around the country.[4] (This figure does not include stoppages by health care employees or by anyone other than municipal workers.) Many of those strikes, and others by public service and public safety employees, have been marred by violence, some of it quite brutal.

In many respects, it is difficult to determine why violence occurs in strikes by public employees. The power and bargaining position these unions derive simply by withholding their services is substantial. Additionally, average wages and benefits for these employees, at least those in the public sector, are generally better than those for equivalent work elsewhere, and job security is good. The work, aside from that of the uniformed employees, is more frequently characterized by tedium than by physical exertion (garbage collecting being an exception), so the environment would not seem to be one conducive to violence. (The uniformed forces are exposed to danger and violence as part of their work, but as trained professionals these individuals should be expected to recognize the evil of violence and abjure its use in strikes.) Finally, interunion rivalry is not great, and because unionization in the public sector is recent, there is no long tradition of class struggle and no roots in either political or industrial revolution. From these factors one might conclude that violence should be unusual in strikes involving public service and public safety employees.

This, however, is not the case. The data on labor violence presented in Chapter III contained records of 139 incidents of violence attributable to government employees other than teachers or public safety employees, and 134 incidents attributable to public safety employees —firemen and policemen—for the six years of the listing, 1975 to 1981.[5] Together, these two groups were involved in more incidents of violence than any other except the combination of the International Brotherhood of Teamsters (Teamsters) and the Independent Truckers Association.

This chapter evaluates several specific examples of violence in strikes by public service and public safety employees, with a view toward establishing not only the fact of the violence but also the reasons for its occurrence. The first example is taken from the experience of the city of Memphis, Tennessee, during the summer of 1978.

---

[4] U.S. DEPARTMENT OF LABOR, BUREAU OF LABOR STATISTICS, HANDBOOK OF LABOR STATISTICS 310 (1977).

[5] *See* Table III–9, *supra.*

MEMPHIS POLICE AND FIREFIGHTERS' STRIKE OF 1978

An example of both the active and the passive aspects of strike violence involving public safety employees was occasioned by a strike of municipal employees—principally firemen, but also policemen and to some extent garbage collectors—of the city of Memphis, Tennessee.[6] A firefighters' strike began during the summer of 1978, and was followed within a few weeks by a police strike which was subsequently joined by another firefighters' strike. Other municipal employees on some occasions honored the picket lines of the striking workers.

The state legislature of Tennessee has never enacted a comprehensive public employee bargaining statute. The task of defining the state's policy toward public sector bargaining has therefore been relegated to the courts.[7] Until the mid-1960s, in order to avoid "government by contract, not by law," and the "illegal delegation of sovereign power" by the government to labor union bargaining,[8] the courts supported the authoritarian position that public employee bargaining in Tennessee was illegal for both the union and the governmental entities involved. In the absence of a statute authorizing public employee labor contracts, the courts tried not to allow public unions.[9] Nevertheless, in the late 1960s, the city of Memphis was no longer able to avoid collectively bargaining with its employees.

The Garbage Strike of 1968

Despite legal prohibitions against public employee bargaining, given the right circumstances public employees' unions can be successful in compelling recognition and collective negotiations.[10] In Memphis, such circumstances occurred in 1968.

---

[6] The fact finding regarding the Memphis police and firefighters' strikes of 1978 was performed by J. Daniel Morgan, J.D., Memphis State University, LL.M. University of Pennsylvania Law School, member, Tennessee Bar. The materials presented here were derived from the same sources as used for the study of the case as published by Northrup and Morgan, *The Memphis Police and Firefighters Strikes of 1978: A Case Study*, 32 LABOR LAW JOURNAL 40–54 (1981).

[7] Weakley County Municipal Electric System v. Vick, 43 Tenn. App. 524, 309 S.W.2d 792 (Tenn. Ct. App. 1957).

[8] City of Alcoa v. IBEW Local 270, 203 Tenn. 12, 308 S.W. 2d 476 (Tenn. Sup. Ct. 1957).

[9] In the Weakley County case, the court of appeals stated that the legislature could authorize public employee bargaining should it choose to do so. 309 S.W.2d at 801.

[10] In tracing the rise of public employee bargaining in the United States, one commentator has stated that ". . . the demonstrated success of initial illegal strikes such as the New York transit strike and some early teachers' strikes became powerful proof that the power to strike was of far greater relevance than the right to strike." Zack, *Impasses, Strikes and Resolutions*, PUBLIC WORKERS AND PUBLIC UNIONS 102 (S. Zakoris ed. 1972).

It rained in Memphis on the day of January 31, 1968. As had happened previously on rainy days, black garbage collectors were sent home from work, whereas white garbage collectors were allowed to remain on the payroll at the shop to be dispatched once again when the rains stopped.[11]

Residual racial discrimination was not an unusual event in 1968, but this instance came at a time when black workers throughout the country were out of patience. The all-black membership of the American Federation of State, County and Municipal Employees (AFSCME), Local 1733, voted to strike in protest against their disparate treatment. Although the union had not heretofore been officially recognized by the city, it demanded an end to racial discrimination, a dues checkoff system, and official recognition as the exclusive bargaining agent of the sanitation workers.[12]

Early in the strike, the city agreed to end racial discrimination but stood firmly against the demands for recognition and dues checkoff. The city adamantly opposed recognition of any union representing municipal employees, insisting that recognition and bargaining were illegal under state law. To the all-black Local 1733, however, the issues of recognition and bargaining had become a struggle "for manhood and dignity."[13]

During the first few weeks of the strike, the level of rhetoric increased,[14] protest marches were held,[15] charges of police brutality were made,[16] and an effective black boycott of downtown retail sales was begun.[17] Memphis became the national focal point of civil rights activity.

On March 28, 1968, seven weeks into the strike, a march led by Dr. Martin Luther King, Jr., ended in much-publicized violence. The climax was reached a few days later when Dr. King was assassinated while preparing to lead another march in support of the strikers. The assassination spawned riots in Memphis and throughout the nation. President Lyndon B. Johnson personally dispatched a high-ranking member of the U.S. Department of Labor to Memphis to serve as a special mediator in the dispute.[18]

Twelve days after the assassination, the city conceded and agreed to

---

[11] Stanfield, *In Memphis: More Than a Garbage Strike*, 95 CURRENT, May 1968, at 11.
[12] *Id.* at 14.
[13] STANFIELD, *in* MEMPHIS: MIRROR TO AMERICA? 1 (1968).
[14] BUSINESS WEEK, Mar. 30, 1968, at 40–42.
[15] Stanfield, *supra* note 11, at 9.
[16] *On the Brink in Memphis*, TIME, Aug. 16, 1968, at 23.
[17] Retail sales in the downtown area dropped to approximately 50 percent of their normal level. See BUSINESS WEEK, Mar. 30, 1968, at 82.
[18] U.S. NEWS & WORLD REPORT, Apr. 29, 1968, at 82.

recognize Local 1733 as the bargaining agent for the sanitation workers, with full rights and checkoff provisions. After an illegal strike of sixty-five days, often punctuated by rioting and violence, the city had recognized its first union.

Impact of the Garbage Strike

Although the strike had begun over issues of discrimination, the real victors of the sanitation strike of 1968 were the public employee unions, black or white. After the garbage strike ended, the city council passed a resolution authorizing the recognition of other unions of city employees upon a show of majority support within a unit. During the next few years, both firefighters and police organized. The International Association of Fire Fighters (IAFF), Local 1784, petitioned for recognition in early August 1971. This was withheld for several months by a dispute over inclusion of a no-strike clause, but in mid-December, the mayor and the union signed a memorandum of understanding which granted official recognition to the union and contained a strict no-strike pledge.[19]

The Memphis Police Association obtained official recognition in July 1973.[20] Its initial agreement with the city included a three-page no-strike clause which narrowly defined the permissible range of union activities. By 1978, the city had recognized and was bargaining with thirteen separate unions representing 4,718 of the city's 9,000 employees.

Negotiations Preceding the 1978 Strikes

When bargaining began for new public employee contracts in 1978, both the firefighters and the police unions had new leadership. There was a general feeling of distrust for the city's administration because of a continuing controversy involving the previous year's negotiations, when the city's final offer was conditioned on projections of a substantial budgetary deficit, which in fact turned out to be a surplus when the books were closed on the year.[21] There were also other factors contributing to the restiveness of the members, particularly the firefighters. The firefighters had lived with a lack of parity with police pay for seven years and were concerned that the present system of wage increases, which were based on across-the-board percentage increases, would widen the gap. Younger members of both protective forces were expressing dissatisfaction with what they termed the paternalistic atti-

---

[19] (Memphis) Commercial Appeal, Dec. 17, 1971, at 1.
[20] (Memphis) Commercial Appeal, July 8, 1973, at 1.
[21] Memphis Press-Scimiter, Aug. 5, 1977, at 1.

tude of city officials, and for a variety of political, economic, and organizational reasons, hard bargaining was expected in the summer of 1978.

The firefighters' negotiations were the first to present problems for the city. The firefighters voted to reject the city's "final offer" on June 30, 1978. The union served notice that it was prepared to strike the following day.

The rejected offer provided for a 6 percent increase in wages immediately, followed by a $30 across-the-board increase in April 1979, and a 7.5 percent increase in October 1979. This was the same "final offer" that had been made to the city's other unions. According to the firefighters, their objection to it was not based on the basic wage package. Rather, the firefighters said they were holding out for a shift differential similar to that paid to other city employees.

City officials denied that the shift differential was actually a substantive issue, maintaining that it had come up in the negotiations only at the eleventh hour. The city's view may have been the more accurate one. Much later, a year after the strike, one fire department official expressed the opinion that the shift differential issue was in reality a device used by the union to regain its loss of parity.[22] Whatever the case, the shift differential became the focus of rejection.

As the negotiations progressed, there was some indication that a coalition of unions was developing. David Baker, president of the Memphis Police Association, stated that: "For the first time since 1968, we have all three of the big ones ready."[23] He was referring to the police, the firefighters, and the sanitation workers. The coalition failed to materialize, however. On July 1, 1978, the day the firefighers were set to go out, the sanitation workers voted to accept the city's offer (by the extremely narrow margin of 558 to 553); and the police and firefighters were unable to coordinate their efforts because of their disparate objectives.

The First Firefighters' Strike

On July 1, 1978, at 6 A.M., the firefighters carried out their threat and walked off their jobs. As the strike began, and 1,400 union firefighters left their posts, only 150 nonunion firemen remained to assist supervisory personnel. Less than one-third of the city's fire companies were available to answer fire alarms. The mayor immediately called for and received National Guard troops. The city also received the assistance of federal firefighters from the National Parks Service (who were experienced as firefighters, but unfamiliar with the geography or

---

[22] Interview with fire department official who did not wish to be quoted. Jan. 22, 1979.
[23] (Memphis) Commerical Appeal, July 11, 1978, at 10.

fire main systems of Memphis). A temporary restraining order was issued by the Memphis chancery court against the pickets' blocking of driveways at fire stations and against mass picketing.

Initial Violence. During the first night of the strike, numerous instances of misconduct and vandalism by striking firemen were reported. Police reports indicated that on that first night, the tires had been slashed on seven fire department vehicles.[24] By morning, only three of the fire department's fourteen ambulances were still in operating condition. The tires on the ambulances had been slashed, their engines tampered with, and their medical equipment damaged. Headlamps on several vehicles were smashed. Pickets reportedly kicked the sides of automobiles driven by National Guardsmen as they reported for duty at the armory.

But the worst violence was not the vandalism or misconduct. Over the weekend of July 2 and 3, fires broke out around the city in far greater than normal numbers. On Saturday, the first day of the strike, 225 alarms of fire were reported, and on the following day, there were about 125.[25] Normally, the city experienced between 70 and 80 alarms of fire on a summer Saturday, and a few less on Sunday.

The fires on this particular weekend were particularly damaging because the hoses were manned by the few nonstriking firefighers, out-of-practice supervisory personnel, and some volunteers. At several of the fire sites, strikers were on hand to taunt the undermanned and increasingly fatigued fire crews.[26] Extensive damage—the estimates ran to $3 million—resulted from the fires, twelve of which were considered serious.

In addition to vandalism of equipment and harassment of fire crews, there were also instances in which striking firemen actively hindered efforts to control the fires. One striking firefighter allegedly parked his pickup truck on the hoses at the scene of a fire. When the police ordered him to remove the truck, he came close to striking a police officer with the truck. That striker was arrested and charged with aggravated assault.[27]

At yet another fire, one National Guardsman reported that the undermanned fire crews needed assistance in bringing the fire under control. When guardsmen were called upon to aid the fire crews, the strikers at the scene angrily objected. "After near physical confronta-

---

[24] (Memphis) Commercial Appeal, July 2, 1978, at 1.
[25] Memphis Press-Scimiter, July 3, 1978, at 1. The numbers vary somewhat in other newspaper accounts, but are all of the same order of magnitude as these.
[26] (Memphis) Commercial Appeal, July 2, 1978, at 1.
[27] Shelby County Crim. Ct., *Jail Book* (1978), at 23.

tion [the] district chief decided that to avoid trouble he would not use guardsmen as fire fighters."[28]

At several fire stations, pickets obstructed the efforts of nonstriking firemen to report for work. One captain was reportedly forced into an automobile when he attempted to cross a picket line.[29] At the central fire station, a small group of strikers broke into the building by smashing a glass door and then physically removed some nonstriking firemen from the building, striking and injuring several in the process.[30]

The unusually large number of fires during the strike prompted charges by city officials that strikers were setting fires. As Mayor Wyeth Chandler put it, "You don't have spontaneous combustion suddenly occur on July 2 and all the unoccupied homes suddenly burst into flames."[31] He was also quoted as saying:

> The blame for these open and notorious acts of violence and threats against their fellow firefighters and the holocaust [which has followed] rests with those members of the firefighters' union—hopefully small in number—who believed that such actions would intimidate this government and its citizens into doing whatever was decided.[32]

The police director, Winslow Chapman, said at a news conference that he believed that firemen were responsible for setting 90 to 95 percent of the fires.[33] The city officials supported their theory that strikers were responsible for many of the fires by referring to the "definite pattern" in which the fires occurred.[34] A number of the fires broke out in areas served by fire companies which were already engaged in fighting fires at other locations within their area of responsibility. Officials speculated that only persons with knowledge of the internal organization of the fire department could set fires in such a strategic pattern.[35] Police Director Chapman stated that:

> If you saw from the air you'd see there was a very definite pattern. Last night [Saturday] was one of the most unreal scenes I've ever seen. It was like a World War II newsreel.[36]

A logbook of the weekend activities made by a National Guardsman tends to support the theory that some of the fires were set by someone

---

[28] (Memphis) Commercial Appeal, July 9, 1978, at 1.
[29] Memphis Press-Scimiter, July 3, 1978, at 3.
[30] (Memphis) Commercial Appeal, Oct. 22, 1978, at 3; Memphis Press-Scimiter, Oct. 11, 1978, at 4.
[31] Memphis Press-Scimiter, July 3, 1978, at 1.
[32] *Id.* at 3.
[33] *Id.* at 1; *Government Employee Relations Report,* No. 787 (July 10, 1978), at 15.
[34] Memphis Press-Scimiter, July 3, 1978, at 1.
[35] *Id.*
[36] *Id.* at 3.

with inside information. While the crew from a fire station was out on call, a house under construction directly across the street from the fire station suddenly burst into flames. Because the firefighters and equipment were at another fire, nothing could be done to save the house. The fire was caused by arson.[37]

Other incidents also tended to indicate the involvement of striking firemen in the arson. One building site was inspected during the strike by a person claiming to be a fire marshal. That night, the building was completely destroyed by arson. From the placement of the incendiary devices in the building, the inference was drawn that the arsonist had knowledge of how the most damage could be inflicted. The building contractor asserts that the spurious fire inspector was "casing" the building.[38] Nonetheless, state investigators have failed to identify the culprit.

In fact, considering the vast number of occurrences of arson during the short strike, remarkably few arrests were made. Two striking firemen were arrested during the first night when, acting on a tip, the police had set up a still-watch near a vacant apartment building and apprehended them following a short chase after the building burst into flames. The firefighters' union posted bond for the two suspects, and vowed to "back them to the hilt."[39] After the strike was over, the two arrested firefighters pleaded guilty to charges of arson and were sentenced to serve two to three years in prison.[40]

Another firefighter was arrested on charges of arson connected with a fire during the strike. This firefighter allegedly set fire to his mother-in-law's home, causing $13,000 in damage. Fire Director Robert Walker described this incident as "a family affair."[41]

Union officials placed the blame for the extraordinary number of fires on "energetic arsonists who know the firemen will be accused of setting blazes,"[42] and in fact, three teenagers who were not known to be associated with the firefighters were arrested during the strike for allegedly trying unsuccessfully to set fire to a vacant building.[43] Nevertheless, city officials have remained firm in placing the blame for the majority of the arson on the striking firemen.

As one official pointed out a year after the strike, there were very few incidents of arson during the joint strike of police and firefighters

---

[37] (Memphis) Commercial Appeal, July 9, 1978, at 6.
[38] Confidential interview, January 24, 1979.
[39] (Memphis) Commercial Appeal, July 3, 1978, at 5.
[40] Shelby County Crim. Ct., *Docket Book,* Entry No. 354661 (1978).
[41] (Memphis) Commercial Appeal, Dec. 21, 1978, at 23.
[42] Memphis Press-Scimiter, July 3, 1978, at 1.
[43] Memphis Press-Scimiter, July 3, 1978, at 3.

which occurred a few weeks subsequent to this first strike. This official reasoned that if random arsonists, pyromaniacs, or nonunionists were truly at fault, there would have been even more arson during the joint strike when the city's defenses were at their weakest, but instead there were far fewer arsons during the later strike. This official believes that the strikers used arson as a strike weapon, and abandoned its use in the second strike only because public opinion had turned so strongly against the union.[44]

The first firefighters' strike ended after three days. A chancery court injunction against the strike was granted on July 3, and the firemen voted to return to work in compliance with it. The city had been ravaged by more than 300 fires causing an estimated 3 million in property damage. Damage to fire equipment and station houses was estimated at between $50,000 and $100,000.[45]

During the strike, the firefighters had received little assistance from the police union. Memphis Police Association officers had instructed their members not to make arrests of pickets, but that was the most substantial support given. To avoid problems of crossing firefighters' picket lines, roll calls for police were held in parking lots away from the precinct houses.

More tangible support was given by the members of the AFSCME Local 1733 (the sanitation workers). Although sanitation workers had ratified a contract with the city the day the firefighters' strike began, by the third day, most were honoring the picket lines, and only 12 of the city's 248 garbage trucks were in operation.

Negotiations Resumed. On July 3, as the firefighters were voting to return to work, the 1,100-member Memphis Police Association was voting to reject the city's "final offer." The members also voted to give their president the authority to call for a "job action."

From this point onward, the focus of attention was on the police union. The firefighters returned to work on July 4, the National Guard left the city, and the curfew that had been in effect the previous night was lifted. The firefighters continued to negotiate with the city under the tutelage of a federal mediator. The police also began negotiations but were more vocal in making their demands known to the public.

Negotiations with both unions continued until July 13, when tentative agreements with the leaders of each were reached. The police agreement was to involve a slight variation from the city's original "final offer"; the firefighters' accord left the city's original "final offer" basically untouched, and called for only minor changes involving

---

[44] Confidential interview, January 22, 1979.
[45] Memphis Press-Scimiter, July 5, 1978, at 1.

longevity pay and bonus day compensation. No mention was made in the firefighters' agreement of the shift differential over which the union had said it struck earlier in the month.

Although the leaders approved the new contract, the firefighters themselves did not hold a formal ratification vote on the tentative accord. Dissatisfaction with the package was evident among the members at a meeting held to explain the terms. The leaders decided not to put the issue to vote, which would probably have resulted in another strike, but decided to wait and see what action the police union would take.

The members of the police union rejected their tentative package on July 15, by a nine-to-one ratio. They did not, however, immediately begin a job action. Over the next several days, the policemen attempted to force arbitration of their demands by appealing to the city council (which declined to get involved in the negotiating process), and participated with the Memphis Education Association to begin a petition drive to recall the mayor (without, however, much success). There is also some evidence that a police slowdown may have been in effect. Throughout the evening of Saturday, July 22, only 96 arrests were reported. On the previous Saturday night, 167 had been made during the same time period. Union leaders denied that a slowdown was in effect, and arrests returned to a normal level very quickly.

The union sought a public debate between its leader and the mayor. The mayor acceded to this request, and during the televised debate, he placed his new "final offer" on the table, similar to one which had been accepted by the Memphis Light, Gas and Water employees earlier in the year. After studying it, however, the executive board of the police union turned it down. The union's president, David Baker, warned that the union was considering some form of job action and set its tentative starting date as August 13.

The choice of the date was a strategic maneuver by the union. The city was expecting a large influx of tourists for the first anniversary of Elvis Presley's death, August 16. A police strike beginning the preceding weekend could be expected to affect significantly the number of tourists coming to the city and, thereby, to have a major impact on business revenues. The union apparently hoped that businesses would apply pressure on the mayor to get the negotiations settled.

The Police Strike

More offers and counteroffers exchanged hands, but on August 9, the police association rejected the city's latest proposal, and voted to strike. The mayor called for National Guard assistance for the second time during the summer, declared another civil emergency, and imposed another curfew on the city.

As the strike began, police supervisory personnel and county deputies patrolled the city while the National Guard remained on call. The city obtained a temporary restraining order against the strike, but it was ignored by the policemen, who were already striking illegally.

The violence began early. During the first night of this new strike, the following incidents were reported:

1. Twenty-five police vehicles were disabled;

2. Roofing nails were placed in the driveways of precinct houses to prevent entry or exit;

3. A tear-gas bomb was detonated in the county administration building, which faced City Hall;

4. Strikers vandalized a fire hydrant across from a police station, and then cut a tire on a water works truck that had been sent to turn off the hydrant;

5. SWAT team members took their specialized equipment with them when they went out, and threatened to throw tear gas into the police station.

As the strike progressed, more vandalism and violence by strikers was to occur.

Several other city unions supported the police with sympathy strikes. The city court system was closed down because clerks refused to cross the police picket lines. During the first days of the strike; firefighters continued to work but refused to cross picket lines. The fire equipment was moved onto the streets so that station house picket lines did not have to be crossed. The sanitation workers offered financial assistance to the striking police, but promised to observe the no-strike clause in their own contract.

On Saturday night, August 12, Mayor Chandler ordered all striking policemen removed from the city payroll. The mayor gave the strikers a twenty-four-hour grace period in which to report for duty. After the grace period, strikers would be rehired only as new employees on probationary status. The city had obtained a chancery court order directing the strikers to return to work or to resign from the force.

During the second and third days of the strike, the police were involved with internal union affairs. The leadership of President Baker was challenged by a more radical member of the executive board who had the support of the activist members and who more nearly reflected the mood of the strikers. The challenge was thwarted only when Baker agreed to abandon the moderate stance he had maintained up to that time and to comply with the wishes of the membership.[46] He announced that he would fully support the continuance of the strike.

On the fourth day, more vandalism was reported:

1. Windows and glass doors were broken by rocks and bricks thrown by large groups of strikers at three precinct houses;

2. Strikers marched around the police stations, many armed with ax handles or clubs. Pickets at several stations physically prevented officers from returning to work;

3. Numerous striking policemen were arrested on charges of curfew violations and breach of the peace;

4. Strikers temporarily disabled three fire trucks.

To prevent further vandalism of fire equipment, many trucks were moved into the shelter of the National Guard armory. The National Guard was ordered onto the streets to serve as support for the county deputies and the police supervisors.

By the end of the mayor's twenty-four-hour grace period, only approximately seventy-five to one hundred strikers had returned to duty. And even these officers were allowed to return home after a large number of phone calls were received which threatened their safety and their families. Callers threatened to "make your families pay," to "take it out on your wife and kids," and "to teach you a lesson."[47] The threatening callers knew the officers who returned to work, knew their work assignments, and knew their families. Although supervisory personnel also received threatening calls, they remained on the job.

The Second Firefighters' Strike

The firefighters joined the police in striking on August 14, when the leaders of that union called for a formal vote on the tentative pact that had been reached on July 8, a pact which the membership, not unexpectedly, refused to ratify. The firefighters' leaders labelled the new strike a wildcat strike, primarily because the union was still subject to the July injunction, and by calling the strike unauthorized, the leaders hoped to avoid citation for contempt of court. (In this, they were successful.) There can be little doubt, however, that the call for a formal vote was but a signal to join the police in striking.

The mayor reacted to the firefighters' strike, as he had to the police

---

[46] (Memphis) Commercial Appeal, Aug. 14, 1978, at 14.
[47] (Memphis) Commercial Appeal, Aug. 8, 1978, at 1.

strike, by discharging the strikers, subject to a short grace period. Few firemen returned to work under this threat, however.

Throughout this strike, the city received over 2,000 applications for positions vacated by the striking police and firemen. But as is often true in public employee strikes, the city was not able to break the strike with replacements. State law in Tennessee requires a considerable period of training—240 hours as a minimum for police officers, for example—before replacements could be used in the protective services. Therefore, as again is so often the case, the firemen saw the city's threat of dismissal as an idle bluff and of no particular consequence.

After the firefighters joined the walkout, Memphis essentially ground to a halt, and the strike began to approach the "general" level. On August 15, the Memphis AFL-CIO Labor Council, representing nearly 60,000 workers in the Memphis area, called for the mayor to submit to binding arbitration and threatened to call all of its members out if a settlement was not soon reached. (Although this threat undoubtedly increased the pressure on the mayor, it was probably in the same category as the mayor's threats of dismissal. It would have been unrealistic to assume that all of the AFL-CIO members in the Memphis area would have violated their various contracts and heeded a call for a general strike.)

Garbage workers honored picket lines that were set up at their stations. On August 15, only 23 of the 1,036 sanitation workers reported for duty. The day before, pickets had chased three sanitation workers from their truck and then thrown away the keys to the vehicle.[48] Additional support for the strikers came from the Memphis Education Association, whose executive board promised to honor picket lines when the city schools were scheduled to open on August 18.

The combination of strike pressures and sympathy strikes prompted the mayor to make another offer, hoping to get negotiations started once again, but the unions rejected this offer because it proposed to let the people decide the issue of wage increases directly through a referendum on the November ballot.[49] The unions apparently knew that people can seldom be counted upon to vote themselves tax increases.

The strike, therefore, continued. On the seventh day, the governor of Tennessee, Ray Blanton, acting out of either fear or ideology, entered the fray on the side of the unionists. At the behest of the Memphis Labor Council and AFL-CIO President George Meany, he proposed that the city submit to binding arbitration. To encourage the city

---

[48] (Memphis) Commercial Appeal, Aug. 15, 1978, at 9.
[49] (Memphis) Commercial Appeal, Aug. 16, 1978, at 1.

toward this end, the governor presented the city with a bill for the services of the National Guard. The bill amounted to over $1 million, and the governor emphasized that each additional day of their use would cost the city another $65,000. This bill included a $630,000 charge for National Guard services during the garbage strike of 1968, ten years previously. To further impress his point, the governor threatened to withhold the city's share of gasoline tax revenues until the bill was paid.

Although the mayor stood firmly against the governor's proposal for binding arbitration, the pressures on him to mollify the strikers had become too great to resist. His new offer called for an immediate end to the strikes and amnesty for all strikers who were not charged with felonies. The city and the unions would then submit their last best offers to a federal mediator, who would determine the amount necessary to fund the difference between them. After this difference was determined, a tax increase referendum would be placed on the November 7 ballot. If voters rejected the tax increase, the city's final offer would continue as the compensation rate. If the voters approved the tax increase, the additional revenues would be used exclusively to fund the unions' final offers.

There was no formal response by the unions to this offer, but negotiations with both unions were resumed, joined by members of the Memphis AFL-CIO Labor Council, by members of the Memphis Chamber of Commerce, and by federal mediators. After long hours of shuttle diplomacy, the impasses were finally broken.

Strike Settlement

The offer that settled the strike was basically the same one that had been on the table at the beginning, except that the mayor agreed to make the second year's increase subject to renegotiation based on the nonbinding report of a fact-finding committee.[50] The mayor also agreed to grant amnesty to all strikers except those charged with felonies. Strikers who were charged with curfew violations and breach of the peace would be fully reinstated.[51]

The memberships of both unions ratified the settlement and the eight-day strike ended. Both sides claimed victory: the mayor had held the line on wages; and the unions had succeeded in altering the city's bargaining structure and forcing it to accept outside intervention.

---

[50] The fact finding provisions of the settlement were superseded by later action by the city council and the voters, as discussed below.

[51] A city court judge later dismissed charges against 130 police and firemen who had been arrested for curfew infractions.

Although the unions were not immediately successful in forcing the mayor to submit to binding arbitration or in involving the city council in negotiations, they were successful in involving the state government and forcing the involvement of a broader range of interests in the settlement process.[52]

Both sides could also claim defeat: the mayor had given up the important (structural) things in order to save the money package, and had allowed his "bluff" of discharging the illegally striking officers to be called; and the unions had so overplayed their hands in the vandalism, arson, and general disregard of the citizenry of Memphis that they had turned public sentiment against their cause and lost, thereby, a powerful ally for the future.

Conclusions

Both of the public safety employees' strikes in Memphis in 1978 were short. The first lasted less than three days, and the second less than eight. Also, relatively few strikers were involved in either one of them. At the maximum, the number of strikers participating did not exceed the number likely to be on strike at a single steel mill or automobile plant. Except for the arson, the strikes were not even noteworthy for the severity of the violence exhibited during them.

Nevertheless, the disruption these strikes occasioned to the functioning of the city and the lives of its citizens was severe and far out of proportion to what might be expected in an industrial walkout of the same size. The reason, of course, is precisely because the strikers were *not* industrial workers, but persons responsible for protecting the public. Such strikes can be expected to be short—they create emergency situations which must be resolved quickly if the community is to survive at all—but should not be expected to be violent beyond the violence inherent in the denial of protection. Nevertheless, many such strikes, including these in Memphis, show violence beyond those expected levels.

The following section contains capsule views of selected other strikes involving firefighters, police, and hospital and health care employees to illustrate, if nothing else, that the situation which prevailed in Memphis was far from unique.

---

[52] The unions were ultimately successful in involving the council in negotiations and in winning an arbitration procedure.

OTHER INSTANCES OF VIOLENCE
INVOLVING FIREFIGHTERS

Not only in Memphis, but throughout the country, the principal weapon used by firefighters in their labor disputes seems to be fire—although vandalism, threats to and harassment of supervisors, management, replacements, and nonstrikers, and other forms of misconduct are also common. When some firefighters' union locals are on strike they add pressure to their bargaining by impeding firefighting by any parties as much as possible, as was the case in Memphis. Others, such as the Kansas City local discussed below, make at least some effort to provide protection to the public in life-threatening situations. Either way, property is unprotected and subject to greater hazard, and the community is at the mercy of the strikers. These factors sometimes drive the general public to panic, putting additional pressure on the city's negotiators to settle on whatever terms will end the crisis. Examples of violence in some recent firefighters' strikes follow.

Kansas City, Missouri: 1975, 1979, and 1980

During the five-year period from 1975 to 1980, Kansas City, Missouri, was subjected to three job actions by Local 42 of the International Association of Fire Fighters (IAFF), each of which left the city without adequate fire protection. The first, in October 1975, lasted for four days, during which firefighting equipment was damaged, life-supporting oxygen tanks were emptied, and other vandalism took place.[53]

The number of fires during the period of the strike was approximately double the average expected for that time of the year,[54] and many of the fires were attributed to arson by strikers.[55] The strike ended with a contract that was largely on the union's terms, but it left strained relations between the union and the city. These emerged into further trouble when the contract next came due in 1979.

Firemen remained at their posts when the contract expired in May 1979, but as a means of applying pressure on the city to sweeten its wage offer, they refused to accept overtime work. The city had offered a 15 percent raise over two years; the firemen wanted 20 percent. The refusal to work overtime resulted in dismissals which themselves became an issue, sparking new violence and a subsequent sickout.

[53] (Pomona) Progress Bulletin, Oct. 5, 1975.
[54] Philadelphia Inquirer, Oct. 7, 1975.
[55] (Houston) Post, Oct. 6, 1975, n.p.

In May, within hours after the first ten firefighters were dismissed for twice refusing to work overtime, the car of the Kansas City fire chief was firebombed and extensively damaged. The fire chief attributed the motive to "revenge" and "probably the work of a radical element in the firefighters' union."[56] Ill feelings continued to fester, and the firefighters continued to refuse overtime work.

In December, with the contract still unresolved, the firemen added a sickout to their no-overtime job action, and also refused to perform administrative tasks or any but their regular fire-related jobs. Within two days, the number of employees present for duty fell by 90 percent, and for the next ten days, National Guardsmen and city policemen were the city's primary defense against fire while the firemen, in defiance of court orders, did not report for work.[57]

Aside from the danger posed by the inexperience of the available firefighters, this phase of the job action was relatively nonviolent. Several fires of suspect origin occurred, including a $5.5 million blaze which gutted a new, but unoccupied, nursing home,[58] but there was no indication of striker involvement.[59] By the end of the job action, in early January 1980, the wage issue was settled (the firefighters were to receive a 21 percent raise over two years—more than they had originally asked for) and the men returned to work; but issues still remained unsettled concerning disciplinary action taken against forty-two firefighters who had been dismissed for refusing to work overtime.

There was also growing unrest within the union between strikers and new recruits hired during the December walkout, and between the strikers and nonstrikers. Both the new recruits and the nonstrikers were ostracized and subjected to threats and harassment.[60]

The problem reached crisis proportions in March 1980, when the third walkout in five years began, in defiance of yet more circuit court restraining orders. This time, the violence was more extreme. Before the walkout began, at least eighteen pieces of firefighting equipment were thoroughly vandalized,[61] other equipment was sabotaged, and a series of grass and trash fires was set.[62]

During the first 48 hours of this strike, 170 fire calls were made, of which 34 were fires in buildings or other structures. Arson was involved in 9 of the fires.[63] The number of fires, the number of fires in

---

[56] Philadelphia Inquirer, May 25, 1979, at 3–A.
[57] Philadelphia Inquirer, Dec. 30, 1979, at 6–A.
[58] Philadelphia Inquirer, Dec. 30, 1979, at 6–A.
[59] New York Times, Dec. 31, 1979, at A–4.
[60] (Kansas City) Times, Feb. 11, 1980, n.p.
[61] Paris (Texas) News, Mar. 30, 1980, n.p.
[62] TIME, Mar. 31, 1980, n.p.
[63] The Kansas City Star, Mar. 23, 1980, at A4.

structures, and the number of cases of arson were all considerably higher than the number normally expected. During this period, 2 firefighters were charged with arson in connection with a series of grass fires,[64] but 4 juveniles and another man unconnected with the strike were also arrested on arson charges.[65]

Only one person was injured in a fire during this strike, and he was, in fact, pulled from his burning house and saved from greater injury by striking firefighters who were members of one of several "flying squads" set up by the union to respond to life-threatening situations.[66] These squads showed that the Kansas City firefighters were more responsive to public needs than were their counterparts in many other cities where strikes had occurred, and also that they were more sensitive to the benefits of retaining public sympathy. On the other hand, the squads did nothing to diminish the growing number of other, more minor, fires that plagued the city.

Although the firefighters denied involvement in a series of these fires that occurred on the last day of the strike, the pattern in which the fires were set made it apparent that the intent of the arsonists, whoever they were, was to keep the replacement and substitute firemen busy while minimizing the actual destruction. During the afternoon of the last day of the strike, for example, while negotiators were holding a nonstop session, grass fires were reported at 12:43 P.M., and again at 12:56, 1:47, 2:05, 2:09, 2:33, 2:35, 2:56, 3:06, 3:15, 3:56, and 4:40.[67] If setting these fires was, indeed, one of the strikers' tactics, it was successful. That evening, the city agreed to terms which preserved the wage increase and provided pardons for the forty-two firemen who had been dismissed during the earlier job actions.

St. Louis, Missouri, and Vicinity, 1977

Although not directly strike-related, a series of incidents around St. Louis involving Local 398 of the IAFF and members of the Fire Protection Board demonstrated that violence by firefighters was not limited to arson and minor vandalism:

  1. December 9, 1976: the tires on the Emergency Vehicle Dispatcher's car were slashed.[68]

  2. December 24, 1976: shots were fired into the Emergency

---

[64] *Id.*
[65] *Id.* at 9A.
[66] *Id.*
[67] *Id.*
[68] St. Louis Post Dispatch, Mar. 20, 1977, n.p.

Vehicle Dispatcher's car, and he received threatening phone calls.[69]

3. March 6, 1977: threatening phone calls were made to a Fire Protection Board member in attempts to make him quit his job; shots were also fired into his car.[70]

4. April 9, 1977: the cars of a Fire Protection Board member were spray painted with the word "quit"; the board member received threats to either resign or be killed.[71]

5. April 12, 1977: after vandalism of cars and home and numerous threats and harassment, the Fire Protection Board member resigned.[72]

6. May 7, 1977: cars belonging to other Fire Protection Board trustees were vandalized, and their tires were slashed.[73]

7. May 1977: the windshield of a board member's car was broken and the tires were slashed.[74]

8. May 17, 1977: the firefighters' union's shop steward fire-bombed the home of the Fire District Director.[75]

9. May 1977: a car owned by the son of a Fire Protection Board member was firebombed.[76]

10. July 27, 1977: the windows of a board member's home were broken.[77]

Chicago, Illinois, 1980

During a strike by firefighters in Chicago in 1980, the city suffered a death toll from fire that was much higher than normal.[78] Striking firefighters were not directly implicated in any of the deaths, or in any incidents except for some relatively minor ones involving harassment and arson.[79] The deaths, rather, were attributed to the inability of the

---

[69] *Id.*
[70] St. Louis Globe Democrat, Mar. 10, 1977, n.p.
[71] St. Louis Globe Democrat, Apr. 12, 1977, n.p.
[72] St. Louis Globe Democrat, Apr. 12, 1977, n.p.
[73] St. Louis Globe Democrat, May 9, 1977, n.p.
[74] St. Louis Globe Democrat, Jun. 17, 1977, n.p.
[75] St. Louis Globe Democrat, Jun. 19, 1977, n.p.
[76] Clipping in the author's file. Source newspaper unidentified. July 25, 1977.
[77] St. Louis Globe Democrat, July 16, 1977, n.p.
[78] Glendora (Illinois) Press, Mar. 13, 1980, n.p.
[79] Three striking firemen were suspected of setting fire to an apartment building, Chicago Sun Times, Mar. 8, 1980; An ambulance driver was beaten by four men who called him "scab," Chicago Tribune, Mar. 27, 1980.

shorthanded and inexperienced fire crews to respond adequately to emergencies—which is one of the natural consequences of a fire-fighters' strike. Some of the more serious incidents included:

1. An apartment building was badly damaged by a fire in which two children died. The deaths might not have occurred if the strike had not been in progress.[80]

2. Five persons died in a house fire. The deaths were blamed on the shortage of nonstriking firemen and their inability to arrive at the fire on time.[81]

3. Overall, during the strike twenty persons died in fires, a much higher than normal death toll.[82]

Other Incidents

1. In Biloxi, Mississippi, arson and false alarms were reported during a strike.[83]

2. In Butte, Montana, a cinderblock and paint were thrown through the window of the town's chief executive.[84]

3. In Yonkers, New York, striking firemen stood by and watched as fires of suspicious origin destroyed several buildings, one of which was thought to be the home of from one to four derelicts.[85]

4. In Dayton, Ohio, of fifteen serious fires that occurred during a strike, only one was *not* arson.[86]

5. In Toledo, Ohio, equipment was vandalized and volunteers were harassed by strikers as they tried to put out a hotel fire. Homes burned down as firemen refused to respond, and a higher than normal number of fires broke out in vacant buildings.[87]

6. In Chattanooga, Tennessee, fire vehicles were sabotaged and disabled, two fire engines were damaged, and shots were fired into the home of the fire chief.[88]

---

[80] Chicago Tribune, Mar. 6, 1980, n.p.
[81] New York Times, Mar. 6, 1980, n.p.
[82] Glendora (Illinois) Press, Mar. 13, 1980, n.p.
[83] Lake Charles (Louisiana) American Press, Sep. 20, 1978, n.p.
[84] Great Falls (Montana) Tribune, Sep. 23, 1978, n.p.
[85] New York Post, Apr. 16, 1981, and Apr. 19, 1981; Standard Star, Apr. 16, 1981.
[86] (Dayton) Journal Herald, Aug. 11, 1977, n.p.
[87] Toledo Blade, July 12, 1979; (Baltimore) Evening Sun, July 3, 1979; Philadelphia Inquirer, July 9, 1979.
[88] (Chattanooga) Daily Times, Feb. 28, 1980; Nashville Tennessean, May 9, 1980.

7. In Huntsville, Alabama, three buildings were set on fire during the strike, and fire trucks were pelted with rocks and sticks thrown by strikers.[89]

8. In Anderson, Illinois, striking firefighters watched as a major blaze destroyed a downtown business block. A fireman picketing a fire station a few blocks away said: "I don't feel guilty in the least as long as no lives are lost. Let it burn to the ground for all I care."[90]

9. In Nashville, Tennessee, before going on strike, firemen sabotaged much of the city's firefighting equipment. Firefighters also slashed the tires of a city hazardous materials vehicle.[91]

VIOLENCE IN POLICE STRIKES

When compared to the level of violence in firefighters' strikes, that found in policemen's and other municipal employees' strikes seems tame. Nevertheless, many such strikes are far from placid even though the essential public services which these strikers hold hostage would seem to give them sufficient bargaining pressure. To illustrate the violence that can occur during strikes by policemen, consider the following incidents from a six-day strike by policemen in San Francisco in 1975:

1. Strikers used inoperable vehicles to block access to the town hall.[92]

2. Police equipment was damaged, including the disabling of the steering mechanism on some patrol cars and the slashing of the tires on others.[93]

3. The tires of a police captain's car were ice picked.[94]

4. The keys to 200 squad cars were stolen from the police department.[95]

5. More than 100 tires on the cars of nonstriking policemen were slashed, and car windows were broken.[96]

[89] Birmingham News, Nov. 12, 1978 and Nov. 25, 1978.
[90] Anderson (Illinois) Herald, Aug. 26, 1979, n.p.
[91] Nashville Tennessean, May 9, 1980, n.p.
[92] (Pomona) Progress Bulletin, Aug. 22, 1975, n.p.
[93] San Francisco Examiner, Aug. 20, 1975, n.p.
[94] (Pomona) Progress Bulletin, Aug. 22, 1975, n.p.
[95] (Oakland) Tribune, Aug. 20, 1975, n.p.
[96] (Pomona) Progress Bulletin, Aug. 22, 1975, n.p.

6. Strikers shot out street lights with rifles and pistols.[97]

7. Nonstrikers were harassed and threatened.[98]

8. A pipe bomb blew up in the entrance to the mayor's home.[99]

In New Orleans in 1979, policemen went on strike and the city was treated to a similar spectacle of the keepers of the law turning to lawlessness to advance their economic position. As in San Francisco, police cars had their tires slashed and their windows broken,[100] nails were strewn in police station driveways,[101] nonstrikers were harassed when they crossed picket lines and cherry bombs were thrown at their cars,[102] and the mayor's home came under vegetal attack, this time with eggs, tomatoes, and onions.[103] Also, as might be expected, the number of burglaries and vandalism reportedly increased during the strike.[104]

STRIKES BY MEDICAL CARE EMPLOYEES

Strikes by medical care employees do not have quite the same impact as those by firemen and policemen. In the first place, their basic services do not involve protecting people from harm, so denial of the service does not increase the potential for violence but only prolongs, or decreases the efficiency of, medical care. Secondly, unionized medical care employees generally have far less of a local monopoly in their segment of society than do policemen or firemen, so alternative sources of help are generally available when they are on strike.

Nevertheless, the reaction of fear among the general public is strong when hospital services are interrupted, and many feel that those who would deny medical services or increase the suffering of the sick or injured in order to gain economic advantage are practicing a special form of barbarism. The same is also true when the victims are the elderly or the feeble in nursing homes whose need for continuous care is interrupted.

Under these circumstances, one might expect unionized medical care employees to be circumspect in their approach to strikes, so as to preserve public sympathy and support, but this is no more the case

---

[97] San Francisco Examiner, Aug. 19, 1975, n.p.
[98] (San Francisco) Sunday Courier & Examiner, Aug. 24, 1975, n.p.
[99] (Oakland) Tribune, Aug. 20, 1975, n.p.
[100] (New Orleans) Times Picayune, Feb. 22, 1979, n.p.
[101] *Id.*
[102] *Id.*
[103] (New Orleans) Times Picayune, Mar. 1, 1979, n.p.
[104] Washington Star, Feb. 10, 1979, n.p.

here than it is with protective service employees. Many strikes in the medical care services are characterized by violence. District and Local 1199 of the National Union of Hospital and Health Care Employees, an autonomous division of the Retail, Wholesale and Department Store Union, is reputed to be the most prone to violence among the various unions in the field. The reputation seems deserved.

District 1199, National Union of Hospital and Health Care Employees

Violent incidents occurring during a lengthy strike by members of District 1199 at the Highlands Medical Center in Prestonburg, Kentucky, in the spring of 1981 illustrate the kind of tactics used by health care employees' unions:

1. As the strike began and picket lines were set up, acid was sprayed on cars that crossed the lines, and patients needing emergency care were turned away.[105]

2. Supply trucks and cars crossing the picket lines were harassed and damaged. They were pelted with eggs, rocks, and pieces of pipe and coal.[106]

3. The hospital itself was attacked. A bullet was shot through one of the windows, and the glass door of the entrance to the emergency room was broken by two union members.[107]

4. Security guards were harassed. Pickets threw rocks at them and at their cars,[108] two of them were hit with a bat and pelted with rocks by union officials,[109] and another was injured when his car window was broken.[110]

5. Nonunion employees and others were also attacked. On one occasion, a nonunion employee was attacked and beaten by union members and union officials,[111] and on another occasion two strikers beat a personnel assistant and hurt a bystander in a store parking lot.[112]

At two different hospitals in Huntington, West Virginia, violence occurred during a protracted campaign by District 1199 to organize the

---

[105] Ashland (Kentucky) Independent, Apr. 1, 1981, n.p.
[106] Prestonburg (Kentucky) Times, Apr. 15, 1981 and May 6, 1981.
[107] Prestonburg (Kentucky) Times, May 6, 1981 and May 27, 1981.
[108] Prestonburg (Kentucky) Times, May 6, 1981, n.p.
[109] Frankfort State Journal, May 29, 1981, n.p.
[110] Lexington Herald, Jun. 1981, n.p.
[111] Paintsville (Kentucky) Herald, May 20, 1981, n.p.
[112] Prestonburg (Kentucky) Times, May 6, 1981, n.p.

hospitals. Paint and acid were thrown on nonstrikers' cars,[113] nonstrikers were assaulted and harassed,[114] a doctor was injured while trying to cross a picket line,[115] a county prosecutor was assaulted on the steps of the hospital,[116] and other acts of aggression occurred.[117]

At Long Island Jewish-Hillside Medical Center, in March 1982, among other instances of violence, the tires of twenty-nine cars parked near a housing complex housing interns and residents were slashed,[118] as were the tires on thirteen taxicabs used to transport dialysis patients to the strike-bound hospital.[119] The main building of the hospital was thoroughly and systematically vandalized, including jamming of door locks, flooding of lavatories and elevators, cutting of phone wires to various departments, destruction of hospital supplies, and disablement of garbage compactors and medical electronic equipment.[120] While the strike was still in progress, one newspaper summed up the violence this way:

> Tires have been slashed, fire hoses have been opened and water sprayed down stairwells and into elevator shafts. Some medical equipment was stolen and a door to a library was cemented shut. Visitors coming to see patients said they were subjected to verbal abuse by strikers.
>
> Several men were chased through a parking lot after a hospital guard watched them try to snip through a fence surrounding storage tanks containing the hospital's supply of highly flammable liquid oxygen. No one was caught.[121]

Although the union consistently denied involvement in these incidents, it is difficult to find another likely cause.

Similar incidents of violence occurred in other strikes involving District 1199, and in strikes by other medical care employees affiliated with the Teamsters or with the AFSCME, but District 1199 seems to be the worst.

CONCLUSIONS

Unionization of hospital and health care employees is a relatively recent phenomenon, and most of the violent strikes involving these

---

[113] Welsh (West Virginia) Daily News, Aug. 12, 1977, n.p.

[114] Welsh (West Virginia) Daily News, Aug. 12, 1977; Wheeling Intelligencer, Nov. 3, 1979; Charleston Mail, Oct. 18, 1979.

[115] Welsh (West Virginia) Daily News, Aug. 12, 1977, n.p.

[116] Charleston Mail, Oct. 18, 1979, n.p.

[117] Wheeling Intelligencer, Sep. 25, 1978; Wheeling News Register, Nov. 2, 1979.

[118] New York Times, Mar. 14, 1982, at 18.

[119] Clippings in the author's file. Source newspaper undetermined, but probably New York Post, Mar. 10, 13, and 18, 1982.

[120] *Id.*

[121] New York Times, Mar. 26, 1982, at B-1.

unions occur at the organizational stage, which is the stage at which violence is most likely in other fields as well. Hospitals and nursing homes are generally unused to collective bargaining, however, and therefore have to gain the experience that industrial firms gained years ago. Many hospital administrations simply are not skilled at avoiding strikes or at handling them once they begin. Nevertheless, there should be no excuse for medical care employees to engage in tactics such as those described above.

The purpose of any strike by vital public service employees is to disrupt the delivery of needed services to the community. In the case of policemen and firemen, "this deprivation of essential services is intended to increase public concern and create pressure upon the city's elected officials to take steps to restore the deprived services—that is, to accede to some or all of the . . . union's demands."[122] The added use of violence during such strikes could be expected to generate greater public concern and commensurately greater political pressure. It might also, as was the case in Memphis, encourage involvement by higher levels of government, or by outsiders who have no responsibility for raising the demanded funds, and who therefore are generally more willing to make concessions to reach a quick settlement.

Of all of the violent tactics used by public safety unions in their strikes, arson has had the greatest impact, not only in terms of the costs involved, but also in terms of the fear and public concern it generates. Whether or not the striking unions are directly responsible for setting large numbers of fires, the responsibility for the property losses may ultimately be placed on them. By authorizing a legal or illegal strike, firefighters' unions deprive the citizens of effective protective services and thereby cause losses which would not be incurred but for the strike.[123]

The fires set by arsonists in these strikes are axiomatically purposeful, but it is difficult to find a rational explanation for them. Perhaps the opinion of the mayor of Memphis is correct: that the fires in that city were set simply as an attempt to increase the pressure on the administration for a settlement.

It is also possible that some of them, either there or elsewhere, have been set to show citizens how important fire protection and firemen are to them. Violence against the public emphasizes the lack of the essential protective services. Finally, some of the fires could have come

---

[122] H. JURIS AND P. FEUILLE, UNIONISM: POWER AND IMPACT IN PUBLIC-SECTOR BARGAINING 88 (1973).

[123] Persons who have suffered property losses during similar strikes have successfully pursued damage suits against unions on this theory. *See, Private Damage Actions Against Public Sector Unions for Illegal Strikes*, 91 HARV. L. REV. 1309.

about simply as a reaction to the psychology of strife and confrontation, wherein move and countermove escalate and intensify until moral restraints erode and finally dissolve.

The use of violent tactics like arson or other terrorist activities as a means of instilling fear in the public to increase the political costs of disagreement is, however, not only morally reprehensible but also a risk to the perpetrator who will defeat his own purposes if discovered or credibly blamed for the violent acts. One analyst of strike strategies in sensitive public services has stated that in order for coercive tactics to be used effectively, it must be

> made clear by the union that they are directed at an uncompromising individual or group . . . and *not* at the community at large. Although such activity, especially job action, will affect the public, the [strikers should] try not to alienate the community any more than is necessary.[124]

The Memphis firefighters failed to follow this advice and lost the support of the public. Others, such as those in Kansas City, were somewhat more careful, and therefore somewhat more successful. All employees in public service jobs should be aware, however, that the public and even members of other unions may well resent the increased bargaining power that employees in sensitive public services attain by the accident of the importance of their jobs to community safety, and, therefore, may support the employer or the city in strikes involving violent confrontation.

Reasons for vandalism of city equipment, breaking windows, slashing tires, and other acts against property are easier to find than are reasons for violence against people. This type of violence increases the economic costs of employers' disagreement and refusal to concede to unions' demands. In addition, these and similar coercive acts may also be explained as attempts to increase the political costs of disagreement. Strikes by police and firemen (and to a lesser extent, by medical care employees), even when not violent, bring to bear a great deal of political pressure. Because "strikes in public employment disrupt important services, a large part of the . . . political constituency will, in many cases, press for a quick end to the strike with little concern for the cost of the settlement."[125]

Other acts of violence may be explained as attempts to make the strikes more completely successful in disrupting essential services.

---

[124] Craft, *Fire Fighter Strategy in Wage Negotiations,* QUARTERLY REVIEW OF ECONOMICS AND BUSINESS, (Autumn 1971), at 68 (emphasis in original).

[125] H. WELLINGTON AND R. WINTER, THE UNIONS AND THE CITIES 25 (1971). *See also* Shaw and Clark, *Public Sector Strikes: An Empirical Analysis,* 2 JOURNAL OF LAW AND EDUCATION 223.

Vandalism of equipment is often designed to assure that services can not be provided with that equipment by nonstrikers or replacements. Blocking driveways, scattering nails, and slashing tires are ways of "getting at" employers or nonstrikers, and of assuring a more complete shutdown of services. Beatings, assaults, and threats against nonstrikers decrease the level of services further, and communicate the cost of not participating with the union to the nonstrikers.

Thus, there are three objective-related explanations of the high level of violence and vandalism that accompanies strikes by policemen, firemen, and medical care employees. Where violence is used, it seems to be directed at increasing the economic costs of strikes, increasing their political costs, and making the disruption of essential services more complete. Other explanations may also exist which are unrelated to the achievement of strike objectives. For example, some violent acts may be explained as the simple result of mob psychology.[126]

Whatever the explanations for the strikers' behavior, the use of violent tactics during strikes directly involving the public safety presents a strong argument for truly effective bans on such strikes. Some observers have argued that strikes in the essential service sector, in and of themselves, give a "disproportionate share of effective power in the process of decision" to the unions.[127] This disproportionate power may threaten the "normal American political process."[128] When violence is used as a tactic to increase the power of the unions, the strike becomes all the more intolerable, and the political process is distorted even further.

In addition to the political consequences, strikes in protective services also have a great impact on the social and economic life of the community. Unlike most other public services, police and fire protection cannot easily be replaced during a strike. The lack of full fire and police protection jeopardizes the safety of the public, and curfews are often imposed which damage the economic and social life of the community. Strikes by police and firefighters are simply too devastating to be tolerated. The experiences illustrated above add further evidence to this seemingly obvious fact.

---

[126] *See, e.g.,* E. CANETTI, CROWDS AND POWER 16–22, 485–495 (1966).
[127] WELLINGTON AND WINTER, *supra* note 125, at 25.
[128] *Id.*

CHAPTER VI

Violence in the Construction Trades[1]

Violence has been a labor relations factor in the construction industry for many years. The physical nature of the work, the vulnerability of the workplace, and the impermanence of employment relationships in construction all make violence likely during organizational efforts or labor disputes. Even early studies of the industry repeatedly take notice of its use.

Shortly after the turn of the century, for example, the United States Commission on Industrial Relations took note of the involvement of the International Association of Bridge, Structural, and Ornamental Iron Workers' Union (BSOIW) in the dynamiting of nonunion construction jobs.[2] Others noted repeated references to bombings and other violence in the Chicago construction industry during the first quarter of the century;[3] the occurence of "over three hundred cases of violence" was found in a single construction strike in San Francisco,[4] and numerous instances of violence perpetrated against construction union members and contractors have occurred in connection with labor racketeering. Even historians sympathetic to construction unions recount violent incidents that accompanied many organizational drives.[5]

In recent years, far from decreasing, the use of violence in the construction trades has actually been rising, sparked in part by a resurgence of open shop firms since the mid-1960s. In 1972, the *Engineering News Record* reported:

---

[1] The discussion herein for the period to 1975 is taken from H. NORTHRUP AND H. FOSTER, OPEN SHOP CONSTRUCTION (1975).

[2] L. GRANT, THE NATIONAL ERECTORS' ASSOCIATION AND THE INTERNATIONAL ASSOCIATION OF BRIDGE AND STRUCTURAL IRONWORKERS (1915).

[3] R. MONTGOMERY, INDUSTRIAL RELATIONS IN THE CHICAGO BUILDING TRADES (1972).

[4] F. RYAN, INDUSTRIAL RELATIONS IN THE SAN FRANCISCO BUILDING TRADES 191 (1936).

[5] H. SEIDMAN, LABOR CZARS: A HISTORY OF LABOR RACKETEERING (1938). See also the useful summaries of the McClellan hearings, in which the Teamsters and Operating Engineers were featured, in J. HUTCHENSON, THE IMERFECT UION: A HISTORY OF CORRUPTION IN AMERICAN TRADE UNIONS (1970); and R. KENNEDY, THE ENEMY WITHIN (1960).

Violence is the gut reaction of unions in some areas to counter the open shop. In recent years violence and property damage have hit nonunion projects in Florida, Maryland, Tennessee, Georgia, Ohio, and Pennsylvania.[6]

Recent statistics on violent incidents in the building trades point up the degree to which the targets have changed during the past few years. Chapter III took note of 319 reports of violence found in the labor violence data base which occurred between 1976 and 1981 and involved building trades unions or councils. Of these, fewer than 100 were directed against employers or involved strikes or contract disputes of the traditional type. The great majority arose out of protests against nonunion or open shop work being done in an area where such work had traditionally been done by union shops.

The geographic extent of violence in construction is wide, and it involves most of the traditional building crafts. During the mid-1970s, the National Labor Relations Board (NLRB) issued complaints on charges of coercive violence against four international construction unions (the Construction and Laborers Union, the United Brotherhood of Carpenters and Joiners of America, the United Union of Roofers, Waterproofers and Allied Workers, and the International Association of Bridge, Structural, and Ornamental Iron Workers), plus state and local union bodies of the Operating Engineeers (in Ohio, Michigan, New Jersey, and Pennsylvania), Ironworkers (in Michigan and Massachusetts), Laborers (in Kentucky), Plumbers (in Michigan), and Roofers (in Pennsylvania), and Building and Construction Trades Councils (in Michigan and New Jersey).[7] In litigation, some of the unions charged—notably those in Michigan—agreed to refrain from further violence as part of consent decrees, and others were found guilty of violent and coercive behavior.[8]

Besides these NLRB cases, considerable other litigation in various parts of the country has involved the issue of violence in the construction trades. The use of violence is both common and extensive in the industry. As examples of its scope and character, summaries of events which have occurred in recent years in four localities (Denver, Philadelphia, Michigan, and the Gulf Coast) are set forth below. These summaries are followed by more brief descriptions of violent activities drawn from other places around the country.

---

[6] G. MANGUM, THE OPERATING ENGINEERS: THE ECONOMIC HISTORY OF A TRADE UNION 181–195 (1964).

[7] *Open Shop, A Growing Force and a Catalyst for Change.* ENGINEERING NEWS-RECORD (November 2, 1972), n.p.

[8] This summary is based on the NLRB's general counsel's press release and *Order Consolidating Cases, Consolidated Complaint* and *Notice of Hearing* in Cases Nos. 8-CB-2112, 22-CB-2598, 1-CB-2316, and 7-CC-757, 7-CB-2834). The full names of the construction trades unions mentioned here and elsewhere in this chapter are found in Appendix A.

FIRES IN DENVER

One of the most frequently used tools of labor violence is fire. Buildings under construction by nonunion contractors, lumber yards supplying them, completed projects built by them, construction offices and trailers, and even the homes of nonunion contractors have been torched at one time or another as a lesson in the added costs of nonunion work. This sort of activity was especially dramatic in Denver during the 1960s and 1970s.[9]

The construction-related fires in Denver involved principally apartment houses and condominiums, but other buildings and lumber yards supplying them were also hit. During the period, about forty such fires were reported which involved open shop builders or contractors who were involved in disputes with construction trade unions. The fires usually occurred when they could do the maximum damage—after a building was closed in, but before internal walls and ceilings were in place, for example—and the total amount of destruction during the period was estimated to be over $10 million.

Investigation of these fires was stymied for a considerable amount of time while attorneys for the Northern Colorado Building and Construction Trades Council vainly sought to suppress evidence obtained through wiretapping. The council appealed all the way to the U.S. Supreme Court, but the wiretap procedures were found to have been legal under Colorado law, and the evidence was eventually admitted. In 1975 and 1976, it, along with other evidence developed by the Colorado Bureau of Investigation, resulted in arson convictions and jail terms for a business agent of the Colorado Building and Construction Trades Council, two business agents of the Cement, Lime and Gypsum Workers' International Union affiliated with that council, and the executive secretary of the New Mexico Building and Construction Trades Council. During the trials, there was considerable evidence that this "arson organizing" extended beyond the Denver area, with Arizona, Kansas, and California all mentioned as other sites where it may have occurred. There have been, however, no related indictments or convictions in those other areas.

---

[9] The Denver fires story appeared regularly in the press there. *See* Rocky Mountain News, July 27, 1972; May 13 and December 14, 1974; April 10, June 26, September 24, and October 29–30, 1975; and January 30, 1976; and Denver Post, July 28 and 31, August 8 and 28, September 7, October 10, and December 29, 1972; March 1 and 2 and June 13, 1973, and December 15, 1974, January 9 and April 14, 1975. *See also* C. Stevenson, *Arson-to-Order in the Building Trades,* READER'S DIGEST, March 1976, n.p.

BRUTALITY IN PHILADELPHIA

Philadelphia, like many of the older cities of the East Coast and Midwest, is a "union town." The construction unions there have been key supporters of several mayors and enjoy a close relationship with City Hall. Philadelphia is also a city where construction union violence has been endemic. One of the most blatant and brutal cases is that of the Altemose Construction Company, which began in 1972.[10]

Altemose Construction Company

Altemose is an open shop general contractor. In the early 1970s, a dispute arose between Altemose and the Building and Construction Trades Council of Philadelphia over Altemose's refusal to sign a "subcontractor's agreement" which would have obligated it to let subcontracts exclusively to firms using only unionized labor. Although Altemose was willing to use union subcontractors if they provided the best bid, it was unwilling to deny bidding rights to otherwise qualified nonunion firms.

The organizational efforts by the building trades council in this case, although different in detail, are similar in intention to some of the efforts by the United Mine Workers (UMW) to organize the coal fields: unionization was to be imposed from the top down by securing an agreement, not with individual workers to join the union, but with employers, to compel union employment.

The Altemose dispute reached its climax during the summer of 1972, after Altemose had been awarded the general contract for the construction of a hotel and office building complex called the Valley Forge Plaza, in the suburbs of Philadelphia. In the words of the U.S. Court of Appeals for the Third Circuit:

> In the morning of June 5, 1972, approximately 1,000 men from the Trades Council arrived at the Plaza construction site in buses chartered by one of the Council's member unions and proceeded to destroy vehicles, equipment and other property belonging to Altemose, causing damage in excess of $350,000. Although Altemose immediately obtained a preliminary injunction in state court prohibiting picketing by members of the Trades Council within one mile of any Altemose site or its office building, a second mob descended the following day on the office of Altemose Enterprises and threatened to burn it down. Violence was prevented only through the combined efforts of state and local police. Subsequently, on August 17, J. Leon Altemose was attacked and beaten by members of the Trades Council in broad daylight, while attempting to enter a bank in downtown Philadelphia.
>
> Members of the Trades Council also put pressure on the employees of the construction site to cease working for Altemose. Edward Fitzpatrick, a

---

[10] Laborers' International Union of North America, 219 N.L.R.B. 142 (1975); *affirmed* 532 F.2d 749 (4th Cir., 1976).

business agent for one of the member unions in the Trades Council, called one of the subcontractors on the site, Richard Czeiner, and told him that the unions would prefer that he not work there. Czeiner refused to quit, however, and subsequently several of his vehicles were destroyed or damaged by fire bombs. Despite strong security measures taken by Altemose, construction on the project was plagued by sabotage.

As a result of the violence and threats, many subcontractors withdrew from the site and Altemose and Energy [Czeiner] had considerable difficulty in obtaining qualified workers willing to risk work there.[11]

About two weeks after the initial violence against Altemose, vandals registered at a Sheraton Hotel in Philadelphia—the same chain for which Altemose was constructing the Valley Forge Plaza—and seriously damaged a number of rooms. After that, other Altemose projects were bombed and other violence occurred, all of it apparently directed toward intimidating present and potential customers of Altemose.

Altemose's suppliers and creditors were also pressured to cease doing business with the company. Users were warned not to put the company on their bid list. (To their shame, several church groups removed the company from bidding.) Altemose completed the Valley Forge Plaza, but the company has faced difficulties ever since, perhaps partly as a result of the weak construction market of the late 1970s and early 1980s but also because the unions have maintained their pressures on all fronts. In 1976, for example, the unions induced the then governor of Pennsylvania, the host for the Governor's Conference that year, to move it away from Valley Forge so that the Altemose-built hotel would not receive the patronage.

The union attack on Altemose has been total, apparently in an endeavor to drive the company out of business. Thus, two plumbers sought employment with Altemose, and after being discharged, filed charges with the NLRB. When the NLRB hearing was held, the hearing room was ringed with demonstrators who threatened the Altemose participants. Yet the NLRB regional director did not order a change of venue and the administrative law judge credited the discharged plumbers, discredited the company witness, and found Altemose guilty of an unfair labor practice, a decision with which the NLRB concurred.

In a decision that was about as critical of NLRB procedure as any

---

[11] The material for the Altemose story, unless otherwise noted, is based on numerous press stories and articles collected over the years. *See,* particularly, for the Altemose Case, the (Philadelphia) Evening and Sunday Bulletin, June 5, 11, 12, 14, 15, 18, 20, and 22, July 16 and 17, August 19, 20, 21, 22, 24, and 29, September 15, 18, 19, 20, 21, and 28, and October 18 and 24, 1972; February 18, June 28, July 19, 24, 25, and 27, September 11, October 23, November 8, 10, 11, 22, and 30, and December 1, 5, and 28, 1973; January 20, February 6 and 9, March 3, April 4, 7, 11, and 14, September 8, October 2 and 20, and November 1 and 29, 1974; and January 14, 17, 21, and 22, and March 12, 1975; and Philadelphia Inquirer, May 26, and June 7 and 14, 1972.

ever written, the Court of Appeals for the Third Circuit reversed this decision and castigated the NLRB for permitting a hearing under such circumstances, pointing out numerous discrepancies which reflected upon the credibility of union witnesses, and questioning several key rulings of the administrative law judge.[12] One point made clear by the court decision was that the unions were not interested in organizing Altemose's employees; their objective was to secure jobs for their members by forcing Altemose or other nonunion companies to hire only union subcontractors in their own specialized trades.

The combined pressures on Altemose were telling. By 1980, the company was considerably reduced in size, and its future as a building contractor was greatly diminished. If the results were a victory for the unions, however, they were not without cost.

The violence and destruction that resulted from the mass picketing at Altemose in 1972 was blatant and undisguised, and it gave rise both to NLRB cases and to criminal charges. The first criminal trial involved a battery of lawyers and cost the Philadelphia Building and Construction Trades Council an estimated $300,000. Nevertheless, in it and in two other trials on related crimes and violence in Norristown, Pennsylvania, eighteen unionists, most of whom were members of Local 30 of the United Union of Roofers, Waterproofers and Allied Workers, were convicted of multiple accounts of violence, and eleven of them served time in jail.[13] The attack on Mr. Altemose in broad daylight in downtown Philadelphia, however, brought no convictions.

Roofers Local 30

It was not surprising to those familiar with labor relations in southeastern Pennsylvania that members of Local 30 were involved in the Altemose case, as that local had long been involved in construction-related violence in the Philadelphia area. Indeed, it so prided itself on its tactics that at one time its members had brutalized open shop builders and workers with baseball bats specially inscribed with the Local 30 insignia. In addition, Local 30's business agent had rented the bus used for the attack on the Altemose construction site.

Injunctions have been issued against Local 30; it has been charged in a number of NLRB complaints;[14] and it has been the subject of feature

---

[12] Altemose Construction Company, et al., v. National Labor Relations Board, 514 F.2d 8 (3rd Cir. 1975).

[13] *Id.*

[14] Besides the eleven who were sent to jail, seven were acquitted, and five received probation after their original convictions were overturned on appeal and they later pleaded guilty. *See* Philadelphia Inquirer, June 12, 1980, at B–4, and November 5, 1980, at 1–F.

articles in Philadelphia newspapers and magazines which documented with remarkable specificity its involvement with violence.[15] Nevertheless, during the early 1970s, with the exception of particularly blatant examples such as the attack on Altemose, its violence and transgressions went largely unpunished.

There can be little doubt but that the political atmosphere of Philadelphia during this time contributed to this neglect. The prounion stance of the then mayor was well known,[16] and union officials were represented on all key city agencies dealing with housing, zoning, or building codes.

An example of the degree to which union violence and intimidation was condoned in Philadelphia at that time is found in an account of a Democratic Party dinner in the city in 1974. The mayor had not been invited to sit on the dais for the dinner because of a dispute with a city party chairman. The following scene evolved:

> While over 4,000 Democrats were gathering at Civic Center to dine and hear speeches, a flying squad of roofers burst into the hall. They overturned tables, beat up a 60 year old . . . [opposition member] and a number of deputy sheriffs who were serving as ushers, while the police looked the other way.
>
> A few minutes after the roofers had set the tone, [the mayor] . . . pulled up in his city limousine. [The business agent of the Roofers, the president of the Building and Construction Trades Council, and the business agent of Teamsters Local 107] were riding with him.
>
> Led by a fife and drum corps, . . . [the mayor] and 500 union toughs stormed into the Civic Center, completely upstaging the Democratic politicians and scaring hell out of everyone there . . . They encircled the diners and dignitaries, chanting obscenities . . . and knocking people down along the way. The union chiefs formed a phalanx around [the mayor], who boasted that it was the greatest night in his life.[17]

With the advent of a new mayor, less beholden to the construction unions but equally anti-open shop, and the successful prosecutions in the courts and by the NLRB, the violent activities of Local 30 quieted somewhat during the late 1970s, at least insofar as they were directed against the nonunion construction industry. Local 30 then turned the focus of its attention to Atlantic City and the burgeoning new market there brought on by legalized gambling. It attempted to establish a

---

[15] The Board found Local 30 emphatically guilty of violence in at least two cases and issued remedial orders. *See* Roofers Local 30 (Associated Builders and Contractors, Inc.), 227 N.L.R.B. 1444 (1977); and Roofers Local 30 and Edward R. Kitson and Martin J. Sobol, 228 N.L.R.B. 652 (1977).

[16] *See* J. Riggio, *The Hardhat's Holy War*, LXIII PHILADELPHIA MAGAZINE (August 1972), at 55–61, 126–138; and the series by L. Ditzen, (Philadelphia) Evening Bulletin, July 15–18, 1974.

[17] (Philadelphia) Evening Bulletin, April 10, 1975, at 6.

guard employees' local subsidiary there. On December 16, 1980, John McCulloch, business agent of Local 30, was murdered in his home by one Willard E. Moran, who was later convicted and sentenced to death. Moran then allegedly divulged information that implicated the business agent of the rival Atlantic City guards' union and a racketeering figure who had also been charged in the killing. Press stories linked McCulloch with the late Angelo Bruno, longtime alleged head of the Philadelphia mafia.[18] Racketeering and violence have often gone hand-in-hand in the construction industry.[19]

Schnabel Associates

With the death of its longtime business agent, Local 30 ceased to be at the cutting edge of violence related to the Philadelphia construction industry, but violence associated with that union has, nevertheless, continued. Its most frequent target in the early 1980s has been the firm of Schnabel Associates, which has grown from a small Philadelphia suburban concern to one operating all over the Eastern Seaboard, and which rose in 1982 to No. 372 on the *Engineering News-Record* list of the 400 largest building contractors. Schnabel has always operated open shop.

As it has grown, this firm has endured picketing and violence in a number of areas, but only since 1980 has it become a prime target of violence. In 1981, Schnabel was building at five sites in the Philadelphia area. The building trades unions picketed at all the sites, interfering with deliveries, harassing and threatening employees, and destroying and stealing equipment. According to the *Engineering News-Record,* the violence was particularly rough during the construction of a $3.3 million home for the elderly in Boothwyn and a middle school in Radnor,[20] but pickets were also very much in evidence at the site of a Haverford condominium and elsewhere.

---

[18] M. Mallows, *You Got a Friend in the Business,* LXV PHILADELPHIA MAGAZINE, (September 1974), at 118–123, 200–213.

[19] According to press stories, Angelo Bruno was murdered along with several of his alleged associates in what was termed a fight with their New York City counterparts over jurisdiction in Atlantic City. Control of the restaurant guards' and related union there is thought to be the key to racketeering control of that obviously lucrative site. *See, e.g.,* the series of articles in the (Philadelphia) Evening Bulletin, June 7–10, 1981; Philadelphia Inquirer, December 17, 18, 21, 1980, and September 8, 9, 10, 1982; and also the series in the New York Times, August 29, 30, 31, and September 1, 1982.

[20] *See* SEIDMAN, *supra,* note 5. In New York City, where violence and racketeering is apparently endemic in construction, this situation has been clear for many years. *See, e.g.,* the series on the subject in the New York Times, April 25, 26, and 27, 1982. These articles have led to an official inquiry by the state of New York. At one of the hearings, testimony was heard concerning violence at construction sites. (*State panel told about violence in construction,* New York Times, June 16, 1982, at B3). A few months later, a

When the problems began at the Boothwyn site, Schnabel began videotaping picketing activity and maintaining a journal of the day-to-day events which transpired at all five of the firm's active work sites around Philadelphia. After viewing hundreds of hours of the tapes, a reporter for *Engineering News-Record* wrote:

> The tapes show pickets beating company employees, spiking and slashing tires, throwing rocks and even a stolen chain saw through the windows of cars and trucks entering the jobsite. In the films, union business agents involved in the picketing appear to be directing part of the activity, and local law-enforcement officials are seen standing idly by as pickets violate court injunctions against mass picketing and violence.[21]

The attorney for the construction unions, who had represented them throughout the period covered by this discussion, made the purpose of this harassment very clear. Again as reported by the *Engineering News-Record:*

> Building trades attorney Bernard Katz says his clients are using the same tactics to fight Schnabel that they have been using against nonunion contractors for "more than 30 years. What we want to do, quite simply is erase the competitive advantage Schnabel has by virtue of his hiring workers at substandard wages."
>
> According to Katz, this is done by several means, all of which "make it difficult for him to do business here." Among the extra costs that Schnabel has to bear, he says, are higher prices for building materials—"no driver wants to cross a picket line"—and a disproportionate amount of money spent on security and legal fees. Even if Schnabel completes the Boothwyn project, says Katz, "We are sure we will see less of him in the future" because of the building trades' efforts.[22]

In light of these comments, it is difficult to disagree with the claim of Schnabel's attorney that the violence perpetrated by the union is "planned and calculated."[23] Schnabel has filed a multimillion-dollar damage suit against the Building and Construction Trades Council of Philadelphia, four local unions, and six union officials, but Attorney Katz states that the construction unions "are not the least bit concerned. Believe me, we lost our lawsuit virginity a long time ago."[24]

Other construction violence occurs from time to time in the Philadel-

---

Teamster official implicated in both violence and racketeering in New York construction was found guilty of seven charges of labor racketeering and tax evasion. (*Key Teamster leader is convicted of labor racketeering by L.I. jury,* New York Times, October 9, 1981, at 1). For other New York racketeering-labor convictions, see New York Times, June 8, 1979, at B-2, and March 25, 1982, at B-8.

[21] *See, Middle school project halted after union pickets close site,* (Ardmore, Pa.) Main Line Times, November 12, 1981, at B-2, 14.

[22] Engineering News-Record, May 27, 1982, at 10.

[23] *Id.* at 11.

[24] *Id.* at 10.

phia area;[25] police protection for the nonunion builder is generally absent in the city, and it is often sparse in the neighboring counties as well. Clearly, the legal proscriptions, both civil and criminal, against those who tried to destroy the business of Altemose and those who use violence to "erase the competitive advantage" of nonunion firms have not deterred resort to such tactics.

"LEGAL EXTORTION" IN MICHIGAN

Although Detroit is very much a "union town," over the past few years, open shop construction has been gaining ground in other areas of Michigan (and there have even been some inroads into Detroit itself). The construction unions responded with violence which reached the height of a crescendo in the early 1970s at Kalkaska and Midland, Michigan.[26]

Kalkaska

The town of Kalkaska is a community of 1,600 inhabitants in the northern sector of Michigan's southern peninsula. In July 1971, the Shell Oil Company announced plans to build a gas processing plant there. Shell awarded the contract to the Delta Engineering Company of Houston, a large open shop builder with considerable experience in this type of construction.

Violence began in February 1973, when 400 union demonstrators did $100,000 of damage at the Kalkaska site and at another open shop construction site, injuring two state troopers in the process. In addition, the construction unions began a series of demonstrations at Shell service stations across the state, aided in some cases by members of the International Brotherhood of Teamsters (Teamsters) and the United Automobile Workers (UAW).

A threatened injunction stopped the picketing of service stations, but 200 to 500 construction workers continued literally to create a reign of terror in Kalkaska for the next several months. During the seige, the state of Michigan had to station as many as 350 state troopers—20 percent of its total force—in this small town to protect Delta Engineering's labor force from the demonstrators, most of whom were from Detroit. The cost to the state's taxpayers for this police protection was about $30,000 per day.

---

[25] *Id.* at 11. *See also, AFL-CIO pickets greet open-shop move across the 'no-no' line into Phila.,* (Philadelphia) Evening Bulletin, December 28, 1981, at B-1, 2.

[26] *See, e.g., SEPTA workers enter Delco construction site,* Philadelphia Inquirer, July 21, 1982, at 1-2-B; and *Picketing is curbed at camp, Id.,* September 5, 1981, at 3-B.

Repeated efforts by Shell and Delta to obtain enforceable injunctions were unsuccessful. Finally, in June 1973, at their request, the NLRB moved, in federal district court, for an injunction against the secondary boycott activities and coercion of individuals on the part of the unions and scheduled a hearing for the issues in July.

The district court judge involved was a former labor mediator. Instead of granting an order, he pushed the parties into mediation sessions. The unions were demanding that the nonunion Delta Engineering Company, although subject to no contracts or agreements with any of the unions involved, pay money into the unions' welfare funds as a condition of settlement. Delta refused to go along with this "legal" form of extortion, but did offer to employ fifty union men in its work force. The counteroffer was refused and negotiations continued.

After being prodded by the judge and by the governor of Michigan, Delta and Shell agreed to donate $250,000—the estimated cost of the union welfare programs—to the Kalkaska Township and to try to employ more workers from within a 100-mile radius. The unions were satisfied by this. The violence was called off, and the construction work remained open shop. As part of the settlement, however, Shell and Delta suspended all legal action, which provided the unions with both a reward and a victory for their use of violence. According to one press report:

> The union said they felt the publicity given to the often violence-marred dispute will reap long-range benefits for union members.
> "I don't think anybody else will try to do this [build a major job with non-union work] again in Michigan," one union source said. "There's no doubt about that."
> He predicted "a hell of a lot of construction in the future in the oil industry in Michigan and I bet it's all going to be union."[27]

According to another union official, "There is no doubt it [the settlement] was good for the union movement. In the last three weeks we signed up 20 to 25 companies."[28] As one press article put it, neither

---

[27] The Kalkaska story is based upon the following press stories: Detroit Free Press, February 20, 21, and 27, April 27, May 2 and 3, June 14, 15, 17, 19, 20, 21, 24, 26, 29 and 30, July 12, 17, and 18; Detroit News, June 16, 17, and 21, and July 17, 1973; Bay City Times, February 20, May 15 and 20, June 2, 19, and 24; Midland Daily News, June 15, 16, 20 and 28, July 13, 17 and 18; Jackson Citizen Patriot, June 18 and 19; Traverse City Eagle, July 11, 12, and 17; Grand Rapids Press, July 26; New York Times, March 25 and July 22; Business Week, July 7, 1973; Construction Labor Report, No. 929, July 25, 1973, at A-6 to A-7; Solidarity, June 1973; Building Tradesman, June 22 and 29. The Midland material, exclusive of the Kalkaska situation, is based upon stories in the Midland Daily News, September 4, 5, 6, 14, 15, 17, 18, 20, 21, 27, 28 and 29, October 2, 6, 8, 9, 10, 13, and 17, November 1 and 11, 1973; January 21, February 12, March 5, September 24, October 30 and 31, and November 1, 1974.
[28] Traverse City Record-Eagle, July 17, 1973, n.p.

Shell nor Delta were ever given the NLRB hearing or court injunction to which they were entitled. Instead they "were coerced by the federal judge and the state government into negotiating with a union organization not involved in their project,"[29] or it might be added, which did not represent their employees.

The judge's rationale for mediating instead of issuing the injunction (that one was warranted is indisputable) was that it would not be enforced, and that he always preferred mediation. Such an approach by a federal judge seems questionable.

> Somehow . . . we cannot help but have misgivings about a settlement which, in effect, has been arrived at because members of the Building Trades Council—in order to achieve their ends—were willing to commit acts of violence and vandalism. . . . That such repugnant methods should be rewarded in any way is troubling indeed.[30]

Since the settlement of this dispute, Shell has not attempted to build nonunion in the Kalkaska area and peace has reigned. Thus the violence and the denial of due process to those upon whom violence was inflicted have saved jobs for union construction workers, and the unions have successfully used violence and the continued threat of violence to force a company to pay out a large sum of money which it otherwise would not have paid and for which it received no benefit other than the cessation of violence—"protection" money, in all but name. The unions thus achieved one of their aims, eliminating the economic advantage of nonunion construction, and equalizing the costs of union and nonunion construction work.

Midland

Having won a victory at Kalkaska, the Michigan construction unions turned their attention to Midland, Michigan, where the Dow Chemical Company is located. Dow lets contracts for construction on its huge complex to either union or open shop builders based solely on the bids and provides separate gates for each on construction sites. Between September 1973 and January 1974, the open shop gate at Dow's complex was picketed by 50 to 200 building tradesmen. Dow received fairly good police protection, but entering workmen were severely harassed.

Mass picketing continued until Dow filed charges with the NLRB and eventually won a consent decree in which the unions agreed to stop the use of violence and agreed to a stipulation which could be enforced

---

[29] *Union Trouble in Kalkaska, Court Bows to Extortion,* syndicated story for North American Newspaper Alliance, August 1973.
[30] *Id.*

by any court of appeals upon NLRB application and with defense waived in advance by the unions.

Although the picketing ended at Dow, violence continued. One of Dow's contractors, the Colinson Construction Company—an open shop contractor that had long been the butt of labor violence—received additional threats and had three of its construction projects not located at Dow damaged by bombs. This violence was stopped by another consent decree and a stipulation similar to that for Dow. The stipulation indicates rather conclusively the tactics that the Michigan trades have utilized:

A. Respondents . . . shall:
1. Cease and desist from:
(a) . . . participating in, directing, authorizing, ratifying, condoning or causing acts of property destruction and vandalism, mass picketing and obstruction of ingress and egress, threats of violence and bodily harm, and similar coercive conduct.
(b) In any other manner, or by any other means, restraining or coercing employees in the exercise of their rights guaranteed by Section 7 of the Act.[31]

The stipulation also prohibited the unions from picketing at non-union gates and from engaging in sympathy strikes and secondary boycotts at the affected sites.[32] Since the time these stipulations were issued, construction violence in Michigan has been reduced considerably, although some outbursts have occurred, and twice, the Michigan State Building and Construction Trades Council has been found in contempt for further violence.[33]

VIOLENCE ON THE GULF COAST

The Gulf Coast, stretching from New Orleans to the Mexican border, is one of the strongest nonunion areas in the country, both in construction and in industry generally. Nevertheless, within this nonunion area, there are some very strong union enclaves. These include parts of Louisiana, the "golden triangle" of Beaumont, Port Arthur, and Orange, Texas, and the Galveston-Texas City area. All of these union strongholds have seen violence erupt when nonunion firms have attempted to handle construction projects.

---

[31] *Editorial,* Grand Rapids Press, July 26, 1973, n.p.

[32] *Michigan State Building and Construction Trades Council, AFL-CIO, et al.,* Settlement Stipulation, N.L.R.B. Case No 7–CB–3030 (February 1975).

[33] National Labor Relations Board v. Michigan State Building and Construction Trades Council and Eugene D. Tolot, U.S.C.A., 6th Cir., April 22, 1977; and *id.,* 665 F.2d 1093 (6th Cir., 1980).

Lake Charles

Lake Charles, Louisiana, is in Calcasieu Parish, near the Texas border. Through the years, it has witnessed its share of labor violence. The Southwest Louisiana Building and Construction Trades Council, which also coordinates construction union activities in several neighboring parishes, is powerful in Calcasieu. Nonunion workers, and those of a rival independent union which is headquartered in Baton Rouge, have been attacked periodically.

When Brown & Root, the country's largest contractor, built a paper mill in the Calcasieu town of DeRidder, mass picketing, violence, bombings, and shootings occurred.[34] Brown & Root, which operates open shop, was forced to bring in personnel and materials by helicopter until order was restored by the state police. In 1975, the American Dredging Company sought an injunction to halt repeated acts of violence by the Laborers' and Operating Engineers' unions there. In one of the incidents, thirty persons wielding clubs, chains, wrenches, and other weapons attacked nonunion workers.[35]

The climax of the violence in this parish came in January 1976 when a mob of 100 persons, led by the head of the local Plumbers' union, and using a large fork lift truck as a tank, overturned gates, and shot their way into a construction site of the open shop Payne & Keller Company. One person was killed, several were wounded or injured, and extensive damage was done. This action was the fourth day of violence at the same site. It was coordinated with an attack on another Payne & Keller site in Houston, where additional violence occurred.[36] In the indictments and trials which followed, the leader of the union attack was sentenced to twenty-two-and-one-half years in jail.

Beaumont-Port Arthur-Orange

In Texas, the area around Beaumont, Port Arthur, and Orange is known as the "golden triangle." With its petroleum deposits, refineries, chemical plants, and other processing industries, it has long been a fertile source of employment and a strong union area. Two incidents

---

[34] *Bomb bridge in Louisiana labor dispute,* Chicago Tribune, September 10, 1968.

[35] Orangeburg (S.C.) Times-Democrat, April 19, 1976. *See also, Ex-Teamster claims attack netted $1,000.* Baton Rouge Advocate, February 4, 1971.

[36] The story of the attack was carried by the various presses in most areas. The New York Times and the El Paso Times stories from the Associated Press on January 15, 1976, are the primary sources used here. At Houston, buildings were set afire and considerable damage was done. Again noting the nexus between corruption and violence, the head of the Plumbers' union in Lake Charles allegedly had interests in contracting concerns, the Laborers' local there has been fined for accepting payments to let nonunion firms work, and the business agents both of the Electrical Workers and the Plumbers have been convicted of taking bribes.

illustrate the tactics of construction unions to keep it a union area.

In 1979, Brown & Root contracted to build part of a dock and shore base facility for offshore oil and gas operations of the Atlantic Richfield Company. The construction site was located on a road known as FM-3322 on the Sabine Ship Channel within the golden triangle. In the words of Brown & Root's subsequent suit for damages:

> On the morning of June 12, 1979, a mob of violent and unruly persons estimated at 1,000, more or less, appeared on FM-3322 at the entrance to the Sabine Site, blocking access to the construction site; blocking free and unrestrained travel on FM-3322; tearing down the fences separating the Sabine Site from the public road; stoning, beating upon and damaging the temporary office building of Plaintiff Brown & Root at the Sabine Site; yelling insults and profanity and threats of bodily harm to the employees of Plaintiff Brown & Root inside the Sabine Site and the temporary office building; and preventing other Brown & Root employees from traveling on the public road and gaining access to their place of work at the Sabine Site. The mob, varying in size and composition, continued such unlawful activities from day to day, from June 12, 1979 until or about August 1, 1979.[37]

In August 1979, an injunction was granted forbidding violence at the site, but it continued nevertheless. Employees of Brown & Root were chased as they left the site and some were driven off the road; the company's equipment was damaged; and "interference, intimidation, blocking of access, riot, and gauntlet on the public road approaching the Sabine Site" continued. As a result

> Brown & Root was compelled to replace some of its employees . . . with pipefitters and piledrivers sent to the job by Defendant Sabine Area Council who worked with a substantially equal number of . . . Brown & Root employees in completing the construction work. Thereafter, Defendants discontinued their acts of intimidation at the Sabine Site.[38]

Brown & Root, unable to obtain sufficient police protection for its employees, gave in to the unions' demands for jobs as the only way to restore order and complete the job. It subsequently filed damage suits against the unions as a result of the violence described above, and several of its employees who were injured or intimidated have also filed suit; but regardless of the success of those suits (at the time of this writing, they had not yet been heard), the unions achieved their objective of forcing their will upon the largest construction firm in the country.

Three years before Brown & Root's difficulties in the golden triangle, the A. W. Cross Construction Company was awarded an $8 million

---

[37] Wilson and Brown & Root, Inc. v. Sabine Area Building and Construction Trades Council, et al., complaint before the U.S. District Court, Southern District of Texas, Galveston Division, 1979.

[38] *Id.* at 8-9.

contract by the United States Army Corps of Engineers to erect the
Alligator Bayou Pumping Station and Gravity Drainage Structure on
the hurricane levee along Taylor's Bayou near Port Arthur. The Cross
company is also an open shop contractor.

On January 15, 1976, the Sabine Area Building and Construction
Trades Council held a meeting at which the nonunion status of Cross
was discussed and plans for a "citizen's protest" meeting were mentioned. Two days after that meeting, a crowd of 300 persons assembled
at the pumping station construction site. Mr. Cross and one of his
supervisors attempted to induce the crowd to leave the site. In the
words of the Court of Appeals for the Fifth Circuit:

> Several vehicles made brief forays up the access road, and their occupants
> confirmed with Cross and Scott [his supervisor] that they were at the Cross
> Construction Company jobsite. The crowd began to get unruly, pushing
> and shoving the remaining Cross workers as they arrived. Nevertheless,
> Cross's employees began work as usual. Then, shortly after 7:00 that morn-
> ing, a group of four pickup trucks, each carrying between twelve and
> eighteen persons, emerged from the crowd gathered at the access road and
> drove onto the jobsite. Plaintiff Scott went out to meet the intruders and to
> request them to leave the area, but one of them approached Scott and said,
> "Man, you all have got to be crazy . . . this is a union town."
> Scott told his interlocutor that they did not want any trouble, and he at-
> tempted to gather together the other employees and to leave the jobsite.
> However, before he could complete his mission, someone stepped out of
> the group and struck him on the head. Suddenly, the mob swarmed over
> the construction site, brutally beating Cross and his employees with iron
> rods and wooden boards, overturning and setting fire to the trailer that
> served as the construction site office, smashing automobile and truck
> windshields, and vandalizing company tools and equipment.
> The entire episode lasted only a few minutes, but the destruction was
> devastating. Cross and his employees were treated for their injuries at a
> local hospital, and work at the construction site did not resume for nearly
> three weeks. Some of Cross's employees, frightened by the possibility of
> repeated attacks at the jobsite, refused to return to work. In addition, the
> violence and vandalism delayed the completion of the project by about six
> months, ultimately causing the Cross Construction Company to default in
> its contractual obligation to the U.S. Army Corps of Engineers.[39]

Three persons were convicted of participation in the riot, two of
whom were given jail sentences.[40] The company and some of its employees also sued individuals and the Sabine council and its constitu-
ents for conspiracy and won a judgment in the United States District
Court and Court of Appeals applying the Ku Klux Klan Act of 1871,[41]

---

[39] Paul E. Scott, et al. v. Bill Moore, et al., 640 F.2d 708 (5th Cir. 1981); *affirmed en
banc,* 680 F.2d 979 (5th Cir. 1982); *reversed,* U.S. Sup. Court, July 5, 1983.

[40] *Texans guilty of labor violence,* Lake Charles American Press, July 19, 1976, n.p.

[41] 42 U.S.C. 1985 (3).

as a "conspiracy designed to deprive nonunion workers of the First Amendment right to freely associate with one another where the conspiracy does not occur in conjunction with legitimate union activity and is perfected by force and violence."[42]

A permanent injunction restraining the Sabine council from engaging in violence at the construction site was won—too late to solve the company's problem—and damages were awarded to the individuals and to the company. The case was reversed by the United States Supreme Court. It thus does not provide a weapon against union violence. But as discussed in Chapter VIII, injunctions are effective only if they are swiftly given and enforced and only if penalties are sufficiently severe to restrain what the judges in this case accurately termed "brutal and unprovoked" attacks by construction unionists.

CONCLUDING REMARKS

The accounts of violence in Denver, Philadelphia, Michigan, and the Gulf Coast region are illustrative of what has occurred in many areas. Because only a small portion of construction-related violence occurs in contract disputes, most of it being directed instead against open shop or nonunion subcontractors, its extent tends to increase with the spread of the open shop movement, which has grown considerably in the last ten years, and which has become significant in many parts of the country that formerly were safe union territory.[43] There are, of course, other motivations for union violence associated with construction work, but in Table VI-1, only samples of violence directed against nonunion employees or firms have been included.

In many of these instances, the purpose of the violence is clear: to frighten contractors and employees from working open shop, and to frighten construction users from awarding contracts to open shop builders, To the question of how they determine where they will bid on work, large open shop contractors readily reply: "Where we can be reasonably sure of police protection." Many users consider the same thing before letting contracts. Violence has thus been effective in many areas in maintaining the union shop, and such violence will undoubtedly continue until effective laws to control it are passed.

---

[42] *Supra,* note 39.

[43] The Wharton Industrial Research Unit later in 1983 will publish a revision and update of its study of open shop construction. Data already gathered show a tremendous expansion of open shop at the expense of union construction.

TABLE VI-1

Selected Incidents of Violence Directed Against
Nonunion Employees or Open Shop Contractors
Involving Construction Trades Unions
1976–1981ᵃ

California	Several nonunion construction projects burned by arsonists; 108 company truck tires damaged.
Connecticut	Nonunion workers harassed by disorderly pickets; rock thrown at truck entering nonunion work site; nonunion entrance blocked by mass pickets; picket protesting nonunion contractor jumped into truck and broke window.
Delaware	Stones thrown; cars kicked and pounded; workers threatened; open shop contractor harassed; nonunion workers severely injured by thrown rocks.
Florida	Traffic blocked; cars damaged; workers threatened; stones thrown; trucks burned; power poles cut; rocks and debris thrown; workers injured; shots fired at company truck; tires slashed; rocks thrown; crane engines filled with sand; equipment damaged; cranes burned; plumbers' union official convicted of plot to burn many nonunion businesses.
Georgia	Employees' cars sprayed with paint; shots fired into truck carrying nonunion employees, two of whom were wounded.
Illinois	Bombs destroyed part of hotel being built nonunion; pickup truck overturned; fences torn down; bat-wielding union members severely beat two nonunion workers; equipment damaged.
Iowa	Cars and homes of nonunion employees vandalized; nails put on road; rocks and eggs thrown at employees; construction site blocked; building under construction damaged.
Louisiana	Four persons injured by a flash fire at nonunion construction site; five nonunion workers wounded, one critically, by club-wielding union members.
Maine	Rocks thrown; road blocked; newsmen and others threatened.
Maryland	Tires slashed; rocks thrown at police; police assaulted.
Massachusetts	Unruly picketing; cement wall torn down, equipment damaged; $2,000,000 worth of damage done to equipment of two nonunion companies by union members; police assaulted.
Michigan	Buildings built by nonunion contractor damaged by explosions; area around nonunion site vandalized.
Minnesota	Wiring of housing project cut and snapped; rocks thrown; company trucks damaged, tires slashed, owner of nonunion firm reportedly hit by union official.
Mississippi	Car windshield broken; nonunion employee injured.
Missouri	Open shop construction site bombed; nonunion workers threatened, harassed, and assaulted; rocks thrown at nonunion employees; thirty engines of heavy construction equipment damaged.
Montana	Shed housing nonunion company's records burned by mob; four nonunion workers assaulted.
Nebraska	Supervisor at nonunion construction site beaten by union members.
Nevada	Car windows smashed, office trailer damaged, employees threatened.

TABLE VI-1 (continued)

New Jersey	Windows of company truck broken; bomb found on nonunion construction site; telephone lines cut and pieces of it taken; tires slashed; employees threatened; office trailer vandalized, telephone lines cut, building plans destroyed; office trailer burned by rioting union members at nonunion site; rocks thrown by pickets at cars and vans entering nonunion jobsite; three nonunion workers beaten by union members; nails put on road; human or animal feces thrown into office trailer; worker beaten; threats made.
New York	Construction site blocked; crane damaged; workers threatened; car windows broken.
Ohio	Car window broken; threats to do damage made; nonunion workers roughed up; security guards attacked; windows broken; entrances blocked; company equipment damaged; structure under construction damaged; workers threatened, assaulted, and injured; vandalism occurred; hotel firebombed with Molotov cocktails; windows of restaurant being constructed with nonunion help broken.
Pennsylvania	Bulldozer damaged; wires cut; windows broken; masked men attempting to bomb a nonunion construction site were caught by security guards, who were then kidnapped, taken to a remote area, and beaten; nonunion employees attempting to cross picket line were threatened and assaulted; $100,000 worth of machinery owned by open shop company damaged; tires slashed; truck windshield broken; driver injured; nails strewn on driveway; employees assaulted; thirty tires slashed and windows broken on employees' cars, company truck firebombed; nonunion contractor's home shot into, contractor threatened with death; employees and guests of hotel harrassed; five nonunion employees beaten with iron pipes and pick handles; owner of nonunion firm and his son beaten by union officials and members; equipment of twelve nonunion contractors damaged; picket with a two-by-four chased and threatened employee.
Tennessee	Entrance to construction site blocked; cars damaged; workers threatened; site closed down; hundreds of rocks thrown by pickets; $50,000 worth of equipment damaged; employees threatened with bodily harm and death; rocks thrown; tires slashed; windows smashed.
Texas	$1,000,000 worth of damage done to nonunion worksite by union members; construction site vandalized; seventeen cases of arson; much equipment damaged; employees threatened; mass picketing; windows of employees' cars smashed; employees threatened and harassed; nonunion employees run off road and threatened.
Washington	Objects thrown at vehicles; windows broken.
W. Virginia	Worker shot at when crossing picket line; tacks spread on road.
Wisconsin	Dynamite found on a crane belonging to a nonunion contractor.

aUnions involved include Building and Construction Trades Councils, Bricklayers, Carpenters, Electrical Workers, Ironworkers, Laborers, Operating Engineers, Painters, or Roofers (see Appendix A for official names of these unions).

The incidents are taken from the National Right to Work Legal Defense Foundation data base (discussed in Chapter III) and are derived from popular press reports. Individual source citations are found in the data base, on file at the Wharton Industrial Research Unit, Philadelphia.

CHAPTER VII

Other Cases in Transportation and Manufacturing

This chapter summarizes incidents of labor violence involving unions in the transportation and manufacturing sectors. The intent here is to demonstrate that although the tactics of violence and its targets vary somewhat from case to case and among organizational or industrial settings, the overall purposes remain about the same—to attain union objectives through the blatant and often unpunished use of force and coercion.

Most of the tactics used have already been illustrated in earlier examples, so in the interests of minimizing redundancy, no attempt will be made here to be comprehensive. Nevertheless, no study of labor violence would be complete without at least some attention to the activities of some of the country's largest labor unions, the International Brotherhood of Teamsters, Chauffeurs, Warehousemen and Helpers of America (Teamsters), the United Automobile, Aerospace & Agricultural Implement Workers (UAW—Autoworkers), the United Steelworkers of America (USW—Steelworkers), and the International Association of Machinists and Aerospace Workers (IAM—Machinists). A few noteworthy incidents involving other unions which have not been previously covered will also be discussed.

THE TEAMSTERS

By any measure, the International Brotherhood of Teamsters is an important force in the American labor movement. Its membership, now about 400,000 less, included as many as 2.3 million members during the late 1970s, and it remains the country's largest union, comprising 742 local unions with more than 7,000 officers and business agents.[1] To achieve its position of power, it has struggled not only with employers and employers' associations but also with the AFL-CIO, from which it is independent, and with individual owner-operators of

---

[1] S. BRILL, THE TEAMSTERS 3 (1978).

trucks, dissident groups within its own ranks, competing unions (particularly in the nontrucking fields), and others. The Teamsters, whose members, in addition to trucking, are involved in fields as diverse as jewelry stores, juke boxes, hamburger buns, hospitals, airlines, and police, has no shortage of enemies.

Under these circumstances, and in the light of what we have already seen in the case of other large unions, it should be no surprise to learn that the Teamsters has a long history of labor violence. Much of the Teamsters' reputation for violence is based on its involvement in extortion and racketeering,[2] but it has also partly been formed by the nature of its participation in strikes, and by the violence it has directed against nonstrikers, nonunion or independent truckers, and internal dissidents.

One early case concerning the Teamsters, for example, involved about 5,000 truck drivers, helpers, and platform men who, during a strike in Minneapolis in 1934, caused rioting that resulted in injuries to dozens, death to one special policeman, significant property damage, and enough trouble that the governor had to call out the National Guard and embargo the movement of most trucks in the state.[3]

The Teamsters are an important force in motor transport. As recently as the late 1970s, of the approximately 1 million persons who drove trucks, some 480,000 were members of the union, and about 300,000 of those were covered by the master freight agreement which is the basis for wages (and tariffs) for most of the raw materials, manufactured, or boxed goods—except food products—that are transported by motor vehicle. (Recently, as a result of the deregulation of the industry which began in July 1980, independent and nonunion truckers have had easier access to business, and these numbers have been reduced. According to one estimate, by January 1983, 8,000 new, independent trucking companies had been chartered since deregulation began, and more than 200 of the previously regulated carriers had gone into bankruptcy.[4] The change in structure, together with the impact of the business recession of 1981–82 which resulted in unemployment rates as high as 30 percent in the trucking industry, reduced the number of Teamster long-haul drivers working to an estimated 180,000 by early 1983.[5])

---

[2] *See, inter alia*, BRILL, *supra* note 1, *passim;* Moldea, *The Hoffa Wars*, PLAYBOY, November 1978, at 141; *Insiders and Mobsters Benefit From Loans By Teamsters Fund*, Wall Street Journal, July 22, 1975, at 1; *Teamster Organizer Is Slain In Phila. Waterfront Office*, (Philadelphia) Evening Bulletin, Feb. 4, 1976, at 1.

[3] H. GRAHAM and T. GURR, 1 VIOLENCE IN AMERICA: HISTORICAL AND COMPARATIVE PERSPECTIVES 270 (1969).

[4] *Hard Times for Truckers*, The New York Times, January 27, 1983, at D1.

[5] *Angered by boost in taxes, truckers gear up for strike*, Philadelphia Inquirer, January 28, 1983, at A-1.

The power of this union to idle a large portion of the motor transport system, on whose uninterrupted operation the jobs of most industrial workers depend, is awesome. Nevertheless, or perhaps even because of it, the power has seldom been exercised in national strikes. In fact, the Teamsters union has had only two nationwide walkouts in its history, and both of them were short. The first, in 1976, lasted only three days, and the second, in 1979, lasted only ten. To the surprise of some, neither event was marked by crisis or by unusual violence.[6]

Actually, there would be no great reason to expect violence during a nationwide Teamsters' walkout. The master freight agreement serves only as the starting point for local negotiations, which are more critical. Overall, Teamsters negotiate about 20,000 contracts every year, or an average of 77 on every working day. These local strikes are where most of the violence occurs.[7]

Teamsters Local 115

The national Teamsters union chartered Local 115 as the United Retail and Wholesale Union in 1955.[8] Since its inception, Local 115 has been under the leadership of John Morris. The size of this local is uncertain, but Morris was quoted by the Philadelphia *Evening Bulletin* in December 1977 as stating that the size was 2,500, having grown from a membership of eight at the time of its establishment in 1955.[9]

This union does not confine its membership to a single industry or skill. Over the years, its membership has included truck drivers and helpers from Goodwill Industries and Philadelphia furniture dealers, publicly employed trash collectors from Cheltenham Township (a suburb of Philadelphia), painters, electricians, and carpenters employed at Drexel University, and housekeepers employed at the University of Pennsylvania. One regional magazine described Local 115 and Morris' duty as follows:

> He was given the task of organizing miscellaneous workers—that meant everybody from telephone operators to sanitation engineers to truck

---

[6] *See, e.g., The crisis that didn't happen,* Philadelphia Inquirer, April 15, 1979, at 1-I and 4-I. Nevertheless, there was at least some violence. In an interview with the authors, an officer with one of the country's largest motor freight lines reported that during the April 1979 strike five men drove up to the company's Toledo headquarters, and without even bothering to hide their faces came into the offices, poured gas around the floor, and ignited it. Fortunately, the building did not burn down. (Interview, January 12, 1982, notes in the author's files.)

[7] *See, however,* the discussion of the Fraternal Association of Steel Haulers (FASH) on pages 189-92, *infra.*

[8] This analysis of Local 115 was originally prepared for the Industrial Research Unit by John A. Brinker, in February 1979.

[9] *Penn Strike Leader Got Harrisburg Help,* (Philadelphia) Evening Bulletin, December 14, 1977, at C-5.

drivers who worked for little outfits . . . Johnny Morris was given the grubby, little bargaining units that the big-shot Teamsters couldn't be bothered with.[10]

Over the years, Morris' personality has dominated Local 115. He is outspoken and unpredictable, and his tactics have made him a familiar figure in the press and one of the most controversial labor leaders in the Philadelphia area. Morris was once described in the Philadelphia *Evening Bulletin* as a "shrewd" and "astute" labor leader, but one "whose strikes always seem to have a measure of property vandalism, threats and other alleged 'violent' tactics."[11]

In 1975 Morris made the following comments concerning the tactics employed by Local 115:

> We have physical men who respond physically. It's our job to organize the unorganized and we're very efficient about what we do. To my way of thinking, the unions are better than government. They give the people what they need, and keep the capitalist employers from walking over them.[12]

In December 1977, Morris denied that his union condoned violence but he did concede that "emotional outbreaks" do occur among members.[13] He also made the following statement:

> Violence is the worst thing for any strike . . . A judge will issue an injunction right away and the employer will be able to cut his expenses by having the courts, the sheriff's office, and the Philadelphia police provide protection.[14]

History has proved, however, that regardless of Morris's claims, violence in the forms of vandalism to private property and physical assaults to employers and nonstriking employees, and threats of violence are common occurrences in Local 115 strikes.

In the following sections, five strikes involving Local 115 which occurred during the 1970s are reviewed. They were all "wage and benefit" strikes, as opposed to organizational efforts, and they illustrate common patterns of violence.

J. L. Popowich & Sons Co. (1971).[15]   J. L. Popowich & Sons is a Philadelphia firm involved in the importation and distribution of watch bands. In 1970 annual sales were about $1.5 million. During July 1971, as reported in the legal records, Teamsters Local 115 began to organ-

---

[10] *The Ordeal of Nochman Neff*, PHILADELPHIA MAGAZINE, May 1975, at 204.

[11] *Penn Strike Leader, supra* 9, at C-5.

[12] *The Ordeal, supra* note 10, at 204.

[13] *Penn Strike Leader, supra* note 9, at C-5.

[14] *Id.*

[15] Facts for this case are taken from National Labor Relations Board v. Local 115, affiliated with the Int. Bro. of Teamsters, 338 F.Supp. 856 (E.D. PA 1972).

ize the Popowich employees. On August 2, 1971, Joseph Yeoman, the union business agent, told Popowich management that he had enough authorization cards signed by employees to make a formal demand for recognition. He informed management that if the firm did not recognize the union, there would be a strike on August 4, 1971, two days later. The company responded by saying that it would recognize the union only if there were an NLRB election.

On August 4, 1971, a majority of the employees formed picket lines. Threats and violence began immediately. Acts of violence were committed against employees who continued to work and against the firm's owners. Two female employees were reportedly attacked on August 9, one being hit in the head with a soda bottle and the other, a sixteen-year-old, being "roughed up." Tires on the cars of nonstrikers were slashed numerous times. Violence continued through September; strike settlement was not reached until early 1972.

Drexel University (1973). As of late 1972, Drexel University employed fifty-eight "maintenance employees," including painters, carpenters, and electricians. On November 3, 1972, these employees voted to join Teamsters Local 115; within a few days thereafter, they demanded a contract containing significant wage and benefit increases, and threatened an early strike if it was not granted.

Negotiations on the contract terms began on December 8, 1972. Eight unsuccessful negotiating sessions took place prior to the start of the strike, which began on January 8, 1973. In a newsletter to faculty and staff members, the university explained the main issues:

> The Teamsters were demanding over a two-year period increases ranging from $3.65 to $5.15 an hour. This would mean, for example, that a general Maintenance Mechanic would receive more than $15,329 a year, and an Electrician, more than $20,000. On average, the Teamsters are asking that by 1975, their Drexel members be paid some $17,527 a year—and that is without overtime.[16]

The strike lasted for twenty weeks and was finally settled on May 23, 1973. An injunction request by Drexel was denied by a common pleas court on April 13, at which time the judge ordered both sides to report to him weekly on the progress of their negotiations. According to *The Drexel Triangle,* the university newspaper, the terms of the new contract provided wages well below the level originally demanded by the union.[17]

Despite claims by Morris that, "we are a law abiding union," significant violence and destruction accompanied the Drexel strike. By

---

[16] *Drexel Factopics,* Office of University Relations, January 18, 1973.

[17] *Teamsters Unanimously Ratify Contract; Men Back to Work as 20 Week Strike Ends,* The Drexel Triangle, May 25, 1973, at 1.

January 19, 1973, only ten days after the strike began, the following incidents had been reported:

1. A campuswide power failure due to sabotage at the main substation occurred.
2. Glue and solder were placed in many doorlocks.
3. Threats were made in person and by telephone to faculty members.
4. Students were harassed by strikers.

As of February 5, the value of damage done to university property was estimated at over $500 for broken windows and at about $25,000 for the damage that resulted from the power failure and related "breakdowns."[18]

Incidents of vandalism continued to occur throughout most of the strike. It was necessary for Drexel to place a twenty-four-hour watch on steam rooms and electrical boards. When the director of security was asked in March 1973 what the effect of the increased security was, he responded,

> The effect is that the place is still running. . . . I feel pretty certain that if we didn't put guards at vulnerable areas, we wouldn't be running.[19]

As is common in Teamsters' strikes, Drexel employees experienced considerable harassment and interference when reporting to or departing from work. Considerable interference with delivery vehicles also occurred. These incidents led to Drexel's attempt to secure an injunction in April. As stated previously, the university was not successful. The strike was not settled until the latter part of May.

Philadelphia Furniture Distributors (1973–1975). Simultaneous with the Drexel strike in 1973, Local 115 was involved in strikes with other employers. Two of these strikes involved two Philadelphia furniture dealers, Philadelphia Furniture Distributors and Nate Ben's Reliable Furniture Store. Both strikes lasted almost two years and were marked by many instances of violence. Another strike which occurred during this period involved the now-defunct Lit Brothers department store. Local 115's involvement in that strike was once summarized as follows:

> One day over 800 hard-hats gathered outside Lits in a show of solidarity with Local 115 and began smashing windows, stopping traffic and firing a volley of bottles and rocks at a parking lot owned by Lits. A car was over-

---

[18] Memorandum from Office of the Vice President and Treasurer to Administrative Officers, Deans and Department Heads, February 5, 1978.

[19] *DU Vandalism Continues as Security Increased,* The Drexel Triangle, March 9, 1973, at 1.

turned and a man was sent to the hospital before heavy police reinforcements narrowly managed to restore order. The Lits debacle went on for months, with Local 115 organizers on bull horns intimidating and insulting any pedestrians in the vicinity of 8th and Market who even looked like they might cross the picket line and hazard a shopping trip into the department store, while police looked the other way.[20]

The strike at Philadelphia Furniture Distributors, a small wholesale furniture dealer, began on November 7, 1973. Local 115 had become involved with this company only during the previous summer. Prior to representation by Teamsters Local 115, the fifteen or so employees at this firm had been represented by the United Steelworkers. The reasons for and circumstances of the affiliation change are not clear. When a new contract agreement was not reached, the Teamsters struck, under the supervision of Local 115 representatives.

During the first year of the strike, considerable property damage, threats, and general harassment ensued. On the first day of the strike, sixteen tires were slashed on cars belonging to the firm's owners, salesmen, and nonstriking employees. Additionally, car doorlocks were jammed with toothpicks, matches, and liquid solder. Warehouse entrances were repeatedly blocked and delivery truck drivers were intimidated.[21] Available information indicates that the Teamsters were unsuccessful in reaching a settlement, and owing partly to the determination of the owner to continue operating and partly to the small number of employees involved, they eventually lost interest in the strike.

University of Pennsylvania (1977). The dispute with Local 115 at the University of Pennsylvania involved 343 housekeepers and janitors who had voted for representation by that union only several weeks prior to the elimination of their positions by the university in a move made for economic reasons. Members formed picket lines in early August 1977, and continued to man them until a settlement was reached between the union and the university four months later.

A consolidated written complaint containing over thirty charges of unfair labor practices against Local 115 was issued by the regional director of the NLRB on November 18. This complaint contained many incidents in which university employees were restrained and coerced. Specific examples included assaults of employees at both the veterinary and law schools and stone throwing at the Levy Tennis Pavillion. Threats of bodily harm to supervisors were alleged on numerous occasions.[22]

---

[20] *The Ordeal, supra* note 10, at 208.
[21] *Id.* at 118-19.
[22] National Labor Relations Board, Region 4 v. Teamsters Local 115, Consolidated Complaint, November 18, 1977.

The following detective's affidavit, written in support of a plea by the University of Pennsylvania for injunctive relief, describes day-to-day activities during the strike and exemplifies the type of harassment that occurs during strikes and which can easily lead to violence borne of frustration directed *against* strikers—although it did not do so in this case.

On Friday, August 12, 1977 at approximately 3:49 p.m. I accompanied a University trash truck by driving a van leading the truck. Another detective . . . also in a van followed the University trash truck. At the medical driveway off University Avenue, the trash truck attempted to turn in to the driveway to pick up trash. Three pickets, all wearing Local 115 signs, stood at the entrance of the driveway and blocked the driveway entrance. They let my van go through then blocked the trash truck. I asked the pickets if they would move, there was no reply. They did not move. I immediately, at 3:52 p.m called the Labor Squad of the Philadelphia Police Department. About 10 minutes later the Labor Squad arrived, the pickets still refused to move. The Labor Squad asked the pickets where the Business Agent was. The pickets said he was coming over. Before the Agent came, the Labor Squad asked if the pickets would allow the truck to be moved onto the driveway so traffic would not be blocked. Traffic had, at this point been blocked for about 20 minutes causing a total jam up. The pickets allowed the truck in off the street. . . .

On August 15, 1977 at 2:30 p.m. I was in an unmarked car following the University trash truck. The trash truck picked up trash at the Fine Arts Building and proceeded south on 34th Street. At 2:46 p.m. the truck was stopped in the middle of the 200 block of South 34th Street by four males— Defendants Joseph Yeoman, Jim Oliver, Crazy Eddie Grey, and an unknown white male—who walked into the street causing the truck to stop. I pulled along side of the trash truck and parked on the sidewalk on the east side of the street and called the Labor Squad, which arrived 2 minutes later. The Labor Squad asked the truck to wait until Yeoman finished his speech. About five minutes later Yeoman was through his speech, and he and the others withdrew and allowed the truck to proceed. The truck went west on Walnut Street and arrived at Houston Hall at 2:55. The four Teamsters followed immediately in a brown Pontiac. The Teamsters stopped behind the trash truck, which had to back into the loading area of Houston Hall to pick up trash. The Teamsters gave verbal abuse to the drivers. I called the Labor Squad (which had told me they were not allowed to follow the trash truck) which arrived at 3:05 p.m. The Labor Squad spoke to the Teamsters, and the Teamsters after shouting obscenities at the University driver, at 3:15 allowed the truck to back into the delivery area. As it was backing in, the Teamsters continued to walk back with the truck. Yeoman said to the driver—"If you run over one of my men it will be the last one you ever run over." The truck only went back a short distance. The truck driver and his helper got out and started to pile trash into the truck. The pickets continued to walk in the back of the truck forcing the men to walk in and through the Teamsters. Yeoman said, "you'd better not get any of that fucking dirt on me." The Teamsters continued to harass the University employees. At 3:55 p.m. the University employees got back into the truck to attempt to go to the next stop. The truck started and immediately stopped. Al Smith, the driver, got out and walked back to us and said they were not going to pick up any more trash today. He later told me he was afraid he would brush against the Teamsters and start a confrontation.[23]

Goodwill Industries (1978–79). This strike began in early October 1978 and lasted for nine months, until early June 1979. It involved approximately twenty Local 115 members who were truck drivers and helpers employed by Goodwill Industries of Philadelphia, a sheltered workshop for the handicapped. (Truck drivers are the only nonmanagerial employees of Goodwill who are not handicapped.) Issues were economic and, as of December 15, 1978, despite the fact that wage increases of 50 to 70 percent over a three-year period were offered, settlement had not been reached.[24]

The locks on five Goodwill buildings were vandalized simultaneously in mid-November 1978. Additionally, two members of management were attacked outside Goodwill stores within several days of the latter incident.[25] A spokesman for Goodwill Industries, when asked whether there was a pattern to the violence, commented that, "when negotiations fail there seems to be vandalism."[26]

The strike did not end until Goodwill, which had been compelled by the strike to lay off 225 of its handicapped workers, filed for bankruptcy as its only alternative if the union did not agree to allow reduction of the driver work force from twenty-four to nine drivers.[27]

Common Tactics. The previous examples span fairly evenly the decade of the 1970s. Various trends can be seen over this period as well as patterns among the strikes surveyed.

1. Recent Representation: In each situation Teamsters Local 115 had become the bargaining agent for the striking employees only a short period before their respective strikes. This is not to imply that strikes do not occur where representation by Local 115 has existed for a long time; however, it does appear that Local 115 views maximum potential in violence and finds newly organized employees most amenable to it.

Local 115 seems to espouse violence by new members because of a desire to show strength to the new employer. Additionally, it appears that union officials are successful in convincing new members that

---

[23] *Affidavit of Michael Carroll,* Trustees of the University of Pennsylvania v. Teamsters Local 115 et al., Court of Common Pleas, August Term, 1977.

[24] *Goodwill for Christmas?* (Philadelphia) Evening Bulletin, December 15, 1978, an editorial by the Goodwill regional director.

[25] *Vandals at Goodwill; tension grows,* Philadelphia Inquirer, November 11, 1978, at 1-B.

[26] Telephone interview with Shella Strasbough, Public Affairs Office, Goodwill Industries, 11401 Roosevelt Blvd., Philadelphia, January 30, 1979.

[27] *Goodwill offers strikers layoffs or bankruptcy,* Philadelphia Inquirer, May 8, 1979, at B-1.

178

Union Violence

considerable increases in benefits will materialize if they follow established union tactics, one of which is violence. Frequently, though, the tactic backfires, and the local finishes by settling for little more, or no more, than was on the table when the strike began.

2. Long Strikes: Another characteristic of Local 115 strikes is that they are long, typically lasting for between sixteen and thirty-six weeks. It is true that Local 115 officials consider length an important ingredient to a successful strike. John Morris made a statement concerning this issue in December 1977: "I tell our members that it is not a good strike until it is 12 weeks old. Sometimes employers can go that long before a strike affects them."[28]

The examples discussed here (as well as other strikes by Local 115) indicate that Morris's idea is being followed. A Local 115 strike, therefore, can be expected to last three months or longer. This characteristic is distressing to employers because in addition to the economic losses of a long strike, much time and energy is wasted on early negotiations.

3. Use of Sympathizers; Local 115 officials have, over the years, effectively used other groups to help promote their cause. As seen in the Lit Brothers' strike, Morris was successful in mustering the support of 800 members of the Building and Construction Trades Council.[29] During the University of Pennsylvania strike, truck convoys by other Teamsters members circled the campus during rush hour on several occasions. Local 115 has also been able to enlist the support of the Jewish Labor Committee and the Negro Trade Union Leadership Council. Both of these groups held campus demonstrations.[30] (In other strikes during this period, Morris was also able to gain the full support of the Southern Christian Leadership Conference, which threatened to form a "Resurrection City" at a Cheltenham Township park if the Local 115 garbage strike there was not settled before a specified date.)[31]

4. Use of Violence: Violence in the form of vandalism and assault and threats of violence to employers and nonstriking employees are tactics used repeatedly by Local 115. The violence seen again and again in these examples cannot be considered spontaneous, but is instead an integral part of each strike. These acts are more than just "emotional outbreaks," as claimed by Morris.

Violence or threats of violence against nonstriking employees or

[28] *Penn Strike Leader, supra* note 9, at C-5.
[29] *The Ordeal, supra* note 10, at 208.
[30] *Teamsters Snarl Rush-Hour Traffic at Penn Campus,* (Philadelphia) Evening Bulletin, October 7, 1977, at C-1.
[31] *Cheltenham Negotiations to Resume,* Philadelphia Inquirer, June 10, 1975, at B-2.

replacement employees can almost always be expected. The union's goal is to keep these employees out so that the employer can feel the full effects of the strike. This tactic is certainly not exclusive to Local 115, but its use of the tactic can be seen clearly.

Blocking of vehicles and personnel trying to enter or leave employer's property is another tactic routinely used by Local 115. The goal is the same—to make the employer feel the full effects of the strike. These actions are directed not only against the employer and nonstriking employees but also against any other contractors or service personnel having business with the employer.

The consolidated complaint by the NLRB against Local 115 during the University of Pennsylvania strike cited at least ten examples in the first month of the strike of blocking the ingress and egress of various vehicles. During the Drexel strike, the following report was made:

> Last week union pickets blocked the cars of administrators when they tried to leave from university garages. Drexel cars and trucks making deliveries were also delayed until the Labor Squad came and told the pickets to leave.[32]

This same tactic worked so well in the 1971 J. L. Popowich strike that suppliers and service companies were scared away and no deliveries were made at that firm.[33] The actions of union members against outside garbage collectors actually made the latter refuse to cross the picket line until a court order was obtained.

Violence and threats of violence against management are other strike tactics commonly used by Local 115; however, they seem to be confined to strikes involving smaller firms. The goal of this violence is unclear but it is probably aimed at making management aware of the seriousness of the strike and the union's demands.

The owner of the J. L. Popowich firm was hit in the head by a striking employee and menaced with a knife during the first week of the strike. The owner of Philadelphia Furniture Distributors was subjected to continued threats, ethnic slurs, and according to him, "24-hour surveillance."[34] The operations director and transportation manager at Goodwill Industries were reported to have been attacked one evening outside a Goodwill store.[35]

Destruction of property is also quite common during a Local 115 strike. Morris once stated:

---

[32] *Drexel Seeks Injunction to Move Teamsters From Campus,* The Drexel Triangle, April 6, 1973, at 1.
[33] *See* note 15, *supra.*
[34] *The Ordeal, supra* note 10, at 208.
[35] *Vandals at Goodwill, supra* note 25, at 1-B.

Kid stuff like breaking glass, slashing tires, that gets you nowhere. The police will be on top of you and the public will turn against you.[36]

Regardless of the veracity of the above statement, slashed tires and broken windows were normal occurrences in strikes by Local 115.

Conclusions. The cases covered here show that the use of violence and threats of violence are established tactics of Teamsters Local 115. Examples of violence extend over the past eight years and involve both the public and the private sectors. Violence is used regardless of the size of the employer struck or the number of employees involved in the strike.

Acts of violence normally occurred first against nonstriking employees and then rapidly extended to owners and managers as well as to outsiders having business with the organization being struck. Vandalism to private property is also common and appears to occur with no predictable regularity.

Teamsters Local 584

Local 584 represents the employees of Dannon, manufacturers of the famous yogurt, at its plant on Long Island, New York. On a commission basis, the drivers from this company were earning over $680 per week when a dispute arose over alleged stealing of products by a union shop steward. He was discharged, a wildcat strike occurred, and violence began. One union member has been charged with attempted murder, physical assaults have been common, products have been destroyed or sabotaged, and supermarkets have been threatened if they carry the popular product. As a result of this violence, which hospitalized at least five persons, the company dismissed the work force of the Long Island facility and is producing the product with supervisory personnel at its Ridgefield, New Jersey, plant and shipping it in to the New York area from plants in other parts of the country. According to the *New York Times,* "some of the incidents of violence include the severe beating of a union member outside the Ridgefield plant and the slashing of tires and puncturing of radiators on Dannon trucks. In one incident, a union member was charged with attempted murder after four shots were fired at two Dannon trucks on the Brooklyn-Queens Expressway."[37]

---

[36] *Penn Strike Leader, supra* note 9, at C-5.
[37] *Union fight with maker of Dannon Yogurt is bitter and violent,* The New York Times, March 11, 1983, p. B7.

Teamsters Strikes in Trucking

When Teamsters go on strike against trucking companies, the most common forms of violence seem to be damage to company trucks, particularly tires or air hoses, and harassment of company officials and nonstriking employees.[38] An example is provided by a six-week strike against Haney's Truck Line, in Washington County, Oregon, by Teamsters Local 162 in early 1977.

Incidents reported from that strike included the following:

1. The tires of more than fifty vehicles were damaged by nails spread on roads around the terminal.

2. The tires of several company trucks and several nonstrikers' cars were slashed, as well as those of one customer.

3. Ignition keys of company trucks were stolen and padlocks were tampered with.

4. The door of a company truck was kicked in and a vehicle was driven into the plant gate. On a later occasion, the gate was destroyed. Eggs and other objects were thrown at company property.

5. Managers of the company had their lives threatened.

6. Two nonstrikers were followed home and threatened by strikers, two others were physically assaulted, and another was forced off the road by strikers, then pulled from his car and beaten.[39]

The incidents associated with this strike were not extraordinary in terms of the quantity or the nature of the violence. In the National Right to Work Legal Defense Foundation incident listing of strike violence (see Chapter III), the Teamsters figured in 384 incidents of violence between 1976 and 1981.[40] Among these were sixty incidents involving physical assaults, beatings, or woundings, fifty-four incidents involving shots fired at persons or property, sixteen incidents of arson or firebombing, and eight incidents involving explosives.

---

[38] These judgments, as are others in this section, are based on analysis of the NRTWLDF Violent Incident Data Base, on file with the Wharton Industrial Research Unit, Philadelphia. (*See* Ch. III, *supra.*)

[39] (Washington County, Oregon) News-Times, March 2, 1977.

[40] This statistic and those which follow in this paragraph apply to all Teamsters, not just those involved in trucking.

The listings also show a high death toll. Teamsters were associated with ten fatalities involving:

1. a striker killed by a nonstriker;

2. a nonstriker killed by a striker;

3. a company owner killed by a striker;

4. another company owner killed by a union organizer;

5. two labor attorneys, one in San Juan and another in Oklahoma City, killed by Teamsters;

6. a vice president of the Boatmen's Union, apparently killed in a jurisdictional dispute with Teamsters;

7. a bus driver killed during a teamsters' municipal employees' strike;

8. and two Teamsters officials murdered, one during a gun battle with Ironworkers, and one in an apparent intraunion power struggle.

Conclusions

The preponderance of the evidence on the use of violence by the Teamsters indicates that their strategies for using violence are different than those of the other major union groups reviewed in earlier chapters. The United Mine Workers, in recent years, seems to have directed violence against nonunion firms during national walkouts in order to make the walkouts more effective. The construction unions have directed their violence mostly against nonunion firms in order to deny them business or to drive up their costs so that they lose their competitive advantage over union firms. Public employees seem bent on terrorizing the general public so that political pressures will be in favor of a quick settlement on the unions' terms.

The Teamsters seem to concentrate mostly on the Teamsters' own employers and on nonstrikers, but not during nationwide strikes. In this regard, the Teamsters' use of violence might be regarded as more traditional than the others.

The tactics used, however, are largely the same in all cases, varying only in the degree of brutality with which they are applied. Mass picketing, vandalism, destruction of property, shootings, assaults, threats, harassment, and attacks on the personal property, cars, homes, and, sometimes, the families of the chosen targets are the main weapons in the arsenal.

MANUFACTURING AND MISCELLANEOUS

The tenor and extent of labor violence in many different industries and individual situations has already been broadly demonstrated in previous chapters, and it is unnecessary to catalog it further here for the manufacturing industries. A few specific points which have not otherwise been covered are, however, illustrated here.

The Slow Process of Civil Litigation: United Aircraft, 1960

Subsequent to the breakdown of contract negotiations, several district lodges of the International Association of Machinists and Aerospace Workers (IAM) began a strike at four locations of the United Aircraft Company's Pratt & Whitney and Hamilton Standard divisions located in Connecticut. Approximately 25,000 production and maintenance workers were represented in the bargaining units. The strike began on June 8, 1960, and continued for two months. It was marred by mass picketing and violence, particularly during the first few days, but also after a restraining order prohibiting mass picketing and limiting the number of pickets was agreed to by the unions on June 13, 1960.

The violence itself in this case might be considered mild in comparison to some that we have already seen. Mostly, it involved incidents arising from mass picketing:

> Films taken by the plaintiff at each gate of its plant, show the pickets adopting extreme measures designed to halt all ingress and egress to the plaintiff's plant. Picketers by the hundreds marched in circular formation shoulder to shoulder. Cars trying to enter the plant were blocked off by masses of pickets. Police forcibly pushed picketers aside to open passageways for cars and trucks entering the premises. Drivers and occupants of cars were subjected to a variety of contemptuous gestures. Employees were physically attacked. Profanities and obscenities were shouted along with threats of physical harm. Strikers ostentatiously noted license numbers and occupants of the cars entering and leaving the plant and other strikers took pictures of the cars and occupants, all in an attempt to intimidate workers. Mirrors and radio antennas were torn off cars. The shoving, kicking, pushing and slapping of cars was commonplace. Hundreds of cars turned back. Law enforcement officers, both state and local, were shoved against and on the hoods of cars. Traffic as a result was snarled and backed up for blocks. Numerous arrests were made. Nails, tacks and other sharp objects were strewn on the highway approaches.[41]

---

[41] United Aircraft Corporation v. International Association of Machinists, et al. (Nos. 133884,5) Hartford County Superior Court, 68 L.R.R.M. 2488 May 31, 1968.

United Aircraft contended that the mass picketing and violence amounted to illegal coercion which intimidated many employees and prevented them from reporting to work, and that the company lost profits and was damaged as a result. It sought compensatory and exemplary damages.

After considerable legal sparring between the company and the unions, the case was brought to trial, first on the issue of liability, then on the issue of damages. These were heard and judgments were rendered in favor of the company (for damages in excess of $1.5 million) in late November 1968—eight years and five months after the strike had begun. The court's findings were embraced in 866 numbered paragraphs covering 247 printed pages.[42] The decision was appealed on various grounds.

The Connecticut Supreme Court upheld the trial court's decisions as to the liability of the unions and upheld the award of punitive or exemplary damages, but remanded the case for reassessment of compensatory damages in March of 1971—ten years and nine months after the strike occurred. On further appeal, the U.S. Supreme Court denied *certiorari.*[43]

The case was given a new hearing in 1973 which involved oral testimony from 135 employees and transcripts of earlier testimony from 73 more, in addition to extensive testimony from expert witnesses.[44] A decision, awarding damages to United Aircraft of about $1.4 million was handed down in September 1973.[45] Thirteen years and three months had passed since the strike took place.

This decision filled 109 printed pages of the record, and was appealed. Finally, the Connecticut Supreme Court again reviewed the case and in a decision handed down in June of 1975, reaffirmed the trial court's decision to award damages of $1.4 million to the company. The U.S. Supreme Court denied *certiorari* once more.[46] In pursuing the litigation, the company (now called United Technologies) made several important points concerning the impact of mass picketing and the liability of a union for the tortious conduct of its members in using violence and coercion to intimidate other workers and keep them off the job. Nevertheless, the whole process required fifteen years and un-

---

[42] United Aircraft Corporation v. International Assn. of Machinists, Hartford County Superior Court, 70 L.R.R.M. 2577 December 3, 1968.

[43] United Aircraft Corporation v. International Association of Machinists, 161 Conn. 79, 285 A.2d. 330 (1971); cert. den. 404 U.S. 1016 (1971).

[44] United Aircraft Corporation v. International Assn. of Machinists, et al. (Nos. 133884,5) Hartford County Superior Court, September 4, 1973 (unreported).

[45] *Id.*

[46] International Association of Machinists v. United Aircraft Corporation, 534 F.2d 422 (1975), *cert. denied,* 429 U.S. 825 (1976).

doubtedly cost the company more in legal fees than it recovered in the settlement award.

Fortunately, not all civil proceedings require this much time, but with the exception of injunctions—which frequently have little or no effect, being widely ignored—such relief as is provided typically is slow, and comes too late to have any impact on the conduct or settlement of the strike.

Nonstrikers as Targets of Violence: The United Steelworkers

It has been pointed out in earlier case studies, but deserves additional emphasis, that the brunt of much of the violence associated with strikes is felt not by companies or their managers and supervisors, but by employees who decide for either economic or philosophical reasons not to participate in strikes called by their unions. The three short cases which follow happen to involve strikes by the United Steelworkers of America (USW) but almost a random choice could be made from the strike violence data base to arrive at similar experiences.

Hot Springs, Arkansas, 1978. In the spring of 1978, the United Steelworkers entered into an economic strike against a National Rejectors Company plant near Hot Springs, Arkansas.[47] Five of the women who were employed at the plant decided to continue to report to work during the strike. Most of the violence they suffered occurred after the strike was terminated and the striking union members returned to work in April 1978.

In the subsequent jury trial, which concluded in May 1980 with damage awards totalling $250,000 to the women, evidence was introduced showing that persecution of the five nonstrikers was orchestrated or at least encouraged by the local union officials in order to put pressure on the nonstrikers and cause them to quit.

Violence directed against the individuals, one of whom was pregnant, included the following:

1. The nonstriking employees were repeatedly cursed, threatened with harm, struck, and chased in their cars; their personal property was vandalized in various ways.

2. The home of one of the women was fired into by a shotgun blast which shattered the bedroom window of one of the children and did damage inside the room. (Fortunately, the child was sleeping at a friend's house.)

---

[47] Materials for this case are drawn from "Five Women, Victims of Union Violence, Win $250,000 in Arkansas Jury Verdict," *National Right to Work Legal Defense Foundation News Release,* May 23, 1980.

3. Thirty to fifty union partisans marched regularly past the work-places of the five at the plant, shouting obscenities and threats.

4. Work stations were sabotaged with grease or glue spread on the women's chairs.

5. The women were at various times pursued in their cars, trapped in company restrooms, assaulted by being slapped and having their hair pulled, and threatened with death.

6. Cars of the women were smashed into, and tires were slashed.

In this particular case, although the union was unsuccessful in forc-ing the women to quit and was ultimately ordered to pay compensatory and exemplary damages, lasting scars undoubtedly remained.

Johnson City, Tennessee, 1979. A similar experience was reported in a strike that took place by the United Steelworkers Local 8042 against Jarl Extrusions in Johnson City, Tennessee, between June 8, 1979, and January 11, 1980.[48] That strike saw repeated incidents of vandalism, threats and harassment of employees, bombings, arson, and shootings. A company guard was shot to death in one incident.

Four of the employees of the struck plant decided to return to work and cross the picket lines established by the union. Violence directed against them by union officials and members included the following:

1. One female employee received phone calls threatening her with rape, had rocks thrown at her car, and had shots fired into both her car and her home.

2. Another female employee was injured and her car was damaged when a striker hurled a concrete slab through the car's wind-shield.

3. A male employee was severely beaten by three strikers and suffered permanent ear damage as a result.

4. Another male employee had his home firebombed and exten-sively damaged by arson while he and his wife slept.

As in the previous case, these employees were apparently being pun-ished in very personal ways by the union for daring to cross the picket lines and return to work at a struck plant. In a subsequent trial on this case decided in late 1980, the four employees were awarded compen-satory and exemplary damages amounting to $116,500, but again, the

---

[48] Materials for this case are drawn from "Steelworkers Union Assessed $116,500 damages for Violence, Coercion Against Employees," *National Right to Work Legal Defense Foundation News Release,* November 26, 1980.

damage awards came long after the strike and were unable to modify behavior during it.

North East, Pennsylvania, 1981. After narrowly winning an election (the vote was 65 to 61) to represent the production and maintenance employees of the Ridg-U-Rak company in the small community of North East, Pennsylvania, Local 9051 of the United Steelworkers of America (USW) began negotiations with the company in late 1979.[49] At issue were union security measures and the ability of the company to subcontract work. The bargaining became stalled, and the union called for an economic strike to begin on June 1, 1980. Violence broke out early in the strike, and was directed principally against those employees who elected to cross the picket lines and continue to work at the struck plant. Video tapes made by the company's security firm recorded several shop employees allegedly being attacked by strikers when they attempted to enter the plant. Cars carrying nonstrikers were attacked by individuals carrying crowbars and, in one instance, a hatchet.

Within the first few days of the strike, the company acquired an old school bus which was outfitted with steel sheeting over the rear and side windows and wheels and plexiglass over the front windshield and used to transport workers to the plant, but the local police department ordered the vehicle off the streets, thus forcing the nonstrikers to run the gauntlet of strikers in their own cars.[50] An injunction limiting the number of pickets was requested and received by the company after the first few outbursts, but its principal effect seems to have been to move some of the violence away from the job site, although it was still directed against the nonstriking employees.

A few of the incidents noted include the following:

1. The car of one nonstriker was destroyed in his driveway by a fire of suspicious origin.

2. At one nonstriker's home, rocks were thrown through the windows of the children's bedrooms while they were sleeping; later, all the windows of the nonstriker's car, which was parked outside his home, were shattered.

3. Several cars and a boat belonging to nonstrikers were defaced with spray paint while they were parked near homes or otherwise away from the plant.

---

[49] Unless otherwise noted, the materials for this case are derived from accounts in the Erie, Pennsylvania Daily Times or the North East, Pennsylvania North East Breeze for the following dates: June 10, 17, 24, 1981, August 12, 26, 1981, September 9, 1981, October 21, 1981, November 24, 1981, January 20, 1982, and April 28, 1982.

[50] *Ridg-U-Rak Strike Rocked by Renewed Violence Tuesday,* North East (Pennsylvania) Breeze, June 10, 1981, n.p.

4. Tires on two cars were slashed or punctured.

5. The windows of a car which had previously been attacked by strikers were again broken when smashed by a baseball bat. A house belonging to a nonstriker which had previously been attacked was again vandalized and damaged.

6. Twenty-eight vehicles suffered flat tires due to nails being thrown onto the roadway near the plant entrance, and windshields in other vehicles were also broken out.

Notations were made at various times of cars being struck by pipes, clubs, rocks, concrete slabs, ball bearings, firebombs, hatchets, axes, baseball bats, crowbars, and knives. The damage done was extensive, and most of it was directed very personally against individual employees who declined to honor the strike. Some of these employees were also threatened, harassed, and slandered in various ways.[51]

Like the two previous Steelworker cases, this one resulted in civil actions against the union and individual members for claims exceeding $90,000 (the case had not been resolved at the time of writing). As was also true in the previous two examples, the violent tactics of the unions seemed to be largely unsuccessful in accomplishing the union's goals. Here, the strike against Ridg-U-Rak continued from June 1981 until late April 1982 when, as a result of a decertification election, the union lost its representation rights and the strike was terminated. Striking employees who tried to return to work were unable to do so because of the downturn in the economy and the diminished market for steel products, but they were placed on a waiting list. Thus, the net result to the union in this case was in fact a significant step backwards.

Although in some of the instances described above, violence directed against nonstriking or nonunion individuals resulted in penalties against the perpetrators, such is not usually the case. Rather, it is

---

[51] In a law suit on the case which was still pending at the time this study was prepared (Ronald Yokom et al., v. Arthur Reid, et al., CA, Court of Common Pleas of Erie County, Pennsylvania, Complaint filed February 26, 1982), the wife of one nonstriker who had been the object of other harassment as well, complained as follows: Plaintiff . . . has earned a reputation in the community as an honest and virtuous woman.

On or about August 27, 1981, defendant . . . in order to further the purposes of Local 9051 and the USWA, and contriving to deprive plaintiff . . . of her good name and reputation, and to bring her into scandal and disrepute among her neighbors and family, did speak and publish of the plaintiff, in the presence and hearing of the plaintiff, her husband, family, neighbors, and numerous other persons, the following false, scandalous, malicious and defamatory words while addressing plaintiff's husband: "Hey Yokom, do you know what your wife is doing while you're working your scabby ass off—she's over here f_____ with this black bastard," thereby meaning and intending, and it was understood by said persons, that the plaintiff . . . had sexual relations with a man not her husband.

probable that in the overwhelming number of cases, the use of violence goes unpunished, and much of it is successful in accomplishing its intended purposes to intimidate nonstrikers or their employees into settling closer to the union's position.

Violence in Jurisdictional Disputes: FASH, 1978

In some circumstances in which violence is used in strikes, it almost seems that any target will serve, and that the medium of violence is its own message. This is especially true when the dispute involves jurisdictional challenges between unions. Such apparently was the case in the flurry of shootings which accompanied a job action by the Fraternal Association of Steel Haulers (FASH) which began in late 1978.

About 30,000 persons make their livelihood by hauling steel in their own trucks. Some are independent, but many others are members of the Teamsters union. The latter have an unusual status within the union because they own their own rigs, and therefore are owner-operators rather than employees. Steel haulers in the union are not paid wages, and are not covered by the master freight agreement. Rather, they are covered by a supplemental agreement and are paid a percentage of the value of the trips they make. The steel haulers pay union dues, but do not receive pension rights or other benefits.

In late 1978, a group of Teamster steel haulers became dissatisfied with their status within the union, where it was said they felt like second-class citizens in the matter of compensation, and they joined with a group which had been in existence for a decade or so, called the Fraternal Association of Steel Haulers (FASH). The dissidents wanted to leave the Teamsters and form a separate bargaining unit, with the FASH as their representative. The Teamsters, of course, took a dim view of this action, which would have resulted in the loss of an estimated 10,000 members. The FASH, therefore, determined to force the Teamsters' hand by bringing indirect pressure to bear on the Teamsters. It called for a strike against steel companies and against trucking firms which handled or brokered steel.

On November 11, 1978, the FASH began a work stoppage which was aimed at halting steel shipments throughout the eastern United States in the hopes that the steel companies would become distressed and add their weight to that of the FASH in forcing the Teamsters to release the dissidents as a separate bargaining unit and thus end the strike.[52] This complex plan required that the shutdown be complete, because otherwise the work stoppage would simply drive the available traffic

---

[52] *Steel Haulers Who Ignore Call to Strike Fear Snipers, Vandals on the Highways*, The Wall Street Journal, December 8, 1978, at 10.

into the hands of nonunion truckers or Teamsters who were satisfied with their existing representation.

When the work stoppage was called, a large number of Teamster steel haulers ignored it, and therefore the stage was set for violence against an unusually broad number of targets: nonunion haulers, steel companies, cartage companies, nonstrikers who were members of the FASH, and Teamster steel haulers who declined to join the FASH were all to be targets simultaneously, because only in this way could the stoppage be effective.

The primary targets quickly became anyone who was hauling steel over the road, especially in the prime steel areas of Pennsylvania, Ohio, and Indiana. Because truck drivers work essentially in isolation, and because police cannot easily protect trucks on the open road, the trucks that continued to operate became easy prey.

Steel haulers who wanted to go on working took a number of defensive measures. Most refused to drive at night; many proceeded only in convoys of six or more, accompanied by armed scouts; they drove fast to minimize their exposure, and they kept in contact by citizens' band radio; many carried weapons.[53]

The violence was not long in coming. In the first four weeks of the strike there were more than sixty shooting incidents in Pennsylvania alone, and over the next two months there were hundreds of incidents of nonstrikers being shot at, wounded, or convincingly threatened, and hundred of incidents of firebombings, vandalism, and property damage.[54] The following are some of the incidents that were reported in the popular press during the last two months of 1978 and the first of 1979:

In Indiana:

1. Tires of a Teamster official's car were slashed; FASH members and an FASH official surrounded the car and threatened the Teamster.[55]

2. Many truck tires were slashed at truck stops throughout the Hammond area.[56]

3. Five shots were fired through the window of a truck hauling steel.[57]

---

[53] *A Day of Warfare for Truckers Moving Steel on Midwest Roads,* The New York Times, December 7, 1978, at 1.
[54] *See, e.g.,* The New York Times, November 14, 1978, n.p.
[55] Hammond (Indiana) Times, October 2, 1981, n.p.
[56] Richmond News Leader, December 7, 1978, n.p.
[57] *Id.*

In Ohio:

1. Beatings, property damage, shootings, vandalism, and broken truck windows were reported throughout the Canton area.[58]
2. A truck driver on the road near Norwalk was shot in the neck.[59]
3. Near Cleveland, a picket was shot in the face.[60]
4. Paint was splattered on the windshield of a moving truck.[61]
5. A truck driver was stopped and threatened by three armed men.[62]
6. Two trucks near Youngstown were shot at while they were driving on the highway.[63]
7. A truck stopped at an intersection was shot at by four strikers.[64]
8. A moving truck was struck by a brick.[65]

In Pennsylvania:

1. In one twenty-four-hour period, seven trucks were hit by gunfire, the windows of trucks were shot out, tires were slashed, and mufflers were damaged.[66]
2. A nonstriker was run off the road by strikers and forced to dump his cargo.[67]
3. Nonstrikers driving down the road were shot at and wounded by a sniper.[68]
4. Truckers were fired at by snipers.[69]
5. Trucks on the highway were hit by gunfire.[70]
6. A trucker was shot at as he drove down the highway near East Liverpool.[71]
7. Shots were fired at a convoy of trucks in Beaver County, and one independent trucker was wounded.[72]
8. A truck windshield was broken by a ball bearing shot from a

---

[58] The Wall Street Journal, December 8, 1978, n.p.
[59] (Saint Louis) Globe Democrat, November 15, 1978, n.p.
[60] Grand Rapids Press, December 6, 1978, n.p.
[61] (Youngstown) Sunday Star Ledger, December 3, 1979, n.p.
[62] *Id.*
[63] *Id.*
[64] The New York Times, December 6, 1978, n.p.
[65] (Youngstown) Sunday Star Ledger, December 3, 1979, n.p.
[66] Grand Rapids Press, November 29, 1978, n.p.
[67] Tulsa World, November 14, 1978, n.p.
[68] Grand Rapids Press, November 29, 1978, n.p.
[69] The Wall Street Journal, November 29, 1978, n.p.
[70] Tulsa World, November 14, 1978, n.p.
[71] Journal of Commerce, November 15, 1978, n.p.
[72] Oil City (Pennsylvania) Derrick, November 29, 1978, n.p.

sling shot; the driver of the truck, mistaken for a nonstriker, was injured by the broken glass.[73]

9. A thirty-car caravan of strikers harassed truckers on a highway.[74]

10. Two truckers were shot at; the radiator of a truck was smashed with an ax; and a truck was set afire in separate incidents around Pittsburgh.[75]

The strike, with its guerrilla warfare, dragged on into the new year and then slowly died of exhaustion. Because the actual target of the strike—the Teamsters Union—was not affected by it, and because the cartage companies and steel firms against whom it was directed were powerless to accede to the concessions the FASH was demanding of the Teamsters, there was no mechanism through which a settlement could be reached. The strike thus devolved into a meaningless exercise whose only point was its violence.

VIOLENCE BY INDEPENDENT TRUCKERS, 1983

Two types of nonunion truck drivers are involved in interstate commerce: those who drive for nonunion carriers licensed by the Interstate Commerce Commission (ICC), and those who are independent owner-operators. The independents own their own tractors and either lease them to licensed carriers or use them to transport goods that are free from economic regulation by the ICC, such as unmanufactured food products or raw newsprint.

The total number of independent owner-operators is unknown, but the number was estimated in early 1983 to be approximately 100,000.[76] The Independent Truckers Association, which is not a labor union but which seeks to influence remuneration and working conditions for its members through concerted work stoppages and other strike-like activities, claims that 30,000 of the independents are among its members.[77]

The Independent Truckers Association had staged short work stoppages in 1974 and 1979 to protest the shortage of deisel fuel, the doubling in price of deisel fuel, and the imposition of the fifty-five mile-per-hour speed limit. Although accompanied by violence (see Chapter III

---

[73] Grand Rapids Press, December 6, 1978, n.p.

[74] Richmond News Leader, December 7, 1978, n.p.

[75] Washington Star, January 5, 1979, n.p.

[76] *Angered by boost in taxes, truckers gear up for strike,* Philadelphia Inquirer, January 28, 1983, at A-1.

[77] *Song of the Open Road Turning Sad,* The New York Times, January 30, 1983, at 16.

for incidents relating to the 1979 strike), these protests found a sympathetic ear in Washington and met with limited success, at least with respect to the quantity of fuel made available to truckers.[78]

In early 1983, the Independent Truckers Association called for a strike to protest increases in fuel taxes, excise taxes, and user fees, which were scheduled by the Surface Transportation Act of 1982 to take effect in the spring of 1983. The object of the protest was to force Congress to rescind the act by withholding delivery of foodstuffs, the majority of which are transported by independent truckers.

To have been effective, it would have been necessary for the work stoppage to have been almost complete, requiring the participation of not only the majority of the members of the Independent Truckers Association, but also of other independent truckers. The use of violence to compel solidarity was anticipated before the strike began. Many independent truckers said they would prefer to operate but planned to keep off the roads anyway, because they feared that violence would be directed against nonstrikers. According to one independent driver, "We don't want to [strike], but I'm too old to get shot."[79]

The strike and the anticipated violence began simultaneously, on January 31, 1983. Within the first few hours of the first day of the strike, the Associated Press reported scattered violence directed against trucks in seven states, including half a dozen rigs struck by rocks thrown from bridges, three instances of trucks being sabotaged in a garage, and nails being spread on a highway.[80] Later in the day, other and more serious violence was reported, including incidents of a truck driver being shot in the chest by a sniper while he was unloading his rig in Utah, shots being fired into a truck repair facility in Pennsylvania three times, and ten tractor-trailer rigs being hit by gunfire in eight states.[81] During the evening hours, the shooting death of a trucker in North Carolina was reported.[82]

By the end of the third day, according to a summary by United Press International, the strike had given rise to more than 430 incidents of violence, including more than 130 shootings, which resulted in one death and twenty-six injuries.[83] By the end of the first week, the Asso-

---

[78] *Why the truckers' strike backfired,* 78 BUSINESS WEEK, February 21, 1983.

[79] *Across U.S., many wary of joining strike called by truckers today,* Philadelphia Inquirer, January 31, 1983, at 6-A.

[80] *Scattered Violence Reported in Independent Truck Strike,* The New York Times, February 1, 1983, at A-10.

[81] *Truck War,* Philadelphia Inquirer, February 1, 1983, at 6-A.

[82] *Violent acts escalate in truck strike,* Philadelphia Inquirer, February 2, 1983, at 1-E.

[83] *Trucker Violence Rises in Strike's 3rd Day But Flow of Goods Only Slightly Disrupted,* The Wall Street Journal, February 3, 1983, at 14.

ciated Press had counted more than 1,100 acts of violence in 38 states,[84] but the number of new incidents was decreasing as police protection improved.[85]

Despite the violence, the strike was not effective in interrupting the movement of trucks or in stopping the flow of food. By the eleventh day, amid signs that the protest was collapsing, the leader of the Independent Truckers Association called off the strike in exchange for assurances from several dozen congressmen that they would examine the scheduled increases in federal fuel taxes and user fees. At the time the strike was called off, the final count of violent incidents, according to the Associated Press, included more than 1,700 trucks damaged (including 560 hit by gunfire), 1 driver killed, 66 persons injured, and 95 persons arrested in connection with the strike.[86]

The massive and widespread violence used by the independent truckers in this strike achieved no useful purpose. It inflicted injuries and economic damage upon other independent truckers, it further tarnished the image of the trucking industry, and it failed to compel enough participation to stop the flow of goods. The strike itself was a failure which achieved none of its stated objectives and left those independent truckers who participated in it no better off for their efforts.[87] The 1,700 instances of violence in this strike were perhaps more nearly meaningless than were any of the others reviewed in this study.

CONCLUDING REMARKS

The materials presented in this and the preceding chapters are illustrative rather than definitive in terms of the pervasiveness of labor union violence. The information presented from a wide variety of sources and pertaining to a broad spectrum of unions in many industries demonstrates the extent of the problem and the need for legal remedies for the victims of violence. In Part IV of this book the panorama of laws and administrative actions which have been utilized in violence matters are described and analyzed and the appropriateness and character of the legal response is assessed.

---

[84] *More Truckers Expected Back on Highways as Police Cut Violence,* Los Angeles Times, February 7, 1983, at I-5.

[85] *Id.*

[86] *11-Day Trucker Strike Called Off Amid Signs Protest Had Collapsed,* The New York Times, February 11, 1983, n.p.

[87] *Strike Did Not Halt Freight; Tarnished Industry's Image,* Transport Topics, February 21, 1983, at 1.

PART FOUR

The Legal Response to Union Violence

CHAPTER VIII

Private Injunctive Relief Against Labor Union Violence[1]

Although the victims of strike, picket line, and other union-related violence may be entitled to recompense or other relief at some time after the violence has taken place, their primary concern is that the violence be brought to an immediate end. A court injunction against the continuance of violence would normally be used to accomplish this, but a number of obstacles must be overcome before an injunction can be issued. The federal Norris-LaGuardia Act has a pervasive influence upon this area of the law,[2] and in addition, other laws affect the availability of labor injunctions in the various state courts.

INJUNCTIVE RELIEF UNDER FEDERAL LAW

Although the exact date is not known, the first labor injunction was probably issued in 1883 or 1884.[3] The criminal conspiracy doctrine was falling into gradual desuetude during this period,[4] because of the influence of *Commonwealth v. Hunt,*[5] a case which narrowly limited the scope of the doctrine and which has been hailed as the Magna Carta of the American labor movement. Then, in 1895, the famous Debs case,[6] in which injunctions were used in the Pullman strike, provided impetus for increase in the use of this remedy as an alternative way of dealing with unionization activities.

Between 1880 and 1932, at least 132 federal and 342 state court

---

[1] Portions of this chapter were originally published as Haggard, *Private Injunctive Relief Against Labor Union Violence,* _____ KY.L.J. (1983).

[2] Norris-LaGuardia Act, §§ 1 to 15, 29 U.S.C. §§ 101 to 115 (1976).

[3] Witte, *Early American Labor Cases,* 35 YALE L.J. 825, 832-33 (1926).

[4] For a general account of the "criminal conspiracy doctrine," *see too* HAGGARD, COMPULSORY UNIONISM, THE NLRB, AND THE COURTS 11-17 (1977).

[5] 45 Mass. (4 Met.) 111 (1842); *see* HAGGARD, *supra* note 3 at 15-17.

[6] *In re* Debs, 158 U.S. 564 (1895).

injunctions were issued in labor disputes.[7] The popularity of injunctive relief can be readily understood, especially in cases of actual or threatened violence, destruction of property, and injury to persons. A later criminal prosecution might well vindicate the public interest, but it would do the victimized employer and employees little material good. An action for tort damages could likewise be considered inadequate: unions were often judgment proof; as unincorporated associations they were sometimes difficult to sue; juries, which might be biased in favor of the union cause, were used in damage actions; and in any event, the relief was not available until long after the dispute was over, at which time the employer might have already capitulated to the union's violence-backed demands.[8] As one commentator stated, "the injunction, however, did not suffer from these handicaps and provided relatively swift and comprehensive relief."[9]

Despite its effectiveness, or indeed perhaps because of it, the labor injunction began to come under increased attack in the late 1800s. The conventional wisdom about this era of labor law is that prior to 1932 the "federal judges were inclined to decide labor controversies according to their own predominantly conservative social and political views, and rendered decisions which were generally hostile to the union's use of economic power."[10] This so-called "government by injunction" was also regarded as a judicial usurpation of the legislative prerogative to establish social policy. Those with progressive or liberal social and political views thus sought to discredit the practice and to show that the courts, in issuing injunctions in labor disputes, were grossly abusing their equity powers.

Substantively, the claim was made that the labor injunctions of this era were often impermissibly broad—prohibiting not only various acts of violence and coercion, but also, allegedly, activities in and of themselves completely peaceful and legitimate.[11] The injunctions were also thought to be overly broad with respect to the class of persons being enjoined from the conduct in question, conduct which if repeated subjected them to contempt penalties.[12]

---

[7] Petro, *Injunctions and Labor Disputes: 1880-1932. Part I: What the Courts Actually Did—and Why,* 14 WAKE FOREST L. REV. 341, 351-52 (1978). This figure reflects the number of *reported* cases. It has been estimated that there may be another 500 to 1000 unreported cases. *Id.* at 351.

[8] *See* Winter, *Labor Injunctions and Judge-Made Labor Law: The Contemporary Role of Norris-LaGuardia,* 70 YALE L.J. 70, 72 (1960).

[9] *Id.*

[10] *Id.* at 71.

[11] *See* Kerian, *Injunctions in Labor Disputes: This History of the Norris-LaGuardia Act,* 37 N.D.L. REV. 49, 51-52 (1961); Winter, *supra* note 7, at 72.

[12] *See* Kerian, *supra* note 10, at 52; Winter, *supra* note 7, at 73.

The primary procedural objection was that temporary injunctions were routinely issued on an *ex parte* basis—without hearings, without notice to the other party, without supporting affidavits, and indeed without anything more specific than a standard "form book" pleading.[13]

It was further claimed that once a restraining order was issued, its effect was usually to break the strike completely, thus rendering, from the union's perspective, all further proceedings and appeals futile, however meritorious the objections to the original order might have been.[14]

And finally, from a policy perspective, it was said that "injunctions were essentially repressive in the sense that they required the employees to desist from using the most effective form of self help but did nothing to solve the underlying problems that drove men first to organize and then to strike."[15]

In 1930, these and other points were raised in a book entitled *The Labor Injunction*.[16] Written by then Harvard law professor and later Supreme Court Justice Felix Frankfurter and a Mr. Nathan Greene, this book purported to prove through empirical data that American courts, especially at the federal level, were abusing their equity powers in the manner in which they issued injunctions in labor disputes, as discussed above. Although serious questions have recently been raised about the selectivity of the data reported in this study as well as the conclusions drawn from it and the ideological impartiality of the authors,[17] *The Labor Injunction* was a highly influential book and marked the successful culmination of a forty-year campaign to bring government by injunction to an end. There had been congressional attempts to accomplish this in 1914,[18] but they had been thwarted by the Supreme Court's narrow interpretation of the Clayton Act in *Duplex Printing Press Co. v. Deering*.[19]

In 1932, however, Congress achieved its objective with the passage of the Norris-LaGuardia Act. In language that leaves little room for doubt, that act severely limits the jurisdiction of the federal courts to issue injunctions in labor disputes. Although it has been noted that "Norris-LaGuardia is not an unqualified prohibition against injunc-

---

[13] *See* Winter, *supra* note 7, at 73.

[14] See Wimberly, *The Labor Injunction—Past, Present and Future*, 22 S.C.L. REV. 689, 690 (1970); Winter, *supra* note 7, at 73.

[15] Cox, *The Role of Law in Labor Disputes*, 39 CORNELL L.Q. 592, 595 (1954).

[16] F. FRANKFURTER & N. GREENE, THE LABOR INJUNCTION (1930).

[17] *See* Petro, *supra* note 6.

[18] Section 20 of the Clayton Act, 29 U.S.C. § 52 (1976), appears to be a broad prohibition against the issuance of injunctions in union antitrust cases.

[19] 254 U.S. 443 (1921).

tions,"[20] the courts have generally agreed that "the exceptions which have been left open to injunctive process may not be treated lightly, . . . but should be viewed restrainedly, as a narrow field of permissive jurisdiction."[21]

This chapter explores whether those circumstances and exceptions include acts of labor union violence, and if so, what jurisdictional, substantive, and procedural requirements must still be satisfied before a federal court can issue an injunction against such violence.

Jurisdictional Requirements

An initial restriction on the power of the federal courts to enjoin labor union violence lies not in the provisions of the Norris-LaGuardia Act, but rather in the fact that unlike state courts, federal courts are of limited jurisdiction.[22] A party seeking relief in the federal forum must, therefore, first establish that the case is within the constitutional competence of the federal judicial system. There are several possible bases for such jurisdiction.

Diversity Jurisdiction. Article III, section 2 of the United States Constitution extends the federal judicial power to all cases "between Citizens of different States."[23] By statute, Congress has further limited diversity jurisdiction to cases where the amount in controversy is at least $10,000.[24]

Diversity is a common method for establishing jurisdiction in labor injunction suits.[25] Apart from the problem of proving that the required amount is in controversy,[26] the only other difficulty one might encounter is in maintaining complete diversity of citizenship between the parties. This may, for example, preclude an employer from including the local union and its officials in the law suit, since complete diversity may ex-

---

[20] Oman Constr. Co. v. International Bhd. of Teamsters Local 327, 263 F. Supp. 181, 183 (M.D. Tenn. 1966).

[21] International Ass'n. of Bridge Workers v. Pauly Jail Bldg. Co., 118 F.2d 615, 176 (8th Cir.) *cert. denied*, 314 U.S. 639 (1941).

[22] C. WRIGHT, LAW OF FEDERAL COURTS 17 (3d edition, 1976).

[23] U.S. CONST. art. III, § 2.

[24] 28 U.S.C. § 1332 (1976).

[25] *See* Lauf v. E.G. Shinner & Co., 303 U.S. 323, 327 (1938) (diversity of citizenship held to be a proper basis for jurisdiction; state law governs substantive rights, but the power of the court to grant relief is limited by federal law).

[26] *See* J.J. Newberry Co. v. Retail Clerks Local 665, 67 F. Supp. 86 (E.D. Mo. 1946) (no proof of amount in controversy). This "jurisdictional amount" requirement can be satisfied, however, by reference to the alleged threatened damage rather than to the value of the property already destroyed at the time the injunction is sought. Tri-City Central Trades Council v. American Steel Foundries, 238 Fed. 728, 730 (7th Cir. 1917), *modified on other grounds*, 257 U.S. 184 (1921).

ist only between the employer and the national or international union.[27] An injunction so limited might, however, be totally inefficacious.

Federal-Question Jurisdiction. The Constitution also provides for federal court jurisdiction over "Cases, in Law and Equity, arising under this Constitution, the Laws of the United States, and Treaties made, or which shall be made, under their authority,"[28] and the relevant statute is similarly worded.[29] In both the Constitution and the statute the key phrase is "arising under." Unfortunately, even after two centuries of litigation and scholarly analysis, "it cannot be said that any clear test has yet been developed to determine which cases 'arise under' the Constitution, laws, or treaties of the United States."[30] It is not surprising, thus, that difficult federal-question jurisdiction issues have also arisen in the context of federal labor injunctions.

At first blush, it might seem that the Norris-LaGuardia Act itself, since it is clearly a "United States law," could provide the necessary federal-question jurisdiction. That, however, misconstrues the primary thrust of the act. As the Fifth Circuit Court of Appeals stated in *Brown v. Coumanis*,[31] the Norris-LaGuardia Act expands neither the substantive rights of an employer to obtain an injunction nor the jurisdiction of the federal courts to grant one; the act, rather, represents a *limitation* on both rights and jurisdiction. Thus, "a suit does not *arise under* that Act because the petitioner asserts that the Act will affect its trial. . . . In order to generate this kind of federal jurisdiction a right or immunity created by the Constitution or laws of the United States must be an essential element of the plaintiff's cause of action."[32] In short, although the Norris-LaGuardia Act *permits* a federal district court to enjoin strike and picket line violence under narrow circumstances, the act itself does not *create the right* to such an injunction and it alone cannot provide the jurisdictional basis for a suit of that nature.[33]

If, however, the plaintiff is an interstate common carrier, then the Interstate Commerce Act[34] might provide the necessary jurisdictional basis for a federal injunction against union violence. Under that act, a common carrier has a statutory duty to furnish adequate transporta-

---

[27] *See* J.B. Michael & Co. v. Iron Workers Local 782, 173 F. Supp. 319 (W.D. Ky. 1959).

[28] U.S. CONST. art. III, § 2.

[29] 28 U.S.C. § 1331 (1976).

[30] C. WRIGHT, LAW OF FEDERAL COURTS 63-64 (3d edition, 1976).

[31] 135 F.2d 163 (5th Cir. 1943).

[32] *Id.* at 164-65 (emphasis added).

[33] *But see,* United Parcel Service, Inc. v. Local 25, Int'l. Bhd. of Teamsters, 421 F. Supp. 452 (D. Mass. 1976) (jurisdiction purportedly based on the Norris-LaGuardia Act, since no other jurisdictional basis is apparent from the reported opinion).

[34] 49 U.S.C. §§ 1-27 (1976).

tion facilities, and it has been held that a suit to enjoin violent interference with that duty is a case arising under a law of the United States, over which the district courts thus have original, federal question jurisdiction.[35]

On the other hand, although the Taft-Hartley amendments to the National Labor Relations Act (NLRA) certainly prohibit union restraint and coercion of employees broadly enough to cover most of the kinds of strike and picket line violence that an employer would want to have enjoined,[36] the courts have generally held that this prohibition cannot serve as the jurisdictional base of a private injunction action. There are two reasons for this. Firstly, the enforcement of this federal prohibition against violence lies within the primary and original jurisdiction of the National Labor Relations Board (NLRB), and not the federal district courts.[37] Secondly, although the statute does give the federal district courts power to enjoin violations pending an administrative determination of the issue,[38] that jurisdiction can be invoked only by the general counsel of the board, and not by private parties.[39]

On the other hand, the federal labor laws do allow for private injunctive relief against some kinds of strikes—and if violence is involved it may be enjoined simply as part of the broader injunction against the strike itself. Section 301 of the NLRA[40] for example, has been construed as permitting an injunction when a union elects to strike rather than to arbitrate a contract dispute—the provisions of the Norris-LaGuardia Act notwithstanding.[41] The Railway Labor Act[42] has been

[35] Chicago & Ill. Midlands Railroad Co. v. Bhd. of Railroad Trainmen, 315 F.2d 771, 774-75 (7th Cir.), *remanded for dismissal because of* mootness, 375 U.S. 18 (1963). Brotherhood of Railroad Trainmen v. New York Central Railroad Co., 246 F.2d 114, 120-22 (6th Cir.), *cert. denied,* 355 U.S. 877 (1957). The Seventh Circuit Court of Appeals had also used the Interstate Commerce Act to establish "federal question" jurisdiction in Toledo, Peoria & Western Railroad v. Bhd. of Railroad Trainmen, 132 F.2d 265, 268 (7th Cir. 1944). Although the Supreme Court ultimately reversed the lower court in that case, it reserved judgment on the jurisdictional issue. 321 U.S. at 50, 66.

[36] NLRA § 8 (b)(1)(A), 29 U.S.C. § 158 (b)(1)(A) (1976), makes it an unfair labor practice for a labor union to restrain or coerce employees in the exercise of their statutory rights. *See generally,* Haggard, *Labor Union Violence as an Unfair Labor Practice,* 34 S.C.L. Rev. 273 (1982).

[37] *See* Norton Coal Co. v. UMW, 88 L.R.R.M. 2701, 2702, (W.D. Va. 1974). *But cf.* Oberman & Co. v. United Garment Workers, 21 F. Supp. 20 (W.D. Mo. 1937) (once the Board's election processes are completed, the doctrine of primary jurisdiction is no longer a bar to federal court jurisdiction; case was decided prior to the amendments making union violence an unfair labor practice and is therefore no longer controlling on the facts).

[38] Labor Management Relations Act § 20(j), 29 U.S.C. § 160(j) (1976).

[39] *See* Lock Joint Pipe Co. v. Anderson, 127 F. Supp. 692, 694 (W.D. Mo. 1955); Hat Corp. v. United Hatters Union, 114 F. Supp. 890, 893 (D. Conn. 1953).

[40] Labor Management Relations Act § 301, 29 U.S.C. § 185 (1976).

[41] Boys Market, Inc. v. Retail Clerk's Union, Local 770, 398 U.S. 235 (1970).

[42] Railway Labor Act §§ 1-208, 45 U.S.C. §§ 150-188 (1976).

similarly,[43] and perhaps even more broadly,[44] construed. The injunction against violence in such a case is, however, merely a necessary incident of the broader injunction against the strike itself; and the parameters of the law in those areas are beyond the scope of the present article.

Pendent Jurisdiction. Under the doctrine of pendent jurisdiction, a federal court has the constitutional power to hear and decide a claim based on state law, over which the court would not otherwise have original jurisdiction, if the state law claim is joined with a federal law claim and both claims "derive from a common nucleus of operative fact."[45] In *United Mine Workers v. Gibbs,*[46] the Supreme Court case from which that test is derived, the plaintiff sued for damages under both section 303 of the NLRA, alleging illegal secondary activity, and under the common law of Tennessee, alleging the commission of various torts. Although the state law claim was held to be subject to the Norris-LaGuardia Act's standard of proof on the agency question, the Supreme Court held that the district court did have the power to hear it.[47]

Gibbs, of course, involved a pendent state claim for damages. But there is no reason why a pendent claim for injunction relief based on state law could not just as easily be joined with the section 303 damage action,[48] and the equity jurisdiction of the federal court, albeit subject to the limits of the Norris-LaGuardia Act, thus established on that basis.[49] Moreover, although "the federal claim must have substance sufficient to confer subject matter jurisdiction on the court,"[50] once

---

[43] Brotherhood of Railroad Trainmen v. Chicago R. & Ind. R.R. Co., 353 U.S. 30 (1957) (injunction against strike over a "minor" dispute, involving the interpretation and enforcement of existing contract terms, which must be submitted to binding arbitration under the Railway Labor Act).

[44] *See, e.g.,* American Airlines, Inc. v. Air Line Pilots Ass'n. 169 F. Supp. 777 (S.D.N.Y. 1958) (injunction against strike over a "major" dispute, involving the negotiation of new contract terms, which must be submitted to mandatory but nonbinding mediation efforts under the Railway Labor Act; there are no equivalent provisions in the Taft-Hartley Act; *see generally,* McGuinn, *Injunctive Powers of the Federal Courts in Cases Involving Disputes Under the Railway Labor Act,* 50 GEO. L.J. 46 (1961).

[45] United Mine Workers v. Gibbs, 383 U.S. 715, 725 (1966); *see generally,* C. WRIGHT, LAW OF FEDERAL COURTS 74-77 (3d edition, 1976).

[46] 383 U.S. 715 (1966).

[47] *See also,* Kayser-Roth Corp. v. Textile Workers Union, 479 F.2d 524 (6th Cir. 1973); *cert. denied,* 414 U.S. 976 (1973); Ritchie v. UMW, 410 F.2d 827 (6th Cir. 1969); Smith v. American Guild of Variety Artists, 368 F.2d 511 (8th Cir. 1966), *cert. denied,* 387 U.S. 931 (1967).

[48] Injunctive relief is not directly available under section 303. Amalgamated Ass'n. of Street Employees v. Dixie Motor Coach Corp., 170 F.2d 902 (8th Cir. 1948).

[49] Iodice v. Calabrese, 291 F. Supp. 592 (S.D.N.Y. 1968); *see* GORMAN, LABOR LAW 293 (1976).

[50] 383 U.S. at 725.

that relatively unrigorous test is met and federal jurisdiction attaches, then the court retains that jurisdiction to try the state law injunction claim even if the federal section 303 damage claim is dismissed on the merits.[51]

Removal Jurisdiction. The discussion of the previous jurisdictional issues has assumed that the plaintiff desired to get into federal court. This, however, is obviously not always the case. Indeed, because of the limitations that the Norris-LaGuardia Act imposes on the power of the federal courts to issue injunctions, a plaintiff will usually want to avoid those strictures by seeking an injunction in state court instead. Such a plaintiff might, however, then discover that the defendant union has removed the case to federal court anyway!

Generally speaking, removal from state to federal courts is available to a defendant whenever the lawsuit would otherwise be within the original jurisdiction of the federal court, as when there is diversity of citizenship or when the suit raises a federal question.[52] Thus, if a plaintiff in state court is seeking an injunction against labor union violence and *could have* invoked federal court jurisdiction on either of those bases, then the defendant union can *usually* remove the case to federal court. Although the existence of original diversity jurisdiction may be relatively easy to ascertain in a removal action, the same cannot always be said of federal-question jurisdiction. A defendant seeking to invoke the jurisdiction of the federal courts naturally has the burden of establishing that the plaintiff's action arises under federal law.[53] In doing this, although the defendant is forced to rely on the plaintiff's complaint as drafted,[54] the plaintiff's failure to allege a specific federal right will not necessarily defeat removal jurisdiction. Rather, "removal is proper where the *real nature* of the claim asserted in the complaint is federal, whether or not so characterized by the plaintiff."[55] On the

---

[51] Federal Prescription Service v. Amalgamated Meat Cutters, 527 F.2d 269 (8th Cir. 1975). In this case, the court of appeals held that it was proper for the district court to retain jurisdiction over the pendent claim even though it had found that the federal section 303 claim "lacked substance and was filed merely to give the Court jurisdiction over the pendent court." *Id.* at 273. The court of appeals relied on considerations of "convenience and sound judicial administration" in holding that the refusal to dismiss the state claim was, even under those findings, still proper. *Id.* at 274.

[52] *See generally,* C. WRIGHT, LAW OF FEDERAL COURTS 148-68 (3d edition, 1976); Comment, *Intimations of Federal Removal Jurisdiction in Labor Cases: The Pleadings Nexus,* 1981 DUKE L.J. 743.

[53] Beacon Moving & Storage, Inc. v. Local 814, Int'l. Bhd. of Teamsters, 362 F. Supp. 442 (S.D.N.Y. 1972).

[54] *Id.*

[55] *Id.* at 445; *see also,* Fristoe v. Reynolds Metals Co., 615 F.2d 1209, 1212 (9th Cir. 1980). (Emphasis added.)

other hand, it has also been said that where a "plaintiff has a choice of relying on state law and does so rely, there can be no removal except on the basis of diversity."[56] Needless to say, the way in which these obscure and slightly conflicting principles will be resolved is not a highly predictable matter in any given case.

The doctrine of pendent jurisdiction applies in removal actions also. Thus, if the plaintiff's state law complaint not only seeks an injunction against violence, but also seeks damages for a breach of the collective bargaining agreement or for illegal secondary activity, there would be original federal court jurisdiction over the two latter claims under sections 301 and 303 of the NLRA, removal would be appropriate, and the plaintiff's state law injunction action would be removed right along with the damage claim,[57] with the limitations of the Norris-LaGuardia Act also coming into play with respect to the issuance of such an injunction.

Finally, although the Norris-LaGuardia Act is couched in terms of a *denial* of jurisdiction, this does not preclude removal where jurisdiction would otherwise attach. The Supreme Court has stated that, "the nature of the relief available after jurisdiction attaches is, of course, different from the question of whether there is jurisdiction to adjudicate the controversy."[58]

The advantages of the removal procedure to a defendant union are obvious. Once the cause of action is removed to federal court, the provisions of the Norris-LaGuardia Act apply and may preclude the issuance of the injunction that would otherwise have been available in state courts. Moreover, if the state court has already issued some kind of restraining order, it will be dissolved once the case is removed to federal court, since "to leave the state court restraining order undissolved would be tantamount to granting the same injunction by this court,"[59] which in most cases would be prohibited by the provisions of

[56] 362 F. Supp. at 445; *see also,* Woodland Nursing Home v. District 1199, Hospital Employees, 91 L.R.R.M. 3003 (S.D.N.Y. 1975).

[57] *See, e.g.,* Iodice v. Calabrese, 291 F. Supp. 592 (S.D.N.Y. 1968).

[58] Avco Corp. v. Aero Lodge No. 735, Int'l. Ass'n. of Machinists, 390 U.S. 557, 561 (1968).

[59] Peabody Coal Co. v. Barnes, 308 F. Supp. 902, 903-04 (E.D. Mo. 1969); *see also,* Miller Parlor Furn. Co. v. Furniture Workers' Industrial Union, 8 F. Supp. 209 (N.J. 1934); *accord,* Crestwood Dairy, Inc. v. Kelley, 222 F. Supp. 614, 617, (E.D.N.Y. 1963) ("The 'jurisdictional' form of the prohibitions of that Act upon granting injunctions are not to be interpreted as tolerating remand to the state court for the purpose of enabling it to grant the injunctions that the Norris-LaGuardia Act would preclude a federal court from granting."). In Avco Corp. v. Aero Lodge No. 735, Int'l. Ass'n. of Machinists, 390 U.S. 557 (1968), the Supreme Court expressly left open the question of whether federal courts, after a removal of a section 301 action, are required to dissolve injunction relief previously granted by the state courts. *Id.* at 561 n. 4.

the Norris-LaGuardia Act. When the removal has been based only on diversity of citizenship to begin with, the plaintiff is left with absolutely no relief after the cause has been removed to federal court and the provisions of the Norris-LaGuardia Act have been attached.

This, however, would seem to be an unintended and undesirable result. In the Norris-LaGuardia Act, Congress did not intend to limit the traditional equity jurisdiction of the state courts.[60] Diversity jurisdiction is also not intended to change the substantive law that governs the dispute between citizens of different states.[61] Both of these unintended effects, however, are achieved once the defendant union's right of removal is added to the equation. As a practical matter, the state court's power to enjoin labor violence in these cases is limited by the requirements of the Norris-LaGuardia Act—*i.e.*, if the state court has any broader power, the union will negate it by simply removing to federal court. Diversity jurisdiction can thus be used as a device to change not only the forum in which the dispute is decided, but also the substantive law that governs the resolution of the dispute.[62]

In spite, however, of the advantages that a defendant obtains by removing a state injunction action into federal court, a plaintiff can usually avoid that result if complete diversity is lacking and the plaintiff's original state court claim is limited to a plea for injunctive relief against union violence, with no attempt to also claim damages on what might be construed as either a breach-of-contract or a secondary-boycott cause of action, which would thus raise a federal question, making removal possible.[63]

Substantive Requirements

Assuming that a federal district court has jurisdiction over an injunction action generally, before such an injunction can be issued the re-

---

[60] *See, e.g.,* Ford v. Boeger, 362 F.2d 999 (8th Cir. 1966), *cert. denied,* 386 F.2d 914 (1967).

[61] Erie Railroad Co. v. Tompkins, 304 U.S. 64 (1938); *see generally,* C. WRIGHT, LAW OF FEDERAL COURTS 253-78 (3d edition, 1976).

[62] An analogous conundrum—involving the interplay between specific enforcement by state courts of no-strike agreements, the requirements of the Norris-LaGuardia Act, and the availability of removal jurisdiction—finally led the Supreme Court to hold that the Norris-LaGuardia Act simply did not apply to suits under section 301 of the Taft-Hartley Act to enjoin strikes over arbitrable issues and which are also in violation of a contractual no-strike agreement. Boys Markets, Inc. v. Retail Clerks Union, Local 770, 398 U.S. 235, 253-54 (1970).

[63] *See, e.g.,* Woodland Nursing Home v. District 1199, Hospital Employees, 91 L.R.R.M. 3003 (S.D.N.Y. 1975); B.F. Goodrich Co. v. Teamsters, Local 804, 79 L.R.R.M. 2888 (E.D.N.Y. 1971); Dow Chem. Co. v. Allied and Technical Workers, District 50, 315 F. Supp. 427 (D. Colo. 1970); Dixie Machine Welding & Metal Works, Inc. v. Marine Engrs. Beneficial Ass'n., 243 F. Supp. 489 (E.D. La. 1965); Hat Corp. v. United Hatters Union, 114 F. Supp. 890 (D. Conn. 1953).

quirements of the Norris-LaGuardia Act must still be satisfied. Section 1 of Norris-LaGuardia provides that no court of the United States shall issue any injunction "in a case involving or growing out of a labor dispute, *except* in a strict conformity with the provisions of this chapter."[64] The existence of a "labor dispute" is thus always the threshold issue insofar as the applicability of the Norris-LaGuardia Act is concerned; in the absence of such a dispute the limitations of the statute simply do not apply.[65] The statutory definition of the term is itself relatively broad,[66] however, and the courts have generally construed it quite liberally.[67] In any event, since most union violence occurs in the context of either organizational drives or strikes and picketing related to failure to reach collective bargaining agreement, the existence of a labor dispute is rarely an issue in such cases.

The generalized prohibition against injunctions in section 1 is then reinforced by section 4,[68] which enumerates nine specific acts that cannot be enjoined under any circumstances. Even if the offending conduct is not covered in section 4, however, an injunction still cannot be issued unless the requirements of sections 7 and 8 are also met.[69] These sections thus provide the substantive content to the "except" clause of section 1. They are as follows.

The Conduct Must Be Unlawful. More specifically, subsection 7(a) says that an injunction cannot be issued except upon a finding "that *unlawful acts* have been threatened and will be committed unless

---

[64] Norris-LaGuardia Act § 1, 29 U.S.C. § 101 (1976). (Emphasis added.)

[65] Ashley, Drew & Northern Railway Co. v. United Transportation Union, 625 F.2d 1357, 1362 (8th Cir. 1980) ("Applicability of the Act's anti-injunction proscription . . . depends solely on whether this was a case involving or arising out of a labor dispute within the meaning of the Act").

[66] Norris-LaGuardia Act § 13 (c), 29 U.S.C. § 113(c) (1976) provides as follows: The term "labor dispute" includes any controversy concerning terms or conditions of employment, or concerning the association or representation of persons in negotiating, fixing, maintaining, changing or seeking to arrange terms or conditions of employment, regardless of whether or not the disputants stand in the proximate relation of employer and employee.

[67] *See, e.g.,* American Federation of Musicians v. Carroll, 391 U.S. 99 (1968); Milk Wagon Drivers' Local 753 v. Lake Valley Farm Prods., Inc., 311 U.S. 91 (1940); New Negro Alliance v. Sanitary Grocery Co., 303 U.S. 552 (1938); Corporate Printing Co., Inc. v. Typographical Union, 555 F.2d 18 (2d Cir. 1977). *But see,* Scott v. Moore, 680 F.2d 979 (5th Cir. 1982) (en banc), *reversed,* U.S. Sup. Court, July 5, 1983. ("unlawful activity not associated with any on-going legitimate union conduct" does not involve a "labor dispute" within the meaning of the Norris-LaGuardia Act); Ashley, Drew & Northern Railway Co. v. United Transportation Union, 625 F.2d 1357 (8th Cir. 1980). The court in *Ashley* eschewed a "literal reading" of section 13 (c) and instead held that union conduct occurs within the context of a "labor dispute" in the statutory sense, "only when the offending activity is furthering the union's economic interest . . . ." *Id.* at 1363.

[68] Norris-LaGuardia Act § 4, 29 U.S.C. § 104 (1976).

[69] Norris-LaGuardia Act §§ 7 & 8, 29 U.S.C. §§ 107 & 108 (1976).

restrained or have been committed and will be continued unless restrained."[70] It is not difficult to satisfy this requirement in a union violence case. Indeed, the subsection refers primarily, if not exclusively, to union violence. In *Brotherhood of Railroad Trainmen v. Central of Georgia Railway Co.*,[71] the fifth circuit court said that

> it is plain from the language and the context that the words "unlawful acts" mean violence, breaches of the peace, criminal acts, etc., and that such terms do not include, they do not constitute a general reference to, anything that may be considered illegal but apply specifically to the acts of violence which authority is calculated to control.[72]

This interpretation of subsection 7(a) as at least including all acts of violence is certainly reinforced by the language of section 1. Three of the acts which that section says cannot be enjoined are qualified by the proviso that they be without or not involve "fraud or violence"[73] or that they be "peaceful."[74] One of the sponsors of the Norris-LaGuardia Act in the House of Representatives stated that

> contrary to the belief of some people, this bill does not attempt to take away from the Federal courts all power to restrain unlawful acts or acts of fraud or violence in labor disputes.
>
> The public is amply protected as the bill is now drawn. It is a mistaken notion that some have that all injunctions are proscribed. There still is left to the Federal courts the right to issue injunctions when there are unlawful acts threatened or committed, when substantial and irreparable injury to complainant's property is done—and when there is no adequate remedy at law in all those cases, the Federal courts will still have the right to issue injunctions. When there is fraud, when there is violence, and when there is crime injunctions may issue. When any of those things are threatened or committed injunctions may ensue.[75]

---

[70] Norris-LaGuardia Act § 7(a), 29 U.S.C. § 107(a) (1976). (Emphasis added.)

[71] 229 F.2d 901 (5th Cir. 1956), *cert. dismissed for mootness,* 352 U.S. 995 (1957).

[72] *Id.* at 905.

[73] Norris-LaGuardia Act § 4(e), (i), 29 U.S.C. § 104(e), (i) (1976).

[74] Norris-LaGuardia Act § 4(f), 29 U.S.C. § 104(f) (1976). In speaking of section 4, the court in Scott v. Moore, 680 F.2d 979 (5th Cir. 1982) (en banc) stated that "there was nothing in this provision denying to federal courts the power to enjoin violence, breaches of the peace, or criminal acts simply because they may be committed by persons participating . . . in a labor dispute." *Id.* at 986.

[75] Quoted in Grace Co. v. Williams, 96 F.2d 478, 481 (8th Cir. 1938); United Electrical Coal Companies v. Rice, 80 F.2d 1, 8 (7th Cir. 1935), *cert. denied,* 297 U.S. 714 (1935). *See also,* Potomac Electric Power Co. v. Washington Chapter of C.O.R.E., 209 F. Supp. 559, 560 (D.D.C. 1962) ("The Norris-LaGuardia Act does not apply to injunctions to prevent the commission of crime or sabotage or destruction or injury to property"). Wilson & Co. v. Birl, 27 F. Supp. 915, 917 (E.D. Pa.), *aff'd,* 105 F.2d 948 (3d Cir. 1939) (Norris-LaGuardia Act only left "a residue of jurisdiction necessary for the protection of property against destruction by violence or fraud").

The eighth circuit court explained the moral dimensions of this interpretation of the statute rather eloquently in *International Assn. of Bridge Workers v. Pauly Jail Building Co.,* [76] as follows:

> The dignity of the State has always demanded that certain forms of conduct be not permitted to become the controlling basis for disposing of individual or social controversies. . . . What Congress accordingly must be regarded as having intended in the situation was to leave the federal courts free to enjoin those permeative acts, falling within the term "fraud or violence," which an unsluggish public conscience and a healthy social order cannot soundly tolerate. . . .[77]

In *Westinghouse Broadcasting Co. Inc. v. Dukakis,*[78] the court defined the ultimate scope of the term "unlawful" by reference to the underlying policy of this exception. The court noted that the term had been held to mean "criminal,"[79] but that it had also been held to refer to "mere 'mischief for mischief's sake' unrelated to any proper labor purpose, but not of itself criminal."[80] After stating that "the nub of jurisdiction left to the district court seems to be the preservation of the peace,"[81] the court concluded that "acts of violence, acts likely to cause violence, and verbal harassment of a non-violent but provocative nature may be enjoined."[82] The court therefore held "that the jostling of the plaintiff's cameramen, the interference with them at very close range, and, in particular, the use of defendants' motor vehicles to interfere with their travel, constitutes a level of harassment and intimidation which not only warrants but requires this Court's intervention."[83]

The Persons Being Enjoined Must Have Committed, Authorized, or Ratified the Unlawful Conduct. Section 7(a) states that "no injunction or temporary restraining order shall be issued on account of any threat or unlawful act excepting against the person or persons, association, or organization making the threat or committing the unlawful act or actually authorizing or ratifying the same after actual knowledge thereof."[84] Also relevant to this issue is section 6 of the statute, which provides that no one "shall be held responsible or liable . . . for the

---

[76] 118 F.2d 615 (8th Cir.), *cert. denied,* 314 U.S. 639 (1941).
[77] 118 F.2d at 617.
[78] 412 F. Supp. 580 (D. Mass. 1976).
[79] *Id.* at 583.
[80] *Id.*
[81] *Id.* at 584.
[82] *Id.*
[83] *Id. But see,* 75 CONG. REC. 5471 (1932) ("Mass picketing, intimidations, trailing, besetting, importuning, libeling and false statements, are to be beyond the reach of injunctive relief").
[84] Norris-LaGuardia Act § 7(a), 29 U.S.C. § (107(a) (1976).

unlawful acts . . . except upon *clear proof* of actual participation in, or actual authorization of, such acts, or of ratification of such acts after actual knowledge thereof." [85]

It is thus generally assumed that before a plaintiff is entitled to an injunction, there must be "clear proof" that the person or persons being enjoined have committed, participated in, authorized, or ratified the conduct or threats of misconduct in question. [86] The few courts that have specifically addressed this narrow issue, however, have consistently reached a contrary conclusion.

In *Charles D. Bonanno Linen Service, Inc. v. McCarthy,* [87] the first circuit court stated that "it is readily apparent that § 106 applies only (by its own terms) to liability for damages or criminal responsibility. Proof of union involvement satisfying § 107(a), and, appropriate for the issuance of an injunction against continued, specified illegal acts" [88] can thus be made through the use of somewhat less compelling facts but which presumably still meet the preponderance of the evidence test normally used in civil litigation. [89]

On the other hand, the second circuit court's detailed discussion of section 6 in *Harlem River Consumers Coop, Inc., v. Associated Grocers of Harlem, Inc.* implicitly assumes the applicability of that section in an injunction situation. [90]

The legislative history and Supreme Court decisions construing section 6 are inconclusive on this issue, since they focus more on what "clear proof" means rather than on what elements of the cause of action it applies to. To be sure, the Supreme Court, in *Brotherhood of*

---

[85] Norris-LaGuardia Act § 6, 29 U.S.C. § 106 (1976) (emphasis added)

[86] Professor Gorman states that unions were given "special protection *in injunction proceedings* under the Norris-LaGuardia Act against liability 'except upon clear proof of actual participation in, or actual authorization of . . . or of ratification of' acts of officers or members." R. GORMAN, BASIC TEXT ON LABOR LAW 218 (1976) (emphasis added). *See also,* W. CONNOLLY & B. CONNOLLY, WORK STOPPAGES AND UNION RESPONSIBILITY 174 (1977).

[87] 532 F.2d 189 (1st Cir. 1976).

[88] *Id.* at 191; *see also,* Mayo v. Dean, 82 F.2d 554, 556 (5th Cir. 1936) (the "clear proof" requirement of § 6 "might prevent punishment for contempt or the recovery of damages, but clearly was not intended to apply to the issuance of an injunction to prevent future acts of coercion in a case where such relief would be proper"); Washington Post Co. v. International Printing Union Local 6, 92 L.R.R.M. 2961, 2969 n. 18 (D.C. Sup. Ct. 1976) (court agreed with the *Bonanno* interpretation, but found the question to be "academic" in that case since the evidence was sufficient to satisfy even the "clear proof" standard).

[89] *Accord,* Ramsey, v. UMW, 401 U.S. 302, 307-11 (1971) (except for matters which section 6 specifically require to be established by "clear proof," other matters in a Norris-LaGuardia Act case are proved by a simple preponderance of the evidence).

[90] 450 F.2d 271 (2d Cir. 1971). *See also,* Cinderella Theater Co. v. Sign Writers Union, 6 F. Supp. 164 (E.D. Mich. 1934); Western Union Telegraph Co. v. IBEW, 133 F.2d 955, 958 (7th Cir. 1943).

Carpenters v. United States,[91] an antitrust action, said that "the limitations of that section [§6] are upon all courts of the United States in *all* matters growing out of labor disputes, covered by the Act, which may come before them."[92] But later in the opinion, again speaking of section 6, the Court stated that "its purpose and effect was to relieve organizations . . . and members of those organizations from *liability for damages* or *imputation of guilt* for lawless acts done in labor disputes by some individual officers or members of the organization, without *clear proof.*"[93] In the later case of *Ramsey v. UMW,*[94] the Supreme Court quoted the "in all matters" language of *Carpenters* and said it was "unexceptionable,"[95] but then immediately qualified it by saying that "the federal courts, of course, must heed §6 in all cases arising out of labor disputes *in which the section is applicable.*"[96] The point of the *Bonanno* case, of course, is simply that the section is not applicable except in damages actions, like *Carpenters* and *Ramsey,* or in contempt proceedings. The Supreme Court, however, did not have this specific issue in mind in either *Carpenters* or *Ramsey,* and one should probably not read too much into this language.

The legislative history is equally unenlightening. There was, on the one hand, considerable concern over the then existing practice of issuing injunctions on the basis of *ex parte* affidavits,[97] a matter which seems to relate, not so much to what facts or relationships give rise to vicarious liability, but rather to the quantum of evidence or degree of proof that should be required in order to establish such facts or relationships. If that were the congressional concern with respect to the use of *ex parte* affidavits, then the section 6 clear proof requirement might be considered the congressional response—which would suggest that the section does apply in injunction proceedings.[98]

That reasoning, however, is rather tenuous. And the requirements in section 7 itself that injunctions be based on the testimony of witnesses

---

[91] 330 U.S. 395 (1947).

[92] *Id.* at 401 (1947) (emphasis added). Taken literally, that statement could also be construed as suggesting that all of the elements of section 7, including the existence of the "unlawful" conduct itself, must be established by "clear proof," a position the Supreme Court expressly rejected in *Ramsey v. UMW,* 401 U.S. 302, 207-11 (1970).

[93] 330 U.S. at 403. (Emphasis added.)

[94] 401 U.S. 302 (1970).

[95] *Id.* at 310.

[96] *Id.* (emphasis added.)

[97] *See, e.g.,* 75 CONG. REC. 4689 (1932).

[98] This nexus between the use of affidavits, the degree of proof that they provide, and the issuance of injunctions on the basis of such affidavits is hinted at in SENATE COMMITTEE REPORT ON NORRIS-LAGUARDIA. S. REP. NO. 163, 72d Cong., 1st Sess. (1932) 20-21.

There has been a distinct conflict of opinion in the courts as to the degree of proof required. Mere ex parte affidavits establishing a certain amount of lawless conduct in the

heard in open court and subject to cross examination would seem to be the more obvious correction of the alleged abuses involving the use of *ex parte* affidavits. Moreover, Representative O'Connor, in explaining what section 6 was designed to correct, identified it in terms of "a grossly unfair practice that has grown up of holding officers and members of unions *liable for damages* for the acts of other members without proof of participation or direction or ratification of such acts."[99]

Although the legislative history and Supreme Court authority are by no means conclusive on the issue, on balance they probably do tend to support the *Bonanno* holding. That holding is certainly consistent with the literal words of the statute. Moreover, as a matter of policy there is no sound reason why clear proof of union participation in or authorization or ratification of acts of past violence or threats of future violence should be considered a condition precedent to the issuance of an injunction against future misconduct by that union.

Congress clearly intended that the federal courts continue to have jurisdiction to enjoin violence and threats of violence;[100] and the imposition of a clear proof requirement would unduly interfere with that function. In an injunction proceeding, the test for vicarious liability spelled out in section 7(a), even if it can be established by a mere preponderance of the evidence rather than by clear proof, is still considerably more strict than the common law agency test.[101] This would seem to be a more than adequate guard against the precipitous issuance of labor injunctions, especially in today's judicial climate. Moreover, the union is being enjoined from engaging only in independently "unlawful" acts—acts which the union should have no inclination to engage in anyway. The injunction itself attaches no guilt

---

prosecution of a strike have been held in some instances to establish a "presumption" that the entire union and its officers were engaged in an unlawful conspiracy. . . . Various examples of these different rulings are quoted in FRANKFURTER and GREENE, THE LABOR INJUNCTION, pp. 74-75.

The cases cited by Frankfurter and Greene on those pages all involve the issuance of injunctions, rather than damages or contempt; the congressional concern here with *ex parte* affidavits clearly relates to the "degree of proof" they provide with respect to union responsibility; and this "degree of proof" problem was dealt with, at least in part, by the "clear proof" requirement of section 6.

[99] 75 CONG. REC. 5463 (1932) (emphasis added); *see also,* S. REP. NO. 163, 72d Cong., 1st Sess. (1932) p. 19. "Section 6 of the bill relates to *damages* for unlawful acts arising out of labor disputes."

[100] *See* text at notes 69-82, *supra.*

[101] Section 7 prohibits the issuance of an injunction against anyone except those "making the threat or committing the unlawful act or actually authorizing or ratifying the same after actual knowledge thereof" (emphasis added). It is generally accepted that under the common law rules of agency authority may be implied or apparent, and the knowledge necessary for ratification may be constructive. *See* W. SAVEY, AGENCY §§ 22, 38 (1964).

and imposes no actual liability; and the *Bonanno* holding concedes that the clear proof requirement would apply in contempt proceedings, where such guilt and liability would be imposed.

Regardless, however, of whether it is by a mere preponderance of the evidence or by something stronger, the question of what must be proved on the agency issue presumably remains the same. In *United Mine Workers v. Gibbs,*[102] the Supreme Court described the necessary proof as follows:

> What is required is proof, either that the union *approved* the violence which occurred, or that it participated *actively* or by *knowing tolerance* in further acts which were themselves actionable under state law or *intentionally* drew upon the previous violence for their force.[103]

In that case, which involved a state law damage action to which the clear proof standard clearly applied, the named defendants were not connected with the original violence, and the Court held that their subsequent involvement in the dispute and their picketing amounted neither to a ratification of that violence,[104] nor to an implicit threat of future violence.[105] In this regard, the Court rejected the more realistic appraisal made of the situation by the Court of Appeals for the Sixth Circuit. That court had stated that "the aura of violence remained to enhance the effectiveness of the picketing. Certainly there is a threat of violence when the man who has just knocked me down my front steps continues to stand guard at my door."[106] The Supreme Court, however, disagreed and also stated that "there can be no rigid requirement that a union affirmatively disavow such unlawful acts as may previously have occurred."[107]

On the other hand, in *Kayser-Roth Corp. v. Textile Workers Union,*[108] which was a damage action against the union and thus also subject to the clear proof standard, there was more than ample evidence to satisfy that or, certainly, any less rigorous requirement. There was testimony that two of the defendant union's officers had instructed the strikers to stop nonstriking employees "by any means they could,

---

[102] 383 U.S. 715 (1966).
[103] *Id.* at 739 (emphasis added).
[104] *Id.* at 738.
[105] *Id.* at 739. *See also,* Donnelly Garment Co. v. Dubinsky, 55 F. Supp. 587 (W.D. Mo. 1944), *affirmed,* 154 F.2d 38 (8th Cir. 1946) (proof that the defendant unionists knew of and condoned strike violence against other employers does not constitute proof that the defendants were engaged in a conspiracy to commit violence against the complainant employer).
[106] 343 F.2d at 616.
[107] 383 U.S. at 739.
[108] 479 F.2d 524 (6th Cir. 1973), *cert. denied,* 414 U.S. 976 (1973).

Union Violence

including stripping off their clothes"; [109] there were numerous acts of
violence during the time these agents were supervising the strike and
picket line; there was testimony that the union agents "observed
groups of strikers while they blocked, stoned, and in some cases overturned vehicles"; [110] the agents admitted that they were aware of the
systematic distribution of nails and glass in the company driveways;
one of them personally directed the strikers to jam buses to prevent
nonstriking employees from entering them; and after two days of especially severe violence, this same union agent "congratulated the
strikers for a job well done in closing down the plant." [111]

The union itself, moreover, promised to protect the strikers against
any criminal charges; it provided bail bonds and lawyers for those who
were arrested; and it continued to pay strike benefits even to strikers
who were guilty of criminal misconduct or who were held in criminal
contempt of the state law injunction; [112] and the union magazine
boasted that "when they get angry enough to do things here in Tennessee they go *all the way*." [113] The court thus concluded that "the
union's contention that the proof on these points is not clear proof is
without merit." [114]

Lying in between the inadequate evidence of *Gibbs* and the more-
than-ample evidence of *Kayser-Roth* are, of course, a wide range of
proofs. It is obviously not necessary to prove explicit authorization of
specific acts of violence. [115] The Second Circuit Court of Appeals once
stated that, "if a union delegates to an agent unrestricted authority going beyond the norms of union conduct, §6 does not immunize it from
liability for his illegal acts. Similarly, if it continues him in a previous
position of high responsibility after knowledge of his illegal activities,
§6 affords no shelter." [116] Moreover, union authorization or ratification
can also be established by circumstantial evidence. [117] Finally, even if

---

[109] 479 F.2d at 527.

[110] *Id.*

[111] *Id.*

[112] *But see* Federal Prescription Service v. Amalgamated Meat Cutters, 527 F.2d 269,
277 (8th Cir. 1975).

[113] 479 F.2d at 527 (emphasis added).

[114] *Id.* at 528.

[115] Brotherhood of Carpenters v. United States, 330 U.S. 395, 409 (1947).

[116] Harlem River Consumers Coop. Inc. v. Associated Grocers of Harlem, Inc., 450
F.2d 271, 274 (2d Cir. 1971).

[117] James R. Synder Co. v. Edward Rose & Sons, Inc., 546 F.2d 206 (6th Cir. 1976);
Ritchie v. UMW, 410 F.2d 827, 833 (6th Cir. 1969); *See also,* Kerry Coal Co. v. UMW,
488, F. Supp. 1080 (W.D. Pa. 1980); Sisco v. McNutt, 209 F.2d 550, 552 (8th Cir. 1954)
("While Sisco did not actually strike the blows that injured the plaintiffs, he had an
understanding with those who inflicted bodily harm upon plaintiffs that blows would be
struck," as was evidenced by the fact he drove them to the scene of the assault, waited
while it took place, and then sped away with the assailants).

the clear proof standard does apply in the injunction context, it is nevertheless limited to the issue of agency (or to the union's responsibility) and not to the other matters that must be proved in order for an injunction to be issued.[118]

There Must Be Proof that Substantial and Irreparable Injury Will Follow.[119] This requirement, like the next two, is simply a codification of what equity jurisprudence would require before issuing an injunction in any event. The requirement, moreover, is fairly easy to satisfy when the violence or threats of violence have substantially interfered with the employer's operation of its business. Loss of actual income,[120] idle-resource losses,[121] liability for default penalities,[122] losses owing to delay when time is of the essence,[123] destruction of the morale of other workers,[124] and even the simple deprivation of the employer's right to use its property[125] have all been found to constitute "substantial and irreparable injury" under the Norris-LaGuardia Act.

The Employer's Injury if the Injunction Were Denied Must Be Greater than what the Union's Injury Will Be if It Is Granted. Specifically, the Norris-LaGuardia Act requires a person seeking an injunction to prove "that as to each item of relief granted greater injury will be inflicted upon complainant by the denial of relief than will be inflicted upon defendants by the granting of relief."[126] This too is a traditional requirement of equity jurisprudence and has not been frequently litigated under the Norris-LaGuardia Act. In *Cater Construction Company v. Nischwitz,*[127] where the defendant unions were attempting to force the employer to hire their members on a construction project, the unions plead the loss of "work, wages, destruction of wage scales and loss of union prestige" if the injunction were granted.[128] The court, however, found this to be "speculative" and not sufficient to overcome the employer's measurable economic losses.[129]

There Must Be No Adequate Remedy at Law.[130] Equitable relief is said to be merely supplemental to the traditional common law reme-

---

[118] *See* Ramsey v. UMW, 401 U.S. 302, 310 (1971); Federal Prescription Service, Inc. v. Amalgamated Meat Cutters, 527 F.2d 269, 275 (8th Cir. 1975).

[119] Norris-LaGuardia Act § 7(b), 29 U.S.C. § 107(b) (1976).

[120] Knapp-Monarch Co. v. Anderson, 7 F. Supp. 332 (E.D. Ill. 1934).

[121] Cater Constr. Co. v. Nischwitz, 111 F.2d 971, 974 (7th Cir. 1940).

[122] *Id.*

[123] Washington Post Co. v. International Printing Union Local 6, 92 L.R.R.M. 2961, 2971 (D.C. Sup. Ct. 1976).

[124] *Id.*

[125] Knapp-Monarch Co. v. Anderson, 7 F. Supp. 332 (E.D. Ill. 1934).

[126] Norris-LaGuardia Act § 7(c), 29 U.S.C. § 107(c) (1976).

[127] 111 F.2d 971 (7th Cir. 1940).

[128] *Id.* at 977.

[129] *Id.*

[130] Norris-LaGuardia Act § 7(d), 29 U.S.C. § 107(d) (1976).

dies, and it is thus generally not available to a plaintiff if a damage or other legal remedy would be adequate.[131] The Norris-LaGuardia Act again simply codifies that requirement. This has not posed any real difficulty in labor injunction cases, however, since money damages for interference with work opportunities and business interests are generally considered inadequate for the purposes of establishing equity jurisdiction.[132] The inadequacy of a damage remedy can also be shown by the fact that the capital resources of many unions would render them effectively judgment proof against an award in any substantial amount.[133] Finally, one court noted with respect to the adequacy issue that subsequent tort and criminal actions would involve a cumbersome and expensive multiplicity of suits against the persons guilty of strike violence.[134]

Local Police Officials Must Be Unable or Unwilling to Furnish Adequate Protection.[135] Of all the substantive requirements of the Norris-LaGuardia Act, this one probably poses the greatest difficulties to a plaintiff seeking to obtain an injunction against union violence.

The congressional purpose behind this requirement "was to leave in the hands of state and local authorities those problems of public order which they [are] capable of handling."[136] While this deference to state authority may have been appropriate in 1932, it seems somewhat anachronistic today. When the Norris-LaGuardia Act was passed in 1932, labor relations were regulated almost entirely by state and local law, with federal district court involvement in the issuance of injunctions thus appearing to be an unwarranted anomaly.

The very opposite, however, is true today. The central premise of modern labor relations law is that labor disputes are truly matters of national or interstate concern which transcend the narrow jurisdictional limits of local authority.[137] Although the states, to be sure, retain jurisdiction over torts and crimes committed within their boundaries,[138] the adequacy or inadequacy of state involvement in no way af-

---

[131] *See* DOBBS, REMEDIES 57-62, 108 (1973).

[132] *Id.* at 59-60; Babcock, *Connecticut State Court Injunctions in Labor Disputes,* 54 Conn. B.J. 37 (1980). *But see,* Richard H. Oswald Co. v. Leader, 20 F. Supp. 876 (E.D. Pa. 1937).

[133] *See* Dean v. Mayo, 9 F. Supp. 459, 462 (W.D. La. 1934), *affirmed,* 82 F.2d 554 (5th Cir. 1936).

[134] Washington Post Co. v. International Printing Union Local 6, 92 L.R.R.M. 2961, 2971 (D.C. Sup. Ct. 1976).

[135] Norris-LaGuardia Act § 7(e), 29 U.S.C. § 107(e) (1976).

[136] Cimarron Coal Corp. v. District 23, UMW, 416 F.2d 844, 847 (6th Cir. 1969), *cert. denied,* 397 U.S. 919 (1970), citing the legislative history.

[137] *See* Labor Management Relations Act § 1, 29 U.S.C. § 141 (1976); R. GORMAN, BASIC TEXT ON LABOR LAW 766 (1976).

[138] Youngdahl v. Rainfair, Inc. 355 U.S. 131, 138-39 (1957).

fects the power of the federal National Labor Relations Board (NLRB) to also deal with such problems when they fall within its jurisdiction.[139] It is not clear why the same should not also be true of the federal district courts.

In any event, the requirement exists, and a person seeking an injunction against labor violence thus has the burden of satisfying it. But, as the court in *Cupples Co. v. A.F.L.* noted,[140] "the question promptly arises: what alleged facts or what proof would be sufficient to establish the fact that local officials are unable or unwilling to furnish adequate protection?"[141] The court in that case, however, outlined three possibilities. Firstly, "if there should be a definite declaration on the part of those officials of unwillingness to act that would be sufficient in that respect."[142] In one case, for example, the plaintiff employer was notified by the sheriff "that he could not incur the expense of deputizing enough persons to give the protection needed."[143] The chief of police had suggested "that the best thing Plaintiff could do to prevent violence would be to accede to the demands of the Defendants' union."[144] And in another case, it was noted that "the Sheriff . . . testified that he could not protect plaintiff's [railroad] line properly because of inadequate force, and he and his deputies did nothing to prevent violence."[145] Presumably, a simple refusal to act serves the same evidentiary function.[146]

The *Cupples* court then continued, secondly, "if, after active cooperation by local officials, bloodshed or violence resulted in spite of that co-operation and assistance, the proof of such facts would be sufficient."[147] In *Bonanno Linen Service Inc. v. McCarthy,*[148] for example, the court found that "the police, though *willing,* were *unable* to afford plaintiffs adequate protection,"[149] citing in this regard the many "in-

---

[139] NLRA § 8(b) (1) (A), 29 U.S.C. § 158(b) (1) (A) (1976), makes union violence an "unfair labor practice." *See generally,* Haggard, *supra* note 4.

[140] 20 F. Supp. 894 (E.D. Mo. 1937).

[141] *Id.* at 899.

[142] *Id.*

[143] Cater Constr. Co. v. Nischwitz, 111 F.2d 971, 973 (7th Cir. 1940).

[144] *Id.*

[145] Toledo P & W. R.R. v. Bhd. of Railroad Trainmen, 132 F.2d 265, 270 (7th Cir. 1942), *rev'd on other grounds,* 321 U.S. 50 (1944).

[146] *See* United Electric Coal Companies v. Rice, 80 F.2d 1 (7th Cir. 1935), *cert. denied,* 297 U.S. 714 (1936); J.B. Michael & Co. v. Iron Workers Local 782, 173 F. Supp. 319 (W.D. Ky. 1959); Lake Charles Stevedores v. Mayo, 20 F. Supp. 698. (W.D. La. 1935) (the district judge noted that the sheriff and the governor, who had both refused to act, were seeking reelection, "and there appears little doubt that this fact accounts for the failure or refusal of these officials to do their duty").

[147] 20 F. Supp. at 899.

[148] 532 F.2d 189 (1st Cir. 1976) (emphasis added).

[149] *Id.* at 190 (emphasis added).

cidents of mass picketing, physical assault, window breaking, tire slashing, blocking of plaintiffs' driveways, and threatening" that had gone on in spite of police attempts to control it.[150] On these facts, the court noted that "there was no need for police admissions of inadequacy."[151]
Thirdly, the court in *Cupples* also noted that

> certainly Congress did not intend that this court should await the declaration on the part of local officers of their unwillingness to perform their duty. Most certainly it did not intend that this court should stand by until actual bloodshed, strife, and violence occur before it should lend its aid to then merely prevent a repetition of what Congress evidently intended should be prevented in the first instance.[152]

The courts, however, seem reluctant to ever act on the basis of such anticipated police unwillingness or inability. The court in *Cupples,* for example, found that the evidence before it failed to create the required "impression" that serious violence would erupt or that the local authorities would be derelict in their duty to curtail it,[153] since they had apparently responded, up to that point, to all of the plaintiff's requests for patrols and escorts.

Likewise, in *Donnelly Garment Co. v. Dubinsky,*[154] the plaintiff presented evidence of inadequate police protection in prior strikes involving this union, together with the testimony of a former member of the Kansas City police force concerning "the impossibility of controlling riotous mobs of women by police action."[155] The court, however, noted that there had been a change in the local government and a complete reorganization of the police force. The court also noted that while the sheriff and chief of police had been notified of the injunction hearing, they had not been called as witnesses by the plaintiff. The court concluded that "their failure justifies, if it does not compel, the inference that the testimony of the absent witnesses would have been against them."[156]

Moreover, it would seem that as long as there is at least some effort that is partially effective, the courts will find the local police protection to be sufficient to defeat federal court jurisdiction—regardless of the obvious volatility of the situation. For example, in *Cimarron Coal Corp.*

---

[150] *Id.*

[151] *Id.*

[152] 20 F. Supp. at 899. For example, in Westinghouse Broadcasting Co. v. Dukakis, 412 F. Supp. 580 (D. Mass. 1976), the court found that the police were unable or unwilling to provide adequate protection because the misconduct, although enjoinable because of its propensity to create violence, was for the most part not criminal in nature.

[153] 20 F. Supp. at 899.

[154] 154 F.2d 38 (8th Cir. 1946).

[155] *Id.* at 42.

[156] *Id.* at 43.

v. District 23, UMW,[157] the union conducted mass picketing outside the plaintiff's mine. The police were called on three different occasions and did manage to clear the roadway each time. But, as was noted by the federal district judge who issued an injunction, "even when they were in the general vicinity . . . two vehicles of employees were turned back."[158] He further concluded that "the public officials made no real meaningful response insofar as escorting or offering to escort or insuring protection to any . . . employee who wished to drive between the parked cars and the large number of defendants' associates there gathered."[159] The Sixth Circuit Court of Appeals reversed the decision, however. It noted that

> the sheriff and some state police did appear and some of the employees did go in to work. From this record it would appear that there was something less than a complete mobilization of law enforcement. There was, however, no failure on the part of the law enforcement officials to respond, no testimony from any law enforcement official . . . pertaining to any breakdown of local or state law enforcement, and no property damage or physical assault upon anyone.[160]

In any event it has been suggested that the necessity of proving the inadequacy of local police protection and the uncertainty that surrounds the resolution of that issue has contributed substantially to the fact that federal injunctions against strike violence are so extremely rare.[161]

The Plaintiff Must Have "Clean Hands." Section 8 of the statute reads as follows:

> No restraining order or injunctive relief shall be granted to any complainant who has failed to comply with any obligation imposed by law which is involved in the labor dispute in question, or who has failed to make every reasonable effort to settle such dispute earlier by negotiation or with the aid of any available governmental machinery of mediation or voluntary arbitration.[162]

Representative O'Connor referred to this as the "clean hands" provision.[163] He explained that "a complainant shall not be entitled to an injunction if he has not complied with any contract or obligation on his

---

[157] 416 F.2d 844 (6th Cir. 1969), *cert. denied*, 397 U.S. 919 (1970).

[158] 416 F.2d at 845.

[159] *Id.* at 845-46.

[160] *Id.* at 845; *see also*, Carter v. Herrin Motor Freight Lines, 131 F.2d 557 (5th Cir. 1942); Kohler Co. v. Sheet Metal Workers Int'l. 468 F. Supp. 1016 (E.D. Tenn. 1979).

[161] Stewart & Towsend, *Strike Violence: The Need for Federal Injunctions*, 114 U. PA. L. REV. 459, 462 (1966).

[162] Norris-LaGuardia Act § 8, 29 U.S.C. § 108 (1976).

[163] 75 CONG. REC. 5464 (1932). This is taken from the maxim of equity that "he who comes into equity must come in with clean hands." D. DOBBS, REMEDIES 45 (1973).

part or has not made every reasonable effort to settle the dispute by the available methods of arbitration or mediation."[164]

In *Brotherhood of Railroad Trainmen v. Toledo, Peoria & Western Railroad*,[165] the Supreme Court concluded that this section of the statute was written in "explicit contemplation of the procedures then existing under the Railway Labor Act,"[166] which requires collective bargaining and establishes machinery for nonbinding mediation or, if the parties agree, for binding arbitration of the dispute.[167] In this case, the railroad had negotiated and had likewise utilized the services of the National Mediation Board; but it had refused to agree to binding arbitration—as was its right under the Railway Labor Act.

The Supreme Court, however, held that by virtue of section 8, the railroad's refusal in that regard disqualified it from being entitled to an injunction against the violence that had erupted when the union went out on strike over the dispute. In so holding, the Supreme Court rejected two theories that the lower court had relied on in finding that the requirements of section 8 were either inapplicable or had been complied with in this case. Firstly, the lower court had held that the section did not apply where an injunction was being sought against violence.[168] Another court which had reached the same conclusion indicated "that Congress did not intend to require an employer to negotiate or mediate a dispute with those who were, by intimidation, coercion and violence, threatening the destruction of its property and the right to work of those under legal contract."[169] The Supreme Court, however, held otherwise, suggesting—with a perverse sort of logic—that satisfaction of that duty might well bring the violence to an end and thus make an injunction unnecessary.[170]

Secondly, the lower court had also held that the requirements of section 8 could be satisfied by either mediation or arbitration,[171] and that

---

[164] 45 Cong. Rec. 5464 (1932).

[165] 321 U.S. 50 (1944).

[166] *Id.* at 58.

[167] Railway Labor Act §§ 5, 7, 45 U.S.C. §§ 155, 157 (1976).

[168] 132 F.2d at 271.

[169] Cater Constr. Co. v. Nischwitz, 111 F.2d 971, 977 (7th Cir. 1940).

[170] 321 U.S. at 65.

[171] 132 F.2d at 271. Similarly, the court in Mayo v. Dean, 82 F.2d 554, 556 (5th Cir. 1936), stated that the plaintiff satisfied section 8 "by availing himself of the services of the mediator of the Department of Labor. He was not obliged to propose both mediation and arbitration. One or the other would be sufficient." That case did not involve a railroad subject to the Railway Labor Act. The court of appeals in the *Toledo* case had relied on *Mayo*, however, as authority for the proposition that "the employer is not compelled to avail himself of all three methods; any one of them will fulfill the requirements." 132 F.2d at 271. Conceivably, when the Supreme Court overruled the court of appeals decision in *Toledo*, it also overruled the authority on which the court had relied with respect to this point. *See* 321 U.S. at 61 n. 19. If that is true, then this would logically sug-

since the railroad in this case had participated in mediation it had thus done all that was required. Again, the Supreme Court disagreed:

> Broadly, the section imposed two conditions. If a complainant has failed (1) to comply with any obligation imposed by law or (2) to make every reasonable effort to settle the dispute, he is forbidden relief. The latter condition is broader than the former. . . . The explicit terms demand "*every reasonable effort*" to settle the dispute. Three modes are specified (negotiation, mediation, and arbitration). . . . And its very terms show they were used . . . with the intent of making their exhaustion conditions for securing injunctive relief, not singly or alternatively, but conjunctively or successively, when available.[172]

Although the Supreme Court in this case indicated that "section 8 is not limited to railway labor disputes," subsequent courts have tended to construe the decision narrowly insofar as it concerns nonrailway labor controversies. For example, in *Bonanno Linen Service, Inc. v. McCarthy*,[173] the union argued that the district court's injunction against strike violence violated the provisions of the Norris-LaGuardia Act because the employers had never offered to submit the collective bargaining dispute to arbitration. The First Circuit Court of Appeals rejected this argument, however. It noted that as construed by the Supreme Court in *Toledo*, "the statute does not speak of any voluntary arbitration, but rather requires resort only to 'any available governmental machinery of . . . voluntary arbitration.' Such machinery does exist in the Railway Labor Act, . . . but there is no parallel machinery in the present context."[174]

This is a reasonable interpretation of the statute. Outside the railroad and a few other industries, so-called "interest arbitration," where the parties agree to be bound by a private third party's determination of new contract terms,[175] is a relatively rare phenomenon; and if an employer were required to offer to so bind itself as a condition of obtaining an injunction against violence, then there would probably be no federal injunctions at all!

---

gest that even non-railroad employers are required to offer to submit a dispute to binding arbitration as a condition of obtaining an injunction against violence that occurs in connection with a strike over that dispute. That, however, is contrary to the literal words of the statute and the weight of current authority. *See* text at notes 117 & 118.

[172] 321 U.S. at 56-58.

[173] 532 F.2d 189 (1st Cir. 1976).

[174] *Id.* at 191; *see* Washington Post Company v. International Printing Union Local 6, 92 L.R.R.M. 2961, 2974 (D.C. Sup. Ct. 1976) ("The arbitration language of Section 8 was clearly intended to apply to labor disputes governed by a law which creates specific governmental machinery for arbitration, such as the Railway Labor Act, ... Neither the National Labor Relations Act . . . nor any other law compels resort to such a remedy here").

[175] *See generally,* D. NOLAN, LABOR ARBITRATION LAW AND PRACTICE 224-37 (1979). (emphasis added.)

On the other hand, "governmental machinery of *mediation*" clearly is available even outside the Railway Labor Act. In particular, the Federal Mediation and Conciliation Service has permissive jurisdiction over a wide range of industrial disputes.[176] The service, for example, had been involved in the *Bonanno* negotiations.[177] Before seeking an injunction against union violence, an employer would probably be required to utilize either this service or an equivalent state or local mediation and conciliation service.

While this may appear to be a desirable policy, the observations of an opponent of the Norris-LaGuardia Act are also pertinent here. Representative Beck, in commenting on section 8, noted that

> although the defendant may, without notice, organize industrial war through fraud, violence, and other unlawful acts, . . . the aggrieved may not defend himself by securing injunctive relief without tolerating the violence until he has gone through various steps of peaceful negotiation. While plaintiff is negotiating, the situation may become beyond any possibility of judicial relief.[178]

Despite the broad reading that the *Toledo* decision generally gives to section 8, most of the courts have also not required an employer, as a condition, of obtaining an injunction, to negotiate or bargain with a union when doing so would constitute a breach of the employer's statutory duty to recognize and bargain with some other union as the exclusive representative of its employees.[179] This, too, is a reasonable interpretation of the statute. It would be anomalous indeed to require an employer to commit an unfair labor practice under the NLRA as a necessary condition of obtaining an injunction under the Norris-LaGuardia Act.

On the other hand, even if a complainant satisfies the specific arbitration/mediation requirements of section 8, it must still also satisfy the broader, nonstatutory aspects of the clean hands principle. For example, in the *Washington Post* case the union claimed that the employer lacked clean hands because it had broken certain "anti-strike breaker laws," had illegally induced union resignations, and had bargained in bad faith.[180] Although such conduct, if proven, might conceivably disable an employer from obtaining relief in a court of equity, in that case the court found the claims to be unsubstantiated.

---

[176] *See* NLRA §§ 202 & 203, 29 U.S.C. §§ 172 & 173 (1976).

[177] 532 F.2d at 190. Similarly, a representative of FMCS had attended all but the first six negotiating sessions in the *Washington Post* case, 92 L.R.R.M. at 2974.

[178] 75 Cong. Rec. 5471 (1932).

[179] J.B. Michael & Co. v. Iron Workers Local 782, 173 F. Supp. 319 (W.D. Ky. 1959); *see also,* Cupples Co. v. American Federation of Labor, 20 F. Supp. 894, 900 (E.D. Mo. 1937). *But see,* Carter v. Herrin Motor Freight Lines, 131 F.2d 557, 561 (5th Cir. 1942).

[180] 92 L.R.R.M. at 2974-75.

Those then are the substantive requirements that must be satisfied before a complainant is entitled to a federal injunction against labor union violence. Since in several particulars they go beyond what is usually required in order to obtain a state court injunction against such violence, the net effect is to actively discourage resort to the federal forum for this kind of equitable relief.

Miscellaneous Procedural Requirements

In addition to the substantive elements of the proof that must be satisfied, the Norris-LaGuardia Act also imposes some rather involved procedural requirements.

Section 107, for example, provides that no temporary or permanent injunction can be issued by a federal judge "except after hearing the testimony of witnesses in open court (with opportunity for cross-examination)."[181] Moreover, "such hearing shall be held after due and personal notice thereof has been given . . . to all known persons against whom relief is sought."[182] On the basis of the testimony and evidence adduced at such a hearing, the judge must then be able to find that the substantive requirements of the Norris-LaGuardia Act which were previously discussed, have been satisfied. Presumably, this was intended to prevent the issuance of injunctions on an *ex parte* basis—one of the alleged abuses that led to the Norris-LaGuardia Act.[183]

The courts, fortunately, have tended to take a realistic view of the requirements that there be an evidentiary hearing with actual testimony and that the judge make formal findings of the relevant facts. As the Sixth Circuit Court of Appeals once stated,

> it is true that if there is no dispute between the parties about the facts, the allegations of a complaint may be accepted as true, thus eliminating the necessity of formal findings. . . . But if the allegations of a complaint are denied by a defendant, he is entitled to a hearing, which includes the right to offer evidence in support of his factual claims. . . . A hearing embodies the right to be heard on the controverted facts, as well as upon the law.[184]

For example, in *Railway Express Agency v. Brotherhood of Railway Clerks,*[185] no witnesses were called at the hearing, the parties stated

---

[181] Norris-LaGuardia Act § 7, 29 U.S.C. § 107 (1976).

[182] *Id.* This apparently means notice in time for the defendant to prepare adequately for the hearing. CeloTex Corp. v. Oil Workers Int'l. Union, 377 F. Supp. 750, 753 (M.D. Pa. 1974), *rev'd on other grounds,* 516 F.2d 242 (3d Cir. 1975). (4 hours notice not adequate).

[183] *See* text at note 12, *supra.*

[184] Carpenters' District Council, United Bhd. of Carpenters v. Cicci, 261 F.2d 5, 8 (6th Cir. 1958); *see* Detroit & Toledo Shore Line R.R. v. Brotherhood of Locomotive Firemen, 357 F.2d 152 (6th Cir. 1966).

[185] 437 F.2d 388 (5th Cir.), *cert. denied,* 403 U.S. 919 (1971).

their positions, stipulated all the crucial facts, and filed briefs and affidavits. The union then claimed that the subsequent injunction was issued in clear violation of the Norris-LaGuardia Act. The Fifth Circuit Court of Appeals disagreed, however. It noted that the resolution of the still disputed facts in the union's favor would not affect the result, and that the union also appeared to have waived oral testimony by witnesses. The court concluded that there was no violation "under these limited circumstances."[186]

In addition, however, to requiring pre-hearing notification to everyone against whom injunctive relief is being sought, the act also requires "due and personal notice . . . to the chief of those public officials of the county and city within which the unlawful acts have been threatened or committed charged with the duty to protect complainant's property."[187] Since an injunction cannot be issued in the absence of a finding that the local police are unable or unwilling to control the situation,[188] Congress apparently did "not want to make that imputation against the officers without giving them the opportunity to reply to it, and so notice is to be given to them that they may come in and say, if they can say so, 'We are perfectly able to take care of the situation.'"[189]

These requirements of notice and the opportunity for an adversary hearing apply, however, only to the issuance of a temporary or permanent injunction; a temporary restraining order can still be obtained without them. In order to obtain such temporary relief, however, a complainant must first allege that without it "a substantial and irreparable injury to the complainant's property will be unavoidable."[190] In other words, as explained by Senator Norris, "it must . . . appear, before a temporary restraining order can be issued without notice, that the giving of the notice would of itself result in irreparable damage to the complainant's property."[191] That explanation thus serves to distinguish the irreparable injury that must be shown here from the irreparable injury that would have to be shown in any event.[192] Secondly, such a temporary order can be issued only "upon testimony under oath,"[193] thus apparently precluding the mere use of affidavits.[194]

---

[186] *Id.* at 395; *see also* Missouri-Kansas-Texas R. Co. v. Brotherhood of Locomotive Engineers, 266 F.2d 335, 339 (5th Cir. 1959), *rev'd on other grounds,* 363 U.S. 528 (1960).

[187] Norris-LaGuardia Act § 7, 29 U.S.C. § 107 (1976).

[188] *See* text at notes 135-161 *supra.*

[189] 75 CONG. REC. 4998 (1932).

[190] Norris-LaGuardia Act § 7, 29 U.S.C. § 107 (1976).

[191] 75 CONG. REC. 4508 (1932).

[192] *See* text at notes 59-66, *supra.*

[193] Norris-LaGuardia Act § 7, 29 U.S.C. § 107 (1976).

[194] *See* 75 CONG. REC. 5464 (1932).

Thirdly, such testimony must be "sufficient, if sustained, to justify the court in issuing a temporary injunction upon a hearing after notice."[195]

If a complainant does obtain a temporary restraining order, the act nevertheless provides that it shall not be effective for longer than five days.[196] In *Toledo, P. & W. Railroad v. Brotherhood of Railroad Trainmen,*[197] the complainant obtained a temporary restraining order, and the required hearing on the temporary injunction was begun within five days. There were, however, many witnesses to be heard and the judge thus found it necessary to extend the temporary order twice; an injunction was ultimately issued. The union argued that the extended temporary restraining order violated the act's five-day limit. The Seventh Circuit Court of Appeals disagreed. It noted that the purpose of the five-day limit was to prevent a defendant from being restrained any longer than that without the opportunity for a hearing on the matter. But once a hearing was begun, that purpose was satisfied; and to allow a resumption of the previously restrained conduct during the pendency of a hearing on the matter would subject the complainant to further irreparable damage and thus destroy the very purpose of the original temporary restraining order.[198]

Finally, in order to obtain either a temporary restraining order or a temporary injunction, a complainant is required by the act to first file a security bond in an amount "sufficient to recompense those enjoined for any loss, expense, or damage caused by the improvident issuance of such order or injunction, including all reasonable costs (together with a reasonable attorney's fee) and expense of defense against the order."[199]

Finally, in any contempt proceedings arising out of violations of a Norris-LaGuardia Act injunction, the defendant is by statute entitled to a trial by jury.[200]

INJUNCTIVE RELIEF UNDER STATE LAW

Because of the jurisdictional, substantive, and procedural obstacles that a complainant faces when attempting to obtain a federal court injunction against labor union violence, the more common source of such relief has been the state and local courts. Although these state forums are thought to be generally more hospitable to suits of this kind, a com-

---

[195] Norris-LaGuardia Act § 7, 29 U.S.C. § 107 (1976).
[196] *Id.*
[197] 132 F.2d 265 (7th Cir. 1942), *reversed on other grounds,* 321 U.S. 50 (1944).
[198] 132 F.2d at 267.
[199] Norris-LaGuardia Act § 7, 29 U.S.C. § 7 (1976).
[200] 18 U.S.C. § 3692 (1976) (originally section 11 of the Norris-LaGuardia Act).

plainant will still often be confronted with a variety of complex issues. The injunction must not be so broad as to intrude upon the constitutional rights of the defendants. Care must be taken to avoid the obscure and shifting pitfalls of the federal preemption doctrine. Even in the absence of more specific statutory requirements, a complainant must still satisfy the general equitable prerequisites for such relief. And when statutory requirements exist, as they do in most states, they too must be satisfied.

Constitutional Limits

At one point in its history, the Supreme Court seemed to be of the view that the manner in which labor unions usually picketed was inherently intimidating and coercive,[201] and that the courts not only had the power but also the constitutional duty to enjoin it.[202] In 1940, however, the Court changed its tune radically and began to regard such picketing as simply another form of speech presumably falling under the broad protective umbrella of the First and Fourteenth Amendments.[203] In the years that followed, the Court was confronted with the task of staking out a middle ground between those two poles of thought. The results, however, have been generally confusing. As one court stated, "He who searches for constitutional principles governing injunctions directed against picketing is destined to conduct his investigation in an area which, at best, must be described as a twilight zone."[204]

Most of the controversy and litigation in this area has focused on the question of whether otherwise "peaceful" picketing can be enjoined simply because it seeks to attain some objective which state law deems offensive.[205] The evolution of the law in this area was traced by the Supreme Court in *International Brotherhood of Teamsters Local 695 v. Vogt, Inc.,*[206] in which the Court concluded that a state could constitutionally enjoin even peaceful picketing "when such picketing was counter to valid state policy in a domain open to state regulation."[207] Subsequently, the narrowing of that open domain by the federal pre-

---

[201] American Steel Foundries v. Tri City Central Trades Council, 257 U.S. 184, 204-05 (1921).

[202] Truax v. Corrigan, 257 U.S. 312 (1921).

[203] Thornhill v. Alabama, 310 U.S. 88 (1940).

[204] United Farm Workers Organizing Committee v. LaCasita Farms, Inc. 439 S.W.2d 398, 401 (Ct. of Civil App., Texas, 1968).

[205] *See generally,* Etelson, *Picketing and Freedom of Speech: Comes the Evolution,* 10 JOHN MARSHALL J. OF PRAC. & PROC. 1 (1976); Samoff, *Picketing and the First Amendment: "Full Circle" and "Formal Surrender,"* 9 LABOR L.J. 889 (1958).

[206] 354 U.S. 284 (1957).

[207] *Id.* at 291.

emption doctrine substantially mooted the issue with respect to constitutionally enjoinable union objectives.[208] In any event, we are not concerned here with peaceful picketing.

The other aspect of the middle ground that the Court was left to define involved the means or manner of picketing. The difficulties here have not proved to be great, however. In *Thornhill v. Alabama,*[209] the case which first formally elevated picketing to a constitutionally protected status, the Court conceded that "the power and the duty of the State to take adequate steps to preserve the peace and to protect the privacy, the lives, and the property of its residents cannot be doubted."[210] Although the Court also suggested that otherwise peaceful picketing could not be enjoined merely on the presumption that it would lead to violence and breaches of the peace,[211] in the following year it identified a situation in which such an injunction would be constitutionally permissible.

In *Milk Wagon Drivers Local 753 v. Meadowmoor Dairies, Inc.,*[212] the Court adhered to the *Thornhill* view that picketing could indeed serve the function of informing and eliciting support, and that as such it had to be recognized as a form of expression protected by the First Amendment. But the Court also went on to say that "utterance in a context of violence can lose its significance as an appeal to reason [which is what the First Amendment, the Court said, was designed to protect] and become an instrument of force. Such utterance was not meant to be sheltered by the Constitution."[213] In that case, there had been violence on a "considerable scale"—windows smashed; trucks wrecked, burned, and pushed into the river; plants damaged by bombs; stench bombs thrown; stores set afire; and storekeepers and drivers threatened, shot at, held at gun point, and beaten.[214] Consequently, a state court had enjoined all subsequent picketing, an order which the Supreme Court held to be constitutional. It noted that "the picketing in this case was set in a background of violence. In such a setting it could justifiably be concluded that the momentum of fear generated by past violence would survive even though future picketing might be wholly peaceful."[215]

On the other hand, the Court also cautioned that "the right of free speech cannot be denied by drawing from a trivial rough incident or a

---

[208] Samoff, *supra* note 214, at 901.
[209] 310 U.S. 88 (1940).
[210] *Id.* at 105.
[211] *Id.* at 106.
[212] 312 U.S. 287 (1941).
[213] *Id.* at 293.
[214] *Id.* at 291-92.
[215] *Id.* at 294.

moment of animal exuberance the conclusion that otherwise peaceful picketing has the taint of force."[216] Other than that, the *Meadowmoor* case left undefined the quantum of prior picket line violence that is necessary before a state court can be constitutionally justified in enjoining *all* subsequent picketing, including its otherwise peaceful aspects. Later Supreme Court cases have not shed a great deal of light on that issue either.

In a 1943 case, for example, the Court merely stated that the *Meadowmoor* "record disclosed abuses deemed not episodic and isolated but of the very texture and process of the enjoined picketing."[217] In *Youngdahl v. Rainfair, Inc.,*[218] the Court referred to *Meadowmoor* as involving "a pattern of violence . . . which would inevitably reappear in the event picketing were later resumed,"[219] while the Court said of the case before it that "what violence there was was scattered in time and much of it was unconnected with the picketing."[220]

The state courts have expressed the *Meadowmoor* doctrine in similar terms. As one court rather aptly put it, "the power of equity totally to proscribe picketing conducted for a lawful purpose is limited to those instances where violence so pervades the texture of defendant's activity 'that peaceful picketing is impossible' . . . or where there exists 'no ray of hope that defendants would engage in other than violent

---

[216] *Id.* at 293. Justice Frankfurter's unfortunate phrase, "animal exuberance" has subsequently been taken out of the context of its origin and has, indeed, assumed doctrinal dimensions of its own. As it was used by Justice Frankfurter, the phrase merely refers to picket line misconduct which is not sufficiently serious to poison the entire picketing endeavor; there is *no* intimation that the "animal exuberance" itself is protected or immune from injunctive or other relief. In later years, however, the phrase has come to mean just that! As used by arbitrators, the NLRB, and the courts—who, like Humpty-Dumpty, can apparently make a word mean whatever they choose it to mean—the phrase "animal exuberance" now serves to identify "minor" picket line rowdyism, intimidation, and misconduct which the law will nevertheless affirmatively protect against even the employer self-help remedy of discharge from employment. *See, e.g.,* Allied Indus. Workers v. NLRB, 476 F.2d 868, 879-80 (D.C. Cir. 1973); Local 19. Hotel Union, 240 N.L.R.B. 240 (1979); Bin-Dicator Co., 143 N.L.R.B. 964 (1963), *enforcement denied in relevant part,* NLRB v. Bin-Dicator Co., 356 F.2d 210, 215-16 (6th Cir. 1966). Southern Bell Tel. & Tel. Co., 26 Lab. Arb. 186, 192 (1956) (McCoy, Arb.). I suspect that Justice Frankfurter would not be pleased with this particular perversion of his terminology.

[217] Cafeteria Employees Union, Local 203 v. Angelos, 320 U.S. 296 (1943). Similarly, in AFL v. Swing, 312 U.S. 321, 323 (1941), the Court stated that "acts of picketing when blended with violence may have a significance which neutralizes the constitutional immunity which such acts would have in isolation."

[218] 355 U.S. 131 (1957).

[219] *Id.* at 139.

[220] *Id.*

picketing."[221] Another court construed *Meadowmoor* as holding that "picketing would be enjoined where it is attended with acts of violence and its continuance excites reasonable fears that violence will be resumed,"[222] with the emphasis being on the threat of future coercion that is implicit in the prior violence.[223]

Whether all picketing can be blamed under the *Meadowmoor* doctrine depends, in the last analysis, however, upon the court's perception of the facts, with such bans being upheld in some cases but not others.[224,225]

Although the *Meadowmoor* doctrine can be used to justify a ban on all picketing, it is also often used by the state courts to justify limits on the number or location of pickets.[226] In one case, for example, the court ordered that there be no more than two pickets within five feet of any entrance or exit.[227] This limit, the court said, was justified by the trial court's finding that union pickets had blocked entrances and driveways and had harassed and intimidated customers of the boycotted stores.[228]

On the other hand, even if the past violence rises to the level required under the *Meadowmoor* doctrine, there are still constitutional limits on what kinds of union activity can be enjoined. This issue arose in what is undoubtedly the most notorious case of union violence in recent times, *Altemose Constr. Co. v. Building & Constr. Trades Council of Philadelphia.*[229] In 1972, as a part of an ongoing program of violence and coercion against nonunionized construction firms in the Philadelphia area,[230] the Building and Construction Trades Council launched what the trial judge referred to as "a virtual military assault" upon a con-

---

[221] Waldbaum Inc. v. United Farm Workers, 383 N.Y.S.2d 957, 969 (Supreme Court, Queens County 1976).

[222] Emery v. Hotel Employees Union Local 556, 161 N.W.2d 842, 847 (Minn. 1968), *cert. denied,* 394 U.S. 455 (1969).

[223] *See also,* United Farm Workers Organizing Committee v. LaCasita Farms, Inc. 439 S.W.2d 398, 402 (Tex. Ct. of Civ. App., 1968).

[224] *See, e.g.,* Trans-Western Express, Ltd. v. Local 17, Int'l. Bhd. of Teamsters, 603 P.2d 959 (Colo. Ct. of Appeals, 1979); United Farm Workers Organizing Committee v. LaCasita Farms, Inc., 439 S.W.2d 398 (Tex. Ct. of Civ. App., 1968); Steiner v. Long Beach Local 128, Oil Workers Int'l. Union, 123 P.2d 20 (Cal. Sup. Ct. 1942).

[225] *See, e.g.,* Walbaum, Inc. v. United Farm Workers, 383 N.Y.S.2d 957 (Supreme Court, 1976); Pueblo Bldg. & Constr. Trades Council v. Harper Constr. Co., 204 P.2d 468 (Colo. 1957).

[226] *See, e.g.,* M Restaurants, Inc. v. San Francisco Local, Joint Executive Board of Culinary Workers, 177 Cal. Rptr. 690 (Ct. of Appeal, 1981); Baton Rouge Coca Cola Bottling Co. v. General Truck Drivers Local 5, 403 So.2d 632 (La. Sup. Ct. 1981); International Molders Union v. Superior Court, 138 Cal. Rptr. 794 (Ct. of Appeal, 1977). *But see,* Eads Coal Co. v. UMW, 327 N.E.2d 115 (Ill. App. Ct., 1975).

[227] PTA Sales, Inc. v. Retail Clerks Local 462, 633 P.2d 689, 692 (N.M. 1981).

[228] *Id.* at 691, 693.

[229] 296 A.2d 504 (Pa. 1972), *cert. denied,* 411 U.S. 932 (1973).

[230] In the preceding six months, members of this confederation of unions had attacked a nonunion employee of another construction company, causing multiple fractures, contusions, lacerations, a concussion and $900 worth of dental damage; they had violated a

struction site where Altemose was building a hotel and office building.[231] Approximately 1,000 militant unionists arrived in union-chartered buses and a caravan of private automobiles and proceeded to dismantle the project.

> Damage was estimated at $300,000 and including the following: 4,000 feet of eight-foot high cyclone fence was leveled; an office building, guard hut, and construction trailer were burned to the ground; bulldozers, graders and pans were set afire, or battered with hammers and bars, and lime was added to the fuel tanks of these vehicles. Two security guards were stoned and their vehicle totally destroyed. Local police were impotent to control the mob, and fire trucks dispatched to the scene were turned back because the safety of the firemen was endangered. Throughout this entire scene of violence and destruction a crowd of members of the Council cheered; not until the state police arrived was order restored.[232]

Subsequently, a state court judge issued a preliminary order which, *inter alia*, enjoined the union (1) from engaging in all acts of violence, coercion, and intimidation; (2) from "having any pickets in front of or in close proximity to any entrance" to Altemose construction sites;[233] and (3) from "congregating or assembling in groups within one mile of any" Altemose construction site.[234]

On appeal, the propriety and constitutionality of the last two elements of the injunction caused an evenly divided split among the members of the Pennsylvania Supreme Court. In an opinion subscribed to by three members of the court,[235] it was noted that "defendants' actions involved more than a few isolated incidents of misconduct; rather it demonstrated a pattern of violence coupled with intimidation, harassment, and fear which would inevitably turn even peaceful picketing to violence."[236] The total ban on *picketing* was thus justified under the *Meadowmoor* doctrine.[237]

On the other hand, the prohibition against all union *assemblies* within one mile of any Altemose location caused even this coalition of the court some difficulty. Relying on the United States Supreme Court's

---

prior court order limiting the number of pickets at a particular construction site, and had even engaged in target practice while on picket duty by firing at tin cans; they had beaten two employees of another contractor into unconsciousness; two employees of a roofing contractor were beaten after one of the affiliated unions had lost an NLRB election; seven trucks of that contractor had been fire bombed; and the president and other employees of Altemose Construction Company had received threats to their lives and to those of their families. 296 A.2d at 509. *See also,* Ditzen, *The Roofers: A Study in Union Violence,* The Evening Bulletin, Philadelphia, Penn., July 15, 16, 17, & 18, 1974.

[231] 296 A.2d at 507.
[232] *Id.*
[233] *Id.* at 508 n.5.
[234] *Id.*
[235] Justices Pomeroy, Jones, and Eagen.
[236] 296 A.2d at 514.
[237] *Id.* at 513.

admonition that "an order issued in the area of First Amendment rights must be couched in the narrowest terms that will accomplish the pin-pointed objective permitted by constitutional mandate and the essential needs of the public order,"[238] they concluded that the one-mile prohibition was too broad. Such a prohibition would cover all union meetings, whether directed at Altemose or not; and depending upon the placements of Altemose construction sites, the defendants' First Amendment liberties could be curtailed over a substantial area of southeastern Pennsylvania.[239] They agreed, therefore, that the order should be modified to prohibit the defendants "from congregating or assembly within 200 yards" of any Altemose construction site.[240]

Three other members of the Pennsylvania Supreme Court thought, however, that such an order was still unconstitutionally broad.[241] In their view, 200 yards was no better than one mile, since "both restrictions place the union essentially out of sight of the focus of its protest and consequently serve to effectively deny the right of meaningful protest."[242] These judges were apparently of the view that *Meadowmoor* was not at all a currently viable doctrine of constitutional law; certainly, if the massive violence against Altemose was insufficient to justify a total ban on further picketing, then it is difficult to imagine what *would* trigger the application of the doctrine. On the other hand, these three justices did concede that some limits were constitutionally permissible—namely, that the picketing be limited to ten pickets, in motion at all times, and spaced not less than fifteen feet apart in a single line.[243]

In conclusion, the dimensions of *Meadowmoor,* as a constitutional law doctrine, remain relatively obscure and unexplored. This is due in part to the fact that the question of how far state courts can go in enjoining labor union activity is now more apt to be resolved under the preemption doctrine than under the First Amendment.

The Preemption Doctrine

By virtue of the Supremacy Clause of the Constitution,[244] the federal laws which extensively regulate the labor-management relationship

---

[238] Carroll v. President and Commissioners, 393 U.S. 175, 183-84 (1968).

[239] 296 A.2d at 515.

[240] *Id.*

[241] Justices Roberts, Nix, and Manderino.

[242] 296 A.2d at 506.

[243] *Id.* The other three members of the court said that "the limited picketing suggested in the separate opinion, while appropriate in many types of mass picketing situations, . . . is not realistic or adequate in a situation such as confronted the chancellor in this case." *Id.* at 515 n. 1/2.

[244] U.S. CONST. art. VI.

operate generally to preempt all state and local regulation in the same area.[245] More specifically, as the Supreme Court stated in *San Diego Building Trades Council v. Garmon,*[246] if conduct is either arguably *prohibited* or *protected* by federal law, then it will be presumed that it was the intent of Congress for such laws to supersede all state and local laws dealing with the same matter. On the other hand, the Court in that case also indicated that such intent will not be so readily inferred with respect to matters "deeply rooted in local feeling and responsibility,"[247] with physical assaults, threats, and general public disorder being perhaps the clearest example of that. As the Court put it in another case, "the States are the natural guardians of the public against violence. It is the local communities that suffer most from the fear and loss occasioned by coercion and destruction."[248]

Thus, although most strike and picket line violence is clearly and affirmatively prohibited by the NLRA,[249] it has long been recognized that state prohibition of such conduct is also allowed—whether it is through the operation of the state's criminal laws,[250] the imposition of compensatory tort damages,[251] administrative proceedings,[252] or the issuance of injunctions.[253] Regarding the latter, there is, however, a problem with respect to the possibility of overly broad injunctive relief. In *Youngdahl v. Rainfair, Inc.,*[254] for example, the Supreme Court upheld those portions of the state court injunction which prohibited physical obstruction, threats, and the provocation of violence; but the Court also held that the injunction's total prohibition against all further picketing and patrolling encroached upon the preempted federal domain.

The employer, on the other hand, had attempted to justify that blanket prohibition by reference to the *Meadowmoor* doctrine of tainted picketing. Significantly, here the Supreme Court merely held that the prior violence in that case did not rise to the necessary level—thus

---

[245] *See generally,* R. GORMAN, BASIC TEXT ON LABOR LAW 766-86 (1976).

[246] 359 U.S. 236 (1959).

[247] *Id.* at 244.

[248] United Automobile Workers v. Wisconsin Employment Relations Board, 351 U.S. 266, 274-75 (1956).

[249] NLRA § 8(b) (1), 29 U.S.C. § 158(b) (1) (1976). *See generally,* Haggard, *Labor Union Violence as an Unfair Labor Practice,* 34 S.C.L. REV. 258 (1982).

[250] *See* United Automobile Workers v. Wisconsin Employment Relations Board, 251 U.S. 266, 272-73 & n.10 (1955); DeGregory v. Gresing, 427 F. Supp. 910, 912 n.1 (D. Conn. 1977).

[251] United Automobile Workers v. Russell, 356 U.S. 634 (1958); United Constr. Workers v. Laburnum Constr. Corp., 347 U.S. 656 (1954).

[252] United Automobile Workers v. Wisconsin Employment Relations Board, 351 U.S. 266 (1956).

[253] Youngdahl v. Rainfair, Inc., 355 U.S. 131 (1957).

[254] 355 U.S. 131 (1957).

perhaps suggesting that if the injunction could pass the *Meadowmoor* constitutional test, it would also escape the strictures of the preemption doctrine.

The logical symmetry of that suggested relationship was, however, subsequently destroyed in *UMW v. Gibbs.*[255] There, the union was sued for damages caused by strike violence. On the preemption issue, it was noted that "this Court has consistently recognized the right of States to deal with violence and threats of violence appearing in labor disputes."[256] But the Court then went on to caution that "the permissible scope of state remedies in this area is strictly confined to the direct consequences of such conduct."[257] The employer, in other words, was entitled to recover damages flowing only from the union's acts of violence, and not from the consequences of otherwise peaceful picketing. The employer here, however, also attempted to rely on the *Meadowmoor* theory of tainted picketing as a ground for recovering additional damages. But the Supreme Court rejected the argument, this time noting that *Meadowmoor* was a constitutional and not a preemption case.[258]

The logical inference, of course, is that although the First and Fourteenth Amendments do not necessarily deny states the power to enjoin picketing that is tainted with prior violence, the Supremacy Clause, operating through the preemption doctrine, does nevertheless have just that effect. In other words, it would appear that the preemption doctrine operates above and beyond the First and Fourteenth Amendment limits on the power of states to enjoin union activities.

If, thus, a state court does issue an overly broad injunction that encroaches upon the preempted federal domain, this may prompt the National Labor Relations Board (NLRB) to obtain a federal court order against the enforcement of the impermissible and preempted aspects of the state degree. In *NLRB v. Nash-Finch Co.,*[259] a state court had issued a very broad restraining order which limited the number of pickets, prohibited loitering and patrolling, enjoined the pickets from distributing handbills and other literature, and otherwise went beyond the mere prohibition of force and violence. The Supreme Court there sustained the NLRB's power and authority to seek an injunction against the state court's intrusion into the regulation of peaceful picketing which, it held, was governed exclusively by the federal agency.

When the exercise of the state's traditional police power is consistent

---

[255] 383 U.S. 715 (1966).
[256] *Id.* at 729.
[257] *Id.*
[258] *Id.* at 731.
[259] 404 U.S. 138 (1971).

with what federal law is also trying to accomplish, as in the prohibition of physical assaults and other forms of picket line misconduct discussed above, the argument in favor of preemption is far from compelling, and the notion of concurrent state and federal (administrative) jurisdiction has thus been an easy one for the courts to accept. On the other hand, when the traditional exercise of the state's police power over coercive conduct arguably conflicts with the provisions of federal law, considerations of federal supremacy clearly come into play and it becomes much more difficult to avoid the conclusion that state law must give way. That kind of conflict can arise, for example, whenever a state court attempts to enjoin the continuing trespass of labor union organizers and adherents onto private, company property.

Although there is an obvious qualitative difference between mere trespass onto property and the violent destruction of that property, in a broader generic or philosophical sense both represent a coercive interference with the rights of another. As such, trespass lies at least on the outer parameters of the subject of this book. Moreover, like physical assault and threats of violence, trespass is a legitimate matter of local concern and well within the police powers of the state to prohibit.

On the other hand, under narrow circumstances, federal labor law grants union organizers an affirmative right of access to an employer's premises.[260] Thus, there is a potential conflict between what state trespass laws prohibit and what federal labor laws permit.

In *Sears, Roebuck & Co. v. San Diego County District Council of Carpenters,*[261] the Supreme Court was faced with just such a conflict. There, the union established picket lines on the company's property. Pickets refused to leave when asked to do so, and the company then obtained a state court injunction against the continuing trespass. This, however, was set aside by the California Supreme Court on the grounds, *inter alia,* that since the picketing was arguably protected by the federal statute, state jurisdiction over the dispute was preempted.

The United States Supreme Court reversed. After a thorough review of preemption theory and precedent, the Court concluded that the conundrum should be resolved as follows: before seeking a state court injunction, the employer must first demand that the union discontinue the trespass. Such a demand will give the union the opportunity to invoke the preemptive jurisdiction of the NLRB, which could then actually decide the question of the union's federal right of access. If the right exists, then the state law is obviously preempted. If, however, the union does not file unfair labor practice charges (or, presumably, if the

[260] *See* NLRB v. Babcock & Wilcox Co., 351 U.S. 105 (1956).
[261] 436 U.S. 180 (1978).

NLRB decides that under the circumstances the union has no right of access), then the Court said that the employer should be free to pursue whatever state remedies are available for this property-rights violation, including an injunction against its continuation, without hindrance from the federal preemption doctrine.[262]

In sum, although the preemption doctrine defines the outer limits of state court power to enjoin strike and picket line misconduct, this does not appear to be a serious obstacle, and the limits are sufficiently broad to enable a state court to restore at least a modicum of peace and order to an industrial dispute that has been marred with acts of violence.

Equitable and Statutory Prerequisites for State Court Injunctions

If strike and picket line misconduct is egregious enough to be neither constitutionally protected nor within the exclusive jurisdiction of federal administrative law, then it follows almost as a matter of course that state court injunctive relief will, unless barred by statute, be appropriate and forthcoming. The details of the law in this area vary, of course, from jurisdiction to jurisdiction; but a general review of the salient judicial principles and statutory provisions is possible.

In the absence of specific statutory prerequisites, the availability of injunctive relief in a labor dispute is governed by the same standards that would apply in any other kind of case.[263] One court recently stated the controlling test as follows:

> For a preliminary injunction to issue, the plaintiff must establish: (1) possession of a certain and clearly ascertained right which needs protection; (2) immediate and irreparable injury if the injunction is denied; (3) probability of success on the merits; and (4) no adequate remedy at law.[264]

In addition, since the issuance of an injunction is a discretionary matter, the court will normally balance the equities before issuing an injunction,[265] and also ascertain whether the plaintiff enjoys clean hands.[266] None of these requirements have seemed to pose any difficult

---

[262] *Id.* at 207 n.4. *See also,* Shirley v. Retail Store Employees Union, 592 P.2d 433 (Kan. 1979). When the *Sears* case was remanded to the California Supreme Court, that court held, however, that the state's Moscone Act deprived the state court of jurisdiction to enjoin "peaceful" but unconsented to (and thus a putative trespass) picketing on private property open to the public. Sears, Roebuck & Co. v. San Diego County District Counsel of Carpenters, 599 P.2d 676 (Cal. 1979), *cert. denied,* 447 U.S. 935 (1980).

[263] Rentner v. Sigman, 216 N.Y.S. 79, 80 (Sup. Ct. 1926), *rev'd on other grounds,* 215 N.Y.S. 323 (Sup. Ct. App. Div. 1926).

[264] Yellow Cab Co. v. Production Workers Union, Local 707, 416 N.E.2d 48, 50 (Ill. App. Ct., 1980).

[265] Turner & Seymour Mfg. Co. v. Torrington Foundry Workers, 18 Conn. Sup. 73 (1952); *see generally,* H. McClintock, Equity 383-90 (2d ed. 1948).

[266] Walter A. Wood Mowing & Reaping Mach. Co. v. Toohey, 186 N.Y.S. 95, 101 (Sup. Ct. 1921); *see generally,* H. McClintock, Equity 59-69 (2d ed. 1948).

obstacles insofar as state injunctive relief against union violence is concerned, however.

The right of an employer to operate and the right of the employee to work, free from the coercive interference of others, are firmly established in our jurisprudence.[267] The business and work opportunities that are lost by union violence are frequently substantial,[268] but they are also generally difficult to measure or ascertain. As one commentator has stated, "In the particular context of labor strikes, . . . a company's temporary and permanent loss of customers, employees and goodwill largely are incalculable in money damages, and thus, make ordinary legal relief inadequate."[269] The equities will rarely, if ever, favor a violence-prone union in these cases;[270] and apart from an occasional case of employer misconduct of an egregious nature, the clean hands doctrine is rarely invoked.[271]

Moreover, in the absence of specific statutory constraints, the state courts often take a relaxed but realistic view of union responsibility for the acts of violence which are now being enjoined. In *Meadowmoor*,[272] the Supreme Court laid down what might be called a "constitutional minimum" on the agency issue. After summarizing the extensive acts

---

[267] *See, e.g.,* General Electric Co. v. Local 997, UAW, 130 N.E.2d 758, 764 (Ill. App. Ct., 1955) (plaintiff's "factory constitutes a property right and the free access to such factory by the plaintiff and its employees in an incident of that right."); Westinghouse Elec. Corp. v. United Electrical Workers, 47 A.2d 734, 737 (N.J. Court of Chancery, 1946) ("Complainant has a property right in its buildings and equipment, the preservation of which requires that it be permitted to bring into the plant such persons as it may determine necessary for this purpose."); Isolantite, Inc. v. United Electrical Workers, 22 A.2d 796, 801 (N.J. Ct. of Chancery, 1941), *modified,* 29 A.2d 183 (N.J. Ct. of Err. & App. 1942) ("It would hardly seem necessary to state that the employees have a right . . . to go to and from their work, freely and without hindrance. . . . And the employer has a corresponding right that his employees be unmolested.").

[268] *See* Turner & Seymour Mfg. Co. v. Torrington Foundry Workers, 18 Conn. Sup. 73, 79-80 (1952).

[269] Babcock, *Connecticut State Court Injunctions in Labor Disputes,* 54 CONN. B.J. 37, 41 (1980). *See* Dugan Oil Co. v. Coalition of Area Labor, 423 N.E.2d 1373, 1379 (Ill. App. Ct., 1981); Rice & Holman v. United Electrical Workers, 65 A.2d 638 (N.J. Sup. Ct., 1949); Phelps Dodge Copper Prod. Corp. v. United Electrical Workers, 46 A.2d 453, 460 (N.J. Ct. of Chancery, 1946), *aff'd sub. nom.* Westinghouse Elec. Corp. v. United Electrical Workers, 49 A.2d 896 (N.J. Ct. of Err. & App., 1946).

[270] *See* Westinghouse Elec. Corp. v. United Electrical Workers, 47 A.2d 734 (N.J. Court of Chancery, 1946); Isolantite, Inc. v. United Electrical Workers, 22 A.2d 796 802 (N.J. Ct. of Chancery, 1941), *modified,* 29 A.2d 183 (N.J. Ct. of Err. & App., 1942) ("How much injury will be inflicted upon the defendants by forbidding them from insulting, threatening or assaulting employees?").

[271] *But see,* Pomonis v. Hotel Local 716, 239 P.2d 1003 (N.M. 1952); David Adler & Sons v. Maglio, 228 N.W. 123, 125 (Wisc. 1929); Walter A. Wood Mowing & Reaping Mach. Co. v. Toohey, 186 N.Y.S. 95, 101 (Sup. Ct. 1921) ("Allen's hands are soiled nearly beyond purification.").

[272] Milk Wagon Drivers Local 753 v. Meadowmoor Dairies, Inc., 312 U.S. 287 (1941).

of violence that had occurred in that case, the Court continued as follows:

> These acts of violence are neither episodic nor isolated. Judges need not be so innocent of the actualities of such an industrial conflict as this record discloses as to find in the Constitution a denial of the right of Illinois to conclude that the use of force on such scale was not the conduct of a few irresponsible outsiders. . . . [A] state is not to be treated as though the technicalities of the law of agency were written into the Constitution. . . . It is true of a union as of an employer that it may be responsible for acts which it has not expressly authorized or which might not be attributable to it on strict application of the rule of *respondeat superior*.[273]

State courts often adopt this test when determining whether an injunction can properly lie against a union involved in a strike or picketing that has been marred by acts of violence.[274]

In the exercise of a traditional equity jurisdiction, the state courts thus routinely enjoin a wide range of intimidating and coercive union conduct—physical assaults, threats, damage to property, plant seizures, followings, general harassment, blocked ingress and egress, mass picketing, disturbing the peace, and related acts of misconduct.[275]

In addition, however, to the standards that the courts themselves have imposed, there are also specific statutory provisions in most states governing the issuance of injunctions in labor disputes. Some of these simply codify the common law requirements and, perhaps, limit the issuance of *ex parte* orders.[276] Others, however, are far more comprehensive; frequently, they will incorporate verbatum some or all of the provisions of the federal Norris-LaGuardia Act and are thus

---

[273] *Id.* at 295.

[274] *See, e.g.,* Capital Bakers, Inc. v. Local 464, Bakery Workers Union, 422 A.2d 521, 524 (Pa. Superior Ct., 1980); United Farm Workers Organizing Committee v. LaCasita Farms, Inc., 439 S.W.2d 398, 403 (Tex. Ct. Civ. App., 1968).

[275] *See, e.g.,* M Restaurants, Inc. v. San Francisco Local, Joint Executive Board of Culinary Workers, 177 Cal. Rptr. 690 (Ct. of Appeal, 1981); Baton Rouge Coca Cola Bottling Co. v. General Truck Drivers, Local 5, 403 So.2d 632 (La. Sup. Ct. 1981); PTA Sales, Inc. v. Retail Clerks Local 462, 633 P.2d 689 (N.M. 1981); State v. Chavez, 601 P.2d 30 (Ariz. Ct. of App., 1979); Trans-Western Express, Ltd. v. Local 17, Int'l. Bhd. of Teamsters, 603 p.2d 959 (Colo. Ct. of App. 1979); Westinghouse Electric Corp. v. International Union of Electrical Workers, 396 A.2d 772 (Pa. Superior Court, 1978); State v. Percich, 557 S.W.2d 25 (Mo. Ct. of App., 1977); International Molders Workers Union v. Superior Court, 138 Cal. Rptr. 794 (Ct. of App., 1977); Eads Coal Co. v. UMW, 327 N.E.2d 115 (Ill. App. Ct., 1975); United Farm Workers Organizing Committee v. LaCasita Farms, Inc. 439 S.W.2d 398 (Tex. Ct. Civ. Appeals, 1968); Fleming v. Terminal Transport Co., 151 S.E.2d 137 (Ga. 1966); Steiner v. Long Beach Local 128, Oil Workers Int'l Union, 123 P.2d 20 (Cal. Sup. Ct., 1942); Chrisman v. Culinary Workers Local 62, 115 P.2d 553 (Cal. Dist. Ct. of App., 1941).

[276] *See, e.g.,* N.M. STAT. ANN §§ 50-3-1 and 50-3-2 (1978).

sometimes referred to as "Little Norris-LaGuardia Acts."[277] As is true
of the federal act, these state statutes pose numerous obstacles which
must be overcome before a complainant can obtain injunctive relief
against labor union violence.

The purpose of these statutes is generally the same as that of the
federal act—namely, to eliminate injunctions as a factor in the resolution of otherwise peaceful economic conflicts between labor and
management and to correct certain perceived procedural abuses in the
issuance of injunctions.[278] Although, as with the federal act,[279] the
courts have consistently held that these statutes do not deprive them of
jurisdiction to enjoin acts of violence and coercion,[280] even with respect
to such injunctions certain statutory prerequisites must still be
satisfied. As under the federal act, those that have posed the greatest
difficulty involve proof of union responsibility, proof that the police are
unable or unwilling to control the violence, and satisfaction of the
mediation/arbitration requirement.

Taken word-for-word from section 7 of the federal Norris-LaGuardia
Act,[281] section 31-115 of the Connecticut statute provides, for example,
that "no injunction or temporary restraining order shall be issued on
account of any threat or unlawful act except against the person or persons, association or organization making the threat or committing the
unlawful act or actually authorizing or ratifying the same after actual
knowledge thereof."[282]

---

[277] *See, e.g.,* CONN. GEN. STAT. ANN §§ 31-112 to 31-121; HAW REV. STAT. §§ 380-1 to
380-14; IDAHO CODE §§ 44-703 to 44-710; IND. CODE ANN. §§ 22-6-1-1 to 22-6-1-12; LA.
REV. STAT. ANN. §§ 23:841 to 23:847; MD. ANN. CODE art. 100, §§ 63 to 75; MASS.
GEN. LAWS ANN. ch. 214, § 6; MINN. STAT. ANN. §§ 185.01 to 185.20; N.J. REV. STAT.
ANN. §§ 2A:15-15 to 2A:15-58; N.Y. LAB. LAW (McKinney) §§ 807 to 808; N.D. CENT.
CODE §§ 34-08-01 to 34-08-13; OR. REV. STAT. §§662.010 to 662 -.130; P.R. LAWS ANN.
tit. 29, §§ 101 to 109; R.I. GEN. LAWS §§ 28-10-2 to 28-10-5; UTAH CODE ANN. §§
34-19-1 to 34-19-13; WASH. REV. CODE §§ 39.32.010 to 49.32.910; WIS. STAT. ANN. §§
103.55 to 103.62; WYO. STAT. ANN. §§ 22-7-102 to 27-7-107.
[278] *See, e.g.,* United States Pipe & Foundry Co. v. United Steelworkers Local 2026, 157
A.2d 542, 549-50 (N.J. Sup. Ct., 1960); Coward Shoe, Inc. v. Retail Shoe Salesman's
Union Local 1115F, 31 N.Y.S.2d 781, 784 (Sup. Ct. 1941).
[279] *See* Text at notes 76-88, *supra.*
[280] *See, e.g.,* Anaconda Co. v. UAW, 382 A.2d 544, 546 (Conn. Sup. Ct., 1977); National
Union of Hospital Employees v. Lafayette Square Nursing Center, Inc., 368 A.2d 1099
(Md. Ct. of Special Appeals, 1977); United States Pipe & Foundry Co. v. United
Steelworkers Local 2026, 157 A.2d 542, 549 (N.J. Sup. Ct. 1960); Isolantite, Inc. v.
United Electrical Workers, 29 A.2d 183 (N.J. Ct. of Err. & App., 1942); Bailer v. Fuchs,
27 N.E.2d 812, 814 (N.Y. Ct. of App., 1940).
[281] Norris-LaGuardia Act § 7, 29 U.S.C. § 107 (1976).
[282] CONN. GEN. STAT. § 31-115. *See also,* HAW. REV. STAT., tit. 21, § 380-7(1); IDAHO
CODE § 44-704; IND. CORE ANN. § 22-6-1-6(a); LA. REV. STAT. ANN. § 23:842; MD.
ANN. CODE art. 100, §66; MASS. GEN. LAWS ANN. ch. 214, § 6; MINN. STAT. ANN. §
185.13(1); N.Y. LAB. LAW (McKinney) § 807(6); N.D. CENT. CODE § 34-08-07; OR. REV.
STAT. § 662.070; PA. CONS. STAT. tit. 43, § 206h; P.R. LAWS ANN. tit. 29, § 104; R.I.

In *United Aircraft Corp. v. International Assn. of Machinists,*[283] the Connecticut Supreme Court was required to construe the similarly worded section of the statute dealing with a union's damage liability.[284] Recognizing that an organization such as a labor union can act only through individual persons,[285] the court went on to hold that the mere participation by certain high-ranking union officials in the various acts of violence that occurred was itself sufficient to implicate the union.[286] Thus, with respect to international union presidents, vice presidents and representatives, district business representatives, and presidents and vice presidents of locals, the court held that their "explicit authority" from the union to participate in the violence was not necessary in order to establish the organization's tort liability.[287] In sum, it would appear that the ordinary principles of agency and *respondeat superior* are applied with respect to the misconduct of high ranking union officers of this kind.[288] Even under that approach, however, it is still not always easy to establish liability since, as one commentator put it, "there rarely are witnesses to the unlawful incidents, and oftentimes even the victims do not know the identity of the perpetrators."[289]

On the other hand, according to the Connecticut court, the union's liability for the misconduct of lesser officers and rank-and-file members is even more difficult to establish. Here, there must be actual authorization or ratification, and the court indicated that this requires

> more than the general agency rules of respondeat superior and more than the general authority with which an officer of the organization is clothed by virtue of his office. We subscribe to the proposition that the statute requires proof by the plaintiff that the acts complained of were either expressly authorized by the organization to be charged or were such that they flowed from that authorization.[290]

GEN. LAWS § 28-10-2(a); UTAH CODE ANN. § 34-19-3; WASH. REV. CODE § 49.32.070; WYO. STAT. § 27-7-107.

[283] 285 A.2d 330 (Conn. 1971), *cert. denied,* 404 U.S. 1016 (1972).

[284] CONN. GEN. STAT. § 31-114. This is the analog of Norris-LaGuardia Act § 6, 29 U.S.C. § 106 (1976), except that the Connecticut statute omits the "clear proof" language.

[285] 285 A.2d at 337.

[286] "[W]e conclude that if representatives of the organization to be charged are proved to have actually taken part in the illegal acts complained of then the organization can be held liable for those acts depending upon the number and status of the persons participating and the extent of the organization's knowledge of and power to control their actions." *Id.*

[287] *Id.* at 340.

[288] Babcock, *Connecticut State Court Injunctions in Labor Disputes,* 54 CONN. B.J. 37, 54 (1980).

[289] *Id.* at 56.

[290] 285 A.2d at 337. *See also,* Rochdale Village, Inc. v. Beverly 410 N.Y.S.2d 508 (Sup. Ct. 1978).

As one commentator stated, however, "explicit authorization by a union for members and other persons to commit unlawful acts probably occurs rarely, and when it does occur, is not susceptible of easy proof."[291]

A recent strike in Rhode Island provides a classic example of how statutory provisions such as these can force state court judges to close their eyes to the realities of industrial violence. Despite extensive evidence of violence, property damage, and near riot-like conditions, a state court judge refused to issue an injunction against a union whose members were engaged in an ecomonic strike. The judge said that the incident that triggered the request for an injunction "was chaos, anarchy, a danger to life and a condition that a civilized society ought not to be expected to endure."[292] But he denied the injunction on the grounds that the company had failed to prove that the union had participated in, authorized, or ratified the misconduct, as required by the Rhode Island statute.[293] Recognizing that the company's inability to stop this kind of violence would inure to the collective bargaining advantage of the union, the union's attorney simply noted that "We're very pleased."[294]

In order to provide what was then thought to be the proper degree of federal deference to state authority,[295] the federal Norris-LaGuardia Act requires a complainant to prove that the local authorities are unable or unwilling to control union violence before a federal injunction can be issued against it.[296] Many of the states that used the federal statute as the model for their own anti-injunction statutes rather unwittingly included this same requirement,[297] even though the justification for it in the federal statute would seem to be lacking at the state level. One state court, however, did attempt to explain it in this fashion:

> The criminal law is a standing injunction against violence and the criminal courts, as an original matter, are the proper forum in which defendants, who have breached the peace, must be charged and heard.

---

[291] Babcock, *supra* note 296, at 54-55.
[292] The Bulletin, Providence, R.I., April 1, 1982.
[293] R.I. GEN. LAWS § 28-10-2 (a).
[294] The Bulletin, Providence, R.I., April 1, 1982.
[295] *See* Text at note 141, *supra.*
[296] Norris-LaGuardia Act § 7(e), 29 U.S.C. § 107(e) (1976).
[297] *See, e.g.,* CONN. GEN. STAT. § 31-115 (e); HAW. REV. STAT. § 380-7(5); IDAHO CODE § 44-706(f); IND. CODE § 22-6-1-6(e); LA. REV. STAT. ANN. § 23:844(6); MD. ANN. CODE art. 100, § 68(f); MASS. GEN. LAW ANN. ch. 214, § 6(e); MINN. STAT. § 185.13(5); N.Y. LAB. LAW (McKinney) § 807(1) (e); OR. REV. STAT. § 662.080(5); PA. CONS. STAT. § 2061(f); P.R. LAWS ANN. tit. 29, 105(e); R.I. GEN. LAWS § 28-10-2(e); UTAH CODE ANN. § 34-19-5(6); WASH. REV. CODE § 49.32.072(5); WIS. STAT. § 103.56(f). The New Jersey anti-injunction statute wisely omits this requirement, and the court in *United States Pipe & Foundry Co. v. United Steelworkers,* 157 A.2d 542, 554-55 (N.J. Sup. Ct. 1960), refused to read it into the provision requiring proof of an inadequate remedy at law, N.J. REV. STAT. § 2A:15-53(d).

To substitute a court of equity in the performance of the duties of a criminal court is a grave responsibility and one to be shunned by a court of equity.[298]

This, of course, ignores the fact that equity and the criminal law serve two very different functions. The criminal prosecution of the perpetrators of strike and picket line violence vindicates the public interest in industrial peace and order, but the benefit to the victim is minor and incidental. An injunction, on the other hand, is designed to protect the private rights of a specific person, and the violation of its terms may require recompense for the losses sustained thereby.[299] Moreover, if the court's reasoning were correct, equity would be deprived of jurisdiction to enjoin *any* misconduct which also happened to be criminal in nature—which is surely not the case.[300] To the contrary, as another court more aptly stated,

> one whose rights are invaded and who is faced with an irreparable injury is not required to seek the grace, or to await the pleasure and consequent delay, of police officers. He is not required to argue his case or to address his importunities to a policeman, nor is such officer to be expected to determine the civil rights of a litigant. The proper forum for such matters is the court.[301]

Nevertheless, the requirement is a common one in state anti-injunction statutes, and complainants attempting to satisfy it are sometimes faced with a difficult burden of proof. One court stated that, "to make such a finding, the record would have to show acts of repeated violence which have gone unpunished or undealt with because of the lethargy or inability of the police to deal therewith."[302] That burden has been satisfied in some cases,[303] but not in others.[304]

---

[298] Miller v. Gallagher, 28 N.Y.S.2d. 606, 610 (Sup. Ct. 1941).

[299] *See* Altemose Constr. Co. v. Building & Constr. Trades Council of Philadelphia, 296 A.2d 504, 517 (Pa. 1972), *cert. denied*, 411 U.S. 932 (1973) ("The purpose of a civil contempt proceeding is . . . in some instances to compensate the complainant for losses sustained.").

[300] To be sure, there is a well-recognized maxim that "equity will not enjoin a crime." DOBBYN, INJUNCTIONS 57 (1974). But what that means is that "equity will not enjoin conduct merely *because* it violates a criminal statute. On the other hand, if the conduct to be enjoined amounts to a nuisance, equity will not be prevented from enjoining it merely because it is criminal activity, as long as it can be shown that the criminal process does not provide an adequate remedy for the petitioner." *Id.* at 58.

[301] Blanchard v. Golden Age Brewing Co., 63 P.2d 397, 407 (Wash. 1936). The court here declared that provision of the Washington anti-injunction statute unconstitutional.

[302] Miller v. Gallagher, 28 N.Y.S.2d 606, 610 (Sup. Ct. 1941).

[303] *See, e.g.,* Miller v. Gallagher, 28 N.Y.S.2d 606, 611 (Sup. Ct. 1941) (violence at employees' homes); Grandview Dairy v. O'Leary, 285 N.Y.S.2d 841, 845 (Sup. Ct. 1936) (intimidation of various customers on delivery route).

[304] *See, e.g.,* Baton Rouge Coca Cola Bottling Co. v. General Truck Drivers Local 5,403 So.2d 632, 637 (La. Sup. Ct. 1981); Lindsay v. Teamsters Local 74, 97 N.W.2d 686, 693 (N.D. 1959) (this requirement was subsequently removed from the North Dakota statute, N.D. CENT. CODE § 34-08-07); Miller v. Gallagher, 28 N.Y.S.2d 606, 610 (Sup. Ct. 1941) (police allegedly responded to every incident that occurred on the picket line).

Finally, just as the federal Norris-LaGuardia Act prohibits an injunction in favor of any complainant who has failed to comply with any legal obligation or who has not made reasonable efforts to settle the dispute through mediation or arbitration,[305] so also do most of the state anti-injunction statutes impose this limitation on the power of the state courts to provide equitable relief against strike and picket line violence.[306]

Although it is apparently a fatal defect for a state court to fail to formally "find" that this requirement has been satisfied before issuing an injunction,[307] the state courts have otherwise generally construed the requirement more loosely than their federal counterparts. One state court explained that, "the statute require[s] no more than a reasonable effort to settle by any one of the three methods named. . . . We say to the complainant, Do not bother the court unnecessarily; talk over the matter first with your adversary and you may be able to reach an agreement."[308] Moreover, the state courts seem to recognize that "it is not incumbent on an employer to stand idly by making repeated efforts to negotiate, mediate, or arbitrate while his business is being destroyed."[309] The duty has been said also not to exist where the matter under dispute is already fixed by contract,[310] or where the picketing union represents none of the employees of the complainant.[311]

On the other hand, in determining whether or not the requirement has been satisfied, courts have on occasion thought it necessary to

---

[305] Norris-LaGuardia Act § 8, 29 U.S.C. § 108 (1976).

[306] *See, e.g.,* CONN. GEN. STAT. § 31-117; HAW REV. STAT. § 380-8; IDAHO CODE § 44-707; IND. CODE § 22-6-1-7; LA. REV. STAT. ANN. § 23:845; MD. ANN. CODE art. 100, § 69; MASS. GEN. LAW ANN. ch. 214, § 6(4); N.J. REV. STAT. § 2A:15-54; N.Y. LAB. LAW (McKinney) § 807(4); OR. REV. STAT. § 662.100; PA. CONS. STAT. § 206k; P.R. LAWS ANN. § 106; UTAH CODE ANN. § 34-19-6; WASH. REV. CODE § 49.32.073; WIS. STAT. § 103.57.

[307] *See, e.g.,* National Union of Hospital Employees, v. Lafayette Square Nursing Center, Inc., 368 A.2d 1099 (Md. Ct. of Special Appeals, 1977); DeWilde v. Scranton Building Trades Council, 22 A.2d 897 (Pa. 1941).

[308] Phelps Dodge Cooper Prod. Corp. v. United Electrical Workers, 46 A.2d 453, 460 (N.J. Court of Chancery, 1946), *aff'd sub. nom.* Westinghouse Elec. Corp. v. United Electrical Workers, 49 A.2d 896 (Ct. of Err. & Appeals, 1946). *See also,* Anaconda Co. v. UAW, 382 A.2d 544, 549 (Conn. Superior Ct. 1977) (willingness to mediate *or* arbitrate will satisfy the statute).

[309] Grandview Dairy v. O'Leary, 285 N.Y.S. 841, 844 (Sup. Ct. 1936). *See also,* Continental Paper Co. v. United Paper Workers, 68 A.2d 564 (N.J. Sup. Ct., 1949) (refusal to continue negotiations in the face of illegal union acts does not deprive plaintiff of right to an injunction); Blanchard v. Golden Age Brewing Co., 63 P.2d 397, 407 (Wash. 1936) (holding this provision of the statute unconstitutional on the grounds that "one who is injured or threatened with irreparable injury is not required to negotiate concerning it or attempt to arbitrate it.").

[310] Rice & Holman v. United Electrical Workers, 65 A.2d 638 (N.J. Sup. Ct. 1949).

[311] May's Furs & Ready to Wear v. Bauer, 26 N.E.2d 279 (N.Y. Ct. of App., 1940).

evaluate the employer's "good faith" in bargaining,[312] and to determine if the contract has been violated.[313] These are complex matters, the resolution of which is inappropriate in the urgent context of a request for an injunction against ongoing union violence and coercion, and in any event, they are an inadequate justification for such misconduct.

If all the equitable and statutory requirements for an injunction are satisfied, and an injunction is issued and subsequently violated, then the defendants can be subjected to criminal or civil contempt proceedings. Generally speaking, criminal contempt must be proved "beyond a reasonable doubt,"[314] while the "preponderance of the evidence" test is used in cases of civil contempt.[315] Because of the nature of the enjoined conduct, it is not always easy to determine whether a contempt proceeding involving strike and picket line violence is criminal or civil in nature. The standard of differentiation, however, has been stated as follows:

> The purpose of a contempt proceeding determines whether it is civil or criminal. If the dominant purpose thereof is to vindicate the dignity and authority of the court and to protect the interest of the general public the contempt proceeding is criminal in nature. But where the dominant purpose of the proceeding and contempt order is primarily for the benefit of a private party, and the order is remedial, and judicial sanctions are imposed (1) to coerce the defendant into compliance with the court's order, and (2) in some instances to compensate the complainant for losses sustained, the proceeding is civil in nature.[316]

Although the terms of an injunction must be specific, it is still not always easy to determine whether the conduct being cited as a violation actually qualifies. In one case, for example, the original injunction was against continued "intimidation, harassment and coercion,"[317] and the question was whether this was violated when union agents followed customers away from the plant. The court held that it was. "The meaning of those terms is clear to one acting in good faith. The court

---

[312] United States Pipe & Foundry Co. v. United Steelworkers, 157 A.2d 542, 563-66 (N.J. Sup. Ct., 1960); Kidde Mfg. Co. v. United Electrical Workers, 99 A.2d 210 (N.J. Sup. Ct. 1953).

[313] Kidde Mfg. Co. v. United Electrical Workers, 99 A.2d 210 (N.J. Sup. Ct. 1953) (nonpayment of vacation benefits as required by contract warrants denial of injunction).

[314] *See, e.g.,* In re Coleman, 526 P.2d 533, 536 (Cal. 1974). *Contra,* Pedigo v. Celanese Corp., 54 S.E.2d, 252, 259 (Ga. 1949).

[315] *See, e.g.,* Wagner v. Commercial Printers, 45 S.E.2d 205, 209 (Ga. 1947).

[316] Capital Bakers, Inc. v. Local 464, Bakery Workers, 422 A.2d 521, 524 (Pa. Super. Ct. 1980). *See also,* Altemose Constr. Co. v. Building & Constr. Trades Council of Philadelphia, 296 A.2d 504, 516-18 (Pa. 1972), *cert. denied,* 411 U.S. 932 (1973).

[317] State v. Percich, 557 S.W.2d 25, 40, (Mo. Ct. of App., 1977).

was not required to denominate every type of prohibited conduct which would intimidate, harass and coerce customers. Use of generic terms are sufficient to give petitioners fair warning."[318]

Finally, although one is generally not entitled to a jury trial in either civil or criminal contempt cases,[319] some of the state statutes, like their federal counterpart,[320] do provide for this.[321]

---

[318] *Id.* This case also contains an excellent discussion of some of the other difficult evidenciary problems that can arise in a contempt proceeding involving labor union violence.

[319] Muniz v. Hoffman, 422 U.S. 454, 475-77 (1975).

[320] 18 U.S.C. § 3692 (1976).

[321] *See, e.g.,* MD. ANN. CODE art 100, § 72(c); MINN. STAT. § 185.16; N.J. REV. STAT. § 2A:15-56.

CHAPTER IX

Application of
Federal Anti-Extortion
Statutes to Union Violence[1]

Following the Norris-LaGuardia Act, the next major involvement of the federal government in the problem of labor union violence arose in the context of the federal anti-extortion statutes. The history of these statutes and the cases construing them provide an excellent example of the kind of legislative point and judicial counterpoint that has left the federal law on union violence in a virtual stalemate. The story continues, however; currently pending before Congress are several proposals which would further alter the law and the extent of its application to acts of union violence. In order to appreciate the purpose and probable effect of these proposals, it is, however, necessary to first review what has already transpired.

THE ANTI-RACKETEERING ACT OF 1934

The Legislative History

The original federal anti-extortion statute, known as the Anti-Racketeering Act,[2] was one of several bills that came out of the extensive investigations of "racketeering" conducted in 1933 by the Copeland Committee, a special subcommittee of the Senate Committee on Interstate Commerce.

As introduced in the Senate,[3] this bill did not specifically include or exclude the activities of labor unions. The Senate report stated, however, that "the provisions of the proposed statute are limited so as not to include the usual activities of capitalistic combinations, bona fide

---

[1] Portions of this article were originally published as Haggard, *Labor Violence: The Inadequate Response of the Federal Anti-Extortion Statutes,* 59 NEB. L. REV. 859 (1980).

[2] Ch. 569, 48 Stat. 979 (1934) (current version at 18 U.S.C. § 1951 (1976)).

[3] S. 2248, 73d Cong., 2d Sess. (1934), 78 CONG. REC. 457 (1934).

labor unions, and ordinary business practices which are not accompanied by manifestations of racketeering."[4] The report also stated that at that time "the nearest approach to prosecution of racketeers as such has been under the Sherman Antitrust Act."[5] It noted, however, the limitations of that act, as construed by the courts, in addressing this particular kind of abusive behavior. It is problematic, of course, whether framers of the Senate bill had in mind any of the cases in which the Supreme Court had found the Sherman Act to be inapplicable to various forms of strike violence.[6]

In any event, it is clear that the Anti-Racketeering Act was intended to go beyond the limitations of the Sherman Act in dealing with the problems of racketeering and violence in interstate commerce. It did this by separately prohibiting four things, as they would affect interstate commerce: (1) acts of violence, intimidation, or injury to person or property, or threats thereof; (2) extortion of money or other valuable consideration; (3) coercion of persons to join associations or make payments thereto; and (4) coercion of persons in the exercise of their rights to do or not to do as they choose.

This version of the bill passed the Senate with little or no debate. Moreover, it appears that the bill had been sent to the House before organized labor awoke to the possible implications insofar as labor activities were concerned. Senator Robinson, in belatedly requesting a reconsideration, stated that "representatives of the American Federation of Labor [AFL] informed me this afternoon that both bills [the Anti-Racketeering Act and a bill dealing with extortion by phone] might be very discriminatory against labor in this country, and that they wanted to be heard respecting them.[7]

It is not altogether clear why the AFL thought the bill was "discriminatory" or unfair to them. It seems unlikely that they believed that labor unions are simply entitled to a blanket exemption from the normal prohibitions against physical violence and extortion. In all probability, labor feared that the historically elusive term "coercion" might be construed broadly to encompass, in addition to overt violence, the traditional labor activities of strikes and picketing, especially when such activities were directed at compelling an employer to recognize the union, to pay union wages, and to stop hiring

---

[4] S. REP. No. 532, 73d Cong., 2d Sess. 2 (1934).

[5] *Id.* at 1.

[6] *See, e.g.,* United Leather Workers v. Herkert & Meisel Trunk Co., 265 U.S. 457 (1924); United Mine Workers v. Coronado Coal Co., 259 U.S. 344 (1922).

[7] 78 CONG. REC. 5859 (1934).

nonunion labor.[8] These objectives would certainly seem to be encompassed by the third and fourth provisions of the bill as summarized above. Moreover, strikes to obtain these objectives had been held to be beyond the reach of the Sherman Act, and organized labor knew that the bill was intended to expand that reach in some unspecified fashion. Thus, the fears of the AFL may not have been totally unwarranted.

The House was apparently receptive to whatever fears labor had concerning the Anti-Racketeering Act. When the bill was reported out of committee,[9] it had been rewritten so as to prohibit: (1) the use of force, violence, or coercion to obtain or attempt to obtain money or other valuable consideration, "not including, however, the payment of wages by a bona-fide employer to a bona-fide employee";[10] (2) the wrongful use of force to obtain the property of another without his consent; (3) conduct in furtherance of a plan or purpose to otherwise violate the act; and (4) conspiracies to engage in conduct otherwise prohibited by the act. A final proviso to the act also stated "that no court of the United States shall construe or apply any of the provisions of this act in such manner as to impair, diminish, or in any manner affect the rights of bona-fide labor organizations in lawfully carrying out the legitimate objects thereof, as such rights are expressed in existing statutes of the United States."[11]

The House report, quoting a letter from the attorney general, noted that

> the original bill was susceptible to the objection that it might include within its prohibition the legitimate and bona fide activities of employers and employees. As the purpose of the legislation is not to interfere with such legitimate activities but rather to set up severe penalties for racketeering by violence, extortion, or coercion, which affects interstate commerce, it seems advisable to definitely exclude such legitimate activities.[12]

Assured that the new bill had the complete approval of organized labor,[13] the House and the Senate passed it without further debate.

Despite the effort of Congress to direct the focus of the act toward organized crime and away from organized labor, some of the first in-

---

[8] Under certain forms of the "conspiracy doctrine," labor activities could be considered actionable or, in legal contemplation, "coercive" if either the ends or the means were impermissible. Thus, nonviolent strikes to obtain a closed shop could be enjoined in some cases. *E.g.,* Plant v. Woods, 176 Mass. 492 (1900); *see* T. HAGGARD, COMPULSORY UNIONISM, THE NLRB, AND THE COURTS 21-24 (1977). Organized labor, which had vigorously and more-or-less successfully opposed the "conspiracy doctrine" in other contexts, may have feared its resurrection in the form of this federal criminal law.

[9] 78 CONG. REC. 11402-03 (1934).

[10] *Id.* at 11403.

[11] *Id.*

[12] H.R. REP. NO. 1833, 73d Cong., 2d Sess. 2 (1934).

[13] 78 CONG. REC. 11482 (1934) (remarks of Sen. Copeland).

248 _Union Violence_

dictments under the act were brought against labor union officials. Thus, it soon became necessary for the courts to clarify the scope of the labor exemption. One such case ultimately wound its way to the Supreme Court.

The Case Law

In _United States v. Local 807, International Brotherhood of Teamsters,_[14] members of the union met trucks as they came into New York City and used threats and violence to obtain from the owners of these trucks the equivalent of a day's wage for driving and unloading the trucks within the city. In some instances the defendant unionists did in fact perform some work for which they nevertheless obtained full payment. In others, the owners paid the money but rejected the offers of the defendants to do the driving and unloading. There were also instances in which the defendants apparently either failed to offer to do the work or refused to do any work when asked.

The issue in _Local 807_ boiled down to whether the unionists were using force to obtain "_wages_ by a bona-fide employer to a bona-fide employee,"[15] thus bringing the events within the act's exception in that regard. Although the _Local 807_ case involved a now-repealed portion of the act, what the courts said in this case is important in evaluating the significance of the congressional repudiation of this interpretation, and in determining the meaning of the act as it is presently written.[16]

A number of competing interpretations were proffered in the opinions of both the court of appeals and the Supreme Court. The interpretation that was most obvious and most reasonable, however, was dismissed out of hand by the court of appeals. Speaking of the exception, the court noted that "theoretically it might indeed apply only to situations in which an employee procured by threats the payment of wages due under a contract which the employer had made without coercion."[17] In other words, a _bona fide_ or uncoerced employment relationship must exist before the exception is even applicable.

Presumably, the unstated predicate of this interpretation was that actual physical violence can never really be considered a legitimate and _bona fide_ labor union activity, insofar as the final proviso to the act is

---

[14] 118 F.2d 684 (2d Cir. 1941), _affd._ 315 U.S. 521 (1942).
[15] Ch. 569, 48 Stat. 979 (1934) (current version at 18 U.S.C. § 1951 (1976)).
[16] For discussion of the Congressional repudiation of _Local 807_ and the current version of the Act, see pp. 399-410 _infra._
[17] 118 F.2d at 686.

concerned,[18] and that the specific exemption with respect to wages should, therefore, be narrowly construed. Limiting the exception to violence used by a real employee to obtain the wages that are legitimately due him recognizes the general prohibition against violence, and at the same time, gives some meaning to the express words of the statute. Moreover, it makes sense to read the statute as recognizing a distinction between the use of force to obtain something that one is not entitled to without the consent of the other party (a wage contract), and the use of force to obtain something that one is actually entitled to (wages due under a previously consented to contract); the former but not the latter falls within the general meaning of the term "extortion,"[19] which was apparently the central concern of Congress in passing the act.

Nevertheless, the court had two objections to that interpretation. Firstly, the court felt that there was no real distinction between using coercion to obtain a contract for wages, and using coercion to obtain the wages owed under an otherwise noncoerced contract. The court, however, was simply wrong in that regard; but the court's willingness to indulge in patently fallacious reasoning to reach that desired result is probably more important than the logical fallacy itself.[20]

More importantly, the court of appeals felt that the suggested interpretation would make the exception too narrow. The court noted that the exception was clearly intended to cover "labor disputes," that "practically always the crux of a labor dispute is who shall get the job and what the terms shall be," and that "to confine the exception to cases where the original contract was voluntary would therefore leave out the great mass of instances in which the issue would ever arise."[21] This, however, simply begs the question of whether, with respect to the use of actual physical violence in contrast to the use of economic power, Congress intended the exemption to be narrow or broad.

In any event, the court of appeals obviously had to give the term *bona fide* some other meaning in order to avoid this particular interpretation.

---

[18] *See* note 11 & accompanying text *supra.*

[19] The common definition of criminal extortion is as follows: "Extortion is a crime when . . . any person extorts that which is not due, or more than is due, or before the time when it is due." BLACK'S LAW DICTIONARY 525 (5th ed. 1979).

[20] In order to demonstrate that there was no distinction between the two, the court noted that "if any employer is coerced into makng a contract, the coercion ordinarily persists until the wages fall due, so that it is proper to speak of them as being 'obtained' by the original threats, or violence. . . ." 118 F.2d at 686. While that assertion may well be true, the converse cannot be inferred, namely that if the wages due are obtained through coercion, this necessarily means that the original contract was obtained in like fashion. Nevertheless, this is what would have to be inferred in order to be consistent with the court's notion that the statute recognized no distinction between these two uses of force.

[21] 118 F.2d at 686.

Accordingly, the majority held that the requirement of *bona fides* was not met and thus, the exception did not apply where the money was paid on a "pretext of service never in fact rendered."[22] Conversely, the exception was said to apply whenever the "employee really did the work for which he was paid."[23] The majority, however, immediately expanded the exception to include payments made to a person who offered to do the work but whose offer was refused by the person being coerced to make the payments. It was on this specific point that the dissent parted company with the remainder of the court.[24] The court noted that while it might be difficult to call such payments "wages," it would nevertheless be nonsensical to assume that Congress wanted to grant immunity to one who used coercion to the point of actually getting the job but, at the same time, penalize another who did not persist "in pressing his unwelcome services upon the employer."[25] The court noted that this would "excuse the more heinous offense, and penalize the more venial."[26]

The majority also felt that interpreting *bona fides*, to include any coercively obtained payments as long as work was performed or tendered was justified by reference to the evil that Congress intended to suppress by this act. The court noted that what Congress had in mind was the "blackmail" that "organized gangs of bandits" had levied upon many small businessmen, especially in New York City.[27] Labor violence, *aimed at the legitimate objectives of obtaining jobs and higher wages,* was said to be an altogether different matter. The court noted that

> Congress might indeed have gone further than it did; it might have included payments extorted by threats for services rendered or offered; that too is a grave evil. But, grave as it is, it is of a different kind from that at which this act was aimed. The history of labor disputes is studded with violence which unhappily is not yet obsolete; but, although the *means* employed may be the same as those here condemned, the *end* is always different, for it is to secure work on better terms.[28]

This notion that the legitimacy of the ends somehow takes otherwise violent means outside the prohibitions of the statute has proved to be persistently appealing insofar as the courts are concerned. Although Congress expressly repudiated the Supreme Court decision which af-

---

[22] *Id.*
[23] *Id.*
[24] *Id.* at 690 (Hand, J., dissenting).
[25] 118 F.2d at 687.
[26] *Id.*
[27] *Id.* at 688.
[28] *Id.* (Emphasis added.)

firmed and restated this idea,[29] the theory was subsequently to reappear. Remarkably, it today represents the prevailing interpretation of the amended statute.[30]

On appeal, the Supreme Court again couched the issue in *Local 807* in terms of finding a correct construction of the wage proviso, and suggested three alternative interpretations. The Court first considered the possibility that "the exception applies only to a defendant who has enjoyed the status of a bona fide employee prior to the time at which he obtains or attempts to obtain the payment of money by the owner."[31] Presumably, this interpretation had been considered and rejected by the court of appeals. The Supreme Court rejected it, in part for the same reason—such a reading would allegedly exclude practically all labor disputes from the exemption, a result which the Court found incompatible with the probable intent of Congress. In addition, the Court found this interpretation inconsistent with the literal wording of the statute. The statute "does not except 'a *bona-fide employee* who obtains . . . wages from a bona-fide employer.' Rather, it excepts '*any person* who . . . obtains . . . the payment of wages from a bona-fide employer to a bona fide employee.'"[32] This is simply a disingenuous distortion of the suggested interpretation. The distinction underlying the interpretation focuses not on *who* uses coercion but *for whom* it is used. Coercion would be within the exception only when the person for whom it is used has an otherwise uncoerced employment relationship under which wages are owed.

The second possible interpretation considered by the Court was that the exception "does not apply if the owner's intention in making the payment is to buy 'protection' and not to buy service, even though the defendant may intend to perform the service or may actually perform it."[33] This was apparently the interpretation argued for by the government. However, the Supreme Court rejected it on the ground that the state of mind of the victim could not properly be decisive of the guilt of the defendant. The Court made it quite obvious that it viewed the exception as clearly contemplating the use of violence in labor disputes, as long as it was for a "legitimate" end.

> For example, the members of a labor union may decide that they are entitled to the jobs in their trade in a particular area. They may agree to attempt to obtain contracts to do the work at the union wage scale. They may obtain the contracts, do the work, and receive the money. Certainly

---

[29] *See pp. 399-410 infra.*
[30] *See* notes 136-37 & accompanying text *infra.*
[31] 315 U.S. at 527-28.
[32] *Id.* at 531.
[33] *Id.* at 528.

Congress intended that these activities should be excepted from the prohibitions of this particular Act, even though the agreement may have contemplated the use of violence. But it is always an open question whether the
employers' capitulation to the demands of the union is prompted by a desire
to obtain services or to avoid further injury or both. To make a fine or
prison sentence for the union and its members contingent upon a finding by
the jury that one motive or the other dominated the employers' decision
would be a distortion of the legislative purpose.[34]

Given later developments in Congress and before the courts, one
cannot overemphasize the critical importance of this language. It clearly suggests that, in the Supreme Court's view, the first principle of the
statute was that it was not intended to apply to violence aimed at at-
taining traditional labor goals. The victim's state of mind was rejected
by the Court as a relevant consideration only because its use might
operate in derogation of that principle. Since the instructions of the
trial judge to the jury had suggested the controlling importance of the
victim's intentions in paying the money, the Supreme Court necessarily found that the conviction had to be set aside, and it, therefore, affirmed the court of appeals.

Finally, the Court discussed a third possible interpretation over
which the court of appeals was divided—namely, whether the trial
judge erred in suggesting that payments for work not actually done
could never be considered "wages," notwithstanding the defendants'
willingness to do the work. In this regard, the Court noted that both the
majority and the dissent below had agreed that the payment of money
to one who refuses to do any work is clearly not within the exception,
but that payments to one who actually does the work clearly are within
the exception. The Court apparently concurred with that view and
stated that "the doubtful case arises where the defendants agree to
tender their services in good faith to an employer and to work if he ac-
cepts their offer, but agree further . . . that he should pay an amount
equivalent to the prevailing union wage even if he rejects their proffered services."[35] The Court resolved the doubt in favor of finding
such payments to be "wages" for the purposes of the statute.

The Court said that in determining whether the exemption applied or
not, "the test must . . . be whether the particular activity was among or
is akin to labor union activities with which Congress must be taken to
have been familiar when this measure was enacted."[36] Referring to the
so-called "'stand-by' orchestra device, by which a union local requires
that its members be substituted for visiting musicians, or, if the pro-

[34] *Id.* at 532-33.
[35] *Id.* at 534.
[36] *Id.* at 535.

ducer or conductor insists upon using his own musicians, that the members of the local be paid the sums which they would have earned had they performed,"[37] the Court concluded that the practice of accepting payments even when the services are refused was within the contemplation of Congress and, therefore, within the exemption.

The Court's holding on this point provides even further evidence of its preoccupation with the notion that if the objective is a traditionally legitimate one from labor's perspective, then conduct aimed at obtaining it does not constitute extortion, no matter how violent it is. This, in sum, seems to be the recurring theme of the *Local 807* decision.

Chief Justice Stone registered a strong dissent in the case. His dissent is important because many in Congress later referred to it expressly as evidencing the proper approach to the problem of labor extortion. Unfortunately, it is difficult to pinpoint exactly where in the analysis the chief justice parted company with his brethren. In his view the elements of an offense under the act were: the defendants used force to compel the payment of money; these payments were made to purchase immunity from violence and for no other reason; and this end was knowingly sought by the defendants. With respect to the specific facts of the *Local 807* case, Chief Justice Stone clearly believed that illegal extortion occurs when an employer is forced to make payments for work not done, even when it is the employer that has elected not to use the services of an otherwise willing worker. He noted that "unless the language of the statute is to be disregarded, one who has rejected the proffered service and pays money only in order to purchase immunity from violence is not a bona fide employer and is not paying the extorted money as wages."[38]

Moreover, the chief justice believed that the performance of some work did not necessarily bring forced payments within the exception. He cited with approval an instruction by the trial judge which stated that "if . . . what the operator was paying for was not labor performed but merely for protection from interference by the defendants with the operation of the operator's trucks, the fact that a defendant may have done some work on an operator's truck is not conclusive."[39] Furthermore, he noted that "the character of what the drivers or owners did and intended to do—pay money to avoid a beating—was not altered by the willingness of the payee to accept as wages for services rendered what he in fact intentionally exacted from the driver or owner as the

---

[37] *Id.*
[38] *Id.* at 540 (Stone, C.J., dissenting).
[39] *Id.* at 542.

purchase price of immunity from assault, and what he intended so to exact whether the proffered services were accepted or not.[40] On the other hand, the chief justice did concede that "the procuring of jobs by violence is not within the Act . . ." and that this may include "the 'stand-by' job where no actual service is rendered . . ."[41]

What one may synthesize from these various assertions is that from Chief Justice Stone's perspective, the critical issue was what constituted the "essential purpose" of the transaction. If the "essential purpose" of the transaction is to exchange money in return for work done (or for someone being available to work, as in a "stand-by" situation), there is no violation of the statute even if violence is used to accomplish the transaction. On the other hand, if the "essential purpose" of the transaction is to exchange money in return for freedom from violence, a violation does exist even if work is done or offered to be performed. However, the chief justice did not suggest specific, objective indicia that can be used in identifying such purposes. He conceded, rather, that this is ultimately to be determined by a jury by reference to the perceived intent of the two parties. Since the instructions of the trial judge were consistent with Justice Stone's interpretation of the law, he believed that the convictions should stand.

The *Local 807* case virtually emasculated the Anti-Racketeering Act of 1934 insofar as its effectiveness as a tool against labor violence was concerned. Whether the case was consistent with the original legislative intent is hard to tell, given the obscurity and brevity of the legislative history on the issue. The intent of the Congress sitting at the time the case was decided is, however, a different matter.

THE HOBBS ACT AMENDMENTS

The Legislative History

Congressional reaction to the *Local 807* case was as swift as it was negative. Bills were introduced in the 77th,[42] 78th,[43] and ultimately the 79th Congress[44] to correct what Congress considered to be an outrageous decision. The legislative solution that ultimately prevailed,

---

[40] *Id.* at 540.
[41] *Id.* at 541.
[42] S. 2347, 77th Cong., 2d Sess. (1942); H.R. 6872, 77th Cong., 2d Sess. (1942); H.R. 7067, 77th Cong., 2d Sess. (1942).
[43] H.R. 653, 78th Cong., 1st Sess., 89 CONG. REC. 3218 (1943).
[44] H.R. 32, 79th Cong., 1st Sess. (1945), becoming Hobbs Act §§ 1-6, 18 U.S.C. § 1951 (1976).

the Hobbs Act amendments to the Anti-Racketeering Act,[45] were originally introduced in the 1943 session.[46] The Hobbs Act passed the House that year,[47] but died in the Senate. It was reintroduced the following year and finally enacted into law.[48]

Fearful that any repetition of the exact language of the 1934 Anti-Racketeering Act would give the Supreme Court an excuse for adhering to the *Local 807* approach, Congress completely rewrote the law and took special pains to eliminate the specific language on which the decision was based. The new act provided that

> whoever in any way or degree obstructs, delays, or affects commerce or the movement of any article or commodity in commerce, by robbery or extortion or attempts or conspires so to do, or commits or threatens physical violence to any person or property in furtherance of a plan or purpose to do anything in violation of this section shall be fined not more than $10,000 or imprisoned not more than twenty years, or both.[49]

The terms "robbery," "extortion," and "commerce" were defined, and the final paragraph of the act, the exact wording of which produced much debate, provided that "this section shall not be construed to repeal, modify or affect" the Clayton Act, the Norris-LaGuardia Act, the Railway Labor Act, or the National Labor Relations Act.[50] Notably absent was anything akin to the wage exception of the Anti-Racketeering Act of 1934. Indeed, an amendment again exempting "wages" from the coverage of the Hobbs Act was rejected on the specific grounds that this would simply open the door to another *Local 807* decision.[51]

---

[45] 18 U.S.C. § 1951 (1976).

[46] *See* note 43 *supra.*

[47] The debates in the House on H.R. 653 were fairly extensive and are as much a legitimate source of legislative history from which probable legislative intent may be deduced as are the debates on the identical bill in the following session. United States v. Enmons, 410 U.S. 396, 404 n.14 (1973).

[48] After passing the House in independent form, 91 CONG. REC. 11922 (1945), the substance of the Hobbs Act was also incorporated into the Case Bill, H.R. 4908, 79th Cong., 2d Sess. (1945), which passed Congress but which was vetoed by President Truman, 92 CONG. REC. 674 (1946). Immediately after the veto, the Senate took up and passed the Hobbs Act as previously approved in independent form by the House, 92 CONG. REC. 7308 (1946), thus making it law in spite of the veto. *See generally* Comment, *Labor Law—A New Federal Antiracketeering Law,* 35 GEO. L.J. 362 (1947); Comment, *The Hobbs Act—An Amendment to the Federal Anti-Racketeering Act,* 25 N.C. L. REV. 58 (1946).

[49] 18 U.S.C. § 1951 (1976).

[50] *Id.*

[51] 91 CONG. REC. 11913-19 (1945). Speaking of the *Local 807* case, Congressman Sumners also said: "It was the purpose of the Judiciary Committee to prevent the rendition of that sort of decision by any court in the future, so the language upon which that holding was based was eliminated." *Id.* at 11909.

The legislative history makes absolutely clear that Congress viewed the *Local 807* case as wrongly decided.[52] Thus, the Anti-Racketeering (Hobbs) Act was at least written to require a contrary result on those identical facts, but how much beyond that Congress intended to go is a matter of speculation.

To determine what impact the Hobbs Act was intended to have upon various kinds of violent labor union activity, one can conveniently break the legislative history down into five categories: (1) congressional interpretations of the holding and the dissent in the *Local 807* case; (2) specific examples of the kinds of conduct the new act was intended to reach; (3) interpretations of the "no repeal" proviso and the suggested alternative; (4) the basis of labor's opposition and the congressional responses thereto; and (5) the assertions of no intended "discrimination" for or against labor.

Interpretations of the Local 807 *Case.* Generally speaking, Congress read the *Local 807* case very broadly. The sponsor of one of the first bills introduced on the matter said the case "in effect, placed the Congress in the position of condoning and authorizing the use of force and violence in enforcing demands so long as such force and violence are practiced by members of labor organizations and unions."[53] Similarly, it was said that the case holds "in effect that the use of force and violence was not incompatible to the lawful settlement of disputes between employers and employees."[54] In the debates on the Hobbs Act as introduced the first time, one congressman said: "I think the intent of the Congress in the 1934 statute was to protect the lawful activities of organized labor. The construction put on it by the Supreme Court would authorize unlawful acts—certainly never intended by this Congress."[55]

In these and other instances the concern of Congress seemed to focus on the fact that the *Local 807* case allowed labor unions to use physical violence to enforce their demands against employers. It was, apparently, of no particular moment that in the *Local 807* case the demands specifically involved payments for unwanted, if not unused, labor. Assuming that the Hobbs Act was intended as a negation of a broad reading of the *Local 807* case, it follows that Congress intended to prohibit the use of all violence in the enforcement of labor union demands regardless of the particular nature of the demands.

---

[52] Congressman Hancock called the *Local 807* case "a gross misinterpretation of the law and a distortion of the intent of Congress." 91 CONG. REC. 11900 (1945). *See also* 88 CONG. REC. 2071, 5334-35 (1942); 89 CONG. REC. 3193, 3201, 3202, 3206, 3206-07, 3220 (1943).

[53] 88 CONG. REC. 2071 (1942) (remarks of Sen. Holman).

[54] *Id.* at 5334-35.

[55] 89 CONG. REC. 3202 (1943) (remarks of Rep. Gwynne).

On the other hand, a somewhat narrower interpretation of the *Local 807* case is reflected in the comments of Congressman Hancock, a proponent of the Hobbs Act. "The Supreme Court," he said, "held that . . . members of Teamsters Union 807 in New York City were exempt from the provisions of that law when attempting by the use of force or the threat of violence to obtain wages for a job *whether they rendered any services or not.*"[56] This suggests that the objectionable aspect of the *Local 807* case that was being legislatively overruled pertained not to the permitted use of violence alone, but to its use to achieve that particular result. Consequently, an intent to negate that aspect of *Local 807* would not support an inference that Congress intended to prohibit all forcibly backed union demands.

Perhaps the clearest indication of what Congress intended by its repudiation of *Local 807* can be found in the fact that the dissenting opinion of Chief Justice Stone was repeatedly referred to in approving terms.[57] Indeed, at one point Congressman Whittington expressly stated that "the real purpose of the bill is to remove any doubt about the interpretation of the act by the Chief Justice being correct."[58] Unfortunately, as has been seen, Chief Justice Stone's opinion is somewhat obscure as to the act's prohibition against violence in the labor context.[59]

Specific Examples of Prohibited Conduct. The examples given of the kind of union conduct the new act was designed to reach are much more helpful than are interpretations of *Local 807* in assessing the legislative intent. The facts of the *Local 807* case were, of course, cited time and time again as being prototypical of the kind of abusive labor conduct Congress wanted to reach through the Hobbs Act,[60] but other examples were also given. Congressman Anderson spoke of where the Teamsters used force in connection with a demand that drivers entering San Francisco either become members of the union or use Teamster drivers while within the city.[61] He also spoke of the situation where, in support of an organizational drive among daily employees, a Teamsters union refused to haul the dairy farmers' milk into the city, resulting in considerable spoilage.[62] This was considered an act of "coercion" in the colloquial sense, and one which the proposed act was intended to reach.[63]

---

[56] 91 CONG. REC. 11900 (1945) (Emphasis added.)
[57] *See, e.g.,* 88 CONG. REC. 2071 (1942); 89 CONG. REC. 3206, 3210, 3217 (1943).
[58] 89 CONG. REC. 3221 (1943).
[59] *See text* accompanying notes 38-41 *supra.*
[60] *See* note 52 *supra.*
[61] 91 CONG. REC. 11904 (1945).
[62] *Id.*
[63] *Id.*

Congressman Baldwin of Maryland cited the example of a strike in Baltimore where sabotage and other acts of violence had been directed against the employer and his property:

> This bill would not have been presented to the House if organized labor had recognized law and order in striking and in establishing their rights, *as they have a right to do.* Everyone can remember the taxicab strike in the city of Baltimore . . . where cabs were overthrown, bricks thrown through the windows endangering the lives of people, innocent victims. . . .
>
> Mr. Chairman, labor has a right to strike, but when labor perpetrates that sort of thing, they are going far beyond the bounds of reason. Certainly, I do not take the position that labor has not the right to organize or to strike, but when they do so they should abide by the . . . laws of decency. If they had done that, we would not have this legislation before the House today.[64]

Thus, it is relatively clear that these members of Congress intended the Hobbs Act to prohibit forms of labor violence other than the kind of "featherbedding" practices that were at issue in *Local 807.* It appears that the proposed act was also intended to prohibit the use of violence and coercion to obtain otherwise legitimate objectives such as the organization of employees, membership in the union, the acquisition of work for union members, or a favorable collective bargaining agreement.

Debate Over the "No Repeal" Proviso.   As drafted by Congressman Hobbs, the bill simply said that the four leading labor laws then in existence were not to be considered repealed, modified, or affected by the new legislation. Congressman Celler, however, proposed and strenuously argued for an amendment which would have provided that "no acts, conduct, or activities which are lawful under [the four acts in question] . . . shall constitute a violation of this act."[65] Congressman Celler felt that as drafted the exception to the bill would not protect labor in the exercise of rights guaranteed by the other statutes; the "no repeal" language, he conceded, would continue to protect the exercise of those rights from prosecution under the former statutes, but not necessarily from prosecution under the proposed Hobbs Act.[66]

Congressman Celler's interpretation of the language was not a reasonable one. Language of this kind would normally be construed to mean that if any of the four labor statutes grant labor unions an affirmative right to engage in a particular kind of conduct, the Hobbs Act should not be construed as taking that right away. It was, however, repeatedly pointed out that none of the four acts gave unions the affir-

---

[64] *Id.* at 11918 (1945) (Emphasis added.)
[65] 89 CONG. REC. 3220 (1943).
[66] *Id.*

mative right to engage in any acts of force and violence prohibited by the Hobbs Act.[67]

On the other hand, Congressman Celler's version of the exception would have seriously limited the scope of the act insofar as labor union activities were concerned. It is reasonably apparent from his explanations of the proposed amendment that he construed the term "lawful" to mean "not illegal."[68] Saying that certain conduct is "not illegal" under a specific statute, as per Celler's version, is vastly different from saying that the statute makes such conduct a matter of "right." The Clayton Act,[69] for example, did not give labor unions an affirmative "right" to use force in the settlement of strikes; but the use of such force had also been held to be "not illegal" under that statute.[70] Arguably, under the Celler amendment it would not be subject to prosecution under the Hobbs Act either.[71] Thus, some labor leaders privately conceded that the Celler amendment would have nullified the Hobbs Act altogether, at least insofar as labor activities were concerned.[72] If an act was not already illegal under one of the four statutes, the Hobbs Act simply would not cover it.

Congressman Hobbs opposed the Celler amendment on slightly different grounds. He feared that if certain things which are generally "lawful" under the labor statutes were declared to be beyond the purview of the Hobbs Act, it would be construed as also excluding the pursuit of these "lawful" ends by "unlawful" means.[73] He said,

> Mr. Chairman, almost any crime may be committed while the perpetrator is engaged in otherwise lawful acts, conduct or activities.
> . . . Because a man is engaged in the perfectly lawful conduct of striking, is he guiltless if he commits rape?
> Picketing is lawful. But does that mean that a picket cannot be punished for stealing?
> The right of collective bargaining is guaranteed by law. Does that give collective bargainers the right to murder? . . . .
>
> Honestly and peaceably seeking employment is not only lawful, but commendable. However, it is equally lawful for one from whom employment is sought to refuse it. Does any sane and reasonable man contend that the right honestly and peacefully to seek employment gives the seeker the right to force employment or to beat the refuser? . . . .

---

[67] *Id.* at 3193, 3202.

[68] *See id.* at 3220.

[69] 15 U.S.C. §§ 12-27 (1974).

[70] *See, e.g.,* Apex Hosiery Co. v. Leader, 310 U.S. 469 (1940) (Court held that labor union activity that was illegal under local law could be legal under the Sherman Antitrust Act).

[71] *See* 89 CONG. REC. 3202 (1943) (remarks of Congressman Gwynne).

[72] *Id.* at 3203, 3224 (remarks of Rep. Baldwin).

[73] *Id.* at 3194-95, 3220-21 (remarks of Rep. Hobbs).

I submit that for these reasons the Celler amendment is dangerous, especially in view of the decision in the Local 807 case, which held that no matter how much violence might accompany a request for employment it was all right and you are perfectly innocent under the antiracketeering law. The same thing is true here. No matter what may be said about the Celler amendment, it still does not require, as do the acts to which it points, that lawful acts, conduct or activities must be done in a lawful and peaceful way. Without that or something like that the amendment should be defeated.[74]

The relevance and importance of this language used by the author of the Hobbs Act cannot be emphasized too strongly. In slightly different terms, what Congressman Hobbs was saying was that the fact that the objective or end is legitimate under one of the general labor statutes does not mean that such objective can be pursued by violent means. Rightly or wrongly, Congressman Hobbs feared that the Celler amendment would have that effect insofar as prosecutions under the proposed anti-extortion statute were concerned. Necessarily, Congressman Hobbs also believed that the statute as he drafted it did not have that effect. The Celler amendment was defeated.[75]

Objections to the Hobbs Act and the Responses. It is significant to note that, on a substantive level, the opposition to the act was not grounded on the fact that it was to be a violation of federal criminal law for labor unions to use actual physical violence in furtherance of their organizational or collective bargaining objectives. The substantive objection, rather, was that the act might be construed in such a way as to also preclude unions from pursuing these legitimate goals by the traditional methods of peaceful strikes and picketing. Congressman Celler, for example, noted that

> there are courts which have held that whenever workers seek to bring about a wage increase or other adjustment of their working conditions by a strike, however peacefully conducted, they are attempting to "force" their employer to grant the wage increase or grant the requested adjustment of their working conditions.[76]

He also feared that even a mere demand for a wage increase might be construed as an implied promise to strike if it were not granted, thus making it an illegal "threat."[77] Congressman Celler, concerned that the Hobbs Act might be similarly construed, also noted that "there are courts which have held that picketing, *however peacefully conducted,* is by its very nature an attempt to force the employer into action which he is not willing to take."[78]

---

[74] *Id.* at 3220-31.
[75] *Id.* at 3225.
[76] 91 CONG. REG. 11901 (1945).
[77] *Id.*
[78] *Id.* (Emphasis added.)

Similarly, Congressman LaFollette said of the terms of the act that: "I think they are broad enough to cover a discussion between employees as to whether or not they shall join a union. Those things are often accompanied by heated discussions which might be called coercion and they would affect the right of labor to organize."[79]

The proponents of the bill, however, consistently denied these charges. It is important to note that the basis of their denial was not that the ends being sought in these examples were legitimate ones, thus putting the means being used to achieve them beyond the purview of the act. Instead, they answered that *otherwise peaceful* strikes and picketing are not acts of force or violence; such acts are specifically protected by federal statute and could not, thus, be considered a violation of the Hobbs Act. This point was made repeatedly. Congressman Hancock, in responding specifically to the claims of Congressman Celler, said: "A moment ago the gentleman said the threat of a strike came within the definition of extortion. This bill merely prohibits the wrongful use of force or threats. That cannot apply to a threatened strike because strikes are lawful, they are not wrongful."[80] Similarly, in giving a negative response to the question of whether a threat to go on strike would constitute a violation under the proposed bill, Congressman Sumners said, "as I . . . understand this bill, there is not a thing in it to interfere in the slightest degree with any legitimate activity on the part of labor people or labor unions, unless somebody thinks it is legitimate for them to rob and extort."[81]

That robbery and extortion were intended to connote acts of physical violence is also evident in Congressman Gwynne's listing of what the government would have to prove in order to obtain a conviction under the statute—namely, that the conduct affects interstate commerce, that there be an actual taking of property, and that this be done "by violence, by personal violence, or by actual threats of personal violence."[82] Likewise, Congressman Fellows noted that "the so-called Hobbs bill is designed to make assault and battery and highway robbery unpopular. Its purpose is to protect trade and commerce [which would certainly include the negotiation of collective labor agreements and most other labor-related activities] against interference by violence, threats, coercion, or intimidation."[83]

---

[79] *Id.* at 11920.
[80] *Id.* at 11902.
[81] *Id.* at 11908.
[82] *Id.* at 11903.
[83] *Id.* at 11907.

Congressman Savage was concerned about the act's effect on a "strike for better working conditions."[84] A response by Congressman Barden distinguished a *peaceful* strike from the type of activity the act was designed to prohibit. Focusing on the means used to accomplish the ends sought, he said:

> Do not talk to me about the man on strike. If he were an honest gentleman, he would not commit such offenses as robbery or extortion while on strike or off strike.
>
> . . . The fact that a man is on strike certainly does not license him to be an outlaw . . .
>
> Good honest men do not commit robbery. They do not commit burglary. They do not beat up innocent people. They do not extort money. Good honest men do not do those things.[85]

A few moments later Congressman Michener said that "this bill will not interfere with legitimate strikes"[86]—presumably referring to strikes which are both peaceful and directed toward an otherwise legal end.

Congressman LaFollette also shared the fears of labor that the proposed Hobbs Act might be construed too broadly. Nevertheless, he did agree that the use of force or violence, *even if it was to obtain wages,* should be clearly prohibited. Thus, he proposed an amendment to that effect and said,

> if we put a construction into this statute which states that a bona fide payment of wages from an employer to an employee *shall not include wages* or the transfer of a thing of value *which is obtained by violence* or the threat of use of violence, then we reach the situation we are attempting to reach . . .[87]

The amendment was rejected presumably because the *Local 807* case caused the majority to avoid the "bona fide wages" language altogether and, instead, couch the prohibitions of the statute in even broader language. It would, however, be incongruous indeed to *now* construe the act as not reaching as far as even its opponents were willing to go.[88]

On the other hand, the most commonly cited indication that the act was not designed to reach mere strike violence is contained in the following exchange:

---

[84] *Id.* at 11841 (remarks of Rep. Savage).
[85] *Id.* (remarks of Rep. Barden).
[86] *Id.* at 11843 (remarks of Rep. Michener).
[87] *Id.* at 11846 (remarks of Rep. LaFollette) (emphasis added).
[88] Nevertheless, such a result was, in effect, reached by the Supreme Court in United States v. Enmons, 410 U.S. 396 (1973), where the Court held that the use of violence to obtain a more favorable collective bargaining agreement (covering, among other things, the payment of wages) was not within the prohibitions of the Hobbs Act. *See* text accompanying notes 150-84 *infra.*

Mr. MARCANTONIO. All right. In connection with a strike, if an incident occurs which involves—

Mr. HOBBS. The gentleman needs go no further. This bill does not cover strikes or any question relating to strikes.

Mr. MARCANTONIO. Will the gentleman put a provision in the bill stating so?

Mr. HOBBS. We do not have to, because a strike is perfectly lawful and has been so described by the Supreme Court and by the statutes we have passed. This bill takes off from the springboard that the act must be unlawful to come within the purview of this bill.

Mr. MARCANTONIO. That does not answer my point. My point is that an incident such as a simple assault which takes place in a strike could happen. Am I correct?

Mr. HOBBS. Certainly.

Mr. MARCANTONIO. That then could become an extortion under the gentleman's bill, and that striker as well as his union officials could be charged with violation of sections in this bill.

Mr. HOBBS. I disagree with that and deny it in toto.[89]

Congressman Gwynne also indicated that the act was not intended to cover "a clash between strikers and scabs during a strike."[90] Presumably, Congressman Hobbs also had this kind of picket line violence in mind. If so, the import of what Congressman Hobbs was saying becomes clear. Based on what he said elsewhere in the record,[91] it is inconceivable that he intended to exempt violence simply because it occurred in conjunction with an otherwise legal strike. Although some of the opponents of the bill felt that "minor altercations on the picket line"[92] should not be treated as felonies, there is no basis for assuming that Congressman Hobbs or any other supporter of the bill intended any distinction between major and minor acts of violence.[93] Rather, Congressman Hobbs' statement must be viewed in the context of the specific crimes the bill purported to prohibit—extortion and robbery. The purpose of most picket line violence is to prevent persons against whom it is directed from entering the employer's premises, not to obtain money from them. It is difficult to see how such violence could be conceptualized as either extortion or robbery. In short, Congressman Hobbs was simply recognizing that the act did not reach all violence, but only that which would fit within the legal definition of extortion or robbery.

The Intent Not to Discriminate For or Against Labor. The fifth category of legislative remarks shedding light on the intended scope of

---

[89] 89 CONG. REC. 3213 (1943).
[90] *Id.* at 3202 (remarks of Rep. Gwynne).
[91] *See* notes 73-74 & accompanying text *supra.*
[92] 91 CONG. REC. 11901 (1945) (remarks of Rep. Celler).
[93] United States v. Enmons, 410 U.S. 396, 410 n.20 (1973).

the Hobbs Act indicates that the act should not discriminate on the basis of whether the violent actor was or was not associated with a labor union. Many congressmen objected to the *Local 807* case because it seemed to grant a special license to labor unions alone to use violence in the pursuit of their goals. For example, Congressman Hobbs said that the case "decided that no matter how much violence a *union* man might use *in seeking employment,* he could not be punished under the 1934 Anti-Racketeering Act."[94] He added,

> I am saying that is the effect of the construction put upon robbery committed while engaged in *otherwise lawful* conduct by the Supreme Court decision. No matter how much force is used, robbery is a perfectly innocent pastime, as Chief Justice Stone said, *if the perpetrator be a labor-union member seeking employment.*[95]

Similarly, it was also said that the *Local 807* case "in effect, placed the Congress in the position of condoning and authorizing the use of force and violence *in enforcing demands* so long as such force and violence are practiced by *members of labor organizations and unions.*"[96] Such favored treatment was clearly not acceptable to Congress; it was the nature of the act and not the status of the actor that Congress thought was of controlling importance, and the Hobbs Act was designed to implement that policy. On this point, the following exchange is revealing:

> Mr. SUMNERS of Texas. There is nothing in this bill dealing with persons connected with organized labor as such. It is just an attempt on the part of the Committee on the Judiciary to bring in a bill that will prevent this type of robbery in interstate commerce.
>
> Mr. MICHENER. That is all there is to it. The only way labor is involved is that if these offenders belong to the union, and by robbery or exploitation collect a day's wage—a union wage—they are not exempted from the law solely because they are engaging in a *legitimate union activity.*[97]

In other words, "all are treated alike and no group is given special permission to violate the law."[98] Moreover, as these remarks demonstrate, the legitimacy of a group's goal or objective is irrelevant.

A fairly clear pattern emerges from this legislative history. Congress did not intend to interfere with otherwise peaceful strikes and picketing. Yet, Congress did intend to prohibit the use of force, violence, and threats as a means of obtaining wages or other things of value from an employer despite the fact that obtaining such benefits

---

[94] 89 CONG. REC. 3195 (1943) (Emphasis added.)
[95] *Id.* (emphasis added).
[96] 88 CONG. REC. 2071 (1942) (remarks of Sen. Holman) (Emphasis added.)
[97] 91 CONG. REC. 11843-44 (1945) (Emphasis added.)
[98] *Id.* at 11844 (remarks of Rep. Michener).

might be otherwise completely legitimate. In other words, as brokers of employee services, labor unions were to be limited in the use of force to the same extent as were other brokers or sellers of commodities; in either instance, the effectuation of the exchange through the use of force was to be prohibited as extortion.

The Case Law

Although even a cursory review of the legislative history clearly indicates that Congress intended the Hobbs Act to prohibit labor from using force or violence as a means of obtaining concessions from employers, the initial judicial reaction was still somewhat hesitant. For example, in *United States v. Kemble*[99] the Third Circuit Court of Appeals was faced with facts not unlike those in *Local 807*. A union official had used actual and threatened violence to cause an employer to hire a union member to unload a truck whenever it made deliveries to an RCA plant. These services were not otherwise desired by this employer. The court had little difficulty in finding that, on these particular facts, a violation existed. The court, however, did hedge somewhat when it stated that

> The conclusion seems inescapable that Congress intended that the language used in the 1946 statute be broad enough to include, in proper cases, the forced payment of wages. We say "in proper cases" advisedly. For it is not necessary that we here consider the great variety of circumstances in which coercion may be involved in the payment of wages. We need not consider the normal demand for wages as compensation for services desired by or valuable to the employer. It is enough for this case, and all we decide, *that payment of money for imposed, unwanted and superfluous services* such as the evidence shows Kemble attempted to enforce here by violent obstruction of commerce *is within the language and intendment of the statute.*[100]

Although the majority decision was cautious in construing the scope of the new act, it still went too far in the opinion of dissenting Judge McLaughlin. Notwithstanding the legislative history, he felt that the disagreement Congress had with the *Local 807* decision was a relatively narrow one. He maintained that the Supreme Court there had held that: (1) the use of force to become a genuine employee (one who actually works and is paid for it) was within the "wage" exception; and (2) the use of force to compel the payment of wages when the services of the would-be employee are refused was also within this exception. According to Judge McLaughlin, Congress' quarrel with the decision and its repudiation thereof pertained only to the second point, and that

---

[99] 198 F.2d 889 (3d Cir.), *cert. denied,* 344 U.S. 893 (1952).
[100] 198 F.2d 891-92 (Emphasis added.)

the defendant's conduct in this case fell within the still exempt first point. As such, it merely represented "a reputable union's genuine attempt to organize a trucking corporation,"[101] which was not the kind of conduct that the Hobbs Act was intended to prohibit. Generally, he felt that the use of violence by a labor union in pursuit of a legitimate goal, such as obtaining work for its members, is not a violation of the Hobbs Act; instead, it is a matter for state and local prohibition.

Judge McLaughlin's theory was rejected not only by the third circuit court in *Kemble* but also, later, by the Supreme Court;[102] but not without first picking up some support elsewhere. In *United States v. Green*,[103] Federal District Judge Adair reversed a conviction on the grounds that the facts as alleged in the indictment did not state an offense under the Hobbs Act. The indictment, tracking fairly closely the language used in the *Kemble* case, charged that the defendant had used "actual and threatened force, violence and fear" to cause "wages to be paid for imposed, unwanted, superfluous, and fictitious services of laborers."[104] In concluding that this did not state an offense under the act, Judge Adair relied on the proviso to the Hobbs Act which states that it was not designed to "repeal, modify or affect the provisions of . . . the Wagner Act."[105]

Given the legislative history of this section,[106] of which Judge Adair purported to have made "a personal investigation as to the intent of Congress,"[107] it is startling indeed to see how the section was used to support the result he reached. Noting that in several cases the Supreme Court had held that "a demand by a Union representative for 'feather-bedding' is not an unfair labor practice"[108] under the Wagner Act, Judge Adair stated, "it seems incongruous that Congress intended that a lawful act"[109] under one statute would be punishable as a felony under another.

This reasoning is remarkable in two respects. Firstly, it proceeds as if the Celler version of the proviso had been adopted rather than the committee or Hobbs version. As previously discussed, Congressman Celler wanted the language to read, "no acts . . . which are lawful"

---

[101] *Id.* at 895 (McLaughlin, J., dissenting).
[102] *See* notes 114-22 & accompanying text *infra.*
[103] 135 F. Supp. 162 (S.D. Ill. 1955), *rev'd.* 350 U.S. 415 (1956).
[104] 135 F. Supp. at 162.
[105] 18 U.S.C. § 1951 (1976).
[106] *See* pp. 403-05 of text *supra.*
[107] 135 F. Supp. at 162-63
[108] *Id.* at 163. Judge Adair was undoubtedly correct in concluding that the union's objective in this case was "not illegitimate." This conclusion, as well as its significance insofar as the current law is concerned, will be discussed subsequently. *See* note 152 & accompanying text *infra.*
[109] 135 F. Supp. at 163.

under the labor statutes shall be considered unlawful under the Hobbs Act, with "lawful" apparently being equivalent to "not illegal."[110] Although Congress expressly rejected that approach, that is exactly the interpretation Judge Adair gave the statute.

In addition, Judge Adair simply ignored the warning of Congressman Hobbs that the "lawfulness" of the ultimate objective could not serve as a justification for the use of force to achieve it.[111] Congress, however, did apparently heed this admonition in that it rejected the Celler version which Hobbs said was susceptible to such a construction.

Nevertheless, Judge Adair concluded that—since obtaining wages, albeit for unwanted services, was within the defendant's "rights and responsibilities as a Union representative"[112]—no violation of the Hobbs Act existed even though violence was used to achieve that end. Instead, a violation is made out only when the end itself is "unlawful," as where the union representative is obtaining money for his own benefit.[113] Thus, on the question of the "legitimacy" of the end serving as an exoneration of violent means, Judge Adair was in line with the dissent in *Kemble.*

The Supreme Court, however, disagreed strongly. With respect to the notion that the act applied only to a union official's attempt to obtain money for his own benefit, the Court simply noted that while the union officials in the *Local 807* case were not attempting to get the money for that purpose, the Congress clearly intended for the Hobbs Act to proscribe what they were doing.[114] Furthermore, the Court noted that "the legislative history makes clear that the new Act was meant to eliminate any grounds for future judicial conclusions that Congress did not intend to cover the employer-employee relationship"[115]—including, one would presume, the primary incidents of that relationship, namely the obtaining of work and the payment of otherwise legitimate wages.

---

[110] *See* note 68 & accompanying text *supra.*

[111] *See* notes 73-74 & accompanying text *supra.*

[112] 135 F. Supp. at 163.

[113] *Id.* Most of the cases under the Hobbs Act have involved attempts by labor union officials to extort money for their own personal use. *See, e.g.,* United States v. Daley, 564 F.2d 645 (2d Cir. 1977), *cert. denied,* 435 U.S. 933 (1978); Anderson v. United States, 262 F.2d 764 (8th Circ. 1959); United States v. Varlack, 225 F.2d 665 (2d Cir. 1955); United States v. Compagna, 146 F.2d 524 (2d Cir. 1944), *cert. denied,* 324 U.S. 867 (1945). In some instances the money was not obtained through the threatened use of physical violence, but through the threatened use of "economic force," *i.e.,* otherwise nonactionable strikes, picketing, and the like. How these cases fit into the conceptual scheme will be discussed at 426-29 of text *infra.*

[114] United States v. Green, 350 U.S. 415, 419-20 (1956).

[115] *Id.* at 419 (footnote omitted).

268 Union Violence

With respect to Judge Adair's reliance on the proviso to the Hobbs Act which stated that it did not affect any of the several labor statutes the Court simply noted that: "There is nothing in any of those Acts, however, that indicates any protection for unions or their officials in attempts to get personal property through threats of force or violence. Those are not legitimate means for improving labor conditions."[116] The Court footnoted five cases that presumably illustrated labor conditions or objectives which the labor statutes did not affirmatively permit a union to seek through "threats of force or violence," and which, therefore, fell within the parameters of the Hobbs Act when those means are used. Significantly, in four of these cases, as in *Green* itself,[117] what the unions were trying to attain was not intrinsically "unlawful" or "illegitimate": in *United Construction Workers v. Laburnum Construction Co.*,[118] the object was to get employees to join the union and to get the employer to recognize it as the employees' representative; *Allen Bradley Local 1111 v. Wisconsin Employment Relations Board*[119] involved employer accession to the union's contract demand and employee observance of the picket line; *NLRB v. Fansteel Metallurgical Corp.*[120] dealt with employer recognition of and negotiation with the union over wages, hours, and working conditions; and in *Kemble*[121] the object was to get the employer to hire certain union helpers. Only *United States v. Ryan*[122] involved an objective that was itself illegal—namely, the payment of money by an employer to the representative of his employees. Thus, it would seem that in *Green,* the Supreme Court was concerned with the use of force and violence to obtain payments, not with the legitimacy or illegitimacy of the payments themselves.

This, certainly, is how the lower courts viewed the matter on remand.[123] Following the Supreme Court decision, the defendants asked that the verdict be set aside on the grounds that it was not supported by sufficient evidence and that the trial judge erred in refusing to submit a particular instruction to the jury. The instruction in question would have been to the effect that if the jury finds that the defendant has a labor dispute of a jurisdictional nature with another union at the time of the alleged threats to compel the payment of wages to its

---

[116] *Id.* at 420 (footnote omitted).
[117] *See* note 108 & accompanying text *supra.*
[118] 347 U.S. 656 (1954).
[119] 315 U.S. 740 (1942).
[120] 306 U.S. 240 (1939).
[121] 198 F.2d 889 (3d Cir.), *cert. denied,* 344 U.S. 893 (1952).
[122] 350 U.S. 299 (1956).
[123] *See* United States v. Green, 143 F. Supp. 442 (S.D. Ill. 1956), *aff'd.* 246 F.2d 155 (7th Cir.), *cert. denied,* 355 U.S. 871 (1957).

members for unwanted services, the matter was beyond the scope of the Hobbs Act.[124]

The Court of Appeals for the Seventh Circuit rejected that argument, noting the Supreme Court's admonition that the four labor statutes referred to in the proviso (which do generally regulate labor disputes) in no way sanction the use of force or violence. The court added:

> We agree with the decisions that this statute encompasses illegal conduct which may be an outgrowth of a labor dispute just as any other criminal conduct may result from activity originally lawful. The mere fact that conduct originates in exercise of a lawful function does not prevent the ramifications and extensions thereof from becoming unlawful.[125]

This exactly reflects the position that Congressman Hobbs took with respect to the act. In sum, the *Green* decision on remand correctly stands for the proposition that the use of violence or threats of violence by labor union officials to enforce their demands, regardless of legitimacy, constitutes extortion under the Hobbs Act.

Despite the Supreme Court's willingness to construe the Hobbs Act broadly and as intended, judicial hostility to the Hobbs Act continued to surface. It was conceded that the express congressional reversal of the *Local 807* case necessarily meant that Congress intended to include a demand for wages for work not done within the prohibition of the act. In addition, the *Green* case necessarily meant that, at the very least, a demand for wages for *unwanted* work was covered. As one court framed it, the final issue was whether the act covered "violence to property as a part of a plan to extort a thing of value in the form of a collective bargaining agreement covering wages, hours and working conditions of *wanted* employees."[126] The issue was ultimately answered in the negative. But the path to that result was strewn with unfortunate distortions of the legislative history and embarrassing contortions of ordinary logic and semantics.

The first major case to reach the result was *United States v. Caldes.*[127] Since the Supreme Court was to later speak approvingly of this decision,[128] a detailed analysis is in order. Firstly, the court took a narrow view of the disagreement between Congress and the Supreme Court's result in the *Local 807* case. It said that Congress thought *Local 807* was wrong in recognizing the union member's willingness to work as

---

[124] 246 F.2d at 160.

[125] *Id.*

[126] United States v. Caldes, 457 F.2d 74, 75 (9th Cir. 1972).

[127] 457 F.2d 74 (9th Cir. 1972). *See generally* Willis, *Labor Violence—The Judiciary's Refusal to Apply the Hobbs Act,* 28 S.C. L. REV. 143 (1976).

[128] *See* United States v. Enmons, 410 U.S. 396, 409 (1973).

an excuse for violence, since this could be construed as also permitting the use of force to "bring about the hiring of unwanted, unneeded employees."[129] This particular result was predicated solely on the Supreme Court's interpretation of section 2(a) (the "wage exception"), and the fact that "the legislative history of the Hobbs Act shows that the deliberate purpose of Congress was to eliminate Section 2(a)."[130] Thus, the court in *Caldes* reasoned that the purpose of the Hobbs Act was merely to compel a contrary result in cases like *Local 807,* where the work is either unperformed or unwanted. The court concluded that,

> by eliminating Section 2(a) however, Congress did not intend to eliminate traditional labor or union activity, albeit militant, which has as its object legitimate ends. The exclusion was not meant to provide impunity to the terroristic and extortionate activities of union members, but to protect union activity directed toward legitimate labor goals even when militantly pursued.[131]

The court then noted that the *Green* case fell within this pattern, since the purpose of violence there was to obtain wages for "imposed, unwanted and superfluous or fictitious services."[132] The court also distinguished other lower court cases which had found that "extortion occurred when a union member tried to *foist* himself or another union member on an employer by threats of force and violence."[133]

What the court seemed to ignore was that Congress did not merely repeal the "wage exception" which was the technical basis of the *Local 807* case. Instead, Congress, entirely rewrote the act for the express purpose of precluding decisions like the one in *Local 807.*[134] This suggests a broad rather than a narrow congressional overruling of the decision. Given the repeated emphasis in the debates on the element of violence, it is more likely that it was this aspect of the *Local 807* facts that Congress found offensive—not just the objective to which the violence was directed.

Moreover, euphemisms and pejoratives are no excuse for sound analysis. Pouring paint on the employer's trucks and the clean laundry he was delivering, as in *Caldes,* is no more acceptable when it is called "militant," (in the court's language) than it is when it is called "the use of violence against property." At a more substantive level, the fact that something can be disapprovingly called "foisting" one's "unwanted and superfluous or fictitious services" on an employer does not necessarily preclude that conduct from also being called a "legitimate

---

[129] 457 F.2d at 77.
[130] *Id.* at 76.
[131] *Id.*
[132] *Id.* at 77.
[133] *Id.* (Emphasis added.)
[134] *See* notes 53-55 & accompanying text *supra.*

labor goal." Thus, the distinction articulated by the court is totally without substance.

A classic example of this is the *Green* case. The union there simply wanted the employer to hire union members to scout ahead of bulldozers and warn the drivers of approaching pitfalls; the employer felt that this was an unnecessary precaution. But whatever the diseconomies of the situation, this kind of job acquisition and work sharing among union members is a traditional, legitimate, and otherwise entirely legal objective and purpose of American labor unions.[135] Stated differently, it was as legitimate for the union in *Green* to want to induce the employer to hire an additional man to walk in front of the bulldozer as it was for the union in *Caldes* to want to induce the employer to enter into a collective bargaining agreement. In short, the court really did not succeed in distinguishing the violence in the case before it from the violence in *Green*—not, at least, by reference to the alleged "legitimacy" of the goal.

The court, however, attempted to justify its distinction on another basis. It noted that the language of the Hobbs Act was derived from the New York extortion statute, and under that statute strikes and picketing had been found not to constitute "extortion" if the purpose was to accomplish some legitimate labor objective, such as organization; but such conduct was actionable when merely "used as a pressure device to exact the payment of money as a condition of its cessation."[136] The Hobbs Act had been similarly construed, the court noted, in a case where a labor leader had threatened to call a strike unless the employer paid him some "under the table" money.[137] From this the court apparently concluded that the illegitimacy of the objective is always a necessary element in a Hobbs Act violation. This reasoning, however, is fallacious.

---

[135] Although the NLRA § 8(b)(6), 29 U.S.C. § 158(b)(6) (1976) contains a so-called "anti-featherbedding" provision, it would not prohibit the kind of conduct that was involved in *Green*. In American Newspaper Publishers Assoc. v. NLRB, 345 U.S. 100 (1953), the Court noted that the NLRA "limits its condemnation to instances where a labor organization or its agents exact pay from an employer in return for services not performed or not to be performed." *Id.* at 110. This conclusion is bolstered by Senator Taft's observation that although the Senate did not approve of featherbedding in the broader sense, it "felt that it was impractical to give a board or a court the power to say that so many men are all right, and so many men are too many." 93 CONG. REC. 6441 (1947). Moreover, a demand for the kind of work that was involved in *Green* would not only be a legitimate subject of bargaining, but also a mandatory one. As the Court in *American Newspaper Publishers* put it, the Act "leaves to collective bargaining the determination of what, if any, work, including bona fide 'made work,' shall be included as compensable services." 345 U.S. at 111.

[136] 457 F.2d at 78.

[137] United States v. Kramer, 355 F.2d 891 (7th Cir. 1966).

The distinction adopted by the New York cases with respect to strikes can be understood only in a historical perspective.[138] At one time in the history of American labor law, under the so-called "conspiracy doctrine," strikes and picketing were sometimes said to be inherently coercive, because of the economic injury-in-fact that they caused the person at whom they were directed. However, even before the matter was almost totally preempted by federal statutory law, some of the common law courts had moved considerably away from that position and had adopted a "means/ends" approach. This approach declared the concerted·activities of labor to be actionable or coercive only if they involved either "unlawful means"—conduct which was itself criminal, tortious, or perhaps even in breach of contract—or "unlawful ends"—a term capable of being construed as including almost anything a judge might find to be offensive.

Although this approach is certainly no longer the primary device for measuring the legality of strikes (that function having been assumed by the various federal labor statutes), ghosts of the theory do sometimes emerge in analogous contexts where the issue is whether an otherwise peaceful strike or picketing falls within the purview of some general statute prohibiting "acts of force" or "coercion." In such a case, if a violation exists at all it must necessarily be because the objective itself is unlawful or illegitimate.

The New York case, relied on by the *Caldes* court,[139] held that the otherwise peaceful picketing (the "means") became a coercive exercise of force only when the objective shifted from attempting to organize the employer (a legitimate "ends") to obtaining money from him as a condition of stopping the strike (an illegitimate "ends"). However, if this holding was merely a reflection of the historically pervasive "means/ends" theory of coercion, it becomes readily apparent that one cannot deduce from it what the *Caldes* court deduced—namely, that no strike can be considered coercive unless the ends are illegitimate. To the contrary, under the "means/ends" approach a violent strike is coercive regardless of its objective; and there is nothing in the New York case to suggest otherwise. Thus, the *Caldes* court's reliance on that authority was misplaced.

Finally, at the policy level, the *Caldes* court simply noted that labor unions should be allowed great latitude in pursuing the interests of their members and that "the expansive interpretation of 'extortion' used in the Hobbs Act as urged by the Government would make

---

[138] *See generally* T. HAGGARD, COMPULSORY UNIONISM, THE NLRB, AND THE COURTS 11-24 (1977), which contains, from a slightly different perspective, a comprehensive overview of the evolution of the "criminal conspiracy" doctrine.

[139] People v. Dioguardi, 8 N.Y.2d 260, 168 N.E.2d 683, 203 N.Y.S.2d 870 (1960).

criminal the activities of many militant labor organizations."[140] The court contended, for example, that a strike in violation of a contractual no-strike clause would be a "'wrongful' use of force"[141] and thus, constitute criminal conduct under the government's view. This is a somewhat puzzling assertion, since it would seem that a strike in violation of a no-strike clause would also be a violation under the court's approach. The objective of such conduct certainly could not be denominated a "legitimate labor goal"; thus, by analogy to the New York cases, a strike to obtain that objective could be considered coercive and, therefore, a violation of the Hobbs Act.

As a second example of the possible overbreadth of the government's approach, the court noted that "spontaneous and sporadic fighting on the picket lines could also be condemned as the use of wrongful force and as extortion if [the government's] view was allowed to prevail."[142] The court then indicated that in the year following passage of the Hobbs Act, Congress passed the Taft-Hartley Act, containing "specific provisions which condemned this action as unfair labor practices."[143] Furthermore, the court noted that during the debates on the Taft-Hartley Act, "no congressman expressed an opinion that the Hobbs Act of the preceding year covered union violence while a strike was in progress."[144]

The court's reasoning here is both obscure and factually incorrect. In the first place, the section of the Taft-Hartley Act to which the court specifically referred primarily prohibits secondary boycotts or union attempts to require a neutral employer to stop doing business with the employer with whom the union has a dispute.[145] Although violence can occur in connection with such boycotts, it is certainly not a necessary element of the offense. Moreover, even if violence did occur in a specific situation, the objective of a secondary boycott is to force the victim to stop doing business with someone else, not to force him to pay the union money or anything else of value, *as is required in order for the crime of extortion to exist.* In short, what the Taft-Hartley Act prohibited and what the Government in the *Caldes* case claimed that the Hobbs Act prohibited were two entirely different things. Thus, even if there had been no mention of the Hobbs Act during the Taft-Hartley Act debates, this would have in no way shown that the government's interpretation of the Hobbs Act was overly broad.

---

[140] 457 F.2d at 78.
[141] *Id.*
[142] *Id.*
[143] *Id.*
[144] *Id.*
[145] *See* NLRA § 8(b)(4)(A), 29 U.S.C. § 158(b)(4)(A) (1976).

As a matter of fact, however, the court was simply wrong in suggesting that during the debates on the Taft-Hartley Act no one referred to the prohibitions of the Hobbs Act insofar as strike violence is concerned. In addition to making secondary boycotts, organizational picketing, and jurisdictional disputes unfair labor practices, the Taft-Hartley Act gave federal courts jurisdiction over private damage suits brought by a person injured as a result of such conduct. Senator Aiken, however, wanted to add an amendment which would also allow for injunctive relief in certain situations. He was specifically concerned with the small farmer who could not deliver his produce because of a labor dispute at the market, and for whom a damage action would be impractical. Senator Pepper, in discussing the proposed amendment said: "I do not recall exactly the terms of it, but last year we passed the Hobbs bill, the so-called anti-racketeering bill, which gave jurisdiction to the federal court to act with respect to interruptions of and interference with people delivering their goods, in the way I think the Senator from Vermont has in mind."[146] Senator Aiken, however, responded:

> It has developed that the Hobbs bill was not worth the paper upon which it was written, so far as affording any protection to the farmer was concerned, because the farmer is not *molested* in taking his crop to the market, but when he arrives there may find that the commission man has an agreement for a closed shop, and the farmer cannot unload his produce, and therefore is turned back.[147]

Discounting the hyperbole, Senator Aiken was saying that the Hobbs Act is inadequate to solve the problem totally because it only applies to situations where the farmer has been "molested." The restraints upon delivery that are caused by certain kinds of agreements, secondary boycotts, or jurisdictional strikes cause just as real an injury to the farmer, but are not covered by the Hobbs Act. However, the correlative of his statement is that the Hobbs Act does, in fact, cover acts of molestation, including those that occur in connection with union activities that were, at the time he made this statement, not otherwise illegal under the existing labor statutes. In short, it would seem that the 1947 Congress was aware that the Hobbs Act applied to acts of violence aimed at achieving ends which were not otherwise illegal. This would tend to support the government's position in the *Caldes* case rather than refute it.

In summarizing its overbreadth argument, the court noted that "it appears to us that acts of vandalism of the type committed by these appellants would be more properly and suitably prosecuted in the state

---

[146] 93 CONG. REC. 4860 (1947).
[147] *Id.* (Emphasis added.)

courts and it is doubtful if Congress intended . . . to elevate this type of conduct to the level of the federal court."[148] The opponents of the Hobbs Act, of course, made exactly the same kind of assertion.[149] However, it was of no moment to the *Caldes* court that the majority of Congress apparently felt otherwise.

As specious as the reasoning in the *Caldes* case was, the same result was eventually reached by the Supreme Court without any firmer basis insofar as legislative history or analysis is concerned. In *United States v. Enmons,*[150] the defendants were indicted for firing high-powered rifles at three utility company transformers, draining the oil from a company transformer, and blowing up a transformer substation owned by the company—all done for the purpose of obtaining higher wages and other employment benefits from the company for the striking employees. The indictment was, however, dismissed by the district court on the theory that the Hobbs Act did not prohibit the use of violence in obtaining "legitimate" union objectives.[151] On appeal, the Supreme Court affirmed, advancing four separate justifications for its conclusion.

First, the Court focused on the fact that the statute prohibited only the "wrongful" use of force to obtain property.[152] The Court noted that Congressman Hobbs intended the term "wrongful" to modify the entire section;[153] if it modified only the term "force" it would be redundant because any force to obtain property is wrongful. Therefore, the Court concluded that " 'wrongful' has meaning in the Act only if it limits the statute's coverage to those instances where the obtaining of the property would itself be 'wrongful' because the alleged extortionist has no lawful claim to that property."[154] The Court then added: "Construed in this fashion, the Hobbs Act has properly been held to reach instances where union officials threatened force or violence against an employer in order to obtain personal payoffs, and where unions used the proscribed means to exact 'wage' payments from employers in return for 'imposed, unwanted, superfluous and fictitious services' of workers."[155]

---

[148] 457 F.2d at 79.

[149] *See, e.g.,* 89 CONG. REC. 3201, 3225 (1943); 91 CONG. REC. 11901 (1945).

[150] 410 U.S. 396 (1973).

[151] United States v. Enmons, 335 F. Supp. 641 (E.D. La. 1971), *aff'd.* 410 U.S. 396 (1973).

[152] Specifically, the Act defines extortion as "the obtaining of property from another, with his consent, induced by *wrongful* use of actual or threatened force, violence or fear . . ." 18 U.S.C. § 1951(b)(2) (1976) (Emphasis added.)

[153] 410 U.S. at 399 n.2.

[154] *Id.* at 400.

[155] *Id.* (footnotes omitted).

There are a number of things critically wrong with the Court's reasoning. Firstly, the dilemma posed by the Court—"either construe the Act this way or make it redundant"—is essentially false since there are other possible interpretations. For example, one court of appeals previously suggested that "wrongful" referred to conduct constituting a breach of the peace in contrast to merely tortious conduct.[156] This interpretation gives the term "wrongful" a meaning as a modifier of the term "force" that is certainly as reasonable as the interpretation suggested by the Supreme Court.

A more compelling explanation of the intended meaning of the term "wrongful" can, however, be found through a thoughtful reading of the legislative history. As previously indicated, many of the opponents of the Hobbs Act were fearful that the act would be construed to prohibit legitimate strikes and picketing.[157] Some of them even suggested that a strike is, by definition, the assertion of a form of force.[158] The Hobbs Act proponents answered, of course, that the right to strike was protected by various federal labor statutes; that the rights affirmatively guaranteed by those statutes were not taken away by the Hobbs Act; but that there was nothing in those statutes which gave unions the right to use violence in the course of the exercise of the right to strike.[159]

It is against this background that Congressman Hobbs' assertion that the term "wrongful" "qualifies the entire section" must be viewed.[160] Congressman Voorhis, who was not an enthusiastic supporter of the bill, wanted to make sure that a simple threat to go on strike for higher wages would not be construed as extortion under the act. He was advised that it would not. He then immediately asked the additional question, "Does the word 'wrongful' apply to entire section?"[161] Presumably he wanted to make doubly sure that a peaceful strike would also not be considered wrongful under the Hobbs Act. Congressman Hobbs, in response to the question, then said that the term wrongful "qualifies the entire section."[162] Congressman Hobbs undoubtedly intended this statement to assuage Congressman Voorhis' fears that the act, notwithstanding the proviso, might be so broadly

---

[156] Bianchi v. United States, 219 F.2d 182 (8th Cir.), *cert. denied,* 349 U.S. 915 (1955).
[157] *See, e.g.,* 89 CONG. REC. 3194, 3218 (1943); 91 CONG. REC. 11901 (1945).
[158] Congressman LaFollette, for example, said that "[o]f course, there is an element of coercion in strikes. It is the only right labor has." 91 CONG. REC. 11920 (1945).
[159] *See* 89 CONG. REC. 3193, 3202 (1943), 91 CONG. REC. 11904-05 (1945).
[160] This assertion, and other matters summarized in the text, occurred in the course of remarks among Congressmen Voorhis, Sumners, and Hobbs, recorded at 91 CONG. REC. 11908 (1945).
[161] *Id.*
[162] *Id.*

construed as to prohibit even peaceful strikes. In other words, Congressman Hobbs was saying that even if strikes are considered a form of coercion or force, they are not "wrongful force" unless accompanied by violence. This interpretation easily removes the redundancy which so concerned the Court.

Even if the court correctly concluded that the operative effect of the term "wrongful" in the statute is to identify the objective toward which the force must be directed in order for it to constitute extortion, the Court's reasoning on this point is still subject to question. It is based on the strange assumption that a person has no "lawful claim" to wages which are paid for unwanted services, as in the *Green* case, but that he does have such a claim to wages higher than those the employer would voluntarily pay in the absence of force "in return for genuine services which the employer seeks,"[163] as in the *Enmons* case. However, the distinction is analytically vacuous. A person has no more "lawful claim" to work at $5.00 an hour for an employer who wants to pay only $4.75 than does another person who wants to work for an employer who does not want this person's services at all. In either case, the would-be employee's "lawful claim" to wages is dependent upon the employer's voluntary or noncoerced agreement to pay such wages. Nevertheless, on the basis of a nonexistent distinction, the Court would apply the statute in one case but not the other.

The Court's second justification is somewhat related to this latter point; the Court simply claimed that "the legislative framework of the Hobbs Act dispels any ambiguity in the wording of the statute and makes it clear that the Act does not apply to the use of force to achieve *legitimate* labor ends."[164] To support this extraordinary proposition, the Court first relied on the fact that Congress undoubtedly wanted to overrule the *Local 807* case which had permitted union members to "use their protected status to exact payments from employers for imposed, unwanted, and superfluous services"[165]—presumably not a "legitimate" labor objective, although the Court does not explain why. Assuming that overruling that aspect of the *Local 807* case was the limited intent of Congress, the Court then inferred an intent not to prohibit violence in the pursuit of "legitimate" objectives. In support of this conclusion, the Court referred to several assertions made during the debates to the effect that the bill was not intended to interfere "with any legitimate activity on the part of labor people or labor unions."[166]

---

[163] 410 U.S. at 400.
[164] *Id.* at 401 (Emphasis added.)
[165] *Id.* at 403.
[166] *Id.* at 404 (quoting 91 CONG. REC. 11908 (1945) (remarks of Rep. Sumners)).

This chain of reasoning is weak at almost every link. For example, the Court did not provide an objective basis for distinguishing "legitimate" labor goals from "illegitimate" ones—a basis which could be used to differentiate the objectives being pursued by the union in *Green* from those being pursued by the labor union in *Enmons.*[167] In neither case were the objectives independently illegal, that is, illegal regardless of the means used to achieve them. Also, while it is undoubtedly true that Congress intended to reverse the *Local 807* case, an impartial reading of the legislative history suggests that Congress was at least as concerned with the means that were being used in that case as it was with the ultimate objective being pursued. Finally, the statements relied upon by the Court to the effect that the act would not affect "legitimate" labor activity must be construed in *pari materia* with the more specific assurances that this result would be accomplished by the proviso guaranteeing that the existing labor statutes would not be modified or repealed. This guarantee was, however, tempered by the repeated reminder that these statutes in no way gave labor unions the right to use force or violence.[168]

In short, from the conclusion that the act was not intended to prohibit "legitimate" labor activities, one simply cannot infer that the legitimacy of the objective justifies whatever means are used to achieve it.

The inference not only does not flow from the legislative history; indeed, it is affirmatively contradicted by it. Congressman Hobbs' single objection to Congressman Celler's amendment was that it would allow conduct which was aimed at "lawful" ends to escape the prohibitions of the act even though the conduct itself was "unlawful."[169] By rejecting the Celler amendment, Congress necessarily also rejected the interpretation given to the act by the Supreme Court in *Enmons:* that the legitimacy of the ends sought remove whatever means are used to achieve them from the prohibitions of the statute. Furthermore, while the Court was correct in saying that the Celler amendment was rejected because it "would have operated to continue the effect of the *Local 807* case,"[170] the Court was grossly incorrect in asserting that it was done "solely"[171] for that reason, and that "undoing the restrictive

---

[167] In *Enmons,* the objective of the violence was simply to obtain a more favorable collective bargaining agreement, an obviously legitimate goal in itself, while in *Green* the objective was to obtain job opportunities for union members, a similarly legitimate and entirely traditional goal of the labor movement. *Cf.* United States v. Green, 246 F.2d 155, 160 (7th Cir. 1957) ("There is no doubt that unions have the right to settle disputes [such as the one involved in that case] peacefully by means of negotiation . . ."); *see also* note 134 *supra.*
[168] *See* notes 156-61 & accompanying text *supra.*
[169] *See* notes 72-73 & accompanying text *supra.*
[170] 410 U.S. at 408.
[171] *Id.*

impact of that case"[172] merely means that violence directed at otherwise "illegitimate" ends is now illegal under federal law. To the contrary, it would appear that the legislative overruling of *Local 807* had a much broader purpose.

The only specific language in the legislative history from which the Court could derive support for its interpretation was a single, obscure dialogue between Congressmen Marcantonio and Hobbs.[173] As previously discussed,[174] however, that exchange cannot be construed as a condonation by Hobbs of violence directed toward achieving a "legitimate" end. The Court's reliance on this exchange in support of its interpretation of the statute is unwarranted if not totally misplaced.

The third justification advanced by the Court scarcely deserves mention. The Court simply noted that "in the nearly three decades that have passed since the enactment of the Hobbs Act, no reported case has upheld the theory that the Act proscribes the use of force to achieve legitimate collective-bargaining demands."[175] The Court, without explanation, here cited *Green* and *Kemble* as cases allegedly involving "illegitimate" labor demands, and cited *Caldes* as a case involving "legitimate" labor demands where the indictment was properly dismissed. These cases, however, are either unpersuasive or simply not supportive of the Court's theory.

Nevertheless, from all this the Court concluded that Congress did not intend to legislate the manner in which labor enforced its various demands, since "it is unlikely that if Congress had indeed wrought such a major expansion of federal criminal jurisdiction in enacting the Hobbs Act, its action would have so passed unobserved."[176] To say the least, this is a rather novel theory of statutory interpretation and one certainly not adhered to in other contexts.[177]

Finally, in justifying its narrow interpretation of the Hobbs Act, the Court trotted out its "parade of horribles." The government's theory, the Court said,

> would cover all overtly coercive conduct in the course of an economic strike, obstructing, delaying, or affecting commerce. The worker who

---

[172] *Id.*
[173] *See* text accompanying note 88 *supra.*
[174] *See* text accompanying notes 88-92 *supra.*
[175] 410 U.S. at 408.
[176] *Id.* at 410.
[177] For example, it apparently "passed unobserved" for roughly a hundred years that in the Civil Rights Act of 1866 Congress intended to prohibit purely private as well as public discrimination. However, this did not prevent the Court from so holding in the first case where the issue was squarely presented. Jones v. Alfred H. Mayer Co., 392 U.S. 409 (1968).

threw a punch on a picket line, or the striker who deflated the tires on his employer's truck would be subject to a Hobbs Act prosecution and the possibility of 20 years' imprisonment and a $10,000 fine.[178]

In the first place, as has been suggested before, a reasonable interpretation of the Hobbs Act need not include within its ambit all violence connected with a strike; in many instances either the victim or the purpose is different than would be required in order to constitute "extortion."[179] Moreover, if it is unlikely that Congress intended to punish severely a person who slices tires in the course of a strike to obtain $.50 more per hour, it is certainly no more likely that Congress intended to impose such punishment when that particular conduct occurs in the course of a strike to obtain additional but unwanted work for union members; yet that result could be reached even under the Court's theory. There is, in short, simply no logical relationship between the Court's concern over excessive punishments and its theory that the act should therefore be limited to conduct having an "illegitimate" objective.

In addition, the Court apparently lost sight of the fact that the Hobbs Act, like many other statutes, merely establishes the maximum possible punishments. While it is true that the opponents of the Hobbs Act thought these sanctions might be potentially excessive if applied to the so-called "milder" forms of labor violence,[180] the majority in Congress either felt otherwise or knew that judges would exercise the discretion inherent in their function and mold the punishment to fit the crime.[181] In any event, the Court's concern that an overzealous tire slasher might be fined to the point of impoverishment and incarcerated for the better part of his life is neither a necessary nor even a proper basis for construing the statute the way the Court did.

In sum, none of the reasons advanced by the Court for its reading of the statute can withstand hard analysis. The Court's distortion of the legislative history is particularly disturbing, and it was primarily this that led Justice Douglas, dissenting, to state:

> At times, the legislative history of a measure is so clouded or obscure that we must perforce give some meaning to vague words. But where, as here, the consensus of the House is so clear, we should carry out its purpose no matter how distasteful or undesirable that policy may be to us.[182]

---

[178] 410 U.S. at 410 (footnotes omitted).

[179] *See* text following note 92 *supra.*

[180] *See, e.g.,* 89 CONG. REC. 3201 (1943), where Congressman Celler voiced the concern that the bill may permit simple assaults to be converted into felonies.

[181] *See* Livers v. United States, 185 F.2d 807, 809 (6th Cir. 1950) ("In the enactment of our national laws against crime, the Congress has vested United States District Judges with wide discretion in assessing punishment within the limits of the various federal statutes.").

[182] 410 U.S. at 418 (Douglas, J., dissenting) (footnotes omitted).

The purpose, which Justice Douglas found evident from a careful review of the legislative history, was simply that "the regime of violence, *whatever its precise objective,* is a common device of extortion and is condemned by the Act."[183] With respect to the majority's position, he bluntly but correctly observed that "the Court today achieves by interpretation what those who were opposed to the Hobbs Act were unable to get Congress to do."[184]

Current Ambiguities in the Law

Although the *Enmons* decision resolved the specific issue that was before the Court, the opinion at the same time created two glaring points of uncertainty. First, the Court's holding that the act does not apply to the enforcement of "legitimate" union demands leaves open the question of what exactly an "illegitimate" union demand might be. At the very least, if the sought-after payment would itself be illegal, whether obtained through force or otherwise, a demand for such payment would potentially be within the purview of the Hobbs Act even under the *Enmons* decision. This would appear to cover certain proscribed payments by an employer to any representative of his employees,[185] as well as employer payments into pension funds, check-off payments, and other such payments when not done according to the strict mandates of the law.[186] Arguably, the payment of wages in excess of either mandatory wage guidelines or the terms of a collective bargaining agreement containing a no-strike clause could be included as well. True "featherbedding" would almost certainly be considered a proscribed objective.[187] An employer's requirement that its employees pay union dues in the absence of a valid union security agreement or each individual's voluntary agreement to pay would also seem to qualify,[188] as would the illegal recognition of a union.[189]

More troublesome, however, are those objectives which are not intrinsically "unlawful" but which are, nevertheless, susceptible to being

---

[183] *Id.* (Emphasis added.)

[184] *Id.* at 413.

[185] *See* United States v. Quinn, 514 F.2d 1250 (5th Cir. 1975), *cert. denied,* 424 U.S. 955 (1976). Under the circumstances of that case, the payment of the money was itself thought by the court to be an independent violation of the Taft-Hartley Act, 29 U.S.C. § 186(a) (1976), which generally prohibits payments by an employer to the representative of his employees, thus making it an "illegitimate" objective under the *Enmons* approach.

[186] *See, e.g.,* 29 U.S.C. § 186(c)(4) & (5) (1976) (pertaining to payments made under check-off authorizations and employer contribution into pension funds).

[187] *See* 29 U.S.C. § 158(b)(6) (1976); United States v. Arambasich, 597 F.2d 609 (7th Cir. 1979); United States v. Callahan, 551 F.2d 733 (6th Cir. 1977).

[188] *See* 29 U.S.C. § 158(a) (3) (1976).

[189] *See* United States v. Jacobs, 543 F.2d 18 (7th Cir. 1976), *cert. denied,* 431 U.S. 929 (1977).

called "illegitimate." The existence of this category is a necessary, though perhaps unintended,[190] corollary of the fact that the Court in *Enmons* clearly reaffirmed the *Green* decision. In point of fact, the objective of the union in *Green* was not independently unlawful. Although the union may have been seeking wages for services which the employer felt he did not need, the union members were apparently willing to actually do the work, and thus *Green* was not a true case of "featherbedding" in the statutory sense.[191] What other kinds of "illegitimate" but not unlawful objectives the Court might have in mind is subject only to speculation.[192]

As has been shown, one source of ambiguity stems from the Court's conclusion in *Enmons* that "illegitimacy" of the objective is a necessary element of a Hobbs Act offense. Another ambiguity which the decision creates is whether physical force or violence is also a necessary element. Under prior case law it clearly was not. One of the recurring issues in the cases involving demands for personal payoffs to union officials was whether such demands, when backed *merely* by threats of strikes, picketing, or other presumably peaceful "labor difficulties," could constitute extortion under the Hobbs Act, or whether either actual force or threatened force was required. The courts had consistently held that "reasonable fear of economic loss was enough to come within the statute."[193] The court in *United States v. Varlack*[194] explained:

> It is . . . clear that it was not the intention of the Congress to interfere with the exertion of peaceful economic pressures by a union through the medium of strikes to achieve *legitimate* labor objectives. But it does not follow . . . that only violence or threats of violence are covered by the Act and that the Act is not violated when union leaders or representatives ob-

---

[190] The Court may have simply misread the *Green* decision, for there is some suggestion in the opinion that the Court viewed the facts in *Green* as substantially similar to those in the *Local 807* case. *See* 410 U.S. at 408. This, however, is not accurate in that, in at least some instances, the union members in *Local 807* did not even offer to do any work, thus making it a case of true "featherbedding," and, under *current* law at least, an illegitimate union objective. *See* note 134 *supra*. There was no suggestion of that in *Green*.

[191] *See* note 134 *supra; see also,* United States v. McCullough, 427 F.Supp. 246 (E.D. Pa. 1977).

[192] In United States v. Warledo, 557 F.2d 721 (10th Cir. 1977), a non-labor case, members of a certain Indian tribe were indicted for attempting to obtain money from a railroad to redress past wrongs against the tribe. Payment by the railroad would not, of course, have been illegal, and they alleged that their belief in the validity of their claim was sufficient to bring them within the *Enmons* exception. The Court of Appeals disagreed. "To say that the pursuit of a payment from the railroad for *alleged* past wrongs is not wrongful taxes the statutory language to a highly unreasonable degree." *Id.* at 730.

[193] United States v. Stirone, 262 F.2d 571, 575-76 (3d Cir. 1958).

[194] 225 F.2d 665 (2d Cir. 1955).

tain . . . personal enrichment by using their . . . influence to instill in the minds of the employers with whom they deal a fear of work stoppages or the prolongation of strikes.[195]

Thus, the case law seemed to stand for the symmetrical proposition that it was extortion if *either* the ends *or* the means were independently illegal.[196] By requiring an "illegitimate" objective in every case, *Enmons* necessarily destroyed this formulation, but it is not clear what the decision provides by way of substitution. There are two alternatives: actual legality of the means used is no longer a relevant factor at all, thus making the "illegitimacy" of the ends both a necessary and a sufficient condition of the violation; or *both* illegitimate ends *and* otherwise illegal means (violence of threats of violence) are now necessary for a violation of the Act.

The Court's statement in a footnote to its discussion of the term "wrongful" in *Enmons* is relevant to this issue:

> The Government suggests a convoluted construction of "wrongful." It concedes that when the means used are not "wrongful," such as where fear of economic loss from a strike is employed, then the objective must be illegal. If, on the other hand, "wrongful" force and violence are used, even for a legal objective, the Government contends that the statute is satisfied.[197]

The government's theory was, of course, consistent with the either/or proposition suggested above. In this footnote the Court was clearly rejecting the proposition that the means alone can render a demand illegal. Whether they were also rejecting the proposition that the ends alone can render a demand illegal, is only problematical. That such was not the Court's intent can perhaps be deduced from the fact that the Court also said that "the Hobbs Act has properly been held to reach instances where union officials threatened force or violence against an employer in order to obtain personal payoffs. . . ."[198] The Court here cited three lower court cases which stand unequivocally for the proposition that fear of economic loss, brought about by otherwise peaceful and not illegal strikes or picketing, can rise to the level of extortion under the Hobbs Act, provided the end being sought is itself an illegitimate one.[199] Presumably, the Supreme Court was of the same view.

---

[195] *Id.* at 669.
[196] Comment, *Featherbedding and the Federal AntiRacketeering Act,* 26 U. CHI. L. REV. 150, 159 (1958).
[197] 410 U.S. at 400 n.3.
[198] *Id.* at 400 (footnote omitted).
[199] United States v. Iozzi, 420 F.2d 512 (4th Cir. 1970); United States v. Kramer, 355 F.2d 891 (7th Cir.), *cert. granted and case remanded for resentencing,* 384 U.S. 100 (1966); Bianchi v. United States, 219 F.2d 182 (8th Cir.), *cert. denied,* 349 U.S. 915 (1955).

On the other hand, there is specific language in the legislative history to suggest that the typical "shakedown," where a union official uses his power to call or prolong strikes as a form of threat to induce an employer to make personal payoffs, is not extortion in the statutory sense. Presumably, Congress intended not to involve itself through the Hobbs Act in otherwise peaceful strikes and picketing. In dialogue supporting this proposition, Congressman Sumner stated: "There have been complaints that in the case of strikes an attorney has gone in and asked an operator something like $15,000 or $20,000 as a shake-down to stop a strike. Is there anything in this bill about that?"[200] Congressman Jennings responded: "Not a thing. This does not have a thing in the world to do with strikes."[201]

Since *Enmons,* there have been a number of cases where the courts have indicated that union officials can be convicted for extorting money or other benefits through threats of "economic harm" to an employer.[202] Apparently, the implications of *Enmons* on this issue and the significance of that bit of legislative history have not been discussed. This, however, is a matter of some concern. Where the end is affirmatively illegal, as in the personal payoff situations, perhaps the threatened use of economic force can be called "extortion" without doing undue violence to the term. However, where the "illegality" flows from the fact that the objective is inconsistent with a previously agreed to contract term, one begins to get a little uneasy. Is it proper to make it a "crime" to strike to achieve such an objective? Regardless of one's judgment on this question, it is quite another matter to label as "extortion" the threatened use of *otherwise* peaceful and legal economic force for the purpose of achieving an end which is itself *merely* "illegitimate," as in the *Green* case. Although it seems unlikely that anyone would ever be convicted of extortion for striking in order to require a railroad to hire a "fireman" for a diesel locomotive, such a result flows logically from the *Enmons* decision. This is because the Court in *Enmons* characterized the objective of the union in *Green* as being "illegitimate" even though it was not in fact affirmatively illegal, and suggested that the use of economic force with respect to such ends can be considered extortionate. On the other hand, if the Court did not intend that result, one is necessarily left with the conclusion that the theoretical underpinnings of *Enmons* are hopelessly ambiguous. In either event, some clarification by the Court is certainly in order.

[200] 91 CONG. REC. 11912 (1945).
[201] *Id.*
[202] *See, e.g.,* United States v. Arambasich, 597 F.2d 609 (7th Cir. 1979); United States v. Nell, 570 F.2d 1251 (5th Cir. 1978); United States v. Daley, 564 F.2d 645 (2d Cir. 1977), *cert. denied,* 435 U.S. 933 (1978).

PENDING LEGISLATION

At the time of the *Enmons* decisions, revisions to the Hobbs Act were already in the process of formulation. In 1966, Congress created the National Commission on Reform of Federal Criminal Laws,[203] commonly called the Brown Commission after its chairman, Edmund G. Brown, former governor of California. The mandate of this commission was to study the existing body of federal criminal laws, including the Hobbs Act, and to make recommendations to Congress for revision and recodification. In 1971 the commission submitted its final report, consisting primarily of a proposed draft of a federal criminal code with brief comments for each section.[204] Under this code, extortion, a separate offense under the Hobbs Act, was simply treated as a form of theft. Section 1732 provides that "a person is guilty to theft if he: . . . (b) knowingly obtains the property of another by deception or by threat with intent to deprive the owner thereof, or intentionally deprives another of his property by deception or by threat. . . ."[205] Section 1741 further provided that

"threat" means an expressed purpose, however communicated, to (i) cause bodily injury in the future to the person threatened or to any other person; or (ii) cause damage to property; or (iii) subject the person threatened or any other person to physical confinement or restraint . . . or (x) bring about or continue a strike, boycott, or other similar collective action to obtain property or deprive another of his property which is not demanded or received for the benefit of the group which the actor purports to represent; or (xi) cause anyone to be dismissed from his employment, unless the property is demanded or obtained for lawful union purposes. . . .[206]

Part (x) of the definition stated that a strike or boycott which is not for the purpose of obtaining benefits for the whole group, as in the typical "payoff" or "shakedown" situation, is to be considered illegal. Presumably this is true even though the strike or boycott is an otherwise peaceful one. It also seems clear from the structure of the definition that violence intended to coerce the settlement of a strike (*i.e.,* causing bodily injury, property damage, or physical restraint to obtain an otherwise legitimate group benefit) is also illegal. Finally, as the comments to this section of the draft make clear, part (xi) was clearly designed to exclude from the coverage of the section any threatened or

---

[203] Act of Nov. 8, 1966, Pub. L. No. 89-801, 80 Stat. 1516, *as amended,* Act of July 8, 1969, Pub. L. No. 91-39, 83 Stat. 44.

[204] *Reform of the Federal Criminal Laws: Hearings Before the Subcommittee on Criminal Laws and Procedures of the Senate Committee on the Judiciary, Part I,* 92d Cong., 1st Sess. 129 (1971) [hereinafter cited as *Hearings, Part I*].

[205] *Id.* at 359.

[206] *Id.* at 373-74.

actual enforcement of a union security agreement as long as the dues received under threat of discharge were used for lawful union purposes.[207] Thus, the Brown Commission draft would not have accomplished any major changes in the Hobbs Act as it had been construed before *Enmons.*

The Brown Committee report was submitted to Congress, where it was referred to the Senate and House Committees on the Judiciary and to the president, who created a Criminal Code Revision Unit within the Department of Justice for further study and revision. The Senate committee's end product, after two years of hearings, was bill S. 1,[208] introduced by Senators McClellan, Hruska, and Ervin on January 4, 1973.[209] Although it was derived from the Brown Committee draft, S. 1 differed from that draft in many ways. With respect to the extortion provisions, S. 1 opted in favor of a return to the carefully hammered out language of the existing Hobbs Act. Section 2-9C3 provided that: "A person is guilty of extortion if he intentionally obtains services or property of another from another person, with the consent of the other person, where such consent is induced by wrongful use of actual or threatened force, violence or fear, or under color of official right."[210]

The section-by-section explanation of S. 1 simply stated that "the language is taken from [section] 1951 to carry forward its judicial construction,"[211] presumably including, insofar as Supreme Court cases are concerned, the *Green* decision. It is significant to note that the *Enmons* decision, appearing on February 22, 1973, had not been handed down at the time this explanation was written.

In the meantime, the Criminal Code Revision Unit of the Justice Department had also been working on a draft criminal code. S. 1400[212] was introduced by Senators Hruska and McClellan on March 27, 1973,[213] after *Enmons* had been rendered, and was clearly drafted with the intent of repudiating the decision. Section 1722(a) provided that: "A person is guilty of an offense if he knowingly obtains property of another by force, or by threatening or placing another person in fear that any person will be subjected to bodily injury or kidnapping or that any property will be damaged."[214] The explanation to this section of

---

[207] *Id.* at 374.
[208] S. 1, 93d Cong., 1st Sess. (1973); *Reform of the Federal Criminal Laws: Hearings on S.1, S. 716, S. 1400, S. 1401 Before the Subcommittee on Criminal Laws and Procedures of the Senate Committee on the Judiciary, Part V,* 93d Cong., 1st Sess. 4211-748 (1973) [hereinafter cited as *Hearings, Part V.*].
[209] 119 CONG. REC. 92 (1973).
[210] *Hearings, Part V, supra* note 207, at 4346.
[211] *Id.* at 4786.
[212] S. 1400, 93d Cong., 1st Sess. (1973), *Hearings, Part V, supra* note 224, at 4862-5197.
[213] 119 CONG. REC. 9634 (1973).
[214] *Hearings, Part V, supra* note 207, at 5966.

the bill said that it was "worded to overcome the adverse effects of a recent Supreme Court opinion construing the legislative intent as to one aspect of the existing statute in an unusually restrictive manner."[215] Presumably, the authors of S. 1400 believed that they accomplished this by the omission of the word "wrongful" in the definition of the crime, since the rationale of the *Enmons* decision hangs fairly heavily on the presence of that word in the Hobbs Act.

Hearings were subsequently held on all three versions of a proposed federal criminal code—the Brown Commission draft, S. 1, and S. 1400. On January 15, 1975, Senator McClellan, for himself and several other senators, introduced a new S. 1[216] which incorporated elements of all three of the proposals. Significantly, this S. 1 adopted the language of S. 1400 insofar as extortion was concerned, and the draft report clearly indicated that the subcommittee intended to overrule the *Enmons* decision.[217] Some doubt was expressed, however, as to whether the language used was capable of having that effect. A statement by the Associated Builders and Contractors suggested that in order to make the matter clear the following be added after the final word "damaged" in section 1722(a): "Notwithstanding that the same acts or conduct may also be a violation of state or local law, and notwithstanding that such acts or conduct were used in the course of a legitimate labor dispute or in the pursuit of legitimate union or labor ends or objectives."[218] The second S. 1, with some amendments, was reported by the Subcommittee on Criminal Laws and Procedures to the full committee on the Judiciary on October 21, 1975, where the bill was allowed to die.

The next step was taken on May 2, 1977, when Senators McClellan and Kennedy introduced S. 1437,[219] the Criminal Code Reform Act of 1977.[220] This bill allegedly represented a compromise on several controversial and important points, the lack of agreement on which had kept prior bills from moving through the legislative process. The extortion offense, however, was again simply defined, as obtaining property of another "(1) by threatening or placing another person in fear that

---

[215] *Id.* at 4847.

[216] S. 1, 94th Cong., 1st Sess. (1975).

[217] SENATE COMMITTEE ON THE JUDICIARY, 94TH CONG., 2D SESS., DRAFT REPORT TO ACCOMPANY S. 1 644-59 (Comm. Print 1975).

[218] *Reform of the Federal Criminal Laws: Hearings on S. 1 Before the Subcommittee on Criminal Laws and Procedures of the Senate Committee on the Judiciary, Part XII,* 94th Cong., 1st Sess. 215 (1975).

[219] 123 CONG. REC. S6831 (daily ed. May 2, 1977).

[220] S. 1437, 95th Cong., 1st Sess. (1977), *Reform of the Federal Criminal Laws: Hearings on S. 1437 Before the Subcommittee on Criminal Laws and Procedures of the Senate Committee on the Judiciary, Part XIII,* 95th Cong., 1st Sess. 9485-792 (1977) [hereinafter cited as *Hearings, Part XIII*].

any person will be subjected to bodily injury or kidnapping or that any property will be damaged; or (2) under color of official right."[221]

The committee report on S. 1437[222] contains an excellent summary of the then existing law with respect to extortion under the Hobbs Act and indicates approval of the judicial decisions holding that "fear" under the statute applies not only to fear of physical violence but also fear of economic harm to the victim's property or business. Moreover, the report is unequivocal in its repudiation of the *Enmons* "legitimate objectives" rationale. Noting that such an exception had not been recognized with respect to extortion by other persons, the committee felt that labor union officials were not entitled to such a privileged treatment:

> The thrust of an extortion statute should be to punish violent extortionate means to obtain the property of another regardless of the legality of the ends sought, and this principle should apply in the collective bargaining context as well as elsewhere. Thus, an employer who blows up a union office or causes a union official to be assaulted in order to instill fear and thereby obtain property of the union ought to be guilty under the Act irrespective of whether the property could have been obtained lawfully through collective bargaining. And the same should be true in the reverse situation. Accordingly, the Committee has proposed in effect to overturn the *Enmons* result by treating the parties engaged in a labor dispute no differently from other persons in terms of the applicable prohibitions under this section, which is limited to extortionate means involving actual or threatened violence.[223]

The committee report, however, also responded to the concern expressed by the *Enmons* Court that minor acts of picket line violence might, but for a narrow reading of the statute, be elevated into a federal felony. The report noted that

> in the Committee's view such acts do not fall within the purview of the Hobbs Act (nor should they be Federally punishable) since there is no intent thereby to obtain the employer's property through the use of force and the acts do not in fact cause the employer to part with his property; in short, such isolated acts of violence do not partake of the nature of extortion.[224]

To ensure that the act would be construed in that fashion, the proposed extortion provision contained an additional section specifically recognizing that "it is an affirmative defense to a prosecution under subsection (a)(1) that the threatened or feared injury or damage was minor and was incidental to peaceful picketing or other concerted ac-

---

[221] *Id.* at 9602.
[222] S. REP. No. 605, 95th Cong., 1st Sess. (1977).
[223] *Id.* at 624-25.
[224] *Id.* at 624.

tivity in the course of a bona fide labor dispute."[225] Senator Kennedy, who introduced S. 1437 in the Senate, explained that "a defense is added to the extortion provision to make it clear that minor incidents occuring in the course of legitimate labor picketing are not punishable under the extortion statute."[226]

Immediately thereafter, however, Senator Kennedy introduced an amendment to the extortion provision which deleted the "affirmative defense" section altogether and substituted the following:

> (b) PROOF.—In a prosecution under subsection (a)(1) in which the threat or fear is based upon conduct by an agent or member of a labor organization consisting of an act of bodily injury to a person or damage to property, the pendency at the time of such conduct, of a labor dispute, as defined in 29 U.S.C. 152(9), the outcome of which could result in the obtaining of employment benefits by the actor, does not constitute prima facie evidence that property was obtained 'by' such conduct.[227]

In Senator Kennedy's view, the amendment simply clarified existing law, which, as he understood it, required proof not only of acts of violence but also of the fact that the violence was done with the intent of extorting. Beyond saying that and restating what the amendment itself said directly,[228] he offered no explanation.

Senator Thurmond's remarks, on the other hand, were considerably more enlightening. In explaining his lack of objection to the amendment, he noted that

> this amendment would add a "proof" subsection designed to prevent a trial judge from holding that, in a case described in the new subsection, mere proof that personal injury or property damage occurred during a labor dispute constitutes a sufficient showing of the causal relationship between the obtaining of property and the threat of fear based on that injury or damage to justify submission of that issue to the jury. It prevents such a holding directly, by providing that proof of the coincidence of the labor dispute and the injury or damage in such a case is not "prima facie evidence" of the causal relationship. It is true, of course, that such a causal relationship sometimes does exist where injury or damage occurs during a labor dispute. This proposed subsection, however, is based on the belief that where there is a cause and effect relationship, or the intent to obtain property by means of a threat or fear resulting from injury or damage, it should be possible to prove, in addition to that coincidence, some other circumstances adding to the strength of the inference of causation.
>
> The proposed subsection does not address the question of which particular additional circumstance or circumstances, when proven along with that coincidence, will suffice to justify the submission of the issue to the jury.

---

[225] *Hearings, Part XIII, supra* note 219, at 9602-03.
[226] 124 CONG. REC. S12 (daily ed. Jan. 19, 1978).
[227] *Id.* at S17.
[228] *Id.* at S17-18.

One which clearly would be sufficient in many cases to avoid a directed verdict is the circumstance that the defendant was, or conspired with, a person negotiating on behalf of the union involved in the labor dispute. The same result might obtain, where the repetitive or systematic nature of property damage, or its exact timing, contributed to an inference, based also on the fact that a labor dispute was pending at the time the damage was done, that the damage was purposeful rather than mindlessly vindictive.[229]

The amendment was adopted,[230] and S. 1437 passed the Senate on January 30, 1978;[231] however, the bill was allowed to die in the House.

Undaunted by this lack of prior success, Senator Kennedy, on behalf of himself and several other senators, reintroduced a proposed recodification of the federal criminal laws[232] in the Criminal Code Reform Act of 1979, S. 1722.[233] As introduced, the extortion provisions of this bill were identical to those contained in S. 1437 as passed by the Senate.

Hearings were again held on this bill, and to at least some of the representatives of management the extortion provisions of the bill were apparently satisfactory. The published comments of the Associated Builders and Contractors, Inc. noted, for example, that the omission of the word "wrongful" in the act properly eliminated the "legitimate objectives" exception read into the Hobbs Act by the Court in *Enmons*.[234] Furthermore, the comment stated that, properly construed, the "proof" provision was acceptable as well. In their view, if the violence was something more than a minor and unrelated incident, and the employer could testify "that there was a direct connection between the violence and his decision to increase benefits,"[235] then the requirements of the section would be satisfied and a *prima facie* case of violation made out.

For the most part representatives of organized labor agreed with this interpretation of the proposed statute and, for that reason, were vehemently opposed to it. They objected to the overruling of the *Enmons* decision by elimination of the term "wrongful" in the definition of extortion on many of the same policy grounds that were advanced by the Court in that case. Witnesses cited numerous reasons why *Enmons* should not be overruled: the danger of making minor picket line misconduct a federal criminal felony; the danger of overactive and politically ambitious prosecutors using this as an excuse to intrude un-

---

[229] *Id.* at S17.
[230] *Id.* at S18.
[231] *Id.* S860.
[232] 125 CONG. REC. S12204 (daily ed. Sept. 7, 1979).
[233] S. 1722, 96th Cong., 1st Sess. (1979), *Reform of the Federal Criminal Laws: Hearings on S. 1722, S. 1723 Before the Senate Committee on the Judiciary, Part XIV,* 96th Cong., 1st Sess. 11090-484 (1979) [hereinafter cited as *Hearings, Part XIV*].
[234] *Hearings, Part XIV, supra* note 232, at 10707.
[235] *Id.*

necessarily into strike situations; the resulting unwarranted incursion of federal jurisdiction into an area traditionally left to the states; the disruption of the balance already struck by Congress in the labor-management relations area; the chilling effect upon the exercise by employees of other federally protected rights; and the existence of other remedies for labor violence.[236]

Moreover, the "proof" provision was regarded by labor as inadequate to guard against the evils that would result from making labor activity generally subject to the statute. Thomas X. Dunn, general counsel for the Building and Construction Trades Department of the AFL-CIO, stated:

> It is clear that section 1722(b) is designed to create an additional burden of proof in prosecutions for misconduct which occur in the course of a labor-management dispute. The Government would be required to establish a nexus between the alleged misconduct and the obtaining of otherwise legitimate employment benefits. As a practical matter, however, this burden of proof could be satisfied easily in almost every economic strike where misconduct occurs. It appears that all that the Government need do to satisfy its burden is present the employer involved in the strike who will testify that the alleged violence or threat of violence was a factor in his decision to agree to workers' demands for higher wages or other employment benefit.
>
> Thus, section 1722(b) would not be an effective means of discouraging the Government from applying the proposed extortion statute to any misconduct which occurs in the course of an economic strike.[237]

Robert M. Baptiste, counsel for the International Brotherhood of Teamsters, expressed a similar sentiment:

> While the amendment was proposed in "recognition that tempers often flare in labor disputes" and all strike-related misconduct should not be a Federal criminal offense, we submit that the proof provisions can so easily be satisfied that virtually all economic strikes where misconduct occurs could be subject to this new Federal extortion penalty.[238]

Lance Compa, Washington representative of the United Electrical, Radio and Machine Workers of America (UE), was fearful of the undesirable consequences that could result if the interpretation advanced by Senator Thurmond[239] was taken as controlling. He stated:

> Furthermore, Senator Thurmond offered a detailed interpretation of the Kennedy Amendment that constitutes dangerous legislative history. Senator Kennedy made no careful explanation of his amendment. Senator Thurmond said the proof requirement would not be necessary if the defen-

---

[236] *Id.* at 10045-48, 10691-92.
[237] *Id.* at 10693.
[238] *Id.* at 10049.
[239] *See* note 228 & accompanying text *supra*.

dant "was or conspired with" a union negotiator or if the damage was "repetitive," "systematic" or "purposeful rather than mindlessly vindictive."

Applying this interpretation would, first of all, chill any contact between a union negotiating committee and the rank and file members. Instead of keeping a firm hand on the strike—which is essential if the committee is to be effective at the bargaining table—a committee will be forced into a "hear no evil, see no evil" position, sequestered from the membership in order to avoid possible prosecutions. Even so, a prosecutor out to nail an aggressive union leader could frighten or entice with promises of immunity a rank and file member to implicate the union official in some damage.

Second, the "purposeful rather than mindlessly vindictive" interpretation effectively removes any protection the Kennedy Amendment might have provided, since any damage in a strike, misguided as it may be, is connected to the purpose of winning the strike.[240]

As drafted, the extortion provisions of S. 1722 represented a compromise which could not be held together because of the strong opposition of organized labor. This, however, opened the door anew to the full range of possibilities including reaffirming the *Enmons* approach in its entirety, on the one hand, or providing no special exemptions for labor, on the other, as well as several intermediate possibilities.

Eventually, a new compromise was hammered out. It was agreed that the basic definition of the offense of extortion would remain the same, but that the "proof" provision would be replaced with a "bar to prosecution" provision; the "grading" and "jurisdiction" provisions remained unchanged. In relevant part, the extortion section, as finally approved and reported out by the Senate Judiciary Committee, reads as follows:

§ 1722. EXTORTION.

(a) OFFENSE.—A person is guilty of an offense if he obtains property of another—

(1) by threatening or placing another person in fear that any person will be subjected to bodily injury or kidnapping or that any property will be damaged; or

(2) under color of official right.

(b) BAR TO PROSECUTION.—It is a bar to prosecution under this section that the offense occurred in connection with a labor dispute as defined in 29 U.S.C. 152(9) to achieve legitimate collective bargaining objectives, unless there is clear proof that the conduct which constitutes the threat or placing in fear required under subsection (a)(1) consists of a felony and the conduct was engaged in for the purpose of causing death or severe bodily injury in order to secure such objectives; and the Attorney General, Deputy Attorney General, or Assistant Attorney General for the Criminal Division certifies in writing that—

---

[240] *Hearings, Part XIV, supra* note 232, at 10764.

(A) the facts establish the existence of the additional elements of the offense required under this subsection;

(B) a federal prosecution should be commenced under this section; and

(C) the State is unable or unwilling to proceed with any equivalent prosecution relating to such conduct.[241]

The committee report summarized the compromise in these terms: "The Committee has concluded over the objection of a substantial minority that, except in the circumstances set forth in subsection (b) of section 1722, for the purposes of this bill the *Enmons* decision should not be modified."[242] The Committee, in other words, was willing to accept the *Enmons* proposition that the "legitimacy" of a union's objective was sufficient to justify even the use of physical violence to achieve it, at least in the sense of rendering the violence not illegal under federal law. "On the other hand, the Committee believes that the thrust of an extortion statute should be to punish violent extortionate means to obtain the property of another regardless of the legality of the ends sought and has carried forward current law to that effect in situations not involving a labor dispute."[243]

That is what the proposed statute said, but what it meant was another matter. For example. S. 1722 did nothing to clarify the two main ambiguities of the existing case law. By carrying forward the *Enmons* rationale of "legitimate" union objectives, the proposed statute also carried forward the ambiguities associated with that rationale.[244] Furthermore, the committee report on the bill did nothing to clarify the ambiguity. At one point the report noted that the committee intended to reaffirm the *Enmons* principle "to the effect that labor officials were not covered for their extortionate activities against employers in the course of a labor dispute, if the objective sought was *a permissible goal of collective bargaining.*"[245] Similarly, in discussing the meaning of the phrase "legitimate collective bargaining objectives," the committee report noted that this "encompasses activities to secure *non-corrupt* labor union objectives even if, as in *Enmons,* those activities would violate other laws and excludes such objectives as efforts to obtain personal payoffs or payments for superfluous services."[246]

The difficulty, as with the *Enmons* decision itself, is in fitting the *Green* facts into such a formulation. Although the objective sought in *Green* was certainly to obtain "payments for superfluous services," in

---

[241] S. 1722, 96th Cong., 2d Sess. (1980) (as reported with amendments).

[242] S. REP. No. 533, 96th Cong., 2d Sess. 645 (1980).

[243] *Id.*

[244] *See* pp. 281-84 of text *supra.*

[245] S. REP. No. 533, 96th Cong., 2d Sess. 649 (1980) (Emphasis added.)

[246] *Id.* at 651 (Emphasis added.)

Union Violence

the colloquial sense, as a legal matter the objective was both "noncor-
rupt" and "a permissible goal of collective bargaining"; yet a violation
was found to exist in that case, undoubtedly because of the presence of
violence. The committee, like the Court in *Emmons,* obviously did not
intend to overrule *Green.* Because the presence of violence is no longer
a sufficient condition for a violation, however, the reconciliation of
results of *Green* with the wording of the proposed statute was somewhat less than obvious.

With respect to the second major ambiguity, the committee report
did make clear that the damage to property referred to in the definition
of extortion included only physical damage to property and did not include mere economic loss or injury. Those kinds of Hobbs Act injuries
were, the committee report noted, intended to be covered by the proposed section on blackmail rather than the extortion section.[247] Section
1723 provided that "a person is guilty of an offense [of blackmail] if he
obtains property of another by threatening or placing another person in
fear that any person will . . . (4) improperly subject any person to
economic loss or injury to his business or profession. . . ."[248] The committee report commented that

> this carries forward . . . the present reach of the Hobbs Act. . . . as inter-
> preted by judicial decisions. It is designed to make clear that this section
> does not reach legitimate activity, such as strikes, boycotts, or picketing ac-
> tivity undertaken in support of such objectives as increased wages or im-
> proved working conditions for employees.[249]

The significance of this language should be readily apparent. The
word "improperly," as used in the proposed section on blackmail, was
obviously intended to have the same connotation as the word
"wrongful" contained in the Hobbs Act and construed by the Supreme
Court. This means that the objective must be an "illegitimate" one. So
construed, the blackmail section tied in nicely with the extortion section. If the objective being sought is other than a "legitimate" one, the
extortion section is relevant if the "means" involve threats of physical
damage to person or property, but if the "means" involve mere threats
of economic injury, the blackmail section is relevant.

With respect to the latter, an unduly broad definition of "illegitimate" (*i.e.,* broad enough to encompass the objective sought by
the union in *Green*) would create some difficult problems. It is highly
unlikely that the committee intended to include within the offense of
blackmail a union's peaceful picketing to cause an employer to add jobs

[247] *Id.* at 648 n.58.
[248] S. 1722, 96th Cong., 2d Sess. (1980) (as reported with amendments).
[249] S. REP. NO. 553, 96th Cong., 2d Sess. 657 (1980) (footnote omitted).

which he considers unnecessary or superfluous. The ambiguities inherent in the central concept of the two sections, however, (namely, the fuzzy notion of "legitimate" versus "illegitimate" ends) made this statute, in theory at least, susceptible to that construction.

In summary, if, under the extortion section, the union's objective were other than a "legitimate" one, whatever that means, it would not be covered by the bar under subsection (b) and a prosecution could commence under the main provisions of the section.[250] On the other hand, even if the union was attempting to achieve "legitimate collective bargaining objectives,"[251] the use of force to that end could still be considered extortion if the requirements spelled out in the "unless" clause of subsection (b) were all met. With respect to these, the committee report, which presumably represented an authoritative interpretation of the language, deserved to be quoted in full, because it added things which are certainly not apparent on the face of the language itself:

> The exception to the bar stated in subsection (b) is intended to spell out the exclusive circumstances which may give rise to a Federal extortion prosecution involving unlawful conduct that occurs during a labor dispute to achieve legitimate collective bargaining objectives. In essence this exception adds two elements to the crime. First, the government must prove that the defendant engaged in conduct against the person which, if there were Federal jurisdiction, would be a felony under the code. This element requires an act and not a mere statement or threat to act. Second, the government must prove that the defendant acted not merely "knowingly" as that term is used in the code but with the preestablished intent to (a) cause death or severe bodily injury, and (b) by so doing to force acceptance of the union's demands. "Severe bodily injury" means protracted disabling or disfiguring bodily injury that precludes the individual from gainfully working.
>
> The phrase "clear proof," which has its origin in Section 6 of the Norris-LaGuardia Act (29 U.S.C. Section 106), as used here imposes on the government the obligation to establish by direct evidence that the conduct against the person included in the exception was undertaken for the purpose specified therein. Without such proof, violence, no matter how serious, during a labor dispute is outside the Federal extortion law.
>
> In order to reinforce traditional principles of federalism the bar is not overcome (and the Federal government may not initiate an investigation or prosecution of the illegal conduct) unless the Attorney General, Deputy Attorney General, or Assistant Attorney General for the Criminal Division certifies in writing that (a) the facts establish the existence of the additional elements of the offense required by the exception to the bar; (b) a Federal prosecution should be commenced under this section; and (c) for reasons other than insufficient evidence the State refuses to proceed with a pro-

---

[250] *See* text accompanying note 240 *supra.*
[251] S. 1722, 96th Cong., 2d Sess. (1980).

secution relating to the conduct against the person specified in the exception to the bar. Such a certification must be based on evidence obtained by or available to the State prior to the Federal government's involvement in the matter; however, once the certification is made, this provision does not limit the Federal government's ability to secure and rely on additional evidence.[252]

Construed in this fashion, it would appear that section 1722 would have resulted in federal prosecution of violence in connection with collective bargaining only in the rarest of situations. The "clear proof" standard has, for example, been a difficult one to meet in Norris-LaGuardia cases, and one could expect it to be a popular and successful ground of defense under the proposed extortion section as well. Similarly, the limits on federal *initiation* of investigations and prosecutions under the extortion section, as suggested by the committee report, would severely hamstring the enforcement of the statute. The exclusion of threats to cause property damage and the definition of "severe bodily injury" in terms of "protracted disabling or disfiguring bodily injury that precludes the individual from gainfully working"[253] further limits the circumstances under which the section could be applied to labor violence. Moreover, insufficiency of the evidence as a basis for nonprosecution by the state is not, according to the committee report, sufficient to permit federal involvement, an ironic limitation since the state's lack of sufficient evidence may well be attributable to its inability to effectively investigate a crime having interstate dimensions. Finally, the requirement of what amounts to an *affirmative* recommendation from someone at the *highest* levels of the Justice Department that a prosecution be commenced seems to create almost a presumption against prosecution, immediately makes the decision a politically sensitive one, and also suggests that the discretion involved there is somewhat broader than that which would exist otherwise. Nevertheless, the Criminal Code Reform Act of 1979, S. 1722, containing the extortion provision thus described, was reported out favorably by the Senate Judiciary Committee. It was, however, allowed to die at the end of the 96th Congress.

When the Criminal Code Reform Act was reintroduced the following year, as S. 1630,[254] the extortion section had been changed once again. The complicated and obscure provisions of the prior section 1722 were replaced with the simple reinsertion of the word "wrongful" in the definition of the offense. The report accompanying the committee bill stated that "the Committee has concluded that for the purposes of this

---

[252] S. REP. No. 553, 96th Cong., 2d Sess. 651-52 (1980).
[253] *Id.* at 651.
[254] S. 1630, 97th Cong., 1st Sess. (1981).

bill the *Enmons* decision should not be modified,"[255] and as drafted this section would thus simply leave the current law unchanged. Although most of the attention was initially focused on the Senate committee hearings, the House of Representatives was at this time also quietly proceeding on the matter of revising and recodifying the federal criminal laws. The Brown Commission draft itself was, for example, introduced in the House as H.R. 300,[256] but no hearings were ever held on it. As the reforms began to solidify in S. 1 and S. 1400, "liberal" representatives, alarmed at the direction the legislation was taking, introduced their own proposed code of federal criminal laws, H.R. 10850[257] in 1975 and H.R. 1250[258] in 1976. One commentator has called these "belated and hastily drafted alternatives"[259] to S. 1, and they do not really warrant any detailed analysis.

The first proposal to receive serious consideration by the House was H.R. 6869.[260] This was the so-called "companion bill" to S. 1437 which omitted the term "wrongful" (thus overruling *Enmons*) and provided an affirmative defense if the threatened injury was "minor and incidental to peaceful picketing."[261] Organized labor was not, however, happy with the wording of this defense. Lance Compa, Washington representative of the United Electrical, Radio and Machine Workers of America (UE) stated that

> H.R. 6869 provides a defense, not a bar to prosecution, that the threatened or feared injury or damage was "minor" and "incidental" to a "bona fide labor dispute." Each of these terms is dangerously unclear. How much damage is minor? What is incidental? Who determines whether there is a bona fide labor dispute? Suppose, for example, what an employer labels a "wildcat" strike is later found by the NLRB to be protected Unfair Labor Practice strike? Where would this leave a prosecution based on the "bona fide" requirement?[262]

The bill was never reported out of committee. That year, however, the Subcommittee on Criminal Justice did report H.R. 13959[263] to the House Committee on the Judiciary. This bill was designed merely to reorganize the federal criminal laws, but not, at that point in time, to change their substance. Thus, it carried forward the law as construed by the Court in *Enmons.*

---

[255] S. REP. NO. 97-307, 97th Cong., 1st Sess. 677 (1981).

[256] H.R. 300, 92d Cong., 2d Sess. (1972).

[257] H.R. 10850, 94th Cong., 1st Sess. (1975).

[258] H.R. 12504, 94th Cong., 2d Sess. (1976).

[259] Schwartz, *Reform of the Federal Criminal Laws: Issues, Tactics, and Prospects,* 41 LAW & CONTEMP. PROB. 12 (1977).

[260] H.R. 6869, 95th Cong., 2d Sess. (1978).

[261] *Id.*

[262] *Hearings, Part XIV, supra* note 232, at 10763.

[263] H.R. 13959, 95th Cong., 2d Sess. (1978).

The next proposed revision to the federal criminal laws appeared in the form of H.R. 6233.[264] As introduced, section 2522 of this bill provided, with respect to the extortion offense that:

> (a) Whoever knowingly threatens or places another person in fear that—
> (1) any person will be subjected to bodily injury or kidnapping; or
> (2) that any property will be damaged; and thereby obtains property of another, or attempts to do so, commits a class C felony.
> (b) It is not a defense to a prosecution for an offense under this section that the conduct constituting the offense was in furtherance of a legitimate objective or activity.[265]

Subsection (b) obviously makes express what the omission of the term "wrongfully" in subsection (a) leaves only implicit—namely, that the *Enmons* approach was to be repudiated in its entirety.

When H.R. 6233 was later reintroduced as H.R. 6915,[266] however, the extortion provision had been changed by the insertion of the term "wrongfully" before the term "obtains" in subsection (a), thus making subsection (a) directly contradictory to the language in subsection (b). Apparently, the legal and logical effect of that was to reaffirm the "legitimate objectives" defense of *Enmons*.[267]

H.R. 6915 was reported out of committee in this form, but it too died without having been acted on at the end of the 96th Congress. Its counterpart in the 97th Congress, H.R. 1647, met a similar fate.

The legislative limbo that these comprehensive revisions of the federal criminal code repeatedly find themselves in suggests that the eventual enactment into law of any one of them is unlikely. In the 97th Congress, members with a more specific interest in *at least* amending the coverage of the Hobbs Act thus introduced separate legislation to accomplish that result. For example, the amendments to the Hobbs Act which were proposed by Senator Thurmond (and others) in S.613[268] specifically state that it is not the intention of Congress to allow an exception simply because the violent misconduct "takes place in the course of a legitimate business or labor dispute or in pursuit of a legitimate business or labor objective." In addition to thus overruling the *Enmons* decision, S. 613 went further and also would have made it

---

[264] H.R. 6233, 96th Cong., 1st Sess. (1979). A "working draft" of this bill was also introduced in the Senate as S. 1723, 96th Cong., 1st Sess. (1979), but with subsection (b) omitted.
[265] *Id.*
[266] H.R. 6915, 96th Cong., 2d Sess. (1980).
[267] One logical, but somewhat unlikely explanation, of this draft was that it made "legitimate objectives" a defense in all cases *except* those involving labor extortion, thus turning on its head the uniquely favored treatment afforded labor unions by the *Enmons* decision.
[268] S. 613, 97th Cong., 1st Sess. (1981).

a federal crime to interfere with interstate commerce by "inflicting, or threatening to inflict, death or serious bodily injury on any person" or by "willfully damaging to the extent of $2,500 or more any property, including real property, used for business purposes."

At hearings before the Subcommittee on Criminal Law,[269] S. 613 received warm support from some groups, strong opposition from others, and only a limited endorsement from the Department of Justice. The fairness and rationality of the special *Enmons* exception,[270] the extent of labor violence in this country,[271] the ability of local authorities to deal with it,[272] the burdens this would impose on federal enforcement agencies,[273] and the propriety of extending federal criminal jurisdiction to cover such acts of misconduct[274] were issues of fact and policy which again divided the various witnesses. The position of the Department of Justice was that the *Enmons* decision should be overruled, but that the expansion of the Hobbs Act to cover non-extortionate violence was unwarranted.[275]

Although the proponents of S. 613 generally conceded that minor picket line incidents would not be covered by the extortion prohibition,[276] it is not clear how the proposed statute effects that result or what the scope of the exclusion would be. The representative from the Department of Justice explained that "conduct in the nature of incidental picket line violence is not in itself designed for the obtaining [of] property from another,"[277] and thus would not even fall within the definition of extortion. However true that may be in the abstract, it provides little guidance to those charged with the enforcement of the statute, and this witness thus urged that appropriate language be drafted to delineate expressly the scope of this exclusion.

In any event, because of the Reagan administration's opposition to S. 613's expansion of federal criminal jurisdiction and the prospect of this bill being bottled up indefinitely in the Judiciary Subcommittee on Criminal Law, Senator Thurmond later introduced S. 2189[278] and assigned it directly to the Judiciary Committee itself, of which he is the chairman. More narrow in scope than the prior proposal, S. 2189 would

---

[269] S. 613, *A Bill to Amend the Hobbs Act: Hearings before the Subcommittee on Criminal Law of the Committee on the Judiciary,* 97th Cong., 1st & 2nd Sess. (1981–82).

[270] *See, e.g., id.* at 18-19, 22, 37-39, 61, 140.

[271] *See, e.g., id.* at 10-12, 17, 21, 41, 62, 135.

[272] *See, e.g., id.* at 7, 14, 17, 21, 72, 151.

[273] *See, e.g., id.* at 6, 9, 16, 18, 36-37, 99-100.

[274] *See, e.g., id.* at 8, 34-36, 39-40, 138-40.

[275] *Id.* at 5-6.

[276] *See, e.g., id.* at 3, 5, 82, 84.

[277] *Id.* at 5.

[278] S. 2189, 97th Cong., 1st Sess. (1981).

Union Violence

have simply overruled the *Enmons* decision by providing that the legitimacy of the objective is no defense in an extortion case. In the House of Representatives, H.R. 450[279] would have both overruled the *Enmons* exception and further expanded the Hobbs Act by prohibiting acts of damage or destruction of property, in excess of $2,000, which interfere with interstate commerce, whether these violent acts are of an extortionate nature or not. No final action, however, was taken on either of these bills.

Proposed amendments to the Hobbs Act continue to be introduced, however. In the 98th Congress, Senator Grassley has introduced a bill, S. 452,[280] which would overrule *Enmons,* but which would also exclude relatively minor picket line violence from its coverage. Conduct that is merely incidental to peaceful picketing in the course of a legitimate labor dispute, that causes bodily injury or damage to property of less than $2,500, or that was not intended to extort property would be excluded.

On the other hand, H.R. 49[281] and H.R. 287[282] go beyond mere extortion and would also prohibit other acts or threats of violence which occur in the context of a labor dispute or in the proximity of the work place.

[279] H.R. 450, 97th Cong., 1st Sess. (1981).
[280] S. 462, 98th Cong., 1st Sess. (1983).
[281] H.R. 49, 98th Cong., 1st Sess. (1983).
[282] H.R. 287, 98th Cong., 2d Sess. (1983).

CHAPTER X

Picket Line and Strike Violence as Grounds for Discharge[1]

Despite the availability of other legal remedies, the "self-help" remedy of discharge from employment is often the most effective response that an employer can take when employees resort to the use of force and violence in labor disputes.

The employer's power to discharge such employees is, however, subject to several limits—firstly, to those imposed by the terms of the employment contract itself (most commonly, a collective bargaining or strike settlement agreement between the employer and the union representing its employees), and secondly, to those imposed by the federal National Labor Relations (Taft-Hartley) Act (NLRA). Despite the almost universal moral condemnation of such conduct by society, the law does not always translate that outrage into an effective remedy insofar as allowing discharge, at least when it occurs within the context of a "labor dispute" between the employer and a labor union.

CONTRACTUAL LIMITATIONS: THE APPROACH OF LABOR ARBITRATORS

When an individual is employed "at will," he may be discharged by the employer for any reason or for no reason at all, and the question of whether one may be terminated for violent misbehavior is thus easily answered.[2] When, however, an individual is employed subject to the terms of a collective bargaining agreement, the employer's liberty to terminate the relationship is almost always more limited. Although

---

[1] Portions of this chapter originally appeared as Haggard, *Picket Line and Strike Violence as Grounds for Discharge,* 18 HOUSTON L. REV. 423 (1981).

[2] *See, e.g.,* General Elec. Co., 45 Lab. Arb. 490, 491 (1965) (Gomberg, Arb.) (in contrast to the need for establishing a rationale for employee discipline under a collective bargaining agreement, "[no] such rationale was needed to justify the discipline of the servant by the master in the antecedent master-servant relationship"); Park v. Southeastern Haulers, Inc., 210 S.C. 18, 30, 41 S.E.2d 387, 393 (1947) (with respect to an employment at will, "the [employer] may discharge the employee without cause (and without duty to furnish him any explanation, recommendation, or what not)").

some collective agreements spell out in some detail the circumstances under which an employer can discharge or otherwise discipline an employee, most agreements merely provide that it must be "for cause," "for just cause," "for good and sufficient cause," or for some similarly described reason,[3] thus raising the question of whether such cause includes acts of violence against person and property. The forum in which that issue is commonly resolved is that of labor arbitration.

In the context of the normal work environment, labor arbitrators tend to take a fairly hard line on violent acts, especially assaults. One commentator has observed:

> Actual violence is almost always dealt with severely. Arbitrators usually consider physical assault unjustifiable even in the face of extreme vocal provocation. Even when an employee strikes a supervisor or other employee, the victim should not overreact to the situation by becoming the aggressor. According to many decisions he is only justified in defending himself, not in retaliating.[4]

Even allowing for the existence of labor arbitrators who might tend to be a bit more liberal in finding exonerating circumstances for "minor acts" of workplace violence, the significant point is that the entire standard of what constitutes just cause for discharge changes whenever the conduct occurs within the context of a labor dispute of some variety. As one arbitrator put it, "What may be called just cause in times of industrial peace is not just cause for discipline during a strike. This is a universal rule among arbitrators."[5] Consequently, many assaults and acts of property damage, which in normal times would clearly warrant discharge from employment, are in times of strike found to be merely grounds for some lesser form of industrial discipline, usually suspension without pay.[6] Although such an approach may be nearly universal among labor arbitrators, the justifications advanced for it differ widely.

---

[3] *See* [1979] 2 COLLECTIVE BARGAINING NEGOTIATIONS AND CONTRACTS (BNA) 40:11-12.

[4] Rettig, *Arbitrations on Discipline,* in ARBITRATING LABOR CASES 86 (N. Levin ed. 1974).

[5] United States Pipe & Foundry Co., 52 Lab. Arb. 1112, 1116 (1969) (Finley, Arb.).

[6] Most arbitrators feel that the "just cause" standard itself implicitly includes a requirement that the penalty be proportionate to the offense and that they, therefore, have the inherent power to reduce or modify a penalty that is too severe. *See generally* F. ELKOURI & E. ELDOURI, HOW ARBITRATION WORKS 628–30 (3d ed. 1973). Since discharge is said to be the "capital punishment" of the industrial relations world, American Enka Corp., 39 Lab. Arb. 441, 442 (1962) (Updegraff, Arb.), this power is generally resorted to in only the most egregious cases of picket line and strike violence. *See, e.g.,* J. R. Simplot Co., 64 Lab. Arb. 1061, 1064–65 (1975) (Collings, Arb.). Suspension without pay is nearly always the substituted lesser punishment. Where the authorized suspension is, however, shorter than the time the employee has *actually* been laid off, reinstatement with partial backpay represents a windfall to the employee, which must

The first rationale for this policy proceeds from the nature of "just cause" itself. One arbitrator has commented that "nothing in the contract endows the employer with the right to invoke the disciplinary function for any reason other than in pursuit of its managerial function during that time when the employee is obligated to contribute to production."[7] Even if in normal times the employer's right is expanded to discipline misconduct which is somehow work related, even though it occurred on neither company time nor company property,[8] in times of strike the justification for employer discipline, according to this argument, is even more attenuated. In the strike situation, the entire employer-employee relationship is in abeyance, the loyalty normally expected of an employee has already been ruptured, the collective bargaining agreement frequently has expired, and considerations of in-plant discipline and order do not exist.[9] In short, a strike represents a form of "economic war" and the standards governing the relationship in times of peaceful production simply are not appropriate. This attitude is clearly reflected, for example, in the decision of Arbitrator McCoy in the *Southern Bell Telephone & Telegraph*[10] case. He said:

> Ordinarily, and in normal times within the plant, when the plant is operating normally, an invitation to a fight addressed to a foreman or other supervisor, is a very serious thing. It is disruptive of discipline. No plant can operate successfully if its foremen are subject to that sort of intimidation. Thus in ordinary times I consider such an incident as very serious. But this was not an ordinary time. Discipline was not threatened in any event, because the normal employee-supervisor relationship was in abeyance during the strike; the incident did not occur in the plant while the Company was trying to operate the plant normally. It occurred in front of the Building where Mr. J_____ had been engaged in a scuffle with a striker. The reasons which impel me to hold an invitation to fight as a serious matter in normal times within the plant do not apply to this situation.[11]

Whatever the legitimacy of the above rationale, it can only be carried so far. Conceivably, it might be used as a justification for a more liberal

---

surely lessen the deterrent effects of the so-called penalty. Indeed, reinstatement even without back pay is susceptible of being construed as arbitral condonation of the conduct. As expressed by one arbitrator, "if H_____ were returned to work by the Arbitrator, it would be a type of visible and highly public vindication, by at least a forgiving third party, of his actions following [a] contested hearing." General Tel. Co., 69 Lab. Arb. 351, 357 (1977) (Bowles, Arb.). The agreement under which the arbitration is conducted may, of course, expressly limit the arbitrator's power to reduce a penalty once it has been found that the employee did in fact engage in conduct warranting *some* discipline. *See, e.g.,* Harvey Aluminum, Inc., 46 Lab. Arb. 949, 955 (1966) (McNaughton, Arb.).

[7] General Elec. Co. 45 Lab. Arb. 490, 492 (1965) (Gomberg, Arb.).

[8] General Tel. Co., 69 Lab. Arb. 351, 357 (1977) (Bowles, Arb.).

[9] *See, e.g., id.* at 352; General Elec. Co., 45 Lab. Arb. 490, 492 (1965) (Gomberg, Arb.); General Elec. Co., 38 Lab. Arb. 1182, 1185 (1961) (Holly, Arb.).

[10] 26 Lab. Arb. 186 (1956) (McCoy, Arb.).

[11] *Id.* at 193.

attitude toward provocative conduct such as picket line profanity and insults of the kind involved in the *Southern Bell* case,[12] and for other acts that would in normal times be considered "disloyal" to the enterprise. Such reasoning surely cannot, however, justify the malicious destruction of company property or even acts of "minor" violence against the employer, its supervisory personnel, other employees, customers, or suppliers. As one arbitrator stated, "Vigorous persuasion does not extend to physical assault, but it most assuredly will include the use of a vocabulary not found in the politer circles."[13] Moreover, physical violence, whether it occurs during a strike or in the normal work enrivonment, should be considered cause for discharge, not because of its negative effect upon production, although that is an additional reason, but simply because this is conduct which no civilized person can be expected to tolerate in those with whom he associates.[14] Thus, as a matter of contract interpretation, unless there is clear evidence of a contrary intent, the canons of both common sense and decency would suggest that the term "just cause for discharge" includes almost any act which violates the physical integrity of another person or his property.

This view is reflected in the opinion of the board of arbitrators in the *Indiana Bell Telephone Co.*[15] case, as follows:

> The Board is cognizant of the gravity of the penalty and that discharge is properly reserved only for the most serious offenses. The Board is mindful of the right of every citizen to be free from physical assault, coercion or duress as to personal freedom, and the wanton destruction of his property. Violence to compel adherence to a cause, whether it be of a political, religious, or ideological nature, is alien to our American system.
>
> The right to strike for lawful purposes is recognized, but that right is restricted by the corresponding duty to respect those rights which are guaranteed to every citizen. The existence of a strike, no matter how just the cause, does not serve to abrogate the basic rights of individuals to be free from bodily harm, restraint of their persons, threats inducing fear, and damage to their property.[16]

Of course, if an employer, motivated by considerations of forgiveness or economics, elects not to terminate the employment relationship

---

[12] Downey Beer Distribs., Inc. 46 Lab. Arb. 378, 379 (1966) (Kotin, Arb.).

[13] General Elec. Co., 45 Lab. Arb. 490, 492 (Gomberg, Arb.).

[14] *See id.,* where the Board noted:
   The employer is not the custodian of public order. He does have the same right as does any other citizen when he has sustained a personal injury to add the sanction of his private power lawfully exercised when the public authority has adjudged the accused guilty of an illegal act in which the employer is the injured party.
Id. at 492.

[15] 22 Lab. Arb. 567 (1954) (Fisher, Horvitz, & Kelliher, Arbs.).

[16] *Id.* at 570.

with such a person, it may exercise that option on an individual basis; but under most collective bargaining agreements there is no warrant for assuming that the employer has contractually bound itself to do this as a general matter.

The second justification that is frequently advanced for treating "labor dispute" violence more leniently than normal work-related violence stems from a recognition of the fact that a strike and picket line create an emotionally charged situation that is by its very nature precipitous of violence even among persons normally not prone in that direction, thus serving to exonerate them from full culpability.[17] The following quotation reflects this attitude:

> Scuffling, jostling and occasional blows on the picket line between pickets and working employees is a common result of labor disputes. Such conduct is not to be condoned. It simply has not been eradicated from the American scene. When emotions are high and tempers are short such flare-ups do occur, human nature being what it is. Courts and Boards have almost uniformly held that conduct of this nature, although reproachful, is not cause for discharge.[18]

Of course, the failure of arbitrators to treat such conduct seriously may well be one reason it has not been "eradicated." Moreover, it must be borne in mind that this environment of tension is created at least in part by the strikers themselves[19] and that the individuals who participate in these mass activities do so of their own accord and with full knowledge of the strike's propensity to evoke emotional and violent reactions.[20] In short, even if in some situations a momentary loss of self-control, brought about by unexpected and unavoidable circumstances, can legitimately be considered as a mitigating factor insofar as personal culpability is concerned, it does not seem that the

---

[17] *See, e.g.,* General Tel. Co., 69 Lab. Arb. 351, 354 (1977) (Bowles, Arb.) ("It is elementary that the incident must be viewed in the context of a long economic strike where tempers flare, resentments are deep, group loyalties become intemperate"); General Elec. Co., 38 Lab. Arb. 1182, 1181 (1961) (Holly, Arb.) ("acts of indiscretion and violence are to be more expected during strikes"); Southern Bell Tel. & Tel. Co., 26 Lab. Arb. 186, 192 (1956) (McCoy, Arb.) (attempt to provoke a fight characterized as "only the sort of angry reaction, sudden flareup of temper, so-called 'animal exuberance,' to be expected in tense situations on the picket line"). The other side of the coin is, of course, that this excuse is not available for strike violence that occurs away from the picket line, an element sometimes noted by arbitrators when considering the evidence. *See, e.g.,* General Tel. Co., 69 Lab. Arb. 351, 360 (1977) (Bowles, Arb.); Southern Bell Tel & Tel. Co., 26 Lab. Arb. 593, 596 (1956) (Alexander, Arb.); Southern Bell Tel. & Tel. Co., 25 Lab. Arb. 556, 561 (1955) (Alexander, Arb.).

[18] Southern Bell Tel. & Tel., 25 Lab. Arb. 767, 769 (1956) (Schedler, Arb.).

[19] Sawbrook Steel Castings Co., 50 Lab. Arb. 725, 733-34 (1968) (Seinsheimer, Arb.).

[20] *But see* General Elec. Co., 38 Lab. Arb. 1191 (1962) (Guthrie, Arb.), where the arbitrator spoke of "the emotional pressures of such a crowd where a striker *finds himself*" *(emphasis added),* as if his presence there was somehow a surprise and quite beyond his control. *Id.* at 1195.

picket line presents such a situation. Rather, individuals must assume full responsibility for their own acts of misconduct, notwithstanding consideration of the "heat-of-the-moment."

A more reasoned view on this matter is reflected in the opinion of Arbitrator Schmidt in the _Westinghouse Electric Corp._[21] case:

> I am not unmindful of the fact that a labor dispute resulting in a strike and picketing creates an atmosphere of tension, and is likely to generate rough conduct and emotional displays. But even in that atmosphere I cannot condone or deal lightly with acts of violence, bodily assaults upon company representatives and non-striking employees, and destruction of property.[22]

This approach, however, seems to be a minority view.

The third justification attempts not only to excuse labor dispute violence by reference to the inherently emotional nature of the situation, but also to shift the blame and responsibility to the employer. Paraphrasing this view does not, however, do justice to it; the full dimensions of the rationale can be fully appreciated only by reference to the actual words of its proponents, of which the following lengthy quotations are exemplars.

In _J.R. Simplot Co._,[23] Arbitrator Collings stated the general proposition in these terms: "Although the Company had a legal right to keep the plant open, its decision to do so gives it some share of responsibility for creating an environment conducive to violence."[24] The evidence and reasoning on which that conclusion was based was summarized as follows:

> [According to an expert on industrial disputes,] violence occurs usually _only_ when management decides to utilize strategies of replacing striking workers and/or deploying armed men. There is seldom violence when the struck plant is shut down, and virtually _always_ violence when management however, legally within its rights, decides to continue operation. Management knows this well and is therefore guilty of "contributory negligence" when it takes on the historical inevitability of violence in choosing to operate. It is a bit like the woman who dresses provocatively, struts in an inciting manner at 2 a.m. in a dubious neighborhood, and then virtuously yells "rape" when attacked.[25]

Presumably, Arbitrator Collings would exonerate the rapist in that situation from any serious criminal liability or, to keep the analogy straight, would at least view with opprobrium any self-help efforts at-

---

[21] 40 Lab. Arb. 1169 (1963) (Schmidt, Arb.).
[22] _Id._ at 1172.
[23] 64 Lab. Arb. 1061 (1975) (Collings, Arb.).
[24] _Id._ at 1065. (Emphasis added.)
[25] _Id._

tempted by the unfortunate woman, a result certainly at odds with the mainstream of American jurisprudential thought.[26]

Similarly, in *United States Pipe & Foundry Co.*,[27] Arbitrator Finley offered the following observations:

> So spotless a capitolist [sic] as Andrew Carnegie is quoted as having said "While public sentiment has rightly and unmistakenly condemned violence even in the form for which there is most excuse I would have the public give due consideration to the terrible temptation to which the working man on a strike is sometimes subjected. To expect that one dependent upon his daily wage for the necessities of life will stand peacefully by and see a man employed in his stead is to expect too much."
>
> The Company contributed to bad feelings on this picket line by sending out a letter afore mentioned in this case while negotiations were in progress [dealing with the terms and conditions of employment that would prevail once the then existing contract expired], then another letter sent out by the Company of October 27th which had been quoted previously in the case as consisting of a back-to-work movement.
>
> These letters, in the opinion of the Referee, contributed to disorder and high tempers on the picket line. Maintaining plant operations places some responsibility on the Company. Since the history of labor conflicts and strikes are very much more prevalent when the plant tries to operate, you must expect trouble and be willing to pay the consequences.[28]

The keystone of this argument—namely Carnegie's patronizing attitude and low estimation of the ability of wage earners to resist the temptation of using physical violence—is an affront to the dignity, intelligence, and moral sensibilities of the entire working class. The refusal to recognize a person as a morally responsible agent, capable of choosing right over wrong and being expected to live with the consequences, represents the ultimate denial of that person's humanness;[29] and excusing the conduct of the few strikers who choose violence as the means for achieving an economic goal does an injustice to them, as well as to the many laborers on the picket line who resist that temptation.

---

[26] *See* Wadlington v. State, 254 Ind. 94, 257 N.E.2d 822, 825 (1970). ("While this court might agree with appellant that for a woman to get out of a car late at night and to walk unaccompanied along a city street might not be a wise course of action, such conduct on the part of the victim is by no means a defense to the commission of the crimes charged [kidnapping, assault with intent to commit rape]"); State v. Overman, 269 N.C. 453, 153 S.E.2d 44, (1967) ("[c]ontributory negligence by the victim is no bar to prosecution by the State for the crime of rape").

[27] 52 Lab. Arb. 1112 (1969) (Finley, Arb.).

[28] *Id.* at 1116.

[29] *See generally,* C. Lewis, *The Humanitarian Theory of Punishment,* in God in the Dock (1970).

Finally, in *General Electric Co.*,[30] Arbitrator Holly, in an often-quoted opinion, summarized the "employer fault" theory in these terms:

> The Company's decision to exercise its right to keep the plant open during the strike and to actively encourage workers to report for work contributed to a situation of historically predictive results. Labor history amply demonstrates that token picketing is practiced if the employer closes the plant during a strike, and that picket line incidents almost inevitably occur when the plant is kept open. It must be presumed that Company officials were aware of this possibility. Although the Company had a legal right to keep the plant open, its decision to do so gives it some share of responsibility for creating an environment conducive to violence. In the real world, it is frequently difficult to equate the rights of the Company to operate during a strike with the rights of strikers to engage in picketing. The truth of the matter is that these two rights are not completely compatible because the successful pursuit of one defeats the other; thus, a conflict situation is created. This fact, of course, does not excuse picket line violence, but it does place some of the responsibility for such on the door stop of the Company.[31]

This notion of "conflicting rights," upon which the conclusion about joint responsibility is partially based, reflects an inadequate conception of the specific rights in question, if not of rights in general, since if properly and fully defined, true rights can never conflict.[32] In any event, the rights in question here certainly do not clash. Absent prior contractual commitments, the right of employers to operate their businesses entails no duty on the part of employees to participate in those operations or to refrain from peacefully picketing; conversely, the right of the employees to strike and picket does not entail a duty on the part of employers to refrain from operating their plants if able.[33] Thus, even if the existence of a conflict of rights could somehow operate in mitigation of the use of violence, at least to the extent of spreading the responsibility for it among each of the parties, the theory has no applicability here. To be sure, the economic interests or desires of the

---

[30] 38 Lab. Arb. 1182 (1961) (Holly, Arb.). For other cases in which the "employer fault" theory has been articulated, see Washington Scientific Indus., Inc., 67 Lab. Arb. 1044, 1046 (1976) (O'Connell, Arb.); American Enka Corp., 39 Lab. Arb. 441, 442-43 (1962) (Updegraff, Arb.); Westinghouse Elec. Corp., 26 Lab. Arb. 836, 844-45 (1956) (Simkin, Arb.). *But see* Sawbrook Steel Castings Co., 50 Lab. Arb. 725, 734 (1968) (Seinsheimer, Arb.).

[31] 38 Lab. Arb. at 1186.

[32] *See generally* Machan, *Prima Facie versus Natural (Human) Rights,* 10 J. OF VALUE INQUIRY 119 (1976).

[33] This is true not only philosophically, but also as a matter of positive law. In NLRB v. Mackay Radio & Tel. Co., 304 U.S. 333 (1938), the Supreme Court noted that although the National Labor Relations Act provided that "'[n]othing in this Act shall be construed so as to interfere with or impede or diminish in any way the right to strike,' it does not follow that an employer, guilty of no act denounced by the statute, has lost the right to protect and continue his business by supplying places left vacant by strikers." *Id.* at 345.

two parties may be in conflict when an employer attempts to operate a plant in the face of a strike, but conflicts of that nature are inherent in any free society, as where one party desires to sell high and the other to buy low. Thus, it would be absurd to suggest that when violence is used to resolve that kind of economic conflict, the victim must share at least a part of the blame with the aggressor.

In a broader vein, moreover, all three quotations display an unfortunate confusion between factual or causal relation, on the one hand, and moral and legal responsibility on the other. The differences between the two are most clearly seen in the context of tort law. As the late Dean Leon Green once asserted, "Whether a victim suffered hurt as a result of defendant's conduct [a matter of causation] is a question . . . wholly apart from whether the defendant should be made to compensate the victim [a matter of responsibility]."[34] The same difference must be recognized here. To be sure, an employer's decision to operate a plant in the face of a strike may occupy an important if not germinal link in the chain of events leading to the assault by a striker upon a nonstriker or supervisor: but for the employer's decision to operate, these persons would not have been entering the plant, the striking employees would not have been enraged by the action, no assault would have taken place, and so on. Therefore, the causal relation issue can be conceded. Whether the employer is somehow "responsible" for the assault, however, even if the effect of such responsibility is merely to impose on the employer the legal disability of not being able to discharge the actual assailant, is an entirely different matter.

Looking again by analogy to tort law, one sees that legal responsibility normally attaches only when it can be said that the causative activity somehow breaches a duty or standard of proper conduct. And, as Dean Green also pointed out, this is inescapably a "policy problem," one which requires the decision maker to look to a wide variety of "administrative, economic, moral, and/or other factors, summed up as justice."[35] When the decision is made that persons ought to be responsible for the injury that their conduct has caused, that conclusion is an assertion that the conduct is to be considered "wrongful"—a value judgment that is unfortunately obscured when a court buries its decision under neutral terms such as "proximate cause."[36]

The same analysis may be applied to the problem at hand. Holding employers partially responsible for labor violence merely because they

---

[34] Green, *The Causal Relation Issue in Negligence Law*, 60 MICH. L. REV. 543, 562 (1962).
[35] *Id.* at 563.
[36] *Id.* at 563 n.55.

310 Union Violence

attempt to continue to operate their plants during the pendency of a strike, though often explained in neutral cause/effect terms and by reference to scholarly studies on the subject, necessarily represents a determination that such conduct is somehow "wrongful." But wrongful with reference to what? With respect to arbitration, the touchstone of the rights and duties of the parties, express or implied, is, of course, the contract between the parties.[37] In determining what rights and duties the employer has under the employment contract, it is essential to keep in mind that the sole reason for the employer's existence as a business entity—indeed, it rises to the level of an affirmative moral, if not legal, obligation owed to the owners of the enterprise—is to produce, sell, and distribute goods and services and to show a profit.[38] Against that background, one cannot easily assume that any employer would consciously agree that any legal disability, in the form of not being able to discharge a person guilty of violent conduct against the business, should flow in whole or in part from the employer's exercise of the power and duty to operate a plant, even in the face of a strike. Furthermore, arbitrators who arrive at that conclusion would appear to be dispensing their own brand of somewhat ersatz industrial justice rather than interpreting and applying the agreement in light of the probable intent of the parties.[39]

Despite the questionable nature of the justifications, however, a distinction is commonly made between labor dispute violence and normal work environment violence, with a more lenient attitude being manifested toward the former. This is not to say that the practice is to fully exonerate all strike and picket line misconduct; some violence still warrants discharge, and even when that sanction is not approved, lesser ones are routinely upheld. Fortunately, the doctrinal underpinnings of the theory of treating picket line violence leniently are more pernicious in articulation than in application.

Nevertheless, some acts of violence are tolerated, and the question thus becomes one of differentiating between those acts which do warrant discipline and those which do not. In order to make such a determination, arbitrators frequently utilize a set of criteria first articulated by Arbitrator Holly in the *General Electric Co.,*[40] case:

---

[37] United Steelworkers v. Warrior & Gulf Nav. Co., 363 U.S. 574, 578 (1960) ("[t]he collective bargaining agreement states the rights and duties of the parties").

[38] *See* H. HENN, LAW OF CORPORATIONS, (1970). "The business corporation is a type of a corporation formed to collect a fund of capital and to dedicate such fund to a more or less definite commercial purpose for profit." *Id.* at 2-3.

[39] *Cf.* United Steelworkers v. Enterprise Wheel & Car Corp., 363 U.S. 593, 597 (1960) ("an arbitrator is confined to interpretation and application of the collective bargaining agreement; he does not sit to dispense his own brand of industrial justice").

[40] 38 Lab. Arb. 1182, 1185-86 (1961) (Holly, Arb.).

1. How serious was the offense in terms of injury to persons or damage to property? In regard to this question it was found that injury to persons is always viewed as more serious than damage to property.

2. Was the act provoked or unprovoked? The consensus of the Arbitrators whose awards bore on this point was that an unprovoked act was more serious than one that was provoked.

3. Was the act a premeditated one of aggression, or was it a spur of the moment reaction to an unanticipated situation? As would be expected aggression and premeditation are viewed as the more serious.

4. Were remedies at law available for the offense, and if so, were they exercised? Was the conduct more properly the concern of civil authorities than the concern of the employer? The exercise of both civil penalties and company discipline obviously raises a question of double jeopardy.

5. Was the conduct destructive of good employee-employer relations? Discipline is generally viewed as more proper when conduct destroyed or worsened relationships.

6. Was the conduct destructive of good community relations? Did the conduct increase community fears and did terror result?

7. What will be the effect of the administration of the discipline? Or, to put it another way, what purposes are to be accomplished by discipline? Will it restore good relations? Will it create a respect for law and order? Or, is the discipline being administered in a spirit of vindictiveness or for the purpose of establishing a "show case"?

8. Was the disciplinary action administered without discrimination? Reasonable uniformity of treatment for similar actions is necessary. It is noted, however, that uniformity of action does not necessarily mean identical or equal action. For example, the discharge penalty would be greater for an employee with 30 years of service than for one of 5 years of service.

9. Was the conduct and its results such that it would be unreasonable to expect that the employee could be reabsorbed into the work force?[41]

Needless to say, when the violence occurs within the context of a labor dispute it is the exceptional case, usually one involving substantial injury to persons or to property, that warrants discharge under the approach taken by most arbitrators. Thus, discharges were upheld in one case where rocks and other missiles were thrown at an office building; paint hit one woman and flying glass injured other employees.[42] Another case where discharges were sustained involved a "screaming and hollering" mob that descended at night upon the home of a nonstriker. Although only eggs were thrown, the arbitrator found that an "atmosphere of terror" existed.[43] A discharge was upheld against a striking employee when he hit a plant guard in the face without warning or provocation.[44] In another case, the discharged

[41] *Id.*
[42] Southern Bell Tel. & Tel. Co., 25 Lab. Arb. 270, 279-280 (1955) (McCoy, Arb.).
[43] Southern Bell Tel. & Tel. Co., 25 Lab. Arb. 410, 412 (1955) (McCoy, Arb.).
[44] *Id.* at 416-17.

employee had threatened a nonstriker with an open knife and said that he had been sent for the purpose of "cutting his guts out."[45] Discharges were also sustained for throwing rocks through the glass doors of the plant and for threatening to "beat the _____ out of" a nonstriking employee.[46] Spraying paint on a nonstriking employee warranted discharge in another case,[47] as did puncturing two tires on a nonstriking employee's car,[48] throwing eggs at close distance and injuring one person,[49] cutting telephone wires,[50] and stealing an expensive part of a coin telephone owned by the company.[51] In another case, cumulative acts of intimidation, rock throwing, assaults, blocking of access, threatening people who crossed the picket line, breaking car windows, and causing other property damage were held to warrant discharge.[52] Similarly, discharges were upheld in another case where striking employees threw rocks at company trucks and nonstriking employees ripped the short wave wires off the truck, broke a camera, and threw rocks at the cameraman. In the same strike, an employee was discharged, and the discharge sustained, for hitting a person inside his car and for tearing his jacket.[53]

On the other hand, in a number of cases arbitrators have reduced the penalty of discharge to mere suspension for varying lengths of time. Driving a car close and fast alongside nonstrikers to "somewhat frighten" them was found to warrant only a two-week suspension.[54] A striking employee who hit a supervisor in the face and shoulder was reinstated with a three-week suspension,[55] while an employee who tripped or kicked a nonstriker and hit her on the head with a handbag was suspended for four weeks.[56] Employees who spit tobacco juice on equipment, used picket signs to interfere with work, and made threatening remarks to nonstrikers were given a six-week suspension.[57] A threat to "get" a nonstriking employee and other verbal abuse warranted only a two-week suspension,[58] as did scratching

---

[45] Southern Bell Tel. & Tel. Co., 25 Lab. Arb. 474, 478-79 (1955) (Alexander, Arb.).
[46] Southern Bell Tel. & Tel. Co., 26 Lab. Arb. 29, 29-30 (1956) (Schedler, Arb.).
[47] Harvey Aluminum, Inc., 47 Lab. Arb. 196, 198-99 (1966) (Block, Arb.).
[48] Southern Bell Tel. & Tel. Co., 26 Lab. Arb. 186, 186-87 (1956) (McCoy, Arb.).
[49] Southern Bell Tel. & Tel. Co., 26 Lab. Arb. 515, 516-17 (1956) (Whiting, Arb.).
[50] *Id.* at 520; Southern Bell Tel. & Tel. Co., 26 Lab. Arb. 742, 742-43 (1956) (McCoy, Arb.).
[51] Southern Bell Tel. & Tel. Co., 25 Lab. Arb. 270, 274-77 (1955) (McCoy, Arb.).
[52] Sawbrook Steel Casting Co., 50 Lab. Arb. 725, 739-40 (1968) (Seinsheimer, Arb.).
[53] Westinghouse Elec. Corp., 40 Lab. Arb. 1169, 1172-73 (1963) (Schmidt, Arb.).
[54] Southern Bell Tel. & Tel. Co., 25 Lab. Arb. 343, 346 (1955) (McCoy, Arb.).
[55] *Id.* at 350.
[56] Southern Bell Tel. & Tel. Co., 25 Lab. Arb. 767, 770 (1956) (Schedler, Arb.).
[57] Southern Bell Tel. & Tel. Co., 26 Lab. Arb. 29, 32-33 (1956) (Schedler, Arb.).
[58] Southern Bell Tel. & Tel. Co., 26 Lab. Arb. 515, 519-20 (1956). (Whiting, Arb.).

cars as they came through the picket line.[59] An employee who followed the car of a nonstriking employee, and who pulled in front of her four times was guilty of "mere harassment" rather than "an actual assault," but was given a two-month suspension.[60] Finally, in one egregious case,[61] the grievant was a part of a group of pickets that "surged out" to confront another group of nonstriking employees who were trying to get into the plant by going around the picket line. The grievant threw a "shoulder block" into a seventy-two-year-old man, who suffered a mild fracture of a vertebra, missed work for a week, and wore a back brace for another six weeks. Nevertheless, the arbitrator held that the grievant had no intent to cause injury, concluded that his conduct "must obviously be rated as a fairly mild form of picket line violence," and reduced the discharge to a one-week suspension.[62]

Finally, in some cases arbitrators have found that strike misconduct does not warrant any discipline at all. In one case,[63] for example, a striking employee had been discharged for blocking a truck entering the plant and preventing employees from leaving the premises; he had also used a slingshot against company property. Because of his long service and "satisfactory work record," however, the arbitrator ordered the employee reinstated with full back pay.[64] In the same case, another employee who had thrown a rock at a photographer was reinstated because he had previously invented something that proved to be quite valuable to the company.[65] This same arbitrator, in ordering the reinstatement of an employee who had attempted to coerce and intimidate other employees, observed that "while D____'s behavior was perhaps not exemplary from the Company's point of view it is not serious enough to warrant discharge."[66]

In conclusion, one would think that employee misconduct which is either criminal or tortious in nature, when directed against the company or its other employees, would be "just cause" for discharge under any definition of that term, and in normal working conditions it is. When such misconduct occurs in the context of a labor dispute, however, a different definition seems to prevail.

It must be borne in mind that, except to the extent to be discussed in the following section, these decisions do not involve the imposition of

---

[59] General Elec. Co., 38 Lab. Arb. 1191, 1199 (1962) (Guthrie, Arb.).
[60] Delta Plate Co., 32 Lab. Arb. 899, 900 (1959) (Wade, Arb.).
[61] Yale & Towne Mfg. Co., 39 Lab. Arb. 1273 (1962) (Gill, Arb.).
[62] *Id.* at 1275.
[63] U.S. Pipe & Foundry Co., 52 Lab. Arb. 1249 (1969) (Mattice, Arb.).
[64] *Id.* at 1253.
[65] *Id.*
[66] *Id.* at 1254.

statutory law on the employer. It is rather a matter of private contract interpretation. If an employer genuinely disapproves of the manner in which labor arbitrators have tended to construe the term "just cause" insofar as strike violence is concerned, then the employer can at least attempt to negotiate different, more restrictive language into the collective bargaining or strike settlement agreement. Although the economic and "political" (vis-à-vis labor/management relations) realities may make such changes difficult, it is an alternative that employers should be encouraged to pursue. It would represent one step, at least, toward the elimination of the violence and lawlessness that too often seem to prevail in picket line and strike situations.

STATUTORY LIMITATIONS: THE APPROACH OF THE NLRB AND THE COURTS

Although the "just cause" provisions of collective bargaining agreements impose a significant limitation on the power of an employer to discharge an employee, there are significant statutory limitations—such as those contained in section 7 of the National Labor Relations (Taft-Hartley) Act (NLRA).

Statutory Background and Early Case Law

Section 7 of the NLRA gives employees "the right to self-organization to form, join, or assist labor organizations, to bargain collectively through representatives of their own choosing, *and to engage in other concerted activities for the purpose of collective bargaining or other mutual aid or protection. . . .*"[67] The employees' exercise of this right, moreover, is protected against employer interference, restraint, or coercion by section 8(a)(1) of the act.[68]

The language of section 7 is broad enough to encompass almost any conduct engaged in by two or more employees aimed at improving their employment situation, from the peaceful submission of grievances to blowing up the plant. On the other hand, although the actual or intended scope of section 7 may be both unclear and disputed in some particulars,[69] it has long been recognized that not all conduct which satisfies the literal words of the statute is necessarily "pro-

---

[67] NLRA § 7, 29 U.S.C. § 157 (1976). (Emphasis added.)
[68] *Id.* § 8(a)(1), 29 U.S.C. § 158(a)(1).
[69] *Compare* Schatzki, *Some Observations and Suggestions Concerning a Misnomer—"Protected" Concerted Activities,* 47 TEXAS L. REV. 378 (1969) *with* Haggard, *Picket Line Observance as a Protected Concerted Activity,* 53 N.C. L. REV. 43 (1974) [hereinafter cited as Haggard, *Picket Line Observance*].

tected" against every kind of employer response.[70] Rather, the ends that can be sought,[71] the means that can be used to obtain them,[72] and exactly what activity is protected against[73] all raise questions, the answers to which must be found in an evaluation of the overall purposes of the statute, the immediate interests of the employees and the employer, and the larger interests of society as a whole.[74]

Whatever the ambiguities with respect to the ultimate dimensions of section 7, the Supreme Court recognized early that the extraordinary protections of the statute would not be extended to protect acts of force and violence against persons and property. In one of the first related cases to come before the Court, *NLRB v. Fansteel Metallurgical Corp.*,[75] the Court made abundantly clear that neither section 7, the specific section 13 guarantee of the right to strike, nor the National Labor Relations Board's (NLRB, or the board) statutory remedial powers could be construed as justifying an infringement upon the employer's common-law right to discharge employees who engage in acts of force against persons or company property.[76] In that case, in response to unfair labor practices by the employer, the employees had engaged in a massive sit-down strike involving the seizure and occupancy of two of the company buildings. Attempts by the sheriff to evict the workers resulted in what the Supreme Court characterized as a "pitched battle."[77] In sustaining the right of the employer to discharge these employees, the Supreme Court noted:

---

[70] "[B]oth the Board and the courts have recognized that not every form of activity that falls within the letter of this provision is protected." Elk Lumber Co., 91 N.L.R.B. 333, 336-37 (1950) (footnote omitted).

[71] For example, a pre-election boycott to force an employer to immediately recognize one of two unions on the ballot had been held to be unprotected because such recognition would itself be illegal under the act. Hoover Co. v. NLRB, 191 F.2d 380, 389 (6th Cir. 1951). Moreover, some matters, though legitimate as objectives, are so remote from the employment relationship as not to be within the ambit of section 7 at all. *See, e.g.,* G & W Elec. Specialty Co. v. NLRB, 360 F.2d 873, 877 (7th Cir. 1966) (protest over decisions of a credit union run exclusively for company employees but operated independently of the company).

[72] In Eastex, Inc. v. NLRB, 437 U.S. 556 (1978), the Supreme Court seemed to adopt a test whereby the "protectedness" of an activity is to be determined by reference to a "sliding scale," the factors of which are the immediacy of the objective to wages, hours, and working conditions and the coerciveness or injuriousness of the activity. *Id.* at 568 n.18. *Accord,* Haggard, *Picket Line Observance, supra* note 69, at 102-06.

[73] A peaceful economic strike, for example, is a concerted activity for mutual benefit that is protected against the employer response of discharge but not against permanent replacement. NLRB v. Mackay Radio & Tel. Co., 304 U.S. 333, 339 (1938).

[74] *See generally* Cox, *The Right to Engage in Concerted Activities,* 26 IND. L. J. 319 (1951); Getman, *The Protection of Economic Pressure by Section 7 of the National Labor Relations Act,* 115 U. PA. L. REV. 1195 (1967).

[75] 306 U.S. 240 (1939).

[76] *Id.* at 250-58.

[77] *Id.* at 249.

The employees had the right to strike but they had no license to commit acts of violence or to seize their employer's plant. We may put on one side the contested questions as to the circumstances and extent of injury to the plant and its contents in the efforts of the men to resist eviction. The seizure and holding of the building was itself a wrong apart from any acts of sabotage. But in its legal aspect the ousting of the owner from lawful posses- sion is not essentially different from an assault upon the officers of an employing company, or the seizure and conversion of its goods, or the despoiling of its property or other unlawful acts in order to force com- pliance with demands. To justify such conduct because of the existence of a labor dispute or of an unfair labor practice would be to put a premium on resort to force instead of legal remedies and to subvert the principles of law and order which lie at the foundations of society.[78]

The Supreme Court's interpretation of the NLRA was apparently consistent with congressional intent. A few years later, when Congress was debating whether to bring labor violence within the coverage of the federal anti-extortion statute, some congressmen expressed the fear that rights protected by the NLRA and other federal labor statutes might thereby be jeopardized. The obvious answer was expressed by Congressman Gwynne, who said that "there is nothing in any of those statutes which authorizes the use of force and violence."[79] Conduct which the Supreme Court in *Fansteel* said was not affirmatively pro- tected against discharge by the NLRA was thus intended to be made affirmatively illegal by the Anti-Racketeering (Hobbs) Act.[80]

In the years immediately following, however, the *Fansteel* decision was substantially ignored by the NLRB[81] and narrowly construed by most of the courts of appeals.[82] Moreover, many of the early cases in- volving acts of violence were prosecuted primarily under section 8(a)(3) rather than under sections 7 and 8(a)(1), the claim being that the employee's participation in the strike itself, and not the alleged acts of strike misconduct, was the true motivating cause of the refusal to reinstate. If retaliation was so motivated, the refusal to reinstate would constitute "discrimination" under section 8(a)(3) regardless of whether

---

[78] *Id.* at 253.
[79] 89 CONG. REC. 3202 (1943).
[80] Although the Supreme Court was to later construe the Hobbs Act differently, it seems clear that this was the original intention of Congress. *See generally* Haggard, *Labor Violence: The Inadequate Response of the Federal Anti-Extortion Statutes,* 59 NEB. L. REV. 859 (1980).
[81] One writer made the following observation about the NLRB:
The Supreme Court gagged at the idea that sit-down strikers or seamen who commit mutiny aboard ship could not be discharged for so doing, but the Board absorbed this defeat in its stride and continued to apply its rule (though perhaps in modified form) that the commission of acts of violence by employees, unless very serious, was not necessarily a bar to their assertion of rights under the act.
Teller, *The Taft-Hartley Act and Government by Injunction,* 1 LAB. L.J. 40, 54 (1949).
[82] *See, e.g.,* NLRB v. Stackpole Carbon Co., 105 F.2d 167, 176 (3d Cir. 1939).

the misconduct was or was not otherwise protected by section 7 and generally the NLRB was not reluctant to find such motivation.[83] It was probably within this context, thus, that the "minor violence" exception had its genesis, for in some cases the board seemed to be saying that the misconduct could not possibly have been the actual cause of the refusal to reinstate whenever the misconduct was "minor" in nature.[84] It was but a short step from that to the assertion that the misconduct, even if it were the true cause of the employer's retaliation, was nevertheless not unprotected. For example, in *Indiana Desk Co.,*[85] the NLRB made the following observation:

> [While the discharged employees] engaged in jostling on the picket line . . . their conduct involved no serious acts of violence, and no arrests were made by the local police authorities. Such disorder, although not condoned by us, can normally be expected in any extensive strike, and it is no warrant for a denial of reinstatement.[86]

The courts of appeals during this period also evidenced some tolerance toward "minor" strike-related violence. The Third Circuit Court of Appeals in *Republic Steel Corp. v. NLRB*[87] expressed this tolerance:

> We think it must be conceded . . . that some disorder is unfortunately quite usual in any extensive or long drawn out strike. A strike is essentially a battle waged with economic weapons. Engaged in it are human beings whose feelings are stirred to the depths. Rising passions call forth hot words. Hot words lead to blows on the picket line. The transformation from economic to physical combat by those engaged in the contest is difficult to prevent even when cool heads direct the fight. Violence of this nature, however much it is to be regretted, must have been in the contemplation of the Congress when it provided in Sec. 13 . . . that nothing therein should be construed so as to interfere with or impede or diminish in any way the right to strike. If this were not so the rights afforded to employees by the Act would be indeed illusory. We accordingly recently held that it was not intended by the Act that minor disorders of this nature should deprive a striker of the possibility of reinstatement.[88]

The misconduct in that case, which the NLRB and court considered so minor as to not warrant the employer's refusal to reinstate, included

---

[83] *See, e.g.,* Ohio Calcium Co., 34 N.L.R.B. 917, 945 (1941); Acme-Evans Co., 24 N.L.R.B. 71, 98 (1940); El Paso Elec., 13 N.L.R.B. 213, 237 (1939).

[84] *See* Ford Motor Co., 23 N.L.R.B. 342, 371-72 (1940).

[85] 56 N.L.R.B. 76 (1944).

[86] *Id.* at 79 (footnote omitted).

[87] 107 F.2d 472 (3d Cir. 1939), *modified,* 311 U.S. 7 (1940).

[88] *Id.* at 479. Previous to this decision, the Board had also determined the reinstatement rights of the strikers by reference to what it considered to be the gravity of their criminal offenses. Republic Steel Corp., 9 N.L.R.B. 219, 392 (1938). *See also* NLRB v. Stackpole Carbon Co., 105 F.2d 167, 176 (3d Cir. 1939).

unlawful obstruction of the United States mail, the discharge of firearms, malicious destruction of property worth less than $300, unlawful interference with telegraph and telephone messages, the transportation of explosives, the interference with and obstruction of railway tracks, carrying concealed weapons, and one case of assault and battery serious enough to warrant a fine of $200, costs, and a suspended sentence of six months.[89]

In still other cases, the NLRB indirectly made acts of "minor" violence protected as a *de facto* matter by simply requiring reinstatement as a part of the remedy for the employer's unfair labor practices. In *Berkshire Knitting Mills,*[90] for example, the NLRB ordered the reinstatement of employees who had been found guilty of such offenses as disorderly conduct, malicious mischief to highways, assault and battery, inciting to riot, riot, unlawful assembly, and resisting arrest.[91] The board said, "We are unable to find that any one of the individuals against whom convictions have been recorded is not a suitable employee or that his or her reinstatement would tend to encourage violence in labor disputes," especially in light of the fact that the strike during which these crimes occurred was in protest of the employer's unfair labor practices.[92]

Even narrowly construed, the original NLRA would have to be interpreted as vastly expanding the legal powers and immunities of labor unions[93] and of simultaneously limiting those of the employer. This expansion and limitation was, moreover, exaggerated by the NLRB's own imaginative and decidedly pro-labor application of the statute, previously described. Nevertheless, by 1947 an increasingly conservative Congress had become convinced that unions, and employees acting on behalf of unionization, had become too powerful and that the NLRB was abusing its discretion by applying the act too liberally in favor of various coercive union activities. Thus, in the Taft-Hartley Act of 1947, Congress attempted to impose curbs on both labor unions and the NLRB. The primary approach of the act was to subject labor unions to various unfair labor practices provisions,[94] including a prohibition against the restraint or coercion of employees in the exercise

---

[89] 107 F.2d at 480.
[90] 17 N.L.R.B. 239 (1939).
[91] *Id.* at 292.
[92] *Id.* at 291-92. The same result was reached in the second decision as well. 46 N.L.R.B. 955, 1002-03 (1943).
[93] *See generally,* Pound, *Legal Immunities of Labor Unions,* in LABOR UNIONS AND PUBLIC POLICY 122 (1958), *reprinted in* 1 J. LABOR RESEARCH, 46 Reprint Series (1979).
[94] NLRA, § 8(b), 29 U.S.C. § 158(b)(1976).

of their right to refrain from union activities;[95] to outlaw the closed shop and allow only the most abbreviated form of compulsory unionism agreement, something equivalent to the agency shop or a service fee arrangement;[96] and to impose certain other specific limits on the board's exercise of its powers.[97]

Labor union violence against employees and employers alike was clearly one of the concerns of the Taft-Hartley Congress. The House Report on Legislation expressed that concern eloquently:

> For the last 14 years, as a result of labor laws ill-conceived and disastrously executed, the American workingman has been deprived of his dignity as an individual. He has been cajoled, coerced, intimidated, and on many occasions beaten up, in the name of the splendid aims set forth in section 1 of the National Labor Relations Act. . . .
>
> The employer's plight has likewise not been happy. . . . He has been required to employ or reinstate individuals who have destroyed his property and assaulted other employees. . . . He has had to stand helplessly by while employees desiring to enter his plant to work have been obstructed by violence, mass picketing, and general rowdyism.[98]

Congress responded to this concern in two ways. In the first place, union violence against employees was made an unfair labor practice. As was indicated above, section 7 was expanded to include a right to refrain from union activities, and section 8(b)(1)(A) was added to prohibit unions from restraining or coercing employees in the exercise of that right. This change was made primarily, if not exclusively, for the purpose of outlawing "mass picketing and the use of violence in the conduct of a strike."[99] Furthermore, Congress apparently had a fairly broad conception of violence in mind; the legislative history suggests

---

[95] *Id.* at §§ 7, 8(b)(1)(A), 29 U.S.C. §§ 157, 158(b)(1)(a). This prohibition was specifically intended to reach various forms of union-inspired violence, as is discussed in the text below. Refer to text accompanying notes 98-111 *infra*.

[96] *See* T. HAGGARD, COMPULSORY UNIONISM, THE NLRB, AND THE COURTS 34-69 (1977).

[97] In addition to an express prohibition against Board orders requiring the reinstatement of employees who have been discharged "for cause," the Taft-Hartley Act also made a specific attempt to limit the Board's tendency to base employer unfair labor practices on the employer's substantive bargaining proposals, NLRA, § 8(d), 29 U.S.C. § 158(d) (1976), and on speeches given by the employer expressing his opposition to unionization, *id.* § 8(c), 29 U.S.C. § 158(c)—two areas in which Congress thought the Board had gone further than it should.

[98] SUBCOMM. ON LABOR OF THE SENATE COMM. ON LABOR AND PUBLIC WELFARE, H.R. REP. No. 245, 80th Cong., 2d Sess., *reprinted in* LEGISLATIVE HISTORY OF THE LABOR MANAGEMENT RELATIONS ACT, 1947, at 295-96 (Comm. Print 1974) [hereinafter cited as LEGIS. HIST. LMRA].

[99] 93 CONG. REC. 6540 (1947) (rem. of Rep. Hartley), *reprinted in* LEGIS. HIST. LMRA, *supra* note 102, at 881-83. *See also* 93 CONG. REC. at 4563 (rem. of Sen. Taft), 6548 (rem. of Rep. Halleck), LEGIS. HIST. LMRA at 1208, 897-98.

that it was intended to include threats,[100] various kinds of picket line harassment and abuse,[101] any kind of conduct covered by local criminal laws,[102] and even conduct merely actionable in tort[103] or against which an injunction could be obtained.[104] Only a union, of course, can be found guilty of a section 8(b)(2) unfair labor practice, but the legislative history repeatedly makes it clear that "any employees participating in these activities may certainly be discharged for cause and are not entitled to reinstatement."[105] In other words, an employee does not engage in a protected concerted activity when he participates in the commission of an act which is an unfair labor practice for the union.

The second way in which the Taft-Hartley Act Congress responded to the problem of labor violence was by limiting the NLRB's power to order reinstatement, thereby redefining the scope of employee activities protected against discharge. The House version of what was to become the Taft-Hartley Act specifically exempted from the protections of section 7 all conduct "constituting unfair labor practices under section 8(b), unlawful concerted activities under section 12, or violations of collective bargaining agreements";[106] section 12, in turn, included as unlawful concerted activities "the use of force or violence or threats thereof" in connection with strikes and picketing.[107] Congress felt that these exemptions from section 7 were necessary because of the inclination of the board "to reinstate with back pay, strikers whom employers discharge for what the board seems to regard as minor crimes."[108] The House Report at this point then cited the board's decisions in both the *Republic Steel*[109] and the *Berkshire Knitting Mills*[110] cases as examples of what it considered to be the board's erroneous approach to the problem.[111]

---

[100] *Id.* at 4142, 4563 (rem. of Sen. Taft), Legis Hist. LMRA at 1025, 1208.

[101] S. Rep. No. 105, 80th Cong., 1st Sess. 50 (1947), *reprinted in* Legis. Hist. LMRA, *supra* note 98, at 456.

[102] 93 Cong. Rec. at 4563 (rem. of Sen. Taft), *reprinted in* Legis. Hist. LMRA, *supra* note 102, at 1208. Indeed, it was on that basis, in part, that some members of Congress opposed also making such conduct an unfair labor practice. *Id.* at 4559, 4563, Legis. Hist. LMRA at 1199-1200, 1208.

[103] *Id.* at A2824, Legis. Hist. LMRA at 905 (rem. of Rep. Landis).

[104] *Id.* at 4563, Legis. Hist. LMRA at 1208.

[105] *Id.* at 7495, Legis. Hist. LMRA at 912, *supra* note 98, at 544, 546, *and* [1947] U.S. Code Cong. & Ad. News 1135, 1164-65.

[106] H.R. 3020, 80th Cong., 1st Sess. 19 (1947), *reprinted in* Legis. Hist. LMRA, *supra* note 98, at 176.

[107] *Id.* at 47, Legis. Hist. LMRA at 204-05.

[108] H.R. Rep. No. 245, *supra* note 98, at 19, Legis. Hist. LMRA at 318.

[109] 9 N.L.R.B. 219 (1938). Refer to note 87 *supra*.

[110] 46 N.L.R.B. 955 (1943). Refer to notes 90-92 *supra*.

[111] H.R. Rep. No. 245, *supra* note 98, at 27, Legis. Hist. LMRA at 318.

In addition, in section 10(c) of the House bill the NLRB's power to order reinstatement was sharply limited; this section stated "no order of the Board shall require the reinstatement of any individual as an employee who has been suspended or discharged, or the payment to him of any back pay, unless the weight of the evidence shows that such individual was not suspended or discharged for cause."[112] The House Report stated that this change was necessary because "in the past, the Board, admitting that an employee was guilty of gross misconduct, nevertheless frequently reinstated him, 'inferring' that, because he was a member or an official of a union, this, not his misconduct, was the reason for his discharge."[113] The report then mentioned critically a board decision[114] which had adopted a line of reasoning previously discussed—namely, that because of the relatively minor nature of the employee's misconduct, the employer must necessarily have been motivated by antiunion considerations and was thus guilty of discrimination under section 8(a)(3).[115] The report noted that "the change made in section 10(e)[sic] on this subject is intended to put an end to the belief, now widely held and certainly justified by the Board's decisions, that engaging in union activities carries with it a license to loaf, wander about the plants, refuse to work, waste time, break rules, *and engage in incivilities and other disorders and misconduct.*"[116] The drafters of the House Report apparently thought that all of those forms of conduct were adequate "cause" for discharge.

As originally reported, the Senate version of what was to become the Taft-Hartley Act contained neither the change in the wording of section 7 nor the addition of section 10(c).[117] As finally passed by both the House and the Senate, however, the Taft-Hartley Act omitted the House amendment to section 7 but included, with only a change in the standard of proof requirement,[118] the House version of section 10(c).

With respect to the omission in the final bill of the previously proposed change in the wording of section 7, the House Conference Report simply stated that it was of the view that later court decisions had effectively repudiated and overruled the approach taken by the

---

[112] H.R. 3020, *supra* note 106, § 10(c), LEGIS. HIST. LMRA at 196.

[113] H.R. REP. NO. 245, *supra* note 108, at 42, LEGIS. HIST. LMRA at 333.

[114] Wyman-Gordon Co., 62 N.L.R.B. 561 (1945), *enforced in part,* 153 F.2d 480 (7th Cir. 1946).

[115] H.R. REP. NO. 245, *supra* note 108, at 42, LEGIS. HIST. LMRA at 333.

[116] *Id.,* LEGIS. HIST. LMRA at 333. (Emphasis added.)

[117] S. 1126, 80th Cong., 1st Sess. (1947).

[118] The "weight of the evidence" language was omitted because "the Board, under the general provisions of section 10, must act on a preponderance of the evidence" anyway. H.R.REP. NO. 510, *supra* note 105, at 55, LEGIS. HIST. LMRA at 559, [1947] U.S. CODE CONG. & AD. NEWS at 1161.

NLRB in cases like *Berkshire Knitting Mills,*[119] "wherein the Board attempted to distinguish between what it considered as major crimes and minor crimes for the purpose of determining what employees were entitled to reinstatement."[120] The report concluded that the change in section 7 was thus no longer necessary, a conclusion which unfortunately did not take into account the board's occasional policy of simply ignoring court of appeals decisions with which it disagreed.

In any event, the House Conference Report also explained that "there was real concern that the inclusion of such a provision [one specifically listing conduct that was not to be considered protected] might have a limiting effect and make . . . conduct not specifically mentioned subject to the protection of the act."[121] That statement suggests that the range of activities to be protected by section 7 should be narrowly rather than broadly defined.

Finally, the House Conference Report suggested that the changes in section 7 were rendered unnecessary by the Senate agreement to the inclusion of section 10(c), which, according to the report, "applies with equal force whether or not the acts constituting the cause for discharge were committed in connection with a concerted activity."[122] More specifically, the report noted that "employees who engage in violence, mass picketing, unfair labor practices, contract violations, or other improper conduct, or who force the employer to violate the law, do not have any immunity under the act and are subject to discharge without right of reinstatement."[123]

This legislative history virtually speaks for itself. Violence, no matter how minor, is not a protected concerted activity, and employees who engage in such conduct and who are discharged because of it are not entitled to reinstatement. As will be shown subsequently, however, the current state of the law does not reflect that legislative intent or anything remotely close to it.

Violence as a Protected Concerted Activity

Critical to an understanding of what the approach of the NLRB and the courts is toward the problem of labor violence is an appreciation of exactly how they frame the issue. Properly, the issue should be framed in this way: at common law, absent contract terms to the contrary, an

[119] 17 N.L.R.B. 239 (1939). Refer to text accompanying notes 90-92 *supra.*
[120] H.R. REP. No. 510, *supra* note 105, at 39, LEGIS. HIST. LMRA at 543, [1947] U.S. CODE CONG. & AD NEWS at 1145.
[121] *Id.,* LEGIS. HIST. LMRA at 543, [1947] U.S. CODE CONG. & AD. NEWS at 1145.
[122] *Id.,* LEGIS. HIST. LMRA at 543, [1947] U.S. CODE CONG, & AD. NEWS at 1145.
[123] *Id.,* LEGIS. HIST. LMRA at 543, [1947] U.S. CODE CONG. & AD. NEWS at 1145.

employer (or the employee, for that matter) could elect to terminate the employment relationship for any reason or no reason at all.[124] The NLRA, however, imposed at the federal level what at the time were properly considered to be some extraordinary limitations of the exercise of that liberty.[125] Under the act, therefore, before an employer's decision to terminate an employee can be considered illegal, it should be shown that the clear purpose and intent of the federal law was affirmatively to protect the employee conduct listed as the cause for the discharge; otherwise, the employer's common-law liberties must be considered to remain intact. The issue, thus, should be whether the extraordinary protections of federal law were intended to be extended to even minor acts of employment-related physical violence, intimidation, and property damage. When framed in that manner, the issue promotes an almost automatic negative response.

That, however, is not how the NLRB and the courts currently frame the issue. With respect to strike-related violence, at least, the board and the courts start with the uncontested proposition that going on strike is a form of concerted activity that the law protects against discharge.[126] When a striker engages in some kind of misconduct during the course of an otherwise protected strike and is discharged for that reason, the issue is whether the egregiousness of what the employee did is "sufficient to remove him from the protection of the Act"[127] or to cause him to be "deprived of reinstatement rights."[128] When the issue is framed in this way, the psychological burden of persuasion clearly shifts to the employer, and results in a less-than-

---

[124] The generally recognized common law rule at the time the National Labor Relations Act was passed was accurately stated in Payne v. Western & A.R.R., 81 Tenn. 507 (1884). The court observed that employers "may dismiss their employees at will . . . for good cause, for no cause, or even for cause morally wrong, without being thereby guilty of legal wrong." *Id.* at 519-20.

[125] In Adair v. United States, 208 U.S. 161, 174-75 (1908), the Supreme Court had recognized that the common law rule was but an incident of the broader constitutional liberty of contract. To ameloriate the impact of the National Labor Relations Act upon this recognized constitutional right of contract, the Supreme Court in NLRB v. Jones & Laughlin Steel Corp., 301 U.S. 1 (1937), observed:

> [T]he Act does not interfere with the normal exercise of the right of the employer to select its employees or to discharge them. The employer may not, under cover of that right, intimidate or coerce its employees with respect to their self-organization and representation, and, on the other hand, the Board is not entitled to make its authority a pretext for interference with the right of discharge when that right is exercised for other reasons than such intimidation and coercion.

Id. at 45-46.

[126] *See, e.g.,* NLRB v. Hartmann Luggage Co., 453 F.2d 178, 181 (6th Cir. 1971).

[127] Star Meat Co. v. NLRB, 105 L.R.R.M. (BNA) 3144, 3145 (6th Cir. Nov. 4, 1980).

[128] Southern Fla. Hotel & Motel Ass'n, 245 N.L.R.B. No. 49, [1979-80] NLRB Dec. (CCH) ¶ 16,355 (Sept. 28, 1979).

automatic or universal condemnation, for the purposes of the NLRA, of otherwise actionable conduct.

The controlling approach for determining what kinds of violence are protected and what kinds are not has been summarized as follows:

> The Board and courts have consistently ruled that not every act of misconduct committed during a strike deprives an employee of the Act's protection. Although an employee may have engaged in misconduct, he or she may not be deprived of reinstatement rights absent a showing that the conduct was so violent or of such a serious nature as to render an employee unfit for future service.[129]

Similarly, the Court of Appeals for the First Circuit recently expressed the same idea in these terms:

> It is well established that serious misconduct during a strike justifies a refusal to reinstate after the strike is over. On the other hand, minor picket line and other misconduct, even though crude or offensive, will not justify discipline, as the right to strike necessarily implies some "leeway for impulsive behavior."[130]

It is significant that both the "minor violence" and "not unfit for future service" tests pre-date the Taft-Hartley Act amendments.[131] The cases articulating both tests were *expressly* criticized by the legislative history of the act,[132] and presumably were overruled by the enactment of section 10(c), a fact to which both the NLRB and the courts currently seem oblivious.

In any event, when trying to determine whether a striker's misconduct is so serious as to render him unfit for future employment, the NLRB and the courts generally apply a totality-of-the-circumstances test. As the board recently noted, "each incident of alleged misconduct must be assessed in light of the surrounding circumstances, including the severity and frequency of the involved employees actions."[133] Buttressed by a principle no more concrete than that, the approach naturally degenerates into a case-by-case adjudication. For the purposes of predicting which discharges will be sustained and which will not, one must look at how the board and the courts generally react to various kinds of recurring fact situations.[134] With respect to some of

---

[129] *Id.,* [1979-80] NLRB Dec. ¶ 16,355, at 30,605.

[130] Associated Grocers of New England, Inc. v. NLRB, 562 F.2d 1333, 1335 (1st Cir. 1977).

[131] Refer to text accompanying notes 88 & 92, *supra.*

[132] Refer to note 112 *supra* and accompanying text.

[133] Advance Pattern & Mach. Corp., 241 N.L.R.B. No. 70, [1978-79] NLRB Dec. (CCH) ¶ 15,754 (Mar. 28, 1979).

[134] *See generally* Erickson, *Forfeiture of Reinstatement Rights Through Strike Misconduct,* 31 LAB. L.J. 602 (1980). For an excellent summary of the Board's view of the law, see Coronet Casuals, Inc., 207 N.L.R.B. 304, 304-05 (1973).

these, one will note a rather marked difference between the attitude of the board and that of the courts of appeals, with the latter consistently taking a less tolerant view of various kinds of strike violence and general misconduct. A brief review of some of these areas, and of the reasons for the disagreement, is thus in order.

One of the current controversies pertains to the use of threats, usually made by persons on a picket line against nonstriking employees. A threat to do physical harm to another is, of course, an actionable offense under both common and criminal law;[135] the issue, therefore, is often whether the words or conduct in question actually rise to the level of being a "threat" in legal contemplation. A similar definitional problem has confronted the NLRB and the courts when the matter arises within the context of a section 7 claim that what the employee did or said was not sufficiently "threatening" to take the action outside the protections of the NLRA.

The NLRB has fairly consistently taken the position that making purely verbal threats, unaccompanied by any physical acts or gestures that would provide added emphasis or meaning to the words, does not constitute strike misconduct of a sufficiently serious nature to warrant discipline.[136] This approach is apparently premised on the belief that since emotions run naturally high in strike and picket line situations, a certain amount of rough talk and hyperbole must necessarily be expected.[137] Thus, in one case, the wife of a nonstriking truck driver was told, "If Walt goes on the run there will be trouble for you."[138] Similarly, an employee was warned not to cross the picket line because "there may be something or someone to stop you."[139] In neither of these cases were the threats accompanied by overt physical acts and discharges were not upheld. On the other hand, discharge was condoned when a striker hit a car with his body, breaking the mirror, and ordered the company president out, saying "I'll kick the _____ out of you."[140] A threat to kill a supervisor, accompanied by physical movements toward him, was likewise held to be unprotected.[141]

---

[135] *See, e.g.,* S.C. CODE ANN. § 22-5-150 (1976)(authorizing the arrest of persons who "utter menaces or threatening speeches"); W. PROSSER, HANDBOOK OF THE LAW OF TORTS 37-41 (4th ed. 1971).

[136] *See, e.g.,* Arrow Indus., Inc., 245 N.L.R.B. No. 179, [1979-80] NLRB Dec. (CCH) ¶ 16,313 (Sept. 28, 1979); Valley Oil Co., 210 N.L.R.B. 370, 375-76 (1974).

[137] *See* Federal Prescription Serv., Inc., 203 N.L.R.B. 975, 977 (1973).

[138] Arrow Indus., Inc., 245 N.L.R.B. No. 179, [1979-80] NLRB Dec. (CCH) ¶ 16,313 (Sept. 28, 1979).

[139] Carraway Geriatric Centers, 243 N.L.R.B. No. 98, [1979-80] NLRB Dec. (CCH) ¶ 16,073 (July 18, 1979).

[140] Hedstrom Co., 235 N.L.R.B. 1198, 1198 (1978).

[141] *Id.*

The courts of appeals generally have taken a tougher stand than the NLRB toward threatening statements. The refusal of the Court of Appeals, Fifth Circuit, for example, to enforce portions of the board's order is illustrated by *NLRB v. Moore Business Forms, Inc.*[142] Among other things, the court refused to enforce a portion of the order which required the reinstatement of an employee who had been discharged for telling two company supervisors as they picked up nails off the parking lot that there would be "two nails at home in your driveway for every one you pick up."[143] Likewise, the board had dismissed as mere "picket line braggadocio"[144] the statement, which was addressed to an employee who had expressed an intention to return to work: "there's ways to keep you from it."[145] The court noted that although *how* this employee was going to be stopped was not expressly stated, "in all the violent behavior surrounding this strike the threat really left nothing to the imagination."[146] Another striker, who had a stick in his hand,[147] told a nonstriking employee not to come in to work the next day. The court again relied on "the violent context of this strike"[148] as the justification for finding the threat to be serious and unprotected. Finally, another striker allegedly asked a nonstriker if his wife and children were safe and then said, "I thought you had more sense than that"[149] with respect to the nonstriker's decision to cross the picket line. The board had found this too ambiguous to constitute a threat serious enough to warrant discharge, but the court of appeals disagreed.[150]

Although the courts of appeals have been fairly consistent in either ignoring or expressly rejecting the NLRB's "overt acts" requirement, some differences still exist among the circuits with respect to the proper alternative for identifying a "threat" warranting discharge. On the one hand, some have focused on the subjective intent of the discharged employee and have held a threat to be unprotected only if the employee *intended* to threaten or intimidate nonstrikers.[151] In *NLRB v. Pepsi Cola Co.,*[152] the Fifth Circuit Court of Appeals denied the reinstatement of a

---

[142] 574 F.2d 835 (5th Cir. 1978). *But see,* Georgia Kroft Co. v. NLRB, 696 F.2d 931 (11th Cir. 1982).
[143] *Id.* at 844.
[144] *Id.* at 845.
[145] *Id.*
[146] *Id.*
[147] The nonstriking employee had testified that the striker shook the stick at her and actually threatened to use it on her if she returned to work, but the Board's administrative law judge found that the striker did not threaten her. *Id.*
[148] *Id.*
[149] *Id.*
[150] *Id.* at 846.
[151] NLRB v. Pepsi Cola Co., 495 F.2d 226 (4th Cir. 1974).
[152] *Id.*

striker who told a prospective employee, "I know where you live, and if you go in there to work, I'll come looking for you."[153] On the other hand, using the same approach, the court in *NLRB v. Hartmann Luggage Co.*[154] decided that a striker's threatening statement to a nonstriker to the effect that " 'it would be a shame for them to have to kill him [or they hated to kill him] because he was too young to die' . . . was made under circumstances which make it incredible that she *intended* it literally, and we regard it as picket line rhetoric."[155]

On the other hand, other courts have focused on the subjective perceptions of the threatened employee and the effect of the threat upon him. Thus, in *NLRB v. Efco Manufacturing, Inc.,*[156] the court held that a striker's threat to beat up a plant manager did not justify a refusal to reinstate because the threat did not put the manager in direct fear of a beating.[157] Conversely, the *NLRB v. Trumbull Asphalt Co.*[158] court found that a threat of bodily harm which so frightened a nonstriker that he left work for five weeks was sufficiently egregious for the employer to deny reinstatement.[159] Similarly, in *Federal Prescription Service, Inc. v. NLRB,*[160] a statement to a nonstriker that his son "just may have an accident" was found to be unprotected because of the threat's effect on the threatened employee.[161]

In what has been regarded as a highly influential opinion in this area, the Third Circuit Court of Appeals expressly rejected the NLRB's "overt acts" requirement. In *NLRB v. W. C. McQuaide, Inc.,*[162] the court noted that "threats are not protected conduct under the Act, and we fail to see how a threat acquires protected status simply because it is unaccompanied by physical acts or gestures."[163] The court, however, also rejected both the "intent" and the "effect" tests of what constitutes an unprotected threat.[164] Instead, the court adopted what it called "an objective standard to determine whether conduct constitutes a threat sufficiently egregious to justify an employer's refusal to reinstate,"[165] namely " 'whether the misconduct is such that, under

---

[153] *Id.* at 228.
[154] 453 F.2d 178 (6th Cir. 1971).
[155] *Id.* at 185 (Emphasis added.)
[156] 227 F.2d 675 (1st Cir. 1955).
[157] *Id.* at 676.
[158] 327 F.2d 841 (8th Cir. 1964).
[159] *Id.* at 844-46.
[160] 496 F.2d 813 (8th Cir.), *cert. denied,* 419 U.S. 1049 (1974).
[161] *Id.* at 818.
[162] 552 F.2d 519 (3d Cir. 1977). *See also* Cabon & Jarin, *The Third Circuit's New Standard for Strike Misconduct Discharges: NLRB v. W.C. McQuaide, Inc.,* 23 VILL. L. REV. 645 (1977-1978).
[163] 552 F.2d at 527 (footnotes omitted).
[164] *Id.*
[165] *Id.* at 527.

the circumstances existing, it may reasonably tend to coerce or intimidate employees in the exercise of rights protected under the Act.'"[166]

The standard expressed in *McQuaide,* of course, was simply the test the same court had previously used for determining whether conduct by a union rose to the level of restraint or coercion in violation of section 8(b)(1)(A). As far as it goes, the approach is consistent with the view, expressed in the legislative history, that coercive conduct which would be an unfair labor practice for a union to engage in is also to be considered unprotected insofar as the individual participants are concerned.[167] Such misconduct, however, was certainly not considered to be the only unprotected union activity, for that interpretation would necessarily exclude violence that is directed only against the employer, violence that coerces employees other than in the exercise of their section 7 rights, and other forms of misconduct which might not amount to the restraint or coercion of anyone in the section 8(b)(1)(A) sense. Presumably, the Third Circuit Court of Appeals intended to borrow only the objective "does it reasonably tend to coerce" aspect of the section 8(b)(1)(A) test, and even then only as one possible indicia of conduct that is unprotected under the act.

Applying this test to the facts before it, the court in *McQuaide* thus concluded that the merely abusive language of one striker and the threatening statement of another striker to an uninjured nonstriker whose windshield had been shattered by a rock did not reasonably tend to coerce or intimidate.[168] On the other hand, the court did find that another striker's threats could reasonably tend to coerce or intimidate, and thus refused to order his reinstatement.[169]

As evidence of its potential influence in this area of the law, the *McQuaide* test was subsequently adopted by the First Circuit Court of Appeals in *Associated Grocers of New England v. NLRB,*[170] where strikers whose reinstatement was at issue had threatened the lives of three job applicants; at least one of the three construed the threat as a serious threat on his life and did not apply for work. Because the threat had been unaccompanied by any physical acts or gestures, however, the

---

[166] *Id.* at 528, *quoting* Local 542, International Union of Operating Eng'rs. v. NLRB, 328 F.2d 850, 852 (3d Cir.), *cert. denied,* 379 U.S. 826 (1964).

[167] Refer to note 105 *supra.*

[168] 552 F.2d at 528.

[169] *Id.* In the words of the Court, this striker "followed non-striker Kring to a delivery point and said he would 'get him,' shook his fist at Inston and said he would 'knock the goddam shit out of [him]' if he drove again, told truckdriver Harris, 'Scab, you're going to get yours,' and partially blocked Harris's egress." *Id.*

[170] 562 F.2d 1333 (1st Circ. 1977).

NLRB had held his conduct to be protected.[171] The court of appeals, however, rejected the board's "overt acts" test and, using the *Mc-Quaide* approach, found that in these circumstances the conduct and words would reasonably tend to coerce or intimidate, and that they were therefore unprotected.[172]

On the other hand, the court was not as certain with respect to the words and conduct of another striker. This striker had approached a neighbor who was planning to apply for a job at the struck plant, informed him that strikebreakers historically had sometimes met with violent retaliation, and that he might expect similar "repercussions."[173] Although the NLRB had found that this was intended as a threat of violence and calculated to intimidate the neighbor, it also found the threat to be within the protection of section 7 simply because the neighbor was neither intimidated nor deterred from filing a job application.[174] The court of appeals, however, held that the neighbor's subjective reaction to the threat could not be controlling and remanded that part of the case to the board for reconsideration under the *McQuaide* approach.[175] On remand the board again determined that the striker was entitled to reinstatement,[176] all of which may suggest that in close cases at least, the use of the *McQuaide* test by the board may not have a significant impact on its conclusions on employee reinstatement rights. Rather, the board's attitude toward strike violence is probably more important than the test it uses to identify unprotected activities; unfortunately, that is something not easily changed by either legislative or judicial instruction.

The legislative history of the Taft-Hartley Act also suggests that mass picketing should not be protected.[177] The objectionable feature of mass picketing is that it physically impedes ingress and egress at the employer's business, thus interfering with the section 7 rights of nonstriking employees. The board and some courts of appeals now take the view, however, that picket line conduct is not unprotected if it merely impedes or makes ingress and egress more inconvenient; only a permanent or substantial blocking, or the additional infliction of significant physical harm, rises to the level of unprotected activity. A typical example of the kind of access impediment the board will

---

[171] *Id.* at 1336.
[172] *Id.* at 1337.
[173] *Id.*
[174] *Id.*
[175] *Id.*
[176] Associated Grocers of New England, Inc., 238 N.L.R.B. No. 11 (1978). *See also,* A. Duie Pyle, Inc., 263 N.L.R.B. No. 92 (1982).
[177] Refer to text accompanying notes 98, 99, & 123 *supra.*

tolerate can be found in *Coronet Casuals, Inc.,*[178] in which several strikers had been discharged for standing in front of cars, thereby causing short delays in and out of the company parking lot. This was often accompanied by abusive language. Cars were sometimes kicked and one was allegedly scratched.[179] In finding the discharges to be an unfair labor practice, the board noted that everyone eventually got in and out of the parking lot, that there was no actual or implied threat of harm, that this had been a strike of long duration, and that the action was a response to the employer's unfair labor practice.[180] Similarly, in *Golay & Co., v. NLRB,*[181] access by cars into the parking lot was blocked by mass picketing for about two hours but employees could and did park their cars outside and enter on foot.[182] A board order requiring reinstatement of the pickets was enforced by the Seventh Circuit Court of Appeals.[183]

On the other hand, slightly more egregious forms of mass picketing, though often tolerated by the NLRB, have generally been looked at with a more jaundiced eye by the courts of appeals. For example, in *NLRB v. Community Motor Bus Co.,*[184] striking employees had prevented any buses from leaving the depot by mass picketing. The buses eventually left with a police escort, but the mass picketing did not stop until the employer got an injunction. In refusing to enforce the board's order calling for reinstatement of the employees who participated in the activity, the court noted that "the mass picketing that blocked the company's gate was organized and persistent."[185] Moreover, "the pickets were not engaged in trivial acts of misconduct, but were interfering with a basic right guaranteed by statute, the right of nonstriking employees to continue working."[186]

Similarly, in *W. J. Ruscoe Co. v. NLRB,*[187] the discharged employee had been involved in a group effort "to push and rock a car and to block its ingress into petitioner's plant."[188] One of the employees had also been a part of a group that pulled a driver out of his truck; someone in the group had thrown a bottle shattering a window in the truck,

---

[178] 207 N.L.R.B. 304 (1973). *See also* Owen Joist Corp., 248 N.L.R.B. No. 76, [1980] N.L.R.B. Dec. ¶ 16,860 (Mar. 29, 1980); E-Systems, Inc., 244 N.L.R.B. No. 36, [1979-80] N.L.R.B. Dec. ¶ 16,179 (Aug. 5, 1979).
[179] 207 N.L.R.B. at 306.
[180] *Id.* at 308.
[181] 156 N.L.R.B. 1252 (1966).
[182] *Id.* at 1260.
[183] Golay & Co. v. NLRB, 371 F.2d 259 (7th Cir. 1966).
[184] 439 F.2d 965 (4th Cir. 1971).
[185] *Id.* at 967.
[186] *Id.* at 966.
[187] 406 F.2d 725 (6th Cir. 1969).
[188] *Id.* at 726.

and the discharged employee had thrown gravel at a supervisor who was attempting to photograph the incident.[189] Although the NLRB had held that this misconduct was not serious enough to warrant a denial of reinstatement rights, the Sixth Circuit Court of Appeals disagreed:

> Those who impede the free flow of traffic into or from a struck plant exceed reasonable limits [i.e. the limits previously discussed on what a striker can do to persuade others to join his cause]. . . . Obviously, one who throws gravel and other debris at those not sympathetic with his views . . . exceeds reasonable limits. . . . This type of behavior clearly lies outside the class of exuberant or impulsive conduct which the Board argues must be protected to carry out the policies of the act.[190]

Somewhat related to both the threat and the ingress/egress cases are the "car chase" cases, for such conduct can result in an impermissible restriction upon nonstrikers' freedom of movement. and can also be construed as posing a threat of serious injury. The Board generally starts with the proposition that merely following the car of a nonstriker or a management official is not unprotected conduct, and, indeed, seems to tolerate even more. For example, in *Advance Pattern & Machine Corp.,*[191] several strikers followed a job applicant after he left the plant. The applicant eventually called the police, who told the strikers to leave, but they again followed him and threw a beer can at his car. The strikers were discharged when the employer learned of the incident.[192] The administrative law judge found that the driver of the car had engaged in "serious misconduct removing him from the statutory and remedial protection of the Act. . . . Moreover, the facts and surrounding circumstances do not reveal a basis for belief that such conduct was that of animal exuberance in response to an existing situation."[193] The NLRB, however, reversed on this point, holding that there was no evidence that the striker "drove dangerously close to Burns or that he attempted to force Burns off the road." The throwing of the beer can was dismissed as "clearly a trivial incident."[194]

On the other hand, where the "following" represents more than mere harassment and is done in a reckless or dangerous manner, the board will often find it to be unprotected. In *Birch Tree Numer One, Inc.,*[195] for example, a group of strikers followed a supervisor and a nonstriker at speeds of 50-55 miles per hour, sometimes drove along the side of the car, and at one point forced the nonstrikers onto the

---

[189] *Id.*
[190] *Id.* at 727.
[191] 241 N.L.R.B. No. 70, [1978-79] NLRB Dec. (CCH) ¶ 15,754 (March 28, 1979).
[192] *Id.,* [1978-79] NLRB Dec. ¶ 15,754.
[193] *Id.,* [1978-79] NLRB Dec. ¶ 15,754.
[194] *Id.,* [1978-79] NLRB Dec. ¶ 15,754.
[195] 243 N.L.R.B. No. 87, [1979-80] NLRB Dec. (CCH) ¶ 16,011 (July 17, 1979).

shoulder of the road. In another incident, strikers passed a nonstriker and then cut sharply in front of the car. Subsequently, the strikers drove in the passing lane next to her car and cut in toward her several times. The NLRB noted that although there was no property damage, the "actions were calculated to have and did have the effect of placing nonstriking employees and others in fear of imminent injury to themselves."[196]

The NLRB and the courts of appeals, however, do not always agree over what additional conduct or circumstances will convert a "mere following" into something for which an employee can be discharged. In *NLRB v. Moore Business Forms, Inc.*,[197] a striker overtook and passed a nonstriker who was driving to work. The striker then slowed his car down in front of the nonstriker, causing him to brake, and swerved into the other lane whenever he attempted to pass. Eventually, the striker stopped his car in the middle of the road and blocked the way. The board found that this conduct was not sufficiently serious to warrant the employer's refusal to reinstate.[198] The Fifth Circuit Court of Appeals, however, disagreed: "As a matter of law, we cannot agree with this conclusion. Bragg had no right to accost, pursue, block, or otherwise interfere with the right of any citizen in the use of the public highway while attempting peacefully and lawfully to go to work."[199]

Similarly, in *Associated Grocers of New England v. NLRB*,[200] two strikers had followed a supervisor in a car for fourteen miles at night. This so frightened the supervisor that he drove past his house so that his wife and children would not be endangered. He finally turned down a lonely dead-end country road, where his egress was blocked briefly by the strikers.[201] The administrative law judge found that although the strikers intended to and did frighten the supervisor, his "fear was soon put to rest, he was never in danger, and he eventually realized this."[202] The First Circuit Court of Appeals, however, using the same objective test that it had borrowed from *McQuaide* for evaluating the legality of verbal threats, found that the conduct of these strikers "reasonably tended to intimidate within the meaning of the standard we have adopted,"[203] and that "the Board exceeded its authority in

---

[196] *Id.*, [1979-80] NLRB Dec. ¶ 16,011.
[197] 574 F.2d 835 (5th Cir. 1978).
[198] *Id.* at 843.
[199] *Id.*
[200] 562 F.2d 1333 (1st Cir. 1977).
[201] *Id.* at 1337.
[202] *Id.*
[203] *Id.*

conferring immunity under the Act upon such obviously frightening conduct."[204]

Another favorite activity of picketers is throwing projectiles. Whether the law will allow an employer to discharge an employee who engages in this kind of activity seems to depend on what is thrown, who or what it is thrown at, whether the object is hit, and whether any damage or injury occurs. Traditionally, the NLRB has been fairly tolerant of egg-throwing incidents. For example, in *MP Industries, Inc.,*[205] strikers threw eggs at buildings and cars.[206] Although the administrative law judge had upheld the discharge, the board disagreed. Following the general approach to issues of this kind, as described in the opening paragraph of this section, the board said that this conduct was "minor and isolated in nature and caused no damage to Respondent's building, the automobiles, or any person. We therefore conclude that this act falls within the category of impulsive, trivial incidents which we have found insufficiently serious to deprive an employee caught up in a lawful strike from the protection of the Act."[207] A similar finding by the board was, however, reversed by the court in *NLRB v. Moore Business Forms, Inc.*[208]

On the other hand, even the NLRB takes a more serious view of rock and brick throwing, presumably because of the inherent risk of damage or injury resulting from such conduct. In *Bryan Infants Wear Co.,*[209] for example, the board upheld the discharge of an employee who had thrown a brick through the window of a nonstriking employee's truck.[210] Throwing rocks at buses carrying strike replacements frequently results in discharge as well.[211] If no damage in fact results from the rock throwing, as in *Southern Florida Hotel & Motel Association,*[212] then the board will sometimes order reinstatement.[213]

---

[204] *Id.*

[205] 227 N.L.R.B. 1709 (1977). *See also* Northfield Cheese Co., 242 N.L.R.B. No. 157, [1979-80] NLRB Dec. (CCH) ¶ 15,906 (June 13, 1979); Jer-Dan Corp., 237 N.L.R.B. 302 (1978).

[206] 227 N.L.R.B. at 1709.

[207] *Id.* at 1710.

[208] 574 F.2d 835 (5th Cir. 1978). Refer to text accompanying notes 215 & 216 *infra. See also* Ostego Ski Club v. NLRB, 542 F.2d 18, 19 (6th Cir. 1976); Oneita Knitting Mills, Inc. v. NLRB, 375 F.2d 385, 391-92 (4th Cir. 1967).

[209] 235 N.L.R.B. 1305 (1978).

[210] *Id.* at 1308.

[211] *See, e.g.,* South Shore Hosp., 245 N.L.R.B. No. 110, [1979-80] NLRB Dec. (CCH) ¶ 16,479 (Sept. 28, 1979); International Harvester Co., 226 N.L.R.B. 166, 169 (1976).

[212] 245 N.L.R.B. No. 49, [1979-80] NLRB Dec. (CCH) ¶ 16,355 (Sept. 28, 1979).

[213] *See id.,* [1979-80] NLRB Dec. ¶ 16,355 at 30,603-04.

Throwing objects at specific people seems to be especially dis-favored,[214] although here again the courts take a dimmer view of such activity than does the NLRB. In *NLRB v. Moore Business Forms, Inc.*,[215] the board had said throwing a small block of wood at a plant guard was mere horseplay, but the court said it was conduct warrant-ing discharge.[216] On the other hand, the board has held that merely throwing bottles and debris onto company property was not grounds for discharge, even though it did cause some unspecified damage.[217]

It is within the context of violence directed at persons attempting to cross a picket line, either on foot or in cars, that the distinction be-tween "minor" and "serious" violence is most often evident. The NLRB, for example, has suggested that "engaging in minor scuffles and disorderly arguments"[218] on the picket line is not unprotected activity. Additionally, it has been said that "implusive behavior on the picket line is to be expected, especially when directed against nonstriking employees and strike breakers."[219] On the other hand, "brutal violence" against nonstrikers has been recognized as constituting grounds for discharge.[220]

In *South Shore Hospital*,[221] thus, the NLRB ordered the reinstatement of a striker who kicked at and attempted to open the door of a car crossing the picket line.[222] On the other hand, in the same case it upheld the discharge of a striker who pushed a woman job applicant up against a fence and put her in fear of physical harm.[223] In another case, however,[224] when a very large striker grabbed a replacement (of smaller size) "by the shoulder with some force and pushed him 4 or 5 feet,"[225] the board said this "pushing incident was impulsive, was minor—not causing any injury and not deterring the strike replacement from going to work—and was a single, isolated incident."[226] After giv-ing the usual disclaimer that "neither we nor the Board condone

---

[214] *See, e.g., id.;* Carlon, 239 N.L.R.B. 495, 498-99 (1978); Bromine Div., Drug Research, Inc., 233 N.L.R.B. 253, 259 (1977); American Beauty Baking Co., 171 N.L.R.B. 700, 718 (1968).

[215] 574 F.2d 835 (5th Cir. 1978).

[216] *Id.* at 844.

[217] American Cyanamid Co., 239 N.L.R.B. 440, 440 (1978).

[218] Coronet Casuals, Inc., 207 N.L.R.B. 304, 305 (1973).

[219] Montgomery Ward & Co., v. NLRB, 374 F.2d 606, 608 (10th Cir. 1967).

[220] NLRB v. Kelco Corp., 178 F.2d 578, 582 (4th Cir. 1949).

[221] N.L.R.B. No. 110, [1979-80] NLRB Dec. (CCH) ¶ 16,479 (Sept. 28, 1979). *See also* Gold Kist, Inc., 245 N.L.R.B. No. 142, [1979-80] NLRB Dec. (CCH) ¶ 16,408 (Sept. 28, 1979).

[222] 245 N.L.R.B. No. 110, [1979-80] NLRB Dec. ¶ 16,479.

[223] *Id.,* [1979-80] NLRB Dec. ¶ 16,479.

[224] Star Meat Cutters, 237 N.L.R.B. 908 (1978).

[225] *Id.* at 908.

[226] *Id.* at 909.

violence, even of a minor nature," the Sixth Circuit Court of Appeals affirmed the board's order of reinstatement.[227] Picket line violence of a somewhat more serious nature was involved in *Bartlett-Collins Co.,*[228] where the board upheld the discharge of a strike who, while attempting to dissuade another employee from returning to work, cursed him and punched him in the face, breaking his jaw.[229]

The NLRB and the Third Circuit Court of Appeals recently disagreed over the egregiousness of picket line misconduct in the case of *Chevron U.S.A. v. NLRB.*[230] A striking employee jumped on the hood of an automobile being driven out of the facility by a company guard; he remained on the hood for 1.3 miles, while repeatedly beating upon the windshield. When the strike ended, this employee was given a ten-day suspension. The board held that this conduct was protected against even this limited sanction, but the Third Circuit Court of Appeals disagreed. "We arrive at this conclusion," the court said, "for a number of reasons. For one thing, the activity occurred away from the picket line, on a public highway. The misconduct was prolonged in duration. More importantly, Legg's behavior consisted not of a verbal threat but of a physical act that could have resulted in serious injury. Finally, while recognizing that it is not dispositive, we note that Legg's intent, throughout the incident, was to harass and intimidate Meeson."[231]

Other kinds of misconduct which seem to recur with some frequency include putting nails and glass in parking lots and driveways,[232] carrying dangerous weapons,[233] and using profane and vulgar language.[234] These acts have sometimes been found to be cause for discharge, and sometimes not.

This somewhat random sampling of primarily recent cases was not designed to be comprehensive nor to provide the basis from which

---

[227] Star Meat Co. v. NLRB, 105 L.R.R.M. (BNA) 3144, 3145 (6th Cir. Nov. 4, 1980).
[228] 230 N.L.R.B. 144 (1977).
[229] *Id.* at 171.
[230] 672 F.2d 360 (3d Cir. 1982).
[231] *Id.* at 361.
[232] *See, e.g.,* NLRB v. Hartmann Luggage Co., 453 F.2d 178, 185 (6th Cir. 1971); Moore Bus. Forms, Inc., 224 N.L.R.B. 393, 394 (1976).
[233] *See, e.g.,* Advance Industries Div.—Overhead Door v. NLRB, 540 F.2d 878, 882 (7th Cir. 1976) (pellet gun); MCC Pacific Valves, 244 N.L.R.B. No. 138 [1979-80] NLRB Dec. (CCH) ¶ 16,294 (billy club); Mosher Steel Co., 226 N.L.R.B. 1163, 1165 (1976) (shot gun on rack in pickup truck parked at the picket line).
[234] *Compare* NLRB v. McQuaide, Inc. 552 F.2d 519, 528 (3d Cir. 1973) ("[I]t is well settled that the use of epithets, vulgar words, or profanity does not deprive a striker of the protection of the Act," *with* NLRB v. Longview Furniture Co., 206 F.2d 274, 276 (4th Cir. 1953) (rude language aimed at humiliating and intimidating nonstrikers held to be unprotected because of the concerted manner in which it was uttered).

some clarifying principle might be synthesized. The cases merely demonstrate the *ad hoc* approach taken by the NLRB and the courts, wherein some kinds of strike and picket line "misconduct" (i.e. conduct otherwise civilly or criminally actionable) are in fact affirmatively protected by the NLRA. Nevertheless, it is often difficult to know in advance what specific acts of misconduct will so qualify.

Closely related to the question of what kinds of misconduct are protected by sections 7 and 8(a)(1) is the question of which party has the burden of proof. In a section 7 case the General Counsel of the NLRB would normally have the burden of proving that the conduct for which the employee was discharged was in fact affirmatively protected by the NLRA.[235] Such is not the case, however, with respect to discharges for strike misconduct.

The Supreme Court addressed this issue in *NLRB v. Burnup & Sims, Inc.*,[236] and as subsequently construed by the NLRB, that decision delineates the accepted allocation of the burden of proof. Initially, the General Counsel is required only to prove that the employees, to the employer's knowledge, were *generally* engaged in a protected concerted activity of some kind, such as an economic strike, and that they have been discharged or denied reinstatement. This constitutes a *prima facie* case of a section 8(a)(1) violation.[237] In the words of the board, "the burden of going forward with the evidence shifts to the Respondent [the employer] to establish that it held an 'honest belief' that the striking employees who were denied reinstatement engaged in misconduct of such a serious character as to justify Respondent in denying them their jobs."[238] As the quotation suggests, the primary burden is on the employer and it consists of two elements. There is, first, the "honest belief" aspect, which apparently means that the employer must have some reasonably reliable and objective evidence that the employees actually engaged in the misconduct with which they were charged.[239] In this regard the board has opined:

> Each striker's eligibility for reinstatement must be judged solely upon incidents in which the striker in question is alleged to have participated. Unauthorized acts of violence on the part of individual strikers are not

---

[235] *See* Krispy Kreme Doughnut Corp. v. NLRB, 635 F.2d 304, 310 (4th Cir. 1980) (Board's burden of proving the concertedness aspect of a section 7 unprotected activity cannot be satisfied through the use of a presumption).

[236] 379 U.S. 21 (1964).

[237] National Steel Corp., 242 N.L.R.B. No. 63, [1978-79] NLRB Dec. (CCH) ¶ 15,838 (May 16, 1979).

[238] *Id.*, [1978-79] NLRB Dec. (CCH) ¶ 15,838.

[239] *See* International Union, UAW v. NLRB, 455 F.2d 1357, 1367 (D.C. Cir. 1971); Bromine Div., Drug Research, Inc., 233 N.L.R.B. 253, 260 (1977).

chargeable to other union members in the absence of proof that identifies them as participating in such violence.[240]

The second aspect of the employer's burden of proof pertains to the "serious character" of the misconduct. This, of course, merely means that the misconduct must be of a truly egregious variety, as illustrated in the discussion above.

If the employer meets this burden, then it is incumbent upon the General Counsel to prove that the employees did not in fact engage in the misconduct in question, notwithstanding the employer's honest belief that they did.[241]

Assuming that the employer has not met his burden of proof and that the General Counsel has met his, then a violation of section 8(a)(1)[242] will be found, and the employees who engaged in the protected misconduct will be entitled to be reinstated with back pay. The amount of the back pay award, however, apparently depends on exactly what the employer's response to the misconduct was. If the employer simply refused to reinstate the employees at the termination of the strike, then the back pay award would normally run from the date of their application for reinstatement.[243] On the other hand, if at the time of the misconduct the employer affirmatively discharged the employees, under a recent NLRB decision their back pay runs from the date of such discharge, even though the employees were on strike at the time. In *Abilities & Goodwill, Inc.*,[244] which itself was not a misconduct case, the board abandoned the prior rule, which required a wrongfully discharged striker to apply for reinstatement with the employer's back pay liability beginning as of the time such application was made. Instead, the board decided to treat a discharged striker like any other discharged employee, for whom a request for reinstatement is not required and whose entitlement to back pay usually begins on the date of the discharge.[245] The board made these observations:

---

[240] Coronet Casuals, Inc., 207 N.L.R.B. 304, 305 (1973). *See also* NLRB v. Sea-Land Servs., Inc., 356 F.2d 955, 966 (1st Cir.), *cert. denied,* 385 U.S. 900 (1966); Gold Kist, Inc., 245 N.L.R.B. No. 142, [1979-80] NLRB Dec. (CCH) ¶ 16,408 (Sept. 28, 1979). However, when the violence is in fact a "group activity," each participant can be discharged regardless of the exact role he happened to play. *See, e.g.,* Alcan Cable West, 214 N.L.R.B. 236 (1974); Giddings & Lewis, Inc., 240 N.L.R.B. 441 (1979).

[241] National Steel Corp., 242 N.L.R.B. No. 63, [1978-79] NLRB Dec. (CCH) ¶ 15,838 (May 16, 1979).

[242] Whether a section 8(a)(3) violation also exists is, however, a separate issue. S₍ NLRB v. Burnup & Sims, 379 U.S. 21, 22 n.2 (1964). Refer to text accompanying not₍ 293-318 *infra.*

[243] *See, e.g.,* National Steel Corp. 242 N.L.R.B. No. 63, [1978-79] NLRB Dec. ¶ 15,8'

[244] 241 N.L.R.B. No. 5, [1978-79] NLRB Dec. (CCH) ¶ 15,634 (March 15, 1979), *forcement denied on other grounds,* 612 F.2d 6 (1st Cir. 1979).

[245] *Id.,* [1978-79] NLRB Dec. ¶ 15,634, at 29,216.

When discharged strikers withhold their services after the date of the unlawful discharge, one cannot really be certain whether their continuing refusal to work is voluntary, i.e., a result of the strike, or whether the reason for not making application for reinstatement is that the employer, by discharging the employees, has unmistakenly impressed on him the futility of making such an application. . . . [B]ecause the uncertainty is caused by the employer's unlawful conduct, we will not indulge in the presumption that the discharge itself played no part in keeping the employees out of work. Rather, it seems to us more equitable to resolve the ambiguity against the wrongdoer and presume, absent indications to the contrary, that the discharged strikers would have made the necessary application were it not for the fact that the discharge itself made such application a futility.[246]

Although it would seem that at best this doctrine represents a windfall for economic strikers who happen to be blessed with an employer so indiscrete as to discharge them for engaging in conduct that is obviously and properly protected by the NLRA, its aplication in the "strike misconduct" cases is totally unwarranted. To begin with, the "protected" character of such misconduct is at least dubious. Apart from that, however, even the NLRB and the courts concede that the law should not affirmatively condone acts of violence, no matter how minor. Yet, by ordering not only the reinstatement of a discharged striker who has engaged in "protected misconduct," but also by awarding back pay from the date of the discharge (rather than the date of the request for reinstatement after the strike is over), the board in effect rewards and encourages such misconduct during a strike. If an employee can precipitate his own discharge during a strike by engaging in some of the milder forms of violence, then he can enjoy what is in essence a "free" or "paid-for" strike at the employer's expense. Despite its weakness, however, the board has applied its new doctrine even in the strike misconduct cases.[247]

In conclusion, it would seem highly unlikely that the drafters of the original NLRA, which was intended to promote the "friendly adjustment of industrial disputes,"[248] intended to provide affirmative protection to acts of agression, coercion, intimidation, and minor violence, even when committed in connection with otherwise legitimate strikes and picketing. Yet, despite an early Supreme Court opinion confirming that impression, the NLRB and the courts of appeals originally pursued a different approach to the matter. This led, in turn, to legislative criticism and an obvious attempt to correct the situation through the

---

[246] *Id.,* [1978-79] NLRB Dec. ¶ 15,634 at 29,216-17. Members Pennello and Murphy registered a vigorous dissent.
[247] *See, e.g.,* Gold Kist, Inc., 245 N.L.R.B. No. 142, [1979-80] NLRB Dec. (CCH) ¶ 16,408 (Sept. 28, 1979) (with Member Murphy again dissenting).
[248] NLRA § 1, *as amended,* 29 U.S.C. § 151 (1976).

Taft-Hartley Act amendments, primarily the addition of section 10(c). Although defining a section 10(c) "cause" for discharge by reference to the current arbitral view on the subject would not produce results appreciably different from those presently being reached by the board and some courts,[249] defining that term by reference to what Congress apparently intended in 1947 definitely would require a reversal of the current approach.

The Right to Be Reinstated Notwithstanding the Unprotected Nature of the Misconduct

Even if a discharged employee engaged in strike or picket line misconduct so eregious that it did not fall within the affirmative protection of section 7, he might nevertheless be entitled to reinstatement. This result is reached if it is found that the employer condoned the misconduct, if the misconduct was merely a pretextual reason for the discharge, or if reinstatement would otherwise effectuate the purposes of the NLRA. These three grounds will be considered in turn.

The Condonation Theory. In *NLRB v. Colonial Press, Inc.,*[250] the theory of condonation was stated succinctly:

> The principle of waiver by condonation used in the context of labor relations is that, if after an employee commits acts of misconduct lawfully justifying his discharge, and thereafter the employer, fully cognizant of the acts, agrees not to discipline him, the employer may not thereafter rely on the same misconduct as the basis for discharging or refusing to reinstate the employee.[251]

The theory of condonation is, as that quotation suggests, sometimes expressed in terms of waiver,[252] but at other times the predominant conceptual influences seem to be estoppel[253] or breach of contract.[254]

---

[249] Indeed, if the Board were also to indulge in the logical fallacy that conduct that is *not* "cause" for discharge under section 10(c) is *necessarily* protected by section 7, then using arbitration decisions as a point of reference would probably result in a substantial liberalization of the kinds of strike misconduct for which an employee cannot be discharged under the act, as it would seem that arbitrators tolerate even more than do the board and the courts. Refer to text accompanying notes 6-70 *supra.*

[250] 509 F.2d 850 (8th Cir.), *cert. denied,* 423 U.S. 833 (1975).

[251] *Id.* at 854.

[252] *See also* Packers Hide Ass'n. v. NLRB, 360 F.2d 59, 62 (8th Cir. 1966); Brantley Helicopter Corp., 135 N.L.R.B. 1412, 1417 (1962).

[253] Packers Hide Ass'n. v. NLRB, 360 F.2d 59, 62 (8th Cir. 1966) ("the doctrine prohibits an employer from misleadingly agreeing to return its employees to work and then taking disciplinary action for something apparently forgiven"); Poloron Prods., Inc., 177 N.L.R.B. 435, 438 (1969)("General Counsel in his brief states the matter in terms of estoppel, arguing that, because the men abandoned their strike on the promise that no reprisal would be visited upon them, the Company 'is estopped from now asserting that the concerted activity of June 13 was unprotected. . . .'").

[254] NLRB v. Colonial Press, Inc., 509 F.2d 850, 856 n.10 (8th Cir.), *cert. denied,* 423 U.S. 831 (1975) ("the Second Circuit's comment that 'the condonation principle . . . is

Since the kind of facts that are relevant under one approach might not necessarily be so under the other two, it undoubtedly would be helpful if the law could settle on one theoretical underpinning, or at least keep the three separate so that the individual requirements of each approach might eventually be worked out. Instead, we have been left with a fairly amorphous concept that is without any clearly defined legal antecedents.

Moreover, as an administrative law judge for the NLRB recently commented, "the doctrine . . . is easier to state than to rationalize."[255] In some instances, for example, the condonation doctrine has been justified in terms of promoting labor peace. In other words, the board has said that the "public policy of encouraging strike settlements requires that the employer be held to his agreement,"[256] and once a dispute has been amicably resolved it should be allowed to remain that way. This justification, which tends to cast the condonation theory in "breach of contract" terms, is most applicable when the reinstatement of employees guilty of strike misconduct is being claimed as an express or implied part of a strike settlement agreement.

The theory, however, has also been explained or justified in terms of depriving the employer of a wrongfully obtained "benefit." This would apply when employees end an otherwise legal and protected strike upon the express or implied assurance that the employer will not retaliate against any strikers who might have acted in an excess of zeal. This justification tends to present the theory as one essentially of estoppel.[257]

Finally, with respect to unprotected "breach of contract" strikes, the NLRB has concluded that since "the original activity lost its protected character *solely* by virtue of a separate document giving the employer an affirmative defense which he could waive," finding such a waiver can be justified as simply another way of vindicating the underlying statutory right, that of going on strike.[258] This justification, obviously, suggests a waiver analysis.

---

more akin to the doctrine of waiver than to the technicalities of contract law . . . should not be taken as an invitation to disregard contract principles entirely."); Poloron Prods., Inc., 177 N.L.R.B. 435, 438 (1969) (the employees returning to work found to be "the immediate *quid pro quo* for the condonation").

[255] 177 N.L.R.B. at 438.

[256] Brantley Helicopter Corp., 135 N.L.R.B. 1412, 1417 (1962). *See also* Jones & McKnight, Inc. v. NLRB, 445 F.2d 97, 103 (7th Cir. 1971); Poloron Prod., Inc., 177 N.L.R.B. 435, 438 (1969) ("the policy of favoring strike settlements, which is the real heart of the condonation doctrine, requires more than just a temporary abandonment of the strike").

[257] Refer to note 253 *supra*.

[258] Brantley Helicopter Corp., 135 N.L.R.B. 1412, 1417 (1962). (Emphasis added.)

Whatever the policy justification for the condonation theory, or the conceptual mode in which it is cast, there is also the problem of fitting the doctrine into the words and the structure of the statute. The trial examiner in *Poloron Products*[259] explained the difficulty in these terms:

> The original activity never was protected; its "protected" nature was forfeited by some characteristic (such as the breach of contracts) which inhered in the activity and accompanied it throughout its existence. Thus if an employee struck in breach of contract, was thereafter reinstated, and then is discharged for the original activity, it is easy to see that the employer's action is a breach of his agreement, but it is somewhat more difficult to find the *statutory* violation, for that must hinge on *protected* activity of the employee.[260]

The difficulty, however, has not proved to be insurmountable. There are basically two ways in which the law fits the condonation theory into the broader statutory scheme. One operates on the assumption that in cases of discharge or refusal to reinstate, the totality of the employee's conduct contains both protected and unprotected aspects. Thus, once the employer has "condoned or waived the unprotected aspect of the activity," it is "thereafter bound as a matter of law to view the activity without regard to its unprotected aspects, i.e., as simply a concerted activity for mutual aid or protection,"[261] and thus not an activity for which the employee can be penalized.

The second way in which the law attempts to reconcile the condonation theory with the statutory scheme is by making the discharge or refusal to reinstate more a violation of the antidiscrimination provisions of section 8(a)(3) than of the anti-restraint prohibition of section 8(a)(1). That is, the NLRB apparently views "condonation" as an implicit admission by the employer that the misconduct of the employee in question does not in fact rise to the level of being cause for discharge. Thus, "once he [the employer] has indicated that the misconduct on which he relied for severing the employment relationship is no longer his true reason for denying reinstatement . . . there can remain only the discriminatory reason for denying such reinstatement,"[262] which thus establishes a violation of section 8(a)(3). Closely related to, but theoretically distinguishable from the cases adopting this approach, are those which allege that the employer has used the misconduct merely as a "pretext" for discharge, with the real reason

---

[259] 177 N.L.R.B. 435 (1969).

[260] *Id.* at 438.

[261] Brantley Helicopter Corp., 135 N.L.R.B. 1412, 1418 (1962). *See also* Poloron Prods., Inc., 177 N.L.R.B. 435, 438 (1969).

[262] Colonial Press, Inc., 207 N.L.R.B. 673, 674 (1973) *enforcement denied in part,* 509 F.2d 850 (8th Cir.), *cert. denied,* 423 U.S. 833 (1975).

for the retaliation being the employee's union activity.[263] The difference is that in the condonation cases the "discrimination" is more or less fictional, while in the pretext cases the discrimination is alleged to exist in fact.

With respect to proving employer condonation, the controlling approach, at least among the courts of appeals, seems to be the one stated by the Fifth Circuit Court of Appeals in *NLRB v. Marshall Car Wheel & Foundry Co.*:[264]

> Where, as here, the strike misconduct is clearly shown, condonation may not be lightly presumed from mere silence or equivocal statements, but must clearly appear from some positive act by an employer indicating forgiveness and an intention of treating the guilty employees as if their misconduct had not occurred. We think respondent correctly asserts that the essential elements of condonation, i.e. forgiveness and the resumption of the former relationship between the strikers and respondent, are patently lacking here.[265]

The application of this test is, however, somewhat uncertain, with the NLRB having a much greater tendency to find condonation than the courts of appeals. In the *Marshall Car Wheel* case, for example, the board had found condonation where an employer failed "expressly to assign their unprotected activity as the reason for [the employees'] discharge"[266] during an emergency created by the strike, plus the fact that this reason was not equivocally asserted as an affirmative defense in the unfair labor practice proceedings. The court of appeals found this to be insufficient evidence of condonation, especially since even the employees who were reinstated were taken back *only* "as new employees,"[267] a fact which the court apparently thought rebutted both the forgiveness and the full resumption of the former relationship requirements.

Similarly, in *Packers Hide Association v. NLRB,*[268] a group of employees had engaged in an unprotected wildcat strike. On the day of the walkout, the employer invited the strikers to return to work, but the offer was declined at that time. The next day, however, the strikers did indicate a desire to return to work. The plant manager consented, but also scheduled a meeting with the employees for the following day.

---

[263]The factual patterns of both the "condonation" and the "pretext" theories are sufficiently similar, however, as to warrant analysis under both in some cases. *See, e.g.,* Plasti-Line, Inc., v. NLRB, 278 F.2d 482, 486-87 (6th Cir. 1960). For a separate discussion of the "pretext" theory, refer to text accompanying notes 293-318 *infra*.

[264] 218 F.2d 409 (5th Cir. 1955).

[265] *Id.* at 414.

[266] *Id.* at 414-45.

[267] *Id.* at 416.

[268] 360 F.2d 59 (8th Cir. 1966).

At that time, an instigator of the strike was discharged.[269] The NLRB found the invitation to return to work, which "made no reservations whatsoever, actual or potential, limiting to the status of the strikers in any respect upon their return to work,"[270] operated as a condonation.[271] The Eighth Circuit Court of Appeals disagreed, saying that the board's conclusion was based on "a misunderstanding of the doctrine of condonation."[272] The applicable standards, the court said, were those stated in *Marshall Car,* and on that basis it found "a lack of evidence in the instant case to demonstrate a willingness on the part of the employer to forgive the improper conduct of the strikers and to 'wipe the slate clean.'"[273] In addition, the court articulated the following important policy consideration:

> The Board's decision, if upheld, would reward the guilty and penalize the victim. Such a conclusion violates the spirit and purpose of the Act in that it is calculated to stimulate and aggravate ill-feeling between management and employees rather than promote industrial peace.[274]

More recently, in *NLRB v. Colonial Press, Inc.,*[275] the Court of Appeals for the Eighth Circuit again reversed an NLRB finding of condonation. After reviewing the prior case law, the court added:

> In applying these principles to the instant case, we think the Board's order is unrealistic as it exaggerates the significance of the . . . somewhat general and ambiguous statements of the Company's representatives soliciting some of the dischargees to come in and talk to them about reemployment. The conversations appearing most frequently in the record utilized the phrase, "the door is always open." This and similar communications can at best amount only to preliminary invitations to negotiate reemployment. . . . The Company made no unconditional offers for dischargees to return to work without penalty. . . . An enlargement of the salutary condonation principle to embrace such nebulous and preliminary overtures toward former employees would be detrimental to the purposes of the National Labor Relations Act to promote more harmonious labor relationships between employers and employees, aside from ignoring contract principles relevant to establishing an employer-employee relationship.[276]

Although, as the above cases indicate, the NLRB has sometimes been quite apt to find condonation under the slightest of circumstances, at other times the board seems as insistent upon specificity as the courts of appeals. For example, in *Southern Florida Hotel & Motel*

---

[269] *Id.* at 61.
[270] *Id.*
[271] *Id.* at 62.
[272] *Id.*
[273] *Id.*
[274] *Id.* at 63.
[275] 509 F.2d 850 (8th Cir.), *cert. denied,* 423 U.S. 833 (1975).
[276] *Id.* at 855-56.

Association,[277] the employer had agreed to reinstate all striking employees pursuant to a strike settlement except those whose jobs had been eliminated or whose departments were still closed at the end of the strike. The administrative law judge held that this action by the employer operated as a condonation of several instances of strike misconduct, since the employees guilty of this misconduct had not been expressly excluded.[278] The board, however, disagreed:

> In our view, Respondents' agreement to return all striking employees does not evince a willingness to wipe the slate clean and to continue the employer-employee relationship because not only was the subject of strike misconduct not raised or discussed by either the Union or the Association, but the record is unclear whether the Association's negotiators possessed knowledge of the incidents of strike misconduct.[279]

The NLRB also noted that "in other instances where the board has found condonation, the employer's conduct usually involves some positive manifestation of a willingness to forgive the specific misconduct involved."[280] Although the board added that a specific and positive assertion of forgiveness was not always necessary, it was of the view, in this case at least, that something more than a general agreement to return strikers to work is required in order to make a finding of condonation.[281]

One issue which has apparently divided the courts of appeals is whether condoning the misconduct of some strikers necessarily requires the reinstatement of all strikers who engaged in the same or similar misconduct. In *Retail Store Union v. NLRB,*[282] the employer refused to reinstate some employees who had engaged in unprotected leafleting. The employer did, however, reinstate other strikers who had also participated in the leafleting. The NLRB held that the reinstatement of these strikers constituted condonation of the misconduct, thus requiring the reinstatement of all employees who had engaged in the conduct.[283] The District of Columbia Court of Appeals agreed.[284]

On the other hand, in *NLRB v. Community Motor Bus Co.,*[285] the employer rehired as new employees six persons who it believed had been innocently involved in illegal mass picketing and distinguished them from those the company believed had purposely engaged in the

---

[277] 245 N.L.R.B. No. 49, [1979-80] NLRB Dec. (CCH) ¶ 16,355 (Sept. 28, 1979).
[278] *Id.,* [1979-80] NLRB Dec. ¶ 16,355 at 30,604.
[279] *Id.,* [1979-80] NLRB Dec. ¶ 16,355 at 30,604.
[280] *Id.,* [1979-80] NLRB Dec. ¶ 16,355 at 30,604.
[281] *Id.,* [1979-80] NLRB Dec. ¶ 16,355 at 30,604-05.
[282] 466 F.2d 380 (D.C. Cir. 1972).
[283] *Id.* at 384.
[284] *Id.* at 387.
[285] 439 F.2d 965 (4th Cir. 1971).

misconduct. The NLRB, however, held that this rehiring amounted to a condonation of the illegal mass picketing itself, thus requiring the reinstatement of all the strikers so involved.[286] The Fourth Circuit Court of Appeals disagreed,[287] and asserted:

> The Company was free to discharge or rehire any or all of the strikers whose misconduct forfeited reinstatement rights. Any other rule, especially in the absence of anti-union animus, would confront the employer with an all-or-none rehiring choice, which is not required by the Act or by the doctrine of condonation.[288]

The approach espoused by the Fourth Circuit Court of Appeals would certainly seem to be the better view. The NLRB itself has recognized that it is legitimate for an employer to single out the instigators or leaders of unprotected conduct and refuse to reinstate only those employees.[289] In addition, one would think that an employer who wants to express his disapproval of (and thus hopefully deter) future misconduct, but who for obvious economic reasons cannot afford to discharge all guilty employees, should be allowed to impose such "punishment" on a selective basis, provided that the employer is not guilty of otherwise impermissible motives.

Finally, although the legal effect of a condonation is normally to preclude the employer from later imposing punishment on the perpetrator of some kind of unprotected misconduct, an exception exists. In *Poloron Products*,[290] a group of employees went out on an unprotected strike; the employer, however, reinstated them and agreed that he would not take any reprisals against them, a clear case of express condonation. A few weeks later, some of the employees again engaged in an unprotected strike. This time, the employer suspended all of the employees who participated, and those who had also engaged in the prior unprotected walkout were discharged.[291] Clearly, the imposition of this stiffer penalty was due to the employees' prior participation in misconduct which the employer had condoned *at that time.* By conceptualizing the condonation theory in "contract" terms, and with the policy of favoring strike settlements being the underlying justification, the NLRB sustained the employer's action:

> To be sure the employees did abandon the June 13 walkout and returned to work, and this was the immediate *quid pro quo* for the condonation. But fair-

---

[286] *Id.* at 966.
[287] *Id.*
[288] *Id.* at 968.
[289] *See, e.g.,* Chesty Foods, 215 N.L.R.B. 388, 393 (1974); Ohio Stone Co., 180 N.L.R.B. 868, 873 (1970).
[290] 177 N.L.R.B. 435 (1969).
[291] *Id.* at 436.

ly implied, it seems to me, was an understanding to remain at work for a reasonable period, and not to walk out again in the immediate future for a similar cause. Of course the Employer was free to invoke penalties against the second walkout, and the complaint here is that by invoking disparate discipline he reneged on his condonation. But by participating in the second walkout, the employees also reneged on their part of the settlement. The policy favoring strike settlements, which is the real heart of the condonation doctrine, requires more than just a temporary abandonment of the strike.[292]

In conclusion, it would seem that the condonation theory is of somewhat uncertain application. The cases often turn very closely on their exact facts; and although the courts are consistently more rigorous than is the NLRB, the resolution of the issue before either forum is probably more a function of effective advocacy than of logic or precedent.

"Pretextual" and "Dual Purpose" Discharges. Even if an employee has engaged in unprotected activities which the employer has not condoned, an unfair labor practice may still exist if the real reason for the discharge is not the misconduct but is, rather, the employee's union status or participation in other protected activities. In such a case, the violation is conceptualized primarily in terms of discrimination which discourages union membership, as prohibited by section 8(a)(3), rather than *only* as restraint or coercion of employees in the exercise of section 7 rights, as prohibited by section 8(a)(1)—the primary difference between these two approaches is that motive normally must be proved in the section 8(a)(3) action, while it is generally irrelevant under section 8(a)(1).[293]

Finding "motive," however, is a tricky business. The NLRB and the courts obviously cannot look into the employer's mind, and absent incriminating employer statements, a finding of impermissible motive must necessarily rest on circumstantial evidence and the inferences that can reasonably be drawn therefrom. In the early days of the NLRA, the board was perhaps overly inclined to infer an impermissible motive, especially when the misconduct alleged by the employer to be the cause of the discharge was of a relatively "minor" nature.[294] The legislative history of the Taft-Hartley Act indicates that there was considerable congressional concern over this approach,[295] but it would not

---

[292] *Id.* at 438.
[293] *Accord,* Textile Workers Union v. Darlington Mfg. Co., 380 U.S. 263, 269 (1965) ("[a] violation of § 8(a)(1) alone . . . presupposes an act which is unlawful even absent a discriminatory motive," a situation which does *not* exist when an employee has in fact engaged in unprotected misconduct for which he has been fired").
[294] Refer to text accompanying notes 83-84 *supra.*
[295] Refer to text accompanying notes 113-116 *supra.*

appear that this had much effect in curbing the board's tendencies in this regard.

A fairly recent case involving picket line misconduct will serve as an adequate example of the problem of "pretextual" or "dual purpose" discharges. In *Federal Prescription Service,*[296] the employer had refused to reinstate an employee who, while on the picket line, had suggested to a nonstriker that her son "just may have an accident."[297] The administrative law judge had found this to be a threat which was not protected by section 7 and that the employer, therefore, had not violated section 8(a)(1).[298] The NLRB did not expressly disagree with that conclusion, but nevertheless found that the employer had violated section 8(a)(3): "Assuming *arguendo* that the remark constituted a threat, the issue remains, whether the Respondent in fact discharged Mrs. Peterson for making the threat or whether Respondent seized upon the threat as a pretext for ridding itself of one of the Union's most vigorous adherents."[299] The board then concluded that the employer was illegally motivated. It noted that the employer had a strong antiunion animus, that the discharged employee was notoriously prounion, that the employer did not investigate the alleged threat or give the employee an opportunity to present her side of the story, that the employer clearly had discriminated against other employees, and that the discharged employee had been an object of earlier unfair labor practices.[300] In addition, the board seemed to feel that the misconduct was of a relatively trivial nature, not to be condoned but understandable under the circumstances of the strike.[301]

Although it was not expressly stated in the opinion, the NLRB in this case was presumably following its "partial motive" test for determining the legality of "pretextual" or "dual motive" discharges. This approach, to which the board adhered for a number of years, provides that if a discharge was motivated in any substantial degree by the protected activities of the employee, the discharge violates the NLRA even though "just cause" was also present and relied on as a ground for the employer's action.[302]

---

[296] 203 N.L.R.B. 975 (1973), *enforced as modified,* 496 F.2d 813 (8th Cir.), *cert. denied,* 419 U.S. 1049 (1974).

[297] *Id.* at 976.

[298] *Id.* at 993.

[299] *Id.* at 976.

[300] *Id.*

[301] *Id.* at 977. In denying enforcement of the board's reinstatement order, the Eighth Circuit treated the case as raising strictly a "protected activities" issue, and completely ignored the pretext/discrimination aspect on which the Board based its decision. 496 F.2d at 818.

[302] *See, e.g.,* Central Casket Co., 225 N.L.R.B. 362, 376 (1976); Broyhill Co., 210 N.L.R.B. 288, 295 (1974); Erie Sand Steamship Co., 189 N.L.R.B. 63, 65 (1971).

Although most of the courts of appeals went along with the NLRB's "partial motivation" test,[303] it was also the subject of much criticism, and other courts, especially in the first circuit, repudiated it in favor of a "dominant motive" or "but for" approach to the problem,[304] or some other variation thereof.[305] The multiplicity of approaches, coupled with the uncertainty of the result in any given factual situation, left the law in a considerable state of confusion.

Apparently recognizing this, the NLRB recently attempted to set things right. In *Wright Line,*[306] after a comprehensive review of its own "partial motivation" test and the alternatives used by the various courts of appeals, the board finally opted in favor of a test articulated by the Supreme Court in *Mt. Healthy City School District Board of Education v. Doyle.*[307] Although the *Mt. Healthy* test was originally formulated for the purpose of determining when the discharge of a public employee is for unconstitutional rather than permissible reasons, the board concluded that the decision was consistent with the purposes and policies of the NLRA as well,[308] and thus adopted it as the statutory test.

Under the *Mt. Healthy* test, as construed by the NLRB and translated into a section 8(a)(3) context, the burden is initially upon the General Counsel to show that the discharged employee had engaged in some kind of protected conduct and that this conduct was a "substantial" or "motivating" factor in the discharge. If the General Counsel sustains the burden, then he has made a *prima facie* case. The burden then shifts to the employer to show that "it would have reached the same decision absent the protected conduct."[309]

That is the controlling test, but what it means is quite another matter. The first circuit, whose "dominant motive" approach had required

---

[303] *See, e.g.,* NLRB v. Gogin, 575 F.2d 596, 601 (7th Cir. 1978); Neptune Water Meter Co. v. NLRB, 551 F.2d 568, 569 (4th Cir. 1977); NLRB v. Southeastern Stages, Inc., 423 F.2d 878, 879 (5th Cir. 1970); Betts Baking Co. v. NLRB, 380 F.2d 199, 203 (10th Cir. 1967); NLRB v. West Side Carpet Cleaning Co., 329 F.2d 758, 761 (6th Cir. 1964); NLRB v. Great E. Color Lithographic Corp., 309 F.2d 352, 355 (2d Cir. 1962).

[304] *See, e.g.,* NLRB v. Eastern Smelting & Ref. Corp., 598 F.2d 666, 669-70 (1st Cir. 1979); Coletti's Furniture, Inc., v. NLRB, 550 F.2d 1292, 1293 (1st Cir. 1977); NLRB v. Billen Shoe Co., Inc., 397 F.2d 801, 803 (1st Cir. 1968); NLRB v. Pioneer Plastics Corp., 379 F.2d 301, 307 (1st Cir.), *cert. denied,* 389 U.S. 929 (1967); NLRB v. Lowell Sun Publ'g Co., 320 F.2d 835, 841 (1st Cir. 1963). *See also,* Western Exterminator Co. v. NLRB, 565 F.2d 1114, 1118 (9th Cir. 1977).

[305] *See, e.g.,* Waterbury Community Antenna, Inc. v. NLRB, 587 F.2d 90, 97-99 (2d Cir. 1978); Edgewood Nursing Center, Inc. v. NLRB, 581 F.2d 363, 368 (3d Cir. 1978).

[306] 251 N.L.R.B. No. 150, [1980] NLRB Dec. (CCH) ¶ 17,356 (Aug. 27, 1980).

[307] 429 U.S. 274 (1977).

[308] 251 N.L.R.B. No. 150 [1980] NLRB Dec. ¶ 17,356. *But see* Federal-Mogul Corp. v. NLRB, 566 F.2d 1245, 1265 (5th Cir. 1978) (Thornberry, J., concurring); Wolly, *What Hath Mt. Healthy Wrought?* 41 Ohio St. L.J. 383, 397-99 (1980).

[309] 251 N.L.R.B. No. 150, [1980] NLRB Dec. ¶ 17,356.

the General Counsel to prove that *but for* the protected activity the employee would *not* have been discharged (in spite of the acts of misconduct), had earlier viewed the *Mt. Healthy* decision as a vindication of its approach.[310] At least one commentator has agreed, calling the two approaches "virtually identical standard[s]."[311]

The NLRB, however, did not read the *Mt. Healthy* approach as being the same as that previously followed by the first circuit. To be sure, the board recognized that both tests reflect a rejection of its prior "partial motivation" test; but while the first circuit approach replaces the General Counsel's rather easy burden of proving partial motivation with a much stricter one, the *Mt. Healthy* approach—according to the board, at least—merely says that the case does not end once the General Counsel has proved the presence of such partial motivation. Rather, the employer also must be given the opportunity to rebut the *prima facie* case that has been made against him.[312] In short, under the *Wright Line* decision, the General Counsel's initial burden of proof remains exactly as before.

Moreover, although the NLRB also conceded that there was a "surface similarity"[313] between the second part of the *Mt. Healthy* test and the approach previously used by the first circuit, it said the two differed with respect to the bearer of the burden, with the *Mt. Healthy* test putting the burden of proof on the employer and the first circuit approach putting it on the General Counsel. Thus, while under the first circuit approach the General Counsel had the burden of proving that the protected conduct was a "necessary condition"[314] of the discharge, the *Mt. Healthy* approach imposes on the employer the burden of proving that the *un*protected conduct was merely a "sufficient condition"[315] of the discharge, which is really what is meant by the requirement that the employer show that it would have reached the same decision in spite of the protected conduct.[316] This formal shifting of the burden may not make any practical difference, however, because it

---

[310] NLRB v. Eastern Smelting & Ref. Corp., 598 F.2d 666, 671 (1st Cir. 1979).

[311] DuRoss, *Toward Rationality in Discriminatory Discharge Cases: The Impact of Mt. Healthy Board of Education v. Doyle Upon the NLRA*, 66 GEO. L.J. 1109, 1113 (1978).

[312] 251 N.L.R.B. No. 150, [1980] NLRB Dec. ¶ 17,356, at 32,467.

[313] *Id.*, [1980] NLRB Dec. ¶ 17,356, at 32,467.

[314] A "necessary condition" refers to a *causal factor* without which a particular *effect* would not occur. *See* B. SKYRMS, CHOICE AND CHANCE—AN INTRODUCTION TO INDUCTIVE LOGIC 85 (2d ed. 1975). Although it is by no means certain that when courts use a "but for" test they always intend this, literally construed the phrase "but for X, no Y" most probably means that "X is a necessary condition of Y."

[315] A "sufficient condition" refers to a *causal factor* the presence of which insures a particular *effect*.

[316] 251 N.L.R.B. No. 150, [1980] NLRB Dec. ¶ 17,356, at 32,466.

would appear that in most cases employers had assumed the responsibility anyway and had, in the first circuit at least, prevailed on that basis.[317] In other words, the cases decided in the first circuit seem to be saying that *because* the employer had demonstrated that the unprotected activity was a sufficient condition of the discharge, it was obvious that the General Counsel had failed to prove that the protected activity was a necessary condition of that discharge.

Regardless of which party has the formal burden of showing that the unprotected activities were or were not a sufficient condition of the discharge, it is very important to determine not only whether the employer has ever imposed similar punishment for similar misconduct in the past, but also whether it has consistently done so.[318] Although making this a controlling factor may limit an employer's flexibility in dealing with employees and cause it to have second thoughts about forgiving misconduct today because of the way in which that may inhibit its responses to misconduct when it occurs again, that may be a desirable result to the extent that it makes violence a less common and acceptable aspect of the employment relationship.

At this juncture, however, it is not clear that the *Wright Line* approach is going to prevail. It has met with mixed reviews from the various federal courts of appeals,[319] and after turning down one opportunity to do so,[320] the Supreme Court did recently agree to review the question of the proper allocation of proof in "pretextual" and "dual purpose" cases.[321]

The Thayer Doctrine: Where Reinstatement Will Otherwise "Effectuate the Policies of the Act"

An employee who has been non-discriminately discharged for engaging in unprotected and uncondoned conduct can nevertheless claim

---

[317] *See, e.g.,* NLRB v. Eastern Smelting & Ref. Corp., 598 F.2d 666, 671 (1st Cir. 1979); Liberty Mut. Ins. Co. v. NLRB, 592 F.2d 595, 602 (1st Cir. 1979). Furthermore, where the General Counsel did prevail, it was often because of direct rather than circumstantial evidence of a controlling impermissible motive. *See, e.g.,* Colleti's Furniture, Inc., 550 F.2d 1292, 1292-93 (1st Cir. 1977). The board found that the employer told the employee, "If you don't stop this talk about striking, I'm going to get rid of you." Colletti's Furniture, Inc., 224 N.L.R.B. 1547, 1550 (1976). *See also* NLRB v. South Shore Hosp., 571 F.2d 677, 683 (1st Cir. 1978).

[318] For a discussion of the formal models for showing the existence of a sufficient condition, see SKYRMS, CHOICE AND CHANCE, *supra* note 314, at 96-107.

[319] In Zurn Industries, Inc. v. NLRB, 680 F.2d 683 (9th Cir. 1982), the court reviewed the status of the *Wright Line* approach in the various circuits and ultimately concluded that is represented what was at least a defensible interpretation of the statute.

[320] Red Ball Motor Freight, Inc. v. NLRB, _____ U.S. _____ (1982) (White, J., dissenting) (denial of certiorari).

[321] NLRB v. Transportation Management Corp., 686 F.2d 63 (1st Cir. 1982), *cert. granted,* _____ U.S. _____ (1982).

reinstatement rights when the misconduct occurs in connection with a strike protesting an employer's unfair labor practices and the NLRB determines that reinstatement of this particular employee would be an appropriate *remedy* for those unfair labor practices. This exercise of the board's statutory power to devise such remedies for unfair labor practices "as will effectuate the policies of this act"[322] is generally refered to as the "Thayer Doctrine" after a case of that name.[323]

In evaluating the propriety of the Thayer Doctrine, one must necessarily return to the Supreme Court's *Fansteel* decision.[324] In that case, the NLRB had argued that even if the persons who had been discharged did not remain "employees" in the statutory sense (because their conduct was not "protected" by the NLRA), the board nevertheless had the power to order their reinstatement as a remedy for the unfair labor practice against which they had struck and of which the employer had been found guilty.[325] The Supreme Court rejected the argument. To be sure, the Supreme Court did not *expressly* say that the board lacked the power to *ever* impose such a remedy;[326] but the underlying policy considerations cited by the Court for denying the board the power in this case would seem to be of a fairly fundamental nature.[327]

Initially, the Court noted that the NLRB's "power to command affirmative action is remedial, not punitive,"[328] with the obvious implication being that affirmatively requiring an employer to reinstate an employee who has been discharged for misconduct merely punishes the employer for its unfair labor practices and does not, in itself, pro-

---

[322] NLRA § 10(c), 29 U.S.C. § 160(c) (1976).

[323] NLRB v. Thayer Co., 213 F.2d 748 (1st Cir. 1954). *See generally,* McDowell & Huhn, NLRB REMEDIES FOR UNFAIR LABOR PRACTICES 135-43 (1976).

[324] NLRB v. Fansteel Metallurgical Corp., 306 U.S. 240 (1939).

[325] *Id.* at 257.

[326] *Id.* at 257-58.

[327] *Id.*

[328] *Id.* at 257. Specifically, the court gave the following explanation:

The Board recognizes that in "many situations" reinstatement or reemployment after discharge for illegal acts would not be proper, but the board insists that it was proper in this instance. For the reasons we have given we disagree with that view. We think that a clearer case could hardly be presented and that, whatever discretion may be deemed to be committed to the board, its limits were transcended by the order under review.

Id. at 258. The Thayer Doctrine is currently bottomed on this quotation's ambiguity regarding the scope of the Court's disagreement with the Board. The proponents of the doctrine taking the view that the Court *merely* said that the Board could not impose the remedy *in that case.* Indeed, one authority cites the case as *affirmatively* holding that the Board has such power. "The Court also held that while the discharges did not violate the act, the board could unless arbitrary and unreasonable require the employer to hire back the strikers as a remedy for the unfair labor practices which triggered the strike." R. GORMAN, BASIC TEXT ON LABOR LAW UNIONIZATION AND COLLECTIVE BARGAINING 312 (1976)

vide a *remedy* for them. More importantly, though, the Court noted that the NLRA's ultimate objective of securing labor peace was supposed to be met through the substitution of legal remedies for various forms of employee "self-help" in response to untoward employer conduct vis-a-vis unionization, a policy which would be thwarted if force and violence were to be justified merely by reference to the fact that an employer's unfair labor practice had occurred.[329] The Court expressed its conclusion in these terms:

> There is not a line in the statute to warrant the conclusion that it is any part of the policies of the Act to encourage employees to resort to force and violence in defiance of the law of the land. On the contrary, the purpose of the Act is to promote peaceful settlements of disputes by providing legal remedies for the invasion of the employees' rights. . . . To secure the prevention of unfair labor practices by employers, complaints may be filed and heard and orders made. The affirmative action that is authorized is to make these remedies effective in the redress of the employees' rights, to assure them self-organization and freedom in representation, not to license them to commit tortious acts or to protect them from the appropriate consequences of unlawful conduct. We are of the opinion that to provide for the reinstatement or reemployment of employees guilty of the acts which the Board finds to have been committed in this instance would not only not effectuate any policy of the Act but would directly tend to make abortive its plan for peaceable procedure.[330]

In the years that followed, although *Fansteel* was more or less ignored, no overt attempt was made by the NLRB to exercise its remedial powers exactly in the way *Fansteel* has proscribed. On the other hand, the board continued to be quite liberal in finding, expressly or by necessary implication, that certain kinds of union-related misconduct were protected against discharge. This, in turn, led to the Taft-Hartley Act amendments, especially the section 10(c) prohibition against the reinstatement of any employee who had been discharged "for cause," but that limitation also was ignored or narrowly construed by the board. It was out of one such case that the Thayer Doctrine ultimately arose, albeit with some ironic twists.

In *NLRB v. Thayer Co.*,[331] the employees had gone out on strike in protest of some allegedly discriminatory discharges. The intensive

---

[329] 306 U.S. at 258.

[330] *Id.* at 257-58. *See also id.* at 252-54 (rejecting, on a similar basis, the argument that the conduct itself was affirmatively protected against discharge because it was in response to the employer's unfair labor practices):

> To justify such conduct because of the existence of a labor dispute or of an unfair labor practice would be to put a premium on resort to force instead of legal remedies and to subvert the principles of law and order which lie at the foundation of society.

Id. at 253.

[331] 213 F.2d 748 (1st Cir. 1954).

picketing, which was eventually enjoined by a state court,[332] was accompanied by several "incidents" consisting of "visits by carloads of strikers to the homes of nonstrikers, and an assault by pickets on a nonstriker."[333] Apart from contending that the strike itself was generally unprotected, the employer asserted that the employees who participated in these "incidents" were not entitled to reinstatement.[334]

The NLRB, however, found that the employer had committed various unfair labor practices, that the strike was a protected unfair labor practice strike, and that the "incidents" were insufficiently serious to justify the employer's refusal to reinstate those employees who had engaged in the questionable activity. The board noted that "none of the individual incidents involved actual restraint, violence, or coercion, or conduct which exceeded the animal exuberance and mutual harrassment characteristics of such strike situations."[335]

The First Circuit Court of Appeals disagreed in part. With respect to the "incidents" described above, the court concluded that they "were coercive in nature and calculated to instill fear of physical harm in the nonstriker victims, and are therefore not activities protected under § 7."[336] Rather than refusing to enforce this portion of the NLRB's order, however, the court remanded, for it was of the view that the analysis should not necessarily end there. That is, the court indicated that in formulating the proper remedy for the case the board should, notwithstanding the unprotected nature of the misconduct, also consider whether the discharges were "for cause"; if they were, then the court apparently recognized that reinstatement would be barred by section 10(c), but if they were not, then the board should consider whether reinstatement would otherwise effectuate the policies of the NLRA.[337]

In explaining why a finding that certain conduct was "unprotected" by section 7 could not necessarily be dispositive of the question of reinstatement rights, the court first had to carefully explain the exact nature of the relationship between section 7 and section 10(c). It did so in the following terms:

> The "for cause" proviso added to § 10(c) in 1947 is applicable where the employee is engaged in collective action as well as where he acts alone, . . . and it would seem that where an employee is discharged because he engaged in collective action and the discharge is found to be "for cause", the action is not the type protected under § 7. . . . However, a determination

---

[332] Thayer Co. v. Binnall, 326 Mass. 467, 95 N.E.2d 193 (1950).
[333] H.N. Thayer Co., 115 N.L.R.B. 1591, 1593 (1956).
[334] *Id.* at 1591.
[335] H. N. Thayer Co., 99 N.L.R.B. 1122, 1133 (1952).
[336] 213 F.2d at 757.
[337] *Id.*

that an employee is not engaged in a § 7 activity does not necessarily mean that, if he is discharged for his participation in the unprotected action, the discharge is "for cause". That depends on the surrounding circumstances. What is *cause* in one situation may not be in another.[338]

As an abstract matter, the court here is absolutely correct. Put differently, if conduct constitutes "cause" for discharge under section 10(c), then by definition it cannot be considered protected under section 7. But the reverse is not necessarily true. Conduct may be considered "unprotected" because it fails to meet either the "concertedness"[339] or "mutuality"[340] requirements, because the objective is not closely enough related to the employment relationship,[341] or because the means used are "irresponsible" but not otherwise affirmatively unlawful.[342] In none of these situations, however, is such conduct *necessarily* cause for discharge under section 10(c).[343]

On the other hand, that observation is of academic interest only insofar as Thayer-type situations are concerned, for when the reason the conduct is unprotected is because the means themselves are unlawfully coercive (rather than for the other reasons listed above), then *by definition* the conduct must also be considered "cause for discharge" under section 10(c). This is especially true in light of the fact that in order to be considered unprotected, the misconduct must be of more than just a "minor" nature.[344] Furthermore, it is clear beyond cavil that Congress intended to include such conduct within its meaning of the term "cause" for discharge.[345] In short, in the particular circumstances of the *Thayer* case, the section 7 issue and the section 10(c) issue *do* collapse into one, with a finding of "unprotectedness" thus being dispositive of the reinstatement issue.

The court, on the other hand, simply did not read section 10(c) in that light. Rather, the court made this observation about reinstatement and the policies of the NLRA:

---

[338] *Id.* at 753 n.6 (citations omitted).

[339] *See, e.g.,* Ontario Knife Co. v. NLRB, 247 N.L.R.B. No. 168 [1980] N.L.R.B. Dec. (CCH) ¶ 16,742 (Feb. 21, 1980).

[340] *See, e.g.,* NLRB v. Illinois Bell Tel. Co., 189 F.2d 124, 129 (8th Cir.), *cert. denied,* 342 U.S. 885 (1951).

[341] *See, e.g.,* Eastex, Inc. v. NLRB, 437 U.S. 556, 567-68 (1978) ("We may assume that at some point the relationship [between the immediate objective of the activity and the employees' interests as employees] becomes so attenuated that an activity cannot fairly be deemed to come within the 'mutual aid or protection' clause.").

[342] *See, e.g.,* NLRB v. Marshall Car Wheel & Foundry Co., 218 F.2d 409 (5th Cir. 1955).

[343] To take a clear but mundane example, assume that an employee was known to have cheered for the Oakland Raiders in the 1980 playoffs and for this reason was discharged by his employer, a rabid Houston Oiler fan. The employee's conduct in no sense meets *any* of the requirements for being protected by section 7, but by the same token, it does not constitute "cause for discharge."

[344] Refer to text accompanying notes 124-249 *supra.*

[345] Refer to text accompanying notes 116 & 123 *supra.*

The trial examiner, in recommending the reinstatement of such strikers, took into consideration the fact that "the strike resulted from the flagrant unfair labor practices of Respondent Companies. This seems perfectly proper . . . in deciding whether or not their discharge was "for cause" and whether their reinstatement would effectuate the policies of the Act.[346]

The court's method of defining misconduct constituting "cause" for discharge by reference, in part, to the fact that it was in response to an unfair labor practice by the employer is not supported in the legislative history. Indeed, since the analysis is inconsistent with the spirit of *Fansteel,* the method presumes that Congress intended to repudiate that portion of the Supreme Court decision—an untenable presumption, since *Fansteel* is one of the few opinions to be mentioned favorably in the legislative history.[347]

On remand, without acquiescing generally to the validity of this approach,[348] the NLRB did as the court of appeals had instructed; that is, although it did not expressly discuss the section 10(c) "cause for discharge" issue, it did reevaluate the facts from the perspective of whether reinstatement would "effectuate the policies of the Act."[349] And, to the undoubted dismay of the employees who had been ordered reinstated under the prior board decision, a board with a different composition now held that "the basic policies of the Act . . . particularly its purpose to settle industrial strife 'by orderly and peaceful procedures,' and to protect the 'rights of individual employees,'"[350] precluded it from ordering the reinstatement of the employees who had participated in the incidents in question.[351] Thus, in its first application, a doctrine which has since come to represent a liberalization of the reinstatement rights of the perpetrators of strike violence was applied in just the opposite manner.

Two members of the NLRB, however, vociferously dissented,[352] and their position is more reflective of both how the Thayer Doctrine is now applied and the rationale behind such an application. The dissent reasoned:

> While the Board must not countenance individual acts of misconduct and should use its influence to discourage unseemly behavior during strikes, it must not in so doing weaken the sanctions of the Act as to unfair labor prac-

---

[346] 213 F.2d at 748, 756 (1st Cir. 1954).
[347] H.R. Rep. No. 245, *supra* note 98, at 27 Legis. Hist. LMRA at 318; S. Rep. No. 105, *supra* note 105, at 28, Legis. Hist. LMRA at 434; 93 Cong. Rec. 6600 (1947), *reprinted in* Legis. Hist. LMRA, *supra* note 98, at 1538.
[348] H.N. Thayer Co., 115 N.L.R.B. 1591, 1593 (1956).
[349] *Id.*
[350] *Id.* at 1596.
[351] *Id.*
[352] *Id.* at 1597-606 (Members Murdock and Peterson, dissenting).

tices. . . . A decision, such as the one the majority has reached in this case, can but encourage employers who would ignore the provisions of the Act and must demonstrate to them that they may successfully avoid the detriment of a reinstatement and back pay order if employees during a strike, either by chance or provocation, engage in less than proper conduct.

While we are in positive agreement with the purpose of our colleagues to discourage intemperate conduct by strikers, we doubt that the remedy they have framed will achieve this purpose. Withholding reinstatement and back pay from the strikers who engaged in misconduct will be of little significance in deterring strikers from the rash acts which commonly arise in the heated atmosphere of a labor dispute, while ordering such affirmative relief would in no wise justify the improper conduct. A reinstatement and back-pay order does not grant a reward to employees; it rather restores the jobs and wages which unfair labor practices caused them to lose.[353]

Apart from the fact that the policy advocated here was one that had already been repudiated both by the Supreme Court (in *Fansteel*) and Congress (in section 10(c) and the other Taft-Hartley Act amendments), the thesis of the dissent is questionable on other points as well. The subtle suggestion that an employer might be encouraged by the majority approach to commit unfair labor practices simply for the purpose of inducing employees to engage in acts of misconduct for which it can then successfully fire them seems somewhat far fetched. The allegation that a denial of reinstatement rights would not serve to deter "strikers from the rash acts which commonly arise in the heated atmosphere of a labor dispute" seems contrary to common assumptions about the deterrent effect of "punishment," even upon the commission of emotional acts.[354] Moreover, most of the misconduct in *Thayer* did not involve merely a flare of tempers on the picket line but was, rather, conduct that had to have been deliberate and

---

[353] *Id.* at 1605-06.

[354] Regardless of whether one could or could not prove a literal and direct deterrent effect in any specific case, consistently allowing employers to discharge employees who engage in violent misbehavior would definitely tend to reinforce the notion that this violent conduct is not an acceptable part of industrial relations, thereby discouraging its occurrence. *See* H. PACKER, THE LIMITS OF THE CRIMINAL SANCTION (1968). Packer observes:

The socializing and habit-forming effects of the threat of punishment are not limited to simple, literal observation of threats being made and carried out. There is heavy symbolic significance in the operation of the criminal sanction; for the process of ascribing guilt, responsibility, and punishment goes on day after day against the background of all human history. The vocabulary of punishment (itself heavily influenced by legal concepts and models) with which we become acquainted beginning in early childhood impresses us—some more than others—with the gravity of antisocial conduct. The ritual of the criminal trial becomes for all of us a kind of psychodrama in which we participate vicariously, a morality play in which innocence is protected, injury requited, and the wrongdoer punished. It is

premeditated. Conversely, the dissent's denial that an order of reinstatement would serve to "justify" or "reward" the employees for their misconduct is by no means convincing; to the contrary, a reinstatement order would seem to have exactly that effect. Finally, conceding that "but for" the employer's unfair labor practice the occasion for the employee's misconduct would never have arisen, it is still not clear why, as a matter of either moral or legal theory, the former serves to exonerate the latter. Indeed, it would seem that it clearly should not, given the qualitative differences between the acts, the overall antipathy of the statute toward violence,[355] the ready availability of peaceable remedies for employer unfair labor practices,[356] and the minimal nature of the employer's response.[357] Moreover, while the "but for" analysis may perhaps legitimately be used to identify a factual "cause" of the misconduct (but not necessarily the moral or legal responsibility for it) when the strike is originally called in protest of an employer's unfair labor practice, the reasoning is far less persuasive, even at this factual level, when the discharged employee enjoys the status of an unfair labor practice striker *only* because of the so-called "conversion doctrine." Under this doctrine, a work stoppage which began as an economic or collective bargaining strike is "converted" into an unfair labor practice strike if the NLRB determines that the employer's unfair labor practice had the effect of prolonging the strike.[358] This finding of prolonga-

---

not simply the threat of punishment or its actual imposition that contributes to the total deterrent effect but the entire criminal process, standing as a paradigm of good and evil, in which we are reminded by devices far more subtle than literal threats that the wicked do not flourish. These public rituals, it is plausible to suppose, strengthen the identification of the majority with a value system that places a premium on law-abiding behavior.

Id. at 43-44.

[355] Refer to text accompanying notes 98-123 *supra.*

[356] Refer to text accompanying note 78 *supra.*

[357] Ironically, the law seems to concede that an employer is free to pursue criminal or civil (damages) relief against an employee guilty of misconduct. Local 833, UAW v. NLRB, 300 F.2d 699 (D.C. Cir. 1961), *cert. denied,* 370 U.S. 911 (1962). In that context it seems highly unlikely that the employer's own unfair labor practice would constitute "provocation" or would even be admissible as a "mitigating circumstance." Yet, when the employer *merely* seeks to terminate an otherwise voluntary relationship because of the employee's misconduct, the Thayer Doctrine (as construed by the dissent and as currently applied) allows the unfair labor practice to operate as a limitation on the exercise of that power. Although it may be possible to explain this by reference to the fact that loss of a job may entail a much greater detriment or "injury in fact" than the imposition of either civil or criminal penalties, the conceptual or philosophical difference between the two responses is enormous. And *if* limits are to be imposed, it should be upon the employer's *active* demand for retribution or recompense rather than upon his merely *passive* attempt to disassociate himself from the miscreant.

[358] *See generally* GORMAN, LABOR LAW, *supra* note 328, at 339 (1976).

tion is, however, a fairly judgmental if not entirely fictional matter.[359] Thus, there is little if any justification for saying that strike misconduct committed after the magical point in time at which prolongation occurred was in any realistic sense "caused" by the employer's unfair labor practice. It is impossible to determine when an unfair labor practice has prolonged a strike, and in many cases it is just as likely as not that the strike would have continued as long as it did anyway, and that the employee would have engaged in the same misconduct. All of this makes the application of the "but for" test very tenuous indeed. In sum, the case for the application of the Thayer Doctrine in the manner envisioned by the dissent is simply not very compelling.

Although the NLRB followed the specific mandate of the court in the *Thayer* case, it ignored the Thayer Doctrine in later cases. This eventually inspired yet another remand by a court of appeals. In *Local 833, UAW v. NLRB*,[360] the employer had discharged employees who, during the course of what was ultimately found to be an unfair labor practice strike, had engaged in "belly-to-back" mass picketing, committed physical assault upon nonstrikers, demonstrated in large and jeering crowds outside the homes of nonstrikers, and blocked, pushed, and shoved applicants who were attempting to enter the plant.[361] The trial examiner found that the misconduct was either not unprotected or it had been condoned by the employer, but the board disagreed and refused to order reinstatement.[362] On appeal, the union argued that, regardless of whether the misconduct was protected or condoned, the board should be required to reconsider the reinstatement issue under the Thayer Doctrine. The District of Columbia Court of Appeals agreed.[363]

The court, rephrasing the test for reinstatement, observed that "where an employer who has committed unfair labor practices discharges employees for unprotected acts of misconduct, the NLRB must consider both the seriousness of the employer's unlawful acts and the seriousness of the employees' misconduct in determining whether reinstatement would effectuate the policies of the act."[364] This restatement of the test is perhaps unfortunate in that it omits any specific reference to the limiting effects of section 10(c), an omission which could only tend to lead the analysis even further away from the rele-

---

[359] Gorman notes,"[o]bviously, there is no litmus-paper test to determine whether a strike would have continued as long as it did even in the absence of the employer unfair labor practice or to determine exactly the date at which the conversation takes place." *Id.*
[360] 300 F.2d 699 (D.C. Cir. 1961).
[361] *Id.* at 702.
[362] *Id.*
[363] *Id.* at 702-03.
[364] *Id.*

vant legislative intent with respect to matters of this kind. Later, however, the court did recognize that the board must take section 10(c) into account, but indicated that in determining whether "cause" existed the board should consider matters "such as the employer's unfair labor practices, each employee's job history, and the relationship between the acts of misconduct and fitness for continued service,"[365] none of which seems to be relevant under the legislative history, given its express condemnation of precisely this kind of employee misconduct in a strike situation.[366]

The court advanced two justifications for its adoption of the Thayer Doctrine. "First, the employer's antecedent unfair labor practices *may* have been so blatant that they provoked employees to resort to unprotected action. Second, reinstatement is the only sanction which prevents an employer from benefitting from his unfair labor practices through discharges which may weaken or destroy a union."[367] As the use of the term "may" indicates, even the court recognized the rather speculative nature of its argument. Even taken as such, though, the court's "speculations" do not seem particularly reasonable or compelling. For example, while it may sometimes be reasonable to assume an employer's unfair labor practice has actually provoked a strike or other concerted activity that is unprotected because of its timing, because it is in breach of contract, or because it is otherwise "indefensible" (as in a slowdown situation), it seems unlikely that such a nexus often exists between employer unfair labor practices and a picket line assault or the other kinds of violent misconduct normally involved in a Thayer Doctrine case. Although the unfair labor practice may *cause* the strike, which then provides the opportunity for the assault (as argued by the dissent in *Thayer*), what literally provokes the violence in those cases is, more often than not, the fact that other employees have not joined the strike or other persons are attempting to take the striking employees' jobs, which is to say that the court's provocation justification does not carry the doctrine very far forward.

Indeed, recognizing that "provocation" constituted a primary justification for the doctrine, one court of appeals recently limited its application accordingly. In *Mosher Steel Co. v. NLRB,*[368] the employer

---

[365] *Id.* at 705.
[366] Refer to text accompanying notes 98-123 *supra*. Conversely, with respect to strikers who were present at the employment office picketing but who did not themselves obstruct applicants, *id.* at 703, an argument could be made that while "unprotected" the conduct was not at the same time "cause" for discharge—a situation to which the balancing test aspect of *Thayer* could then be applied without doing damage to the spirit of the act.
[367] *Id.* (Emphasis added).
[368] 568 F.2d 436 (5th Cir. 1978).

had discharged three unfair labor practice strikers for threatening physical violence against a nonstriker who was attempting to cross the picket line, for hitting a nonstriker with a cue stick in a neighborhood bar, and for kicking and damaging a motorcycle belonging to a nonstriker.[369] The NLRB, however, ordered the reinstatement of all three.[370]

On appeal, the court noted that under the balancing test of the Thayer Doctrine[371] "it is almost as if employer unfair labor practices gave a 'self-defense' claim to the worker dismissed for unprotected conduct."[372] The court, moreover, apparently espoused the view that "self-defense" justifies action against the original aggressor but not against innocent third parties. Thus, the court noted that "in the instant case, in retaliation to employer unfair labor practices, violent conduct was directed not at management, but against fellow workers who also suffered from employer misconduct."[373] And since the purpose of the NLRA is to protect individual employees in the exercise of their right to strike or not, the court concluded that the reinstatement of employees who directed physical violence at fellow employees would in no sense be consistent with the policies of the act.[374] Construed in this fashion, the Thayer Doctrine will have a small role to play in the violent misconduct cases, as a large percentage of them do involve employee-to-employee rather than employee-to-management violence. The construction is, however, a reasonable one.

The second justification of the Thayer Doctrine proffered by the *Local 833, UAW* case was that reinstatement "is the only sanction which prevents an employer from benefitting from his unfair labor practices through discharges which may weaken or destroy a union."[375] Although it is certainly possible that selective discharges of

---

[369] *Id.* at 439.

[370] *Id.* at 438.

[371] The case also illustrates how easy it is for the section 10(c) "cause" element of the original *Thayer* case analysis to be subsumed entirely but erroneously into the broader balancing approach. In *Thayer*, the court had put the test this way: "The actual questions in this case are whether under the circumstances the strike conduct was cause for discharge, *and, if not,* whether reinstatement would effectuate the policies of the Act." 213 F.2d at 754 (emphasis added). In *Mosher Steel*, however, the court treated the fact that the conduct was cause for discharge, not as a total bar to reinstatement, as section 10(c) properly requires and the original Thayer Doctrine implicitly recognizes, but rather as merely that which must then be balanced against the employer's own misconduct. 568 F.2d at 441. For example, the Court said that *"because* we hold that the conduct . . . was sufficient to cause dismissal it is then necessary to determine whether their reinstatement would further the policies of the Act." *Id.* (emphasis added).

[372] *Id.*

[373] *Id.* at 442. The court did, however, order the reinstatement of one of the employees on the ground, *inter alia,* that his discharge had been illegally motivated. *Id.* at 441.

[374] *Id.* at 442.

[375] 300 F.2d at 703.

this kind might directly or indirectly undermine a union's effectiveness or even majority strength, the probability of that happening in large numbers of cases is too remote for it to serve as a general justification for the doctrine. To the contrary, most of the cases involve the discharge of only a few employees whose presence or absence in the work force will not affect organizational and bargaining strength. Moreover, if those discharged are in fact leaders of a union whose tacit policy is to engage in violence against employees not sympathetic to the cause, then it would seem that the legitimate benefit these employees gain from being free of their coercion more than offsets the possible illegitimate benefit the employer gets in being free of a union.

Again, when viewed in the context of discharges for violent strike and picket line misconduct, the explanations advanced for the Thayer Doctrine do not seem particularly compelling. Nevertheless, in light of this judicial insistence, and coincidental with a change in its membership, the NLRB eventually accepted the Thayer Doctrine. On the other hand, it is also significant to note that the board first accepted the doctrine in *Blades Manufacturing Co.*,[376] where the unprotected response to the employer's unfair labor practice consisted of partial or intermittent strike activity.[377] The board specifically noted that "the strike activity of the employees was not in violation of any law. It was at all times peaceful."[378] It is submitted that the application of the Thayer Doctrine to unprotected activity of that kind is far easier to justify than its application to acts of violence, as the latter, but not necessarily the former, clearly constitutes "cause" for discharge in the statutory sense. Notwithstanding the legitimacy of its initial application by the board, however, the doctrine was soon applied in the violent misconduct cases as well.

Within that context, the application of the doctrine is somewhat unpredictable, with the results turning on innumerable factual variations and the often unstated but rather obviously present subjective feelings of the different administrative law judges, NLRB members, and federal judges who are forced to confront these rather unpleasant matters. One rather good attempt to distill from all the cases some controlling general principles occurred, however, in the administrative law judge's decision in *Fibreboard Paper Products Corp.*,[379] as follows:

> In applying the various indicia established by the decisions discussed above, and synthesizing their holdings, it would appear that in determining

---

[376] 144 N.L.R.B. 561 (1963).
[377] *Id.* at 566.
[378] *Id.* at 567.
[379] 180 N.L.R.B. 142 (1969).

whether the employee's conduct is so aggravated as to bar reinstatement, the following factors should be weighed in reaching a judgment:

(1) The employer's provocation, if any, in the context of reinstatement having as its primary purpose the prevention of discriminatory discharges for union activities;

(2) The post-reinstatement job contract between the employee and employer;

(3) Whether reinstatement would exacerbate the future employment relationship so as to result in decreased business efficiency or serious maladjustments to the employer's work force and its relations with its employees;

(4) Whether the employee's conduct is so unlawful that his continued employment by reinstatement should not be forced on the employer because the nature of the dischargee's misconduct renders harmonious employer-employee relations improbable; and

(5) Whether the employee's conduct was so flagrant as to render him unfit for further employment so that it would not only be unreasonable to require his reinstatement but it would also not "effectuate the policies of the Act" nor "preserve industrial peace."[380]

Applying those criteria to the facts before him, the administrative law judge in *Fibreboard Paper Products* ordered the reinstatement of an employee who had thrown a vial of paint at a car which other pickets had overturned on the picket line; but he did deny reinstatement to two other strikers who had violently shoved and threatened an official of another union, blocked access to cars into the plant, rammed one car with a truck, and hit a management attorney in the mouth as he was attempting to enter the plant.[381]

---

[380] *Id.* at 173.

[381] *Id.* at 170-71. In other cases the Board has denied reinstatement rights. *See, e.g.,* Beaver Bros. Baking Co., 198 N.L.R.B. 327 (1972) (employees threatened lives of nonstrikers, vandalized cars, sabotaged company property, threw rocks at company officials, forcibly interfered with deliveries and pick-ups, damaged trucks, and attempted to provoke fights with nonstrikers); Lewis Bus. Forms, Inc., 180 N.L.R.B. 1695 (1969) (employees displayed clubs, chains, broken bottles, a hammer, and a baseball bat at their tent on the picket line and threatened a truck driver with a metal bar); Sea Land Serv., Inc., 146 N.L.R.B. 931 (1964) (employees knifed a nonstriker and threatened another employee with physical harm if he testified for the company); Laura Modes Co., 144 N.L.R.B. 1592 (1963) (employee followed a management official as he left the plant and identified the official for eight men who beat him up); Philip Carey Mfg. Co., 140 N.L.R.B. 1103 (1963) (employees followed nonstrikers home and physically assaulted them, provoked a fight with nonstrikers at a restaurant, and blocked the ingress of a truck by threatening the driver with a rock). As the date of the *Philip Carey* case indicates, although the Board did not use the Thayer Doctrine as an *affirmative* justification for ordering reinstatement until later, it did cite *Local 833, UAW* as precedent for refusing to order reinstatement. *Id.* at 1132 n.81.

In contrast, in other cases the Board ordered reinstatement under the Thayer Doctrine. *See, e.g.,* Allied Indus. Workers v. NLRB, 476 F.2d 868 (D.C. Cir 1973) (employees followed a nonstriker's car for some time, threatened to "get" a nonstriking employee, and impeded access into the plant); Coronet Casuals, Inc., 207 N.L.R.B. 304 (1973) (employee threw cherry bombs on the plant premises); O'Daniel Oldsmobile, Inc., 179 N.L.R.B. 398 (1969) (employee on picket line pulled sharp metal object from belt and

Although it is theoretically unnecessary to even reach a Thayer Doctrine issue unless the conduct is in fact "unprotected," there seems to be no real difference between what the NLRB has held to be unprotected in a section 8(a)(1) context and what it finds to be so egregious that reinstatement cannot be ordered as a part of a Thayer Doctrine remedy. Indeed, it is sometimes difficult to determine the statutory perspective from which the board is considering the issue.

In any event, like the NLRB's expansive reading of section 7, the Thayer Doctrine does serve to protect employees from being discharged for the commission of various kinds of strike and picket line misconduct.

---

gestured for a nonstriking employee to get out of his car); J.P. Stevens & Co., 163 N.L.R.B. 217 (1967) (employee threatened and cursed a manager); Oneita Knitting Mills, Inc., 153 N.L.R.B. 51 (1965) (employees twice opened the door of a car crossing the picket line, hit cars with fists, threatened a nonstriker at her home, and threw eggs and tomatoes at a car); Elmira Mach. & Speciality Works, Inc., 148 N.L.R.B. 1695 (1964) (employees temporarily delayed access to plant, rocked cars, followed nonstrikers as they left the plant, and damaged a truck crossing the picket line); R.C. Can Co., 144 N.L.R.B. 210, 218 (1963) (employee threatened to "kick hell" out of the plant manager).

CHAPTER XI

Labor Union Violence as an Unfair Labor Practice[1]

As construed by the National Labor Relations Board (NLRB) and the courts, the National Labor Relations (Taft-Hartley) Act (NLRA) *seems* to project two somewhat inconsistent approaches to the problem of labor union violence. On the one hand, as discussed in the preceding chapter, the act imposes significant limits on the power of an employer to discharge an individual employee who has committed acts of picket line and strike violence. On the other hand, the act specifically makes it an unfair labor practice "for a labor organization or its agents . . . to restrain or coerce . . . employees in the exercise of rights guaranteed in section 7,"[2] particularly the right to refrain from certain union-sponsored activities. The NLRB and the courts have, moreover, evidenced a consistent willingness to include within this prohibition a wide range of violent and coercive misconduct. Unfortunately, the rigor of prohibition is diluted significantly by the inadequacy of the remedies that are allowed for its violation. The apparent inconsistency, in short, seems to have been resolved in favor once again of a somewhat passive if not implicitly tolerant attitude toward the problem of labor union violence.

---

[1] Portions of this chapter originally appeared as Haggard, *Labor Union Violence as an Unfair Labor Practice*, 34 S.C.L. REV. 273 (1982).

[2] Labor Management Relations Act § 8(b)(1)(A), 29 U.S.C. § 158(b)(1)(A)(1976). A second part of this section makes it an unfair labor practice for a labor union to "restrain or coerce . . . an employer in the selection of his representatives for the purposes of collective bargaining or the adjustment of grievances . . . ." Labor Management Relations Act § 8(b)(1)(B), 29 U.S.C. § 158(b)(1)(B) (1976). The "restraint" or "coercion" that occurs most often under § 8(b)(1)(B) consists not of physical violence, but of otherwise peaceful strikes and picketing or the imposition of union discipline on members who also happen to be company supervisors. *See generally* R. GORMAN, LABOR LAW 405-06, 689-94 (1976). Moreover, in cases where the restraint or coercion of the employer in the selection of his collective bargaining representative consists of violent assaults upon management or supervisory personnel, it is likely that such conduct will also indirectly restrain or coerce employees in violation of section 8(b)(1)(A). *See, e.g.*, Broadway Hospital, Inc., 244 N.L.R.B. 341 (1979). The "violence" aspects of a section 8(b)(1)(B) violation do not, thus, warrant separate discussion.

At any rate, this chapter explores in detail this affirmative federal prohibition against the use of violence by labor unions and their agents and supporters.

HISTORICAL BACKGROUND AND LEGISLATIVE HISTORY

In the years preceding the passage of the original National Labor Relations (Wagner) Act (NLRA), much of the violence perpetrated by, or in the name of, labor unions was allegedly in response to the refusal of employers to recognize and bargain with those unions as the exclusive representatives of their respective employees.[3] This refusal was not illegal at the time; employers simply believed it to be an exercise of their constitutional rights.[4] Proponents of unionization did not share this view. They considered this legal employer intransigence to be a violation of *their* fundamental liberties of speech, association, and of some obscurely defined right to an "industrial democracy."[5] As is often the case when two sides are vigorously asserting mutually inconsistent "rights," the conflict readily and repeatedly produced violence.[6]

The impact of this violence was not, of course, limited to the parties themselves. It resulted in disruptions of production and commerce that ultimately disadvantaged and inconvenienced the population at large. Inevitably, the pressure on Congress to do something about it became compelling. In the early days of the New Deal, after an unsuccessful and unconstitutional experiment in regulating labor relations under the Industrial Recovery Act,[7] Congress finally responded with the passage of the NLRA.[8] In essence, the NLRA codified most of

---

[3] In *NLRB v. Jones & Laughlin Steel Corp.*, the Supreme Court noted that:
   experience has abundantly demonstrated that the recognition of the right of employees to self-organization and to have representatives of their own choosing for the purpose of collective bargaining is often an essential condition of industrial peace. Refusal to confer and negotiate has been one of the most prolific causes of strife. This is such an outstanding fact in the history of labor disturbances that it is a proper subject of judicial notice and requires no citation of instances.
301 U.S. 1, 42 (1937).
   [4] Since the Supreme Court of this era was a rather vigorous proponent of the "economic" due process doctrine, this belief was by no means an unwarranted one. *See generally* B. SEGAN, ECONOMIC LIBERTIES AND THE CONSTITUTION 126-55 (1980).
   [5] See generally M. DERBER, THE AMERICAN IDEA OF INDUSTRIAL DEMOCRACY, 1865-1965 (1970); J. AUERBACH, LABOR AND LIBERTY (1966).
   [6] *See generally* S. LENS, THE LABOR WARS (1973); NATIONAL COMMISSION ON THE CAUSES AND PREVENTION OF VIOLENCE, VIOLENCE IN AMERICA 288-89 (1969); J. BECHER, STRIKE! (1972); Taft & Ross, *American Labor Violence: Its Causes, Character, and Outcome, reprinted in* HISTORY OF VIOLENCE IN AMERICA 281-395 (1969).
   [7] National Industrial Recovery Act, Pub. L. No. 73-67, 48 Stat. 195 (1933), declared unconstitutional in Schechter Poultry Corp. v. United States, 295 U.S. 495 (1935).
   [8] National Labor Relations Act, Pub. L. No. 74-198, 49 Stat. 449 (1935).

the rights that the labor unions had previously claimed and proscribed employer interference with those rights. In particular, the act made it an "unfair labor practice" for an employer to interfere with the organizational activities of its employees,[9] to dominate or interfere with the formation or activities of labor unions,[10] to discriminate against employees on matters related to unionization,[11] or to refuse to recognize and bargain collectively with the union selected by its employees.[12] There were no corresponding union unfair labor practices.

Although the expressly stated purpose of the NLRA was to end strikes and other more egregious forms of industrial warfare,[13] that purpose was apparently not fully served by the legislation. To be sure, the number of employees being represented by labor unions in collective bargaining rose dramatically,[14] but so did the number and intensity of strikes.[15] In 1946, with the inhibiting effects of World War II finally removed, the nation was again inundated by a wave of long and sometimes bitter triangular confrontations between labor unions,

---

[9] *Id.* §§ 7, 8(1).
[10] *Id.* § 8(2).
[11] *Id.* § 8(3).
[12] *Id.* § 8(5).
[13] *Id.* § 1, *see also,* A. COX, D. BOK & R. GORMAN, LABOR LAW—CASES AND MATERIALS 72-77 (9th ed. 1979).
[14] Between 1930 and 1940, union membership as a percentage of all employees in nonagricultural establishments rose from 11.6% to 26.9%. G. BLOOM & H. NORTHRUP, ECONOMICS OF LABOR RELATIONS 61 (7th ed. 1973).
[15] The Bureau of Labor Statistics Work Stoppage figures for the twenty years between 1927 and 1947 are as follows:

[Worker and days idle in thousands]

| | | Stoppages beginning in year | | |
| | | Average duration (calendar days) | Workers involved | |
Year	Number		Number	Percent of total employed
1927	707	26.5	330	1.4
1928	604	27.6	314	1.3
1929	921	22.6	289	1.2
1930	637	22.3	183	.8
1931	810	18.8	342	1.6
1932	841	19.6	324	1.8
1933	1,695	16.9	1,170	6.3
1934	1,856	19.5	1,470	7.2
1935	2,014	23.8	1,120	5.2
1936	2,172	23.3	789	3.1
1937	4,740	20.3	1,860	7.2
1938	2,772	23.6	688	2.8
1939	2,613	23.4	1,170	3.5

nonunion employees, and management.[16] These confrontations led to a growing public sentiment that unions were perhaps abusing the powers granted them by the NLRA. It was felt that legal constraints were necessary to restore the proper balance and to insure some degree of industrial order. A conservative Congress was apparently sympathetic to this viewpoint and responded in 1947 by passing the Taft-Hartley Act, which amended the NLRA in several particulars. The most important amendment was the addition of a list of *union* unfair labor practices paralleling, to some extent, those previously applied to employers.

Congressional concern over what many said was an abuse of a union's statutorily enhanced bargaining, organizational, and other economic powers was reflected in the new provisions. The NLRA made it an unfair labor practice for unions to refuse to bargain in good faith with employers,[17] to involve so-called "secondary employers" in labor disputes not of their own making,[18] or to engage in organizational or recognitional picketing.[19] A similar concern is evidenced in the prohibition of the "union shop" and of peaceful union efforts to obtain and enforce these restrictive arrangements.[20]

Congress, however, was concerned with more than merely figurative "coercive" union conduct. The legislative history clearly indicates

[Worker and days idle in thousands, cont'd. from p. 367]

		Stoppages beginning in year		
		Average duration (calendar days)	Workers involved	
Year	Number		Number	Percent of total employed
1940	2,508	20.9	577	1.7
1941	4,268	18.3	2,360	6.1
1942	2,968	11.7	840	2.0
1943	3,752	5.0	1,980	4.6
1944	4,956	5.6	2,120	4.8
1945	4,750	9.9	3,470	8.2
1946	4,985	24.2	4,600	10.5
1947	3,693	25.6	2,170	4.7

U.S. DEP'T OF LABOR, BUREAU OF LABOR STATISTICS, HANDBOOK OF LABOR STATISTICS 508 (1978). Apologists for the Wagner Act, of course, explain these statistics by reference to factors other than a failure of the underlying policy. *See, e.g.,* I. BERNSTEIN, THE NEW DEAL COLLECTIVE BARGAINING POLICY 143-45 (1975).

[16] *See* J. BRECHER, STRIKE! 276-80 (1972).

[17] NLRA § 8(b)(3), 29 U.S.C. § 158(b)(3)(1976).

[18] NLRA § 8(b)(4), 29 U.S.C. § 158(b)(4)(1976).

[19] NLRA § 8(b)(7), 29 U.S.C. § 158(b)(7)(1976).

[20] NLRA § 8(a)(3), (b)(2), 29 U.S.C. § 158(a)(3), (b)(2)(1976); *see generally* Haggard, *A Clarification of the Types of Union Security Agreements Affirmatively Permitted by Federal Statutes,* 5 RUT.CAM. L.J. 418, 439-44 (1974).

equivalent dismay over the many reported instances of actual physical violence and intimidation that labor union supporters had directed against both employers and employees not sympathetic to the union cause.[21] In the case of violence directed toward employers, Congress simply reaffirmed what it thought should have been clear under the NLRA as originally passed: that employee acts of personal intimidation toward supervisors and damage to company property are not a form of "concerted activity" protected by section 7. Rather, they are acts for which that employee can be discharged.[22] Congress went further in the case of violence directed toward employees and made it an unfair labor practice for a labor organization or its agents to commit acts of violence directed at the employer's other employees.

In many respects, the original House version of the Taft-Hartley Act was more stringent than the final bill. It made it an unfair labor practice for any employee, "by intimidating practices," to interfere with the section 7 rights of other employees.[23] Similarly, the original House version made it an unfair labor practice for a labor organization "to interfere with, restrain, or coerce individuals in the exercise of rights guaranteed in section 7(b)."[24] The section defining "unlawful concerted activities" specifically described the kinds of conduct which the authors of the bill apparently intended to prohibit, namely:

> By the use of force or violence or threats thereof, preventing or attempting to prevent any individual from quitting or continuing in the employment of, or from accepting or refusing employment by, any employer; or by the use of force, violence, physical obstruction, or threats thereof, preventing or at-

---

[21] *See, e.g.,* Labor Management Relations Act, Ch. 120, Pub. L. No. 101 (1947)(codified at 29 U.S.C. §§ 141-187 (1976)), *reprinted in* SUBCOMMITTEE ON LABOR OF THE SENATE COMM. ON LABOR AND PUBLIC WELFARE, 93d Cong., 2d Sess. LEGISLATIVE HISTORY OF THE LABOR MANAGEMENT RELATIONS ACT OF 1947, at 456, 882, 898, 905, 912, 1025, 1207-08 [hereinafter cited as LEGIS. HIST. LMRA]. The House Committee Report on an early version of what was to eventually become the Taft-Hartley Act explained:

> For the last 14 years, as a result of labor laws ill-conceived and disastrously executed, the American workingman has been deprived of his dignity as an individual. He has been cajoled, coerced, intimidated, and on many occasions beaten up, in the name of the splendid aims set forth in section 1 of the National Labor Relations Act. . . .
>
> The employer's plight has likewise not been happy. . . . He has been required to employ or reinstate individuals who have destroyed his property and assaulted other employees. . . . He has had to stand helplessly by while employees desiring to enter his plant to work have been obstructed by violence, mass picketing, and general rowdyism.

Id at 295-96.

[22] *See generally* Haggard, *Picket Line and Strike Violence As a Grounds For Discharge,* 18 HOUS. L. REV. 444-48 (1981) [hereinafter cited as Haggard, *Picket Line*].

[23] LEGIS. HIST. LMRA at 52.

[24] *Id.* at 52-53.

> tempting to prevent any individual from freely going from any place and entering upon an employer's premises, or from freely leaving an employer's premises and going to any other place; or picketing an employer's place of business in numbers or in a manner otherwise than is reasonably required to give notice of the existence of a labor dispute at such place of business; or picketing or besetting the home of any individual in connection with any labor dispute.[25]

Persons injured by these activities were authorized to sue in federal court to recover the damages sustained as a result thereof.[26]

The committee report adds little to this, except perhaps to suggest that mass picketing was a form of intimidation that was of special concern. It alone is cited as an example on several occasions.[27] The House debates on the original House bill are not particularly enlightening either. They refer to the problem of employee intimidation by labor union officials in general terms only.[28]

In comparison to its House counterpart, the bill as originally introduced in the Senate was more moderate in its delineation of union unfair labor practices. In fact, it did not include any prohibition against union coercion of employees in the exercise of their statutory rights. Four members of the Senate Committee which introduced the bill proposed to correct that omission by floor amendments. In their supplemental views which were attached to the Senate Report, they indicated that "the committee heard many instances of union coercion of employees such as that brought about by threats of reprisal against employees and their families in the course of organizing campaigns; also direct interference by mass picketing and other violence."[29] Accordingly, Senator Ball introduced a floor amendment adding a provision similar to the one in the House version making it an unfair labor practice for a labor organization "to interfere with, restrain, or coerce employees in the exercise of the rights guaranteed by section 7."[30]

The debate on this amendment was fairly extensive and is enlightening in several aspects. Among other things, the proponents of this amendment gave some fairly specific examples of the kinds of union conduct they intended to prohibit. As in the House debates, mass picketing was a repeated example.[31] The use or threatened use of ordinary physical violence as a means of forcing employees to support

---

[25] *Id.* at 78.
[26] *Id.* at 79.
[27] *Id.* at 296, 297, 335.
[28] *See, e.g., id.* at 647, 649, 677.
[29] *Id.* at 456.
[30] *Id.* at 1018.
[31] *Id.* at 1020, 1032, 1199, 1202.

the union during an organizational or recognitional drive was frequently cited as an evil to which the amendment was directed. Senator Ball, for example, referred to a letter from a small employer in New York:

> He is a wholesaler, and he tells how a goon squad from Union Local No. 65 of the CIO on several occasions sent gangs of men into his plant. They pushed his employees around and threatened them if they did not join the union. Finally, in desperation, many of them said, "We do not want to be beaten up, so we will join," even though it was not their free choice.[32]

He also referred to a case where the union "several times threatened, jostled, and beat up one of the employees as he was going to work."[33] There are many other less specific references to beatings, threats, physical violence, and similar kinds of "goon squad" tactics.[34]

The debates, however, also make it clear that the prohibition was intended to extend beyond coercive conduct that might otherwise be actionable under state criminal or civil law. Senator Ball, for example, noted that "if the unions, in their organizing drives cannot persuade a majority to join voluntarily, they place a picket line in front of the shop, make scurrilous remarks about the employees as they go to work, and subject them to all kinds of abuse, even verging on physical violence, but very often not reaching the point where State laws would come into effect."[35] The opponents of the amendment, on the other hand, feared that the prohibition might indeed reach too far. In particular, they were concerned that the phrase "interfere with" might be construed so broadly as to limit union organizers in making vigorous but peaceful appeals on behalf of the union cause.[36]

As a matter of logic, the opponents' fears may not have been totally unfounded. The "interfere with, restrain, or coerce" language of the amendment was identical to the equivalent NLRA (Wagner) prohibition against employer conduct. Senator Ball clearly stated that "the purpose of the amendment is simply to provide that where unions, in their organizational campaigns, indulge in practices which, if an employer indulged in them, would be unfair labor practices, . . . the unions also shall be guilty of unfair labor practices."[37] At one time, the NLRB and some courts had indeed taken a narrow view of what an employer could *say* in opposition to unionization without committing an

---

[32] *Id.* at 1018.
[33] *Id.* at 1019.
[34] *Id.* at 1020, 1024, 1025, 1028, 1031.
[35] *Id.* at 1019-20. *See also, id.* at 1018, 1031.
[36] *Id.* at 1023, 1138.
[37] *Id.* at 1018. *See also, id.* at 1021, 1025, 1031, 1203.

unfair labor practice.[38] In any event, without conceding that it materially changed the scope of the prohibition, the proponents of the amendment finally agreed to drop the phrase "interfere with,"[39] and the amendment passed.[40]

Even with the elimination of the arguably vague notion of interference, the prohibition against union restraint and coercion of employees remained fairly broad and was certainly intended to at least encompass any conduct even colorably tortious or criminal in nature. This suggests that the so-called "milder forms" of labor-related violence, tolerated by the law in other contexts,[41] were clearly intended to be considered an unfair labor practice when perpetrated by those acting on behalf of labor organizations.

Proving that the perpetrators of violence were acting on behalf of a labor union, and that a labor union was thus legally responsible for the conduct, was a difficulty recognized by both the opponents and proponents of section 8(b)(1). Senator Pepper, for example, doubted that making this conduct a union unfair labor practice would really solve the problems being referred to:

> I wonder if, in the main, the abuses to which the Senator [Ball] refers are not acts which are consummated by individuals and which, if wrong, are their individual responsibility, but which cannot fairly be charged against the organization, the union, itself. Seldom would it be possible to find any resolution on the part of the union, or any action by the executives or authoritative agents of the union, directing that the acts complained of be committed.[42]

Senator Ball, however, apparently believed that the responsibility of unions could be proved by somewhat less direct evidence:

> I am sorry that I cannot agree with the Senator. I think that when there are mass picket lines, which usually produce acts of violence, which are

---

[38] *See, e.g.,* NLRB v. Federbush Co., 121 F.2d 954, 957 (2d Cir. 1941)("What to an outsider will be no more than the vigorous presentation of a conviction, to an employee may be the manifestation of a determination which it is not safe to thwart," thus making such a presentation a prohibited form of "interference."). On the other hand, the fears of the opposition were perhaps unfounded in light of the further proposed addition to the statute of section 8(c), which was to severely limit the kinds of speech that could be considered an unfair labor practice by employers or unions. *See* NLRA § 8(c), 29 U.S.C. § 158(c) (1976). *See also* LEGIS. HIST. LMRA at 1023 (in which Senator Taft contended that the hypotheticals posed by the opposition could not be considered a prohibited form of interference because of the proposed free speech provision).

[39] LEGIS. HIST. LMRA at 1138-39.

[40] *Id.* at 1216-17.

[41] *See generally* Haggard, *Picket Line, supra* note 22, at 448-66.

[42] LEGIS. HIST. LMRA at 1020.

organized in front of the entrance of a plant, it is virtually always the union leaders who organize them. Sometimes it may be a small minority of the union.[43]

Senator Taft also conceded that "it may be difficult to prove the responsibility of a union"[44] for certain kinds of coercive conduct, such as telephone threats. Congress, however, apparently thought it was not an insurmountable difficulty—certainly not a reason for rejecting the proposed prohibition—and adopted the ordinary common law rules of agency for establishing union responsibility.[45]

Unlike the House version, the Senate bill did not contain a provision making it an unfair labor practice for individual employees to intimidate other employees in the exercise of section 7 rights. Nor did the Senate bill contain an equivalent of the House section on "unlawful concerted activities" which allowed for private damage actions by the victims of union violence. Because of these and other substantial differences between the House and the Senate bills, a joint conference committee was appointed.

The bill eventually reported out by the joint committee followed the Senate version in most material respects.[46] Insofar as acts of union violence were concerned, the committee version followed the Senate amendment to section 8(b)(1) to the letter.[47] The House conference report, wherein the House members of the joint committee explained the differences between the House bill as originally passed and the committee (Senate) version and the reasons for their acceptance of the latter, does not say a great deal about section 8(b)(1)(A). The report does, however, express the view that the kinds of conduct generally described in the "unlawful concerted activities" section of the House bill were now effectively proscribed as an unfair labor practice.[48] Although private remedies were not made expressly available by the committee bill, the report noted that since section 301(b) made unions generally liable to suit, "unions that engage in these practices to the injury of another may subject themselves to liability under ordinary principles of law."[49] The report also noted the availability of injunctive relief, if requested by the NLRB, against violent conduct in violation of this section.[50]

---

[43] *Id.* at 1020.
[44] *Id.* at 1026-27.
[45] *See* text accompanying note 58, *infra.*
[46] For a detailed comparison of the Senate and committee bills, see Legis. Hist. LMRA at 1536-44.
[47] *Id.* at 1539.
[48] *Id.* at 546.
[49] *Id.*
[50] *Id.* at 546-47.

The report's explanation of omitting the "interference with" language comports generally with the above discussion. It noted the concern that the term might not be construed as it had been in the employer unfair labor practice section (as being no broader than the words "restraint" and "coercion"), and the term was thus omitted.[51] The use of this reasoning implies that the omission is otherwise without substantive significance.

With respect to the standard to be used in holding a union responsible for the violent conduct of individuals acting on the union's behalf, the committee report noted substantial agreement between the House and the Senate bills. The original House bill had specifically stated that the Norris-LaGuardia Act was not to apply to the "unlawful concerted activities" section.[52] Under the Norris-LaGuardia Act, no labor organization or its officials could be held responsible for the acts of an individual member or official "except upon clear proof of actual participation in, or actual authorization of, such acts, or of ratification of such acts after actual knowledge thereof."[53] In one case,[54] at least as it was construed by Senator Taft,[55] the Supreme Court had held that the liability of a union under the act's definition was more limited than would be the case under the normal rules of agency. Senator Taft made it clear that the term "agent" in the proposed section 8(b) was not to have a similarly constricted meaning; but it was not to automatically include every individual who might happen to be a member of the union:

> I think the word "agent" used here, as used in the contract section, and as used in other places in the bill, means an agent under the ordinary rules of agency, an agent of the labor union, the organization, as such. The fact that a man was a member of a labor union in my opinion would be no evidence whatever to show that he was an agent.[56]

In order to clearly express this intention, the "definitions" section of the committee bill contained the following provision: "In determining whether any person is acting as an 'agent' of another person so as to make such other person responsible for his acts, the question of whether the specific acts performed were actually authorized or subsequently ratified shall not be controlling.[57]

The House committee report summarized the above background and concluded that "hence, under the conference agreement, as under the

---

[51] *Id.* at 547.
[52] *Id.* at 79-80.
[53] Norris LaGuardia Act § 6, 29 U.S.C. § 106 (1976).
[54] United Bhd. of Carpenters v. United States, 330 U.S. 395 (1947).
[55] Legis. Hist. LMRA at 1599.
[56] *Id.* at 1204-05.
[57] NLRA § 2(13), 29 U.S.C. § 152(13) (1976).

House bill, both employers and labor organizations will be responsible for the acts of their agents in accordance with the ordinary common law rules of agency (and only ordinary evidence will be required to establish the agent's authority.)''[58]

The House debates on the committee (Senate) bill add little to the committee report explanation. Strike violence is generally referred to several times.[59] Mass picketing is again singled out as one particular kind of union conduct section 8(b)(1)(A) was designed to prohibit.[60] One speaker also referred to "sit down strikes" as a form of union unfair labor practice under this section.[61] Some members of the House had apparently expressed misgiving over the adequacy of the penalties under the committee (Senate) bill. In response, Congressman Landis detailed them as follows: "On violence, mass picketing, and other intimidation and coercion, the penalties are, first discretionary injunction by the Board, second, possible suit for damages, third, cease-and-desist order of the Board, and fourth, employee discharged therefor not entitled to reinstatement."[62] The final Senate debates on the committee bill add no further enlightenment on section 8(b)(1)(A).

It is against this background that the current NLRB and court decisions must be viewed.

THE ELEMENTS OF A SECTION 8(B)(1)(A) VIOLATION

There are three basic elements of a section 8(b)(1)(A) violation. First, the conduct that is to be sanctioned must fall within the legal definitions of "restraint" or "coercion." Second, the restraint or coercion of employees must be in the exercise of their section 7 rights. And third, the conduct must have been committed by a labor organization or its agents. These elements will be discussed more fully in turn.

The Meaning of Restraint and Coercion: General Legal Principles

Several important issues concerning the exact scope of section 8(b)(1)(A) have arisen over the years. There was the question of whether recognitional picketing, although a peaceful and not otherwise illegal nature, could nevertheless constitute "restraint" or "coercion"

---

[58] LEGIS. HIST. LMRA at 540; *see also id.* at 1537.

[59] *Id.* at 882, 898, 927.

[60] *Id.* at 882, 905, 912, 927. *But cf., id.* at 1202-03 (recognizing that unfair labor practice proceedings would be "a completely impractical way of dealing with a mass picket line" and declaring, thus, that this was not a "major objective" of the section).

[61] *Id.* at 912.

[62] *Id.* at 905.

under section 8(b)(1)(A). The Supreme Court ultimately decided this issue in the negative.[63] An important aspect of the theoretical relationship between section 8(b)(1)(A) and other union unfair labor practice provisions was resolved when it was finally decided that violations of other provisions did not also *necessarily* amount to restraint or coercion under section 8(b)(1)(A).[64] A controversy still exists over the extent to which a union can fine or otherwise discipline its current (or former) members without restraining or coercing them.[65] In a dispute over the fundamental nature and intended scope of section 8(b)(1)(A), the District of Columbia Circuit Court of Appeals recently reversed an NLRB finding that a union does not restrain or coerce an employee when it refuses to allow him to post materials critical of the union on the union's inplant bulletin board.[66]

However cloudy the ultimate dimensions of section 8(b)(1)(A), one thing is absolutely clear from the case law: the section *does* prohibit violence, physically intimidating conduct, and threats thereof. In one case, the Supreme Court reviewed the legislative history and observed that "the note repeatedly sounded is as to the necessity for protecting individual workers from union organizational tactics tinged with violence, duress or reprisal."[67] Similarly, in an early case, the NLRB noted that in this section "Congress sought to fix the rules of the game, to insure that strikes and other organizational activities of employees were conducted peaceably by persuasion and propanganda and not by physical force, or threats of force, . . ."[68] Indeed, given the legislative history, no other conclusion is possible.

The NLRB and the courts adhere fairly consistently to an objective approach in identifying specific union conduct that falls within the above descriptions and which does, thus, restrain or coerce. The question is not whether a union agent subjectively intended to restrain or coerce. Nor is it whether any employees were in fact restrained or

---

[63] NLRB v. Local 639, Int'l Bhd. of Teamsters, 362 U.S. 274 (1960).
[64] National Maritime Union (Texas Co.), 78 N.L.R.B. 971, 982-87 (1948), *enforced*, 175 F.2d 686 (2d Cir. 1949), *cert. denied*, 338 U.S. 954 (1950), *overruled on other grounds*, 119 N.L.R.B. 307, 308 n.3 (1957), *see* IBEW v. NLRB, 341 U.S. 694, 701-03 (1951). This is to be contrasted with the theoretical relationship between section 8(a)(1) and other *employer* unfair labor practices. Commission of any of the latter will necessarily also be a "derivative" form of "interference, restraint, and coercion" under the former. *See generally* R. GORMAN, LABOR LAW 132 (1976); Oberer, *The Scienter Factor in Sections 8(a)(1) and (3) of the Labor Act: Of Balancing, Hostile Motive, Dogs and Tails*, 52 CORNELL L.Q. 491 (1967).
[65] *See* Machinists Local 1327 (Dalmo Victor), 263 N.L.R.B. No. 141 (1982). *See generally* R. GORMAN, LABOR LAW 677-89 (1976).
[66] Helton v. NLRB, 656 F.2d 883 (D.C. Cir. 1981).
[67] NLRB v. Local 639, Int'l Bhd. of Teamsters, 362 U.S. 274, 286 (1960).
[68] Perry Norvell Co., 80 N.L.R.B. 225, 239 (1948).

coerced.[69] The test, rather, "is whether the misconduct is such that, under the circumstances existing, it may reasonably tend to coerce or intimidate employees in the exercise of rights protected under the Act."[70] In the words of the first circuit, "a violation is established if the natural tendency of the coercive misconduct is to deter the exercise of § 7 rights by the employees who either witness it or learn of it."[71] Similarly, "that no one was in fact coerced or intimidated is of no relevance. The test of coercion and intimidation is not whether the misconduct proves effective."[72] Thus, a violation can be made out even if the employees against whom the violence is directed nevertheless successfully persist in the exercise of their section 7 rights.[73]

Against this background, it is not too surprising to find that the NLRB and the courts have been willing to include a wide range of strike, picket line, and organizational campaign misconduct within the prohibitions of section 8(b)(1)(A). Indeed, some apparently believe that the law imposes an unreasonably high standard of conduct. One trial examiner rather sarcastically noted that "it may seem unrealistic to require that a picket line shed the sweetness and charm of Vassar's daisy chain or that it maintain the dignity of the procession of cardinals (although so close a formation would not be tolerated), but that appears to be the trend of Board decisions."[74]

Such hyperbole aside, there is obviously a threshold level of coerciveness to which the misconduct must rise, and not every form of harrassment, nonprivileged touching, or verbal abuse qualifies. The NLRB recognizes, for example, that some misconduct is simply "too

---

[69] United Steelworkers Local 1397, 240 N.L.R.B. 848, 849 (1979); *cf.* United Rubber Workers Local 796 (Tennessee Wheel & Rubber Co.), 166 N.L.R.B. 165, 171 (1967)(the union agent's "motive" is likewise irrelevant). *But cf.* Millwrights Local 1421, United Bhd. of Carpenters (Jervis B. Webb Co.), 156 N.L.R.B. 94, 98 (1965)(the trial examiner conceded that the union agent's conduct "was bound to fill them [the employees] with some apprehension. . . . But I cannot conclude that Carter [the union agent] consciously intended to terrify them, or that they were actually terrified, or that either of them fled in fear of his life.").

[70] Local 542, Operating Eng'rs v. NLRB, 328 F.2d 850, 852-53 (3d Cir. 1964), *cert. denied,* 379 U.S. 826 (1964).

[71] NLRB v. Unión Nacional de Trabajadores, 540 F.2d 1, 7 (1st Cir. 1976), *cert. denied,* 429 U.S. 1039 (1977).

[72] Local 542, Operating Eng'rs v. NLRB, 328 F.2d at 852.

[73] *See, e.g.,* Local 3887, United Steelworkers (Stephenson Brick & Tile Co.), 129 N.L.R.B. 6, 10 (1960), *enforced,* 290 F.2d 587 (5th Cir. 1961); Local 761, Int'l Union of Elec. Workers (Gen. Elec. Co.), 126 N.L.R.B. 123, 124-25 (1960), *enforced,* 287 F.2d 565 (6th Cir. 1961); United Furniture Workers Local 309 (Smith Cabinet Mfg. Co.), 81 N.L.R.B. 886, 888 (1949); International Longshoremen's Union Local 6 (Sunset Line & Twine Co.), 79 N.L.R.B. 1487, 1505 (1948)("It is immaterial that this conduct failed to deter the non-striking employees from returning to work. It was reasonably calculated to accomplish that end, and its inefficacy in this particular instance is no defense to the charge that it was violative of the Act.").

[74] Local 235, Lithographers Union (Henry Wurst, Inc.), 187 N.L.R.B. 490, 495 (1970).

trivial to be regarded as restraint or coercion."[75] Other misconduct has been dismissed as mere "'picket line horseplay' devoid of sinister purpose."[76] And in one case, the board characterized some minor misconduct on the picket line in terms of "exuberance short of coercion."[77]

Nevertheless, the range of misconduct falling within this "trivial" or *"de minimus"* exception is relatively narrow. Its absolute outer limits are probably marked by the facts of *Service Employees International Union, Local 50 (Evergreen Nursing Home):*[78]

> Here, in the course of a number of days of picketing, we have two instances of employees being impeded in their entry to work . . . , one employee being grabbed at by an unidentified picket provoked by being called a "damned nigger," two chairs placed on the sides of one of two driveways, and two trucks briefly impeded from leaving the area and one truck briefly impeded from entering. No one was injured, nothing was thrown, no one was prevented from going to work or leaving, and no vehicle was harmed or excluded from the premises.[79]

The trial examiner in *Evergreen Nursing* was "not disposed to equate conduct such as this, either instance by instance or in its totality, with the sort of conduct that section 8(b)(1)(A) was designed to prevent."[80] Thus, the complaint was dismissed.

On the other hand, if the misconduct in question is found to be more than trivial or *de minimus,* then the fact that it was a single, isolated, and nonrecurring incident will usually not be recognized as a defense. In one case, the union resisted enforcement of the NLRB's order on the grounds that "the alleged violation consisted of the single statement that 'somebody might get hurt.'"[81] The District of Columbia Circuit Court of Appeals, however, did not agree that a threat of physical violence should be disregarded because the evidence did not show it was repeated.[82] Similarly, in response to a union claim that its misconduct was only an "isolated incident," the Second Circuit Court of Ap-

---

[75] International Longshoremen's Union Local 6 (Sunset Line & Twine Co.), 79 N.L.R.B. 1487, 1506 (1948)(union agent opened car door and "dared" nonstriking employee to come out); *see also* United Mechanics Union Local 150-F (American Photocopy Equip. Co.), 151 N.L.R.B. 386, 391 (1965); Joint Board, Cloak Makers Union (Free-Play Togs, Inc.), 140 N.L.R.B. 1428, 1434-35 (1963). *But see* International Bhd. of Carpenters Local 1092 (Walsh Constr. Co.), 219 N.L.R.B. 372 (1975); United Steelworkers (Wright Line Div. of Barry Wright Corp.), 146 N.L.R.B. 71 (1964); UMW Local 7083 (Grundy Mining Co.), 146 N.L.R.B. 176 (1964).

[76] Central Mass. Joint Board, Textile Workers Union (Charles Weinstein Co.), 123 N.L.R.B. 590, 606 (1959).

[77] General Iron Corp., 224 N.L.R.B. 1180, 1189-90 (1976).

[78] 198 N.L.R.B. 10 (1972).

[79] *Id.* at 12.

[80] *Id. See also* TKB Int'l Corp., 240 N.L.R.B. 1082, 1099 (1979).

[81] Highway Truck Drivers Local 107 v. NLRB, 273 F.2d 815, 818 (D.C. Cir. 1959).

[82] *Id.*

peals noted that "it would be a sorry state of affairs if such improper conduct should be condoned and encouraged by a ruling that only unsuccessful and repeated mass picketing, attended by physical exclusion of employees from their place of work, should be considered sufficiently substantial to warrant [the finding of a violation]."[83]

Even though a union's misconduct may not be trivial or isolated enough to keep it from being considered an illegal form of restraint and coercion, it can still be argued that it is sufficiently minor that the NLRB should refrain from issuing a remedial order. This argument was accepted and became a board doctrine which was spelled out in detail in the *Jimmy Wakely Show* case.[84] It is premised on the notion that in situations of this kind, issuance of a cease and desist order would not serve any good purpose, and that the board's limited resources should be directed toward matters having a more significant impact in effectuating the purposes of the NLRA.[85] Although the doctrine is not unique to section 8(b)(1)(A), it has been occasionally invoked in that context with varying results. In *Southwest Regional Joint Board, Amalgamated Clothing Workers (Finesilver Manufacturing Co.)*,[86] for example, the administrative law judge said that even if he believed the threats had been uttered,

> remedial relief nevertheless would not be warranted. Such relief would do little if anything to effectuate the policies of the Act. In a unit of 600 to 800 employees I would regard the two statements . . . as coercive, but, as having been made to a single employee in such a large unit, I would consider the remarks as too insignificant and isolated to warrant remedial relief.[87]

On the other hand, in *General Iron Corporation*,[88] the NLRB disagreed with its administrative law judge and found that the threats in question there *were* "sufficiently flagrant and coercive to necessitate a

---

[83] NLRB v. Local 140, United Furniture Workers, 233 F.2d 539, 540 (2d Cir. 1956); *see also* NLRB v. United Mine Workers, 429 F.2d 141, 145 (3d Cir. 1970); International Bhd. of Pottery Workers (Homer Laughlin China, Inc.), 217 N.L.R.B. 25, 27-28 (1975); Pacific Abrasive Supply Co., 182 N.L.R.B. 329, 336 (1970); United Rubber Workers Local 796 (Tennessee Wheel & Rubber Co.), 166 N.L.R.B. 165, 171 (1967); United Steelworkers Local 2118 (Worcester Stamped Metal Co.), 153 N.L.R.B. 1561, 1566 (1965). *But see* Congreso de Uniones Industriales de Puerto Rico (National Packing Co.), 237 N.L.R.B. 1406, 1408 (1978) ("Standing alone, under the circumstances this statement made by a minor representative of the Respondent might be viewed as an isolated incident and one which would not warrant the finding of a Section 8(b)(1)(A) violation.").

[84] American Fed'n of Musicians (Jimmy Wakely Show), 202 N.L.R.B. 620 (1973).

[85] *Id.* at 621.

[86] 216 N.L.R.B. 644 (1975).

[87] *Id.* at 646 n.7 *Accord* Local 463, United Cement Workers Union (Trinty Concrete Prod. Co.), 190 N.L.R.B. 567 (1971); Taxi-Drivers Union (Morse Taxi & Baggage Transfer, Inc.), 174 N.L.R.B. 1 (1969); ILGWU (Twin-Kee Mfg. Co.), 130 N.L.R.B. 614 (1961).

[88] 218 N.L.R.B. 770 (1975).

remedy."[89] The two cases are certainly distinguishable;[90] but it is unlikely that acts of union violence and intimidation will escape the sanctions of the board if they are found to constitute restraint and coercion.[91] The current disfavor of the *Wakely* doctrine makes this especially true today.[92]

Unions sometimes attempt to defend against section 8(b)(1)(A) violations by reference to the employer's own alleged unfair labor practices. The defense can be conceptualized in terms of either "provocation" or "clean hands" (since the employer is usually the charging party in the section 8(b)(1)(A) case). But regardless of how the defense is conceptualized, it has been consistently rejected. As one trial examiner stated, "the fact that an employer may be violating the Act is no justification for proscribed conduct by a union, either in retaliation or in defense."[93] The proper response, rather, is for the union to institute

---

[89] *Id.* at 770; *accord* General Teamsters Local 298 (Schumacher Elec. Corp.), 236 N.L.R.B. 428 (1978); United Steelworkers (Vulcan-Cincinnati, Inc.), 137 N.L.R.B. 95, 97 (1962).

[90] In *General Iron,* the Board noted that the threats were also tied in with the company's own illegal attempts to keep a rival union out of the picture. The threats were made to the chief activist for the rival union, and although the threats were made to a single employee they "were likely to be disseminated to the small unit of 25 employees. . . ." 218 N.L.R.B. at 770.

[91] Even though a cease and desist order may appear to be an unnecessary formality where the misconduct complained of is of an "isolated" nature, there is another valid reason for issuing the order. If the misconduct should recur, the order can be used as some evidence, at least, of the union's propensity to violate the Act. In turn, this may justify a broader remedial order in the subsequent case. *See* text accompanying notes 466-88 *infra.* Since the Board's remedies for section 8(b)(1)(A) violations are inadequate, at best, any doctrine which would tend to limit them even further should be strenuously avoided.

[92] *See generally* United States Postal Serv., 253 N.L.R.B. 1203 (1981); Coca-Cola Bottling Co., 250 N.L.R.B. 1341 at n.13 (1980); Container Corp. of America, 244 N.L.R.B. 318, 324 (1979); United States Postal Serv., 242 N.L.R.B. 228 (1979); United Steelworkers Local 1397, 240 N.L.R.B. 849 (1979); General Motors Corp., 232 N.L.R.B. 335 (1977); Retail Clerks Int'l Ass'n, 226 N.L.R.B. 1393 (1976); Stanislaus Imports, Inc., 226 N.L.R.B. 1190, 1192 (1976).

[93] United Mine Workers (Chapel Coal Co.), 160 N.L.R.B. 913, 915 (1966); *see also* United Mine Workers (Solar Fuel Co.), 170 N.L.R.B. 1581, 1592 (1968), *enforced,* 418 F.2d 240 (3d Cir. 1969); Amalgamated Ass'n of Street Employees (Plymouth & Brockton Street Railway Co.), 142 N.L.R.B. 174, 178 n.2 (1963); United Furniture Workers Local 309 (Smith Cabinet Mfg. Co.), 81 N.L.R.B. 886, 888 (1949). On the other hand, under the so-called "Thayer Doctrine," NLRB v. Thayer Co., 213 F.2d 748 (1st Cir. 1954), *cert. denied,* 348 U.S. 883 (1954), an employer's unfair labor practices may serve as a "justification" of sorts for individual acts of violence. An employee who is guilty of such misconduct during the course of an unfair labor practice strike may be ordered reinstated, despite the unprotected nature of his activity, if the Board determines this would effectuate the policies of the Act. The rationale for the doctrine is, in part, that "the employer's antecedent unfair labor practices may have been so blatant that they *provoked* employees to resort to unprotected action." Local 833, UAW v. NLRB, 300 F.2d 699, 703 (D.C. Cir. 1962), *cert. denied,* 370 U.S. 911 (1962) (emphasis added). *See generally* Haggard, *Picket Line, supra* note 22, at 479-93.

the peaceful procedures of the law by filing an unfair labor practice charge against the employer.[94] Moreover, the NLRB has noted that what is at stake in a section 8(b)(1)(A) case are the rights of employees. Since "unlawful conduct on the part of the Company, if established, would neither extinguish the right of its employees to be free of union restraint and coercion, nor justify the Respondent Unions' alleged infringement of that right,"[95] the defense is simply not meritorious. Finally, in allocating responsibility, the causal relationship between the mere commission of an unfair labor practice by the employer and the use of physical violence by the union is factually and conceptually questionable.[96] An administrative law judge once noted in reference to this point, "while it is understandable that one may return a punch, this is not the case here because there is a distinct dichotomy in time, and one type of misconduct as such does not warrant unrelated conduct of the type developed here."[97] Of course, the board recognizes literal or direct provocation by an alleged victim, whether an employee or agent of the employer, as a defense to a section 8(b)(1)(A) violation.[98] But even in such situations, the board has cautioned against union "self help" remedies.[99]

In most section 8(b)(1)(A) cases, the coercion in question is aimed at nonstriking employees and it operates upon them directly. The section is not limited to those two particulars, however. The NLRB and the courts have held that even employees who are willingly participating in the strike or other concerted activity can be coerced by union violence and, similarly, that employees can be coerced even if the violence is directed in the first instance at someone else.

As to indirect coercion, physical violence against management personnel and company property is not itself an unfair labor practice under the statute except in the infrequent case where it is designed to affect the employer's selection of collective bargaining represen-

---

[94] Communications Workers (Ohio Consol. Tel.), 120 N.L.R.B. 684, 686-87 (1958), *enforced,* 266 F.2d 823 (6th Cir. 1959) (per curiam), *aff'd,* 362 U.S. 479 (1959)(per curiam).

[95] International Longshoremen's Union, Local 6 (Sunset Line & Twine), 79 N.L.R.B. 1487, 1492 n.6 (1948).

[96] *See* Haggard, *Picket Line, supra* note 22, at 486-87.

[97] ILGWU (Elsing Mfg. Co.), 186 N.L.R.B. 342, 343 n.1 (1970).

[98] *See, e.g.,* General Iron Corp., 224 N.L.R.B. 1180, 1191 (1976); General Bldg. Laborers Local 66 (Courter & Co.), 198 N.L.R.B. 125, 128 (1972); Brewers Union, Local 6 (Falstaff Brewing Corp.), 141 N.L.R.B. 448, 457-58 (1963); District 65, Retail Store Union (I. Posner, Inc.), 133 N.L.R.B. 1555, 1557 (1961). Alternatively, these cases can be read as saying that since the violence in question is a response to the employees' own provocative conduct or speech instead of their failure to support the union, there has been no coercion of employees *in the exercise of their section 7 rights*—an essential element of a section 8(b)(1)(A) violation. *See* text accompanying notes 339-83, *infra.*

[99] *See* Peninsula Shipbuilders' Ass'n (Newport News Shipbuilding & Dry Dock Co.), 239 N.L.R.B. 831, 834 (1978).

tatives.[100] The NLRB and the courts, however, have consistently held that such violence can be said to indirectly restrain or coerce employees in the exercise of their rights. The theory is that the employees, upon learning of such violence, will reasonably assume that they can expect similar treatment if they, like the employer, are so brazen as to oppose the union. The board once put it rather graphically:

> When a gang of men, led by two union officials, assaults and seriously injures a middle-aged president of an employer, and the union officials are known to the persons assaulted, it can hardly be urged that the assailants should not have foreseen that their assault would be the subject of considerable publicity and police action, and of necessity inevitably come to the attention of nonstriking employees. . . . [U]nder such circumstances nonstriking employees might have reasonably regarded such incidents as a reliable indication of what would befall them if they sought to work during the strike.[101]

The Second Circuit Court of Appeals added:

> But for the fact that someone called out "the cops," the beating would probably have continued until [the company president] and his son were left bleeding and unconscious in the doorway, as a gruesome warning to those who otherwise might wish to continue to work for their employer.[102]

The critical fact in indirect coercion cases is that the violence against nonemployees occurs in a context where it is likely that the employees will learn of it.[103] Violence which does not meet that requirement is usually of a fairly minor nature, occurs away from the picket line, and is not witnessed by any employees.[104]

---

[100] Section 8(b)(1)(B) makes it an unfair labor practice for a labor organization to "restrain or coerce . . . an employer in the selection of his representatives for the purposes of collective bargaining or the adjustment of grievances; . . ." Labor Management Relations Act § 8(b)(1)(B), 29 U.S.C. § 158(b)(1)(B) (1976). Most of the violations of this section involve various nonviolent attempts by unions to control the employer's selection of his bargaining representative. *See generally* R. GORMAN, LABOR LAW 405-06 (1976). Occasionally, however, actual physical violence is used in this regard. *See, e.g.,* Broadway Hospital, Inc., 244 N.L.R.B. 341 (1979); Unión de Trabajadores (Puerto Rico Corset & Brassiere Assoc.), 174 N.L.R.B. 489 (1969).

[101] Local 140, United Furniture Workers (Brooklyn Spring Corp.), 113 N.L.R.B. 815, 822 (1955), *enforced,* 233 F.2d 539 (2d Cir. 1956); *see also* NLRB v. Unión Nacional de Trabajadores, 540 F.2d 1 (1st Cir. 1976), *cert. denied,* 429 U.S. 1039 (1977); National Union of Marine Cooks (Irwin-Lyons Lumber Co.), 87 N.L.R.B. 54 (1949); United Furniture Workers Local 309 (Smith Cabinet Mfg. Co.), 81 N.L.R.B. 886, 888-89 (1949).

[102] 233 F.2d at 541.

[103] NLRB v. Unión Nacional de Trabajadores, 540 F.2d 1, 6 (1st Cir. 1976), *cert. denied,* 429 U.S. 1039 (1977).

[104] *See, e.g.,* Teamsters Local 695 (Wisconsin Supply Co.), 204 N.L.R.B. 866, 870 (1973); International Ass'n of Machinists (General Elec. Co.), 183 N.L.R.B. 1225, 1232 (1970); *see also* General Truck Drivers Local 5 (Union Tank Car Co.), 172 N.L.R.B. 137, 144 (1968)(Board declined to decide the issue of whether day-to-day roughhousing,

The employees being coereced by union violence against nonemployee third parties are usually employees who have declined to support the strike or join in the other concerted activities of the union. A separate question is whether striking employees can also be coerced by such violence. The NLRB and the courts have held that they can be indirectly coerced. The theory is that violence, even though certainly not directed at voluntary participants in the strike, may nevertheless operate to deter them from ever abandoning their support of the union.

For example, in *NLRB v. International Woodworkers of America*,[105] the union had committed various acts of violence against supervisory employees and independent contractors who were performing "struck work." The acts were committed only in the presence of striking employees who were manning the picket line. The union argued that once an employee joins the picket line a presumption exists that this employee will stay out of the plant for the duration of the strike. It follows that it is conceptually impossible for any acts of violence against third persons to be considered the operative cause of an already striking employee's decision not to return to work. Therefore, the violence does not restrain or coerce such an employee. The NLRB and the fifth circuit rejected the suggested presumption and a proposed requirement of proving that any specific employee on the picket line was actually deterred from returning to work:

> We think it comports with common sense to find that out of a shifting mass of from twenty-five to fifty pickets that may have been on duty during the several days on which the acts of violence occurred, there were some whose adherence to the cause of the strike, especially in the light of the extreme methods used by their leaders, might well, but for these acts of violence by which they were cautioned against such a step, have joined the other employees who remained at work in the face of the strike.[106]

On the other hand, in *Taxi-Drivers Union (Morse Taxi & Baggage Transfer, Inc.)*,[107] a union agent threatened to beat up a supervisor for allegedly discouraging employees from supporting the union. The trial examiner thought that the theory behind cases of violence against supervisors "is that employees may reasonably regard such threats as a reliable indication of what would befall them if they refrain from sup-

---

horseplay, and harassment of management officials could ever be said to indirectly "restrain" or "coerce" employees; the trial examiner held that it could not), *enforced in part,* 410 F.2d 1344 (5th Cir. 1969).

[105] 243 F.2d 745 (5th Cir. 1957).

[106] *Id.* at 747; *see also* International Ass'n of Machinists (General Elec. Co.), 183 N.L.R.B. 1225, 1231 (1970); Local 888, Int'l Union, UAW (Miami Plating Co.), 144 N.L.R.B. 897, 903 n.15 (1963).

[107] 174 N.L.R.B. 1 (1969).

porting the Union, as is their right under Section 7."[108] That trial examiner, however, concluded that the union agent's "conduct posed no threat to those rights; rather, it purported on its face to be in aid of other Section 7 rights, namely the right to support the Union."[109] He apparently did not consider it a compelling possibility that such violence might deter employees from withdrawing support.

Such are generally the theoretical parameters of restraint and coercion under section 8(b)(1)(A). Examples of specific kinds of conduct that have been found to be illegal and some of the theoretical problems that exist with respect to identifying such conduct are discussed in the following section.

Specific Kinds of Misconduct that "Restrain" or "Coerce"

Union misconduct that has been found to restrain or coerce includes the usual range of tortious and criminal activity—threats, assault and battery, property damage, blocking of egress and ingress, plant seizures, and other miscellaneous forms of intimidation.

Threats and Threatening Statements. The most common form of restraint and coercion consists of threats of physical violence or threatening statements which suggest the possibility of such violence. Almost every section 8(b)(1)(A) case contains a few instances of this particular form of misconduct.

The NLRB's attitude toward threats apparently depends on the legal context in which the threats are considered. When the issue is whether a striking employee loses the protection of section 7 and thus may be discharged for making threatening statements towards nonstriking employees, the board tends to treat such statements with some degree of tolerance.[110] Indeed, no matter how egregious the words themselves may be, the board has taken the position that, when uttered within the context of an otherwise legitimate strike, they are not "unprotected" unless accompanied by overt physical acts or gestures.[111] In contrast,

---

[108] *Id.* at 3.
[109] *Id. But see* Unión Nacional de Trabajadores (Macal Container Corp.), 219 N.L.R.B. 429 (1975), *enforced,* 540 F.2d 1 (1st Cir. 1976), *cert. denied,* 429 U.S. 1039 (1977). There, the union agent assaulted the company president in an attempt to induce him to reinstate some employees. Rather than saying that this conduct could not coerce employees because it was on their behalf, as in the *Morse Taxi & Baggage* case, the Board reverted to the normal theory about the effect of assaults on management. "That Respondents would resort to such tactics in enforcing their demands would, in the circumstances of this case, tend to have a coercive effect upon employees regarding their own exercise of rights guaranteed by the Act." 219 N.L.R.B. at 429.
[110] *See generally* Haggard, *Picket Line, supra* note 22, at 450-52.
[111] *See, e.g.,* Arrow Indus., Inc., 245 N.L.R.B. 1376 (1979); Bartlett-Collins Co., 230 N.L.R.B. 144 (1977); Valley Oil Co., 210 N.L.R.B. 370, 376 (1974). *But see* NLRB v. W.C. McQuaide, Inc., 552 F.2d 519, 527 (3d Cir. 1977).

when the issue is whether a union agent has restrained or coerced employees, the board views threatening remarks in a much less favorable light.

The most obvious kind of threat refers specifically to various kinds of physical injury or property damage that may be visited upon those who refuse to support the union. The NLRB has had no difficulty finding that such statements have the tendency to restrain or coerce. The following list is merely a representative sample of the thousands of threats that have been uttered over the years. It is not intended to titillate or embarrass. It is simply intended to give the uninitiated a good dose of the kind of vulgar brutality that dominates this sordid little corner of industrial relations. In light of the assaults and actual violence that will be described in subsequent sections, these threats, despite their apparently exaggerated nature, should not be taken lightly. Consider the following examples:

"The next time I catch you in that plant I am going to give you a whipping."[112]

"We're going to crack your head."[113]

Employee was told that a union agent "was going to get the hell beat out of him."[114]

"I only have one leg but I can beat the hell out of you."[115]

Union agent said that the mine will stay union, "if it takes bloodshed to do it."[116]

Union agent told employees that they intended to organize the store and that "wives and children of employees had better stay out of the way if they didn't want to get hurt."[117]

Union agent told employee that "he would see to it that Brown was beaten up until no one could recognize him and what was left would be dumped in the river."[118]

"When this thing is over . . . you are going to be a dead son-of-a-bitch."[119]

Union agent threatened to " 'take the camera and jam it' where cameras are not customarily encased."[120]

---

[112] Perry Norvell Co., 80 N.L.R.B. 225, 235 (1948).

[113] *Id.* at 236.

[114] *Id.* at 237.

[115] International Longshoremen's Union Local 6 (Sunset Line & Twine Co.), 79 N.L.R.B. 1487, 1498 (1948).

[116] Randolph Corp., 89 N.L.R.B. 1490, 1492 (1950), *enforced in part,* 187 F.2d 298 (7th Cir. 1951).

[117] United Mine Workers (Union Supply Co.), 90 N.L.R.B. 436, 437 (1950).

[118] Local 595, Int'l Ass'n of Bridge Workers (Bechtel Corp.), 108 N.L.R.B. 1070, 1075 (1954), *enforced,* 218 F.2d 958 (6th Cir. 1954).

[119] United Steelworkers, 114 N.L.R.B. 532, 535 (1955).

[120] Communications Workers (Ohio Consol. Tel. Co.), 120 N.L.R.B. 684, 696 (1958), *enforced,* 266 F.2d 823 (6th Cir. 1959)(per curiam), *aff'd,* 362 U.S. 479 (1959)(per curiam).

Nonstriking employee told he was "'liable to wind up' in a funeral home."[121]

Union agent threatened to have the "_____ kicked out of" certain employees.[122]

Nonstriking employee told he would "get a punch in the nose."[123]

"I am going to smear you up."[124]

"I will break your goddam legs."[125]

Nonstriking employee told he would not "get out alive" if he went back to the plant.[126]

Nonstriking employee told he "would never reach the age of 21" if he kept working.[127]

"If I had a gun I would shoot you."[128]

"You are going to wind up in the hospital."[129]

"If I see you again in any of the buildings, I'm going to break your head."[130]

"We'll kill you."[131]

Employee favoring a rival union told he was "looking for trouble and [was] going to get hurt."[132]

"Kill the SOB's."[133]

"You are going to be dead."[134]

Union agent told supervisor, who was using a stick with a magnet on it to pick up nails, that he "was going to stick that stick up [his] rear." A picket on the same occasion threatened to "wrap the stick around his head."[135]

---

[121] United Packinghouse Workers, 123 N.L.R.B. 464, 469 (1959), *enforced,* 274 F.2d 816 (5th Cir. 1960).

[122] Subordinate Lodge No. 169, Int'l Bhd. of Boilermakers, 129 N.L.R.B. 1003, 1009 (1960).

[123] Industrial Union of Marine Workers (Bethlehem Steel Co.), 130 N.L.R.B. 412, 423 (1961).

[124] Checker Taxi Co., 131 N.L.R.B. 611, 645 (1961), *enforced in part,* 99 L.R.R.M. 2903 (D.C. Cir. 1978).

[125] *Id.*

[126] Local 316, United Cement Workers Union (National Gypsum Co.), 133 N.L.R.B. 1445, 1448 (1961).

[127] Local 542, Operating Eng'rs (Giles & Ransome, Inc.), 139 N.L.R.B. 1169, 1172 (1962), *enforced,* Local 542 Operating Eng'rs v. NLRB, 328 F.2d 850 (1964), *cert. denied,* 379 U.S. 826 (1964).

[128] United Furniture Workers (Jamestown Sterling Corp.), 139 N.L.R.B. 1279, 1282 (1962).

[129] Local 3, IBEW, 144 N.L.R.B. 1089, 1100 (1963), *enforced,* 340 F.2d 71 (2d Cir. 1965).

[130] *Id.*

[131] *Id.*

[132] United Sugar Workers Union Local 9 (American Sugar Co.), 146 N.L.R.B. 154, 159 (1964).

[133] UMW Local 7244 (Grundy Mining Co.), 146 N.L.R.B. 244, 246 (1964).

[134] *Id.*

[135] United Steelworkers (Wright Line Div. of Barry Wright Corp.), 146 N.L.R.B. 71, 73 (1964).

"You keep on insisting on getting your back broken."[136]

Union agent made a threat to an employee to "beat your damn brains out [with an iron pipe] for going to work."[137]

An employee said to a union agent, in reference to employees who did not join the strike, that "we will mash their heads down."[138]

Employee asked if he would like a "roughing up."[139]

Union agent said he would "knock your god-damn brains out."[140]

"If you come back tomorrow, you get your ass kicked in."[141]

Union agent told employees that some men were out looking for the rival union organizer and that they were going to "jerk his head off."[142]

"We are going to mess up your pretty face one of these days."[143]

Employee told that "he might be pulled off the road one night and get his brains knocked out."[144]

Employee told that "his wife and children might wind up dead."[145]

Union agent said he was going to have employee "killed and shipped back to the country in a pine box," that he would have his head "mashed in," and have him "beat up."[146]

Union agent told employee he would "kick the stuff out of him" and "wipe the streets with him."[147]

Union agent told employee he would "put him in a meat grinder and grind him up."[148]

Union agents said they would "break heads and beat people" if necessary to get them to join the union.[149]

Union agent threatened to "whip up on" nonstriking employee.[150]

Union agent threatened to "break open" nonstriking employee's head.[151]

---

[136] Cleveland Local 24-P, Lithographers Union (Akron Engraving Co.), 160 N.L.R.B. 949, 951 (1966).

[137] Teamsters Local 115 (E.J. Lavino & Co.), 157 N.L.R.B. 1637, 1640 (1966).

[138] General Truck Drivers Local 5 (Union Tank Car Co.), 172 N.L.R.B. 137, 138 (1968), *enforced in part,* 410 F.2d 1344 (5th Cir. 1969).

[139] General Drivers & Dairy Employees Local 563 (Fox Valley Material Suppliers Ass'n), 176 N.L.R.B. 386, 398 (1969), *enforced,* 76 L.R.R.M. 3002 (2d Cir. 1971)(per curiam).

[140] Teamsters Local 327 (Whale, Inc.), 178 N.L.R.B. 422, 423 (1969), *enforced in part,* 432 F.2d 933 (6th Cir. 1970).

[141] General Drivers & Dairy Employees Local 563 (Northern Contractors Supply, Inc.), 183 N.L.R.B. 1023, 1025 (1970).

[142] General Truck Drivers Local 5 v. NLRB, 410 F.2d 1344, 1346 (5th Cir. 1969).

[143] Local 115, Int'l Bhd. of Teamsters, 186 N.L.R.B. 56, 60 (1970).

[144] Local 235, Lithographers Union (Henry Wurst, Inc.), 187 N.L.R.B. 490, 492 (1970).

[145] *Id.* at 493.

[146] Brewers Local 6 (Custom Packaging Corp.), 192 N.L.R.B. 1263, 1265 (1971).

[147] Isaac Putterman (Rockville Nursing Center), 193 N.L.R.B. 959, 976 (1971).

[148] *Id.*

[149] Nationwide Plastics Co., 197 N.L.R.B. 996, 1005 (1972).

[150] Plastic Workers Local 929 (Doughboy Recreational, Domain Ind., Inc.), 200 N.L.R.B. 419 (1972).

[151] Local 810, Steel Fabricators Warehousemen (Scales Air Compressor Corp.), 200 N.L.R.B. 575, 579, 583 (1972).

"We are going to bomb you."[152]

Union agent indicated a desire to "bust" nonstriking employee or her husband in the mouth.[153]

Woman picket told business manager that "they would hang his 'ass' from a pole and use the pole as his backbone."[154]

Nonstriking employee asked if she wanted to be a "bloody mess."[155]

Nonstriking employee told she "was the mother _____ they wanted to get, a nigger, and they would like to mess [her] up good."[156]

Union agent told employee he would not drive a truck again if the agent "had to break his arms and legs."[157]

Employee testified that he was told that he "might get a block along side [his] head."[158]

Union agent asked employee who refused to honor the picket line, "Do you know you could have bodily harm done to you? Did you know you could have your husband—do you know things could happen to your friends and your family?"[159]

Union agent invited employee outside where agent said "he would kick him in the ass."[160]

Union agent told employee that if he did not stop circulating a decertification petition they would find him "floating face down in the river."[161]

Union agent, while holding a brick over the employee's head, threatened to "bust [the employee's] brains out."[162]

"I'll just knock your ass over this gas pump."[163]

Union agent told employee that he would have to leave the job and that he could go "either peaceful or in a coffin."[164]

Union agent said "he was going to wipe [employee's] ass up with the floor."[165]

Union agent said union would "beat your f_____ ass with a baseball bat."[166]

[152] Teamsters, Local 695 (Wisconsin Supply Co.), 204 N.L.R.B. 866, 868 (1973).
[153] Coopers Int'l Union (Independent Stave Co.), 208 N.L.R.B. 175 (1974).
[154] Service Employees Int'l Union, Local 50 (Our Lady of Perpetual Help Nursing Home, Inc.), 208 N.L.R.B. 117, 119 (1974).
[155] *Id.* at 122.
[156] *Id.*
[157] Truck Drivers Local 705 (Associated Transp., Inc.), 209 N.L.R.B. 292, 307 (1974), *enforced*, 532 F.2d 1169 (7th Cir. 1976), *cert. denied*, 429 U.S. 1022 (1976).
[158] Local 275, Laborers Int'l Union (S.B. Apartments, Inc.), 209 N.L.R.B. 279, 287 (1974).
[159] Local 723, IBEW, 213 N.L.R.B. 1, 2 (1974).
[160] International Bhd. of Pottery Workers (Home Laughlin China, Inc.), 217 N.L.R.B. 25, 27 (1975).
[161] *Id.*
[162] Freight Drivers Local 557 (Liberty Transfer Co.), 218 N.L.R.B. 1117, 1122 (1975).
[163] Laborers Int'l Union Local 245 (Apex Contracting, Inc.), 219 N.L.R.B. 142, 145 (1975), *enforced*, 91 L.R.R.M. 2559 (4th Cir. 1976).
[164] *Id.*
[165] International Bhd. of Carpenters Local 1092 (Walsh Constr. Co.), 219 N.L.R.B. 372, 377 (1975).
[166] *Id.*

Employee told he would be "one dead mother f_____."[167]

Union agent said he would "beat in [employee's] f_____ brains."[168]

Employee told that "he would be taken out in a box" if he remained in the state.[169]

Employee told to get out of the state or "I'll kill you."[170]

Union agent said "I will tear his goddamned head off his shoulders."[171]

Union agent, while raising an automatic pistol in his pocket, said "Shut up or I'll blow your goddam head off."[172]

Subcontractor told that if he were caught out by himself his "ass was going to be filled with so much lead that he was not going to be able to walk."[173]

"We are going to blow your head off."[174]

Employee testified that a union agent threatened "to get her little girl" who was in the car with her.[175]

Employee told that if he went to work he "would not have a pickup [truck] left."[176]

Employee asked "if we would like to have our house blown up."[177]

"You don't think too much of your life do you buddy?"[178]

As employee crossed the picket line, union agent called out, "Peggy's dead."[179]

"You f_____ bitch, I am going to f_____ kill you."[180]

As employee crossed the picket line, union agent called out, "you are a dead man."[181]

"I will bust your f_____ head."[182]

Union agent told six-year-old child of nonstriking employee "that they intended to burn her mother and cut her."[183]

---

[167] *Id.*

[168] *Id.*

[169] IBEW, Local 1547 (M & M Elec. Co.), 225 N.L.R.B. 331, 333 (1976), *enforced,* 96 L.R.R.M. 3413 (D.C. Cir. 1977).

[170] *Id.*

[171] Alberici-Fruin-Colnon, 226 N.L.R.B. 1315, 1323 (1976), *enforced,* 567 F.2d 833 (8th Cir. 1977).

[172] *Id.*

[173] Local 30, United Slate, Tile and Composition Roofers (Associate Builders & Contractors), 227 N.L.R.B. 1444, 1446 (1977).

[174] Local 30, United Slate, Tile and Composition Roofers (Kitson Bros., Inc.), 228 N.L.R.B. 652, 656 (1977).

[175] Amalgamated Meat Cutters (Iowa Beef Processors, Inc.), 233 N.L.R.B. 839, 842 (1977).

[176] *Id.*

[177] *Id.* at 844.

[178] Local 810, Int'l Bhd. of Teamsters (Russell Plastics Technology, Inc.), 235 N.L.R.B. 40, 41 (1978).

[179] *Id.* at 42.

[180] *Id.*

[181] Maywood Plant of Grede Plastics, 235 N.L.R.B. 363, 380 (1978), *enforced in part,* 628 F.2d 1 (D.C. Cir. 1980).

[182] Broadway Hosp., Inc., 244 N.L.R.B. 341, 344 (1979).

[183] *Id.* at 347.

Union agent attacked employee, saying "I'm going to beat your m_____ f_____ head off."[184]

"With a few broken bones, you won't be able to drive that truck."[185]

In the foregoing examples, both the intended victim and the nature of the harm are rather expressly stated. One hardly needs background or context to recognize them as illegal threats. Other statements are perhaps somewhat more ambiguous at face value, but take on decidedly sinister overtones when uttered during a strike or organization drive dominated by acts of violence and intimidation. In this context, the following statements have also been found to restrain and coerce:

"While no heads were broken last time . . . things could be different now."[186]

"I hate to think what would happen if you walked in there."[187]

"You better not try it [cross the picket line] or there will be trouble."[188]

Employee told that "there may be trouble later" if she did not sign a union authorization card.[189]

"If you go in [the plant] you gotta come out," said in a harsh tone.[190]

"Lay off the union business or your ulcers will be bothering you."[191]

"Let him go *this time.*"[192]

Union agent told nonstriking employees that "We are going to get your women next."[193]

"You're a family man, aren't you?"[194]

Employee told "not to come into work because something could happen to [his] family."[195]

"We'll get you."[196]

"We'll take care of you."[197]

[184] Pipeline Local 38 (Hancock-Northwest, J.V.), 247 N.L.R.B. 1250 (1980), *enforced,* 108 L.R.R.M. 2816 (D.C. Cir. 1981).
[185] General Teamsters Local 959 (Frontier Transportation Co.), 248 N.L.R.B. 743, 744 (1980).
[186] United Sugar Workers Union Local 9 (American Sugar Co.), 146 N.L.R.B. 154, 159 (1964).
[186] United Furniture Workers Local 309 (Smith Cabinet Mfg. Co.), 81 N.L.R.B. 886, 906 (1949).
[188] *Id.* at 900.
[189] United Mine Workers (Union Supply Co.), 90 N.L.R.B. 436, 438 (1950).
[190] Local 5367, United Steelworkers, 123 N.L.R.B. 216, 224 (1959).
[191] Checker Taxi Co., 131 N.L.R.B. 611, 620 (1961), *enforced in part,* 99 L.R.R.M. 2903 (D.C. Cir. 1978).
[192] Dressmakers Joint Council, ILGWU (Susan Evans, Inc.), 146 N.L.R.B. 559, 561 (1964), *enforced,* 342 F.2d 988 (2d Cir. 1965).
[193] Teamsters Local 327 (Coca Cola Bottling Co.), 184 N.L.R.B. 84, 91 (1970).
[194] Allou Distributors, Inc., 201 N.L.R.B. 47, 54 (1973).
[195] United Rubber Workers Local 796 (Tennessee Wheel & Rubber Co.), 166 N.L.R.B. 165, 168 (1967).
[196] Street Employees (Plymouth & Brockton Street Railway Co.), 142 N.L.R.B. 174, 179 (1963).
[197] *Id.*

"You shouldn't try to work today because somebody is really going to get hurt bad."[198]

"You never know what is going to happen at home if you work."[199]

"We'll get you sooner or later."[200]

Nonstriking employee told it would be "unhealthy" for him to drive the company president's car.[201]

"[W]here's your wife? When you get home tonight you better make sure your children are there, where exactly is your wife right now?"[202]

"You f_____ bitch, we know who you are and we will get you."[203]

"We will fix her so she won't work permanently."[204]

Employee testified that union agent threatened "to *fix me to where I would not be filing no more charges.*"[205]

Statements might be considered too ambiguous to rise to the level of a threat when the identity of the person or persons who are supposed to inflict the anticipated injury is unclear. A legally recognized threat requires intimations by the speaker that he or his agents intend to cause pain, injury, or harm to the person being addressed. It should thus be distinguished from mere warnings or predictions that some third party, over whom the speaker has no control, might engage in such conduct. Since the latter is not a threat, it would probably not rise to the level of restraint or coercion. This issue arose in *International Brotherhood of Teamsters, Local 745.*[206] An employee named Brown had been distributing literature on behalf of the Professional Drivers Council (PROD), a group of dissident Teamsters. He was approached by Henry, an agent of the Teamsters local, and asked to join Democrat Republican Independent Voter Education (DRIVE), the political arm of the Teamsters. Brown refused. According to the administrative law judge:

> Henry then told Brown, "Well, I can't help you then . . . Let me state, I circulate with some pretty rough people. . . . The word is out." Brown asked "Well, what word?" and Henry responded that he (Brown) was in danger. Brown asked what kind of danger and was told, "Well, PROD, they have done used you enough. They don't need you anymore because you are going

---

[198] District 11, UMW (S & S Coal Co.), 235 N.L.R.B. 757, 759-60 (1978).

[199] District 50, UMW (Tungsten Mining Corp.), 106 N.L.R.B. 903, 922 (1953).

[200] Perry Norvell Co., 80 N.L.R.B. 225, 238 (1948).

[201] Local 810, Fabricators & Warehousemen (Scales Air Compressor Corp.), 200 N.L.R.B. 575, 583 (1972).

[202] Local 30, United Slate, Tile and Composition Roofers (Kitson Bros., Inc.), 228 N.L.R.B. 652, 656 (1977).

[203] Amalgamated Meat Cutters (Iowa Beef Processors, Inc.), 233 N.L.R.B. 839, 843 (1977).

[204] *Id.* at 846.

[205] Pipeline Local 38 (Hancock-Northwest, J.V.), 247 N.L.R.B. 1250 (1980), *enforced,* 108 L.R.R.M. 2816 (D.C. Cir. 1981) (emphasis in original).

[206] 240 N.L.R.B. 537 (1979).

too far and they are going to get rid of you." Brown asked Henry what he meant and Henry said, "I mean completely." When Brown asked "You mean kill me?" Henry said, "Right." Henry further elaborated by saying, "How about some morning would you like to go out and your motor is missing out of your car . . . you start your car and blow your car up or maybe the side of your house might be blowed out, or something like that."[207]

Board member Murphy felt that the union, through its agent Henry, was merely suggesting that some third party (over whom Henry had absolutely no control) might take violent action against Brown. Thus, the statement could in no measure be construed as a threat by the respondent union to take such action.[208] The majority of the NLRB panel, consisting of members Penello and Truesdale, disagreed. They noted that

> such a position ignores the obvious import of Henry's message: namely, that Henry, and those "rough" people with whom he circulated, would make sure, through violence if necessary, that Brown discontinued his anti-Teamster activities. In this respect, our dissenting colleague concedes that Henry had no knowledge or involvement with PROD, and that Brown himself, an active PROD member, knew that Henry could not and did not speak for that organization. Thus, Brown could only have believed that Henry, not PROD, was threatening him with violence if he failed to join Respondent Local and abandon his PROD activities.[209]

Similarly, in another case, the union agent told employees who were crossing the picket line that "the people who had gone out on strike were not going to hurt them but that outsiders would and that he was telling them as a friend."[210] The administrative law judge construed this as a coercive warning.[211] In another case, a union agent admitted that she asked a nonstriking employee "if she had thought what might happen to her small children if she crossed the line," as there had been some talk of burning the homes of such employees. The agent claimed "that she asked the question from friendship and concern, not malice,"[212] an explanation which this administrative law judge accepted.

Statements that might appear to be threatening have been held otherwise in a number of cases. In some instances, it is simply because the statement does not unambiguously refer to physical violence; the statement can also be construed as indicating that the union intends to

---

[207] *Id.*

[208] *Id.* at 538.

[209] *Id.* at 537.

[210] General Teamsters Local 959 (Frontier Transp. Co.), 248 N.L.R.B. 743, 745 (1980).

[211] *Id.* at 746. *See also* Warehouse & Distribution Workers Union, Local 688 (Coca-Cola Bottling Co.), 115 N.L.R.B. 1506, 1511 (1956).

[212] Plastic Workers Local 929 (Doughboy Recreational, Domain Indus., Inc.), 200 N.L.R.B. 419, 422 (1972).

make some perfectly legal response to what the dissident employee is doing. In one case, for example, union agents said they would get two employees "off the job, one way or the other."[213] The general counsel argued that such language threatened the use of violent and illegal as well as legal means. The NLRB disagreed, saying that it was simply too ambiguous.[214] In another case, the union president said of a member who was causing some internal trouble, "I don't know what I am going to do with O'Brien, but I'll get him in my own way." That language was found to be too ambiguous to be construed as a threat of illegal retaliation.[215]

The *Taxi Maintenance Corporation*[216] case probably contains the largest number of this kind of allegedly ambiguous statements. The union agent's statement to dissidents that he would "get them one at a time"[217] was, for example, construed as merely an indication that he intended to bring charges against them before the union executive committee. A statement that the union agent would make an employee "eat his words" was characterized as "a symbolic metaphor referring only to inducing a retraction of the insulting name calling"[218] that the employee had engaged in. "We have just started to fight and you are not going to like what is going to happen"[219] was found not to be a threat of violence. Even the following statement was allowed: "This is war, we're going to get you. We are going to get every one of you."[220] The administrative law judge noted that "although the term 'war' as a specific activity is associated with violence, in modern parlance it can refer to any all-out contest short of violence and does not necessarily connote bodily harm."[221]

Sometimes what the union agent says he will do is so improbable or exaggerated that the NLRB and the courts feel warranted in not treating it as a serious threat. In one case, for example, a union dissident testified that a union agent had said "he could see himself obtaining a Norden bomb sight and flying over my home."[222] In another case,

[213] Mill & Smeltermen Union, Local 16A, 170 N.L.R.B. 578 (1968).
[214] *Id.*
[215] Operating Eng'rs Local 150 (Builders Ass'n of Chicago), 165 N.L.R.B. 159, 160 (1967); *see also* J. Ziak & Sons, Inc., 152 N.L.R.B. 380, 382 (1965)(union official said he would "take care of" or "get" some dissidents; held to be too ambiguous).
[216] New York City Taxi Drivers Union Local 3036 (Taxi Maintenance Corp.), 231 N.L.R.B. 965 (1977).
[217] *Id.* at 968.
[218] *Id.*
[219] *Id.* at 970.
[220] *Id.*
[221] *Id.* at 971.
[222] The Buffalo Newspaper Guild Local 26 (Buffalo Courier-Express, Inc.), 220 N.L.R.B. 79, 85 (1975).

the First Circuit Court of Appeals dismissed as mere hyperbole a statement by the union president that the union "would tear down the gates" if the company closed them "and that not even the police could stop" them.[223] And in *NLRB v. United Papermakers,*[224] the Sixth Circuit Court of Appeals refused to treat as a threat of actual physical harm a statement by a union agent that he would "bring in the big boys from New York" and "chop up" an employee if he tried to obtain a board decertification election.[225] The court noted that "such a threat literally read would be an extraordinary one. This record presents no pattern of violence, let alone chopping into little pieces."[226]

Occasionally the NLRB refuses to treat a statement as a threat of violence simply because the recipients themselves did not regard it seriously. In one case, for example, a company guard testified that a union agent had said "the next scab that walks across that picket line, they would work him over [so] that we would have to pack him back over."[227] The board held that there was no violation because the guard to whom this statement was made apparently did not believe that the person who made it was "the kind" who could carry it out.[228] In another case, the union agent doubled up his fist and said, "I'll use that if it's necessary. If you ain't damn careful, I'll use that on you."[229] The statement was found not to be a violation because it was not "intended or taken as more than a bluff."[230]

Finally, one case must simply be considered an aberration insofar as NLRB law is concerned. An employee was told by a union agent that "if the strike keeps on it might indulge in physical violence and you just might get hurt."[231] The board, over Member Leedom's dissent,[232] said this was "an ambiguous statement which we . . . cannot construe as a warning that the strikers would resort to violence if nonstrikers continued to work."[233] That case, however, is an exception to an otherwise good Board record in treating threatening statements for what they are, an unwarranted restraint and coercion of employees in the exercise of their workplace rights.

---

[223] NLRB v. Unión Nacional de Trabajadores, 540 F.2d 1, 10-11 (1st Cir. 1976), *cert. denied,* 429 U.S. 1039 (1977).
[224] 397 F.2d 153 (6th Cir. 1968).
[225] *Id.* at 154.
[226] *Id.*
[227] International Woodworkers Local 3-3 (Western Wirebound Box), 144 N.L.R.B. 912, 924 (1963).
[228] *Id.*
[229] Perry Norvell Co., 80 N.L.R.B. 225, 234 (1948).
[230] *Id.* at 242.
[231] District 65, Retail Store Union (I. Posner, Inc.), 133 N.L.R.B. 1555, 1556 (1961).
[232] *Id.* at 1557 n.3.
[233] *Id.* at 1556-57.

Assaults Upon Persons. Physical assaults upon management employees and personnel is another kind of union misconduct which occurs with a high degree of frequency in reported cases and is perhaps the most literal form of restraint and coercion. These assaults range from being highly aggravated to relatively technical.

The assault described in the *Higbee Company*[234] case is typical of the more serious kinds of beatings that occur. The assault, upon an employee (Vitko) as he approached the picket line, was committed by an "unidentified stranger" but for whom the union was legally responsible:

> The stranger . . . struck Vitko in the face and knocked him to the ground. As Vitko attempted to rise, the stranger either kicked or delivered a violent blow to the back of Vitko's head. . . . A policeman arrived and gave assistance to Vitko, who began vomiting and shortly thereafter "passed out." He was taken to the hospital and several hours later to his home. He remained at his home about a month under the care of a doctor and suffered continuous headaches. Around Thanksgiving time, he was hospitalized again for approximately a week and subjected to X-rays, examinations, and four spinal taps.[235]

Similarly terrifying and brutal are the assaults described in the *L.E. Cleghorn*[236] case. One hundred to one hundred and twenty-five men invaded a mine site cursing and threatening employees, throwing rocks, and forcing them to discontinue their work.[237] During the course of this:

> Mrs. Starcher, a clerk employed in the scale house, attempted to record the license numbers of some of the pickets' automobiles. Several of the pickets assaulted her, took her notes from her, and threw her against the screen door leading to the scale house, breaking the door. She was then forced into the scale house where she was imprisoned by the pickets. Cleghorn attempted to go to her rescue and about 15 or 20 pickets assaulted him, striking him on the head and face, knocking off his eyeglasses, beat him to the ground, and then kicked him, and finally rolled him down an embankment onto the railroad siding about 75 feet from where the assault began. At the time of the hearing, about a year after the assault, there was still a small lump on his back where he was kicked by the pickets.[238]

---

[234] Painters Dist. Council No. 6 (Higbee Co.), 97 N.L.R.B. 654 (1951), *enforced,* 202 F.2d 957 (6th Cir.), *cert. denied,* 345 U.S. 995 (1953).

[235] 97 N.L.R.B. at 661-62.

[236] UMW Dist. 31 (L.E. Cleghorn), 95 N.L.R.B. 546 (1951), *enforced,* 198 F.2d 389 (4th Cir. 1952), *cert. denied,* 344 U.S. 884 (1952).

[237] 95 N.L.R.B. at 560.

[238] *Id.*

396   *Union Violence*

There are, unfortunately, other reported instances of equally brutal attacks.[239] Relatively less serious beatings, punchings, slappings, kickings, and assaults with various objects seem almost commonplace in the case law.[240] Persons have been fired upon[241] and every conceivable kind of missile has been hurled at nonstriking employees, management personnel, and vehicles that have attempted to enter a plant during a strike.[242] Pickets have caused a wide range of damage to

---

[239] *See, e.g.,* Local 810, Int'l Bhd. of Teamsters (Russell Plastics Technology, Inc.), 235 N.L.R.B. 40, 41 (1978) (during a strike, job applicant was hit in the head by a striker with a rock in his hand; he fell to his knees and was then kicked); Local 612, Int'l Bhd. of Teamsters (Deaton Truck Line), 146 N.L.R.B. 498, 500-03 (1964)(described as a "cruel beating"); Operating Eng'rs Local 513 (Long Constr. Co.), 145 N.L.R.B. 554, 558 (1963)(employee on job site was beaten into unconsciousness and hospitalized for four days; his jaw was broken in two places, he had to buy false teeth to replace his own that were knocked out during the assault, and he was out of work for almost two months); United Furniture Workers, Local 309 (Smith Cabinet Mfg. Co.), 81 N.L.R.B. 886, 912-13 (1949)(*inter alia,* a 71 year old man was struck behind the right ear and suffered a concussion).
[240] *See, e.g.,* UAW Local 552 (Delavan Corp.), 239 N.L.R.B. 312, 314, 317 (1978) (security officer jabbed in neck with a picket sign; nonstriking employees hit with rubber hose, kicked in face, and hit with picket sign; nonstriking employee jabbed with a picket sign, fracturing two ribs); Newport News Shipbuilding & Dry Dock Co., 233 N.L.R.B. 1443, 1453-54 (1977), *enforced,* 85 L C #11073 (4th Cir. 1979); Unión de Operadores y Canteros (Puerto Rican Cement Co.), 231 N.L.R.B. 171, 174 (1977)(5 foot, 165 pound employee beaten by a 200 pound striker); Local 30, United Slate, Tile and Composition Roofers (Associated Builders & Contractors), 227 N.L.R.B. 1444, 1448-49 (1977) (roofer struck and knocked off garage); District 1199, Hosp. Health Care Employees (Southport Manor Convalescent Center, Inc.), 227 N.L.R.B. 1732, 1734 (1977) (striker reached into car and slapped lady in the face); IBEW Local 1547 (M & M Elec. Co.), 225 N.L.R.B. 331, 333 (1976)(union agent scratched employee with a hammerclaw, drawing blood), *enforced,* 96 L.R.R.M. 3413 (D.C. Cir. 1978); Edward Kraemer & Sons, Inc., 203 N.L.R.B. 739 (1973)(union agent hit employee with a pistol and his fists); International Bhd. of Teamsters Local 327 (Det. Distrib. Co.), 201 N.L.R.B. 787, 791 (1973)(assault upon president of rival union); Local 3, IBEW, 144 N.L.R.B. 1089, 1101 (1963)(employee hit in the face with a pair of steel pliers), *enforced sub nom,* New Power Wire & Elec. Corp. v. NLRB, 340 F.2d 71 (2d Cir. 1965); United Steelworkers, 114 N.L.R.B. 532, 535 (1955)(while getting into car to go to work, employee seized and knocked unconscious); Perry Norvell Co., 80 N.L.R.B. 225, 237 (1948)(woman employee was hit in the face, suffered a bloody nose, had her hair pulled, and was knocked down).
[241] *See, e.g.,* District 11, UMW (S & S Coal Co.), 235 N.L.R.B. 757, 759 (1978); UMW Local 7083 (Grundy Mining Co.), 146 N.L.R.B. 176, 179 (1964); Local 316, United Cement Workers Union (National Gypsum Co.), 133 N.L.R.B. 1445, 1449 (1961); United Mine Workers (Union Supply Co.), 90 N.L.R.B. 436, 449 (1950).
[242] *See, e.g.,* Broadway Hosp., Inc., 244 N.L.R.B. 341, 346 (1979)(shoe); UAW Local 552 (Delvan Corp.), 239 N.L.R.B. 312, 314 (1978)(eggs, rocks, soda water); Philadelphia Ambulance Serv., 238 N.L.R.B. 1070 (1978)(lit cigarette, dousing with skunk perfume); General Teamsters Union Local 298 (Schumacher Elec. Corp.), 236 N.L.R.B. 428, 434 (1978)(rocks); Amalgamated Meat Cutters (Iowa Beef Processors, Inc.), 233 N.L.R.B. 839, 842 (1977) (blocks of wood); Unión de Operadores v. Canteros (Puerto Rican Cement Co.), 231 N.L.R.B. 171, 172 (1977)(beer cans, rocks); District 1199, Hosp. Health Care Employees (Southport Manor Convalescent Center, Inc.), 227 N.L.R.B. 1732, 173435 (1977) (coffee, hot chocolate); Warehouse Employees Local 590 (Southern States Coop.), 211 N.L.R.B. 807, 808 (1974)(stones); Oil Workers Int'l Union, Local 1-591 (Snelson, Inc.), 208 N.L.R.B. 296, 298 (1974)(crowbar); Local 918, Int'l Bhd. of

vehicles[243] and occasionally personal injury to the occupants.[244] The pickets have used their own hands and feet as well as a variety of other objects.[245] Pickets have also scratched cars with sharp objects as they pass through the picket line.[246] A more terrifying practice is violently rocking cars back and forth[247] and occasionally even turning them over.[248]

Buses carrying nonstriking employees seem to be an especially attractive target of union violence. One truly egregious assault of this kind occurred in the *General Electric*[249] case:

Teamsters (Tale-Lord Mfg. Co.), 206 N.L.R.B. 382, 385 (1973)(eggs, rocks); Teamsters Local 327 (Whale, Inc.), 178 N.L.R.B. 422, 424-25 (1969)(rocks), *enforced in part,* 432 F.2d 933 (6th Cir. 1970); Drivers Local 695 (Tony Pellitteri Trucking Service, Inc.), 174 N.L.R.B. 753, 758 (1969)(unidentified object, eggs); Teamsters Local 327 (Hartmann Luggage Co.), 173 N.L.R.B. 1403, 1404-05 (1968)(eggs, rocks, six-inch iron bolt), *enforced in part,* 419 F.2d 1282 (6th Cir. 1970); Teamsters Local 115 (E.J. Lavino & Co.), 157 N.L.R.B. 1637, 1641, (1966)(lawn chair); Teamsters Local 536 (Connecticut Foundry Co.), 165 N.L.R.B. 916, 920 (1967) (fire cracker); Teamsters Local 783 (Coca-Cola Bottling Co.), 160 N.L.R.B. 1776, 1778 (1966)(beer bottle); United Steelworkers Local 2118 (Worcester Stamped Metal Co.), 153 N.L.R.B. 1561, 1570-72 (1965)(fire crackers, eggs); ILGWU (F.R. Knitting Mills, Inc.), 145 N.L.R.B. 10, 15 (1963)(rocks); Local 346, International Leather Goods Union (Baronet of Puerto Rico, Inc.), 133 N.L.R.B. 1617, 1628 (1961)(bottles, rocks); Local Union 5367, United Steelworkers, 123 N.L.R.B. 216, 224 (1959)(bricks, bats, rocks).

[243] *See, e.g.,* Maywood Plant of Grede Plastics, 235 N.L.R.B. 363, 385 (1978)(shattered windshield, dents), *enforced in part,* 628 F.2d 1 (D.C. Cir. 1980); Local 810, Int'l Bhd. of Teamsters (Russell Plastics Technology, Inc.), 235 N.L.R.B. 40, 42 (1978)(dents, shattered windshield, vinyl top ripped); Puerto Rico Newspaper Guild Local 225 (El Mundo, Inc.), 201 N.L.R.B. 423, 425 (1973)(dents, cracked windshield, vinyl top ripped); International Woodworkers, Local 3-3 (Western Wirebound Box Co.), 144 N.L.R.B. 912, 916-21 (1963)(tailpipe and taillight broken; rearview mirror, windshield wipers, antenna, and chrome strip torn off).

[244] *See, e.g.,* UAW Local 552 (Delavan Corp.), 239 N.L.R.B. 312 (1978); Laborers' Int'l Union (Apex Contracting Co.), 219 N.L.R.B. 142 (1975), *enforced,* 91 L.R.R.M. 2559 (4th Cir. 1976).

[245] *See, e.g.,* UAW Local 552 (Delavan Corp.), 239 N.L.R.B. 312, 314 (1978)(fists, picket signs); Amalgamated Meat Cutters (Iowa Beef Processors, Inc.), 233 N.L.R.B. 839, 841-42 (1977)(small log, branch of tree, piece of firewood, a 2 x 4); Local 248, Meat & Allied Food Workers (Milwaukee Indep. Meat Packers Ass'n), 222 N.L.R.B. 1023, 1028 (1976)(meat hook), *enforced,* 84 L C #10826 (7th Cir. 1978); International Union Local 245 (Apex Contracting, Inc.), 219 N.L.R.B. 142, 145 (1975) (shovels), *enforced,* 91 L.R.R.M. 2559 (4th Cir. 1976); Puerto Rico Newspaper Guild Local 225 (El Mundo, Inc.), 201 N.L.R.B. 423, 425 (1973)(fists, sticks, picket signs).

[246] *See, e.g.,* Amalgamated Meat Cutters (Iowa Beef Processors, Inc.), 233 N.L.R.B. 839, 842-43 (1977); Local 248, Meat & Allied Food Workers (Milwaukee Indep. Meat Packers Ass'n.), 222 N.L.R.B. 1023, 1027-28 (1976).

[247] *See, e.g.,* District 11, UMW (S & S Coal Co.), 235 N.L.R.B. 757, 760 (1978); Puerto Rico Newspaper Guild, Local 225 (El Mundo, Inc.), 201 N.L.R.B. 423, 425 (1973); Brotherhood of Locomotive Firemen (Phelps Dodge Corp.), 130 N.L.R.B. 1147, 1148 (1961), *enforcement denied in part,* 302 F.2d 198 (9th Cir. 1962).

[248] *See, e.g.,* United Auto Workers (American Metals Prod. Co.), 146 N.L.R.B. 1349, 1354 (1964); United Furniture Workers, Local 309 (Smith Cabinet Mfg.), 81 N.L.R.B. 886, 912-13 (1949).

[249] International Ass'n of Machinists (General Elec. Co.), 189 N.L.R.B. 50 (1971).

Among the women on the second bus were nonstriking employees Monserrate Fuentes, Carmen Maria Diaz, and Luz A. Martinez. The composite testimony of these three employees show that as their bus neared the church, Nicolas Matta, the aforementioned right-hand man of strike leader Maldonado, threw a can of inflammable fluid into the bus through its door and a nearby open window, drenching it and a number of its occupants. Immediately, another striker, William Rosario, who was standing next to Matta, threw a lighted object at the part of the bus that had been drenched with the liquid. The bus immediately burst into flames. At least four identified nonstrikers in the bus, besides other unidentified persons, were burned as a result of the flames which engulfed the inside of the bus. One employee, Zelmina Gonzales Matta, was seriously burned on her shoulders, back, and neck, while another nonstriking employee, Paulina Ramos Fuentes, was still hospitalized at the time of the trial herein, some 3 months after the incident, as a result of the burns received in the bus. As the occupants fled from the burning bus, they were chased by strikers carrying sticks and stones. Several sought refuge in nearby houses where they became captives because of the taunting threats of physical violence from strikers if they came out. Finally they were evacuated under police protection about 7 p.m. that night.[250]

As the NLRB once stated, "certainly this type of criminal and tortious conduct is the very type of activity intended to be banned by Section 8(b)(1)(A)."[251]

Furthermore, the NLRB has even evidenced concern over "technical" kinds of assault; assaults referred to as "minor picket line and other misconduct" in other contexts.[252] The board has found employees and management personnel to have been illegally grabbed,[253] pushed,[254] tripped,[255] jostled,[256] pinched,[257] jabbed,[258]

---

[250] *Id.* at 56.

[251] United Mine Workers (Union Supply Co.), 90 N.L.R.B. 436, 450 (1950).

[252] Associated Grocers v. NLRB, 562 F.2d 1333, 1335 (1st Cir. 1977); *see also* Southern Fla. Hotel & Motel Ass'n, 245 N.L.R.B. 561 (1979). The "minor violence" doctrine holds that an employee who is otherwise engaged in a legitimate strike does not lose his protected status and thus cannot be discharged when he engages in certain of the less egregious forms of strike and picket line misconduct. Thus, such misconduct is a "protected concerted activity" under the statute. *See generally* Haggard, *Picket Line, supra* note 4, at 448-50. The Board's approach in those cases is, however, logically inconsistent with the tougher approach that it takes in the section 8(b)(1)(A) context. The legislative history of the Taft-Hartley Act makes it clear that conduct which is an unfair labor practice when engaged in by a union agent is definitely *not* a "protected concerted activity" when engaged in by a mere employee acting on his own. LEGIS. HIST. LMRA at 544, 546, 912.

[253] *E.g.,* Broadway Hosp., Inc., 244 N.L.R.B. 341, 349 (1979); Checker Taxi Co., 131 N.L.R.B. 611, 619 (1961); United Steelworkers, 114 N.L.R.B. 532, 535 (1955); UMW, District 50 Local 12824 (Eagle Mfg. Co.), 112 N.L.R.B. 74, 78 (1955); Perry Norvell Co., 80 N.L.R.B. 225, 235 (1948).

[254] *E.g.,* Maywood Plant of Grede Plastics, 235 N.L.R.B. 363, 379 (1978), *modified,* 628 F.2d 1 (D.C. Cir. 1980); Dressmakers Joint Council, ILGWU (Susan Evans, Inc.), 146 N.L.R.B. 559, 561 (1964), *enforced,* 342 F.2d 988 (2d Cir. 1965); Painters Dist. Council No. 6 (Higbee Co.), 97 N.L.R.B. 654, 661 (1951), *enforced,* 202 F.2d 957 (6th Cir. 1953),

shoved, [259] bumped,[260] spat upon,[261] wrestled with,[262] and elbowed.[263] They have also had their hair pulled,[264] their hands[265] and heels[266] stepped on, and their feet stomped.[267] Indeed, even the systematic harassment, jostling, and taunting of an employee while he works has been held to constitute illegal restraint and coercion.[268] Although these kinds of misconduct most often occur in the context of other, more serious acts of violence, it would seem that the board also views them as an independent violation of section 8(b)(1)(A).[269]

Hindering Egress and Ingress. A great deal of the union violence previously described is aimed at preventing employees from going to work during a strike. Another method pickets use to accomplish that same objective is to physically obstruct or block egress and ingress to the employer's business. This may be done in mass, in some tight formation, or by other obstacles. The legislative history makes it clear that this was one of the principal evils section 8(b)(1)(A) was intended

---

cert. denied, 345 U.S. 995 (1953); Essex County Council of Carpenters, Number 10 (Fairmount Constr. Co.), 95 N.L.R.B. 969, 997 (1951).

[255] *E.g.,* Central Mass. Joint Board, Textile Workers Union (Charles Weinstein Co.), 123 N.L.R.B. 590, 591 (1959); Essex County Council of Carpenters, Number 10 (Fairmount Constr. Co.), 95 N.L.R.B. 969, 997 (1951).

[256] *E.g.,* Maywood Plant of Grede Plastics, 235 N.L.R.B. 363, 379 (1978), *modified,* 628 F.2d 1 (D.C. Cir. 1980); Painters Dist. Council No. 6 (Higbee Co.), 97 N.L.R.B. 654, 661 (1951), *enforced,* 202 F.2d 957 (6th Cir. 1953), *cert. denied,* 345 U.S. 995 (1953).

[257] Central Mass. Joint Board, Textile Workers Union (Charles Weinstein Co.), 123 N.L.R.B. 590, 591 (1959).

[258] Industrial Union of Marine Workers (Bethlehem Steel Co.), 130 N.L.R.B. 412, 423 (1961).

[259] *E.g.,* UAW Local 552 (Delavan Corp.), 239 N.L.R.B. 312, 316 (1978); IBEW Local 309 (R. Dron Elec. Co.), 212 N.L.R.B. 409, 411 (1974); ILGWU (F.R. Knitting Mills, Inc.), 145 N.L.R.B. 10, 14 (1963).

[260] IBEW Local 309 (R. Dron Elec. Co.), 212 N.L.R.B. 409, 411 (1974).

[261] Broadway Hosp., Inc., 244 N.L.R.B. 341, 346, 349 (1979).

[262] *E.g.,* Local 888, Int'l Union, UAW (Miami Plating Co.), 144 N.L.R.B. 897, 899 (1963); District 65, Retail Store Union (Eastern Camera & Photo Corp.), 141 N.L.R.B. 991, 993 (1963).

[263] Perry Norvell Co., 80 N.L.R.B. 225, 236 (1948).

[264] Local 1150, United Elec. Workers (Cory Corp.), 84 N.L.R.B. 972, 995 (1949).

[265] *E.g.,* International Union of Elec. Workers (Sperry Rubber & Plastics Co.), 134 N.L.R.B. 1713, 1723 (1961); *see also* United Steelworkers (Wright Line Div. of Barry Wright Corp.), 146 N.L.R.B. 71, 73 (1964).

[266] District 1199, Hosp. Health Care Employees (Southport Manor Convalescent Center, Inc.), 227 N.L.R.B. 1732, 1734 (1977).

[267] Dressmakers Joint Council, ILGWU (Susan Evans, Inc.), 146 N.L.R.B. 559, 561 (1964), *enforced,* 342 F.2d 988 (2d Cir. 1965).

[268] Newport News Printing Pressmen's Union Local 288 (The Daily Press, Inc.), 188 N.L.R.B. 475, 480 (1971)(trial examiner said the conduct "manifest[s] many of the clodish features of a carnival fun house and low level vaudeville," *id.* at 478-79).

[269] *But see* Joint Board, Cloak Makers Union (Free-Play Togs, Inc.), 140 N.L.R.B. 1428, 1434 (1963)(nudging, pushing, and shaking a hand in front of an employee's face were, in the absence of any other acts of violence, held not to constitute a violation).

to eliminate,[270] and the NLRB and the courts have generally respected that intent. Although the board is willing to tolerate a little inconvenience in crossing a picket line, it has held that "blocking an entrance or exit even for a short period of time constitutes restraint and coercion within the meaning of the Act."[271] The board has condemned delays of "from a few seconds to a few minutes"[272] and of "one to five minutes."[273] It has, however, refused to find a violation where the picketing merely caused nonstriking employees "to 'deviate' from their usual route in order to detour around the pickets."[274] In one case, the board said that an alleged illegal blocking by a single automobile that pulled out into the middle of a street "strain[ed] at a gnat."[275] On the other hand, the board has consistently held that an attempt to block ingress and egress need not be actually successful in order for a violation to occur.[276]

A number of techniques have been used to block ingress and egress. The most effective has been so-called "mass picketing." Although the NLRB has been reluctant to label this a *per se* violation,[277] the presence of a large number of pickets may nevertheless make entrance physically impossible. It may at least create such a coercive atmosphere that no one would be inclined to even attempt entrance. As the Third Circuit Court of Appeals once put it:

> the massing of large numbers of men . . . was itself violative of Section 8(b)(1)(A) strictures. It is well settled that picketing which interferes with or blocks the ingress or egress of employees and others at a place of employment, or which, in effect, forces employees to "run a gauntlet," is inherently coercive and in contravention of the Act.[278]

---

[270] *See* text accompanying notes 25, 27, 29, 31, and 60 *supra*.

[271] Shopmen's Local 455 (Stokvis Multi-Ton Corp.), 243 N.L.R.B. 340, 346 (1979); *see also* Service Employees Local 254 (M.I.T.), 218 N.L.R.B. 1399, 1401 (1975)(ingress found to have been impeded even though pickets allowed in any cars that so "insisted"), *modified*, 535 F.2d 1335 (1st Cir. 1976). *But cf.* United Elec. Workers Local 813 (Ryan Constr. Corp.), 85 N.L.R.B. 417, 435 (1949)(locking gate held not to be a violation because it was promptly opened on request), *overruled on other grounds*, 126 N.L.R.B. 905, 906 (1960).

[272] Lithographers Int'l Union (Holiday Press), 193 N.L.R.B. 11, 15 (1971).

[273] Metal Polishers Union Local 67 (Alco-Cad Nickel Plating Corp.), 200 N.L.R.B. 335, 336 (1972); *see also* United Furniture Workers, Local 472 (Colonial Hardwood Flooring Co.), 84 N.L.R.B. 563, 564 (1949)(car blocked for three or four minutes).

[274] Central Mass. Joint Board, Textile Workers Union (Charles Weinstein Co., 123 N.L.R.B. 590, 606 (1959); *see also* Perry Norvell Co.), 80 N.L.R.B. 225, 237-38 (1948).

[275] General Iron Corp., 224 N.L.R.B. 1180 (1976).

[276] *See, e.g.*, Local 761, Int'l Union of Elec. Workers (General Elec.), 126 N.L.R.B. 123, 124-25 (1960), *enforced*, 287 F.2d 565 (6th Cir. 1961).

[277] *See, e.g.*, United Steelworkers (Vulcan-Cincinnati, Inc.), 137 N.L.R.B. 95, 98 (1962); Local 1150, United Elec. Workers (Cory Corp.), 84 N.L.R.B. 972, 976-77 (1949).

[278] NLRB v. United Mine Workers, 429 F.2d 141, 146 (3d Cir. 1970).

Cases in which ingress and egress have been prevented "through the sheer force of massed numbers,"[279] or by what might better be called simple "mob action," are fairly numerous. What transpired in the *Grundy Mining Company*[280] case is illustrative of this particular technique:

> after Poor's passenger car turned into Pocket Road, the large, surging mob of men completely blocked and sealed off that road, for practical purposes precluding travel thereon and, therefore, access to the minesite where they worked. . . . [T]he second convoy vehicle, driven by John Higgins, was unable to proceed down Pocket Road, since Pocket Intersection and Pocket Road to a distance of about 50 to 75 feet was "completely blocked off" by about 300 men "hollering and squalling and whooping and cussing and doing most anything," and who "threatened and cussed" John Higgins and told him "that they'd been fooling with him long enough, to get out of there they were going to kill every one of the damn son-of-a-bitches.[281]

Moreover, even if the mass of pickets does not actually block ingress and egress, the presence of large numbers of union demonstrators may be sufficiently threatening to deter nonstriking employees from risking retaliation.[282] In the *Weirton Construction Company* case, the pickets did not physically bar access to the mine. However, the NLRB noted that "the presence of a large group of men milling about on the road, without identifying signs and possessed of a considerable numerical advantage over the 15 . . . employees located at the mine site would tend, when taken together with the remarks made by the pickets, to chill the desire of employees to cross the picket line and come to work."[283]

Although ingress and egress may be directly or indirectly blocked by the mere presence of a mass of pickets, a lesser number can accomplish the same result through the technique of "close formation"

[279] Industrial Union of Marine Workers Locals 5 & 9 (Bethlehem Steel Co.), 130 N.L.R.B. 412, 422 (1961).
[280] UMW Local 7083 (Grundy Mining Co.), 146 N.L.R.B. 176 (1964).
[281] *Id.* at 178-79; *see also* Unión de Operadores y Canteros (Puerto Rican Cement Co.), 231 N.L.R.B. 171, 172 (1977); ILGWU (F.R. Knitting Mills, Inc.), 145 N.L.R.B. 10 (1963); UMW, District 31, (Bitner Fuel Co.), 92 N.L.R.B. 953, 954 (1950). *enforced,* 190 F.2d 251 (4th Cir. 1951); UMW, District 23 (W. Ky. Coal Co.), 92 N.L.R.B. 916, 936 (1950), *enforced,* 195 F.2d 961 (6th Cir. 1952), *cert. denied,* 344 U.S. 920 (1952); International Longshoremen's Union Local 6 (Sunset Line & Twine Co.), 79 N.L.R.B. 1487, 1500 (1948).
[282] Local 275, Laborers Int'l Union (S.B. Apts., Inc.), 209 N.L.R.B. 279, 286 (1974).
[283] United Mine Workers (Weirton Constr. Co.), 174 N.L.R.B. 344 (1969). *But see* North Elec. Mfg. Co., 84 N.L.R.B. 136 (1949), where the trial examiner's suggestion that an unfair labor practice is committed by "mass picketing . . . and the creation of the general atmosphere inducing a belief that going to work would be at the risk of sustaining physical injury," *id.* at 155, was apparently rejected by the Board, *id.* at 136 n.2.

picketing.[284] Another technique is simply refusing to move from in front of an entrance or gate.[285] The nonstriking employee who desires to enter the plant is unwittingly compelled to initiate the contact with the union pickets and thereby risk retaliatory assaults of the kinds previously described.[286] Most of those assaults occurred in just this context. Nonstriking employees who attempt to enter in vehicles face an additional dilemma when confronted by pickets who refuse to move out of a driveway. As the NLRB put it in one case, "the car drivers were faced with the choice of running down the pickets, at the risk of inflicting serious injury, or driving away. This interposition of passive force to prevent employees from going to work is, we believe, a form of restraint proscribed by section 8(b)(1)(A)."[287]

Finally, vehicular ingress and egress is often hindered or blocked by the placement of various obstacles in the roadway[288] or by the time-honored tactic of scattering nails in the path of on-coming cars and trucks.[289] Reflecting sunlight into the eyes of drivers is another annoy-

---

[284] *See, e.g.,* Service Employees Local 254 (M.I.T.), 218 N.L.R.B. 1399, 1401 (1975) (pickets in driveway 5 to 7 feet apart), *enforced in part,* 535 F.2d 1335 (1st Cir. 1976); International Longshoremen's Union Local 6 (Eureka Chem. Co.), 164 N.L.R.B. 1158, 1160 (1967)(20 to 30 pickets walking 2 to 10 inches apart in a close circle in front of the door; so-called "back-to-belly" picketing), *enforced,* 420 F.2d 957 (9th Cir. 1969); International Woodworkers, Local 3-3 Western Wirebound Box Co., 144 N.L.R.B. 912, 917 (1963). *But cf.* United Elec. Workers Local 813 (Ryan Constr. Co.), 85 N.L.R.B. 417 (1949) ("Although there were as many as 20 pickets before a 23 foot wide entrance on occasion, none of the pickets at any time engaged in any violence or threats, overt or implicit," and employees were told they could pass through), *overruled on other grounds,* 126 N.L.R.B. 905, 906 (1960).

[285] *See, e.g.,* Metal Polishers Union, Local 67 (Alco-Cad Nickel Plating Corp.), 200 N.L.R.B. 335 (1972)(union agent stood in front of door); Local 235, Lithographers Union (Henry Wurst, Inc.), 187 N.L.R.B. 490, 495 (1970)(two pickets walked in front of car; one of them jumped on the hood); Teamsters Local 115 (E.J. Lavino & Co.), 157 N.L.R.B. 1637, 1639-40 (1966) (pickets blocked entry by walking and standing in front of cars); International Union of Elec. Workers (Sperry Rubber & Plastics Co.), 134 N.L.R.B. 1713, 1722 (1961)(pickets refused to move out of driveway).

[286] *See* text accompanying notes 234-69 *supra.*

[287] International Longshoremen's Union Local 6 (Sunset Line & Twine Co.), 79 N.L.R.B. 1487, 1506 (1948).

[288] *See, e.g.,* Unión de Operadores y Canteros (Puerto Rican Cement Co.), 231 N.L.R.B. 171, 172 (1977)(metal drums); Local 761, Int'l Union of Elec. Workers (General Elec. Co.), 126 N.L.R.B. 123, 124 (1960)(concrete blocks, milk bottle crates, water buckets, lawn chairs), *enforced,* 287 F.2d 565 (6th Cir. 1961); United Furniture Workers, Local 309 (Smith Cabinet Mfg. Co.), 81 N.L.R.B. 886 (1949)(automobiles, railroad ties, raised gutter plates); *see also* International Ass'n of Machinists (General Elec. Co.), 183 N.L.R.B. 1225, 1231 (1970)(chaining gate shut).

[289] *See, e.g.,* District 34, Int'l Ass'n of Machinists (Wolf Mach. Co.), 254 N.L.R.B. 282 (1981); Amalgamated Meat Cutters (Iowa Beef Processors, Inc.), 233 N.L.R.B. 839, 844 (1977); District 50, Allied & Technical Workers (Austin Co.), 198 N.L.R.B. 1184, 1186 (1972), *enforced,* 83 L.R.R.M. 2455 (6th Cir. 1973); Local 235, Lithographers Union (Henry Wurst Co.), 187 N.L.R.B. 490, 494 (1970) (employer paid $700 to have the tires of nonstriking employees repaired); ILGWU (Elsing Mfg. Co.), 186 N.L.R.B. 342, 345 (1970).

ing and potentially dangerous tactic.[290] But, regardless of how it is accomplished, physically preventing people from freely entering and leaving a place of business has consistently been held to be an illegal form of restraint and coercion.

Invasions and Seizures of Company Property. Not content to just intimidate nonstriking or nonunion employees as they attempt to enter the employer's premises, some labor unions have carried their violence into the workplace itself. Such invasions of company property, and the attendant coercion of working employees by various threats and assaults, were a common occurence in the mine fields during the 1950s. Roving bands of from a few hundred to over two thousand unionists would converge upon a particular mine, effectively shutting it down. What happened next, in several instances, was described by the Sixth Circuit Court of Appeals:

> The project had been carefully organized and planned, for in each mine visited, while the union agents were ordering the management to bring the men up out of the shafts and pits, the union men who followed Suver and Chaney proceeded in a definite pattern of operation. They rounded up all the nonunion men working above ground and herded them with force and constant abuse to a place designated by the union agents for speeches. The union men encircled the non-union men so that they were hemmed in by the overwhelming number of the union group. The union agents then declared that the mines would be closed and the men would not be allowed to work until they had joined the union and collective bargaining contracts had been signed by the management. The non-union men were ordered to raise their hands to show that they would comply with these conditions. When some hands were not raised, abusive epithets were hurled at the non-union men and they were threatened.[291]

Vicious assaults, destruction of company property, and threats of violence occurred in several of the other cases of mine invasion and seizure that were litigated during this period.[292] The United Mine Workers (UMW), however, has not been the only union to engage in

---

[290] *See, e.g.,* District 50, Allied Technical Workers (Austin Co.), 198 N.L.R.B. 1184, 1186 (1972); United Steelworkers Local 2118 (Worcester Stamped Metal Co.), 153 N.L.R.B. 1561, 1568 (1965).

[291] NLRB v. UMW, 195 F.2d 961, 961-62 (6th Cir. 1952), *cert. denied,* 344 U.S. 920 (1953).

[292] *See, e.g.,* UMW District 2 (Fetterolf Coal Co.), 103 N.L.R.B. 1572 (1953), *enforced,* 210 F.2d 281 (3d Cir. 1954); UMW District 2 (Mercury Mining & Constr. Co.), 96 N.L.R.B. 1389 (1951), *enforced,* 202 F.2d 177 (3d Cir. 1953); UMW District 31 (L.E. Cleghorn), 95 N.L.R.B. 546 (1951), *enforced,* 198 F.2d 389 (4th Cir. 1952), *cert. denied,* 344 U.S. 884 (1952); UMW District 31 (Bitner Fuel Co.), 92 N.L.R.B. 953 (1950), *enforced,* 190 F.2d 251 (4th Cir. 1951); *see also* Allou Distrib., Inc., 201 N.L.R.B. 47, 55-56 (1973)("invasion" of a warehouse area and threats of violence).

this particular form of organizational activity. In *Susan Evans, Inc.,*[293] fifteen to twenty-five men of the International Ladies Garment Workers Union (ILGWU) stormed into a shop. In the words of the board, "there ensued a wild melee. The raiders ran in screaming and yelling, 'This place is on strike, everybody out.'"[294] The employer ordered them to leave, but they refused. One employee was forcibly prevented from phoning the police. Another employee was pushed around and punched in the chest. Yet another was threatened with being hit on the head with a coke bottle. The employees left the premises. The union agents then "forcibly escorted them to the ILGWU office"[295] to have them join the union. A similarly violent invasion occurred in *Hotel La Concha,*[296] where "a group of people came bursting into the hotel lobby armed with metal pipes, sticks, and clubs, shouting 'to the casino' and heading for the casino door."[297] They beat up a security officer who tried to stop them. Once inside, "the casino was thrown into an uproar of shouting, violence, and confusion. . . ."[298]

Needless to say, the NLRB and the courts have no difficulty in finding violent conduct of this nature to be illegal restraint and coercion. The illegality of a union invasion and seizure of company property does not, however, necessarily turn on the violent acts that usually accompany it. The board first began defining the parameters of this doctrine in the *District 65, Retail Store Union*[299] case. The organizing tactic used there was described by the board as follows:

> they entered the premises of the employer without invitation or permission, and after entering went to the work stations of various of the employees, remained there for brief periods . . . against the will and over the protest of the employer, and while at such work stations either engaged the employees in conversation, or gained their attention while informing the

---

[293] Dressmakers Joint Council, ILGWU (Susan Evans, Inc.), 146 N.L.R.B. 559 (1964), *enforced,* 342 F.2d 988 (2d Cir. 1965).

[294] 146 N.L.R.B. at 563.

[295] *Id.* at 564.

[296] Union de Tronquistas Local 901 (Hotel La Concha), 193 N.L.R.B. 591 (1971).

[297] *Id.* at 595.

[298] *Id.* An equivalent kind of misconduct, involving an invasion and violent disturbance of a union dissidents' meeting, is reported in Local 57, UAW (Louis R. Miller), 102 N.L.R.B. 111 (1953).

[299] District 65, Retail Store Union (B. Brown Assoc., Inc.), 157 N.L.R.B. 615 (1966), *enforced,* 375 F.2d 745 (2d Cir. 1967). In a much earlier case, Gimbel Brothers, 100 N.L.R.B. 870 (1952), the union used the following tactic to convince employees to join: "surround them on the selling floor—together with the customers they were trying to serve—and . . . maintain a loud, continuing commotion, including name-calling." *Id.* at 876. Although this was unattended by any actual physical obstruction, the Board concluded without much discussion that "this kind of indoor picketing is the equivalent of physical coercion." *Id.* at 877.

employees either orally, or by handing out literature, concerning the Union, and . . . in this manner prevented the employees from engaging in their normal work.[300]

The union apparently used this tactic in several different stores. In some, there were threats of physical violence which were obviously illegal. In at least one store, however, there were no accompanying threats or acts of violence. The NLRB was thus confronted with the issue of whether the above-described conduct could alone be considered a form of restraint or coercion. The board held that it could:

> In these cases . . . , the mass of union representatives, by sheer force of moving bodies, impose the union's will over that of the protesting employer, on its own premises, and in the presence of its employees. Such conduct I find and conclude was reasonably calculated to coerce the employer. Coercive conduct directed against an *employer* in the presence of his employees is deemed to be coercive of the *employees* under a well-established Board principle. . . Implicit in this rule is the valid assumption that employees, observing that the employer cannot withstand the force of the union, naturally conclude, or would be inclined to conclude, that they too should yield to the union's wishes.[301]

Subsequently, the *District 65* case was more or less limited to its facts. The touchstone of the doctrine was further clarified in *Levitz Furniture*[302] wherein four to six union agents came into the store's employee luncheonette to distribute literature and solicit union membership. They refused to leave when asked, and even argued with the police about this for over an hour. The NLRB found this conduct not to be a section 8(b)(1)(A) violation. It noted that in *Levitz,* unlike the *District 65* case, there was no mob of union agents; the few that entered occupied only a limited area of the store; and there was no disruption of the business. The board concluded that such conduct "did not result in the imposition of the Respondent's will over the Company and its premises so as to constitute restraint and coercion. . . ."[303] It is now clear that not every trespass or uninvited entry onto company property by union agents necessarily rises to the level of demonstrating to the employees that the union "can impose its will over the company and its premises. . . ."[304] Rather, it would seem that

---

[300] 157 N.L.R.B. at 617.
[301] *Id.* at 623.
[302] Retail Store Employees Local 1001 (Levitz Furniture Co.), 203 N.L.R.B. 580 (1973).
[303] *Id.* at 581.
[304] New York Typographical Union Local 6 (Artintype, Inc.), 213 N.L.R.B. 925, 929 (1974). Although there were some instances of physical shoving in that case, the administrative law judge found them to be minor. No one was hurt; there was no disruption; and the union agents were not successful in gaining entry. Thus, the judge concluded that the *Levitz* factor, the imposition of the union's will over the employer, simply was not present.

some significant degree of disruption must occur before an otherwise
nonviolent invasion can be said to represent an imposition of the
union's will over the employer.[305]

Destruction of Company Property. Just as assaults upon management
personnel and seizures of the plant premises have been construed as
methods of indirectly restraining and coercing employees, the NLRB
and the courts have similarly condemned the damage or destruction of
company property by union agents. As the Second Circuit Court of Appeals once explained it, "destruction of the employer's property
restrains the employees in the exercise of their rights under Section 7
by threatening their jobs and by creating a general atmosphere of fear
of violence."[306] Union agents have been found guilty of a section
8(b)(1)(A) violation for vandalizing company trucks,[307] smashing windows,[308] throwing firebombs,[309] and otherwise causing damage to company property, buildings, and equipment.[310]

Other Menacing Conduct on the Picket Line. Although the mere
maintenance of a picket line has been described as a "coercive technique,"[311] it is obviously not illegal under section 8(b)(1)(A) unless
something more is involved. That something more, however, need not
rise to the level of express threats or actual assaults in order for a violation to occur. Rather, the NLRB has recognized that various other
kinds of menacing conduct on the picket line can serve to illegally
restrain or coerce employees in the exercise of their rights.

For example, in one case picketing employees carried "ax handles,
iron bars, signs, and boards with large nails protruding from them."[312]

---

[305] *See* Bartenders Local 2 (Zim's Restaurants, Inc.), 240 N.L.R.B. 757 (1979). In *Zim's
Restaurants,* thirty to forty union agents entered the restaurant and approached
employees who were on duty. On the union's instruction, the employees subsequently
left their duty stations to attend a five to ten minute meeting in a banquet room. In
another incident, from twelve to seventeen union agents invaded the kitchen and remained there for twenty minutes "making noises by clanging pots and pans and by
shouting, screaming and swearing." *Id.* at 774. The judge found this conduct to easily fall
within the *District 65* doctrine.

[306] New Power Wire & Elec. Corp. v. NLRB, 340 F.2d 71, 72, n.1 (1965).

[307] *See, e.g.,* Local 30, United Slate, Tile and Composition Roofers (Associated Builders
& Contractors, Inc.), 227 N.L.R.B. 1444, 1446 (1977).

[308] *See, e.g.,* Broadway Hosp., Inc., 244 N.L.R.B. 341, 346 (1979); Teamsters Local 327
(Whale, Inc.), 178 N.L.R.B. 422, 423 (1969), *enforced in part,* 432 F.2d 933 (6th Cir.
1970); North Electric Mfg. Co., 84 N.L.R.B. 136, 151 (1949)(more than 443 window
panes broken).

[309] *See, e.g.,* Teamsters Local 327 (Whale, Inc.), 178 N.L.R.B. at 423.

[310] *See, e.g.,* Teamsters Local 695 (Wisconsin Supply Corp.), 204 N.L.R.B. 866 (1973);
Teamsters Local 327 (Coca-Cola Bottling Co.), 184 N.L.R.B. 84 (1970); American
Newspaper Guild (Vindicator Printing Co.), 151 N.L.R.B. 1558 (1965); UMW District 2
(Mercury Mining & Constr. Corp.), 96 N.L.R.B. 1389 (1951), *enforced,* 202 F.2d 177 (3d
Cir. 1953); North Elec. Mfg. Co., 84 N.L.R.B. 136 (1949).

[311] Printing Specialties Union, 82 N.L.R.B. 271, 292 (1949).

[312] Brotherhood of Railway Carmen, Local 543, 248 N.L.R.B. 285, 288 (1980).

The NLRB characterized this as an "implicit threat of physical violence."[313] Similarly, carrying or displaying guns and rifles,[314] and the conspicuous use of knives to whittle on sticks,[315] have been held to be inherently coercive. Possession of explosive devices in a truck parked near the picket line has also been held to be a violation.[316]

Under certain circumstances, even attempts by the union to identify those who are crossing the picket line can be considered sufficiently menacing to be a violation. For example, in one case the NLRB noted that

> during the mass picketing, automobile license numbers of nonstriking employees were recorded by the pickets at the Respondent's instructions. At the same time threats were voiced by pickets that: "We will get you" and "We have your license number. . . ." In the context of the threats and violence on the picket line it would have been reasonable for the nonstriking employees who were not cooperating with the strikers to have anticipated that the taking of the license numbers was for the purpose of identifying them for reprisals.[317]

Similarly, "photographing of nonstrikers has been found by the Board to be 'calculated to instill in [employees'] mind[s] a fear of retribution, because of [their] refusal to join the strike, . . . particularly when coupled with other conduct such as the pickets' actions here in blocking certain vehicles and appearing to take down license plate

---

[313] *Id. See also* Unión de Operadores y Canteros (Puerto Rican Cement Co.), 231 N.L.R.B. 171, 173 (1977)("'shovels, sticks, rakes, and other equipment susceptible of being used as a weapon"); Oil Workers Int'l Union Local 1-591 (Snelson, Inc.), 208 N.L.R.B. 296, 297 (1974)("clubs resembling baseball bats or ax handles"); Local 235, Lithographers Union (Henry Wurst, Inc.), 187 N.L.R.B. 490, 493 (1970)(sticks held in a threatening manner); General Truck Drivers Local 5 (Ryder Truck Lines, Inc.), 161 N.L.R.B. 493, 50102 (1966)(pieces of lumber or sticks), *enforced,* 389 F.2d 757 (5th Cir. 1968); International Woodworkers (Region 5)(Pioneer Lumber Co.), 140 N.L.R.B. 602, 605 (1963) (brandishing of clubs); Hermandad de Trabajadores de la Construccion (Levitt Corp.), 127 N.L.R.B. 900, 913 (1960)(broken bottle); United Packinghouse Workers, 123 N.L.R.B. 464, 465 (1959) ("heavy sticks and clubs"), *enforced,* 274 F.2d 816 (5th Cir. 1960)(per curiam); North Electric Mfg. Co., 84 N.L.R.B. 136, 151 (1949)(sticks, clubs, stones); United Furniture Workers Local 309 (Smith Cabinet Mfg. Co.), 81 N.L.R.B. 886, 900-01 (1949)(sticks or clubs; bricks were also broken up and put in piles along the picket line).

[314] *See, e.g.,* Local 918, Int'l Bhd. of Teamsters (Tale-Lord Mfg. Co.), 206 N.L.R.B. 382, 383-84 (1973)(exhibition of hand gun); Teamsters Local 695 (Wisconsin Supply Corp.), 204 N.L.R.B. 866, 868 (1973)(union agent appeared on picket line carrying a partially covered rifle); *accord* General Truck Drivers Local 5 v. NLRB, 410 F.2d 1344, 1346 (5th Cir. 1969) (display of revolver at union meeting).

[315] UMW Local 7083 (Grundy Mining Co.), 145 N.L.R.B. 247, 254 (1963).

[316] Unión de Operadores y Canteros, 231 N.L.R.B. 171, 176 (1977).

[317] Local 761, Int'l Union of Electrical Workers (General Elec. Co.), 126 N.L.R.B. 123, 124 (1960), *enforced,* 287 F.2d 565 (6th Cir. 1961); *see also* Local 235, Lithographers Union (Henry Wurst, Inc.), 187 N.L.R.B. 490, 495 (1970); United Steelworkers (Vulcan-Cincinnati, Inc.), 137 N.L.R.B. 95, 96 (1962); Local 316, United Cement Workers Union (National Gypsum Co.), 133 N.L.R.B. 1445, 1449 (1961).

numbers."[318] These same acts, however, have been allowed in the absence of an otherwise coercive atmosphere.[319]

Section 8(c), another Taft-Hartley Act amendment to the NLRA, provides that "the expressing of any views, argument, or opinion . . . shall not constitute . . . an unfair labor practice under any of the provisions of this subchapter if such expression contains no threat of reprisal or force."[320] The NLRB has taken the position that, without more, mere "name calling" does not violate section 8(b)(1)(A) and is privileged under section 8(c).[321] In the *Charles Weinstein Company*[322] case, for example, the trial examiner noted that "although the atmosphere was not that of a Sunday-school picnic, the language repeatedly used was mostly familiar picket-line jargon."[323] This included the use of such words as "scabs," "whore," "sluts," "whoremaster," "bags," "tramps," "dirty rats," "bums," "bastards," "dirty pigs," and "sons-of-bitches." Used less frequently were "dried-up-redhead," "Christ-killer," "f_____ Jew," "white nigger," "herring choker," and "cockroach."[324] On the other hand, when name calling occurs in an otherwise coercive atmosphere, it can become a violation. In *West Kentucky Coal Company*[325] for example, the board noted that the union's verbal abuse was "an integral part of the coercive conduct, and cannot be dismissed or disregarded, in view of the circumstances under which they were uttered, as being mere expressions of views, arguments, or opinions, or as merely name calling, or as momentary exuberance of spirit."[326]

[318] NLRB v. Service Employees Int'l Union Local 254, 535 F.2d 1335, 1337 (1st Cir. 1976).
[319] *See, e.g.,* Service Employees Int'l Union, Local 50 (Our Lady of Perpetual Help Nursing Home, Inc.), 208 N.L.R.B. 117, 119 (1974); *cf.* Laborers' Int'l Union Local 245 (Apex Contracting, Inc.), 219 N.L.R.B. 142, 147 (1975), *enforced,* 91 L.R.R.M. 2559 (4th Cir. 1976).
[320] NLRA § 8(c), 29 U.S.C. § 158(c) (1976).
[321] *See, e.g.,* International Longshoremen's Union Local 6 (Sunset Line & Twine Co.), 79 N.L.R.B. 1487, 1505 (1948); Perry Norvell Co., 80 N.L.R.B. 225, 242 (1948).
[322] Central Mass. Joint Board, Textile Workers Union (Charles Weinstein Co.), 123 N.L.R.B. 590 (1959).
[323] *Id.* at 604.
[324] *Id.* at 602-03.
[325] United Mine Workers (West Kentucky Coal Co.), 92 N.L.R.B. 916 (1950), *enforced,* 195 F.2d 961 (6th Cir. 1952), *cert. denied,* 344 U.S. 920 (1953).
[326] 92 N.L.R.B. at 949. The Court of Appeals also noted that "[i]t is true that the calling of names under certain circumstances may not amount to coercion; but in the degree to which it was exhibited here it expressed overwhelming hostility." 195 F.2d at 962. *See also* Taxicab Drivers Union Local 777 (Crown Metal Mfg. Co.), 145 N.L.R.B. 197, 204 (1963) ("The loud use of profanity and obscenity in the public streets directed to an employer and to police whose duty it is to preserve order at the scene of a strike is, when committed in the presence of employees going to work and employees on strike, an act of coercion in itself"), *enforced,* 340 F.2d 905 (7th Cir. 1964).

Restraint and Coercion Away From the Picket Line and Work Site. Violence between those who are working and those who are not might possibly be explained as a momentary loss of control in the emotionally supercharged atmosphere of a picket line confrontation.[327] That explanation, however, becomes increasingly strained the further the misconduct is from the actual scene of the labor dispute.[328] Of course the NLRB has condemned the same kinds of misconduct found to restrain and coerce on the picket line when that misconduct occurs away from the picket line. There are, however, also some unique kinds of restraint and coercion that occur away from the picket line.

Following nonstriking employees as they leave work has been found to be coercive conduct under certain circumstances. In *Sunset Line & Twine*[329] for example, some employees were followed by a large group of strikers who were yelling, swearing, using profane language, and blowing automobile horns. The NLRB said that

> the conduct of the strikers and their companions, quite apart from the words they used, in trailing the greatly outnumbered little group of strikebreakers for a considerable distance through the town was clearly intimidatory. This pursuit away from the plant by an inimical superior force clearly conveyed the unspoken threat that the strikebreakers might well be subjected to bodily harm. As such it was hardly less coercive within the meaning of Section 8(a)(1) than an express threat of physical violence.[330]

Employees driving to and from work are also frequently "harassed" by strikers in automobiles: following bumper-to-bumper,[331] cutting in

---

[327] Courts, the Board, and labor arbitrators frequently take this into account when determining whether a striking employee who has engaged in so-called minor picket line misconduct thereby has lost the protections of the statute and can be discharged for cause. *See, e.g.,* Associated Grocers of New England, Inc. v. NLRB, 562 F.2d 1333, 1335 (1st Cir. 1977) ("'[M]inor picket line and other misconduct, even though crude or offensive, will not justify discipline, as the right to strike necessarily implies some 'leeway for impulsive behavior.'"); Indiana Desk Co., 56 N.L.R.B. 76, 79 (1944) ("jostling on the picket line . . . can normally be expected in any extensive strike"), *enforced in part,* 149 F.2d 987 (7th Cir. 1945); Southern Bell Tel. & Tel. Co., 26 Lab. Arb. (BNA) 186, 192 (1956)(McCoy, Arb.)(attempt to provoke a fight characterized as "only the sort of angry reaction, sudden flareup of temper, so-called 'animal exuberance,' to be expected in tense situations on the picket line").

[328] Labor arbitrators certainly take a more serious view of misconduct occurring away from the picket line. *See, e.g.,* General Tel. Co., 69 Lab. Arb. (BNA) 351, 360 (1977)(Bowles, Arb.); Southern Bell Tel. & Tel. Co., 26 Lab. Arb. (BNA) 593, 596 (1956) (Alexander, Arb.).

[329] International Longshoremen's Union Local 6 (Sunset Line & Twine Co.), 79 N.L.R.B. 1487 (1948).

[330] *Id.* at 1505; *see also* Drivers Local 695 (Tony Pellitteri Trucking Serv., Inc.), 174 N.L.R.B. 753, 755 (1969). *But see* Lumber Workers Union, Local 1407 (Santa Ana Lumber Co.), 87 N.L.R.B. 937, 938 (1949)(merely following company trucks to see destination of deliveries was not coercive).

[331] Plastic Workers Local 929 (Doughboy Recreational, Domain Indus., Inc.), 200 N.L.R.B. 419, 421 (1972).

front of the nonstriking employees' cars and suddenly slowing down,[332] zigzagging in front of them,[333] attempting to force them off the road,[334] pushing them when stopped at an intersection,[335] and other forms of assault with a vehicle.[336] Needless to say, the NLRB has had no difficulty in finding such dangerous and intimidating conduct to be illegal under the statute.

Finally, the NLRB has also taken a fairly tough stance on picketing and demonstrations in front of the homes of nonstriking employees and management officials. In one case, for example, the union and a large group of strikers picketed in front of nonstriking employees' residences with signs accusing them, by name, of "scabbing." There was also a lot of shouting and the wife of one nonstriker became hysterical with fear. Ignoring the union's first amendment claim, the board found that this conduct "constituted a coercive force" which "held the nonstrikers up to ridicule and sought public condemnation for their failure to join the strike."[337] Therefore, it was held to be illegal under the statute.[338]

The Section 7 Rights That are at Issue. In the majority of section 8(b)(1)(A) cases, the restraint and coercion occurs in the context of either an organizational campaign, a work stoppage, or a strike. It is directed at employees who choose not to participate in these particular union activities. It is readily apparent from both the legislative history[339] and the case law that such a refusal is included in the section 7 rights to refrain from union concerted activities.[340] This issue warrants little further discussion.

---

[332] Metal Polishers Union, Local 67 (Alco-Cad Nickel Plating Corp.), 200 N.L.R.B. 335 (1972); Teamsters Local 536 (Connecticut Foundry Co.), 165 N.L.R.B. 916, 918 (1967).

[333] Local Union 5367, United Steelworkers, 123 N.L.R.B. 216, 224 (1959).

[334] UMW District 50 (Eagle Mfg. Co.), 112 N.L.R.B 74, 78 (1955).

[335] Amalgamated Meat Cutters (Iowa Beef Processors, Inc.), 233 N.L.R.B. 839, 845 (1977).

[336] *See, e.g.,* Local 810, Fabricators & Warehousemen (Scales Air Compressor Corp.), 200 N.L.R.B. 575, 583 (1972); ILGWU (Elsing Mfg. Co.), 186 N.L.R.B. 342, 347-48 (1970); Local 456, Int'l Bhd. of Teamsters (Strauss Paper Co.), 149 N.L.R.B. 49, 57 (1964).

[337] United Mechanics Union Local 150-F (American Photocopy Equip. Co.), 151 N.L.R.B. 386, 393-94 (1965).

[338] *Id. See also* District 34, Int'l Ass'n of Machinists (Wolf Mach. Co.), 254 N.L.R.B. 282, 284 (1981)(car full of union supporters shouting obscenities and threats drove back and forth in front of non-striking employee's home); Communications Workers (Ohio Consol. Tele.), 120 N.L.R.B. 684, 685, 695 (1958)(8 to 10 strikers followed manager and congregated in front of his house), *enforced,* 266 F.2d 823 (6th Cir. 1959) (per curiam), *modified and aff'd,* 362 U.S. 479 (1959)(per curiam).

[339] *See* text accompanying notes 32 and 35 *supra.*

[340] *See* text accompanying notes 67, 68 *supra.* In NLRB v. International Woodworkers, 243 F.2d 745 (5th Cir. 1957), the court expressly noted that "the right to work in the face of a strike" is a right protected by section 7, *id.* at 747 n.3.

Insofar as the *affirmative* exercise of section 7 rights is concerned, employee participation in the collective bargaining process certainly should be protected.[341] In addition, the exercise of other rights under the statute, such as the filing of decertification petitions[342] or unfair labor practice charges against the union,[343] should easily come under the umbrella of section 7 insofar as retaliatory measures by the union are concerned. Indeed, almost any kind of dissident activity or opposition to the union would seem to be protected. Voicing objections to the manner in which the hiring hall is run,[344] holding "rump" meetings to discuss working conditions,[345] voicing opposition to specific union leaders,[346] and attempting to have them removed from office[347] have all received protection.

In order for criticism of and opposition to specific union leaders to be considered protected, however, the union related purpose must somehow be disclosed. In the *Bethlehem Steel Corporation* case,[348] for example, the assaulted employee had been vocally critical of a grievance committeeman who had refused to support a particular grievance. The trial examiner found that what the employee did and said "was not criticism of union policies at a union meeting seeking to reverse union policy. . . . This was criticism of Harmon to other employees for some *undisclosed purpose.*"[349] Similarly, even when an employee is assaulted or threatened during an organizational cam-

---

[341] *Accord* Brewers Local 6 (Custom Packaging Corp.), 192 N.L.R.B. 1263 (1971). In that case, some employees apparently were not happy with the way in which the union was conducting the bargaining for a new contract; the employees took the initiative themselves in dealing with the employer and in formulating a counterproposal. The trial examiner found this to be a protected concerted activity. The Board, probably because it felt this conduct may well have been in derogation of the union's statutory role as the exclusive bargaining representative, chose not to rely on this finding but upheld the violation on a different theory. *Id.* at n.2. *See* text accompanying notes 378-83, *infra.* Clearly, however, an employee's *legitimate* participation in the collective bargaining process would be considered protected in the *full* sense of the word.

[342] Painters' Dist. Council No. 6 (Higbee Co.), 97 N.L.R.B. 654, 66266 (1951), *enforced* 202 F.2d 957 (6th Cir.), *cert. denied,* 345 U.S. 995 (1953).

[343] Truck Drivers Local 705 (Associated Transp., Inc.), 209 N.L.R.B. 292, 307 (1974), *enforced,* 532 F.2d 1169 (7th Cir.), *cert. denied,* 429 U.S. 1022 (1976).

[344] International Ass'n of Bridge Workers Local 433 (Associated Gen. Contractors of Calif., Inc.), 228 N.L.R.B. 1420 (1977), *enforced,* 600 F.2d 770 (9th Cir. 1979), *cert. denied,* 445 U.S. 915 (1980).

[345] Local 57, UAW (Louis R. Miller), 102 N.L.R.B. 111, 118 (1953).

[346] General Truckdrivers Local 5 (Ryder Truck Lines, Inc.), 161 N.L.R.B. 493 (1966), *enforced,* 389 F.2d 757 (5th Cir. 1968).

[347] *Cf.* New York City Taxi Drivers Union Local 3036 (Taxi Maintenance Corp.), 231 N.L.R.B. 965 (1977).

[348] United Steelworkers Local 2610 (Bethlehem Steel Corp.), 225 N.L.R.B. 310 (1967).

[349] *Id.* at 314 (emphasis added). *Accord* NLRB v. IBEW Local 1229, 346 U.S. 464 (1953) (public criticism of employer that did not disclose its connection with a labor dispute held not to be protected against discharge by the employer).

paign, a strike, or while participating in intraunion activities, the general counsel must prove that the restraint and coercion are related to these matters rather than something else. The "something else" that is occasionally found to exist is a purely personal animosity that has flared into violence, often because of the employee-victim's own provocative words or conduct. When personal animosity is the reason for the violence, the violence does not amount to restraint or coercion of employees *in the exercise of their section 7 rights.* The factual distinction is a fine one to draw in some cases. For example, in *Ryder Truck Lines,*[350] the trial examiner concluded that "the incident was an outgrowth of the hostility between the two men, the exchange of insults between them, and Albin's movement toward Partin which could reasonably have been interpreted by Partin as a threatening move."[351] The NLRB, however, construed the facts differently, concluding that the threat "was caused by Albin's opposition to Partin's leadership of the Respondent [Union]."[352] In several other cases, the board has agreed that the assaults were the result of personal animosities instead of union related behavior.[353] Therefore, no violation of the statute occurred.

A more difficult theoretical problem exists when a union restrains or coerces during the course of a jurisdictional or work assignment dispute. The NLRB generally finds a violation in this situation by using a broad conception of what constitutes a protected concerted activity. In *Edward Kraemer & Sons,*[354] for example, the union objected to the fact that a member of another union was driving a truck on the job and proceeded to pistol whip him. The board simply noted that the "assault . . . was in furtherance of the Union's claim to all truckdriving work and its opposition to Curtsinger's driving a truck on the project. Therefore, we conclude that such action was coercion and restraint of an individual employee on the basis of union related considerations."[355]

By stating the test for "protectedness" broadly, the Board shifted the focus of the section 7 analysis from the conduct of the individual (which is the usual one made) to the conduct and purpose of the union.

---

[350] General Truckdrivers Local 5 (Ryder Truck Lines, Inc.), 161 N.L.R.B. 493 (1966), *enforced,* 389 F.2d 757 (5th Cir. 1968).

[351] *Id.* at 499.

[352] *Id.* at 494 n.1.

[353] *See, e.g.,* New York Typographical Union Local 6 (Artintype, Inc.), 213 N.L.R.B. 925, 930 (1974); General Bldg. Laborers Local 66 (Courter & Co.), 198 N.L.R.B. 125, 128 (1972); Carpenters Dist. Council of Sabine Area (Miner-Dederick Constr. Corp.), 195 N.L.R.B. 178, 181 (1972)(racial animosity); Hotel Employees Union Local 466 (Treadway Inn), 191 N.L.R.B. 528, 533 (1971); ILGWU (Twin-Kee Mfg. Co.), 130 N.L.R.B. 614, 615 (1961); Strauss Stores Corp., 94 N.L.R.B. 440, 463 (1951).

[354] Edward Kraemer & Sons, 203 N.L.R.B. 739 (1973).

[355] *Id.* at 740.

This approach gives the individual, and properly so, an open ended sort of section 7 right to be free of any union related violence. It obviates the necessity of closer inquiry into whether what the employee was doing (or refraining from doing) fits into one of the traditional section 7 activity molds.

A much narrower conception of the scope of section 7 was articulated by Board Member Murdock in *Rufus M. Tackett*,[356] a case which also centered around a jurisdictional or work assignment dispute between two unions. In dissent, he said that "normally, employees engage in concerted activity to secure some benefit from their employer. Other employees may be satisfied to continue or begin working without that benefit. Section 8(b)(1)(A) protects the latter from restraint or coercion by the former.[357] He then intimated that the union's purpose in *Tackett*, by contrast, was simply to drive the members of another union out of the mine; that the union was certainly not asking them to act in concert with this "demand for their own liquidation";[358] and that the violence that was directed against them could not be because they were *refraining* from so acting, in a section 7 sense. Rather, he noted that "the demand in this case was the very essence of a dispute between two labor organizations and, in my opinion, had nothing to do with the concerted activities of either."[359] This narrower conception, however, has not prevailed.[360]

The most controversial section 7 issue to confront the NLRB and the courts in a section 8(b)(1)(A) context concerns employees who engage in conduct in violation of a collective bargaining agreement and who are assaulted or threatened by the union for doing so. This issue first arose in *Abe Meltzer, Inc.*[361] wherein union agents blocked ingress and physically attacked two employees who had performed overtime work in another shop in violation of the collective bargaining agreement. The board found this to be a section 8(b)(1)(A) violation:

> We believe that the Union's action in requiring employee compliance with the overtime provisions of the contract reflected a union policy having mutual aid and protection as its objective. The determination by Zweig and Abravaya to work notwithstanding the Union's general "spread the work" policy constituted a refusal on their part to assist the Union in effectuating that policy. . . . We do not, as our dissenting colleague contends, condone

---

[356] Local 6281, UMW (Rufus M. Tackett), 100 N.L.R.B. 392 (1952).
[357] *Id.* at 396.
[358] *Id.* at 396-97.
[359] *Id.* at 397.
[360] *Accord* Dover Corp., 211 N.L.R.B. 955 (1974), *enforced in part*, 535 F.2d 1205 (10th Cir.), *cert. denied*, 429 U.S. 978 (1976).
[361] 108 N.L.R.B. 1506 (1954), *enforcement denied*, NLRB v. Furriers Joint Council, 224 F.2d 78 (2d Cir. 1955).

employee breaches of contractual obligations. We find only that where, as here, there is a conflict between union policy and the action of individual employees refraining from promotion of that policy, the statute does not permit resort to violence by a union to enforce the policy. For it is well settled that section 8(b)(1)(A) outlaws, without qualification, all union violence against employees which has the effect of interfering with their statutory right to refrain from assisting labor organizations or engaging in concerted activities.[362]

Board Member Peterson dissented and his position was subsequently adopted by the Second Circuit Court of Appeals. It noted that "section 8(b)(1)(A) was not intended to confer on the Board general power covering all acts of violence by a Union."[363] Rather, the section only covers acts of violence directed at the exercise by employees of their section 7 rights. The court thus concluded that once a union policy, such as that of "spreading the work," becomes incorporated in a contract between the union, as the exclusive bargaining representative, and an employer, the individual employee no longer has a section 7 right to ignore that policy or violate the contract in which it appears. To hold otherwise, the court noted, would not be "consistent with the underlying purpose of the Act to promote the consummation of collective bargaining agreements as 'the effective instrument of stabilizing labor relations and preventing, through collective bargaining, strikes and industrial strife.'"[364] The court concluded that the object of the violence did not pertain to the exercise of section 7 rights and, thus, no section 8(b)(1)(A) violation had occurred.

Several years later, the NLRB adhered to the court's view that an employee does not have a section 7 right to violate the terms of a collective bargaining agreement. The alleged section 8(b)(1)(A) violation consisted merely of the union's attempt to have the employee discharged.[365] It was not until 1971 that the board was again confronted with a case of violence.

In *Penntruck Co.,*[366] a union agent assaulted an employee who was engaged in a work stoppage, allegedly in violation of the no-strike provision of the union-employer contract. After a careful review of competing policy considerations, legislative history, and the theoretical construct of section 7 itself, the NLRB decided to adhere to the position it took in *Abe Meltzer:* that such conduct does in fact violate the NLRA.

---

[362] 108 N.L.R.B. at 1508-09.
[363] 224 F.2d at 80.
[364] *Id.*
[365] Millwrights Local Union 1102 (Planet Corp.), 144 N.L.R.B. 798, 801 (1963).
[366] Teamsters Local 729 (Penntruck Co.), 189 N.L.R.B. 696 (1971).

The NLRB's conclusion is ultimately founded on an abstract, but apparently correct, proposition that "protected activity" and its converse, "unprotected activity," are not static concepts.[367] The status of a particular kind of conduct does not remain the same "for all purposes and in all contexts, . . . regardless of the nature of the coercion applied against that employee conduct."[368] Rather, in a section 7 case, one must also ask, "protected against what?" The answer may vary. For example, the fundamental section 7 activity of going on an economic strike is certainly protected against an employer response of discharge; but it is not protected against permanent replacement.[369] The difference flows from the fact that one response can be justified by the employer's legitimate interest in keeping its business going,[370] but the other cannot. That is only one of innumerable factors that must be included in the analytical equation used to resolve section 7 issues.

In *Penntruck*, the NLRB conceded that an individual's work-stoppage despite a contractual no-strike clause would not be protected against a union response requesting that the employer discharge such an employee, nor against discharge itself.[371] Thus, the board's task was simply to identify the element in the equation that would protect the discharge of an employee but not protect a union's response of physical violence. The element it relied on was the limited nature of a union's power to waive the individual's section 7 rights.

In *Penntruck*, the employee was striking to protest the discharge of fellow employees. This is almost prototypical section 7 activity, with respect to both the objective and the means being used to achieve it. What would render it unprotected, however, is the fact that the union has waived the employees' right to engage in this activity in the exercise of its statutory power as the exclusive bargaining representative of the employees. Although the policy of exclusive representation is central to the structure of the NLRA, the power of such a representative to waive an individual employee's section 7 rights must be limited by other policy considerations.[372]

---

[367] Indeed, with respect to some kinds of conduct, the fluidity of the concept is such that it is difficult if not impossible for employees, employers, labor union, or practitioners to ever predict with certainty whether this conduct will or will not be held to be protected under the facts of their respective cases. *See, e.g.,* Haggard, *Picket Line Observance as a Protected Concerted Activity,* 53 N.C.L. REV. 43, 84-85 (1974). The holding in *Penntruck,* however, would not seem to raise this difficulty.

[368] 189 N.L.R.B. at 698-99.

[369] NLRB v. Mackay Radio & Tel. Co., 304 U.S. 333 (1938).

[370] *Id.* at 345-46.

[371] 189 N.L.R.B. at 699.

[372] *See, e.g.,* NLRB v. Magnavox Co., 415 U.S. 322 (1974) (union cannot contractually waive individual employee's section 7 solicitation rights).

In *Penntruck,* The NLRB looked to the abhorrent nature of what the employee was allegedly "waiving": the right to be protected against physical violence.[373] The board read the legislative history of section 8(b)(1)(A) as requiring a "blanket prohibition upon all forms of violence, [without] qualification or exception."[374] It noted the absence of a parallel congressional concern about the union response of requesting discharge.[375] Under the facts, discharge would have been a permitted response. Violence was not. The board concluded:

> An employer and a union acting on behalf of his employees may waive, to a limited extent, the Section 7 protection of those employees by agreeing, in effect, that certain activity otherwise shielded by Section 7 will be subject to the imposition of job or internal union discipline; no contract, however, can surrender the right of employees to be protected against violence directed at their participation in what are essentially acts of "mutual aid or protection."[376]

Finally, the NLRB did not find compelling the countervailing policy consideration relied on by the second circuit in the *Abe Meltzer* case: the importance of achieving industrial peace and stability through the inviolability of collective bargaining agreements. The board simply noted that

> the withholding of the sanctions of the Act in a case such as this—in effect, tolerating the use of violence in the context of a labor dispute—hardly promises to foster a reduction of "industrial strife." And it would be the rare employee, indeed, who, when contemplating whether to breach a contractual provision, would be encouraged to do so by the possibility that any physical assaults perpetrated against him by his union might be found to be violative of Section 8(b)(1)(A).[377]

Meltzer and *Penntruck* dealt with employee conduct that would normally be considered unprotected because it breached the collective bargaining agreement. It was nevertheless found to be protected against violent union reprisals. The logic of those decisions can, however, be extended to cover another kind of conduct. In the *Custom Packaging Corp.* case,[378] several employees engaged in bargaining activities with the employer, arguably in derogation of the union's status as the statutory and exclusive bargaining representative. That conduct

---

[373] Indeed, the mere suggestion that a union, which may be the individual employee's bargaining agent *only* by operation of federal law and without his express consent, should ever have the power to waive the rights of such a "principal" against the agent itself would be outrageous—especially if the waiver concerns the fundamental right to be free of physical violence.

[374] 189 N.L.R.B. at 699.

[375] *Id.* at 700 n.9.

[376] *Id.* at 699.

[377] *Id.* at 698.

[378] Brewers Local 6 (Custom Packaging Corp.), 192 N.L.R.B. 1263 (1971).

would not normally be considered protected.[379] The NLRB, nevertheless, found that the union had violated section 8(b)(1)(A) when it resorted to physical violence against one of these employees.

Of course, employees have an express section 7 right to bargain collectively. That right, however, is limited by the section 9 concept of exclusive representation. A union that is selected by a majority of the employees becomes the exclusive bargaining representative of those employees.[380] Individual agreements are without force and effect.[381] In fact, an employer violates its own duty to bargain in good faith when it deals directly with employees in circumvention of the union.[382] Yet just as a union's power to redefine protectedness through the exercise of its right of exclusive representation (*i.e.*, by waiving certain rights in a contract with the employer) is limited by the overriding consideration that union violence must be condemned, so also should the concept of exclusive representation itself be similarly limited. In short, collective bargaining activities by individual employees in derogation of the union's status as exclusive representative should, nevertheless, be protected against union violence.

The *Custom Packaging* case arguably stands for that proposition. The NLRB, unfortunately, did not put it in precisely those terms. The trial examiner held that the conduct was protected in the conventional sense, and proceeded with the normal analysis. Affirming the trial examiner's decision, the board, however, did not rely on that finding. Citing the *Penntruck* decision, the board said, "assuming, *arguendo*, that his conduct was unprotected within the meaning of Section 7 of the Act, we would, nonetheless, find that the Respondent's resort to violence in the circumstances set forth herein violated Section 8(b)(1)(A) of the Act."[383] Such a statement is, however, conceptually and linguistically confusing. It is one thing to say that certain conduct is protected but only against union violence; it is quite another to say that it is unprotected but that union violence will nevertheless be considered a violation of section 8(b)(1)(A)—a section which only prohibits the restraint and coercion of employees who are engaged in protected conduct. Nevertheless, the bottom line seems to be that union violence against employees in performing the union's normal functions restrains

---

[379] Emporium Capwell Co. v. Western Addition Community Org., 420 U.S. 50 (1975) (attempt to bargain separately for a minority group held to be in derogation of the authority of the exclusive bargaining representative and thus not protected against the employer's reprisal of discharge).

[380] National Labor Relations Act (NLRA) § 9(a), 29 U.S.C. § 159(a) (1976).

[381] J.I. Case Co. v. NLRB, 321 U.S. 332 (1944).

[382] *See generally* R. GORMAN, LABOR LAW 381-85 (1976).

[383] 192 N.L.R.B. at 1263 n.2.

or coerces employees in the exercise of their section 7 rights. Put differently, employees have an unqualified section 7 right to be free from such violence.

The Agency Question

Frequently, the most contested issue in a section 8(b)(1)(A) case is whether the restraint and coercion of employees in the exercise of their section 7 rights has in fact been committed by a labor organization or its agents rather than someone simply acting on his own. The tests for establishing such responsibility vary, depending on whether only the local union has been charged or whether the national or international union has also been named as a respondent.

Proving the Responsibility of the Local Union. The burden of proving that the union entity is legally responsible for the violent acts of its employees, members, or others acting on its behalf is, of course, on the general counsel.[384] As a matter of general agency law, responsibility can be established by proof that the acts were previously authorized, that they were committed within the individual's "scope of employment" with the union, or that they were subsequently ratified.[385] There does not appear to be any section 8(b)(1)(A) cases where the general counsel was able to show that the union, acting formally in its institutional capacity, ever gave specific prior authorization or subsequent ratification to acts of violence[386]—although the systematic and obviously well-coordinated use of force by some unions strongly suggests the existence of a deliberately conceived policy in that regard. In any event, union responsibility is nearly always established by showing that the acts of violence were committed "within the scope of employment" of some agent or subagent of the union. In *Sunset Line & Twine,*[387] the NLRB states the test this way:

> A principal may be responsible for the act of his agent within the scope of the agent's general authority, or the "scope of his employment" if the agent is a servant, even though the principal has not specifically authorized or indeed may have specifically forbidden the act in question. It is enough if

---

[384] International Longshoremen's Union Local 6 (Sunset Line & Twine Co.), 79 N.L.R.B. 1487, 1508 (1948).

[385] United Furniture Workers Local 472 (Colonial Hardwood Flooring Co.), 84 N.L.R.B. 563, 583 (1949).

[386] *But cf.* Unión de Tronquistas Local 901 (Hotel La Concha), 193 N.L.R.B. 591, 598 (1971) (union found to have condoned assault by declaring assailants "not guilty" without investigating the matter and by giving two of the assailants jobs with the union).

[387] International Longshoremen's Union Local 6 (Sunset Line & Twine Co.), 79 N.L.R.B. 1487 (1948).

the principal actually empowered the agent to represent him in the general area within which the agent acted.[388]

Union offers, business agents, and stewards have general authority to conduct the affairs of the union. When they are individually responsible for an act of violence, then the union itself is nearly always responsible as well.[389] In one case, for example, the union job steward (Allen) was given general authority to police a shopping center job, report any nonmembers he found working there, and attempt to secure their removal. He secured the latter by physical assault. The NLRB found that the "Respondent Union is chargeable with Allen's resort to violence in his zeal to carry out Respondent Union's policy of reserving the work . . . for its members."[390]

Insofar as strike and picket line violence is concerned, the acts of strike committees and picket line captains are nearly always found to be acts for which the union is legally responsible.[391] As the Second Circuit Court of Appeals once stated, "a union cannot leave the direction of a strike and picketing to a 'strike committee' and escape liability for the activities of the committee."[392] Indeed, in one case the union was held responsible for picket line violence because of its failure to disavow one individual's assumption of the role as spokesman for the union on the picket line.[393] The union was not held responsible for his conduct away from the picket line.

In 1951, the NLRB expressly declined to "pass upon the question of whether individuals engaged in picketing activities become, *per se,* agents of the sponsoring labor organizations." Subsequently, the board

---

[388] *Id.* at 1509.

[389] *See, e.g.,* District 34, Int'l Ass'n of Machinists (Wolf Mach. Co.), 254 N.L.R.B. 282 (1981) (chief steward and business representative); Industrial Union of Marine Workers (Bethlehem Steel Co.), 130 N.L.R.B. 412, 424 (1961) (officers and stewards); Local 1150, United Elec. Workers (Cory Corp.), 84 N.L.R.B. 972, 977-78 (1949) (stewards); International Longshoremen's Union Local 6 (Sunset Line & Twine Co.), 79 N.L.R.B. 1487, 1507 (1948) (business agent and the vice president of the local), *Contra* NLRB v. Dallas General Drivers Local 745, 264 F.2d 642, 648 (5th Cir. 1959), *cert. denied,* 361 U.S. 814 (1959).

[390] United Bhd. of Carpenters Local 55 (Grauman Co.), 100 N.L.R.B. 753, 754 (1952), *enforced,* 205 F.2d 515 (19th Cir. 1953).

[391] District 34, Int'l. Ass'n of Machinists (Wolf Mach. Co.), 254 N.L.R.B. 282 (1981) (picket line captain); Industrial Union of Marine and Shipbuilding Workers (Bethlehem Steel Co.), 130 N.L.R.B. 412, 424 (1961) (picket captains); Perry Norvell Co., 80 N.L.R.B. 225, 244 (1948) (strike committee). *But see* District 1199, Health Care Employees (Frances Schervier Home & Hosp.), 245 N.L.R.B. 800, 804 n.6 (1979) (members of the negotiating committee not "agents" of the union insofar as strike violence was concerned).

[392] New Power Wire & Elec. Corp. v. NLRB, 340 F.2d 71, 73 (2d Cir. 1965).

[393] National Union of Marine Cooks (Irwin-Lyons Lumber Co.), 87 N.L.R.B. 54, 55, 77-78 (1949).

has determined that the union is at least responsible for the acts of *"authorized pickets."* In the *Coca-Cola Bottling Works* case,[394] the board noted that:

> it is well known that in authorized strikes unions are normally responsible for the acts of authorized pickets. Threats and the employment of force on a picket line, even though forbidden, are reasonably to be expected, and so "within the scope of employment of pickets for which the labor organization is responsible."[395]

In another case, the trial examiner noted that "the sanctioning of a strike by a labor organization's agent . . . makes the participants in strike activities (such as picketing) the subagents of the labor organization in such activities."[396] The board, however, has refused to find that the acts of rank and file members, without more, are necessarily the acts of the union itself.[397] The second circuit has criticized this position as a "rather narrow conception of who constitute[s] the union."[398]

If a labor organization is to be held responsible for breaches of a statutory duty committed by its agents while acting within the scope of their employment, the next step is to determine the exact parameters of that duty. Obviously, it prohibits the agent from personally engaging in any of the acts of violence previously described.[399] If an agent does commit such an act, neither a prior prohibition[400] nor a subsequent repudiation[401] by the union will serve as a defense. The agent, however, is obligated to do more than just refrain from violence himself.

---

[394] Teamsters Local 327 (Coca-Cola Bottling Works of Nashville), 184 N.L.R.B. 84 (1970).

[395] *Id.* at 94; *see also* Local 612, Int'l Bhd. of Teamsters (Deaton Truck Line, Inc.), 146 N.L.R.B. 498, 503 (1964) ("[I]t is well settled that a labor organization is responsible for violence in which its pickets engage at a picket line."). But even if authorized pickets are not agents per se, the union can still be held responsible for this misconduct on the theory that the union has an affirmative duty to control what they do. *See* text accompanying notes 402-03 *infra.*

[396] United Furniture Workers Local 472 (Colonial Hardwood Flooring Co.), 84 N.L.R.B. 563, 585 (1949).

[397] New Power Wire & Elec. Corp. v. NLRB, 340 F.2d 71, 72 (2d Cir. 1965). The Board's position would appear to be consistent with the legislative history. *See* text accompanying note 56 *supra.*

[398] 340 F.2d at 72.

[399] *See, e.g.,* Freight Drivers Local Union 557 (Liberty Transfer Co.), 218 N.L.R.B. 1117 (1975); ILGWU (Elsing Mfg. Co.), 186 N.L.R.B. 342 (1970); Perry Norvell Co., 80 N.L.R.B. 225 (1948).

[400] Local 235, Lithographers Union (Henry Wurst, Inc.), 187 N.L.R.B. 490 (1970) (Instructions not to commit violence "are not sufficient to absolve a labor organization of responsibility for acts of violence committed by . . . agents of the union during the course of an unauthorized strike).

[401] United Bhd. of Carpenters Local 55 (Grauman Co.), 100 N.L.R.B. 753, 755 (1952) (A statement by another union official "at the scene of the assault that the Respondent Union disapproved of, and regretted, the assault was [not] sufficient to relieve the Respondent Union of responsibility therefor), *enforced,* 205 F.2d 515 (10th Cir. 1953).

In *Tony Pellitteri Trucking Service, Inc.*,[402] the trial examiner advanced the theory that union officials have an affirmative duty to insure that strike and picket line violence do not occur. He said:

a union which calls a strike and authorizes picketing must retain control over the pickets in whatever manner it deems necessary, in order to insure that they do not act improperly. If a union is unwilling, or unable, to take the necessary steps to control its pickets, it must then bear responsibility for their misconduct.[403]

In most cases, however, the NLRB relies on a closely related but perhaps somewhat narrower theory for holding the union responsible for the violent misconduct of pickets. Union responsibility can be established through the principle of tacit ratification even if the misconduct of subagents is not deemed to be within the scope of their "employment" as pickets (for which the union would be directly responsible).[404] When misconduct occurs in the presence of a union's primary agent who does nothing to repudiate or stop it, the law routinely treats it as a form of ratification.[405] As the board put it in one case, "the principal's

[402] Drivers Union, Local 695 (Tony Pellitteri Trucking Serv., Inc.), 174 N.L.R.B. 753 (1969).

[403] *Id.* at 758. *See also* Local 30, United Slate, Tile and Composition Roofers (Associated Builders & Contractors), 227 N.L.R.B. 1444, 1450 (1977); Teamsters Local 783 (Coca-Cola Bottling Co. of Louisville), 160 N.L.R.B. 1776 (1966) (liability of the union based "on the fact that Respondent, which authorized the strike, knew of the acts of misconduct and violence but took no steps reasonably calculated effectively to stop such acts").

[404] *See* text accompanying notes 395 and 396 *supra.*

[405] *See, e.g.,* NLRB v. Unión Nacional de Trabajadores, 540 F.2d 1, 9 n.7 (1st Cir. 1976) ("silent approbation"), *cert. denied,* 429 U.S. 1039 (1977); International Ass'n of Bridge Workers Local 433 (Associated Gen. Contractors of Calif., Inc.), 228 N.L.R.B. 1420, 1425 (1977) (union agent "acquiesced in those threats through his silence"), *enforced,* 600 F.2d 770 (9th Cir. 1979), *cert. denied,* 445 U.S. 915 (1980); Local 30, United Slate, Tile and Composition Roofers (Kitson Bros., Inc.), 228 N.L.R.B. 652, 653 (1977); Teamsters Local 783 (Coca-Cola Bottling Co. of Louisville), 160 N.L.R.B. 1776 (1966); International Woodworkers Local 3-3 (Western Wirebound Box Co.), 144 N.L.R.B. 912, 915 (1963); Local 542, Operating Eng'rs (Giles & Ransome, Inc.), 139 N.L.R.B. 1169, 1175 (1962), *enforced,* 328 F.2d 850 (3d Cir. 1964), *cert. denied,* 379 U.S. 826 (1964); Bonnaz Embroideries Trucking & Pleating Union Local 66 (V. & D. Machine Embroidery Co.), 134 N.L.R.B. 879, 880-81 (1961); Local 346 International Leather Goods Union (Baronet of Puerto Rico, Inc.), 133 N.L.R.B. 1617, 1628, 1632 (1961) (local politician incited and led a riot against the plant: "No evidence was offered by Respondents that they publically disassociated themselves from the speaker's conduct or statements"); Central Mass. Joint Bd., Textile Workers Union (Charles Weinstein Co.), 123 N.L.R.B. 590, 591 (1959). *But see* NLRB v. Service Employees Local 254, 535 F.2d 1335, 1338 (1st Cir. 1976) (assault, which occurred in first week of strike, was the only act of violence, no union officers were present, and only 3 or 4 pickets were present; the court found "no recurrence, nor anything indicating Union acquiescence in or approbation of the assault."); NLRB v. Dallas General Drivers, Local 745, 264 F.2d 642, 648 (5th Cir. 1959) (board found union responsible because of steward's failure to repudiate threats made in his presence; the court, however, refused to presume the authority of a steward to acquiesce in and to adopt, on behalf of the Union, threats made by union members who were not themselves officers), *cert. denied,* 361 U.S. 814 (1959).

consent, technically called authorization or ratification, may be manifested by conduct, *sometimes even passive acquiescence,* as well as by words.''[406] In other words, a union has an affirmative duty to disassociate itself from violence. Breach of this duty by one of its primary agents renders the union responsible.

One notable exception to the theory of ratification by silence concerns threatening statements made by members during the course of a union meeting. In *Union Tank Car,*[407] the NLRB explained:

> we do not think that each and every remark made from the floor which goes unrenounced by the presiding [sic] officer can be held to be a statement of union policy . . . *To hold the union responsible, absent any positive evidence of ratification or approval, for every course of conduct suggested from the floor goes beyond any reasonable presumption of acquiescence by silence.*[408]

Of course, prior instructions to pickets not to engage in violence do not relieve the union of responsibility when an agent nevertheless acquiesces in such violence.[409]

Another theory under which a union may be held responsible for acts of violence committed in the presence of its agents is predicated on the legal maxim that "in mob action, the acts of one may in legal contemplation justifiably be regarded as acts of all."[410] The duty and responsibility of the union and its agents is not limited, however, to acts of violence committed by or in the presence of these agents. On the contrary, when a union agent has committed or acquiesced in various acts of violence, this may be said to have instigated the perpetration of similar misconduct. The NLRB, in *Bethlehem Steel,*[411] put it this way: "Where authorized union agents, by their misconduct, set an example for rank-and-file pickets, thereby instigating the similar type of misconduct engaged in by such pickets, the Union is equally liable for such latter misconduct which occurred in the absence of authorized

---

[406] International Longshoremen's Union Local 6 (Sunset Line & Twine Co.), 79 N.L.R.B. 1487, 1508 (1948) (emphasis added).

[407] General Truck Drivers Local 5 (Union Tank Car Co.), 172 N.L.R.B. 137 (1968).

[408] *Id.* at 138 (emphasis in original); *see also* District 1199, Hosp. Health Care Employees (Southport Manor Convalescent Center, Inc.), 227 N.L.R.B. 1732, 1733-34 (1977) (Board found no "positive evidence as to show ratification or approval. . . .[I]t would be unreasonable to hold the Union responsible for such remarks made by employees in the confused and emotional atmosphere of such union meetings.").

[409] *See, e.g.,* Local 235, Lithographers Union (Henry Wurst, Inc.), 187 N.L.R.B. 490 (1970); Teamsters Local 327 (Whale, Inc.), 178 N.L.R.B. 422, 427 (1969), *enforced in part,* 432 F.2d 933 (6th Cir. 1970); Local 379, Bldg. Material & Excavators (Catalano Bros.), 175 N.L.R.B. 459, 470 (1969).

[410] UMW Local 7083 (Grundy Mining Co.), 146 N.L.R.B. 176, 182 (1964); *see also* UMW Dist. 2 (Mears Coal Co.), 173 N.L.R.B. 665, 669 (1968), *enforced,* 429 F.2d 141 (3d Cir. 1970).

[411] Industrial Union of Marine Workers (Bethlehem Steel Co.), 130 N.L.R.B. 412 (1961).

agents."[412] Similarly, with respect to violence that is committed by individuals away from the picket line, one trial examiner rather eloquently noted that "in this situation, it may be said that the ugly flower of unlawfulness which blossomed away from the picket line resulted from the seed of defiance planted and nurtured at the picket line" by union agents.[413]

The union, however, can apparently cut off its liability for subsequent misconduct by repudiating the prior acts of its agents and by taking steps to insure that they are not repeated. The NLRB has held that such repudiation will prevent the imputation of any "subsequent similar misconduct committed by [non-officials to the local] without a specific showing of their express or implied sanction."[414]

Proving the Responsibility of the National or International Union. Although the matter is obviously affected by the specific terms of the constitution and bylaws of the two bodies,[415] a national or international union and its local affiliates are generally considered to be separate legal entities.[416] Thus, proof that a local union is legally responsible for acts of violence does not necessarily implicate the parent organization. Its responsibility must be separately proved.

Responsibility, of course, is proved if a personal agent of the national or international, operating generally within the scope of his assigned duties, participates or acquiesces in acts of violence.[417] Responsibility of the national or international may also be predicated on the theory that the local union which was legally responsible for the violence was the agent of the national or international union. Although a local union will usually be considered the agent of the national or international only in the context of the local's negotiation or enforcement of the collective bargaining agreement with the employer,[418] an agency of broader scope has been found in some cases. In the *Personal Products Corp.*

---

[412] *Id.* at 424 n.8; *see also* Local 810, Int'l Bhd. of Teamsters (Russell Plastics Technology, Inc.), 235 N.L.R.B. 40, 46-47 (1978); International Ass'n of Machinists (General Elec. Co.), 183 N.L.R.B. 1225, 1233 (1970); UMW Dist. 2 (Solar Fuel Co.), 170 N.L.R.B. 1581, 1592 (1968), *enforced,* 418 F.2d 240 (3d Cir. 1969); International Union of Elec. Workers (Sperry Rubber & Plastics Co.), 134 N.L.R.B. 1713, 1724 (1961).

[413] District 50, UMW (Tungsten Mining Corp.), 106 N.L.R.B. 903, 922 (1953).

[414] General Iron Corp., 224 N.L.R.B. 1180, 1191 (1976).

[415] *See* United Furniture Workers Local 472 (Colonial Hardwood Flooring Co.), 84 N.L.R.B. 563 (1949) (close relationship between local and the international, under the latter's constitution, was relied on in part by the Board in finding both units to be jointly responsible for acts of violence).

[416] United Mine Workers (Blue Diamond Coal Co.), 143 N.L.R.B. 795, 797 (1963).

[417] *See, e.g.,* United Furniture Workers, Local 472 (Colonial Hardwood Flooring Co.), 84 N.L.R.B. 563, 583-85 (1949); United Furniture Workers, Local 309 (Smith Cabinet Mfg. Co.), 81 N.L.R.B. 886, 889-91 (1949).

[418] *Accord,* United Mine Workers (Blue Diamond Coal Co.), 143 N.L.R.B. at 797 (local's agency limited to enforcement of the contract, and thus no responsibility for interna-

case,[419] for example, the trial examiner found that "the International duly constituted Local 1172, its admitted administrative agency, as its agent for the purpose of representing employees of the Company *and engaging in the various concerted activities* set forth below, instigated by the Local within the scope of said agency, and that is, as well as the Local, is responsible for such conduct."[420] The concerted activities in question included various threats and the blocking of entrances into the plant.

In most cases, however, the national or international has been held liable on the theory that the strike and related conduct is a joint venture between it and the local union. For example, actual participation by an agent of the national or international in acts of violence has been held to render the parent union liable for the agent's misconduct and for the misconduct of the local union and its agents. The theory is that his participation converts the strike into a common undertaking.[421] A joint venture relationship has also been found to exist in a case where the international fully identified itself with the local in calling and conducting the strike, the strike was conducted for the purpose of protecting the interests of members of both units, and the international joined with the local in pleading certain affirmative defenses without differentiating itself in any way.[422] The international can also be found liable on a joint venture theory if it jointly sponsors the strike by providing strike benefits.[423] Finally, in one case the NLRB relied on the fact that the international had urged the need for a "united front" among all its affiliate locals in conducting the strike against this employer. It had publicly endorsed the strike, it had used its official publication to solicit financial support for the local, and it had acknowledged in its answer to the unfair labor practice complaint that it was a party to the strike.[424] Whether a national or international union

---

tional's acts of violence unrelated to that function). *But see,* NLRB v. International Longshoremen's Union, 210 F.2d 581, 584-85 (9th Cir. 1954) (local found to be agent of the international in negotiating an illegal hiring hall contract).

[419] Textile Workers Union (Personal Products Corp.), 108 N.L.R.B. 743 (1954), *enforced in part,* 227 F.2d 409 (D.C. Cir. 1955), *cert. denied,* 352 U.S. 864 (1956).

[420] 108 N.L.R.B. at 755 (emphasis added).

[421] United Furniture Workers Local 472 (Colonial Hardwood Flooring Co.), 84 N.L.R.B. 563, 582-87 (1949); Local 1150, United Elec. Workers (Cory Corp.), 84 N.L.R.B. 972, 977-78 (1949); United Furniture Workers Local 309 (Smith Cabinet Mfg. Co.), 81 N.L.R.B. 886, 890-91 (1949).

[422] International Longshoremen's Union Local 6 (Sunset Line & Twine Co.), 79 N.L.R.B. 1487, 1513 (1948).

[423] United Rubber Workers Local 796 (Tennessee Wheel & Rubber Co.), 166 N.L.R.B. 165, 167 (1967).

[424] International Woodworkers (W.T. Smith Lumber Co.), 116 N.L.R.B. 507, 508 (1956), *enforced,* 243 F.2d 745 (5th Cir. 1957).

and its local will be found to have engaged in a joint venture in conducting a strike is, thus, essentially a factual matter. It appears that it does not take much to implicate the national or international under this theory.[425]

REMEDIES FOR SECTION 8(B)(1)(A) VIOLATIONS

As the above discussion indicates, the NLRB and the courts have adopted a definition of restraint and coercion that is certainly broad enough to encompass most ordinary kinds of violent criminal or tortious conduct. In applying section 8(b)(1)(A), they have construed the phrase, "in the exercise of the rights guaranteed in section 7," to include almost anything an employee might do in connection with his work or in his relationships with the union. They have also taken a broad but realistic view of union responsibility for the violence that occurs incident to unionization activities.

But legal prohibitions, and identification of conduct that falls within those prohibitions, is a meaningful exercise of sovereign power only to the extent that an effective sanction or remedy is provided. Otherwise, the entire process—from the legislative enactment itself, to the long and costly administrative trials that are conducted for the purpose of establishing the existence of a violation, to the ultimate review by already overburdened federal circuit courts of appeals—is simply an exercise in futility,"full of sound and fury, signifying nothing."[426] The prohibition against union violence contained in section 8(b)(1)(A) comes perilously close to that. In the blunt words of one trial examiner, "the powers of the Board . . . are *inadequate* to cope with violence."[427]

Successive general counsels have attempted to obtain more effective remedies for labor union violence—only to be stymied by the recalcitrance of administrative law judges, the NLRB, or sometimes even the courts. In any event, the remedies that the board does order, those it does not, and the parameters of the debate surrounding these various issues are all discussed below.

---

[425] *But see* Local 30, United Slate, Tile and Composition Roofers (Associated Builders & Contractors), 227 N.L.R.B. 1444, 1451-52 (1977) (failure of international to take corrective action does not render it liable); National Union of Marine Cooks (Irwin-Lyons Lumber Co.), 87 N.L.R.B. 54, 57 (1949) (no sponsorship of the strike or participation in the misconduct by the longshoremen's union).

[426] Shakespeare, *Macbeth*, Act V., Sc. 5, line 19.

[427] Taxicab Drivers Union Local 777 (Crown Metal Mfg. Co.), 145 N.L.R.B. 197, 205 (1963) (emphasis added), *enforced*, 340 F.2d 905 (7th Cir. 1965); *accord*, Local 612, Int'l Bhd. of Teamsters (Deaton Truck Line, Inc.), 146 N.L.R.B. 498, 506 & n.12 (1964) (listing of more effective remedies which the trial examiner, under Board precedent, found he lacked the power to order). *See generally* Note, *Strike Violence: The NLRB's Reluctance to Wield Its Broad Remedial Power*, 50 FORDHAM L. REV. 1371 (1982).

426 _Union Violence_

The Board's Remedial Powers Generally[428]

The statutory power of the NLRB to devise remedies for unfair labor practices is contained in section 10(c), which states that if the board finds a violation of the statute then it

> shall state its findings of fact and shall issue and cause to be served on such person an order requiring such person to cease and desist from such unfair labor practice, and to take such affirmative action including reinstatement of employees with or without back pay, as well effectuate the policies of this [Act]. . . .[429]

Through this broadly worded statutory mandate, Congress apparently intended to give the board discretion to formulate such remedies as it, in the exercise of its expertise and experience in labor relations, should deem appropriate.[430] The corollary of that broad discretion is that the courts of appeals should exercise extremely limited review over the board's performance of its remedial functions.[431]

Since discretion is subject to abuse, the NLRB's remedial orders are by no means totally immune from judicial scrutiny. The claim most commonly made on appeal is that a particular board order goes beyond one of the two broad constraints the courts have recognized: the order must consist only of that "which can fairly be said to effectuate the policies of the Act,"[432] and it must be limited to the requirement of affirmative action that is purely "remedial, not punitive."[433]

One commentator has suggested that the first of these limitations simply means that the remedy in question must neither be in conflict with any one of the primary objectives of the statute nor attempt to achieve ends other than those contemplated by those objectives.[434] The prohibition against "punitive" orders is, on the other hand, a bit more difficult to pin down.[435] It has been suggested that it is simply another term used to describe orders which attempt to achieve ends other than those contemplated by the statute.[436] Since the broad pur-

---

See generally D. McDowell & K. Huhn, NLRB Remedies For Unfair Labor Practices 6-15 (1976) [hereinafter cited as McDowell & Huhn].

NLRA § 10(c), 29 U.S.C. § 160(c)(1976).

See, e.g., NLRB v. Seven-Up Bottling Co., 344 U.S. 344, 346 (1953); Republic Aviation Corp. v. NLRB, 324 U.S. 793, 800 (1945); International Ass'n of Machinists v. NLRB, 311 U.S. 72, 82 (1940).

See, e.g., Phelps Dodge Corp. v. NLRB, 313 U.S. 177, 194 (1941); Amalgamated Local Union 355 (Russell Motors, Inc.) v. NLRB, 481 F.2d 996, 1006 (2d Cir. 1973).

Virginia Elec. & Power Co. v. NLRB, 319 U.S. 533, 540 (1943).

Consolidated Edison Co. v. NLRB, 305 U.S. 197, 236 (1938).

McDowell & Hunt, _supra_ note 434 at 9.

See Note, _NLRB Damage Awards,_ 84 Harv. L. Rev. 1670, 1679-83 (1971) (highly critical of the alleged remedial-punitive distinction).

McDowell & Huhn, _supra_ note 428 at 12-13.

pose of NLRB remedies is to dissipate the effects of the prohibited conduct, remedies which neither deprive the violator of the fruits of his illegal conduct nor make the victim whole have sometimes been considered punitive in nature.[437] Similarly, remedies of a purely deterent nature have been called punitive.[438] Since an unfair labor practice is not a crime, the Supreme Court has suggested that it is inappropriate for the board to compensate injuries allegedly suffered by the body politic.[439] And finally, in one case, the Supreme Court apparently believed that the unfair labor practice was probably not the operative cause of the activity the board sought to remedy. Consequently, the Court concluded that the remedy was punitive or confiscatory.[440]

Although judicial review of NLRB orders that allegedly go too far is thus necessarily limited, there is room for the courts to "modify"[441] these orders by simply striking out the objectionable portions. When the converse issue arises—a board order that allegedly does not go far enough—the reviewing and modifying powers of the courts are somewhat more circumscribed.

When the NLRB refuses to grant a remedy because it believes that it lacks statutory authority to do so, a question of law is raised over which the courts of appeals can and do exercise a relatively expansive review function.[442] If the court disagrees with the board's interpretation of the law, then the appropriate judicial response is apparently to remand the case to the board for it to decide, within the limits of its newly defined discretion, whether it will exercise the statutory power that the court has bestowed upon it.[443] Similarly, the Supreme Court has said that "when a reviewing court concludes that an agency invested with broad discretion to fashion remedies has apparently abused that discretion by omitting a remedy justified in the court's view by the factual circumstances, remand to the agency for reconsideration, and not enlargement of the agency order, is ordinarily the reviewing court's

---

[437] *See* Local 60, Carpenters v. NLRB, 365 U.S. 651, 655 (1961).

[438] *See* Republic Steel Corp. v. NLRB, 311 U.S. 7, 12 (1940).

[439] *Id.* at 10.

[440] *See* Local 60, Carpenters v. NLRB, 365 U.S. at 655-56.

[441] Section 10(f) gives the appropriate federal court of appeals the power to review Board orders and "to make and enter a decree enforcing, modifying, and enforcing as so modified, or setting aside in whole or in part the order of the Board." NLRA § 10(f), 29 U.S.C. § 160(f) (1976).

[442] For example, in Ex-Cell-O Corp., 185 N.L.R.B. 107 (1970), *enforced on other grounds,* 449 F.2d 1058 (D.C. Cir. 1971), the Board refused to advise an economic "make whole" remedy for employer bad faith bargaining on the grounds, *inter alia,* that it lacked the statutory authority to do so. 185 N.L.R.B. at 108-09. The District of Columbia Court of Appeals, on the other hand, engaged in a fairly exhaustive evaluation of this issue in the related case of IUE v. NLRB (Tiidee Products, Inc.), 426 F.2d 1243, 1251-53 (D.C. Cir. 1970), *cert. denied,* 400 U.S. 950 (1970).

[443] *See, e.g.,* IUE v. NLRB, 426 F.2d at 1253.

proper course."⁴⁴⁴ Affirmative modification by a court would thus appear to be appropriate only in "the exceptional situation in which crystal clear board error renders a remand an unnecessary formality."⁴⁴⁵

It is against this background that NLRB orders in the section 8(b)(1)(A) context will be viewed.

Cease and Desist Orders

The most common remedy for an unfair labor practice of any kind is, of course, the cease and desist order. Although the party charged with an unfair labor practice may have already completed or stopped its illegal conduct by the time the NLRB issues its order, how the board defines or describes what the guilty party is to "cease and desist" from is nevertheless an important issue. Board orders are not self-enforcing. If enforcement by a federal court of appeals is sought and obtained, the order of the board becomes the order of the court. The order can then be enforced, if necessary, through contempt proceedings. It goes without saying that the broader the original cease and desist order, the greater the likelihood of a subsequent contempt citation. Since what a union might be required to do to purge itself of contempt could far exceed anything the board could have originally required,⁴⁴⁶ the exact scope of the cease and desist order is a matter of some significance.

In the section 8(b)(1)(A) context, there are four general levels of conduct from which a union may be ordered to cease and desist. At the narrowest level, the union will simply be ordered to cease and desist from the specific conduct which has been found to restrain or coerce employees of a particular employer. For example, in one case the union was ordered to "cease and desist from . . . [t]hreatening any employee of Frontier Transportation Company or the family of such an employee with physical injury because that employee refuses to strike or honor said Union's picket line. . . ."⁴⁴⁷

In slightly broader terms, the union guilty of an unfair labor practice will also be ordered to "cease and desist from . . . *any like or related*

---

⁴⁴⁴ NLRB v. Food Store Employees Local 347, 417 U.S. 1, 10 (1974). If persistent, the Board usually will prevail. The *Tiidee* case is the classic confrontation over the "make whole" issue. On remand in *Tiidee,* the Board conceded its statutory *power,* but nevertheless again declared itself incapable of calculating such a remedy, ultimately forcing the court to acquiesce in the Board's refusal to grant additional relief. Tiidee Products, Inc., 194 N.L.R.B. 1234 (1972), *enforced,* 502 F.2d 349 (D.C. Cir. 1974), *cert. denied,* 421 U.S. 991 (1975).

⁴⁴⁵ 417 U.S. at 8.

⁴⁴⁶ *See* text accompanying notes 613-23, *infra.*

⁴⁴⁷ General Teamsters, Local 959 (Frontier Transportations Co.), 248 N.L.R.B. 743, 746 (1980).

manner [of] restraining or coercing employees in the exercise of the rights guaranteed them in Section 7 of the Act."[448] Cease and desist orders routinely use such language.

A third level of conduct from which a union may be ordered to cease and desist concerns the restraint and coercion, not only of the employees of the particular employer involved in the case, but also the employees of any employer. As one trial examiner explained it:

> Unless successive and unending consent court decrees, each assuring only one employer freedom from this type of unlawful tactic by this Union, are to be accorded no further substantive meaning, it is time that the Respondent be effectively enjoined from committing unfair labor practices of this kind with respect to any and all other employers situated within its geographic area of jurisdiction.[449]

Shortly after the Taft-Hartley Act amendments, a broad, "of any employer" kind of cease and desist order against a union was approved by the Supreme Court in *IBEW, Local 501 v. NLRB.*[450] In that case, the union had induced the employees of one subcontractor to strike. The union hoped to thereby cause the general contractor to stop doing business with another subcontractor, the one with whom the union had its primary dispute. This conduct is clearly declared illegal by section 8(b)(4)(A) of the amended NLRA and the NLRB ordered the union to cease and desist from inducing either the employees of this particular subcontractor or "any employer."[451] The union challenged the order as being too broad but the Court affirmed. It noted that to do otherwise would expose the primary employer to exactly the same kind of unlawful pressure from this union, albeit through other "comparable channels"[452]—namely, through anyone else who might also happen to be doing business with him directly or indirectly.[453]

Similar attempts by the NLRB to issue this kind of broad order in section 8(b)(1)(A) union violence cases were initially met with disfavor by the courts. In *Communications Workers v. NLRB,*[454] the Supreme Court explained that the union agents "were not found to have en-

---

[448] *Id.* (emphasis added).

[449] Teamsters Local 327 (Greer Stop Nut Co.), 160 N.L.R.B. 1919, 1923 (1966). In that case, however, the Board found the order to be inappropriate because the facts did not establish the necessary "proclivity" on the union's part to violate the act. *Id.* at 1920.

[450] 341 U.S. 694 (1951).

[451] *Id.* at 698, 705.

[452] *Id.* at 705-06.

[453] The court also suggested the same justification for a broad order in the case of a secondary boycott. In NLRB v. Brewery & Beer Distrib. Drivers Local 830, 281 F.2d 319 (3d Cir. 1960), the court suggested that "the danger of the occurrence of the prohibited conduct is much wider than inducements confined to employees of the specifically mentioned secondary employers." *Id.* at 323.

[454] 362 U.S. 479 (1960) (per curiam).

gaged in violations against the employees of any employer other than
Ohio Consolidated and we find neither justification nor necessity for
extending the coverage of the order generally by the inclusion therein
of the phrase 'any other employer.' "[455] The Court also explained that
the mere fact that employees loaned from other telephone companies
"were included within the ambit of petitioners' coercive acts plainly
does not evidence such a generalized scheme against all telephone
employers, for it was only the employment of such employees at the
struck plant that brought them within the scope of the union's activities."[456]

The Supreme Court has thus suggested that the "of any employer"
order is appropriate only when the circumstances or objectives of the
violence against the employees of one employer make it likely that
similar violence will be directed against the employees of other
employers unless restrained.

The classic example arose in *United Mine Workers, District 31 (M &
T Coal Co.)*,[457] in which the union was found guilty of assorted assaults,
threats, mass picketing, and the blocking of ingress and egress at the
mine sites of five different coal companies. The union was
simultaneously engaged in organizational efforts at four other mines,
and its ultimate goal was to organize all nonunion mines in the area.
The NLRB concluded that "in view of these facts, . . . we believe that
the conduct of the Respondents evidences . . . a generalized scheme
against all nonunion mines within the jurisdiction of District 31 which
can be remedied only by the entry of a broad order."[458] The court of
appeals agreed.[459] In sum, given the scope of the union's proven
misconduct (against the employees of five different employers) and its
ultimate objective (unionization of all the mines within its jurisdiction),
it was likely that similar violence against other employees would occur
unless it too was covered by the restraining order.

After *M & T Coal Co.*, the doctrine gradually evolved into one
whereby a likelihood of recurring violence is identified primarily by
reference to a somewhat broader concept of the union's so-called "proclivity" to engage in that particular kind of misconduct.[460] The

---

[455] *Id.* at 480.
[456] *Id.* at 481. *Accord* NLRB v. Taxicab Drivers Union Local 777, 340 F.2d 905, 909
(7th Cir. 1964); Highway Truck Drivers v. NLRB, 273 F.2d 815 (D.C. Cir. 1959).
[457] 129 N.L.R.B. 146 (1960), *enforced,* 299 F.2d 441 (D.C. Cir. 1962).
[458] *Id.* at 149.
[459] 299 F.2d at 444.
[460] *See, e.g.,* International Bhd. of Teamsters Local 327 (Det. Distrib. C.), 201 N.L.R.B.
787, 792 (1973); Teamsters Local 327 (Coca-Cola Bottling Works of Nashville), 184
N.L.R.B. 84, 96 (1970); Teamsters Local 327 (Hartmann Luggage Co.), 173 N.L.R.B.
1403, 1407 (1968), *remanded,* 419 F.2d 1282 (6th Cir. 1970); Teamsters Local 327 (Greer

necessary proclivity can be established by reference to prior cases of similar misconduct by the same union, or sometimes simply by reference to the outrageous facts of the case in which the broad order is being issued.[461] Where the prior violation had occurred some fifteen years earlier, however, the NLRB said that "in view of the length of time that has elapsed since the last previous Board adjudication of unlawful conduct,"[462] the broad order was not justified. Furthermore, the board has held that an administrative law judge cannot base a finding of proclivity on prior cease and desist orders enforced through consent decrees containing nonadmission clauses.[463]

In *NLRB v. Teamsters, Local 327*,[464] the sixth circuit generally sustained the NLRB's proclivity justification for cease and desist orders covering the employees of "any other employer,"[465] but cautioned that such orders would have to satisfy the normal requirements of specificity. The order in that case did not:

> First, this order is addressed to mortal human beings, yet it has no limitation in time. Second, the order is both too broad and too vague in relation to persons expected to obey it[466] (presumably on pain of contempt proceedings). Third, the order does not define the jurisdiction of Local 327 and thus it provides no means of defining the people for whom protection is sought.[467]

These requirements, however, have not posed any insurmountable obstacles to the board. The jurisdiction of the local union can usually be defined geographically with some degree of precision.[468] The board has also simply identified it as "the area in which Respondent Local purports to represent employees. . . ."[469] The "successors and

---

Stop Nut Co.), 160 N.L.R.B. 1919, 1923 (1966); *accord* Local 30, United Slate, Tile and Composition Roofers (Kitson Bros., Inc.), 228 N.L.R.B. 652, 653 (1977) (the word "proclivity" was not actually used, but the justification advanced for the issuance of a broad order was essentially the same).

[461] Unión Nacional de Trabajadores (Jacobs Constructors Co.), 219 N.L.R.B. 405, 411-12 (1975), *enforced,* 540 F.2d 1 (1st Cir. 1976), *cert. denied,* 429 U.S. 1039 (1977).

[462] Local 810, Steel Fabricators (Scales Air Compressor Corp.), 200 N.L.R.B. 575, 575 n.3 (1972).

[463] Teamsters Local 327 (Greer Stop Nut Co.), 160 N.L.R.B. 1919, 1920 (1966).

[464] 419 F.2d 1282, 1284 (6th Cir. 1970); *see also* NLRB v. Teamsters, Local 327, 432 F.2d 933 (6th Cir. 1970).

[465] 419 F.2d at 1283-84.

[466] The reference here is to the fact that the order went not only to the union and its agents but also to its "successors and assigns." *Id.* at 1283.

[467] *Id.*

[468] *See, e.g.,* International Bhd. of Teamsters Local 327 (Det. Distrib. Co.), 201 N.L.R.B. 787, 788 (1973); Unión de Tronquistas Local 901 (Hotel La Concha), 193 N.L.R.B. 591, 599 (1971); Teamsters Local 327 (Coca-Cola Bottling Works of Nashville), 184 N.L.R.B. 84 (1970).

[469] Local 30, United Slate, Tile and Composition Roofers (Kitson Bros., Inc.), 228 N.L.R.B. 652, 658 (1977).

assigns" language has been dropped from orders, although as one administrative law judge stated, "I cannot help but believe, . . . that the Sixth Circuit overlooked the limited meaning of 'successors and assigns' and its implicit presence in limited form anyway in enforcement orders, . . . [thus] making the change of little or no significance."[470] The requirement as to time has simply been ignored. As noted by one administrative law judge, "it seems to me that a time limitation is something too difficult to tailor in advance, but must be determined by the Respondent's future conduct."[471]

In the fourth and broadest kind of cease and desist order, the NLRB orders a union to cease and desist from restraining employees of the charging party (and of any other employers, if the facts warrant it), not only in the ways specifically named, but also in any other manner. Although broad orders of this kind are certainly not unique to section 8(b)(1)(A) violations, the courts have generally viewed them with caution.[472] In one case, for example, the District of Columbia Circuit Court of Appeals refused to enforce an order requiring the union to cease and desist from restraining or coercing employees in any manner. It felt that "peaceful, valid activities should not be inhibited by a cease and desist order which, though its purpose is to reach only illegal conduct, is framed so broadly as to cause petitioners to refrain from that which is legal for fear of violating the order or court decree enforcing it."[473] The board will nevertheless issue such an order under appropriate circumstances.

In the past, the NLRB seemed to focus on one of two somewhat overlapping criteria. In some cases, the board has predicated a broad order on the fact that the violation went "to the very heart of the Act."[474] Although this criteria was occasionally used in the section 8(b)(1)(A) union violence context,[475] the board has generally used the same test that it employs in evaluating the propriety of an "any employer" remedial order. That approach focuses more on the union's apparent disregard for statutory rights in general rather than on the rights being violated in the immediate case.[476] In *Hickmott Foods,*

[470] Unión de Tronquistas Local 901 (Hotel La Concha), 193 N.L.R.B. 591, 598 n.5 (1971).

[471] Teamsters Local 327 (Coca-Cola Bottling Works of Nashville), 184 N.L.R.B. 84, 96 n.14 (1970).

[472] *See generally* McDOWELL & HUHN, *supra* note 428 at 19-24.

[473] United Mine Workers v. NLRB, 299 F.2d 441, 445 (D.C. Cir. 1962).

[474] *See* Hickmott Foods, Inc., 242 N.L.R.B. 1357 (1979), and cases cited at 1357 n.3.

[475] *See, e.g.,* Pipeline Local 38 (Hancock-Northwest, J.V.), 247 N.L.R.B. 1250, 1263 (1980) (ALJ's decision); Centac Corp., 179 N.L.R.B. 313, 322 (1969).

[476] *See, e.g.,* Pipeline Local 38 (Hancock-Northwest, J.V.), 247 N.L.R.B. 1250, 1252 (1980), *enforced,* 108 L.R.R.M. 2816 (D.C. Cir. 1981).

Inc.,[477] the board recently abandoned the "heart of the act" analysis altogether—in violence cases and elsewhere. It stated that an "in any manner" cease and desist order would be warranted "only when a respondent is shown to have a proclivity to violate the act, or has engaged in such egregious or widespread misconduct as to demonstrate a general disregard for the employees' fundamental statutory rights."[478] Thus, just as an "any other employer" order can be justified by reference to the probability of the union expanding the scope of its victims, the "in any other manner" order has been justified by reference to the probability of the union expanding the scope or nature of its misconduct.[479] Evidence of the latter proclivity can be found in the seriousness and extent of the proven misconduct, in the immediate case or in other cases.[480] The board, however, has held that neither settlement agreements[481] nor administrative law judge decisions to which exceptions are not taken[482] can be relied on as evidence of a proclivity to violate the act.

Posting Notices

In addition to requiring that a respondent cease and desist from further violations of the NLRA (however broadly defined they may be), NLRB orders also traditionally require that signed notices of compliance be posted at appropriate places. This includes the union's "business office and meeting halls . . . in conspicuous places, including all places where notices to members are customarily posted."[483] Fur-

---

[477] 242 N.L.R.B. 1357 (1979).

[478] *Id.* Thus, in Local Lodge 5, Int'l Bhd. of Boilermakers (Regor Constr. Co.), 249 N.L.R.B. 840 (1980), even though the administrative law judge viewed the union violence as "serious and striking at the heart of the act," *id.* at 851, he refused to issue a broad order because the prior cases involved either the International Union or other locals, and he felt that those violations did not show a proclivity for violence by this particular local.

[479] *See* Teamsters Local 327 (Hartmann Luggage Co.), 173 N.L.R.B. 1403 n.1 (1968), (broad order denied because facts of the case did not rise to the level required by this test), *remanded on other grounds,* 419 F.2d 1282 (6th Cir. 1970).

[480] In Hickmott Foods, Inc., 242 N.L.R.B. 1357 (1979), the Board noted that where "violations of the Act are proved and it can be further shown that a respondent, either previous to or concurrently with the [violations thus proved], engaged in other severe conduct violative of [the Act], a broader order may be warranted." *Id.* at 1357.

[481] Local 248, Meat & Allied Food Workers (Milwaukee Independent Meat Packers Ass'n), *enforced,* 84 Lab. Cas. (CCH) ¶ 10826 (7th Cir. 1978), 222 N.L.R.B. 1023 (1976) (broad order nevertheless justified in light "of the extensive pattern of serious strike-associated misconduct and the Respondent's failure to take any serious consequential steps to stop or curtail such activity. . . ."); Local 612, Int'l Bhd. of Teamsters (Deaton Truck Line, Inc.), 146 N.L.R.B. 498, 506 (1964).

[482] Broadway Hosp., Inc., 244 N.L.R.B. 341, 341 n.7 (1979).

[483] *See, e.g.,* General Teamsters Local 959 (Frontier Transp. Co.), 248 N.L.R.B. 743, 746 (1980).

thermore, the union is required to supply copies for the company to post on its employee bulletin boards, provided the "company is willing to post them."[484] On the other hand, a broader dissemination of the union's *mea culpa* is sometimes required. When, for example, the union violence has had a pervasive effect on a widely dispersed group of employees, the board has required the union to mail copies of its notice either to all of its members or to all of the employees of the affected employers.[485]

An additional requirement that the union arrange to have its notice published in a newspaper of general circulation has had a more difficult time gaining acceptance.[486] In *NLRB v. Unión Nacional de Trabajadores*,[487] however, the court sustained both mailing and publication requirements on the following basis:

> The Board clearly has the power to fashion its orders in a manner that will insure that their contents are communicated to all employees whose rights are affected. Widespread communication is aimed at counteracting the coercive effects of the § 8(b)(1)(A) violations. . . . Here, where many of the victims of the unlawful Union activities were not Union members, the remedy of ordering merely that copies of the notices be posted at the Union offices and meeting places would plainly be inadequate. The mailing requirement is an appropriate device to help insure that the victims of the Union's wrongdoing learn of the Board's actions.
>
> The further requirement that the notices be published in all newspapers of general circulation helps insure that all interested persons will receive notice. . . . Moreover, where the violations are flagrant and repeated, the publication order has the salutary effect of neutralizing the frustrating effects of persistent illegal activity by letting in "a warming wind of information and, more important, reassurance."[488]

Finally, where the perpetrator of the violence is a particular union official, the board has at times specifically required him to sign the notices.[489]

---

[484] *Id.*

[485] *See, e.g.,* Pipeline Local 38 (Hancock-Northwest, J.V.), 247 N.L.R.B. 1250 (1980), *enforced,* 108 L.R.R.M. 2816 (D.C. Cir. 1981); Local 248, Meat & Allied Food Workers (Milwaukee Indep. Meat Packers Assoc.), *enforced,* 84 Lab. Cas. (CCH) ¶ 10826 (7th Cir. 1978), 222 N.L.R.B. 1023 (1976); International Bhd. of Teamsters Local 327 (Det Distrib. Co.), 201 N.L.R.B. 787 (1973); Teamsters Local 327 (Whale, Inc.), 178 N.L.R.B. 422 (1969), *enforced in part,* 432 F.2d 933 (6th Cir. 1970).

[486] The following cases rejected the publication remedy: United Mine Workers v. NLRB, 299 F.2d 441, 445 (D.C. Cir. 1962); Truck Drivers Local 705 (Associated Transp., Inc.), 209 N.L.R.B. 292 (1974), *enforced,* 532 F.2d 1169 (7th Cir.), *cert. denied,* 429 U.S. 1022 (1976); Teamsters Local 327 (Coca-Cola Bottling Works of Nashville), 184 N.L.R.B. 84, 96 (1970); Teamsters Local 327 (Whale, Inc.), 178 N.L.R.B. 422, 427 (1969), *enforced in part,* 432 F.2d 933 (6th Cir. 1970).

[487] 540 F.2d 1 (1st Cir. 1976), *cert. denied,* 429 U.S. 1039 (1977).

[488] 540 F.2d at 11-12.

[489] *See, e.g.,* Teamsters Local 695 (Wisconsin Supply Corp.), 204 N.L.R.B. 866 (1973); General Truckdrivers, Local 5 (Ryder Truck Lines, Inc.), 161 N.L.R.B. 493, 504 (1966), *enforced,* 389 F.2d 757 (5th Cir. 1968).

Remedies Which Affect the Union's Bargaining Status

A union that has been found guilty of section 8(b)(1)(A) violence may find its status as a bargaining representative affected in a variety of ways. First, if the violence occurred during the pendency of a representation election which the union won, the NLRB may refuse to certify the union as the winner and order a new election. The board will take this action in the exercise of its section 9 powers to regulate the election process, whenever the conduct at issue has violated the so-called "laboratory conditions." Conduct violates the laboratory conditions when it interferes with the free and untrammeled choice of the employees in the selection of a bargaining representative, whether or not such conduct rises to the level of an unfair labor practice.[490] Of course, if the conduct does in fact restrain or coerce employees in the exercise of their section 7 rights, that constitutes grounds for setting aside the election almost as a matter of course.[491]

The matter becomes a bit more complicated, however, when both the employer and the union engage in unfair labor practices or other disruptive conduct in an election. In a nutshell, the law is this: if the employer's unfair labor practices have so undermined the union's majority strength and so tainted the atmosphere with coercion that a fair and free election (or reelection) is no longer possible, then the board may simply order the employer to bargain with the union rather than proceed with an election (or reelection); however, if the union's acts of violence and intimidation outweigh the employer's unfair labor practices, then the board may withhold the issuance of a bargaining order in favor of that union. The full meaning and significance of this legal principle can be understood only against its historical background.

In *Herbert Bernstein (d/b/a Laura Modes Co.),*[492] a union claiming to represent a majority of employees demanded that the employer recognize and bargain with it. The employer requested a "few days" for consultation with its attorney, and the union agreed. In the meantime, the employer engaged in illegal interrogation of employees, threatened reprisals if the employees continued their support of the union, and evidenced an intent to *never* recognize or bargain with the union. Subsequently, several union agents invaded the employer's premises, viciously assaulted him, and "pushed around" a female office employee. Section 8(b)(1)(A) charges were brought against the union and it agreed to a settlement. The employer, however, was found guilty of illegal restraint, interference, and coercion under section 8(a)(1).

---

[490] *See* General Shoe Corp., 77 N.L.R.B. 124, 126 (1948).

[491] *See* Sindicato Puertorriqueno de Trabajadores (Cayey Indus., Inc.), 184 N.L.R.B. 538, 541 (1970).

[492] 144 N.L.R.B. 1592 (1963).

The employer was also found guilty of failure to recognize and bargain with the union in violation of section 8(a)(5) because it lacked a good faith doubt of the union's majority status. At the time of the case, the normal remedy for a section 8(a)(5) violation of this kind would have been an affirmative order requiring the employer to recognize and bargain with the union. In the words of the NLRB:

> We do not, however, deem it appropriate to give the Charging Union the benefit of our normal affirmative bargaining order in the circumstances of this case. For we cannot, in good conscience, disregard the fact that . . . the Union evidenced a total disinterest in enforcing its representation rights through the peaceful legal process provided by the Act in that it resorted to and/or encouraged the use of violent tactics to compel their grant. . . . We recognize of course that the employees' right to choose the Union as their representative survives the Union's misconduct. But we believe it will not prejudice the employees unduly to ask that they demonstrate their desires anew in an atmosphere free of any possible trace of coercion.[493]

The board thus withheld its bargaining order until the union could establish its majority status through a board-conducted election.

In the context of its origin, the *Laura Modes* doctrine is relatively uncomplicated. If it is possible that a union obtained the authorization cards supporting its claim of majority status by violence or threats of violence, or if it is possible that the union's violence caused previously consenting employees to change their minds about representation, then court-ordered bargaining is unwarranted. Despite the lack of a subjective good faith doubt on the employer's part about the union's majority status, it makes sense to withhold the benefit of a bargaining order from such a union and instead require it to establish its claim through the preferred and more accurate processes of an NLRB-conducted election. That presupposes, of course, that the employer's unfair labor practices have not been so extensive as to make a fair and free election impossible. Where that occurs, an exception was soon recognized. The Second Circuit Court of Appeals put it this way:

> It is exceedingly hard to believe that Congress meant to authorize the Board to require bargaining with a union having a bare card-count majority which has attempted to increase this or to enforce its claim to representation by hitting other employees or the employer on the head. . . . *The only cases where arguably a union's resort to serious violence to enforce its demands might be disregarded would be when the employer's conduct has rendered a fair election impossible.*[494]

That exception to the *Laura Modes* defense has become very important because of the Supreme Court's subsequent decision on the pro-

---

[493] *Id.* at 1596.
[494] NLRB v. United Mineral & Chem. Corp., 391 F.2d 829, 841 (2d Cir. 1968) (emphasis added).

priety of NLRB bargaining orders generally. In *Linden Lumber Div., Summer & Co. v. NLRB*[495] the Supreme Court held that an employer's section 8(a)(5) duty to recognize and bargain with a union is not activated by a mere showing that the union possesses authorization cards from a majority of the employer's employees, and that a bargaining order is normally appropriate only under the circumstances previously spelled out by the Court in *NLRB v. Gissel Packing Company.*[496] In *Gissel,* the Court held that when an employer engaged in unfair labor practices that have a tendency to undermine the union's majority strength *and make the election or new election impossible,* the board may issue a bargaining order as a remedy to those unfair labor practices.[497] This, however, creates an anomaly. Since the *Laura Modes* defense to a bargaining order apparently does *not* apply where the employer has committed unfair labor practices of this kind, and since under *Gissel* a bargaining order will be issued only where these kinds of unfair labor practices have occurred, it would appear that the *Laura Modes* defense has no further application or vitality in a bargaining order case of this kind.

However, the *Laura Modes* defense continues to be recognized as a defense to a *Gissel* bargaining order, though the rationale for its continued application is a bit strained. In the typical *Gissel* bargaining situation, an employer has engaged in unfair labor practices which make a fair and free election impossible. That unfortunate state of affairs is certainly not corrected by the fact that the union has also engaged in coercive misconduct. As the NLRB stated in *Donelson Packing Co.*:[498]

> Union unfair labor practices arising in the same situation [where the employer has also engaged in them] can hardly be said to detract from the coercive atmosphere in which an election must be run. In the minds of prospective voters, misdeeds by competing parties do not erase or neutralize each other, as an alkali neutralizes an acid. Indeed, such conduct by a union, where found, compounds rather than nullifies employer misconduct, and minimizes rather than improves the likelihood that an election will produce a free and untrammeled employee choice.[499]

For this reason the approach used by the board in applying the *Laura Modes* defense in a *Gissel* bargaining order context "is one of a general balancing of the equities rather than a calibrated measuring of the im-

[495] 419 U.S. 301 (1974).
[496] 395 U.S. 575 (1969).
[497] *Id.* at 614. *See generally,* Note, *The Gissel Bargaining Order, the NLRB, and the Courts of Appeals: Should the Supreme Court Take a Second Look?,* 32 S.C. L. REV. 399 (1980).
[498] 220 N.L.R.B. 1043 (1975), *enforced,* 569 F.2d 430 (6th Cir. 1978).
[499] *Id.* at 1060.

pact upon voters, point and counterpoint, of the various acts of coercion and interference which have occurred on all sides."[500] There is, of course, no fixed formula for determining exactly where this "balance of equities" should be struck. The presumption, however, seems to be against the employer. The more serious his unfair labor practices, the less likely it is that the NLRB will view the case as one in which the "extraordinary and unusual" *Laura Modes* defense will be recognized.[501] Moreover, the union misconduct itself must at least be actionable under section 8(b)(1)(A)[502] and also be of a fairly egregious nature before it will trigger the application of the *Laura Modes* defense. For example, in *Donovan v. NLRB*,[503] both the board and the Second Circuit Court of Appeals held that a bargaining order should be issued even though the union and its agents had engaged in the following misconduct:

> forcibly entering the employer's premises; following nonstriking employees to and from work; repeatedly threatening them with physical harm and property damage; calling in a bomb scare to the employer's nursing home; mass picketing, blocking ingress and egress of nonstrikers, and banging on cars; kicking a car, cursing and threatening management; attempting to run a company representative off the road; throwing small rocks and pebbles at a supervisor's car; assaulting a nonstriker and damaging his property; threatening, following, and harassing management representatives attempting to enter and leave the facility; and even before the strike, repeatedly attempting to enter the nursing home without permission.[504]

On the other hand, in *NLRB v. United Mineral & Chemical Corp.*,[505] there were numerous threats of physical violence. An automobile carrying nonstriking employees was stoned; several of these employees were removed from cars and beaten up. Stones and

---

[500] *Id.*

[501] General Iron Corp., 224 N.L.R.B. 1180, 1194 (1976) (in addition to unfair labor practices, the employer "engaged in further provocations by resorting to gross physical violence against Local 455 officials.").

[502] Delchamps, Inc., 244 N.L.R.B. 366, 378 n.17 (1979), *enforced,* 653 F.2d 225 (5th Cir. 1981).

[503] 520 F.2d 1316 (2d Cir. 1975), *cert. denied,* 423 U.S. 1053 (1976).

[504] The trial examiner summarized these forms of misconduct in General Iron Corp., 224 N.L.R.B. 1180, 1195 (1976). *See also* Pace Oldsmobile, Inc., 256 N.L.R.B. No. 111 (1981); Martin Arsham Sewing Co., 244 N.L.R.B. 918 (1979); International Union of Operating Eng'rs (Oklahoma Osteopathic Hosp.), 238 N.L.R.B. 1113, 1114 n.5 (1978), *enforced,* 618 F.2d 633 (10th Cir. 1980); Philadelphia Ambulance Serv., Inc., 238 N.L.R.B. 1070 n.6 (1978); Maywood Plant of Grede Plastics, 235 N.L.R.B. 363, 363-66 (1978), *enforced in part,* 628 F.2d 1 (D.C. Cir. 1980); Paramount Gen. Hosp., Inc., 223 N.L.R.B. 1017 (1976), *enforced,* 81 Lab. Cas. (CCH) ¶ 13305 (D.C. Cir. 1977); Triumph Army Center, 222 N.L.R.B. 627, 633 (1976), *enforced,* 571 F.2d 462 (9th Cir. 1978); Black Angus of Lauderhill, 213 N.L.R.B. 425, 434 (1974); Federal Prescription Serv., Inc., 203 N.L.R.B. 975, 999 (1973), *enforced in part,* 86 L.R.R.M. 2185 (8th Cir. 1974).

[505] 391 F.2d 829 (2d Cir. 1968).

tomatoes were thrown, and an assault on the owner resulted in a fractured leg and his incapacitation for five months. This union misconduct was deemed serious enough to warrant the withholding of a bargaining order.[506]

Beyond comparing the seriousness of the union's misconduct with that of the employer in deciding whether to issue a bargaining order in the face of a *Laura Modes* defense, the NLRB also looks for evidence of the union's general willingness to use the orderly processes of the law. In *United Mineral & Chemical Corp.,*[507] for example, the board noted that "the Union evidenced a total disinterest in enforcing its representation rights through the peaceful legal process provided by the Act in that it resorted to and/or encouraged the use of violent tactics to compel their grant."[508] Similarly, in *Joseph H. Bliss,*[509] the trial examiner noted that the record "presents a sordid picture of disregard of the law, violence, and misconduct, and their failure to compel or seek recognition by following through on the normal procedures of Board action available to them under the law."[510]

Finally, although the "agency" requirement obviously must be satisfied in order for there to be a section 8(b)(1)(A) violation, the NLRB seems to require an even higher degree of official union participation in the *Laura Modes* setting. In *Highland Plastics, Inc.,*[511] the administrative law judge noted that "the direct participation of Union officials in violent acts or, at the very least, their presence and acquies[c]ence when significant violence occurs is an essential factor to justify the extraordinary remedy of withholding an otherwise appropriate bargaining order."[512]

Those, then, are the factors the NLRB and the courts take into account in applying the *Laura Modes* defense in the *Gissel* bargaining order context—*i.e.,* where union violence is relied on as a grounds for denying that particular remedy for employer unfair labor practices. The *Laura Modes* doctrine, however, also recognizes union violence as a possible defense to a straightforward "refusal to bargain" claim.[513] In

---

[506] *Id.* at 839 n.15 *See also* NLRB v. World Carpets, 463 F.2d 57 (2d Cir. 1972).

[507] 155 N.L.R.B. 1390 (1965), *enforced,* 391 F.2d 829 (2d Cir. 1968).

[508] *Id.* at 1396.

[509] 174 N.L.R.B. 737 (1969).

[510] *Id.* at 741. *See also* International Union of Operating Eng'rs Local 948 (Oklahoma Osteopathic Hosp.), 238 N.L.R.B. 1113, 1121-22 (1978), *enforced,* 618 F.2d 633 (10th Cir. 1980); Pacific Abrasive Supply Co., 182 N.L.R.B. 329, 331 (1970).

[511] 256 N.L.R.B. 146 (1981).

[512] *Id.* at 163.

[513] In the *Gissel* context, there is no underlying section 8(a)(5) refusal-to-bargain violation, and the bargaining order is simply a remedy for the employer's section 8(a)(1) (restraint, interference, and coercion of employees) and section 8(a)(3)(discrimination) violations. Linden Lumber Div., Summer & Co. v. NLRB, 419 U.S. 301 (1974). A non-

Unión Nacional de Trabajadores,[514] for example, the union had won the election and had been certified as the collective bargaining representative. But negotiations between the union and the employer were marked with threats and acts of violence by the union. The employer refused to meet further with the union until the violence ended. Assurances were given that it would not recur. Subsequently, the employer was charged with an illegal refusal to bargain. Relying on the *Laura Modes* doctrine, the board held that the refusal was justified. The board found that "the record clearly establishes that . . . the Union engaged in violence and made threats which were unprovoked, pervasive in character, and destructive of an harmonious bargaining relationship. We would not expect or require an employer to sit down and bargain with a union guilty of such misconduct absent adequate assurances against continuation thereof."[515] Again, however, the union violence must be fairly egregious before it will operate as a defense to a section 8(a)(5) refusal-to-bargain charge.[516]

In *Homer Laughlin China,*[517] another section 8(b)(1)(A) remedy affecting the bargaining status of an incumbent union was rejected. The employer argued for an exception to the "contract bar" doctrine:[518] if the contracting union has been found guilty of violence, then its contract with the employer should not be recognized as a bar to holding a decertification election. The trial examiner, however, balanced the "minor" nature of the union violence against the general statutory policy of promoting stability in bargaining relationsips reflected in the "contract bar doctrine." He concluded that an excep-

---

Gissel bargaining order may, however, also be issued where an employer clearly does have a section 8(a)(5) bargaining duty which has been breached, subject, of course, to the availability of the *Laura Modes* defense.

[514] 219 N.L.R.B. 862 (1975), *enforced in part,* 540 F.2d 1 (1st Cir. 1976), *cert. denied,* 429 U.S. 1039 (1977).

[515] *Id.* at 863. *See also* Broadway Hosp., Inc., 244 N.L.R.B. 341, 355 (1979); Dow Chem. Co., 216 N.L.R.B. 82 (1975); Allou Distrib., Inc., 201 N.L.R.B. 47 (1973) (employer illegally withdrew recognition from incumbent union, refused to bargain, and caused a decertification petition to be filed; but because of the union's own violations of section 8(b)(1)(A) in trying to coerce employees to withdraw the petition, the Board opted to order an election rather than issue a bargaining order against the employer).

[516] The Board also refused to recognize the *Laura Modes* defense in the following cases: Condon Transp., Inc., 211 N.L.R.B. 297, 303 (1974); J.C. Penney Co., 205 N.L.R.B. 1043, 1047 (1973), *enforced,* 86 L.R.R.M. 2152 (3d Cir. 1974); Ramona's Mexican Food Prod., Inc., 203 N.L.R.B. 663, 685 (1973), *enforced,* 531 F.2d 390 (9th Cir. 1975); Quintree Distributors, Inc., 198 N.L.R.B. 390, 404-05 (1972).

[517] International Bhd. of Pottery Workers (Homer Laughlin China, Inc.), 217 N.L.R.B. 25 (1975).

[518] Under this doctrine, "the Board will dismiss as untimely an election petition which is filed during the term of a collective bargaining agreement (having a definite termination date) which has a duration less than three years, or which is filed during the first three years of an agreement of longer fixed duration." R.GORMAN, LABOR LAW 54 (1976).

tion was not warranted under the facts of the case.[519] Nevertheless, the possibility is left open that such a remedy might indeed be appropriate in cases of more serious union violence.

That possibility is certainly suggested by the extreme action taken by the NLRB against the infamous *Unión Nacional de Trabajadores*. In the *Carborundum Company* case,[520] as a part of its remedial order against extensive and serious violence by this union, the board ordered that the union be decertified as the collective bargaining representative. The board further denied it the right to even invoke the statutory processes in aid of its demand for renewed recognition until the coercive effects of its violence were dissipated and another election was held. The factual predicate of this particular remedy was the union's total disregard for the peaceful processes of the statute and the board's authority in enforcing them, the union's use of violent self-help measures, and the resulting destruction of any hope of constructive bargaining or effective representation by such a union.[521] In short, it seems that the board was simply outraged at the union's abuse of its certification status and was determined to revoke it.

On appeal, that part of the remedy was allowed to stand, but only because the first circuit found that it lacked jurisdiction to directly review a decertification order.[522] The court did, however, proffer some gratuitous comments about the general propriety of this kind of order. Noting the extreme importance of the majority's right to be represented by the union duly selected by them in a prior NLRB-conducted election, the court suggested that "a decertification order is an extreme measure and should be entered only when the Board has

---

[519] 217 N.L.R.B. at 29.

[520] Unión Nacional de Trabajadores (Carborundum Co.), 219 N.L.R.B. 862 (1975), *enforced in part,* 540 F.2d 1 (1st Cir. 1976), *cert. denied,* 429 U.S. 1039 (1977).

[521] The Board suggested that this union:

has evinced an intent to bypass the peaceful methods of collective bargaining contemplated in the Act. . . . It has consistently exhibited an utter disregard for the orderly and lawful processes available under the Act, and has instead deliberately resorted to self-help through violence. This Union . . . evidence[s] a total disinterest in furthering the Act's policies of promoting collective bargaining and industrial peace. Indeed, it has infected the bargaining process.

While we recognize the importance of the right of employees to be represented by their duly selected bargaining representative, we cannot continue to certify as a qualified bargaining representative a labor organization such as the Respondent Union which does not lawfully pursue its representation rights and is openly defiant of the authority of the Board and the teaching and purposes of the Act. Due to the atmosphere of fear and coercion generated by the Union's unlawful conduct, no constructive bargaining on behalf of the employees it represents is feasible. Thus, this [u]nion has corrupted and frustrated the representative scheme of bargaining envisaged by the Act.

219 N.L.R.B. at 863-64.

[522] 540 F.2d at 12-13.

first demonstrated that there are no equally effective alternative means of promoting the objectives of the Act."[523] More specifically, the court suggested that if the issue were to arise again, the board should perhaps be more analytical in its approach:

> First, it should consider the effect of the Union's misconduct *at the Carborundum plant* on the operation of the representational and collective bargaining processes. If it finds that constructive bargaining is not feasible, it should then consider whether the objectives of the Act could be promoted equally well either by an order excusing the employer of his bargaining obligations until the Union has provided adequate assurances that the misconduct will not recur or by normal § 8(b)(1)(A) remedies. At this point, it will be proper to consider the evidence of the Union proclivity for unlawful conduct since it is relevant as to the likelihood that less drastic measures will be effective. We emphasize that, because of the important employee interests that are at stake the focus should be on promoting peaceful collective bargaining and not on fashioning sanctions to deter Union misconduct. We recognize that the two may often be hard to separate.[524]

The circumstances under which decertification might be an appropriate remedy for section 8(b)(1)(A) violations, and the analytical framework for dealing with that issue, have not, however, been litigated to any further extent.

Back Pay Awards

In *Phelps Dodge Corp. v. NLRB*,[525] the Supreme Court suggested that "making the workers whole for losses suffered on account of an unfair labor practice is part of the vindication of the public policy which the Board enforces."[526] Nevertheless, the NLRB and the courts have always recognized some limits on the kinds of monetary awards that the board, as an administrative agency, is empowered to order. In the section 8(b)(1)(A) context, the board has consistently refused to order unions to compensate employees who have incurred hospital or medical expenses as a result of union violence.[527] It has likewise refused to order monetary awards covering union damage to company property and equipment.[528] This refusal is apparently consistent with legislative history which suggests that the board was not intended to

---

[523] *Id.* at 13.
[524] *Id.* at 15 (Emphasis in the original.)
[525] 313 U.S. 177 (1941).
[526] *Id.* at 197.
[527] Local 612, Int'l Bhd. of Teamsters (Deaton Truck Line, Inc.), 146 N.L.R.B. 498, 506 n.12 (1964), Operating Eng'rs Local 513 (Long Constr. Co.), 145 N.L.R.B. 554, 562-63 (1963).
[528] Local 30, United Slate, Tile and Composition Roofers (Associated Builders & Contractors, Inc.), 227 N.L.R.B. 1444 (1977).

have the general power to award damages in the conventional or common-law sense of the word; remedies of that kind were left to the discretion of the courts.[529] Indeed, in listing the remedies that would be available for a section 8(b)(1)(A) violation, Congressman Landis specifically referred to a "possible *suit* for damages"[530]—thus suggesting a judicial rather than an administrative source of the particular remedy.

The impropriety of back pay awards, however, is not so clear. That award consists of back pay to employees who have lost work because of the union's violent misconduct—either because of a disabling injury or the simple inability of the employee to get into the plant. Despite the strong and cogently reasoned dissents of several NLRB members over the years, the board has consistently refused to grant such relief.[531] The courts of appeals have, sometimes reluctantly, acquiesced in this policy.[532] The board's reasons for the policy warrant careful scrutiny, because this is one remedy, unlike those discussed above, that is likely to be taken seriously by unions bent on violating the act.

---

[529] *See* LEGIS. HIST. LMRA at 1371; National Maritime Union (Texas Co.), 78 N.L.R.B. 971, 989-90 (1948), *enforced,* 175 F.2d 686 (2d Cir. 1949), *cert. denied,* 338 U.S. 954 (1950), *overruled on other grounds,* 119 N.L.R.B. 307, 308 n.3 (1957).

[530] LEGIS. HIST. LMRA at 905 (Emphasis added.)

[531] Unión Nacional de Trabajadores (Macal Container Corp.), 219 N.L.R.B. 429, 430 (1975), *enforced,* 540 F.2d 1 (1st Cir. 1976), *cert. denied,* 429 U.S. 1039 (1977); Unión Nacional de Trabajadores (Catalytic Indus. Maint. Co.), 219 N.L.R.B. 414 (1975), *enforced,* 540 F.2d 1 (1st Cir. 1976), *cert. denied,* 429 U.S. 1039 (1977); Unión Nacional de Trabajadores (Jacobs Constr. Co.), 219 N.L.R.B. 405 (1975), *enforced,* 540 F.2d 1 (1st Cir. 1976), *cert. denied,* 429 U.S. 1039 (1977); Unión de Tronquistas Local 901 (Lock Joint Pipe & Co.), 202 N.L.R.B. 399 (1973); Local 235, Lithographers Union (Henry Wurst, Inc.), 187 N.L.R.B. 490, 491 n.5 (1970); United Steelworkers (Inspiration Consol. Copper Co.), 174 N.L.R.B. 189 (1969); UMW (Blue Diamond Coal Co.), 143 N.L.R.B. 795 (1963); Local 983, United Bhd. of Carpenters (Burke Co.), 115 N.L.R.B. 1123 (1956); UMW, District 31 (Bitner Fuel Co.), 92 N.L.R.B. 953, 955 n.5 (1950), *enforced,* 190 F.2d 251 (4th Cir. 1951); UMW (West Ky. Coal Co.), 92 N.L.R.B. 916, 921 (1950), *enforced,* 195 F.2d 961 (6th Cir.), *cert. denied,* 344 U.S. 920 (1952); Local 1150, United Elec. Workers (Cory Corp.), 84 N.L.R.B. 972, 1014 (1949); United Furniture Workers Local 472 (Colonial Hardwood Flooring Co.), 84 N.L.R.B. 563, 565 (1949); International Union, UAW (North Elec. Mfg. Co.), 84 N.L.R.B. 136, 157 (1949).

[532] Drobena v. NLRB, 612 F.2d 1095, 1098 (8th Cir. 1980), ("It is not too much to say that the members of this panel of this court do not think highly of the Board's policy that has been described as that policy applies to the alleged facts of this case"), *cert. denied,* 449 U.S. 821 (1980); United Ass'n of Journeymen of Plumbing v. NLRB, 553 F.2d 1202, 1205-06 (9th Cir. 1977); NLRB v. Oil Workers Union, 476 F.2d 1031, 1037 (1st Cir. 1973); National Cash Register Co. v. NLRB, 466 F.2d 945, 966 (6th Cir.) ("[W]e entertain doubts about the validity of the *Colonial Hardwood* rule. . . ."), *cert. denied,* 410 U.S. 966 (1972). In UAW v. Russell, 356 U.S. 634, 641 n.5 (1958), the Supreme Court noted the Board's policy and acknowledged petitioner's argument that the Court's more recent decisions mandating broad remedial relief for unfair labor practices superceded the policy, but found it unnecessary to pass on the issue in that case.

Initially the NLRB took the position that it simply lacked the statutory power to award back pay to employees who lost work because of union violence. In the first case in which the matter was raised, the trial examiner treated it as merely another claim for "money damages," which Congress did not give the board the power to assess.[533] Clearly, as is implicit in the wording of the statute itself, an unqualified characterization of back pay in those terms is unwarranted.

Accordingly, the NLRB predicated its "lack of power" argument on a slightly narrower basis. Section 10(c) of the statute authorizes the board to order parties who have been found guilty of an unfair labor practice "to take such affirmative action including reinstatement of employees with . . . back pay, as will effectuate the policies of this Subchapter: *Provided,* that where an order directs reinstatement of an employee, back pay may be required of the employer or labor organization, as the case may be, responsible for the discrimination suffered by him. . . ."[534] From this language the board concluded that a back pay award was appropriate *only* when an employee had been illegally discharged and was being reinstated, and that a union was liable for such back pay only when that union had *caused* the discharge in violation of section 8(b)(2).[535] By necessary implication, a back pay award against a union was not authorized when the loss of work was merely the result of a section 8(b)(1)(A) violation rather than a union-induced discharge.[536]

Such a literal and narrow reading of section 10(c) was grossly inconsistent with both its own and the Supreme Court's prior decision in *Phelps Dodge Corp. v. NLRB.*[537] In *Phelps,* the NLRB had required the company to hire and make whole for their loss of earnings persons whom the company had discriminatorily refused to hire. The company argued that a literal reading of the statute authorized a back pay order only in conjunction with a reinstatement order. Since the persons in question had never been employed by the company, the make whole remedy was inappropriate. The Supreme Court rejected this interpretation:

> To attribute such a function to the participal phrase introduced by "including" is to shrivel a versatile principle to an illustrative application. We

---

[533] International Union, UAW (North Elec. Mfg. Co.), 84 N.L.R.B. 136, 157 (1949).

[534] NLRA § 10(c), 29 U.S.C. § 160(c)(1976).

[535] NLRA § 8(b)(2), 29 U.S.C. § 158(b)(2)(1976). This section prohibits a union from causing or attempting to cause an employer to discriminatorily encourage or discourage union activity in violation of section 8(a)(3).

[536] *See* United Furniture Workers Local 472 (Colonial Hardwood Flooring Co.), 84 N.L.R.B. 563, 565-66 (1949).

[537] 313 U.S. 177 (1941).

find no justification whatever for attributing to Congress such a casuistic withdrawal of the authority which, but for the illustration, it clearly has given the Board. The word "including" does not lend itself to such destructive significance.[538]

The same kind of narrow reading of section 10(c) was the basis of the NLRB's asserted lack of power to award back pay as a remedy for section 8(b)(1)(A) violence cases in *West Kentucky Coal.*[539] Member Reynolds registered the first of several strong dissents to this policy. He argued that the board had the broad power to "take whatever affirmative action it believes will effectuate the policies of the Act."[540] That power included a back pay award against a union that "through the exercise of illegal coercive tactics which rendered civil authority helpless, caused a temporary hiatus in the tenure of employment of the employees . . . thereby causing them a loss in pay."[541] On the question of the board's power to grant such relief, Member Reynolds clearly seems correct. Section 10(c) specifically authorizes back pay as the obvious ancillary to a reinstatement order. Furthermore, the broader concept of "affirmative action" would also seem to authorize the back pay remedy in other situations.

---

[538] *Id.* at 189. Subsequently, in Radio Officers v. NLRB, 347 U.S. 17 (1954), the Supreme Court made clear that a reinstatement order is not a precondition to the award of back pay against a union. In *Radio Officers,* a union had caused the employer not to hire someone, and only the union was charged with an unfair labor practice. The union was found guilty and ordered to reimburse the person for the wages he would have received but for the unfair labor practice. Since the employer was not joined in the complaint, no reinstatement order was issued. In response to the union's argument that back pay was available only as an incident to a reinstatement order, the Supreme Court stated that the authority conferred by section 10(c) was:

> not to limit, but merely to illustrate, the general grant of power to award affirmative relief. . . . The purpose of Congress . . . was not to limit the power of the Board to order back pay without ordering reinstatement but to give the Board power to remedy union unfair labor practices comparable to the power it possessed to remedy unfair labor practices by employers.

Id. at 54. In nonsection 8(b)(1)(A) contexts, the Board has retreated from its original insistence that a back pay award is appropriate only as an adjunct to a reinstatement order remedying an illegal discharge. In Graves Trucking, Inc., 246 N.L.R.B. 344 (1979), *enforced as modified,* 111 L.R.R.M. 2862 (7th Cir. 1982), an employer physically assaulted an employee, rendering him unfit to work. In ordering back pay but no reinstatement, the Board noted that "while Nash [the employee] was never discharged per se, he suffered the monetary consequence of discharge without the physical capacity to mitigate his loss." *Id.* at 345. The same would be true if a union agent had committed the assault.

[539] UMW (West Ky. Coal Co.), 92 N.L.R.B. 916 (1950), *enforced,* 195 F.2d 961 (6th Cir. 1952).

[540] 92 N.L.R.B. at 922. The proviso quoted in the text accompanying note 542 *supra* was not in the statute at the time section 10(c) was being construed by the Supreme Court in *Phelps Dodge,* although as Member Reynolds noted, it "is likewise merely illustrative of the Board's power, it follows that the proviso does not delimit the Board's remedial power." *Id.*

[541] *Id.* at 925-26.

Coincident with the NLRB's assertion of lack of power has been its alternative assertion that granting such relief would not in fact effectuate the purposes and policies of the act. In recent years it has increasingly justified its position on that basis.[542]

Although the NLRB has never clearly articulated its basis for this, it apparently sees some intrinsic difference between an employee's loss of work occasioned by section 8(b)(2) "discrimination" and a loss of work occasioned by section 8(b)(1)(A) coercion. In *Colonial Hardwood*, for example, the board noted that

> an award of back pay [in the latter situation] would be in the nature of *damages* to the employee for an *interference with his right of ingress to the plant,* as contrasted with compensation to him for *losses in pay* suffered by him because of *severance of or interference with the tenure or terms of the employment relationship between him and his employer* in the ordinary case in which back pay is awarded. . . .[543]

That linguistic distinction is without a substantive difference. It is obvious that when an employee has been coerced into supporting a strike, the union's "interference with his right of ingress to the plant" also causes a "severance of or interference with the tenure or terms of the employment relationship between him and his employer." Indeed, the back pay award serves only to compensate him for that severance rather than for the antecedent and independent interference with his right of access—interference for which he may still be entitled to compensatory damages in a common-law tort action.[544]

Put differently, from the perspective of the employee who has lost work because of his unwillingness to support the union, it is immaterial

---

[542] *See* Drobena v. N.L.R.B., 612 F.2d 1095, 1097 (8th Cir.), *cert. denied,* 449 U.S. 821 (1980).

[543] 84 N.L.R.B. at 565-66 (emphasis added). The trial examiner in that case drew a distinction on the basis that a "[d]iscriminatory discharge clearly operates as a continuing exclusion from further employment by the particular employer with a resulting loss of earnings," a loss which the employee has no way of avoiding until a Board order of reinstatement is obtained. On the other hand, "[e]xclusion from work in a plant by a striking labor organization on a particular occasion may or may not have such a continuing effect," since "employees physically excluded from work by a labor organization may immediately secure entrance to the plant with such protection as may be needed, through the police." *Id.* at 589. Apart from its gross overestimation of the adequacy of police protection in cases of this kind, this distinction fails for apparently expecting employees to risk life and limb resorting to a form of self-help vindication of section 7 rights. The Board, fortunately, did not proceed on that basis.

[544] The Board clearly recognized this in Graves Trucking, Inc., 246 N.L.R.B. 344 (1979), *enforced as modified,* 111 L.R.R.M. 2862 (7th Cir. 1982). In *Graves Trucking,* the Board noted that "contrary to Respondent's suggestion, such a monetary award [back pay to compensate an employee for lost work caused by an employer assault] is not reparation for the physical injury suffered by Nash, but a necessary remedy to vindicate the purposes of the Act." *Id.* at 345. The Board recognized other forums in which the employee could recover damages for personal injuries. *Id.* at 345 n.8.

whether the loss results from a union-induced discriminatory discharge or union-sponsored violence. The Supreme Court has said that one central "policy of the Act is to insulate employees' jobs from their organization rights."[545] Sections 8(a)(3) and 8(b)(2) effectuate that policy by protecting employees against employer and union discrimination which cause interference with the employee's job. The remedy is a back pay order. But as the Supreme Court noted in *Scofield v. NLRB*,[546] section 8(b)(1)(A) is a part of that very same protective web. Indeed, its primary purpose is to prevent *coercive* interference with the employee's right to work and hold a job.[547] If loss of wages is the consequence of any form of illegal interference, the employee should be made whole regardless of whether it is union discrimination or union coercion that is the ultimate cause. On the question of the appropriate remedy for the interference, it simply should not make that much difference which subsection of the statute the case happens to fall under.

This is especially true in light of the liberality the NLRB has shown in finding section 8(b)(2) violations. In one early case, *Randolph Corporation*,[548] two employees were threatened off the job by union agents. The board found that the employer was aware of this and therefore guilty of a "constructive discharge" in violation of section 8(a)(3) "by failing to disavow such expulsion of these employees from the plant." Since it was all caused by the union, the union was guilty of a section 8(b)(2) violation as well. The board called for a make whole award of lost wages for which the employer and the union were jointly and severally liable. The Seventh Circuit Court of Appeals refused to accept the board's "constructive discharge" theory, apparently because of the obvious inequity of making the employer even partially liable in such a situation.

After the Supreme Court held that it was not necessary to allege a section 8(a)(3) violation or join the employer in order to proceed against a union for a section 8(b)(2) violation,[549] the NLRB was able to continue its expansive reading of section 8(b)(2) without implicating an otherwise innocent employer in the violation. For example, in the *Stuart Wilson*[550] case, several employees had been laid off from work and sent

[545] Radio Officers Union v. NLRB, 347 U.S. 17, 40 (1954).

[546] 394 U.S. 423, 428-30 (1969).

[547] Indeed, the emphasis in *Scofield* upon the protection of job rights as the primary purpose of the section 8(b)(1)(A) prohibitions led the Sixth Circuit to cast doubt on the continued validity of the *Colonial Hardwood* doctrine. National Cash Register Co. v. NLRB, 466 F.2d 945, 965 n.20 (6th Cir.), *cert. denied,* 410 U.S. 966 (1972).

[548] 89 N.L.R.B. 1490 (1950), *enforcement denied in relevant part,* 187 F.2d 298 (7th Cir. 1951).

[549] Radio Officers Union v. NLRB, 347 U.S. 17 (1954).

[550] Local 212, Int'l Bhd. of Teamsters (Stuart Wilson, Inc.), 200 N.L.R.B. 519 (1972).

home by the employer because of threats of union violence against them if they continued working. The board held that it was not necessary for the general counsel to show that the union made an express demand or request that the employer get rid of these employees since the conduct which violated section 8(b)(1)(A) was obviously directed toward that end.[551] The board likewise held that "the Act does not require a showing of discharge or complete separation from employment to establish discrimination under Section 8(b)(2)."[552] The union was required to make these employees whole for their loss of wages.

To be sure, the employees' loss of pay in *Radio Officers* was caused by the union *working through the employer*—which satisfies at least the formal requirements of a section 8(b)(2) violation. But it seems clear that the employer participation and the section 8(b)(2) violation itself were merely incidental to the real cause of the loss—namely, the illegal threats comprising the section 8(b)(1)(A) violation.[553] It is thus not at all clear why employer "involvement" should be absolutely required in establishing union liability for back pay to employees who lost work because of such violence.

The remote or indirect participation of employers in the exclusive union hiring hall cases further demonstrates the almost fictional nature of this requirement in a section 8(b)(2) context and the lack of any significant factual difference between a violation of section 8(b)(2) and section 8(b)(1)(A). If a prospective employee visits an exclusive hiring

---

[551] *Id.* at 522.

[552] *Id.* at 521.

[553] Indeed, the Board dropped the requirement of a section 8(b)(2) joinder altogether in a section 8(b)(1)(A) case *not involving violence.* In Warehouse Union Local 860 (The Emporium), 236 N.L.R.B. 844 (1978), *enforced,* 652 F.2d 1022 (D.C. Cir. 1981), the union negotiated a collective bargaining agreement including terms that caused the employer to close a portion of his operation. The union's prior knowledge of this possibility and its failure to advise the employees that this might occur was found to be a breach of the duty of fair representation and therefore a violation of section 8(b)(1)(A). The administrative law judge held as follows:

> It is recognized that an 8(b)(2) violation is not alleged. It is further recognized that the record does not show a direct causal relationship between Respondent's 8(b)(1)(A) violation and the loss of jobs suffered by clerical employees. Finally, there is no way to know whether, had they been given by Respondent the information they were entitled to, the clerical employees would have adopted an all-or-nothing bargaining position, although such is most unlikely and unnatural. Nonetheless, those employees were entitled to make their own decision, and they were deprived of that right by Respondent's knowledgeable silence. Under such circumstances, the employees' plight was Respondent's intentional creation, and equity demands that Respondent remedy that dereliction. Consequently, it will be recommended that Respondent make whole all SB-4 clerical employees who lost their jobs on October 15, 1977, as a result of Respondent's unfair labor practices.

Id. at 851.

hall but is violently thrown out because of his nonmembership in the union, then section 8(b)(1)(A) is violated.[554] Yet no back pay remedy would be currently available on that basis alone. On the other hand, even though the employer is involved only to the extent that it was a party to the contract giving the union the otherwise legal power to act as the employer's exclusive hiring agent, the discriminatory nature of the union's conduct will cause it to be treated as a section 8(b)(2) violation. Then the union will be required to make the employee whole for any loss of pay he may have suffered as a result of its unlawful conduct.[555] The availability of the remedy thus turns more on which section the conduct is conceptualized under than on any material fact.

The critical factual similarity between a section 8(b)(2) violation and a section 8(b)(1)(A) violation is that union conduct causes a loss of work for the employee victims. The factual difference is that a section 8(b)(2) violation apparently requires some degree of employer participation, however remote, while section 8(b)(1)(A) does not. It would seem, however, that insofar as a make whole or back pay remedy is concerned, the similarity is far more significant than the difference. Therefore, this remedy should be available regardless of which section of the statute happens to be applicable. The NLRB's rather facile presumption of some intrinsic difference between section 8(b)(2) and section 8(b)(1)(A) violations in issuing back pay orders is totally without basis.

Apart from the dubious distinction between "discriminatory" and "coercive" interference with an employee's work opportunities, the NLRB has advanced other so-called "policy" reasons for its refusal to ever include back pay as a remedy for a section 8(b)(1)(A) violation. Several of those reasons where rather neatly cataloged by the board in the *Long Construction Company*[556] case.

First, the NLRB noted that the "cease-and-desist order, in conjunction with the utilization of the contempt procedures provided in the Act, is well designed to prevent the recurrence of the unfair labor practices and to vindicate public rights."[557] The board's reasoning here is

---

[554] *Cf.* Piledrivers Local 438 (Ernest Constr. Co.), 234 N.L.R.B. 1301 (1978); IBEW Local 1547 (M & M Elec. Co.), 225 N.L.R.B. 331 (1976), *enforced,* 96 L.R.R.M. 3413 (D.C. Cir. 1977); Local 138, Int'l Union of Operating Eng'rs, 123 N.L.R.B. 1393 (1959), *enforced,* 293 F.2d 187 (2d Cir. 1961).

[555] *See* Printing Pressmen Local 284 (Las Vegas Sun, Inc.), 230 N.L.R.B. 1104, 1104 & n.3 (1977).

[556] International Union of Operating Eng'rs Local 513 (Long Constr. Co.), 145 N.L.R.B. 554 (1963).

[557] *Id.* at 556. On the contrary, Member Kennedy correctly noted that "[a] notice is no substitute for lost wages." Unión Nacional de Trabajadores (Catalytic Indus. Maint. Co.), 219 N.L.R.B. 414, 417 (1975), *enforced,* 540 F.2d (1st Cir. 1976), *cert. denied,* 429 U.S. 1039 (1977).

Union Violence

highly questionable. It is wrong in its factual premises. Even a casual reading of section 8(b)(1)(A) cases will reveal a high degree of recidivism among certain unions. The board itself has recognized that fact through its "propensity for violence" test in issuing broader (but equally hollow, insofar as the already injured employees are concerned) cease and desist orders.[558] The board's assertion also flies in the face of repeated observations by its own trial examiners and administrative law judges that cease and desist orders and the other standard remedies are totally inadequate as a response to the problem of labor union violence.[559]

A remedy such as a cease and desist order, which is designed only to "prevent the recurrence of the unfair labor practices,"[560] may be a fair and intelligent way for the law to deal with conduct of previously uncertain illegality that caused no demonstrable harm to anyone. Such a remedy, however, is inadequate when patently illegal conduct has caused a tangible injury of the kind the labor statute was designed to prevent. Here, a command to cease and desist is obviously necessary and important,[561] but the primary objectives of the remedial order in such a situation should be restoration, compensation, and correction of the injury. It would certainly include the payment of lost wages when employees have been unable to work because of a union's section 8(b)(1)(A) violence. As the Supreme Court noted, back pay is "a reparation . . . designed to vindicate the public policy of the statute by making the employees whole for losses suffered on account of an unfair labor practice."[562] The NLRB has certainly recognized and implemented that policy insofar as equivalent employer unfair labor practice violence is concerned. In *Graves Trucking, Inc.,*[563] a supervisor became so annoyed by an employee's exercise of protected rights that he grabbed the employee around the neck and violently choked him, causing injuries which kept this employee from work. Nowhere in that case did the board suggest its *Long* rationale that a mere cease and desist order would be "well designed to prevent the recurrence of the unfair labor practices and to vindicate public rights."[564] On the contrary, the board concluded that this kind of unfair labor practice was more appropriately remedied by a back pay order. It noted that

---

[558] *See* text accompanying notes 460-82, *supra.*
[559] *See, e.g.,* Local 612, Int'l Bhd. of Teamsters (Deaton Truck Line), 146 N.L.R.B. 498, 506 & n.12 (1964); Taxi-cab Drivers Local 777 (Crown Metal Mfg. Co.), 145 N.L.R.B. 197, 205 (1963), *enforced,* 340 F.2d 905 (7th Cir. 1965).
[560] 145 N.L.R.B. at 556.
[561] *See* text accompanying notes 446-82, *supra.*
[562] NLRB v. J.H. Rutter-Rex Mfg. Co., 396 U.S. 258, 263 (1969).
[563] 246 N.L.R.B. 344 (1979), *enforced as modified,* 111 L.R.R.M. 2862 (7th Cir. 1982).
[564] 145 N.L.R.B. at 556.

like other Board remedies, backpay is intended to dispel the effect of unlawful conduct, whether in response to protected concerted activities or union activities, by restoring discriminatees as nearly as possible to the economic position they would have enjoyed in the absence of the unlawful conduct.

. . . The only way to restore Nash [the choked employee] as nearly as possible to the economic position he would have obtained, but for Responsent's unlawful conduct, is to make him whole for compensation lost as a result of Respondent's unfair labor practice. . . . Were we to withhold backpay in these circumstances we would allow Respondent to escape all liability for loss of wages Nash suffered because of factors Respondent unlawfully caused. Such a result would clearly be contrary to the remedial purposes of the Act.[565]

Secondly, the NLRB gave another reason in *Long* for denying back pay to employees who lose work because of union violence:

to the extent that the Board has power to award backpay to employees injured by Respondent's violent conduct, such power derives from the effect of such conduct on the employee's employment relationship; yet the employee's loss of pay may be only a small part of the total required to make him whole, which total may well include medical expenses as well as compensation for physical injury and pain and suffering.[566]

If all that verbiage makes any sense at all, it seems only to say that because the board cannot award common law tort damages and thus fully compensate an employee for his physical injuries, it also cannot restore to the employee the wages he lost as a consequence of these injuries and the union's coercive interference with his right to work. That is simply a *non sequitur* of classical dimensions. To say the least, such fallacious reasoning did not deter the board in the *Graves* case from issuing a back pay order against an employer whose violent unfair labor practice kept an employee from working—even though the physical injury itself was left uncompensated under the board order.[567]

The third justification advanced by the NLRB in *Long* was:

to the extent that satisfaction of individual claims which are primarily private in nature may also serve to further the public interest in obtaining the peaceful resolution of labor disputes, such interest is equally well served by the individual's resort to those remedies traditionally used to process claims resorting from another's tortious conduct.[568]

To begin with, one must note that the board's refusal to award back pay is not limited to situations of coercive interference with a single employee's right to work. Those cases might perhaps be accurately

---

[565] 246 N.L.R.B. at 345.
[566] 145 N.L.R.B. at 556.
[567] 246 N.L.R.B. 344 (1979), *enforced as modified,* 111 L.R.R.M. 2862 (7th Cir. 1982).
[568] 145 N.L.R.B. at 556.

characterized as merely involving "individual claims which are primarily private in nature."[569] Rather, the board has refused to provide this remedy even in cases where the union violence is so massive as to border on civil riot.[570] This suggests that the board's overall policy in this regard is not really predicated on this third justification at all.

Furthermore, the NLRB's argument simply proves too much. If no significant public interest is served by a board-ordered back pay award in one of the "individual claims" cases, then why is there not a similar lack of public interest in all the other remedies as well, or, indeed, a lack of interest in recognizing such union conduct as a section 8(b)(1)(A) violation at all? If carried to its logical conclusion, the board's argument would seem to suggest a form of reverse preemption. State remedies would become the exclusive source of relief in "individual claims" cases. That result, however, is clearly inconsistent with the intent of Congress. Congress was obviously aware that much of the union violence that it was proscribing under section 8(b)(1)(A), whether directed at single individuals or whole groups of employees, was already actionable under state law.[571] Congress, however, was also apparently of the view that the public interest in labor peace was not adequately served by the mere fact that state court relief was available to employees who might choose to pursue it. Although the legislative history is silent on this, one may surmise that this was because too few employees had the resources and stamina to vigorously prosecute a complicated and time-consuming tort action against a labor union. Thus, Congress recognized that the public interest in stopping these sometimes isolated but persistently recurring instances of union violence required public prosecution of the claims through the agency of the NLRB.

The process of prosecution is of course complicated and costly. It requires investigation of the alleged violation, issuance of a complaint, an oftentimes lengthy hearing before an administrative law judge, and ultimate review by a panel of the NLRB itself. It is a travesty of justice, a virtual waste of precious administrative resources, and serves neither the interests of the public nor the affected employee to go through that elaborate process at the public expense, find that a labor union has in

---

[569] *Id.*

[570] *See supra* note 537 and cases cited therein (particularly the *Unión Nacional de Trabajadores* cases).

[571] Indeed, because conduct made illegal by section 8(b)(1)(A) already was actionable under state common and/or criminal laws, some authorities opposed the Taft-Hartley Act amendments, arguing that state remedies should remain the exclusive sources of relief. *See, e.g.,* LEGIS. HIST. LMRA at 373-74, 1191-93.

fact interferred with an employee's right to earn a living, and then deny that employee any recoupment of his monetary losses on the grounds that he should relitigate the issues in state court.[572] Next in the *Long Construction Co.* case catalog of reasons why the make whole remedy is inappropriate in section 8(b)(1)(A) cases is the NLRB's assertion that "the numerous and complicated factual questions involved in settling such claims are not such questions as fall within the Board's special expertise, but do fall within the special competence of judge and jury."[573] That is utter and complete nonsense. There is probably no tribunal in the world with greater expertise in dealing with back pay issues than the NLRB. As the board itself recognized in the *Graves Trucking* case, "a back pay order is one of the remedial devices adopted to attain just results in diverse, complicated situations" and "the Board has thus employed the back pay remedy in multifarious circumstances."[574] Although a back pay order can be a complex remedy, the board has developed a wide array of principles, doctrines, rules, and formulas over the years that are designed to deal with the various kinds of back pay issues that arise.[575] There is absolutely no reason why this body of established law could not be used in the section 8(b)(1)(A) context in the same way it is used in other cases where back pay is an appropriate remedy.

Undoubtedly, it may be difficult to determine exactly which employees are honestly entitled to a back pay award in some cases. As one trial examiner noted, "it is impossible to determine from the record which employees remained away from work in response to peaceful persuasion by pickets, which, as a consequence of restraint and coercion, and which, for reasons unconnected with the strike."[576] The NLRB, however, is constantly faced with factual determinations of equal or greater difficulty and complexity. It has always managed to devise evidentiary tests for coping with such matters. Indeed, one rule that could be applied in section 8(b)(1)(A) cases, stated by the sixth circuit, is that "once an intital showing of substantial and widespread coercion is made, it is incumbent on the union or employer, as the case

---

[572] *Accord,* MCDOWELL & HUHN, *supra* note 428, at 99-100 (1976).
[573] 145 N.L.R.B. at 556.
[574] 246 N.L.R.B. at 345. Despite its familiarity with back pay awards, the Board argued in Drobena v. NLRB, 612 F.2d 1095, 1098 (8th Cir.), *cert. denied,* 449 U.S. 821 (1980), "that computation and enforcement of such awards [as a remedy to section 8(b)(1)(A) violations] would unduly tax the facilities of the Board. . . ."
[575] *See generally* MCDOWELL & HUHN, *supra* note 428 at 81-99 (1976); Parker *Monetary Recovery Under the Federal Labor Statutes,* 45 TEX. L. REV. 881, 882-94 (1967).
[576] Local 1150, United Elec. Workers (Cory Corp.), 84 N.L.R.B. 972, 1014 (1949); *see* Unión Nacional de Trabajadores (Catalytic Indus. Maint. Co.), 219 N.L.R.B. 414 (1975), *enforced,* 540 F.2d 1 (1st Cir. 1976), *cert. denied,* 429 U.S. 1039 (1977).

may be, to come forward with evidence that specific employees were not coerced."[577] In a section 8(b)(1)(A) union violence case, the specific indicia or evidence of a noncoercion (or of coercion, should the above presumption be inapplicable in a given situation) required could be worked out on a case-by-case basis without a great deal of difficulty on the board's part.

The fifth and final justification advanced by the NLRB in the *Long Construction Co.* case for refusing to recognize back pay awards as a legitimate part of a section 8(b)(1)(A) remedial order was that "our exercise of such authority as may reside in the Board to award compensatory relief might well exert an inhibitory effect on the exercise of State authority, and would, in any event, complicate and confuse the issue, to the possible detriment of the employees whose rights we seek to protect."[578] The board's theory of an "inhibitory effect" is, however, based on pure conjecture; indeed, it seems contrary to the more common experience of state courts, being happily oblivious to the witty diversities of federal labor law and the subtle nuances of the preemption doctrine.[579] It is difficult to see why the board could not deal with the alleged complication and confusion in the same way it tackles other knotty problems. In the *Graves* case, for example, the injured employee had received workmen's compensation, and the board merely noted that "to the extent that this award was in replacement for lost wages, it shall be deducted from his gross back pay."[580] That computation would surely have been no more complicated or confusing had the assault been by a union agent rather than the employer. Thus, this complication factor cannot explain or justify the board's refusal to issue a back pay award against a union under similar circumstances. Finally, it would seem obvious that the real and immediate loss an employee suffers as a consequence of the board's refusal to issue back pay awards in section 8(b)(1)(A) cases far outweighs a merely "*possible* detriment" that might flow from highly speculative inhibitions and confusions envisioned by the board.

The reasons listed in the *Long Construction Company* case are so patently specious that the NLRB subsequently found it necessary to advance an entirely different policy justification for its refusal to award back pay in section 8(b)(1)(A) cases. In *Lock Joint Pipe & Company*[581] the board refused to impose back pay liability on a union. It first reviewed the remedies for union violence that are available, including

---

[577] National Cash Register Co. v. NLRB, 466 F.2d 945, 969 (6th Cir. 1972).
[578] 145 N.L.R.B. at 556.
[579] *Cf.* HAGGARD, COMPULSORY UNIONISM, THE NLRB, AND THE COURTS 172 (1977).
[580] 246 N.L.R.B. at 345 n.11.
[581] Unión de Tronquistas (Lock Joint Pipe & Co.), 202 N.L.R.B. 399 (1973).

the usual cease and desist order, section 10(j) injunctions, possible contempt actions, and the denial of a bargaining order. The board then
continued:

> To do more, in our opinion, runs the risk of inhibiting the right of
> employees to strike to such an extent as to substantially diminish that right.
> For the misconduct of a few pickets may be sufficient to find the union in
> violation of Section 8(b)(1)(A) and enough to intimidate many employees.
> The Board would then be required, under the logic of our dissenting col-
> leagues, to seek backpay for all intimidated employees. Faced with this
> financial responsibility, few unions would be in a position to establish a
> picket line. In our opinion, union misconduct of this nature, while serious,
> does not warrant the adoption of a remedy so severe as to risk the diminu-
> tion of the right to strike, a fundamental right guaranteed by Sections 7 and
> 13 of the Act.[582]

If the reasons listed in *Long Construction Company* are disturbing for
their total lack of cogency, the justification advanced in *Lock Joint Pipe*
is doubly disturbing because of the insight it provides to the NLRB's
values and priorities. The decision warrants close analysis.

The place to begin is the NLRB's conception of what the protected
activity of going on strike really means. In another part of the decision,
the board made explicit its assumption that going on strike and
picketing, in the statutory sense, *necessarily* entail the strong possibility that unpreventable (by union officials) violence will occur. The
board stated that:

> The extension of backpay liability to a situation where, as here, only picket
> line misconduct has occurred involves important considerations going to
> the heart of the right to strike under Sections 7 and 13 of the Act. Those
> sections of the Act have been called the safety valves of labor management
> relations. Emotions run high among those for and those against the union.
> Regrettably, sometimes there is violence and the threat of violence.[583]

If the protected right to strike includes conduct and activities having
this "regrettable" propensity for violence, then there is an internal inconsistency in the statute. What is encompassed by the protections of
some part of the statute is prohibited by other parts. To resolve this inconsistency, the NLRB decided to achieve a balance. It did this by

---

[582] *Id.* at 400.
[583] *Id.* at 399. The Board, however, has not limited its refusal to award back pay merely
to "those occasional situations in which tempers flare on the picket line and strikers
momentarily engage in what has been euphemistically referred to as 'mere animal exuberance.'" The Board has in addition refused to grant back pay even against, "a labor
organization which denounces the laws applicable to its conduct and which systematically threatens the lives of any and all individuals who dare to act in any manner contrary to
its self-interest." Union de Trabajadores (Catalytic Indus. Maint. Co.), 219 N.L.R.B. 414,
(1975) (Member Kennedy, dissenting), *enforced*, 540 F.2d 1 (1st Cir. 1976), *cert. denied*,
429 U.S. 1039 (1977).

recognizing that the violence associated with strikes is an unfair labor practice but also by withholding any remedy for the violation that might jeopardize the financial solvency of labor organizations and their willingness to establish picket lines.[584]

Accepting at face value the NLRB's conception of what the rights to strike and picket really mean, and the statutory inconsistency that this conception entails, the balance that the board reached is nevertheless subject to criticism. It could be argued that the right of an individual to be free from acts of physical aggression in the pursuit of his livelihood is far more fundamental and morally significant than the right of other employees to band together for the purpose of economically coercing their employer.[585] It is a curious distortion of values to leave violations of the former right unvindicated (as far as the employee is concerned) due to a speculative fear that the remedy might somehow "chill" the exercise of the latter right.

An alternative balance would leave the statutory right to strike and picket fully protected against both employer interference and any tendencies of the law to render the purely peaceful aspects of it affirmatively illegal. But it would also make the unions engage in these violence-prone activities "at risk," at least to the extent of being held responsible when the activities do in fact become violent and cause employment-related injuries to individuals whose right not to be injured is supposedly protected by the NLRA. Putting unions to such a risk might chill their institutional willingness to sponsor strikes and maintain picket lines. Yet as the Fourth Circuit Court of Appeals put it in another context, "it is indisputable that the thrust of the NLRA is not the protection of the union, not the protection of the employer, but rather the protection of the employee."[586] If the adequate protection of the employee requires putting either a union or an employer "at risk" when it engages in nominally protected conduct, then so be it.[587]

---

[584] The Board's concern for the financial condition of labor unions apparently was stressed in Drobena v. NLRB, 612 F.2d 1095 (8th Cir.), *cert. denied*, 449 U.S. 821 (1980). In *Drobena*, the General Counsel was quoted as arguing "that such an award may bring about the financial ruin of a local union resulting from the irresponsible acts of one or a few members surcharged with the emotions that labor strife can produce," 612 F.2d at 1098.

[585] *Compare* Haggard, *The Right to Work—A Constitutional and Natural Law Perspective*, 1 J. SOC. & POL. AFF. 215, 220-26 (1976) (suggesting that the right to work free from acts of aggression by others is one of our fundamental natural law rights), *with* Haggard, *Right to Work*, 11 REASON N. 1, May 1979, at p. 34, 36 (suggesting the difficulty of defining the right to strike in traditional natural law or libertarian terms).

[586] Mosher Steel Co. v. NLRB, 568 F.2d 436, 442 (5th Cir. 1978).

[587] NLRA § 10(c), 29 U.S.C. § 158(c)(1976), for example, protects the employer's right to express his views on unionization "if such expression contains no threat of reprisal or force or promise of benefit." In NLRB v. Gissel Packing Co., 395 U.S. 575 (1969),

One can also take exception to the NLRB's notion that protected strikes and picketing necessarily include conduct that is apt to produce unavoidable violence. As a factual matter, that is not the case.[588] Many strikes and picketing are carried out without any union-related violence or even serious threats of such violence. This is because responsible union officials have consciously elected not to engage in any violence or dangerously provocative conduct themselves and have taken additional steps to insure that rank-and-file members conduct themselves in an entirely peaceful and noncoercive manner. Conversely, it would seem that the emotionally supercharged situations which do often lead to violence are situations which have been deliberately contrived or consciously tolerated by the labor union officials in charge. If violence-prone strikes can be conceptually distinguished from strikes not having that tendency, then the chilling thesis makes sense only if one assumes that the board is legitimately concerned with avoiding even the slightest interference with strikes falling in the violence-prone category. Such a concern, however, would not be consistent with the intent of Congress.

In the Taft-Hartley Act, Congress recognized a clear distinction between *purely* noncoercive strikes and picketing and conduct which does restrain and coerce the exercise of employee rights. The former is all Congress intended to protect in sections 7 and 13, and it conclusively intended to prohibit the latter in section 8(b)(1)(A).[589] Such a reading also obviates the inconsistency in the statute falsely perceived by the NLRB. The entire thrust of the Taft-Hartley Act amendments was, in fact, to repudiate the notion that violence is a necessary incident of strikes that must be tolerated to some degree lest the statutory right to

---

however, the Supreme Court adopted a fairly broad if not obscure test for distinguishing illegal threats of economic reprisal from mere predictions of economic consequences. *Id.* at 618-19. The Court's test clearly puts an employer at risk and may similarly chill what is the exercise of not only a statutory but also a first amendment right. The Court emphasized the right of employees to be free of the coercive impact of dangerously ambiguous statements, and suggested that the employer "can easily make his views known without engaging in 'brinksmanship' when it becomes all too easy to 'overstep and tumble [over] the brink,' . . ." *Id.* at 620 (quoting Wausau Steel Corp. v. NLRB, 377 F.2d 369, 372 (7th Cir. 1967)). (The same can be said of strike related violence and of a union's liability for the loss of pay caused by the violence of its employees.)

[588] The notion that violence is an inevitable and unavoidable incident of strikes is, however, a recurring fallacy in industrial relations law and has even been used by labor arbitrators to exonerate employees who were discharged because of such misconduct. *See* Haggard, *Picket Line, supra* note 22 at 423-31.

[589] *See generally,* text accompanying notes 21-41 *supra;* Haggard, *Picket Line, supra* note 22 at 439-48. For a specific example of the kind of violence-prone but not itself violent strike misconduct with which Congress was concerned, see the remarks of Senator Ball, LEGIS. HIST. LMRA at 1019-20.

strike be impeded or diminished.[590] The board is on shaky ground indeed in resurrecting such a philosophy as justification for its refusal to grant full and adequate relief to what is clearly a violation of rights protected by the statute.

Notwithstanding its tenuous basis, the NLRB's position on back pay liability has not been reversed by the courts of appeals.[591] This is probably due to the courts' limited power to compel the board to grant a remedy that the board has refused to grant as a matter of policy[592] rather than an affirmative judicial approval of the policy in question.[593] It would thus appear that relief must come either through a change in board membership or philosophy, or by an amendment to the statute.

Additional Judicial Remedies

All of the foregoing remedies, though not legally effective until enforced by a court, nevertheless *originate* in an NLRB order. There are, however, two additional remedies for section 8(b)(1)(A) violations that are purely judicial in their character and origin.

Section 10(j) Injunctions. Section 10(j) gives the NLRB upon the issuance of an unfair labor practice charge, the discretionary power to immediately petition a United States District Court "for appropriate temporary relief or restraining order." It also authorizes the court to grant such relief "as it deems just and proper."[594]

Under 10(j), the NLRB's petition must allege that the following conditions exist:

(1) an unfair labor practice charge has been filed; (2) a complaint has been issued; (3) the facts presented support the charge; (4) there is a likelihood

---

[590] One of Congress' specific concerns in passing the Taft-Hartley Act was the extent to which the Board and the courts had protected employees involved in strike violence from discharge. In Republic Steel Corp. v. NLRB, 107 F.2d 472 (3d Cir. 1939), *modified,* 311 U.S. 7 (1940), the court justified its tolerance of strike misconduct on the following basis:

Rising passions call forth hot words. Hot words lead to blows on the picket line. . . . Violence of this nature, however, much as it is to be regretted, must have been in the contemplation of the Congress when it provided in Sec. 13 . . . that nothing therein should be construed so as to interfere with or impede or diminish in any way the right to strike.

107 F.2d at 479. Congress, however, repudiated that approach to the statutory reinstatement rights of employees who have been discharged for strike violence. *See* Haggard, *Picket Line, supra* note 4 at 43948. Apparently the Board's similarly based approach to the issue of back pay liability was also implicitly repudiated.

[591] *See* cases cited in note 526 *supra.*

[592] *See* text accompanying notes 443-45, *supra.*

[593] Indeed, two courts of appeals have registered express doubts about the wisdom and validity of the policy. *See* cases cited in note 526 *supra.*

[594] NLRA § 10(j), 29 U.S.C. § 160(j) (1976).

that the unfair labor practice will continue unless restrained; (5) the district court has jurisdiction; and (6) the persons sought to be restrained are subject to the Act. Of course, the primary prerequisites are whether the unlawful conduct, as a matter of law, constitutes an unfair labor practice and whether the record shows a reasonable probability that the acts alleged were in fact committed.[595]

In *Muniz v. Hoffman*,[596] the Supreme Court held that the procedural and substantive limitations of the Norris-LaGuardia Act do not apply to injunctions sought by the NLRB under section 10 of the Taft-Hartley Act. Therefore, union liability and responsibility for the acts of violence being enjoined is established under common-law agency standards rather than under the stringent standards of the Norris-LaGuardia Act.[597] Judicial power under section 10(j) includes the power to issue temporary restraining orders.[598] In appropriate cases, a preliminary injunction can be issued even though an evidentiary hearing has not been held.[599]

The legislative history clearly indicates that section 10(j) injunctions were intended to be one of the preliminary remedies available in the section 8(b)(1)(A) context.[600] Similarly, in *Squillacote v. Local 248, Food Workers*,[601] the court said with respect to violence and threats of violence that

> few, if any, types of violations would present a more compelling case for immediate injunctive relief. Prevention of labor violence is one of the basic purposes of the federal labor acts. Violence has a severe coercive effect on employees' section 157 rights. It is completely contrary to the public interest, and it can quickly give the party willing to engage in such wrongful conduct an advantage.[602]

Accordingly, the NLRB has made use of this power to a limited extent.[603]

In 1979, the general counsel issued a report on section 10(j) injunction proceedings during the prior four year period; he also outlined the criteria his office used in deciding whether to seek a preliminary injunction in unfair labor practice cases.[604] With respect to section

---

[595] McDowell & Huhn, *supra* note 428 at 253-54.
[596] 422 U.S. 454 (1975).
[597] Squillacote v. Local 248, Food Workers, 534 F.2d 735, 743-44 (7th Cir. 1976).
[598] *Id.* at 743.
[599] *See, id.* at 749-50 (declined to decide if hearing was necessary in that case).
[600] *See* text accompanying note 62, *supra.*
[601] 534 F.2d 735 (7th Cir. 1976).
[602] *Id.* at 744.
[603] *E.g.,* Price v. Laborers Local 383, 108 L.R.R.M. 3270 (D. Ariz. 1981); Wilson v. UAW, 97 L.R.R.M. 2013 (S.D. Iowa 1977); Hendrix v. Meat Cutters, 95 L.R.R.M. 2706 (D. Neb. 1977); Vincent v. Local 301, Elec. Workers, 73 L.R.R.M. 2136 (N.D.N.Y. 1969); Potter v. Cement Workers Union, 48 L.R.R.M. 2965 (E.D. Tex. 1961).
[604] NLRB Case Handling Manual (CCH) ¶ 30,162 at 10,348 (1979).

8(b)(1)(A) cases in particular, the report indicates that an injunction should be sought only if three requirements were met. Firstly, it must be shown that "there is a substantial amount of physical coercion or violence and/or the threat of such coercion."[605] An earlier general counsel report on the same subject had similarly stated that the remedy is only available where "the misconduct involved is generally serious, repeated and widespread and connected with a labor dispute of a nature that raises the expectation that, absent injunctive relief, it will continue."[606] Secondly, union responsibility must be clearly established. And thirdly, it must be shown that "the charging party has sought the assistance of state or local authorities and that these authorities are unable or unwilling to control the situation."[607] The general counsel further reported that using injunctive relief against mass picketing and violence had been sought in only thirteen cases during the four year period.[608]

One member of the chairman's task force on the NLRB had previously criticized the general counsel's adherence to a conservative policy with respect to section 10(j) injunctions against violence. The task force's 1976 interim report[609] noted that member's suggestions that the board act more frequently and more promptly in seeking section 10(j) injunctions for union violence; that regional directors be delegated the power to petition for such injunctions; and that they be required to do so in all section 8(b)(1)(A) cases "involving labor organizations 'which have a known proclivity for coercion and violence . . . regardless of the alleged degree of the effectiveness of the police or other law enforcement agencies.'"[610] This member also suggested that such an injunction "include restoration of the status quo by an award to employees of all wages lost as a result of the respondent union's activities."[611] The task force, however, merely recommended a minor procedural change designed to expedite the processing of regional director requests for authority to seek section 10(j) injunctions.[612]

Although section 10(j) injunctions could be an effective tool for providing immediate relief to the victims of union violence, it appears that the NLRB has not taken full advantage of this potential remedy.

Contempt Proceedings. Once an NLRB order has been enforced by a

---

[605] *Id.* at 10,348.
[606] NLRB Case Handling Manual (CCH) ¶30,019 at 10,154 (1976).
[607] NLRB Case Handling Manual (CCH) ¶30,162 at 10,348 (1979).
[608] *Id.* at 10,349.
[609] CHAIRMAN'S TASK FORCE ON THE NLRB, INTERIM REPORT AND RECOMMENDATIONS, LABOR RELATIONS YEARBOOK 1976 (BNA) at 327-88 (1977).
[610] *Id.* at 363.
[611] *Id.*
[612] *Id.*

court of appeals, it becomes a judicial decree that can be further enforced through contempt proceedings. If a party is found in contempt, then a court is empowered to "impose what ever sanctions are necessary under the circumstances to grant full remedial relief, to coerce the contemnor into compliance with [the] court's order, and to fully compensate the complainant for losses sustained."[613] In the words of one study, "this makes available powerful sanction beyond the purely remedial power of the Board."[614]

In *Squillacote v. Local 248, Food Workers,*[615] for example, the union was found in contempt for continuing acts of violence through the conduct of its picket captains. The court, accordingly, ordered these captains removed from the picket line for the duration of the restraining order.[616]

In *NLRB v. Unión Nacional de Trabajadores,*[617] the union was found in contempt of an order which, *inter alia,* required that the union cease and desist from threatening employees and that it publish a notice of intended compliance in a newspaper of general circulation. The union published the required official notice, but the union also ran a "side notice" adjacent to the official notice which, in essence, "destroyed the substance and purpose of the required notice"[618] because it "expressed the Union's intention to threaten and use violence in the future."[619] The court found this to be contumacious and ordered the union to republish the official notice—this time without the illegal side notice. The union was also found in contempt for two subsequent threats against persons who refused to cooperate with the union's demand that they not work during the strike.

In addition to the republication requirement, the court ordered the union to reimburse "the Board for all its expenses, including attorneys' salaries, and all costs and expenditures incurred in the investigation, preparation, presentation, and final disposition of this proceeding to adjudge the Union and Arturo Grant in civil contempt."[620] Finally, to deter future violations, the court ordered that the union be fined "$10,000 for each and every future violation of the decree and $1,000 per day for each day such violation continues."[621]

---

[613] NLRB v. Vander Wal, 316 F.2d 631, 634 (9th Cir. 1963).
[614] McDOWELL & HUHN, *supra* note 428 at 246.
[615] 534 F.2d 735 (7th Cir. 1976).
[616] *Id.* at 739.
[617] 611 F.2d 926 (1st Cir. 1979).
[618] *Id.* at 930.
[619] *Id.*
[620] *Id.* at 934.
[621] *Id.* The union president was also ordered to pay $1,000 for each future violation and $500 for each day that the violation continued. *Id.*

Although the imposition of fines for future violations only is not unusual,[622] it is not clear why the court in a blatant case of contempt should not impose fines in the first instance as well. Similarly, it would seem that the *Unión Nacional* should have been a prime candidate for criminal as well as civil contempt.[623] The employees coerced by the union in violation of the original decree had apparently suffered no loss of wages. If they had, it would have been an ideal situation for the court, in the exercise of its own inherent judicial powers, to require the union to make these employees whole for their losses.

In sum, although the remedies that are available under the exercise of the contempt power will only be resorted to infrequently, they should be applied as rigorously as possible in a proper case.

---

[622] *See* McDowell & Huhn, *supra* note 428 at 246-47.

[623] "[I]f it can be shown that the respondent 'knowingly, willfully and intentionally' violated the court's decree, the Board may petition the court to find the respondent criminally liable for his conduct. Sentences for criminal contempt include monetary fines and imprisonment." *Id.* at 248.

CHAPTER XII

Other Criminal and Civil Sanctions for Labor Violence

The Anti-Racketeering (Hobbs) Act, the state and federal Norris-LaGuardia Acts, decisions under labor arbitration agreements, and unfair labor practice proceedings under the National Labor Relations (Taft-Hartley) Act (NLRA) all represent somewhat specialized responses to the problem of labor union violence. They are important to this study, however, either because they have been (and some continue to be) the focus of considerable public controversy, or because they provide the largest number of reported decisions dealing with misconduct of this nature.

But the law also provides other responses. Although they are not as controversial or as widely reported, the imposition of criminal penalties and damage awards on the perpetrators of union violence probably represent the most fundamental of all possible responses. A brief discussion of some of the legal issues that arise in this context is thus in order.

CRIMINAL LAWS

The criminal law was the vehicle first used in this country to express societal disapproval of certain labor union excesses, namely through the so-called criminal conspiracy doctrine.[1] And although our idea of what, in the labor context, should be regarded as criminal misbehavior has narrowed somewhat since those early days, the criminal law remains an appropriate if not essential means of dealing with labor-related acts of physical violence, threats, intimidation, coercion, and destruction of property. In this regard, the legal and political issues have not been whether such misconduct should not be criminally actionable; the issues, rather, have mainly been whether it should be a matter of state rather than federal law and whether certain criminal laws of general application do in fact apply to labor violence.

---

[1] *See generally,* T. HAGGARD, COMPULSORY UNIONISM, THE NLRB, AND THE COURTS—A LEGAL ANALYSIS OF UNION SECURITY AGREEMENTS 11-17 (1977).

State Criminal Laws

It would appear that the general criminal laws of most states would at least be adequate to deal with the problems of strike, picket line, and labor-related violence. Although the terminology of the law varies from state to state, the Illinois criminal code, which may be taken as fairly typical, proscribes the following acts, all of which could easily occur in a labor dispute: murder,[2] voluntary manslaughter,[3] involuntary manslaughter and reckless homocide,[4] kidnapping,[5] unlawful restraint,[6] assault,[7] battery,[8] reckless conduct,[9] intimidation,[10] home invasion,[11] arson,[12] possession of explosives,[13] damage to property,[14] trespass,[15] unlawful use of weapons,[16] unlawful possession of firearms,[17] mob action,[18] disorderly conduct,[19] armed violence,[20] and looting.[21]

Moreover, many states have criminal laws dealing specifically with labor violence. These laws typically make it either a misdemeanor or sometimes even a felony for any person, by force or by violence, to coerce employees to join labor organizations, to prevent employees from engaging in lawful vocations and enjoying the right to work, to obstruct egress and ingress, to coerce employers to hire or not to hire certain persons, to compel persons to strike or to honor picket lines, to interfere with the normal operation of a business, or, in general, to use such tactics in the course of any labor dispute.[22]

When issues of strike violence are litigated in the context of a discharge arbitration or an unfair labor practice proceeding, the results

---

[2] ILL. ANN. STAT. ch. 38, § 9-1 (Smith-Hurd) [The following citations are to section number only.]
[3] Section 9-2.
[4] Section 9-3.
[5] Section 10-1.
[6] Section 10-3.
[7] Section 12-1.
[8] Section 12-3.
[9] Section 12-5.
[10] Section 12-6.
[11] Section 12-11.
[12] Section 20-1.
[13] Section 20-2.
[14] Section 21-1.
[15] Section 21-3.
[16] Section 24-1.
[17] Section 24-3.1.
[18] Section 25-1.
[19] Section 26-1.
[20] Section 33A-1.
[21] Section 42-1.
[22] *See, e.g.,* ARK. STAT. ANN. § 81-206; GA. CODE 54-801 to 54-805; MICH. COMP. LAWS § 750.352; S.C. CODE § 41-7-70; S.D. CODIFIED LAWS §§ 60-8-1, 60-8-2, 60-10-10, 60-10-12, 60-10-13.

are generally published—thus providing the raw data from which conclusions can be drawn about the incidence of such labor violence and the efficiency of these remedies in dealing with it. Unless an appeal is taken, however, the results of most criminal trials are never reported in published form. The information, of course, could be gleaned from the official records of each of the thousands of state courts; but apart from that, it is simply impossible to tell how often these state criminal statutes, of either the general or the specific variety, are being invoked against the perpetrators of industrial-relations violence or what the results of these prosecutions are. Some observations of a very general nature are however, in order.

One of the major problems that a criminal prosecution encounters is that of proving, beyond a reasonable doubt, that the defendants actually committed the alleged wrongs. Victims may be unable or unwilling to identify their assailants; the defendants' fellow union members are often the only other witnesses, and they may be reluctant to testify; phone threats are usually anonymous; and sabotage and destruction of company property is frequently carried out in the dark of night.

Moreover, and somewhat ironically, the problem of identification is especially acute in just those cases where the imposition of criminal sanctions would appear to be most warranted—namely, where there has been mob violence and widespread destruction of property. A criminal prosecution arising out of the union assault on the Altemose Construction Company is typical in this regard.[23] In *Commonwealth of Pennsylvania v. Reeves*,[24] several members of the Philadelphia Building and Trades Council were convicted of various charges, ranging from riot, riotous destruction of property, malicious destruction of fences, conspiracy, and assault. But the convictions were reversed in part. The court held as a matter of law that without proof of actual participation or encouragement, mere presence at the scene of a riot is not adequate proof of the offense. In this case, labor unionists had trampled down thousands of feet of cyclone fencing. The prosecution had a photograph of one of the defendants running alongside of the fence which was being destroyed. The prosecution's theory was that the defendant "had been alternatively jumping onto and from the fence, and that the cameraman happened to take the picture while the defendant was only running beside the fence."[25] This, coupled with the defendant's membership in a local roofers union, was said to be sufficient to support the jury's verdict.

---

[23] For a more complete description of the events from which this case arose, see pp. 152-54, 299-31, *supra.*

[24] 98 L.R.R.M. 3031 (Pa. Super. Ct., 1978).

[25] *Id.* at 3032.

The court, however, disagreed. It concluded that from this evidence "one could also conjecture that he was running along the fence urging his comrades to dismount it and stop breaking the law. In any event, this is precisely the kind of guesswork or conjecture in which the law prohibits a jury from engaging."[26] The court also discounted some photographs of another defendant, noting that they merely demonstrated his presence at the scene after the destruction had occurred, but not his actual participation in or encouragement of the destruction. The dissent, on the other hand, by reference to these photographs and the lengthy testimony explaining the events that they depicted, more realistically concluded that this was sufficient to establish the defendant's participation in the riotous destruction.

Federal Criminal Laws

Although it is primarily a concern of the states, criminal activity can also fall within the purview of federal jurisdiction if it affects interstate commerce. In addition to the Hobbs Act,[27] which was discussed earlier,[28] there are also several other federal criminal statutes, of either general or specific application, which can be considered for inclusion in the arsenal of legal responses to the problem of labor union violence.

One such statute—whose potential in this regard has not, however, been realized—is 18 U.S.C. § 241, which is part of the post-Civil War civil rights legislation. This section makes it a federal crime to "conspire to injure, oppress, threaten, or intimidate any citizen in the free exercise or enjoyment of any right or privilege secured to him by the Constitution or laws of the United States."[29]

In *United States v. DeLaurentis,*[30] a labor union engaged in a sit-in in an attempt to force the employer to grant recognition. During the course of the sit-in, violence or threats of violence were allegedly directed against employees who refused to participate. Eventually, the labor unionists were indicted for a conspiracy to violate the federal statutory right of those employees—specifically, the right guaranteed by Section 7 of the NLRA to refrain from union concerted activities. They were convicted of the charge.

The United States Court of Appeals for the Second Circuit reversed the conviction, however, and ordered the indictment dismissed. The court concluded that the rights specified in Section 7 of the NLRA

---

[26] *Id.*
[27] 18 U.S.C. § 1951 (1976).
[28] See Chapter IX, *supra.*
[29] 18 U.S.C. § 241 (1976).
[30] 491 F.2d 208 (2d Cir. 1974). See also, United States v. Bailes, 120 F. Supp. 614 (S.D.W. Va. 1954).

must be vindicated exclusively through the procedures set forth in the act and that a union's violation of these rights may not, thus, serve as the basis for a prosecution under section 241. The court advanced three reasons for this conclusion. Firstly, it noted that in the Taft-Hartley Act, Congress had specifically declined to make this unfair labor practice criminally punishable, or even subject to civil damage suits. Secondly, it pointed out that what is a section 7 "right" and whether it has been violated are issues which Congress entrusted to the expertise of an administrative agency and that they are "hardly issues that are best resolved by a jury in a criminal trial."[31] Thirdly, the court noted that when Congress has intended to make labor union activity a crime, it has done so specifically and deliberately.

To the extent that the *DeLaurentis* decision is predicated on the fact that the *only* federal right that was being asserted there was a right created specifically by the NLRA, the court's conclusion about the intended exclusivity of the unfair labor practice remedy is probably sound. The case should not, however, be read as having any broader significance, even though some of the reasons advanced by the court make the case susceptible to that. Specifically, it should not be read as precluding a section 241 prosecution against labor union officials who violate other federal rights—*i.e.* rights for which Congress has not otherwise provided an exclusive statutory remedy.

Although most federal statutory rights do have their own specific statutory remedy and would thus fall within the exclusivity principle of *DeLaurentis*,[32] this is not true of the more broadly based constitutional rights which section 241 also purports to protect against conspiratorial violence. Unfortunately, a problem other than exclusivity of other remedies presents itself here. Traditionally, the Supreme Court has narrowly construed the section 241 phrase, "right or privilege secured . . . the Constitution or laws of the United States." In *United States v. Williams*,[33] for example, the Court explained that this "includes rights which arise from the relationship of the individual and the Federal Government," but it does not include "those rights which the Constitution merely guarantees from interference by a State."[34] Thus, although the right to work is commonly recognized as a fundamental

---

[31] 491 F.2d at 213.

[32] *See* United States v. Berke Cake Co., 50 F. Supp. 311 (D.N.Y. 1943), *appeal dismissed,* 320 U.S. 807 (1943) (an alleged section 241 conspiracy to prevent employees from enforcing their rights under the Fair Labor Standards Act; held that FLSA provided the exclusive remedy).

[33] 341 U.S. 70 (1951).

[34] *Id.* at 77.

constitutional right,[35] the Court has apparently regarded it as being one of the latter types of right and thus not covered by section 241. In *Hodges v. United States,*[36] the Court held that the section did not apply to acts of force which were designed to prevent Negro citizens from working in a sawmill, in that the plaintiff's alleged Thirteenth Amendment right to be free of the disabilities of slavery could be violated only by conduct which actually enslaves and not by mere personal asault. Subsequently, in the *Williams* case, the Court cited *Hodges* as involving a typical "nonfederal" kind of constitutional right for section 241 purposes.[37]

The specific holding of *Hodges* was, however, overruled in *Jones v. Alfred H. Mayer Co.,*[38] and the nonfederal characterization which the Court in *Williams* placed upon the right to work is arguably inconsistent with later section 241 cases. In *United States v. Guest,*[39] for example, the Court held that the implicit constitutional right to travel had a sufficient nexus with exclusive federal jurisdiction over interstate commerce to make it the kind of right section 241 was designed to encompass. There is no reason why the right to work in interstate commerce should not be similarly treated. Violence aimed at preventing out-of-state applicants from competing in the local job market bears the closest analogy to *Guest.* But the fact that the enterprise itself is in interstate commerce should not be sufficient to satisfy the "federal nexus" requirement of section 241. Certainly, if the commerce clause is broad enough to warrant legislation granting employees a federal right to work free from union violence,[40] then it is also broad enough to convert the constitutional right to work into one involving the relation-

---

[35] Although the parameters of this constitutional right are ill defined and its vindication probably inadequate under current law, *see* Haggard, *The Right To Work—A Constitutional and Natural Law Perspective,* 1 J. SOC. & POL. AFFAIRS 215 (1976), the right has long been recognized to exist. *See* Barsky v. Board of Regents, 347 U.S. 472 (1953) (Douglas, dissenting) ("The right to work . . . [is] the most precious liberty man possesses."); Butchers' Union Slaughter-House & Livestock Landing Co. v. Crescent City Co., 111 U.S. 746, 762 (1884) (Bradley, concurring) ("The right to follow any of the common occupations of life is an inalienable right." In re Tiburcio Parrott, 1 Fed. 481 (1880) ("The right to labor is, of all others, after the right to live, the fundamental, inalienable right of man."); Opinion of the Justices, 247 Mass. 589, 597 (1924) ("The right to labor and to do ordinary business are natural, essential, and inalienable, parting of the nature both of personal liberty and private property.").

[36] 203 U.S. 1 (1906).

[37] 341 U.S. at 77, 80.

[38] 392 U.S. 409, 441-43 n.78 (1968).

[39] 383 U.S. 745 (1966).

[40] Section 8(b)(1)(A) of the National Labor Relations Act, 29 U.S.C. § 158(b)(1)(A), which is predicated on the commerce clause of the constitution, creates a statutory right of employees to be free of labor union violence. *See* Chapter XI, *supra.*

ship between the individual and the federal government, and thus protected by section 241.[41]

There are, however, other federal criminal statutes capable of dealing with certain kinds of union violence, and some of them have indeed been so utilized. The Travel Act, for example makes it a federal crime to travel in interstate commerce with intent to commit violence or engage in any unlawful activity, such as arson.[42] Another section of the federal code prohibits the use of explosives to damage or destroy any building, vehicle, or other property;[43] and the Racketeer Influenced and Corrupt Organization Act (RICO) makes it an illegal conspiracy to operate a union by means of a "pattern of racketeering activity," a term which includes "any act or threat, involving murder, kidnaping, . . . arson, robbery . . ." etc.[44]

In *United States v. Thordarson*,[45] several officers and employees of a local Teamsters union were indicted under these three statutes for damaging or destroying the trucks of an employer against whom they had called a strike. The federal district court, however, dismissed the indictments on the grounds that labor unionists cannot be prosecuted under federal criminal law for violent activity which occurs during the course of an otherwise legitimate labor dispute.

The Court's authority for that rather extraordinay proposition of law was, of course, *United States v. Enmons*,[46] which involved a similar construction of the federal anti-extortion statute (the Hobbs Act). The district court in *Thordarson* concluded that the Travel Act, like the Hobbs Act, was concerned with labor racketeering, not with labor violence; that criminal statutes "must be strictly construed, with any ambiguity being resolved in favor of lenity;"[47] that in the absence of

---

[41] This would certainly seem to be consistent with the legislative history of the Thirteenth and Fourteenth Amendments and the post-Civil war civil rights statutes taken as a whole. *See, generally,* Vieira, *Of Syndicalism, Slavery and the Thirteenth Amendment,* 12 WAKE FOREST L. REV. 515, 674-95 (1976).

[42] 18 U.S.C. § 1952 (1976).

[43] 18 U.S.C. § 844(i)(1976).

[44] 18 U.S.C. §§ 1962(d), 1961(1)(1976).

[45] 646 F.2d 1323 (9th Cir. 1981), *cert. denied,* 102 S.Ct. 601 (1981).

[46] 410 U.S. 396 (1973). For a detailed and critical analysis of the *Enmons* decision, *see* Chapter IX, *supra* at 275-84.

[47] 487 F. Supp. 991, 993 (D. Calif. 1980). Under the normal rules of statutory interpretation, if the language of a statute has a plain and unambiguous meaning, it is presumed that this is what the legislature intended and a court is not justified in relying on other indices of legislative intent to reach a result that runs counter to that meaning. *See* R. DICKERSON, THE INTERPRETATION AND APPLICATION OF STATUTES 214 (1975). In the federal courts, however, it would seem that the rule is being increasingly observed by its breach. This case is a particularly egregious example of it. The district court conceded that the provisions of the statute as written "arguably apply" to the conduct for which

explicit language to that effect, the court would not assume that Congress intended to either intrude upon the traditional criminal jurisdiction of the states or "put the Federal Government in the business of policing the orderly conduct of strikes;"[48] and that in any event the controlling federal law in labor controversies was the National Labor Relations Act (NLRA).[49]

The Ninth Circuit Court of Appeals disagreed. It pointed out that the *Enmons* decision was predicated on an interpretation of the term "wrongful" in the Hobbs Act and on the specific legislative history of that statute. The court found nothing in either the language or the legislative history of the Travel Act to suggest a similar interpretation.

With respect to *Enmons* policy of not involving the federal government in the routine policing of strike activity, the court concluded that this too was unique to the statute being construed there. Since extortion theoretically embraces *any* threat or act of violence that is used to obtain the property of another, even minor acts of strike or picket line misconduct could fall within its prohibitions. To avoid converting such routine misconduct into a federal felony, which was said to be inconsistent with the legislative intent, the *Enmons* court engrafted onto the statute an exception for all violence which occurs during an otherwise legitimate strike. The *Thordarson* court concluded, however, that such an exception was unnecessary with respect to the crimes encompassed by the Travel Act. "The destruction of vehicles used in interstate commerce by means of explosives and travel in interstate commerce to commit arson are hardly the sorts of minor picket line violence that the *Enmons* Court feared would be transformed into federal crimes under the Hobbs Act."[50] Similarly, although the *Enmons* Court decided that in the Hobbs Act, Congress did not intend to intrude upon the states' prerogative in regulating routine strike violence, the *Thordarson* court noted that the Travel Act was a direct response to the perceived lack of local control over the interstate use of explosives.

With respect to the preemption argument, the court simply noted

---

the defendants were indicted; but the court then relied on the legislative history to dismiss the indictments, not because it found in that history any evidence of an affirmative intent on the part of Congress to *exclude* this kind of conduct from the general statutory prohibition, but rather because it simply failed to find evidence of specific intent to *include* it! *Id.* at 994-95. The dangers that this technique of statutory interpretation pose for the principle of separation of powers is discussed in Walker, *The Exorbitant Cost of Redistributing Injustice: United Steelworkers of America v. Weber,* 21 B.C.L. Rev. 1, 59-67 (1976).

[48] 487 F. Supp. at 993, quoting *Enmons.*

[49] The court concluded that the prosecution in this case, like the prosecution in *DeLaurentis,* was an unjustifiable attempt "to convert an unfair labor practice into a criminal conspiracy." *Id.* at 995.

[50] 646 F.2d at 1329.

that since the unfair labor practice provisions of the NLRA do not preempt state criminal law prohibiting some of the same kinds of misconduct, they certainly do not preempt the equivalent federal laws either.[51]

In sum, the *Thordarson* court limited *Enmons* to the specific criminal statute at issue there, and refused to read the case as establishing a general, federal criminal law immunity for all labor violence that happens to occur in the context of an otherwise legitimate labor dispute.[52] In addition to the reasons expressly stated by the court, another consideration supports that conclusion very strongly: the *Enmons* decision itself is of dubious validity[53] and properly deserves to be construed no more broadly than the doctrine of precedent would absolutely require. The *Thordarson* case so treats it, and thus leaves open a federal avenue of relief against labor union violence—subject, of course, to the willingness of federal district attorneys to pursue it.

There are, of course, other federal criminal statutes of general application which might cover certain kinds of labor union violence. In *Langel v. United States,*[54] for example, striking unionists dynamited several company trucks and were subsequently convicted of possession of an untaxed and unregistered "firearm" (a bomb).

On the other hand, section 530 of the Landrum-Griffin Act[56] is of specific rather than general applicability insofar as labor union violence is concerned. That section provides criminal penalties for the use or

---

[51] In this regard, the court also noted that the defendants' reliance on *DeLaurentis* was misplaced, in that the substantive right allegedly violated there was a right created by the National Labor Relations Act itself, with the presumption being that Congress intended for that act to also provide the exclusive remedy, whereas that could not be said of the right at issue here. 646 F.2d at 1331.

[52] The same conclusion was reached by the court in United States v. Chambers, 515 F. Supp. 1, 3 (N.D. Ohio, 1981), as follows:

The defendants would have the Court interpret *Enmons* to create an immunity from federal prosecution for union members for any acts, otherwise unlawful, committed in the course of a labor dispute. To state such an argument is to refute it. The end does not justify the means. If a labor dispute makes arson lawful, does it not make murder also unlawful, since the former frequently ends in the latter? This court rejects such an expansive reading of the *Enmons* case.

See, United States v. Parker, 586 F.2d 422 (5th Cir. 1978), *cert. denied,* 441 U.S. 962 (1979); United States v. Love, 482 F.2d 213 (5th Cir.), *cert. denied,* 414 U.S. 1026 (1973).

[53] *See* Chapter IX, *supra,* at 281-84.

[54] 451 F.2d 957 (8th Cir. 1971).

[55] This was in violation of 26 U.S.C. §§ 5821, 5871 (1976); 18 U.S.C. § 371 (1976). The following statutes might also be used in appropriate circumstances: 18 U.S.C. §§ 33 (destruction of motor vehicles and motor vehicle facilities), 921 thru 928 (firearm laws), 1111 (murder), 1112 (manslaughter), 1231 (interstate transportation of persons hired to use force or violence against employees in the exercise of their Section 7 rights), and 2101 (riot).

[56] 29 U.S.C. § 530 (1976).

threatened use of force or violence against union members in the exercise of their membership rights under that particular statute. Unlike its civil damages counterpart,[57] the criminal prohibition applies not only to union officials but also to "any person" who coercively violates a member's rights. Persons thus have been convicted for viciously assaulting members in the exercise of their right to attend and participate in union meetings[58] and to complain about union elections.[59]

DAMAGE ACTIONS

A fundamental maxim of common law jurisprudence—and one, indeed, which flows directly from the canons of natural justice—is that a person who has wrongfully injured another should be required to compensate the victim for the damages suffered thereby. It is not surprising, thus, that both state and federal law allow an action for damages against the perpetrators of strike and picket line violence.

State Law

Whatever else it may be, labor union violence—assaults, trespass, damage to property, preventing egress and ingress, and the other forms of misconduct previously discussed—is also nearly always a common law tort, for which the injured party can sue to recover compensatory damages. When the defendant in such a suit is another private individual, the issues are basically no different than they would be in any tort action—proving the elements of the tort (whatever they happen to be under state law), proving that the defendant committed the tort, and proving damages.

Although this kind of law suit may provide a relatively adequate remedy in simpler cases, complications arise when there has been massive violence and the damages are extensive. A class action[60] or a conspiracy suit[61] against all the participants is often difficult to maintain, and the individual defendants may in any event be virtually "judgment proof" in regard to the enforcement of the award. In this kind of case, thus, the victims of strike and picket line violence have more

---

[57] 29 U.S.C. § 412 (1976).

[58] United States v. Bertucci, 333 F.2d 292 (3d Cir.), *cert. denied,* 379 U.S. 839 (1964); United States v. Roganovich, 318 F.2d 167 (7th Cir. 1963), *cert. denied,* 375 U.S. 911 (1963).

[59] United States v. Kelley, 545 F.2d 619 (8th Cir. 1976), *cert. denied,* 430 U.S. 933 (1977).

[60] *See generally,* Forkosch, *The Legal Status and Suability of Labor Organizations,* 28 TEMPLE L.Q. 1 (1954).

[61] For a case applying the conspiracy theory to a picket line assault, see Hall v. Walters, 85 S.E.2d 729 (S.C.), *cert. denied,* 349 U.S. 953 (1955).

often demanded compensation for their injuries from the labor union conducting the strike or other activity during which the violence occurred. A suit of this nature is also not without its difficulties, however. Generally speaking, in legal contemplation, labor unions are mere "unincorporated associations," an entity unknown to the common law—which also originally meant that they could neither sue nor be sued as separate entities.[62] This old common law rule, however, has been abrogated by statute in most states,[63] and by judicial decree in others.[64] Just recently, for example, in *Diluzio v. United Electrical Workers Local 274,*[65] the Supreme Judicial Court for the Commonwealth of Massachusetts overturned that state's common law rule, and held that labor unions should be treated as legal entities capable of suing or being sued. In that case, the plaintiff sued the union and two individual members for mental suffering and damage to her automobile resulting from an assault upon her as she drove through a picket line at her place of employment. The court noted that

---

[62] *See, e.g.,* Baskin v. United Mine Workers of America, 234 S.W. 464 (Ark. 1921); Picket v. Walsh, 78 N.E. 753 (Mass. 1906).

[63] *See, e.g.,* ALA. CODE §§ 6-7-80, 6-7-81; ARIZ. REV. STAT. ANN. § 23-1323 (1971); CONN. GEN. STAT. § 52-76 (1981); DEL. CODE ANN. tit. 10, § 3904 (1974); FLA. STAT. § 447.11 (1979); GA. CODE ANN. § 3-117 - 3-121 (1975); HAWAII REV. STAT. 634-3 (1976); KAN. STAT. ANN. § 44-811 (1981); LA. CODE CIV. PRO. ANN. art. 738 (West 1960); MD. CTS. & JUD. PROD. CODE § 6-406 (1980); MICH. COMP. LAWS § 612.12 (1981); MINN. STAT. §§ 540.151, 540.152, 540.154 (1980); MONT. CODES ANN. § 25-5-104 (1981); NEB. REV. STAT. § 25-313 (1979); NEV. REV. STAT. § 12.110 (1979); N.H. REV. STAT. ANN. c. 510, § 13 (1968); N.M. STAT. ANN. §§ 53-10-5, 53-10-6 (1981); N.Y. GEN. ASS'NS LAWS §§ 12-13 (McKinney 1942); N.C. GEN. STAT. §§ 1-69, 1A-1, Rule 4(j)(8) (1969 & Cum. Supp. 1981); OHIO REV. CODE ANN. §§ 1745.01, 1745.02 (Baldwin 1982); OKLA. STAT. tit. 12, § 182 (1971); R.I. GEN. LAWS §§ 9-2-12, 9-2-14 (1970); S.C. CODE §§ 15-5-160, 15-9-330 (1977); S.D. CODIFIED LAWS §§ 60-9-1 - 60-9-3 (1978); TENN. CODE § 20-20202 (1981); VT. STAT. ANN. tit. 12, § 814 (1973); VA. CODE § 8.01-15 (1977).

[64] In some states, the courts have done this by court rule. *See, e.g.,* ALASKA R.C.P. 17(b) (1981); COLO. R.C.P. 17(b) (1977); IND. R.C.P. 17(b) (1973); 42 PA. CONS. STAT. ANN. Rule 2153 (Purdon 1975); UTAH R.C.P. 17(d) (1977); WYO. R.C.P. 17(b) (1979). Other courts have held that unions may sue and be sued by implication from other statutory authority. *See* Lockridge, v. Amalgamated Ass'n of St. Elec. Ry. & Motor Coach Employees, 84 Idaho 201, 204 (1962); Jackson v. International Union of Operating Eng'rs, 307 Ky. 485 (1948); Varnado v. Whitney, 166 Miss. 663 (1933); Donnelly v. United Fruit Co., 40 N.J. 61 (1963). Still other courts have declared labor unions to be legal entities. *See* Marshall v. International Longshoremen's & Warehousemen's Union, Local 6, 57 Cal. 2d 781 (1962); Keith Theatre Inc. v. Vachon, 134 Maine 392 (1936); Pushor v. Hilton, 123 Maine 225 (1923); Brawner v. Sanders, 244 Or. 302, 304 (1966); Borden v. United Ass'n of Journeymen & Apprentices, 316 S.W.2d 458 (Tex. Civ. App. 1958), *rev'd on other grounds,* 373 U.S. 690 (1963); Arnold v. National Union of Marine Cooks & Stewards Ass'n, 42 Wash. 2d 648 (1953), *aff'd,* 348 U.S. 37 (1954). Finally, other courts have gotten around the rule by allowing representative suits against individual defendants but with *recovery* against the union as an entity. *See* Thomas v. Dean, 245 Ark. 446 (1968); United Packing House Workers Local 38 v. Boynton, 240 Iowa 212 (1949).

[65] _____ N.E. 2d _____ (Mass. 1982).

474 Union Violence

at the time the common law rule was established, labor unions were strug-
gling for their existence and for recognition. Now "unions have become
endowed with great privileges and responsibilities as representatives of
their members. Existence of such privileges must be accompanied by a correlative duty not to misuse them to the injury of [the public or] individual
union members. Immunity for liability for misuse is inconsistent with basic
notions of justice." . . . "It would be unfortunate if an organization with as
great power as [a labor union] has in the raising of large funds and in directing the conduct of [its] members in carrying on, in a wide territory, industrial controversies and strikes, out of which so much unlawful injury to
private rights is possible, could assemble its assets to be used therein free
from liability for injuries by torts committed in course of such strikes.[66]

Although in most jurisdictions a labor union is thus now an entity
capable of being sued, its liability necessarily depends on the acts of its
officers and members. Establishing the union's legal responsibility for
these acts is sometimes difficult, however. In some cases, plaintiffs
have proceeded on the theory that the union and its members were
engaged in a conspiracy and that the union, thus, was responsible for
the violent acts of its co-conspirators whether it knew about them or
not.[67] Conspiracy, however, is not a favored theory in labor relations,[68]
and in most states the liability of a labor union for acts of violence is
normally established on some other basis.

Generally speaking, a labor union can be held vicariously liable for
the tortious acts of its agents under either the theory of consent or of
respondeat superior.[69] Consent may be in the form of either authorization or ratification, and it may be actual or implied. It is, of course, hard
to obtain proof that a union official with authority to do so actually or
formally authorized an act of violence, although it is sometimes possible to establish that on the basis of circumstantial evidence.[70] For the
purposes of establishing union liability, the equivalent of actual
authorization is also commonly said to exist when that official personally participates in the tortious misconduct. For example in *United Air-*

---

[66] *Id.* at _____ (brackets in original).
[67] *See, e.g.,* International Union, UAW v. Russell, 88 So. 2d 175 (Ala. 1956), *aff'd,* 356
U.S. 634 (1958). *See also,* United Electrical Coal Companies v. Rice, 22 F. Supp. 221
(E.D. Ill. 1938) (discussion of Illinois law).
[68] *Accord,* United Mine Workers v. Gibbs, 383 U.S. 715, 732 (1966).
[69] *See generally,* Comment, *Tort Liability of Labor Unions for Picket Line Assaults,* 10 U.
MICH. J. LAW REFORM 517 (1977); Comment, *The Liability of Labor Unions for Picket
Line Assaults,* 21 U.C.L.A. L. Rev. 600 (1973). Myers, *State Damage Suit by an Employer
Against a Labor Union for Injuries Incurred Through Violence During a Strike,* 34 TENN.
L. REV. 609 (1967), Evans, *The Law of Agency and the National Unions,* 49 KY. L.J. 295
(1961). The common law rules of agency are also discussed extensively at pp. 418-25,
supra.
[70] *See* International Union of Operating Engr's v. Lassitter, 295 So. 2d 634 (Fla. Dist.
Ct. of App. 1974).

craft Corp. v. International Ass'n of Machinists,[71] the president and vice president of the union local, two business representatives of the district, the district organizer, and the international representative were all found to have participated in mass picketing, assaults upon persons and automobiles, and other tortious acts; their participation thus provided the basis for the liability of both the local and the international union.

On the other hand, with respect to the tortious acts of lesser union functionaries or mere members, since actual authorization of the literal sort can again rarely be proved, union liability here is sometimes based on a theory of implied authorization. For example, in *McDaniel v. Textile Workers Union,*[72] a local union was held to have implicitly authorized an assault because its officers were present when the assault occurred and apparently encouraged it, even though they did not participate directly.

It is more common, however, to base a finding of union consent on the fact that it subsequently approved of or ratified the violence. Ratification, for example, has been found where the union arranged bail and paid the fine of a member who committed the assault and failed to expell other pickets who had threatened the victim.[73] Conduct that has been found to constitute ratification under the NLRA—such as a failure to disavow known violence or prevent its recurrence—should also be considered adequate to show ratification in a damage action, since the federal law on that issue is merely an application of common law principles of agency.[74]

Although liability on the basis of consent thus requires either authorization or ratification by the union, liability can also be established under the doctrine of *respondeat superior*. Here, liability attaches even if the misconduct *was* previously prohibited or subsequently disapproved. The doctrine does, however, require two things: that the equivalent of a master-servant relationship exist between the union and the person who actually committed the violence, and that this person was acting within the "scope of his employment" when the misconduct occurred.

---

[71] 285 A.2d 330, 339-41 (Conn. Sup. Ct. 1971). For an additional discussion of this case, see p. 239, nn. 283-88, *supra. See also* UMW v. Patton, 211 F.2d 724 (4th Cir. 1954), and other cases cited in Evans, *supra* note 72, at 302 n.19.

[72] 254 S.W.2d 1 (Tenn. 1952).

[73] *See, e.g.,* Coats v. Construction & Gen. Laborers Local 185, 93 Cal. Rptr. 639 (1971); UAW v. American Metal Prods. Co., 408 S.W.2d 682 (Tenn. 1964); Hall v. Walters, 85 S.E.2d 729 (S.C.), *cert. denied,* 349 U.S. 953 (1955).

[74] For a discussion of the NLRA cases involving tacit ratification by silence, see pp. 419-22, *supra.*

It is generally recognized that ranking officers of a local or national union have a master-servant relationship with the union. The president, vice president, secretary-treasurer, business agents, organizers, and field representatives of such unions are thus frequently regarded as agents for the purpose of imputing liability to the union.[75] On the other hand, although a person is not an agent of the union merely by virtue of his membership in that union,[76] the doctrine of *respondeat superior* has sometimes been applied to pickets who commit acts of violence.[77] Since pickets are often recruited by the union for this duty, assigned to specific stations, equipped with picket signs, put under the supervision of picket line captains, and sometimes even paid for performing this duty, it is not at all inconsistent with the general principles of the master-servant relationship to treat these pickets as agents of the union.[78]

Before the union can be held vicariously liable for the acts of even an agent, it is still necessary to show, however, that those acts were committed "within the scope of the agent's employment." Under general agency law, this is generally determined by factors such as the time, place, and purpose of the actions, and whether the unauthorized conduct is similar in quality to acts which have been authorized.[79] The first of these factors would appear to be satisfied with respect to assaults and property damage that occur during a strike or union organizational drive, that take place on the picket line or at some place to which a nonstriking employee has been followed, and which are designed to induce employees to support the union or the employer to capitulate to its demands. Moreover, since the line between "peaceful" and "coercive" picketing is apparently as unclear as it is frequently crossed, the second factor would similarly seem to be satisfied in most cases of industrial relations violence. As a National Labor Relations Board (NLRB) trial examiner put it in another context, "threats and the employment of force on a picket line, even though forbidden, are

---

[75] *See* Evans, *The Law of Agency and the National Unions,* 49 Ky. L.J. 295, 313 & nn. 62, 63 (1961).

[76] Similarly, for the purpose of charging a union with an unfair labor practice, the acts of rank-and-file members are not necessarily the acts of the union itself. *See* text at p. 420 & n. 396, *supra.*

[77] *See, e.g.,* Titus v. Tacoma Smeltermen's Local 25, 383 P.2d 504 (Wash. 1963); United Bhd. of Carpenters v. Humphreys, 127 S.E.2d 98 (Va. 1962), *cert. denied,* 371 U.S. 954 (1963). *See also,* Teamsters Local 327 (Coca Cola Bottling Co. of Louisville), 184 N.L.R.B. 84 (1970) (union responsible for the acts of "authorized pickets").

[78] *Accord,* Comment, *The Liability of Labor Unions for Picket Line Assaults,* 21 U.C.L.A. L. Rev. 600, 616-17 (1973).

[79] *See* Evans, *The Law of Agency and the National Unions,* 49 Ky. L.J. 295, 315-19 (1961).

reasonably to be expected, and so 'within the scope of employment of pickets for which the labor organization is responsible.' "[80] Likewise, in *United Brotherhood of Carpenters v. Humphreys,*[81] a Virginia court stated that "the assaults were not committed to satisfy any personal motives of the assailants, but were caused by some emotion which naturally grew out of and was incident to the performance of strike activities."[82]

These common law principles of agency are controlling, however, only in the absence of more specific statutory standards. In states with so-called "Little Norris-LaGuardia Acts," a much higher standard of proof is commonly required.[83] In *United Aircraft Corp. v. International Ass'n. of Machinists,*[84] for example, the Connecticut Supreme Court held, at least with respect to subordinate union officials, that proving liability on the union's part requires "more than the agency rules of *respondeat superior* and more than the general authority with which an officer of the organization is clothed by virtue of his office. We subscribe to the proposition that the statute requires proof by the plaintiff that the acts complained of were either expressly authorized by the organization to be charged or were such that they flowed from that authorization."[85]

On the other hand, two states have construed their statutes as requiring a higher standard of proof *only* in injunction cases. The Washington statute, for example, rather unequivocally states that no labor organization "shall be held responsible or liable in any court of the state of Washington for the unlawful acts of individual officers, members, or agents, except upon clear proof of actual participation in, or actual authorization of, such acts, or of ratification of such acts after actual knowledge thereof."[86] In *Buchanan v. International Brotherhood of Teamsters,*[87] however, the Washington Supreme Court reaffirmed a prior decision limiting the applicability of this section to cases involving restraining orders, injunctions, and contempt proceedings. The court concluded from the title description of the statute that this was

[80] Teamsters Local 327 (Coca Cola Bottling Co. of Louisville), 184 N.L.R.B. 84, 94 (1970).
[81] 127 S.E.2d 98 (Va. 1962), *cert. denied,* 371 U.S. 954 (1963).
[82] 127 S.E.2d at 103.
[83] *See generally,* pp. 235-44, *supra.*
[84] 285 A.2d 330 (Conn. 1971), *cert. denied,* 404 U.S. 1016 (1972).
[85] 285 A.2d at 337.
[86] WASH. REV. CODE § 49.32.070 (1979).
[87] 617 P.2d 1004 (Wash. 1980). *See also,* Titus v. Tacoma Smeltermen's Union, 383 P.2d 504 (1963); *see generally,* 57 WASH. L. REV. 193 (1981).

478   *Union Violence*

the narrow concern of the legislature, and thus held that normal rules of agency law were intended to remain applicable in determining a union's vicarious tort liability.[88]

Once a defendant's tort liability is established, the plaintiff is normally entitled to recover all damages that are a natural and proximate result of the tortious acts. In cases of picket line and strike violence, successful plaintiffs are obviously entitled to recover for personal injury and property damage,[89] for the emotional distress they have suffered,[90] and, in proper cases, a punitive award as well.[91]

When union violence has caused a disruption in the normal operation of a business, the economic losses suffered by employers and employees alike can also be recovered. In one case, for example, the employer recovered various excess labor and operating costs that were attributable to the misconduct.[92] Where violence has shut down a plant altogether, the employer is entitled to recover lost profits[93] and the employees their lost wages[94]—subject, of course, to proof that these losses were in fact attributable to the union violence itself and not to the otherwise peaceful aspects of the strike. As the Supreme Court put it in *UMW v. Gibbs,* "the permissible scope of state remedies . . . is strictly confined to the direct consequences of such [violent] conduct."[95]

In addition to the common law right to recover damages, in some states there is also a statutory right to recover damages for violations of various laws prohibiting the use of violence in the labor context.[96]

---

[88] *See also,* Nelson v. Haley, 111 N.E.2d 812 (Ind. 1953). The holdings in these state court cases should be compared with *Charles D. Bonnano Linen Service, Inc. v. McCarthy,* 532 F.2d 189 (1st Cir. 1976), which held that the proof provisions of the federal Norris-LaGuardia Act applied only to liability for damages or contempt. *See* text at pp. 200-44, *supra.*

[89] *See, e.g.,* International Brhd. of Boilermakers v. Newman, 158 S.E.2d 298 (Ga. 1967) (dynamite exploded in plaintiff's bar); United Bhd. of Carpenters v. Humphreys, 127 S.E.2d 98 (Va. 1962), *cert. denied,* 371 U.S. 954 (1963) (assault); Hall v. Walters, 85 S.E.2d 729 (S.C. 1955), *cert. denied,* 349 U.S. 953 (1955) (assault); McDaniel v. Textile Workers Union, 254 S.W.2d 1 (Tenn. 1952) (shooting).

[90] Gentry v. United Steelworkers Local 6178 (Garland County, Arkansas, Circuit Court) (unreported decision; $125,000 awarded for emotional distress).

[91] *See, e.g.,* UMW v. Meadow Creek Coal Co., 263 F.2d 52 (6th Cir. 1959); UAW v. American Metal Prod. Co., 408 S.W.2d 682 (Tenn. Ct. App. 1964).

[92] Overnite Transportation Co. v. Teamsters Union, 125 S.E.2d 277 (N.C. 1962).

[93] *See* United Aircraft Corp. v. International Ass'n of Machinists, 84 L.R.R.M. 2341 (Conn. Super. Ct. 1973); UAW v. American Metal Prod. Co., 408 S.W.2d 682 (Tenn. Ct. App. 1964).

[94] Titus v. Tacoma Smeltermen's Local 25, 383 P.2d 504 (Wash. 1963) (pleadings raised an issue of fact about whether work was actually available to these plaintiffs).

[95] 383 U.S. at 729.

[96] *See, e.g.,* Ariz. Rev. Stat. § 1306; Neb. Rev. Stat. § 613. 290.

Federal Law

There is, of course, no federal common law of torts. State law tort claims may be litigated in federal court on the basis of either diversity[97] or pendent jurisdiction,[98] but in such cases the court is still bound by the limitations of the federal Norris-LaGuardia Act.[99] For example, suits brought under section 303 of the NLRA, which allows damages for illegal secondary boycotts,[100] also frequently include a claim for damages based on state law.[101] Liability under section 303 is based on common law agency rules,[102] while the "clear proof of participation, authorization or ratification" standard applies to the state law claim.[103] It is to a plaintiff's advantage, thus, to include as many of his damage claims as he can under the section 303 violation, and thus to avoid the Norris-LaGuardia Act's more strict standard of proof.[104]

Violations of the Landrum-Griffin Act[105] can also be the basis of a private action for damages. Section 412 of that statute provides that "any person whose rights secured by the provisions of this subchapter have been infringed by any violation of this subchapter may bring a civil action in a district court of the United States for such relief (including injunctions) as may be appropriate."[106] In *Tomko v. Hilbert,*[107] the Third Circuit Court of Appeals held that since the purpose of the legislation was to protect the *union*-member relationship, section 412 should be construed as imposing civil liability only upon labor unions or persons acting in the capacity of an official or agent of a labor union, and not upon persons acting in a purely private capacity. That agency relationship, however, is determined by reference to the

---

[97] *See, e.g.,* Sisco v. McNutt, 209 F.2d 550 (8th Cir. 1954).

[98] *See, e.g.,* Ritchie v. UMW, 410 F.2d 827 (6th Cir. 1969).

[99] United Mine Workers v. Gibbs, 383 U.S. 715 (1966).

[100] Labor Management Relations Act § 303, 29 U.S.C. § 187 (1976).

[101] Labor Management Relations Act § 301(e), 29 U.S.C. § 185 (1976), provides that "in determining whether any person is acting as an 'agent' of another person so as to make such other person responsible for his acts, the question of whether the specific acts performed were actually authorized or subsequently ratified shall not be controlling." *See* Carbon Fuel Co. v. UMW, 444 U.S. 212, 217 n.6 (1979) (common law doctrine of respondeat superior applies).

[102] *See, e.g.,* United Mine Workers v. Gibbs, 383 U.S. 715 (1966); Federal Prescription Service v. Amalgamated Meat Cutters, 527 F.2d 269 (8th Cir. 1975); Ritchie v. UMW, 410 F.2d 827 (6th Cir. 1969).

[103] *See, e.g.,* Kerry Coal Co. v. UMW, 488 F. Supp. 1080, 1097-88 (W.D. Pa. 1980).

[104] Suing under the pendent state law claim may be necessary, however, if the plaintiff wants to hold individual defendants partially liable for the damages, since only "labor organizations" can be sued under the Section 303 claim; punitive damages similarly cannot be recovered under Section 303. Teamsters Local 20 v. Morton, 377 U.S. 252 (1964).

[105] 29 U.S.C. §§ 401 to 531 (1976).

[106] 29 U.S.C. § 412 (1976).

[107] 288 F.2d 625 (3d Cir. 1961).

common law rules rather than the stricter standards of Norris-LaGuardia.[108] In *Shimman v. Frank,*[109] the court thus allowed recovery against the two union members who actually administered the beating, as well as against the local union itself whose officers had instigated the beating and who had otherwise failed to curb the abusive conduct that had been directed against the union dissidents.[110] The plaintiffs in that case recovered their medical bills, lost wages, damages for pain and suffering, attorneys' fees, and punitive damages.

Another federal statute which has recently been used as a vehicle for obtaining civil damages against the perpetrators of union violence is 42 U.S.C. §1985(3).[111] This section, which is a part of the post-Civil War rights statutes, allows the recovery of damages against persons who conspire to deprive any other person or class of persons of the equal protection of the laws. In *Scott v. Moore,*[112] the fifth circuit (en banc) held that the victims of union violence could, under proper circumstances, state a cause of action and recover civil damages under this section. In that case, a construction company that hired without regard to union affiliation and which did not have a collective bargaining agreement with any union had been the object of repeated threats and protest demonstrations by officers and members of the Sabine Area Building and Construction Trades Council. Finally, one morning "the mob swarmed over the construction site, brutally beating Cross and his employees with iron rods and wooden boards, overturning and setting fire to the trailer that served as the construction site office, smashing automobile and truck windshields, and vandalizing company tools and equipment."[113]

In evaluating the elements of a section 1985(3) cause of action, the court in *Scott* easily found that a conspiracy existed, that the violence occurred in the furtherance of that conspiracy, that these acts of violence were indisputably illegal apart from section 1985(3), and that they resulted in personal injuries, property damage, and economic loss.

---

[108] Shimman v. Frank, 625 F.2d 80 (6th Cir. 1980).

[109] 625 F.2d 80 (6th Cir. 1980). *See also,* Parker v. Steelworkers Local 1466, 106 L.R.R.M. 3038 (5th Cir. 1981).

[110] The court, however, held that the plaintiff had failed to establish that either the assailants or the local union were acting as agents of the international union in this incident, and the court therefore exonerated the international from all liability. 625 F.2d 80.

[111] 42 U.S.C. § 1985(3) (1976). *See generally,* Lanery, *Conspiratorial Violence at Picket Lines: Actionable Under § 1985(3) and § 1981,* 5 SAN FERNANDO VALLEY L. REV. 227 (1976).

[112] 680 F.2d 979 (5th Cir. 1982) (en banc), *reversed,* U.S. Sup. Court, July 5, 1983. *But see,* Bova v. Pipefitters Local 60, 554 F.2d 226 (5th Cir. 1977); Iowa Beef Processors v. Gorman, 476 F.Supp. 1382 (N.D. Iowa, 1979).

[113] 680 F.2d at 984.

The only element of the offense that required analysis was the requirement that the conspiracy be for the purpose of depriving a person of the equal protection of the laws. This requirement, the court further indicated, has two components: "(1) the violation of some protected right and (2) a class-based, invidiously discriminatory animus motivating the violation."[114]

With respect to the first element, the court had no difficulty in finding that the object and effect of the defendants' conspiratorial violence was to deprive the plaintiffs of their First Amendment right to associate with their fellow nonunion employees.

On the other hand, the second element was not to be satisfied so easily. The defendants had argued that since section 1985(3) was originally aimed at the Ku Klux Klan's acts of violence against the then-recently freed slaves, the section applied only when the discrimination or unequal treatment was based on the *racial* classification of the victims. The court, however, reviewed the legislative history of the section and concluded that it was not so limited and that at least *some* nonracial classes fell within its ambit as well. The question then became whether the particular class of which the plaintiffs were a part—namely, nonunion employees—were one of the classes covered by the statute's protective cloak. The court determined that they were.

The court noted tht the section was apparently intended to protect associations of both a political and a religious character, classes similar to one defined in terms of union membership. The court noted that extending protection to this class of persons would be consistent with other federal legislation. And the court also noted that association was a fundamental right, with classifications based on the exercise of that right thus being especially suspect.

Having thus held that the plaintiffs were denied the equal protection of the law because they chose to associate with other nonunion employees, the court then went on to narrow its holding somewhat. It noted that "our decision does not imply that every union-nonunion controversy can create a Section 1985(3) cause of action. . . . Neither unionism nor nonunionism suffices to create a covered class."[115] The determinative element in this case was apparently the fact that there was no campaign to organize employees or other legitimate union activity going on at the time.[116]

The final issue that the court here had to confront was that of determining what the proper standard of proof was with respect to the

---

[114] *Id.* at 988. See note 112, *supra.*
[115] *Id.* at 996.
[116] *See id.* at 996 & n.13.

defendant unions. The unions contended that since the controversy arose out of a "labor dispute," the clear-proof standard of the Norris-LaGuardia Act should apply. The court, however, concluded that in the absence of any legitimate union activity, there simply was no "labor dispute" within the meaning of the Norris-LaGuardia Act, and the clear-proof standard thus did not apply. Nevertheless, the court did hold that involvement of some of the defendant unions could not be established even under the ordinary, common law standards for determining vicarious liability.

PART FIVE

Summary and Conclusions

CHAPTER XIII

Conclusions: Incidence and
Motivations of Union Violence

From the evidence presented in this study, there can be no remaining doubt that labor violence is a real and continuing problem. Its presence is a blight on industrial relations that arises with distressing frequency during organizational drives and strikes.

Approximately 3,000 accounts of labor violence have been given here, some of them compendia of hundreds of individual incidents which occurred during the period bounded by 1975 and 1981. These, however, are merely a representative sample of the violence that actually occurs: despite general recognition that labor violence is a problem, no central collection of statistics on it exists, and therefore, there is no realistic way of assessing its true extent. This in itself is a problem, and not simply one for researchers. Lack of consistent reporting serves to disguise the comprehensive nature of labor violence, and diverts from it the legislative attention that it needs.

The incidents reported here, derived mostly from newspaper reports, are often lacking in both consistency and specificity. Many of them, for example, say no more than that "vandalism to company property" occurred during some particular strike, or that "violence erupted on the picket line." They give little or no indication of whether the vandalism involved a wall being defaced by paint or a $100,000 crane being destroyed, or whether the violence on the picket line involved name calling or dynamiting.

In some cases, however, more specific information is available. The labor violence data base, from which Chapter III was derived, embraces some 2,600 records of incidents over a six-year period:

It includes accounts of 49 deaths directly attributable to labor violence;

It covers $15,233,000 worth of estimated damage to company plants and equipment for the 27 instances in which such estimates were made public. (There were approximately 155 other damage reports involving such things as warehouses, hotels, offices, construction projects, heavy equipment engines, and coal trucks for which no dollar estimates were made.);

It identifies at least 2,732 instances of damage to tires, windshields, or bodywork of automobiles;

It lists 229 instances of vandalism which include such items as 40,000 quarts of milk burned; 143 gas valves sabotaged; 20 acres of lettuce ruined; 71 hydraulic lines cut; 2-1/2 miles of fence pulled down; 300 shots fired into a plant; 21 parking meters sabotaged; 20 tons of TNT exploded; 14 plate glass store windows shattered; 300 fires set; 18 fire trucks disabled; 2 railroad trestles damaged; a hand grenade thrown into company headquarters—incidents that are impossible to quantify in dollar terms;

It covers hundreds of injuries or woundings, thousands of shots being fired, and innumerable instances of threats and harassment;

It lists 133 cases in which the homes of company managers or supervisors or the homes of nonunion employees or nonstrikers were shot at, firebombed, or vandalized;

It also includes accounts of attacks on every type of moving vehicle (with the possible exception of unicycles and submarines) including subway trains, tugboats, cabin cruisers, boxcars, tank trucks, locomotives, and earthmoving equipment, as well as thousands of cars and trucks;

It shows that electrical wires, gas lines, telephone lines, water mains, sewage systems, computer cables, and oxygen supplies were tampered with, interrupted, or destroyed in various strikes;

It is a persistent myth that labor violence is an aberrent, rather than a commonplace event that has been blown out of proportion by journalistic sensationalism. That myth is simply unsupportable. Despite the limitations of our data base and its lack of comprehensiveness, it provides ample evidence that violence in labor disputes is a pervasive, wisespread, and continuing problem.

CAUSES OF LABOR VIOLENCE

Other persistent myths about labor violence pertain to its causes. Common belief seems to hold that it arises out of frustration over managerial intransigence, is the spontaneous outgrowth of confrontation, or is the defensive reaction to management's economic or physical initiatives. Again, the recent case record simply does not support this myth. One does not hang the dog of a nonunion employee and attach to it a sign reading, "This happens to scabs," as a defensive reaction to management. Nor does one leave a severed pig's head on a nonunion employee's porch, shoot the dogs of a nonstriking prison guard or the horses of a company supervisor, abduct a nonstriker in fifteen degree temperature and tar and feather him, pull a company foreman from his truck and paint him yellow, or remove the name tags from fifty corpses at the county morgue out of frustration with an intransigent company management, yet all these incidents have occurred during strikes. The overwhelming majority of strikers retain their sensibilities during strikes, but the hostility of strike situations, the protective cover of mass action, and the general "neutrality" of authorities during labor disputes allows a few people the license to commit atrocities which a civilized society should not have to tolerate. In some strikes, patients in hospitals have been denied care, firebombs have been found on the roofs of psychiatric wards, busloads of handicapped and emotionally disturbed children have been attacked, city water supplies have been poisoned, and hundreds of fires have been set in a single city on a single day; the cars, the homes, and the children, spouses, parents, in-laws, and even neighbors of supervisors, nonstrikers or nonunion employees have been threatened, harassed, or attacked.

These incidents cannot conceivably be attributed to frustration or defensive reaction, and they are too numerous to be ascribed to the actions of madmen. Their particular motivations are, of course, unknown, but their general purpose is almost certainly to engender fear and to use that emotion to augment the economic pressures on the employer and thus hasten the settlement of a dispute.

A review of the listings reveals that the most common violent incidents are those which arise from mass picketing, where the protective cover of the mob allows individuals to act with less fear of reprisal. Automobile tires are the most frequently vandalized objects. In thousands of instances they have been stabbed, ice-picked, slashed, cut, punctured, or deflated during the course of strikes.

Damaging automobile tires or other parts of cars is not, of course, an end in itself, but is instead a means of conveying a message to the owner. Usually the message pertains to the evils of crossing a picket line to work at a struck plant. Some attacks on automobiles are more-or-less random in nature, and do arise out of picket line confrontations. Others are more personal and, therefore, more frightening. Excluding for a moment the obviously heinous crimes (such as murder and assault with intent to kill), the most chilling forms of violence during labor disputes, are those which single out the victims as individual targets, particularly when the violence occurs away from the workplace. When one's car is firebombed in one's garage, when a shotgun blast comes through the bedroom window in the dead of night, when the phone rings once every twenty-five minutes for four days and delivers anonymous threats—those are the times that try men's souls, and cause them to ask themselves whether freedom is worth its price.

Deterrents other than moral arguments against such forms of violence and threats are few. Guerrilla tactics are always difficult to interdict, and psychological intimidation is not even illegal in some cases. But the judge who excuses this form of strike violence as the "normal give and take of confrontation" or "a step beyond horseplay" and who discounts the impact it has on individuals threatened or attacked at home, is either disingenuous or uninformed as to its intimidative effect.

To remedy this sort of violence there are no panaceas other than recognizing it and proceding against it as vigorously as the law allows. It is clear, however, that if the scope of permissible strike activities were reasonably circumscribed, the pervasive atmosphere of violence and hatred that accompanies so many labor disputes might be ameliorated (see Chapter XV).

The Targets of Violence

Many persons continue to conceptualize strikes as confrontations between the management of a company and its employees. This, however, is not the most common situation. Many violent incidents noted arise out of confrontations between striking unionists (sometimes with the aid of outsiders from other bargaining units) and a wide variety of third party targets, some of whose relationships to the disputes are tenuous at best. Unionized mineworkers, for example, direct their violence against nonunion mines, hoping to close them down and shut off the flow of coal, thereby bringing pressure on coal users to put pressure on unionized mine operators to settle with the union. Striking dissident steel haulers direct their violence against other unionized steel haulers in order to drive them off the road, thus pressuring their employers to pressure the Teamsters union into acceeding to the demands of the dissidents. Striking construction workers direct their violence against the users of construction built by nonunion firms so that those users will remember the troubles when comissioning work in the future and pressure their future general contractors into agreeing to hire only union subcontractors. Striking firefighters direct their violence against the general public so the general public will bring pressure to bear on state or national officials to, in turn, pressure the local officials into agreeing to the unions' demands.

Where the targets are not these third parties they tend overwhelmingly to be nonstrikers or nonunion individuals who wish to continue working, as is alleged to be their right, during the dispute. These individuals, in strike after strike, must bear the taunts and jeers of the strikers, the opprobrium of the press, the inaction of police authorities, and the brunt of the violence. They are called "scabs" and strikebreakers and minions of management. In addition, even though they choose not to participate in work stoppages either for economic or for moral reasons, final settlement of the strike usually depends on them.

In many instances, company managers and supervisors and the company's plant and equipment can be protected to some degree by guards and security forces; but individual nonstrikers or nonunion employees are too numerous and geographically scattered to be protected in the same way. When confronted in the neighborhood bar, at the picket line, or at home by angry and threatening strikers, such individuals are usually left to their own devices. The average citizen facing such circumstances is not, however, a reliable agent to defend his own rights, and he should not be required to do so.

Again, short of prohibiting strikes or completely reorganizing the system of labor relations, there is no sweeping cure for this problem. Men persist in failing to accord to others basic human rights and the freedom to disagree. But insofar as the right to work and earn a living is a more basic one than the right to be supported in abstaining from work; insofar as the right *not* to join in a common cause is one of our basic freedoms; and insofar as individuals who try to exercise such rights are being impeded from doing so by coercive, intimidatory, and illegal means, they deserve more protection from laws and authorities.

In sum, violence is a fact of life in labor relations; its effects are death, personal injury, property damage, lost work opportunity, and lost production. Its use in strikes is not decreasing with the passage of time; and its use will undoubtedly continue unabated unless actions are taken to curtail it by modifying the ground rules under which strikes can take place and by fixing the responsibility for violence where it belongs.

CHAPTER XIV

Summary of the Legal Response

Over the years, the law has responded in a variety of ways, either directly or indirectly, to the problem of labor union violence.

The first federal law to have a major effect on this phenomenon was the Norris-LaGuardia Act of 1932. Designed to correct what was perceived at the time to be certain abuses in the issuance of injunctions in labor disputes, the Norris-LaGuardia Act severely limits the jurisdiction of the federal courts to grant equitable relief against concerted union activities. Although "unlawful acts" can certainly still be enjoined (assuming that federal jurisdiction otherwise exists), stringent requirements must still be satisfied before even the most egregious acts of violence can be the object of federal injunctive relief. The common law standards of vicarious liability have been replaced with the requirement that the persons to be enjoined must have actually authorized or ratified the violence; there must be proof that local police officials are unable or unwilling to protect the person seeking federal relief; and such a plaintiff must also show that, in spite of the violence being used against him, he has nevertheless made every reasonable effort to settle the dispute peacefully. In addition, a party who seeks federal injunctive relief against union violence must satisfy the normal common law requirements of proof of substantial and irreparable injury, show that this injury is greater than that which the union would suffer if the injunction is granted, and also demonstrate that there is no adequate remedy at law. Finally, the Norris-LaGuardia Act imposes some rather involved procedural requirements that must be satisfied before an injunction can be issued—including prior notice to the persons to be enjoined as well as to the local police officials, a hearing in open court, the posting of a security bond, and the requirement of certain specific findings by the court issuing the injunction. In addition, there are limits even on the issuance of a temporary restraining order.

Although the Norris-LaGuardia Act only limits the jurisdiction of federal courts, the power of the state courts to issue injunctions against union violence is limited by other facets of federal law. The First and Fourteenth Amendments to the Constitution protect peaceful picketing to some extent, and in *Meadowmoor* the Supreme Court attempted to identify the point at which such picketing becomes so imbued with violence as to lose its constitutional protection. The federal preemption doctrine also imposes limits on the power of state courts to issue injunctions in labor disputes.

Insofar as violence is concerned, the more serious limitations are, however, those imposed by the states themselves. After Congress passed the federal Norris-LaGuardia Act, many local legislatures determined that they too should impose some limits on the power of their state courts to issue injunctions in labor disputes. These so-called "Little Norris-LaGuardia Acts" contain provisions similar to those of the federal act, thus often making it as difficult to obtain relief there as in the federal forum.

The next major federal involvement in the problem of union violence arose as a congressional response to a Supreme Court interpretation of the Anti-Racketeering Act of 1934—an interpretation which virtually removed violent labor racketeering from the coverage of the act. Congress responded, however, by passing the Hobbs Act amendment to the Anti-Racketeering Act in 1946. Although the legislative history of this act may be obscure in *certain* respects, it is clear that Congress *did* intend to proscribe union violence aimed at extorting wage increases, benefits, and other concessions from unwilling employers. In spite of this, the Supreme Court has nevertheless construed the statute in such a way as to virtually emasculate its effect on union violence. In *United States v. Enmons,* the Court created a special exception, apparently applicable only to acts of union violence, which excuses such violence as long as it is used in pursuit of otherwise "legitimate" union objectives.

Congress has responded indecisively to the *Enmons* decision. Amendments to the existing statute, some of which have been incorporated in the various proposed versions of a new and comprehensive federal criminal code, have ranged from an express adoption of the *Enmons* approach to a broad prohibition against all serious industrial violence, whether of the extortionate variety or not, which interferes with interstate commerce. At the present time, however, the Hobbs Act remains unchanged and the *Enmons* interpretation of that statute continues to be the controlling one.

In addition to limiting its own response, the law has also posed something of an obstacle to employers who attempt to use the self-help remedy of discharge in dealing with strike and picket line violence by employees. As a matter of private contract law, such misconduct must rise to the level of being "just cause" for discharge before it can be sustained. Labor arbitrators, who are charged with the responsibility of defining that term, have tended to be rather tolerant of certain forms of strike and picket line misconduct, thus providing affirmative legal protection to the guilty employees.

Similarly, the National Labor Relations (Taft-Hartley) Act (NLRA) imposes important statutory limits on the power of an employer to discharge an employee who has participated in strike or picket line misconduct. Strikes and picketing are themselves protected, concerted activities under the statute, and under current interpretations of the law, a striking employee does not lose his otherwise protected status unless he engages in conduct so violent or so serious as to render him totally unfit for future employment—even though the misconduct may otherwise be criminal or tortious in nature.

And even if the misconduct is so egregious as to be "unprotected," the National Labor Relations Board (NLRB) still has a number of theories under which an employer can be required to reinstate the guilty employee. The employer, for example, may be found to have inadvertently "condoned" the misconduct, thus making discharge impermissible. Alternatively, the misconduct might be characterized as a mere "pretext" and the employee's union allegiance found to be the "substantial" or "motivating" factor in the discharge, thus rendering the employer guilty of illegal discrimination. And finally, if the employer himself has committed other unfair labor practices, which theoretically have thus provoked the unprotected violence, then reinstatement of the discharged employee may be ordered under the so-called "Thayer Doctrine."

Although the NLRA thus seems to be rather solicitous of individual employees who succumb to the temptation to use physical force and threats during an industrial dispute, its attitute toward union-sponsored violence is markedly different—or so it would appear at first blush. One of the union unfair labor practices that was added to the statute by the Taft-Hartley Act amendments was section 8(b)(1)(A), which makes it illegal for the union or its agents to restrain or coerce employees in the exercise of their statutory rights.

For the most part, the NLRB and the courts have liberally construed this prohibition. They have adopted a definition of restraint and coercion that includes the full panoply of criminal and tortious misconduct, plus some. Employees are protected against such violence in virtually all of their normal employment and union relationships; and union responsibility is judged by reference to the more realistic common law standards of vicarious liability, rather than those mandated by the Norris-LaGuardia Act. But having found a violation, the board and the courts are unfortunately unable *(or unwilling)* to devise effective remedies for it. During the pendency of unfair labor practice proceedings, the general counsel of the NLRB has authority to request an injunction against the continuation of the violence—although this authority is sparingly exercised. Once a violation is found, a cease and desist order, the dimensions of which may vary, will be issued—and this can be ultimately enforced through contempt proceedings. The union will normally be required to post and sometimes publish notices of its violation. Occasionally, the violence that a union has committed will also operate to deprive it of a bargaining order it might otherwise be entitled to. In truly extreme cases, the board will revoke the certification of a union whose propensity for violence is blatant and recurring.

The remedy that would most effectively vindicate the rights of the employee-victims of this violence, and at the same time deter the union from future misconduct, is, however, a remedy that the NLRB has steadfastly refused to order—namely, a back pay award to compensate employees who have lost work because of the union's unfair labor practices. Although such a back pay award is routinely issued against an *employer* whose violent interference with employee rights has resulted in lost pay, the board's concern that financial accountability might unduly "chill" unionization activities has led it to deny that remedy in the section 8(b)(1)(A) context.

There are, of course, many other laws that touch upon the problem of labor union violence. The criminal laws of each state, as well as a few federal criminal statutes of general application, necessarily encompass much of the violence that occurs in industrial disputes. Moreover, the victims of this violence can always sue to recover personal injury and other consequential damages, under either a common law tort theory or under some specific statute authorizing such suits.

In sum, the law's response to the problem of union violence is extremely varied. How effective it has been is, however, another matter.

CHAPTER XV

Recommendations

Union violence is essentially a moral problem. In the last analysis, it will be "solved" only when labor unionists conscientiously adhere, more than they have in the past, to the conventional ethical norm against the initiation of physical violence. Neither the legitimacy of their ultimate goals nor the intransigence of those who oppose them provide one scintilla of moral justification for the assaults, threats, property damage, and other assorted forms of violence that disgrace the pages of the history of the American labor movement.

Other, if less fundamental, solutions are, however, the focus of this study; and in that regard, the response of the law to this phenomenon of union violence can certainly be improved in several respects. What appears most basically needed is an attitudinal change on the part of those who are charged with writing and enforcing our nation's laws. The constantly recurring theme—evident in legislative histories as well as in the reported decisions of labor arbitrators, the National Labor Relations Board (NLRB), and both state and federal court judges—is that a certain amount of violence is to be expected in labor disputes, and that such violence, although to be decried, is thus more or less "justified." Misconduct which, if committed under different circumstances would be clearly censurable, is, when it occurs in the context of a labor dispute, glibly referred to as mere "animal exuberence"—not to be approved, but not to be taken too seriously either. Even the more egregious forms of violence are seemingly viewed as an unfortunate but inevitable part of otherwise legitimate union activities to which the law should thus react with some restraint lest the imposition of meaningful sanctions somehow "chill" the exercise of these activities.

One should not underestimate the corrosive effect of this general attitude upon industrial peace. The law's tacit approval of "minor violence" only serves to guarantee its recurrence. The theory that even serious acts of violence are an integral part of industrial relations becomes a self-fulfilling prophecy; and the special deference that is sometimes shown toward violence, but only when it occurs in the con-

495

text of a labor dispute, simply perpetuates the myth that union coercion is uniquely privileged—which thus encourages its further exercise.

In sum, one cannot expect the would-be violators to take prohibitions against union violence seriously when the authoritative voices of the legal community—the legislators, judges, administrative officials, arbitrators, and public prosecutors—themselves view it with some degree of tolerance and understanding. Until the legal community adopts a consistent attitude of moral outrage at the use of *any* violence in labor disputes and translates that attitude into an appropriate legal response, any specific alterations of what is already "written" in the law books will be pretty much an exercise in futility.

Nevertheless, assuming that such an attitudinal change were to occur, it might then further manifest itself in several specific modifications of existing law and theory. A primary and particularly frustrating obstacle to obtaining effective legal relief against union violence is the Norris-LaGuardia Anti-Injunction Act, enacted in 1932, and its state law counterparts. The Norris-LaGuardia Act was a product of its time, reflecting a congressional distrust of the federal judiciary and the belief that "law served no useful purpose in labor disputes, save possibly to protect tangible property and preserve public order"[1]—and with federal injunctions properly being hard to obtain even with respect to the latter.

Today, however, the act is a hoary anachronism. The federal district courts are no longer bastions of antiunionism, if they ever were. The so-called policy of "unqualified laissez faire in labor relations,"[2] which the Norris-LaGuardia Act was said to reflect, has been superceded since the 1935 enactment of the National Labor Relations (Wagner) Act (NLRA) by a federal policy of thoroughgoing regulation of the labor-management relationship. And "judicial usurpation" of the legislative power to define that relationship is no longer the problem that it allegedly was in 1932.

In sum, the purposes, policies, and objectives of the Norris-LaGuardia Act have been almost totally eclipsed by subsequent events. Nevertheless, that act continues to have the residual effect of making it difficult for a private party to obtain injunctive relief against labor union violence. Indeed, that would now seem to have become the primary remaining function of the statute.

Congressional reevaluation of the Norris-LaGuardia Act and of the role of the federal courts in enjoining labor union violence is thus long

---

[1] A. COX, LAW AND THE NATIONAL LABOR POLICY 5 (1960).
[2] *Id.* at 8.

overdue. The use of violence to obtain economic and organizational objectives is contrary to the fundamental policies of federal labor law; existing statutory remedies for such misconduct are generally regarded as being inadequate; immediate injunctive relief is of critical importance where there are on-going acts of violence and intimidation; and the need for a uniform federal law is presumably as pressing here, if not greatly more so, as it is in the other areas of labor-management relations.[3] It would seem, therefore, that federal law should *encourage* resort to the federal courts for injunctive relief against union violence, rather than actively *discourage* it, as does the Norris-LaGuardia Act.

Like their federal counterpart, the state "Little Norris-LaGuardia Acts" also address a problem that no longer exists. Many of the injunctions that they prohibit their courts from issuing, involving peaceful labor activities, are beyond the power of the states in any event—because of subsequently developed doctrines of constitutional law and federal preemption. Burdening the labor injunction process with rigorous procedural and evidentiary requirements can no longer be justified by reference to the alleged partnership of state court judges with management or their presumed tendency to act precipitously in such matters.

To the contrary, the "abuses" in the labor injunction process that exist today consist primarily in the fact that the provisions of these outdated state statutes often serve as a protective shield over acts of violence and intimidation that no civilized society should have to endure. Moreover, for those judges who view at least the "milder" forms of union violence as an unfortunate but traditional part of the industrial conflict, these statutes provide a ready excuse for them to deny injunctive relief against misconduct which, in any other context, would clearly be within the concern of a court of equity.

In sum, the time has come for the state legislatures to reevaluate their anti-injunction statutes. The objective of any legislation in this area should not be to curtail injunctive relief against strike and picket line violence, but rather to facilitate its availability through procedures which are speedy, uncomplicated, and essentially fair to all concerned—with the practical realities of this kind of social dysfunction

---

[3] *See* Teamsters Local 714 v. Lucas Flour Co., 369 U.S. 95 (1962). Indeed, it was both the importance of being able specifically to enforce no-strike agreements and the need for a uniform law on this subject that led, in part, the Supreme Court to hold ultimately that the Norris-LaGuardia Act thus simply did not apply to such law suits. Boys Markets, Inc. v. Retail Clerks Local 770, 398 U.S. 235 (1970). An equally desirable act of judicial legerdemain is clearly not possible, however, in freeing the federal district courts from the limits of the Norris-LaGuardia Act in a suit to enjoin a labor union from committing acts of violence, intimidation, coercion, and property destruction—thus necessitating a legislative response.

being always kept in mind. Against that objective, everything else is secondary.

Repeal of the Norris-LaGuardia Act and related state laws would have a substantial impact on union violence. By way of contrast, the various proposed amendments to the Anti-Racketeering (Hobbs) Act—and the strident opposition that they have aroused among labor union supporters—are probably more symbolic than they are substantive. Most labor union violence is not easily conceptualized in terms of "extortion," at least not in the conventional sense of the word. An anti-extortion statute is, thus, a rather awkward way of dealing with this unfortunate phenomenon. But even in its symbolic mien, the controversy is an extremely important one.

The Supreme Court's *Enmons*[4] decision is an affront to American jurisprudence. The "legitimate objectives" rationale of that case is not only inconsistent with the Court's prior decisions, but it also ignores the overwhelming evidence of a contrary legislative intent. The reasoning in the opinion is weak in other respects as well, and one must share the late Mr. Justice Douglas's suspicion that the Court's own predelictions about labor policy played a more instrumental role in the decision than the traditional tenets of statutory construction, thus creating, as he also recognized, serious separation-of-powers problems.[5] Specifically, it would appear that the Court used the judicial process to achieve a political result that probably could not have been achieved by the legislative process and which, as indicated by the current status of pending legislation, probably cannot now be reversed by the legislative process.[6]

At the substantive level, the *Enmons* creation of a doctrinal exception that is applicable *only* to the agents of organized labor raises serious and far reaching questions about the quality and the equality of federal criminal justice in this country. Congressman Hobbs said of the Hobbs Act that "this bill is grounded on the bedrock principle that crime is crime, no matter who commits it; and that robbery is robbery and extortion extortion, whether or not the perpetrator has a union

---

[4] United States v. Enmons, 335 F.Supp. 640 (E.D. La. 1971), aff'd. 410 U.S. 396 (1973).

[5] Mr. Justice Douglas noted that "[w]hile we said in . . . [case citation ommitted] that it is 'retrospective expansion of meaning which properly deserves the stigma of judicial legislation' the same is true of retrospective contraction of meaning." 410 U.S. at 419 (Douglas, J., dissenting).

[6] The *Enmons* decision is, of course, only one example of this rather curious phenomenon. For an insightful analysis of the underlying constitutional (separation of powers) problems posed by this particular use, or abuse, of the judicial process, see Walker, *The Exorbitant Cost of Redistributing Injustice: A Critical View of America v. Weber and the Misguided Policy of Numerical Employment.* 21 B.C.L. Rev. 1 (1980).

card."[7] The *Enmons* view, however, is that this is not necessarily so. Instead, that view seems to be that criminality under federal law is as much a matter of the actor's status as it is of his conduct, and that the status of a labor union official is an especially privileged one in our society.

Clearly, Congress should amend the Hobbs Act to eliminate at least the indefensible gloss placed upon that statute by the *Enmons* decision. The inadequacy of an extortion statute in dealing with labor union violence in a comprehensive sort of way suggests, however, that an even broader statutory solution to the problem might also be in order.

A bill introduced in 1981 in connection with the other Hobbs Act amendments, S. 613, would have made it a federal crime for a labor union or anyone else to interfere with interstate commerce by "inflicting, or threatening to inflict, death or serious bodily injury on any person" or by "willfully damaging to the extent of $2,500 or more any property, including real property, used for business purposes."[8]

Serious labor union violence would seem to be a uniquely appropriate subject of federal criminal law. Since the 1930's, the fundamental premise has been that industrial relations affects interstate commerce almost by definition. National unions, whose jurisdiction extends over many states, are frequently implicated when serious and widespread violence occurs. Even if the violence is otherwise local in its origin and focus, it nevertheless affects the union's organizational and collective bargaining strength, which in turn has a significant impact on interstate commerce. To say the least, union violence sufficiently affects national concerns to make it an unfair labor practice under federal law, and there is no good reason why it should not also be subject to federal criminal sanctions. To be sure, the states should retain concurrent jurisdiction over violence which occurs within their borders, and some kind of comity would have to be worked out between local and federal prosecutors. That, however, is not a serious obstacle.

An equally significant improvement in the law would involve the removal of certain contractual and statutory limits on the liberty of an employer to discharge employees who have committed strike and picket line violence. At the contractual level, it seems unlikely that labor arbitrators are likely to change the trend of their decisions holding so-called "minor violence" not to be grounds for discharge under usual "just cause" provisions. Thus, it devolves upon employers to attempt to negotiate collective bargaining or strike settlement

---

[7] 89 Cong. Rec. 3217 (1943).
[8] S. 613, 97th Cong., 1st Sess. (1981); *See also,* H.R. 450, 97th Cong., 1st Sess. (1981).

agreements which expressly guarantee them the right to deal with these miscreants in an appropriate fashion.

That, however, is a solution which may not adequately protect the real victims of this violence—the employees who attempted to work in the face of the strike, or who otherwise came into contact with picket lines, and who were deterred from doing so by the picket line misconduct. The union, in negotiating a "reinstatement of strikers" clause and in arbitrating grievances arising under it, is obviously not interested in vindicating the rights of these "scabs." And the employer, who is the only other party to the process, may have economic interests which dictate the reinstatement of employees notwithstanding their propensity to use violence against fellow workers. This, of course, is simply another instance where the interests of the individual employee get lost in the grandiose scheme of "industrial democracy" which Congress has created.

With respect to the removal of limits which the NLRB has imposed through its interpretations of the National Labor Relations (Taft-Hartley) Act (NLRA), this could be accomplished either by a reversal of policy on the NLRB's part or by legislative fiat. The former would be the far more effective solution, given the difficulty one would face in drafting unambiguous statutory language to deal with this problem and the board's adroitness in ignoring "obscure" congressional mandates with which it disagrees.

In any event, it is clear that federal labor law must depart from the notion that a certain amount of abusive behavior is to be expected in a strike or picket line situation and that such misconduct remains a part of the employee's "protected concerted activities" unless it rises to a fairly high level of egregiousness. The legislative history of the NLRA negates any intent on the part of Congress to extend *affirmative* statutory protection to union rowdiness or any other form of "minor" coercion. Therefore, unless the board retreats from its current interpretation of the act, Congress should reaffirm its intent in that regard in language that cannot be ignored.

Perhaps even more objectionable are the theories which the NLRB has developed for ordering the reinstatement even of employees who have otherwise engaged in seriously violent acts and other unprotected misconduct. The condonation theory, for example, cannot be explained in coherent or consistent terms, it lacks any compelling policy justifications, and its incorporation into the statutory scheme is a strained one at best. The board would be well advised either to narrow or to abandon it altogether.

Similarly disturbing are the cases where the NLRB presumes to find that an employee was discharged, not because of his unprotected picket line violence, but rather because of his otherwise legitimate union activities. The problem of proving the "real" reason for a discharge is a troublesome one in any context, and the Supreme Court is expected to speak to the issue soon. But whatever test is adopted for dealing with "pretextual" or "dual purpose" discharges in general, it is suggested that the general counsel's proof be rigorously scrutinized whenever the asserted reason for the discharge is the employee's proved or admitted participation in strike or picket line violence. Such an approach would be consistent with the concern of the Taft-Hartley Act Congress that an employee's union affiliation never be allowed to become a license to commit acts of violence and intimidation against fellow employees. Indeed, Congress should consider the possibility of amending the statute to provide that such a person automatically looses his status as an employee—thus obviating the need for a difficult "motive" analysis altogether. This is an approach which the law has taken with respect to employees who engage in peaceful strikes, but ones which violate the prohibitions of section 8(d). Such an approach is even more compelling in the context of employee violence, especially against fellow employees.

Finally, the NLRB should repudiate the Thayer Doctrine—or be required by Congress to do so. An employee who has engaged in unprotected violence should not be entitled to reinstatement *simply* because he happened to commit that violence in the context of what is ultimately determined to be an "unfair labor practice strike." Reinstatement of such an employee cannot be rationally justified by reference to any legitimate statutory policy. To the contrary, it places a premium on the use of violence in precisely those situations where the statute attempts to encourage the use of peaceful legal processes. Again, a "loss of status" provision in the statute might be the best way for Congress to deal with this particular problem.

The one bright spot in the federal law dealing with union violence is the section of the NLRA that declares this to be an unfair labor practice. Unfortunately, this prohibition is more theoretical than real because of the lack of effective remedies. There are, however, several things that could be done about this. In the first place, the general counsel of the NLRB could be far more aggressive in seeking temporary injunctive relief once a section 8(b)(1)(A) charge has been filed. Alternatively, Congress could make it mandatory for the general counsel to seek injunctive relief in such situations, as it has done with respect to other kinds of unfair labor practices. In a similar vein, there should be a more vigorous policing of cease and desist orders and the increased use of contempt proceedings as an enforcement device.

To be sure, a labor union that has been found guilty of section

8(b)(1)(A) violence should not be automatically declared an "outlaw," forever and anon. On the other hand, it would seem that a union with a long history of, and an obvious propensity for, violence should, at some point, lose the special statutory privileges which it enjoys to be an exclusive bargaining representative. Thus, the board should use the loss of certification and denial of bargaining status remedy more than it has in the past. The countervailing policy consideration, that the employees should not be deprived of their chosen bargaining representative, is without merit, in that employees simply do not have the right to be represented by a union which resorts to the use of force in the performance of its functions, and can easily choose another bargaining agent.

Finally, the NLRB must retreat, or be required by Congress to do so, from its refusal to include a "back pay" award as a part of its section 8(b)(1)(A) remedial orders. The board's position on this question is supported by neither law nor policy. Clearly, it has the statutory power to grant such an award, and its refusal to do so represents a gross distortion of priorities and values, in that it reflects a greater concern for the speculative "chilling effect" monetary liability might have on the union's willingness to engage in borderline coercion than it does for the concrete interest which a victimized employee has in recovering at least a part of what he has lost as a result of union violence.

In conclusion, although these recommended changes in the law would not eliminate union violence from the industrial relations scene, they would more adequately express society's disapproval of such misconduct; they would, it is hoped, prevent a substantially greater portion of it; and they would provide more adequate relief to those who are victimized by union violence.

APPENDIX

Appendix A

FULL UNION NAMES
AND THEIR ACRONYMS
AS USED IN THIS STUDY

Full Name of Union or Organization	Acronym Used in This Study
Air Traffic Controllers Organization; Professional	PATCO
American Federation of State, County and Municipal Employees	State, County, and Municipal Employees (AFSCME)
Asbestos Workers; International Association of Heat and Frost Insulators and	Asbestos Workers (HFIA)
Automobile, Aerospace & Agricultural Implement Workers; United	Autoworkers (UAW)
Automobile Machinists Union[a]	Auto Machinists
Automobile Mechanics Union[a]	Auto Mechanics
Bakery, Confectionary and Tobacco Workers' International Union	Bakery Workers (BCTW)
Barbers, Beauticians and Allied Industries International Association[b]	Barbers
Beer Bottlers Union[a]	Beer Bottlers
Boatmen's Union; Inland[a]	Inland Boatmen
Boilermakers, Iron Ship Builders, Blacksmiths, Forgers and Helpers; International Brotherhood of	Boilermakers (BBF)
Brewery, Flour, Cereal, Soft Drink and Distillery Workers of America; International Union of United	Brewery Workers
Bricklayers and Allied Craftsmen; International Union of	Bricklayers (BAC)
Broadcast Employees and Technicians; National Association of	Broadcast Employees (NABET)
Building and Construction Trades Councils[c]	Building Trades Councils

505

Full Name of Union or Organization	Acronym Used in This Study
Butchers, Food Handlers and Allied Workers Union, Ind.	Butchers
Cabinet Makers and Millmen[a]	Cabinet Makers
Cannery Workers Union[a]	Cannery Workers
Carpenters and Joiners of America; United Brotherhood of	Carpenters (CJA)
Cement, Lime and Gypsum Workers International Union; United	Cement, Lime and Gypsum Workers (CLGW)
Cement Masons Union[a]	Cement Masons
Chemical Workers Union; International	Chemical Workers (ICW)
Clothing and Textile Workers Union; Amalgamated	Clothing and Textile Workers (ACTWU)
Communication Workers of America	Communication Workers (CWA)
Culinary Bartenders' Union[a]	Culinary Bartenders
Die Sinkers Conference; International	Die Sinkers (DSC)
Education Association; National	Teachers (NEA)
Electrical, Radio and Machine Workers; International Union of	Electrical Workers (IUE)
Electrical, Radio and Machine Workers of America; United	Electrical Workers (UE)
Electrical Workers; International Brotherhood of	Electrical Workers (IBEW)
Farm Workers of America; United	Farm Workers (UFW)
Fire Fighters; International Association of	Firefighters (IAFF)
Firemen and Oilers; International Brotherhood of	Firemen and Oilers (IBFO)
Food and Commercial Workers International Union; United	Food and Commercial Workers (UFCW)
Furniture Workers of America; United	Furniture Workers (UFWA)
Garment Workers' Union; International Ladies'	Ladies' Garment Workers (ILGWU)
Glass and Ceramic Workers of North America; United	Glass and Ceramic Workers
Glass Bottle Blowers' Association of the United States and Canada[d]	Glass Bottle Blowers (GBBA)
Glass Workers Union; American Flint	Flint Glass Workers (AFGW)
Government Employees; American Federation of	AFGE
Government Employees; National Association of	NAGE
Grain Millers; American Federation of	Grain Millers (AFGM)
Graphic Arts International Union	Graphic Arts (GAIU)

Full Name of Union or Organization	Acronym Used in This Study
Hospital and Health Care Employees; National Union of	Hospital and Health Care Employees
Hotel and Restaurant Employees and Bartenders International Union	Hotel and Restaurant Workers (HERE)
Industrial Workers; International Union of Allied	Allied Industrial Workers (AIW)
Industrial Workers Union; National	Industrial Workers (NIW)
Iron Workers; International Association of Bridge, Structural and Ornamental	Iron Workers (BSOIW)
Laborers' International Union of North America	Laborers (LIUNA)
Laborers Union; Construction and General	General and Construction Laborers
Laundry Workers, Dry Cleaners, and Dye House Workers' International Union	Laundry Workers (LWUI)
Letter Carriers; National Association of	NALC
Longshoremen's Association International (AFL-CIO)	Longshoremen (ILA)
Longshoremen's and Warehousemen's Union; International	Longshore and Warehousemen (ILWU)
Machinists and Aerospace Workers; International Association of	Machinists (IAM)
Mailers' Union; International[e]	Mailers
Maintenance of Way Employees; Brotherhood of	BMWE
Mason Tenders Union[a]	Mason Tenders
Meatcutters and Butcher Workmen of America; Amalgamated[f]	Meatcutters
Mine Workers of America; Progressive	Progressive Mine Workers
Mine Workers of America; United	Mine Workers (UMW)
Molders and Allied Workers Union; International	Molders (IMAW)
Moving Picture Machine Operators Union[a]	Motion Picture Operators
Musicians; American Federation of	Musicians (AFM)
Newspaper Guild; The	Newspaper Guild
Office and Professional Employees International Union	Office and Professional Workers (OPEIU)
Oil, Chemical and Atomic Workers International Union	Oil, Chemical and Atomic Workers (OCAW)
Operating Engineers; International Union of	Operating Engineers (IUOE)

Full Name of Union or Organization	Acronym Used in This Study
Painters and Allied Trades of the United States and Canada; International Brotherhood of	Painters (PAT)
Paperworkers' International Union; United	Paperworkers (UPIU)
Patrolmen's Benevolent Association	Policemen
Pilots Association; Air Line	Airline Pilots (ALPA)
Plastic Workers Union[a]	Plastic Workers
Plumbing and Pipe Fitting Industry of the United States and Canada; United Association of Journeymen and Apprentices of the	Plumbers (PPF)
Postal Workers Union, American	APWU
Pottery and Allied Workers; International Brotherhood of[d]	Pottery Workers
Printing and Graphic Communications Union; International	Printing and Graphics Workers (PGCU)
Production Service and Sales Union; International	Production Workers (PSS)
Professors; American Association of University	University Professors (AAUP)
Public Service Employees Union[a]	Public Service Employees
Pulp and Paper Workers; Association of Western	Pulp and Paper Workers (Western)
Railway, Airline and Steamship Clerks; Brotherhood of	Railway Clerks (BRAC)
Railway Carmen of the United States and Canada; Brotherhood of	Railway Carmen (BRC)
Retail Clerks International Association[f]	Retail Clerks
Retail, Wholesale and Department Store Union	Retail and Wholesale Trade (RWDSU)
Roofers, Waterproofers and Allied Workers; United Union of	Roofers (RWAW)
Rubber, Cork, Linoleum and Plastic Workers of America; United	Rubber Workers (URW)
Service Employees International Union	Service Employees (SEIU)
Sheet Metal Workers' International Association	Sheet Metal Workers (SMW)
Shipbuilders Union[a]	Shipbuilders
Social Workers Union; Community and[a]	Social Workers
Southern Labor Union	Southern Labor Union (SLU)
Steel Haulers; Fraternal Association of[c]	Steel Haulers (FASH)
Steel Workers of America; United	Steelworkers (USW)
Taxi Drivers; Guild of[a]	Taxi Drivers

Full Name of Union or Organization	Acronym Used in This Study
Teachers; American Federation of	Teachers (AFT)
Teamsters, Chauffeurs, Warehousemen and Helpers of America; International Brotherhood of	Teamsters
Theatrical Stage Employees and Moving Picture Machine Operators; International Alliance of	Theatrical Employees
Transit Union; Amalgamated	Transit Workers (ATU)
Transport Workers Union of America	Transport Workers (TWU)
Transportation Union; United	Transportation (UTU)
Truckers Association; Independent[c]	Independent Truckers
Tunnel Workers; Compress and Open Air Caisson Subway Underpinning Foundation and	Tunnel Workers
Typographical Union; International	Typographical Workers (ITU)
Upholsterers' International Union of North America	Upholsterers (UIU)
Woodworkers of America; International	Woodworkers (IWA)

[a]The names of these organizations are taken directly from the NRTWLDF Violence Data Base. They have not been confirmed, and the incidents of violence associated with them may be misallocated.

[b]Merged into United Food and Commercial Workers International Union (UFCW), September 1, 1980.

[c]These organizations are not labor unions as such but do share characteristics with labor unions and engage in strikes.

[d]Merged in August 1982 to form Glass, Pottery, Plastics and Allied Workers International Union. (GPPAW)

[e]Merged into the International Typographical Union (ITU), January 1, 1979.

[f]Merged to form United Food and Commercial Workers International Union (UFCW), June 7, 1979.

Index of Cases

Subject Index

Anti-Injunction Act. *See* Norris-LaGuardia Act
Anti-Racketeering Act of 1934, 21, 245–54, 255–64, 492. *See also* Hobbs Act
acts prohibited by, 246
case law, 248–54
Hobbs Act amendments to, 16, 254–85, 463, 466, 469–70, 499–500
labor reaction to, 246–48
legislative history of, 245–48
provisions of, 492–93
APWU. *See* American Postal Workers Union
Association of Western Pulp and Paper Workers
NRTWLDF violent incident data base listing, 60
Atlantic Richfield Company, 163
ATU. *See* Amalgamated Transit Union
automobile industry
union violence in, 66
Automobile Machinists Union
NRTWLDF violent incident data base listing, 61
Automobile Mechanics Union
NRTWLDF violent incident data base listing, 61
A.W. Cross Construction Company, 163

BAC. *See* Industrial Union of Bricklayers and Allied Craftsmen
back pay awards, 442–58, 502
Baker, David, 130, 131
Bakery, Confectionary and Tobacco Workers' International Union (BCTW)
level of violence by, 63
NRTWLDF violent incident data base listing, 60
Barbers, Beauticians and Allied Industries International Association (Barbers)
NRTWLDF violent incident data base listing, 62
BBF. *See* International Brotherhood of Boilermakers, Iron Ship Builders, Blacksmiths, Forgers and Helpers
BCOA. *See* Bituminous Coal Operators Association
BCTW. *See* Bakery, Confectionary and Tobacco Workers' International Union
Beer Bottlers Union
NRTWLDF violent incident data base listing, 60
Bituminous Coal Operators Association (BCOA), 90, 99, 100, 116
Blantan, Ray, 133

Blue Ridge Coal Corporation, 85–86
BLS. *See* Bureau of Labor Statistics
BMWE. *See* Brotherhood of Maintenance of Way Employees
BRAC. *See* Brotherhood of Railway, Airline and Steamship Clerks
Brewery Workers. *See* International Union of United Brewery, Flour, Cereal, Soft Drink and Distillery Workers of America
Brotherhood of Maintenance of Way Employees (BMWE), 54
Brotherhood of Railway, Airline and Steamship Clerks (BRAC)
NRTWLDF violent incident data base listing, 61
representative acts of violence by, 74
Brown, John, 114
Brown, R.R., 116
Brown & Root, 162, 163
Bruno, Angelo, 156
BSOIW. *See* International Association of Bridge, Structural and Ornamental Iron Workers
Building and Construction Trades Councils
of Colorado, 151
level of violence by, 64
of New Mexico, 151
NLRB complaints against, 150
NRTWLDF violent incident data base listing, 55, 56, 57, 61
of Philadelphia, 152, 157, 229–31, 465–66
representative acts of violence by, 71
of Sabine area, 164, 480–81
of Southwest Louisiana, 162
Bureau of Labor Statistics (BLS), 121
Butchers, Food Handlers, and Allied Workers Union
NRTWLDF violent incident data base listing, 62

Cabinet Makers and Millmen
NRTWLDF violent incident data base listing, 60
Cannery Workers Union
NRTWLDF violent incident data base listing, 60
Cement, Lime and Gypsum Workers International Union (CLGW)
and construction-related violence in Denver, 151
NRTWLDF violent incident data base listing, 60
Chandler, Wyeth, 127, 131, 132–33, 134

Racial Policies of American Industry Series

1. *The Negro in the Automobile Industry,*
   by Herbert R. Northrup.   1968
2. *The Negro in the Aerospace Industry,*
   by Herbert R. Northrup.   1968
3. *The Negro in the Steel Industry,* by Richard L. Rowan.   1968
4. *The Negro in the Hotel Industry,* by Edward C. Koziara
   and Karen S. Koziara.   1968
5. *The Negro in the Petroleum Industry,* by Carl B. King
   and Howard W. Risher, Jr.   1969
6. *The Negro in the Rubber Tire Industry,* by Herbert R.
   Northrup and Alan B. Batchelder.   1969
7. *The Negro in the Chemical Industry,*
   by William Howard Quay, Jr.   1969
8. *The Negro in the Paper Industry,* by Herbert R. Northrup.   1969
9. *The Negro in the Banking Industry,*
   by Armand J. Thieblot, Jr.   1970
10. *The Negro in the Public Utility Industries,*
    by Bernard E. Anderson.   1970
11. *The Negro in the Insurance Industry,* by Linda P. Fletcher. 1970
12. *The Negro in the Meat Industry,* by Walter A. Fogel.   1970
13. *The Negro in the Tobacco Industry,*
    by Herbert R. Northrup.   1970
14. *The Negro in the Bituminous Coal Mining Industry,*
    by Darold T. Barnum.   1970
15. *The Negro in the Trucking Industry,* by Richard D. Leone. 1970
16. *The Negro in the Railroad Industry,*
    by Howard W. Risher, Jr.   1971
17. *The Negro in the Shipbuilding Industry,* by Lester Rubin. 1970
18. *The Negro in the Urban Transit Industry,*
    by Philip W. Jeffress.   1970
19. *The Negro in the Lumber Industry,* by John C. Howard.   1970
20. *The Negro in the Textile Industry,* by Richard L. Rowan.   1970
21. *The Negro in the Drug Manufacturing Industry,*
    by F. Marion Fletcher.   1970
22. *The Negro in the Department Store Industry,*
    by Charles R. Perry.   1971
23. *The Negro in the Air Transport Industry,*
    by Herbert R. Northrup et al.   1971
24. *The Negro in the Drugstore Industry,* by F. Marion Fletcher. 1971
25. *The Negro in the Supermarket Industry,*
    by Gordon F. Bloom and F. Marion Fletcher.   1972
26. *The Negro in the Farm Equipment and Construction
    Machinery Industry,* by Robert Ozanne.   1972
27. *The Negro in the Electrical Manufacturing Industry,*
    by Theodore V. Purcell and Daniel P. Mulvey.   1971
28. *The Negro in the Furniture Industry,* by William E. Fulmer. 1973
29. *The Negro in the Longshore Industry,* by Lester Rubin
    and William S. Swift.   1974
30. *The Negro in the Offshore Maritime Industry,*
    by William S. Swift.   1974
31. *The Negro in the Apparel Industry,* by Elaine Gale Wrong. 1974

Order from: Kraus Reprint Co., Route 100, Millwood, New York 10546

STUDIES OF NEGRO EMPLOYMENT

Vol. I. *Negro Employment in Basic Industry: A Study of Racial Policies in Six Industries (Automobile, Aerospace, Steel, Rubber Tire , Petroleum, and Chemicals),* by Herbert R. Northrup, Richard L. Rowan, et al.   1970

Vol. II. *Negro Employment in Finance: A Study of Racial Policies in Banking and Insurance,* by Armand J. Thieblot, Jr., and Linda Pickthorne Fletcher.   1970

Vol. III. *Negro Employment in Public Utilities: A Study of Racial Policies in the Electric Power, Gas, and Telephone Industries,* by Bernard E. Anderson.   1970

Vol. IV. *Negro Employment in Southern Industry: A Study of Racial Policies in the Paper, Lumber, Tobacco, Coal Mining, and Textile Industries,* by Herbert R. Northrup, Richard L. Rowan, et al.   1971

Vol. V. *Negro Employment in Land and Air Transport: A Study of Racial Policies in the Railroad, Airline, Trucking, and Urban Transit Industries,* by Herbert R. Northrup, Howard W. Risher, Jr., Richard D. Leone, and Philip W. Jeffress. 1971. $13.50 [*]

Vol. VI. *Negro Employment in Retail Trade: A Study of Racial Policies in the Department Store, Drugstore, and Supermarket Industries,* by Gordon F. Bloom, F. Marion Fletcher, and Charles R. Perry.   1972

Vol. VII. *Negro Employment in the Maritime Industries: A Study of Racial Policies in the Shipbuilding, Longshore, and Offshore Maritime Industries,* by Lester Rubin, William S. Swift, and Herbert R. Northrup.   1974

Vol. VIII. *Black and Other Minority Participation in the All-Volunteer Navy and Marine Corps,* by Herbert R. Northrup, Steven M. DiAntonio, John A. Brinker, and Dale F. Daniel.   1979

Order from University Microfilms, Inc.
Attn: Books Editorial Department
300 North Zeeb Road
Ann Arbor, Michigan 48106

[*]Order this book from the Industrial Research Unit, The Wharton School, University of Pennsylvania, Philadelphia, Pennsylvania 19104.